VOLUME 2

HEBREWS TO NEGROES 2

Wake up Black America!

RONALD DALTON JR.

Cover Design: Brittany Jackson

Book Images used are Public Domain and Free Stock Photos

Published by G Publishing, LLC

Library of Congress Control Number: 2015913566

ISBN: 978-0-9971579-1-8

Printed in the United States of America

TABLE OF CONTENTS

CHAPTER 1 5
FROM HEBREWS TO BEING CALLED "NEGROES", THE SAGA CONTINUES!............5
CHAPTER 2 21
DNA EXPLAINED 101: Y-DNA (PATERNAL), MITOCHONDRIAL DNA
(MATERNAL) AND AUTOSOMAL DNA. 21
CHAPTER 3 34
THE LEMBA-YEMEN CONNECTION TO THE "BANTUS NEGRO PEOPLE", THE
BLACK ARAB ISHMAELITES AND THE SHEMITES. 34
CHAPTER 4 63
PROVING THE "COHEN MODEL HAPLOGROUP" TO BE A "FALSE" ISRAELITE
MARKER USING GENETICS AND "CRITICAL THINKING". 63
CHAPTER 5 82
WHITE MOROCCAN JEWS VS BLACK MOROCCAN JEWS. WHO IS THE REAL JEW
AND WHO IS A "CONVERT" TO JUDAISM? WHO WERE THE REAL JEWS WHO
WERE BANISHED FROM IBERIA? 82
CHAPTER 6 99
THE NAMES CHANGE, BUT THE "FALSE GOD" AKA SATAN, STAYS THE SAME.
SATAN'S DECEPTION WAS AROUND BACK THEN AND IT STILL IS AROUND
TODAY..99
CHAPTER 7 106
WHERE DOES THE WHITE RACE COME FROM? DOES ANYBODY KNOW?...........106
CHAPTER 8 145
BEWARE OF EGYPTOLOGISTS, KEMETIANS, "NEW AGE" AFRICAN
SPIRITUALISTS AND PEOPLE PREACHING "UNIFICATION OF RELIGIONS". 145
CHAPTER 9 171
HOW MANY DIFFERENT "AGENDAS" HAS SATAN PUT IN PLACE FOR "GOD'S
CHOSEN PEOPLE" AKA "THE ISRAELITES"?...171
CHAPTER 10 221
IT'S IN OUR BIBLE! THE CURSES OF ISRAEL IS ABOUT US! 221
CHAPTER 11 286
ARE THE INDIGENOUS "INDIANS" HAMITES? IF NOT, ARE THEY SHEMITES? ..286
CHAPTER 12 308
WHO ARE THE REAL HEBREWS? WHICH ONE OF THESE RACES/NATIONS ARE
GOING THROUGH THE CURSES OF ISRAEL AS LISTED IN DEUTERONOMY 28:15-
68? 308
CHAPTER 13 319
THE PUNISHMENT MUST FIT THE CRIME! IT IS WRITTEN IN THE TORAH! 319
CHAPTER 14 333
KNOW THYSELF AND ALSO YOUR SWORN ENEMIES (CAIN & EDOM). WHERE
ARE THEY AT?..333
CHAPTER 15 353
MODERN DAY ISLAM AND MODERN DAY TALMUDIC JUDAISM: HOW IS IT
DECEIVING BLACKS? WHAT IS THE TRUTH? 353
CHAPTER 16 366
ARE TODAY'S JEWS AND ARABS SIMPLY EUROPEANS WHO CONVERTED TO
JUDAISM OR ISLAM? THERE CAN ONLY BE ONE TRUE ARAB AND ONE TRUE
JEW (ISRAELITE)..366

CHAPTER 17 392
SYNAGOGUE OF SATAN: MASTERS OF DECEPTION! THERE IS MORE THAN
MEETS THE "EYE". 392
CHAPTER 18 403
THE NORTHERN HOUSE OF ISRAEL: WHERE DID THEY GO? DID SOME MAKE IT
TO THE "NEW WORLD" AND THE "CARIBBEAN"?................................403
CHAPTER 19 432
THE NORTH AFRICAN, MOORISH, ISRAELITE AND LATINO CONNECTION. 432
CHAPTER 20 457
EXPLAINING HAPLOGROUPS ALL OVER AGAIN. WHAT CAN DNA TELL US?...457
CHAPTER 21 462
FINDING EDOM AND HIS Y-DNA....REQUIRES DIGGING DEEP INTO HIS
HISTORY. "THIS IS YOUR LIFE EDOM!" 462
CHAPTER 22 486
ARE LATINOS/HISPANICS ISRAELITES? HOW CAN ALL THE ISRAELITES BE
"AFRICAN-LOOKING" PEOPLE WHEN THE BIBLE SAYS THE ISRAELTES "MIXED"
WITH MANY NATIONS?..486
CHAPTER 23 502
WHO ELSE FALLS INTO THE Y-DNA "R1B" HAPLOGROUP THAT SCIENTISTS SAY
IS PROOF THAT LATINOS ARE MOSTLY EUROPEAN? 502
CHAPTER 24 545
DID THE ANCIENT EGYPTIANS-HEBREWS ALSO OCCUPY WESTERN EUROPE?
DID THEY LEAVE THEIR GENETIC "MARK" THERE?.....................................545
CHAPTER 25 573
WHERE DO THE MACCABEES COME FROM? WHEN DID THE "GENTILES" INSERT
THEMSELVES INTO BIBLE HISTORY? 573
CHAPTER 26 585
WHAT HAPPENED NEXT IN BIBLICAL HISTORY LEADING UP TO THE FINAL
"GENTILE" EXPANSION OF ISRAEL BY THE GREEKS? 585
CHAPTER 27 593
IS THERE ANY MORE DNA PROOF TO PROVE THAT THE EUROPEAN JEWS ARE
NOT THE DESCENDANTS OF THE BIBLICAL HEBREW ISRAELITES? 593
CHAPTER 28 601
THE "GENTILE HEIST" OF ISRAEL...601
CHAPTER 29 617
THE IDENTITY HIJACK OF ISRAEL'S HIGH PRIESTHOOD. WITHOUT A "TRUE"
LEGITIMATE PRIESTHOOD ANY BUILDING OF ANOTHER JEWISH TEMPLE IS A
SHAM. 617
CHAPTER 30 631
EDOM AND THE GENTILES, CAN THEY WIN TOGETHER?................................631
CHAPTER 31 648
WHAT IS THE MARK OF THE BEAST? HAS IT ALREADY COME OR IS IT AROUND
THE CORNER? DON'T BE FOOLED! 648

CHAPTER 1

FROM HEBREWS TO BEING CALLED "NEGROES", THE SAGA CONTINUES!

In this Second volume edition of "**Hebrews to Negroes 2**" I'm picking up where I left off, which is revealing the "**Truth**" about who the "**Real Children of Israel**" is according to the Bible. The European Jews today are steady looking for the "**10 Lost Tribes of Israel**" so that they can bring them back to Israel in hopes it will hasten the return of their Messiah. Oddly enough, they are bypassing the continent of Africa and focusing on countries to the East of Israel (**i.e. India, Afghanistan, Pakistan, China, Saudi Arabia**). However, they never talk about finding Israelite Tribes in Africa. They know that if they acknowledge that there are other tribes of Israel in Africa that it will raise questions as to how can "White Jews" be akin to "Black Jews". The question European Jews will ask will be, "If Blacks are blood descendants of Jacob, then their DNA should be connected to ours." The sad reality is that it is not. For this reason, many European Jews do not openly accept that the Ethiopian Jews are blood descendants of the Hebrew Israelites. The Jews do on the other hand like to always bring up the "Ethiopian Jews" whenever someone tells them that according to the Old Testament the Real Israelites should be "**People of Color**". They come up with many "Ethiopian Jewish origin theories" such as the Ethiopian Jews being "**converts**" to Judaism or that "White Jews" scattered into Africa after the fall of the 2nd Temple in 70 A.D. only to intermarry with native Hamitic Ethiopian people. These are all poor attempts to justify that the "Original Jews" could not have been a "People of Color". But as you will soon see in the next two volumes, this is a big fat lie. Christians worldwide listen to their Pastor or Priest preach out the bible on Sunday commonly mentioning the words "**Israel**" but do the people really know who "**Israel**" is? Sadly, the answer is **No**. Many Churches will say that it is not important who Israel is today or what color the Messiah was but if it wasn't important why would Europeans and Arabs hid this information from the world? It is a known fact that 2,000 years ago and even during the time Islam was born people knew that the Hebrew Israelites were a "**People of Color**". They knew who the "**People of the Book**" were, they just didn't want us to know this information today. This is why it was important for the Europeans to wipe out as many Native Americans as possible. This is why the Europeans had to commit genocide and slavery practices to the people of the "**New World (i.e. The Americas-Caribbean)**" and the "**Dark Continent (i.e. Africa)**". This is why they needed to change the **language**, the **customs**, the **religion** and the identity of the people they enslaved. This is why the Europeans had to allow 2-3 generations to pass before teaching their slaves the Bible. In the same instance, they had to disconnect the older slaves from the younger slaves so that none of their ancestral history or language could be taught. The slaves had to forget their language and their heritage first before listening to the stories of the Bible from the White man's mouth. If the slave knew his heritage, he would recognize that the Bible was about his ancestors as most Africans already knew about the Old Testament stories before the Europeans/Arabs set foot in their land.

Fact: *In the Americas, prior to Christopher Columbus arrival, there have been found engraved on rock pictures depicting the "**Great Flood**", "the **Ten Commandments**" and the "**Story of Moses in the Exodus**". Many of these relics are in Paleo-Hebrew/Phoenician and not Modern "Block" Hebrew which the European Jews use today.*

This is why the Catholic Church had to convert as many "**Negroes**" and "**Indians**" as they could. That was part of the "**brainwashing**" step to erase our identity. This is why Islam has spread to encompass more than half of the population of Africa. This is why the Europeans promoted race-mixing with the people they conquered and lived amongst as a way to "**whiten-out**" the color of the land. This was called the "**Spanish Mestizaje**", and the Portuguese practiced this method as well in **Brazil**, **Angola**, **Guinea-Bissau**, on the **Cape Verde Islands** and the Island of **Sao Tome** (amongst other Portuguese colonies) near Equatorial Guinea to erase any history of the Black Jews that were living in Iberia before the **Spanish Inquisition** in 1492.

King Manuel I along with **King John II** of Portugal exiled the Black Jews of Portugal to the small African islands of **"Sao Tome"**, **"Principe"** and **Equatorial Guinea** which sits off the coast of West Africa in the **Bight of Biafra** (Below Nigeria).

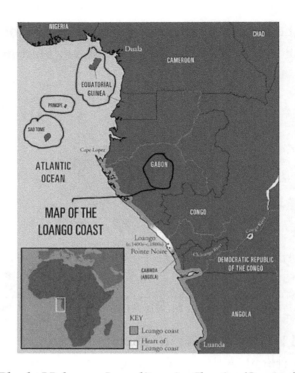

(**Above**) The Black Hebrew Israelites in Iberia (Spain/Portugal) that "overstayed" their welcome in Iberia despite the "Alhambra Decree/Edict of Expulsion" in 1492 were exiled back to Africa. Others were imprisoned as slaves to be dropped off in Spanish/Portuguese colonies abroad (i.e. Jamaica, Brazil, Puerto Rico). In 1492 the Spanish laid their law down and in 1497 the Portuguese laid their law down. King John II of Portugal gave the Black Israelites a chance to convert to Christianity or be sold into slavery. Per history, King John II got tired of the Black Israelites disobeying his order and thus took the children of these Black Israelites and sent them to Portuguese Islands in the heart of the Bight of Biafra below Nigeria. **So why would the Portuguese send so-called White Sephardic Jewish children to Islands in Africa?** Because they were "Black" like the Hamitic inhabitants of Africa. European history books say that these children sent to the Islands of Sao Tome, Principe, Equatorial Guinea were eaten up by giant lizards or died of starvation. European History also states that when **King John II** of Portugal died, his successor, **King Manuel I** allowed the Black Israelites in Portugal to leave on boats to North Africa (Morocco)

8

around 1497. Some however, sailed around Africa using the Atlantic Ocean to get to modern day Nigeria. In Nigeria, according to the Yoruba Jews who are known by their brethren in Nigeria as "**Strange People-Emo Yo Quaim**" their passed down oral history states that they traveled on boats to be with their Hebrew Israelite brothers that they knew were in "**Proper Guinea**" also known as "**Negroland**". The **Sao Tome Island** is the most South Island in the Bight of Biafra. The small island of "**Principe**" is north of Sao Tome. Above "**Principe**" is **Equatorial Guinea**. To the right is the African country of **Gabon**. Since we know people can swim and make boats to get from an island to the mainland, we can assume that the Black Israelites inhabitants of these Islands made their way **Gabon, Cameroon, Angola and the Congo**. So could there still be evidence of these exiled "Black Jews" from Portugal today in Nigeria?

Fact: *In 2016, I talked to a Nigerian Pastor in Detroit who was half-Yoruba/half-Igbo and he acknowledged that there were a community of Black Jews in Yorubaland who were considered "**strange**" by everyone else because they practiced a "**different religion**" with "**different customs**" than the majority of people in Yorubaland (which is either Muslim or Christian). He said that they tell people whenever they ask about their "strange customs", that they are descendants of the Jews in Iberia who were exiled some 500 years ago. What is even more interesting that I found out is that these Black Jews living in Yorubaland known as the "**Bnai Ephraim**" have the same Y-DNA "**E1b1a**" as the other people in Nigeria (**Igbo, Yoruba, including African-Americans etc.**).*

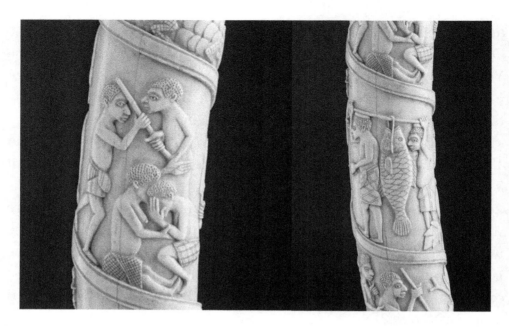

(**Above**) Ancient staff from **Gabon**, Africa. As you can tell by looking at the staff the people of Gabon where black people. They also were good fishermen as were the Cameroonian people who lived to the North of them. Different travelers came through the western coast of Gabon which in Ancient times was the "**Kingdom of Loango**". Here is what one traveler had to say:

"A fact worthy the attention of travelers is, that, according to Oldendorp, The Kingdom of Loango contains Black Jews, scattered throughout the country; they are despised by the Negroes who do not even want to eat with them; they are occupied in trade, **and keep the Sabbath so strictly that they do not even converse on that day**; they have a separate burying ground, very far from any habitation. **The tombs are constructed with masonry, and ornamented with Hebrew inscriptions**..."

How is this possible? How are Black so-called "Africans" in Gabon practicing Jewish customs with the knowledge of the language of "Hebrew"? Did anybody teach them this? Did they attend "Hebrew Schools" staffed by Ashkenazi Jews? The answer is **NO**! Someone clearly has some explaining to do.

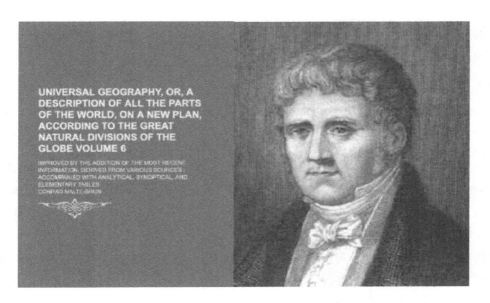

UNIVERSAL GEOGRAPHY, OR, A
DESCRIPTION OF ALL THE PARTS
OF THE WORLD, ON A NEW PLAN,
ACCORDING TO THE GREAT
NATURAL DIVISIONS OF THE
GLOBE VOLUME 6

IMPROVED BY THE ADDITION OF THE MOST RECENT
INFORMATION, DERIVED FROM VARIOUS SOURCES;
ACCOMPANIED WITH ANALYTICAL, SYNOPTICAL, AND
ELEMENTARY TABLES
CONRAD MALTE-BRUN

(**Above**) **Conrad Malte-Brun** was a Dutch-French geographer and journalist who wrote about his travels in Africa. He noted that there were many Black Jews in the coast of West/Central Africa, most notably the "**Kingdom of Loango**" in **Gabon**. He lived from **1755-1826 A.D.**

In his book he quotes the following:

"M. Ehr mann, finding it impossible to explain the origin of these Jews, doubts the reality of the fact; Busching, however, Michaelis, and Zimmermann, do not hesitate to admit their existence; Bruns considers them as descendants of the Falashas of Habesh (West Coast of Arabia), or Abyssinia (Ethiopia); and **Sprengel wishes them to be considered as the DESCENDANTS OF PORTUGUESE JEWS BANISHED IN 1492, who, having quitted their country, are no longer afraid to profess openly the religion (Judaism) of their fathers.**"

"A system of universal geography: or A description of all the parts of the world, on a New Plan, According to the Great Natural Division of the Globe." *By Conrad Malte-Brun, Jean-Jacques-Nicolas Huot, PG 101.*

11

Fact: *The "Habesha" people today mostly consist of* **Amharas** *and* **Tigrayans** *in* **Ethiopia/Eritrea**.

Here is more attestation that the Blacks in Gabon off the Loango Coast were considered to be Hebrew Israelites. This time by European Jewish people themselves!

"It is stated that the Falashas (of Ethiopia) are not the only Jews of the **Negro race**. Bastian speaks of Negro Jews living on the Loango Coast in Western Africa. They are called there "**Mavambu**" or "**Judeos**". "They are, on the whole, a fair looking race," says Bastian. "They are more serious and restrained than the rest of the negroes. **Although in other places they are despised, here they take a dominating position**, or at least such as to be respected and partly even feared, because they are rich and have most of the commerce in their hands." The same author claims that though they are of the Negro race, still he detected Semitic facial features in their physiognomies. **Even in Madagascar a traveler has discovered Jews**. Sibree mentions that in **Ambohipeno**, on the east coast of that island, he met natives who called themselves "**Zafy Ibrahim**," or descendants of Abraham, and who claim to be altogether Jews. "But I could not detect any difference in colour, features, or dialect between them and the other people of the eastern coast," comments the author.

Jews, Race and Environment, by Maurice Fishberg. Pg. 149.

But wait! There is more.

(**Above**) Ancient King of Loango Kingdom, Gabon.

"Oldenthorp, a missionary in the Kingdom of Loango, on the western coast of Africa, says, **that many Jews are settled in that country, who retain still their religious rites, and keep themselves distinct from other nations. Though separated in this manner from the African population, they are quite black, and resemble the other Negroes in every respect as to physical character**. It must be admitted that these variations in the Jewish people from the blue eyes and flaxen (straight) hair of Germany, to the dark complexion of **Cochin** (Jews of Kerala, South India) and **Loango** (Gabon), have a most important bearing upon the present question. Another instance of this influence of climate is afforded us in the changes which have taken place in the Hindoos (Indians).

The Dublin Review, Vol 19 (September 1845) Part 2, pg. 86. edited by Nicolas Patrick Wiseman.

AGAIN, here is the big question. Why would the "**White Portuguese**" people exile so-called White "**Sephardic Jews**" to an African Island off the coast of Nigeria, Cameroon, Gabon and Equatorial Guinea? If this is the case, we should see nothing but Sephardic Jews on the Island of

Sao Tome and if not we should see overwhelming "**Sephardic**" Jewish DNA passed down to their descendants that might be still living on the Island. But unfortunately there is no evidence of white Sephardic Jews ever being there. There is no **Paternal DNA** or **Maternal mtDNA** found in the black people of Sao Tome to suggest that at one time they were all Sephardic Jews. As you will read further in the book, even if White Sephardic Jewish men intermarried or raped Black African women living on the island of Sao Tome, their "**Y-DNA**" mark would be imprinted in the DNA of these mulatto children, even if these mulatto children started marrying **only** "black people" in the following generations.

So is there more evidence that the Original Jews were Black in Ancient Africa? But of course!

The Jews of the "**Bilad al-Sudan**" are currently West Africans whose ancestors were connected to the known "**Black Jewish**" communities located in the Middle East (Yemen), North Africa, or Iberia (Spain/Portugal). Numerous historical records attest to their presence 500-1,700 years ago in the Ancient Ghana, Mali and Songhai Empires.

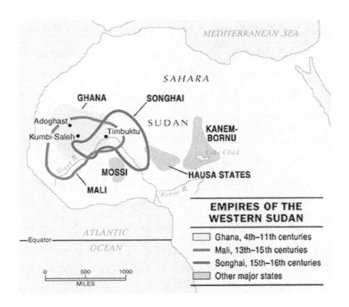

(**Above**) Map of the Ancient Israelite Empires (Ghana, Mali, Songhai).

In Ancient times the territory of the Ghana Empire (300 A.D.-1000 A.D.), Mali Empire (1200 A.D.-1400 A.D.) and Songhai Empire (1400 A.D.-1500 A.D.) was known by the Arabs as "**Bilad al-Sudan**" which means in Arabic, "**Land of the Blacks**". Before this it was nicknamed, "**So-Yuda**" or "**Land of Judah**". The Black Jews from Spain, Portugal and Morocco formed colonies in Senegal, Gambia, Guinea Bissau and the Cape Verde Islands. The Black and White Arabs knew from oral passed down history that the Ten Tribes of Israel were also driven into Africa after the Assyrian Invasion in 700 B.C. Others were driven into Arabia (**Habesha Falashas, Lemba Jews, etc.**) while others traveled further East from Assyria, Syria and Medes/Persia into Asia (**these are your so called "Indians" or Mongloid-looking people**). The Arabs and Jews believed that the famous "**River Sambation**" was also in Africa. Sambation was a place that the descendants of Moses (**Levites/Aaronites**) were supposed to have lived in peace separated by a "**Supernatural**" river/creek that supposedly stopped flowing/babbling every Sabbath day.

Fact: *The Hausa Nigerians (**Northeast Nigerian Muslims**) at one point were ruled under the **Sokoto Caliphate**, led by Black Muslim leader **Sultan***

15

Mohammed Bello. *Mohammed* *kept records stating that the people living in the territory of the Ancient West Africa Empires (**Ghana, Mali, Songhai**) were Hebrew Israelites before the Muslims (under "**Askia Muhammad**") changed up the scene and religion. These Israelites were also known as the **Towrood/Taurud** people and the **Soninke people** (also called Sarankaly/Sarankali). The Soninke people and Songhai people with their dialects can still be seen today in **Mandinka** people (**including the Bambara tribe**), which are a branch of the **Mende** people of the area now known as Mali, Senegal-Gambia, Guinea Bissau, Ghana, Burkina Faso, Mauritania and the Ivory Coast. Today only about 1 million Soninke people are left. They were one of the first Israelites deceived to accept Islam many years ago in West Africa. The **Fulani/Fulbe Tribe in West Africa** were also one of the first people in Africa to convert to Islam. It is believed by Ancient Arabs, that the **Fulani were half-Israelites/half-Shemitic Arabs**. When the Ancient Ghana empires ended many of these Soninke people dispersed to "**Wangara**" which is now "**Nigeria**".*

The land of Wangara is to the East of Lam-Lem. This would be East Nigeria or Igboland. Southwest Nigeria would be Yorubaland. Northwest Nigeria would be Fulani Territory.

Many Africans from Senegal/Gambia are from the Wolof or Mandika/Mandingo Tribe. **They all know about the Soninke and Songhay people in their area, which whom they lived amongst**

(Senegal, Gambia, Guinea, Mauritania, Mali). The Soninke and Towrood/Taurud people claimed to have come from the area between the **Nile River** and the "**Great River**" aka "**The Euphrates**". This was also known by the 2nd Sultan of the Sokoto Nigerian Caliphate, Muslim ruler **Mohammed Bello** (ruled north Nigeria from 1815 A.D. to 1837 A.D.). Mohammed Bello quoted himself in writing through a man named **Hugh Clapperton**:

"**The Towrood or Taurud people, it is said, were originally Jews**, others say Christians; that they came from the land between the two rivers, the Nile and the Euphrates, **and established themselves next to the Jews who inhabited the Cape Verde Islands**; and that whenever they oppressed or encroached upon the Jews, the latter had always recourse (help) to the protection of the officers of the Sehabat (the immediate friends and officers of Mohammed Bello), who then ruled over them.
Journal of a Second Expedition into the Interior of Africa, from the Bight of Benin to Soccatoo, 1829. London: Forgotten Books.

In this book it also states:

"The **Kingdom of Malee (Mali-Guinea)** is an ancient flourishing country, and comprises two other provinces: one is **Bambara**, which contains rivers, woods, sands, a gold mine, and is occupied by the Soodan, who are still infidels, and possess great power; the other, on the west of it, is **Foota**, which is inhabited by the **Towrood, and the Sarankali (Soninke), or Persians.**"

In the translation of the word "**Persians**" in this 1800's text it is found that the word actually used is "**ajam**" which in Arabia was used by Black Arabs to define those who were viewed as "**alien**" or "**outsiders**". These "outsiders" practiced a different religion with different customs (Jewish customs). This most often was the Jews, such as the Jews that came from Arabia to Yemen and from Yemen crossed over into the Horn of Africa (**Ethiopia, Somalia, Kenya**). This is why most Bantus Kenyans and Tanzanians claim their ancestors came from Northeast

Africa, including Ethiopia. The **Lemba Jews** that lived in **Sana'a/Saan'a**, an area in Yemen were eventually harassed by the Arabs and forced to leave Yemen into Ethiopia. Some stayed in Ethiopia known as "**Falashas**" while others traveled down the East coast of Africa all the way down to South Africa (**Zimbabwe, Malawi, Mozambique**). The Lembas story is also similar to the history of the initial founders of the Ghana, Mali and Songhai Empires who were also Black Jews who crossed over from Yemen in Africa.

Fact: *The **Soninke-Sarankali (Israelite)** people still practice **circumcision** today and call it "**birou**". They eventually left the Mali Empire and settled in the fertile lands of the Niger River. The Soninke people, like Gambian Mandingo Tribesmen are a sub-sect of the **Mende Tribe** who all carry the same Y DNA "E1b1a", just like Ghanaians, Nigerians and African-Americans. The **Soninke-Sarankali Tribe** today live in Burkina Faso, the Ivory Coast, Mali, Mauritania, Senegal, Gambia, Ghana, and Guinea-Bissau. Their Y-DNA ranges from "E1b1a" to "R1b". **The most common Y-DNA of Latinos today is "R1b".** Later in the Book, I will explain why many Western Europeans in Spain, Portugal, Wales, Scotland, and Ireland also carry a sub-group of the "R1b". It will indeed give you a "shock". The Bambara people of Mali, Guinea and most Senegalese Wolof/Mandingos are also carriers of the **Y DNA "E1b1a".***

(**Left**) Map of Songhai Empire. (**Right**) Ismael Diadie Haidara is an author, historian and overseer of the "**Kati Manuscripts**" which have belonged to his family (**Kati Tribe**) for centuries. The Kati collection contains over 12,000 manuscripts written by Arabs and Jews (Israelites). Among his notable manuscripts is the "**Tarikh al-fattash**", which talks about the Israelite Songhai Empire in West Africa.

Fact: *In 1853 the German scholar and explorer **Heinrich Barth** visited Timbuktu on behalf of the British government. During his stay he consulted a copy of the "**Tarikh al-Sudan" and the "Tarikh al-fattash"** in his investigation of the history of the **Songhay Hebrew Israelite empire.** The Tarikh al-Sudan and The Tarikh al-fattash are West African chronicles written in Arabic in the second half of the 17th century. It provides an account of the Hebrew Kingdom called Songhay from the reign of **Za el Yemeni** the First ruler 300 A.D to Sonni Ali (ruled 1464-1492 A.D) up to the down fall to the Arabs in 1599 with a few references to events in the following century. According to records such as the **Tarikh al-Sudan and Tarikh al-fattash** the first recorded **HEBREW** presence in West Africa may have occurred with the arrival of the first Za ruler of Koukiya and his brother, located near the Niger River. He was known as **Za el Yemeni (also Zuwu Alyaman) which means "He comes from Yemen"**. History states that **Za el Yemeni** came to Kukiya about 300 A.D.; an ancient abode of the Songhai tribe. He established a line of kings known as the Za, Dja, or the Dia Dynasty. This founder of the first **Soudanic Dynasty** in Western Africa was a Black Hebrew man. The **Tarikh al-Sudan**, states that there were 14 Za rulers of Koukiya after Za el Yemeni before the rise of Islam in the region. In the Tarikh*

19

*al-fattash it also describes a Hebrew community called the "**Bani Israel**" that existed around the 1400's A.D. in Tirdirma, Mali along the Niger River.*

So how do we know that these Hebrews from Yemen were related to Negroes? Let's look at the Genetic Composition of the people in Yemen and the Lemba Jews who lived in Yemen until crossing over into the Horn of Africa. But first, we need a basic introduction lesson to genetics to understand. (I also break this down further in the Book "Hebrews to Negroes 2: Volume 3").

CHAPTER 2

DNA EXPLAINED 101: Y-DNA (PATERNAL), MITOCHONDRIAL DNA (MATERNAL) AND AUTOSOMAL DNA.

autosomes   sex chromosomes

Every human being has 23 pairs of chromosomes. We have 22 pairs of Autosomal chromosomes and 1 pair of Sex chromosomes. Our chromosomes are the blueprint for our DNA, which makes us who we are, from the number of fingers we have on each hand to our skin color. For each pair of chromosomes, 1 chromosome comes from our mother and 1 chromosome comes from our father. Humans have 22 pairs of "autosomal chromosomes". The final "23rd" pair is our "Sex Chromosome". All men have an "X" and a "Y" sex chromosome. Women only have an "X" chromosome. If "mad scientists" ever tried to make man out of using the DNA of woman, they couldn't do it because the woman lacks the sex chromosome "Y" which makes babies male and not female. This is likely the reason why God made Adam first and then made woman (Eve) out of his rib. Adam's rib contained his DNA which included his Autosomal chromosomes and his Sex chromosome "XY", which had the building blocks to make male and female. This is the reason why human beings did not start with the woman. God made man first "In his image" for a reason. Now because only men carry the "Y" Chromosome, a man only inherits his father's Y chromosome "**unmixed with his mother's DNA**". The only thing a man (and a woman) inherits from their mother is an "X" chromosome (i.e. X**X-female,** XY-male). With the help of our father's last name or slave master's last name (aka surname) we can use "Y-Paternal DNA testing" to trace back our lineage/ancestors to a certain time period and figure out where our ancestors come from. In the case of African-Americans and Caribbean Blacks because of slavery, the surname/last name of our ancestors from the 1400's to the 1800's obviously will have a change. This is why most Genetic DNA testing companies cannot tell a person with 100% accuracy what tribe they are from, especially past the year 1000 A.D. when it is said that traditional surnames/last names (i.e. Smith, Johnson, Kelly) didn't exist. In theory, African-Americans paternal line should consist of more "Black" fathers than "White" fathers if they were to go back in time, prior to the slave trades. Before the Europeans came to West Africa to enslave black people, the paternal lineage of West Africans going back 20 generations (i.e. 300-500 years) would most likely be Black.

PATERNAL Y-DNA TESTS

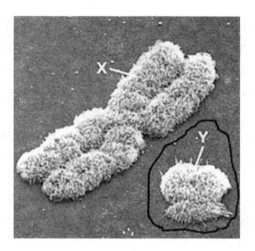

(Above) This is what our **sex chromosomes** look like under an electron microscope. As you can see the male "**Y**" Sex Chromosome is very small compared to the "**X**" Sex Chromosome which both man and woman share.

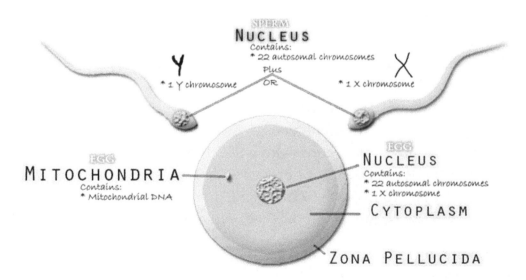

(Above) The nucleus of a man's sperm can only carry a "**Y**" sex chromosome or an "**X**" sex chromosome. The nucleus of every woman's eggs on the planet have **ONLY** a "**X**" sex chromosome. So if a sperm carrying a "**Y**" sex chromosome fertilizes an egg the sex of the child will end up being a **boy**. If a sperm carrying a "**X**" sex chromosome fertilizes an egg the sex of the child will end up being a **girl**. **Y-DNA** testing **ONLY** tests the male "**Y**" sex chromosome following the **PATERNAL** line of your father, and his father, and his father, and so on. It **DOES NOT** test your grandfather on your mother's side or the paternal line through your mother's side of the family. So in essence, as far back as geneticists can go, that beginning man, be him **white or black** leaves his "**genetic mark**" on **ALL** the son's that come after him, even if that beginning man was the **ONLY** "white-appearing man" on the family tree going back 10-20 generations. This "genetic mark" **ONLY** changes when for instance an invading group of men (**Hebrews, Egyptians, Arab Ishmaelite's**) appear on the scene and start having kids with foreign women (**i.e. as in Europe**). Then these men (**Hebrews, Egyptians, Arab Ishmaelite's**) will set their "**genetic Y-DNA mark**" on every son that is born from that point on.

Note: This **DOES NOT** mean that after 2,000 years of race mixing that all the offspring from one man can still be labeled as "Hebrew", "Egyptian" or "Arab Ishmaelite" for instance because of their Y-DNA "genetic mark" which can be seen in the **Y-Haplogroup R**. For this reason, I believe that Haplogroups (Y-DNA/mtDNA) reveal migratory (**travel**) patterns of different people groups which can be used to determine "**who is who**" and "**who is NOT who**". This is one of the **MOST IMPORTANT** things I had to understand when studying the different Haplogroups of the world in relation to the question, "**Where are the Hebrew Israelites**"? This I will explain later.

Paternal Y-DNA testing using Family Tree research of Surnames can sometimes go back as far as 10 generations (200-300 years) to find a common ancestor or country you are from. Using the biological sample (cheek/saliva swab) of your oldest living grand-parent may help you trace your ancestry further back in time using DNA testing + Surnames but most standard DNA tests cannot trace an ancestor match/tribe with "**pinpoint**" accuracy from over 1,000 years ago. Part of the reasoning behind this is that don't have the "**Physical Dead Bodies/Mummified Skeletons**" of Ancient peoples such as the Levites, the Children of Judah, the Children of Ephraim, the Ishmaelite's, the Joktanites, the Moabites, the Ammonites, the Canaanites, the Chaldeans, or even the Priestly Aaronites.

Note: This is why it is **IMPOSSIBLE** *for anyone to claim that genetic studies can prove they are descendants of the Aaronite High Priests in the Bible from over 2,400 years ago (**i.e. the European Jews and their famous Cohen Model Haplogroup theory**).*

Since we are on the topic of DNA testing, one should know that some Y-DNA tests will tell you your "**predicted**" Haplogroup while others will tell you your "**actual**" Haplogroup. This depends on "**STR's (short-tandem repeats)**" which are "**less specific**" in determining "**actual/factual**" Haplogroup placements and "**SNP (Single-Nucleotide Polymorphism)**" markers which are "**more specific**" in determining which DNA Haplogroup we fall into. When Geneticists use the word "**Haplogroup**" they simply mean the "**people groups**" of the entire world who are related (**i.e. Native American Haplogroups, Asian Haplogroups, African Haplogroups, Arab Haplogroups, European Haplogroups**). This I will explain further.

SHORT TANDEM REPEATS (STR'S)

TGTGTTGTTGTTGTTGTTGTTGTTGTTGTTGTTGTTGTTGAC

(**Above**) This is an example of a "**Short Tandem Repeat**" or "**STR**".

Short Tandem Repeats are the most common way DNA tests tell us who we are related to. Most DNA tests use a **12-marker STR test**. So for instance on a person's Chromosome there are different locations/positions which are called in the scientific world a "**gene locus**". "**Alleles**" are variants of **DNA sequences (like the STR segment above)** on specific positions (**loci**) on a chromosome. The human genome is full of "**repeated**" DNA sequences. These repeated DNA sequences can be **very long** or **short**. Short Tandem Repeats are "**short sequences**" of DNA Nucleotide Bases (**Cytosine-C, Guanine-G, Thymine-T, Adenine-T**) which are "repeated" numerous times. DNA testing is easier if these "repeats" are not too long. The repeated "**TGTGTT...**" above is an example of a form of "**DNA sequence**" that could easily be the trait for "**Brown eyes**" or something else. Multiple "**short sequences**" are grouped together in "**alleles**" which are found on different positions (**loci**) located on a particular Chromosomes (numbered from 1 to 23). For instance, in the Genetic world, "**D7S280**" is a specific "loci-position" found on **Chromosome 7**.

SINGLE NUCLEOTIDE POLYMORPHISMS (SNP'S)

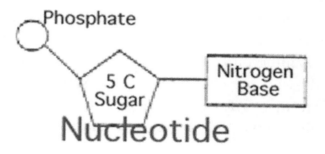

(**Left**) DNA double-helix consists of a sugar (deoxyribose), a phosphate backbone and different pairs of nitrogenous bases (**Cytosine-C**), (**Thymine-T**), (**Adenine-A**), and (**Guanine-G**). Together all of these components are called a **Nucleotide.**

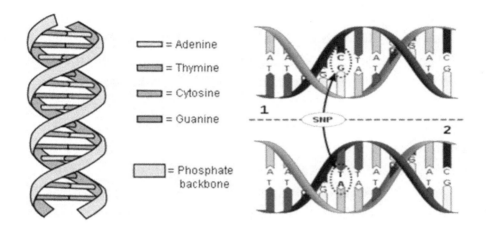

= Adenine	
= Thymine	
= Cytosine	
= Guanine	
= Phosphate backbone	

(Above) **Single Nucleotide Polymorphisms** (SNP's) are "**specific variations**" in a DNA Nucleotide base pair found at specific positions on our human genome that is "**unique**" and seen in only certain select populations.

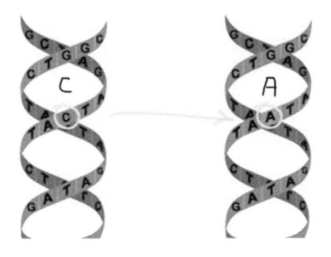

(**Above**) Cell Mutation in our bodies sometimes makes mistakes. This can be equated to "**SNP's**" or **Single Nucleotide Polymorphisms**. In "normal cell division", the Nitrogen Base **Adenine** pairs with **Thymine** and **Cytosine** pairs with **Guanine**. For example, a **SNP** may replace the Nucleotide "**Cytosine-(C)**" with the Nucleotide "**Adenine (A)**" in a certain part of our DNA. This subtle change can make a child's hair "**red**" in a family while everyone else has black hair. SNP's occur normally in everyone's DNA but they can occur as frequent as once in every 300 nucleotides on average, adding up to a possible 10 million SNP's that can be found on the average human genome. Geneticists use these SNP's as "**markers**" to categorize all the people living on the earth into different "**related groups**" called "**Haplogroups**". For instance, the majority of Chinese, Japanese and Filipino people fall under the **Y-DNA Haplogroup** "**O**" based on their similar "**SNP's**". Studies show that "STR's" can be used to "**estimate**" what Haplogroup an individual may fall into, while "SNP's" are used to give us a more definite answer as to what "Haplogroup" we belong to.

Beware though! DNA tests will only reveal information about a small percentage of your human genome (**your DNA blueprint**). If a DNA test goes back **8-10 generations**, there can be as many as **1,024 ancestors** in the Family Tree that over time resulted in making "**You**".

MATERNAL mtDNA TESTS

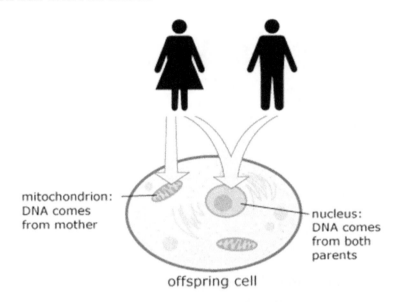

mitochondrion:
DNA comes
from mother

nucleus:
DNA comes
from both
parents

offspring cell

Mitochondrial DNA tests come from the Mitochondria which are the cell's powerhouse to provide the body with energy. The Mitochondria is however outside of the cell's nucleus. For both sexes (male and female), mitochondrial DNA is inherited **ONLY** from the mother. Men inherit the mtDNA from their mother but do not pass it on to their children. Women have their mother's mtDNA and pass it down to both son and daughter. This means that the mothers mtDNA is "**unmixed**" **with the father's genes, therefore allowing a woman to determine** using mtDNA testing if she shares a common maternal ancestor from a certain country or perhaps Tribe.

AUTOSOMAL (NUCLEUS) DNA TESTING

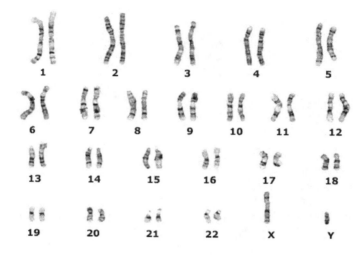

(Above) Our **Autosomal Chromosomes** are listed from **1-22**. The last Chromosome (23rd) is our Sex Chromosome. The Sex Chromosome determines our sex. **MtDNA** and **Y-DNA** testing uses the 23rd Chromosome, not the other 22 remaining Autosomal chromosomes.

Autosomal DNA, X chromosomal DNA, and in males, **Y-chromosomal DNA** are all found in the nucleus of a cell. Autosomal DNA is the rest of your DNA, meaning those other 22 chromosomes inside the cell Nucleus that **ARE NOT "Sex Chromosomes"** or **"Mitochondrial DNA"**. Autosomal DNA gives us traits like our father's nose, our mothers eyes, our fathers skin color, or our father's height. Autosomal DNA takes into account all our other ancestors in the family tree, not just our father, our mother, our grandfather, and our grandmother.

Where do we get our DNA from?

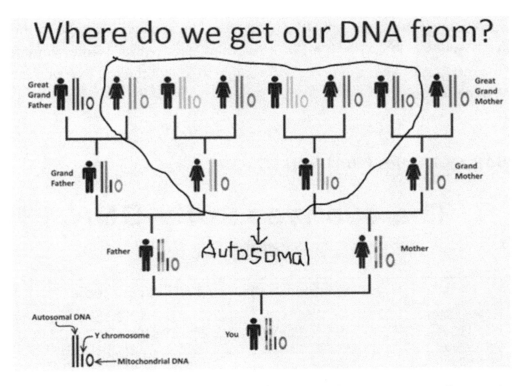

(**Above**) **Autosomal DNA** takes into account "**everyone's**" genetic contribution to "**you**", not just your father, his father or your mother. This is a "**True**" test of how much a "**Person**" is of a certain heritage.

During normal fertilization of a female's egg by a man's sperm and the development of a fetus, we experience a "**watered down**" effect of the ancestral genes as each ancestor's Autosomal DNA gets divided in half with each coming generation on the family tree. Since Autosomal DNA gives us our "**physical appearance**" and "**traits**" through "**random gene expression**" someone who is African-American can have a significant "**European**" presence in their family tree but still end up having a "**dark brown**" skin complexion. This is why a family can appear to change "**Black**" or "**White**" after 3-4 generations depending on if both parents who may be biracial have children who also marry biracial, white or black persons. **This is not the case with Y-DNA or mtDNA. Y-DNA and mtDNA does not change unless there is "outside" race mixing going on.** Meaning if a Black woman marries an Arab man and has sons (the Y-DNA of his sons will change to the Arab man's Y-DNA) or if a Black man has kids with a White woman (the mtDNA of their offspring will change to that of the mtDNA of their White mother).

HAPLOGROUPS, WHAT'S THAT?

The two types of y-DNA test

	STR tests	SNP ('snip') tests		
metaphor:	"individual leaves on a tree"	"branches and twigs"		
used for:	comparing genetic signatures	building phylogenetic tree		
Sequencing	Sanger	Sanger		Next Generation
quantification expressed as	analogue counts of markers	binary e.g. L21+ or L21-		probabilistic quality of base pairs
FTDNA y- tests	12/25/37/67/111 markers	Single SNP	SNP Pack	BigY
use in Surname projects:	main tool	haplogroup confirmation	BigY support	advanced tool
secondary data	haplogroup prediction			STR and mt data

Based on the results of our DNA Tests using "**STR's**" or "**Short-tandem repeats**" or "**SNP's**" or "**Single Nucleotide Polymorphisms-Mutations**", we can be classified into Genetic Haplogroups. **STR's** and **SNP's** are just "**specific markers**" on our DNA that DNA tests look at when comparing our DNA to a huge database of the DNA of all ethnicities to determine what "**Haplogroup**" we "**fit-in**" with. All mankind has been categorized into "**Paternal**" and "**Maternal**" Haplogroups, which basically is like telling us what group of people you come from or are related too. These Haplogroups cannot pin-point our ancestors to say for instance, to the biblical "**Tribe of Dan**" or the "**Tribe of Reuben**". Prior to 1999, finding this information out about what "Haplogroup" we belong too was not possible. Jewish descent, **Bennett Greenspan** founded "**Family Tree DNA**" in 2000 and allowed the public to have access to finding out their **DNA Haplogroups**. Mysteriously, around this time a study was also done at the University of Arizona, which Jews claim proved that they were the descendants of the Israelites, more specifically, the Priestly tribe of Levi (Aaron). This is what the Jews call the "**Cohen Model Haplogroup**". People specializing in "Population movement patterns" called "**Population geneticists**" use these types of DNA evidence (i.e. Haplogroups) to predict how and when groups of people migrated. For instance, they can predict that the Haplogroup, "**E1b1a**" which is specific for "**Bantus Africans**" migrated from Israel/Canaan (Northeast Africa) into Arabia and different parts of Africa. They can predict the route pattern the ancestors of the "**Native Indians**" came from to get to the "**New World**" or the "**Caribbean**".

So now that we have gone over the "basics" of Genetics and DNA testing, let's move further to look at groups of people (White, Black, Arab) who claim to be Jews/Israelites. Using **DNA testing**, the **Bible**, knowledge of **Ancient history** and "**Critical Thinking**" we should be able to make an "educated guess" as to who is Israel and who is not. After all, if Europeans, Arabs, Asians and Indians can claim to be descendants of the Biblical "Children of Israel", why can't blacks claim the same heritage?

CHAPTER 3

THE LEMBA-YEMEN CONNECTION TO THE "BANTUS NEGRO PEOPLE", THE BLACK ARAB ISHMAELITES AND THE SHEMITES.

Genetic studies on regular Yemeni people have shown that they carry a small percentage of DNA influence from Sub-Saharan "**Bantus**" people. The Yemeni women exhibit mostly **L0, L1, L2, L3, L4, L6** but have a higher amount of a "newer" **L6** maternal mtDNA group. The mtDNA "**L**" Haplogroup is typically only seen in the "**Bantus**" people of Africa. Ethiopian women also exhibit maternal DNA (mtDNA) in the "**L**" group (**mostly L2a**) but they also exhibit mtDNA "**M**" which is seen in South Arabians and Near East people. Yes, the Near East! **Maternal mtDNA "M" is seen in high frequencies in India, Bangladesh, Sri Lanka, China, Japan, Nepal, Tibet and some populations in Siberia + the Americas**). So here we see a "**potential**" migration pattern of people that left Northeast Africa (**i.e. Israel**) who over time migrated through the Middle East and Asia, eventually ending up in the Americas. Could this be the "**Missing Link**" to the migratory pattern of the 10 Northern Tribes of Israel lead by "**Ephraim**"? It is a known fact that the mtDNA "**L3**" is the ancestor of the mtDNA "**M**". The most common mtDNA in West Africans (**i.e. Nigeria, Ghana, Cameroon, Congo**) and African-Americans is "**L3**".

Scientists call this the "**Out of Africa**" theory but also state these finding of mtDNA "**M**" is due to the mixture of Ethiopians with other invading nations from the East (Arabs), the migration of people from Northeast Africa (i.e. Israel) and also the East African "Arab" Slave trade which normally took more women than men at a ratio of 2:1.

Source: "Ethiopian Mitochondrial DNA Heritage: Tracking Gene Flow Across and Around the Gate of Tears.", *American Journal of Human Genetics. (Nov 2004), 75(5), pg. 725-770.*

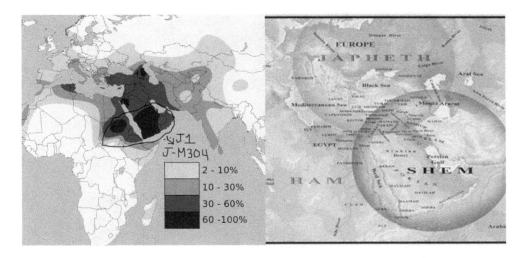

(**Left**) Map of the occurrence (**in frequencies**) of the **Y-DNA J1 gene** (**Haplogroup**). It is believed that the **J1 gene** is a "**Semitic**" gene and could possibly represent a "**marker**" for the **Ancient Arab Ishmaelite's, the Moabites, the Ammonites, the Sons of Keturah or the Sons of Joktan**. It is a known fact that as we get closer to South Arabia, Yemen, Oman and Qatar we see darker, more "**Black**" appearing Arabs, or just straight looking "**Black Arabs**" altogether. This is because the original Arab Ishmaelite's, Sons of Keturah and Shemites (**Children of Shem**) were Black. They had for the most part wooly hair or soft curly hair. (**Right**) Map of where most of Shem's descendants lived in Biblical times with the exception of **Lud (Western Turkey)**. The highest frequency/carriers of the J1 gene are in South Arabia, Yemen, Oman, Qatar, the Black Bedouin Tribes of the Negev Desert in South Israel, the Black Bedouin Arabs in Jordan, and the Amhara/Tigray Ethiopians. To a lesser extent (30% and less) you will see this J1 gene in Palestinians, Iraqis, Ashkenazi, Sephardic Jews and some North African Arabs. It's oldest form, "**J-M304**" is seen in the Black Lemba Jews of South Africa, Yemenites, Omanis and Qataris.

(**Above**) **Lemba Jews of South Africa** who claim to be Israelites who left Israel around 700 B.C. to 500 B.C. around the times of the Assyrian and Babylonian invasion of Israel. The escaped into Arabia, making their way into South Arabia and then into Yemen in a city called "**Sana'a/Senna**". They claim to have not mixed with other African tribes or Arabs living amongst them as it goes against their Jewish customs. But yet it was found that the Lemba Jews have a significant amount of Bantus Negro "**E-M2/E1b1a**" **DNA** in their genetic make-up (**roughly about half**). The other half of the Lemba Jews DNA is "**J1c**". Now here is where it gets interesting. The Lemba Jews claim that they did not mix with any of the other Africans (including the Bantus Africans) when they crossed the over the Gulf of Aden/Red Sea into Ethiopia (Horn of Africa). Eventually they settled into Zimbabwe and supposedly were responsible for the ancient "**Great Zimbabwe City**" centuries ago. The Lemba Jews are also found **in South Africa (Limpopo Province), Malawi, Botswana, and Mozambique**. Despite practicing Jewish customs they still speak a "**Bantus**" language that is found among the Shona people, the Venda people and the Kalanga people (Zimbabwe/Botswana). But where did the Lemba Jews get their "**E-M2/E1b1a**" Bantus gene if they didn't mix with the "locals"? It is a known fact that the majority of regular Yemeni people (including

Yemenite Jews) carry the Y DNA "**J1c**". So what "**sets apart**" the Yemeni Jews from the regular Yemeni Arabs if they both fall into the "J1c" Y-DNA Haplogroup? The only other place with higher number of "J1c"carriers per population is the Black Arab Africans in **Khartoum, Sudan**. Just about every last one of them is brown-black just like their other African neighbors. So what happened and why is the Negro "**E-M2/E1b1a**" gene still seen in small frequencies in Yemen? Is this the result of the Arab East African Slave Trade or perhaps these are Hebrew Israelites that left Israel for Arabia during the Assyrian/Babylonian Invasions in B.C. times. We know according to old Arab historians the Hebrew Israelites that scattered into Arabia were the "minority" amongst the Black Arabs. We also know that they traditionally kept to themselves, often hiding from the Black Muslim Arabs. When the Black Muslim Arabs began to terrorize and cause problems for the Black Jews during the the early beginnings of Islam (**i.e. Battle of Khaybar**) in Arabia/Yemen, the Israelites had to move or continue to be persecuted. Of course when the Arabs attacked the living areas of the Jews, they killed the men, taking the Black Israelite women and children for spoil. This is most likely where the Black Arab "**J1c**" gene was introduced into the community of Lemba Jews while they were in Arabia and Yemen. This unfortunate outcome would cause the the Lembas to be essentially a people of "**Israelite-Arab Shemitic**" ancestry.

Many Arabs from Yemen even theorized that the Lemba Jews were really "**Black Arabs**" or the Semitic "**Sons of Joktan**" from the Arab customs they practiced along with Hebrew customs. Now it is also a known fact that Sudan was a hot-spot for invasion by the Black Arabs during the early "**Westward**" Islamic conquest of Judea, Egypt, Libya, Tunisia, Algeria, Morocco, including parts of North Sudan which is below Egypt in Nubia Territory as the capital city of Nubia was **Meroe, Sudan** in ancient times.

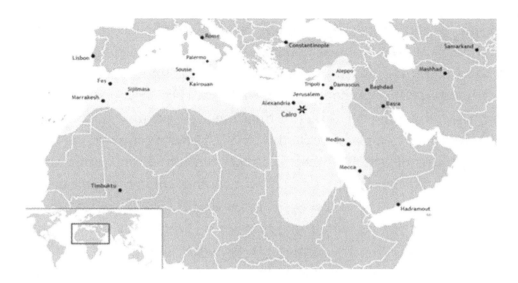

(**Above**) The Black Arab "**Umayyad Caliphate**" took over **Judea-Israel, West Arabia, Egypt, Sudan, Nubia and the rest of North Africa** (i.e. the light shaded area on the map) shortly after the creation of "**Islam**" by Muhammad and his wife **Khadi-YAH**. The Black Arabs were victorius over the White Roman "**Byzantime Empire**" who ruled much of this area prior to the rise of Islam. During the wave of the Black "**Ishmaelite**" Arab conquests through North Africa, they recruited Black Libyan Phuttites and some Black Hebrew Israelites. They would collectively be known as the "**Moors**" who would eventually conquer Spain/Portugal and parts of Western Europe from around 700 A.D. to **1492 A.D.**, when the White Catholic Church banished the Moors along with the Black Israelites from Europe.

During the beginnings of Islam in the 7th Century A.D. the first Black Arab Islamic Caliphate to take over the Judea, the Middle East, Persia and North Africa was the "**Umayyad Caliphate (661 A.D.-750 A.D.)**". The next was the "**Abbasid Caliphate (750 A.D.-1250 A.D.)**". By the latter part of the 1000's A.D. the "White" Non-Black Ishmaelite Arabs were in power changing the face of the Middle East lighter. During the "**Fatimid Caliphate (909 A.D.-1171 A.D.)**" the Black and White Muslims invaded North Sudan, with the **Black Arab men** bringing their "**J1c**" gene with them. Prior to this Africa didn't have the "J1c" present in its land except for maybe in Ethiopia (**because of their mixture with the Semitic Sabaeans who dwelt among the Black Arabs in Arabia**). The majority of Africa at this time was flooded with **Hebrew Israelites** carrying the "E" Y DNA Haplogroup. The reason why the Lemba Jews had half of their men test positive for the Bantus "**E-M2/E1b1a**" gene is because the "**E-M2/E1b1a**" gene was carried by small groups of Israelites that had scattered into Arabia after leaving Israel. The Black Israelites were obviously the "minority" amongst the Black Arab "J1c" carriers because Arabia is still for the most part a "J1" Haplogroup-carrying country. The Black Arabs that were there in Arabia/Arabia Felix (aka. Yemen) in the beginning passed their "J1c" gene down though women into the male seed. So even if the Black Arab had sons from a light-skinned Arab woman or a White woman, their light-skinned or dark-skinned son would still carry the "J1c" gene. The Y-DNA "J1" Haplogroup would still persist in the Middle East, Arabia, Yemen and the Negev Desert (South Israel) even after the invasion by " White Japhetic Arab Turks/Kurds". So even though we see the J1c strongly (>50% frequency) in the dark-skinned Bedouins of the Negev Desert, the Bedouins of Jordan, in brown-skinned Yemenites and Khartoum Sudanese people we know that Lemba Jews did not originally carry the "J1c" gene when they left Israel. Reason being is that the "E-M2/E1b1a" gene is not typically found in Arabia. It is found mainly in Africa where most of the Bantus Hebrew Israelites were scattered at. Africa is the continent where a great number of Israelites scattered into after leaving Israel. The others scattered to the "East", never returning back to Africa or Israel.

Fact: *The Bedouin Black Arabs like the **Tarabin-Azazme Bedouin Tribe**, with their leader, "**Uncle Abu Awaad**" prove in the short-film documentary "**Secrets of the Desert**" by filmmaker **Stephen Graham** that the Ancient Hebrews, which their forefathers knew of, **WERE BLACK**! In the documentary they talk about the "**Battle of Auja al-Hafir**" aka the "**Battle of Auja**" in 1948 which displaced the "former residents" of the land into Arabia and Egypt. The City Auja al-Hafir was an old road that was near water* *wells. The land here was the grazing land for the Azazme Bedouin tribe. The documentary proves that the "Black Ishamelite Arabs" in Negev, South Israel were the original inhabitants of the area before the British and European Jews came on boats. After the creation of the State of Israel in 1948, many of the Black Tarabin Tribes had to leave their land, their homes and families to seek refuge in Jordan, Egypt and Iraq. During the documentary, Sheikh Aied provides further proof that the original Arabs of the Middle East, including the Hebrew Israelites of old, were Black.*

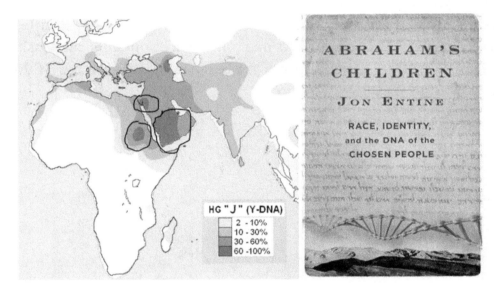

(**Above**) Is the science of "**DNA**" proving the European Jews to be "**imposters**" and not the "Real" Blood DNA descendants of the original Israelites aka "**The Chosen People?**". On the above map, it is easy to see that the **Y-DNA J1c** frequencies is highest in the people living in Khartoum, Sudan, South Arabia, Yemen, Qatar, Oman and Negev Desert, Israel. But even though these nations carry the infamous "**Cohen Model Haplogroup-CMH J1c gene**" they all don't go around calling themselves "**Jews**" from the Priestly Tribe of Levi (Aaron). What lies are we being fed? The "**J1c**" gene does not make you an "**Israelite**".

So we know the people in Khartoum (Sudan), Yemen, Negev Desert (South Israel) and Saudi Arabia do not all profess to be "Jews" despite them all carrying the Y DNA Haplogroup "J1c". However, the Ashkenazi Jews claim that the Y-DNA "J1" (**more specifically the J1c-J1e**) gene makes them Jews, and even more, the descendants of Aaron, the brother of Moses from the Tribe of Levi. They call this gene the "**Cohen Model Haplogroup**". Prior to the year 2000, they had no clue about this "J1c" gene and was not using it to defend their "Jewishness". However, the Ashkenazi Jews genetic make up is **<30% Y-DNA "J1"**. The other 60-65% is European and the majority left is "**Edomite DNA**". Yes, "Edomite DNA". This means that most of the Ashkenazi Jews have mostly European DNA, and only trace amounts of possible "**Semitic**" DNA stemming from Arabia/Arabia Felix or the Middle East.

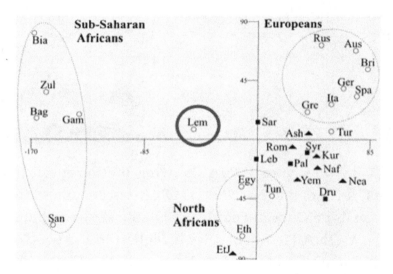

(**Above**) During Genetic studies it was found that the **Lemba Jews** of South Africa fit right "**In the Middle**" when plotted on a graph comparing the Y -DNA chromosomes of Sub-Saharan Africans, Europeans and North Africans. What is interesting is the distance the Lemba Jews (**LEM**) are "**genetically**" from the Bantus "**Mandinka**" Gambians (**GAM**) and Ashkenazi Jews (**ASH**). Based on the graph (**above**), they are in the middle of being Arab-European and Sub-Saharan African (Bantus). But we know the Lembas are Black. The reasons the Lembas exhibit this genetic feature is because "collectively" as a group they are Half-Israelite and, either half-Black Arab Ishmaelite, or perhaps half-the Sons of Joktan/Ammon/Moab.

Fact: *University of Arizona Scientist **Michael Hammer** conducted a study in 2000 proving that Ashkenazi Jews, Sephardic Jews, Middle Eastern Arabs and Europeans were essentially all "**apart**" of the same "**Genetic Cluster**". This means "**genetically**" Arab Middle Easterns, Ashkenazi Jews and Europeans are **ALL BROTHERS**, all having most of their "**genetic stock**" from **Japheth** (Europe).* But the Bible already confirmed this! We just were not paying attention.

Genesis 10:2-5 "The **SONS OF JAPHETH**; Gomer, and Magog, and Madai, and Javan, and Tubal, and Meshech, and Tiras. And the Sons of Gomer, Ashkenaz (**Ashkenazi Jews**), and Riphath (**Turks, Scythians, Balkan people, Sephardic Jews, Ukraine, South Russia**), and Togarmah (**Turks/Kurds/Armenia**).

Note: *Research the Riphatheans-Sarmatians and their connection to the people of the Eurasia (Balkan countries, Ukraine, South Russia, Middle Iran). Herodotus wrote about the Scythians. Paul mentioned these "**Scythians**" in Colossians 3:11 after the word "**Barbarian**" in his famous "**Neither Greek nor Jew**" scripture. Was Paul secretly telling us what "**Gentiles**" were already converts to Judaism during the times of Christ and thus were known at that time as Jews? These people would still be considered "Jews" today...........that is unless someone was to "expose" them as "**Imposters**".*

Colossians 3:11 "Where there is neither **GREEK** nor **JEW**, circumcision nor uncircumcision, **BARBARIAN, SCYTHIAN**, bond nor free: but Christ is all, and in all"

Why did Paul emphasis the word "**Greek**", "**Barbarian**", and "**Scythian**" in this scripture with the word "**Jew**"? We already know the Maccabeans were Greeks. We already know about Hellenistic

43

Judaism. We know that Barbarians back in those days rode horses into battle. This was something that the Turkish and Kurdish Arabs used to do when riding into Judea for **"invasion"** during the **"Crusades"** of the Holy City of Jerusalem. It is a known fact that following the Spanish Inquisition in 1492 (**by King Ferdinand and Queen Isabella**), many of the white Sephardic Jews migrated back into Europe making their way into the Balkan Countries where there was a heavy population of Sephardic Jews.

The **Balkan Countries** are:

- Albania
- Bulgaria
- Bosnia and Herzegovina
- Kosovo
- Macedonia
- Montenegro
- Croatia
- Greece
- Italy
- Serbia
- Slovenia
- Romania
- Turkey

For 450 years (1492-1942) the Sephardic Jews lived in the Balkan Countries and Turkey which were dominated by the Ottoman Empire at the time during Medieval Times. Their most populous cities in the Balkans were **Sarajevo** (10,000 Jews) and **Salonkia/Thessalonkia** (53,000+ Jews). It is reported that by 1940, 150,000 Sephardic Jews lived between Sarajevo and Thessaloniki.

Note: A person **CANNOT** be "**Anti-Semitic**" if the victimized people are not "**Semitic**". The correct term for modern day "Anti-Semitism" is really **"Anti-Japheth-tism."**

So Michael Hammer's study revealed that Arabs and Jews (Sephardic/Ashkenazi) were all related to Europeans. For this reason, many people have now given the Arabs and Jews the name "**Eurasians**". Michael Hammer's study did prove that the Lemba Jews had **WAY MORE** frequencies of the "J1" Haplogroup than most Arabs in the Middle East.

Michael Hammer's 2000 study showed that when a group of Remba/Lemba Jews were tested, almost half of the Lemba/Remba Jews Y-DNA came back positive for "**E-M2**", also known as "**E1b1a**". The other 40-45% of the Lemba/Remba Jews Y-DNA was a mixture of "**J1-M304/M267**" and "**J2-M172**". Even the "**Venda**" people they lived amongst in "**Zimbabwe-South Africa**" tested positive for "**EM2-E1b1a**".

Source:

"**Lemba origins revisited: Tracing the ancestry of Y chromosomes in South African and Zimbabwean Lemba**", *South African Medical Journal, Molecular Genetics. Volume 103, #12, December 2013.*

"**Jewish and Middle Eastern non-Jewish populations share a common pool of Y-chromosome biallelic haplotypes.**" *Proceedings of the National Academy of Sciences. 97:6769-6774. Hammer MF, Redd AJ, Wood ET, Bonner MR, Jarjanazi H, Karafet T, Santachiara-Benerecetti S, Oppenheim A, Jobling MA, Jenkins T, Ostrer H, and B Bonne-Tamir. 2000.*

"**The geographic distribution of human Y chromosome variation. Genetics, 145:787-805**". *Hammer MF, Spurdle AB, Karafet T, Bonner MR, Wood ET, Novelletto A, Malaspina P, Mitchell RJ, Horai S, Jenkins T, and SL Zegura. 1997.*

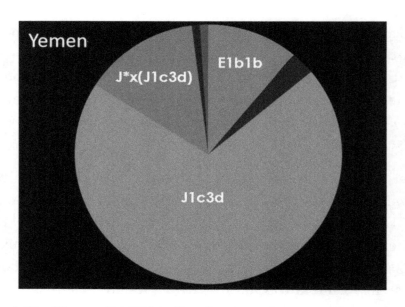

(**Above**) Pie Chart of Y-DNA distribution of **Yemenite Jews**. Notice the predominance of the Y-DNA Haplogroup **J1**, like the Lemba Jews who claimed to have come from Saan'a, Yemen.

According to several genetic studies using **Autosomal DNA**, Yemenite Jews are genetically related to **Saudi Arabians, Palestinians, Black Bedouin Tribes in Negev Desert, South Israel, Qatar, Oman and the United Arab Emirates**. But the people in these countries are not going around calling themselves "**Jews**". The people in these countries are all somewhat related because of their high frequency of **Y-DNA Haplogroup J1 (J1c3d)**. Their second most frequent Y-DNA Haplogroup is **E1b1b**, specifically **E-M35 and E-M81, which Ethiopian Jews, nor Ethiopians fall under**. E-M81 is the most common Paternal Haplogroups seen in White North African Arabs (**Morocco, Tunisia, Algeria, Libya**). Overall, only **TWO** Y Haplogroups (**A3b2, J1- J2**) are shared by Ethiopian Jews and Yemenite Jews. Haplogroup "**A**" represents the Hamitic Sons of Cush (**i.e. Dinka Tribe in Sudan, half of the Ethiopian Jews DNA, native Ethiopians**).

The Black "**Akhdam**" Yemeni people in Saan'a, Yemen who are called the "**Untouchables**" have been reported to have up to a 48% frequency rate of the mtDNA "**L3**", which is seen in **Bantus West Africans, East**

Africans, African-Americans, Caribbean Blacks, Afro-Latinos and the Black Siddis in India/Pakistan. Back as early as 300 A.D. (some say even earlier), the Yemen city of Aden was a major slave port in which many Bantus East Africans were sold throughout the East via the Indian Ocean for over 1,600 years. Per history, many of the Akhdam say they are descendants of Ethiopians who crossed over the Gulf of Aden to Arabia/Arabia Felix in the early years after the birth of Christianity to convert the pagan Arabs to the Christian faith before Islam was born around the 7th century. They say that when Islam was started, Muslim armies drove them back across the Gulf of Aden to Ethiopia. Those that were captured or remained in Yemen were subject to slavery and extreme poverty.

(Left) Veddoid-type indigenous people of the Malabar Coast of South India (Kerala, Karnataka). Notice that some of these men have curly-wooly hair, suggesting "**Negroid**" ancestry. According to Gentile Jewish Convert Benjamin Tudela (1100 A.D.) the people he encountered off the Malabar Coast in Kerala, India during his travels claimed to be **Israelites**. Benjamin noted in his literary work, that the Israelites he encountered in South India were "**Black**" and "**Negroid**" in appearance like the rest of the people in the land. The mtDNA of people in South India, Sri Lanka, Yemen, and East Africans are all the

47

same (**Haplogroup M**). The common ancestor of mtDNA "**M**" is mtDNA "**L3**". The mtDNA Haplogroup "**L3**" is primarily seen African-Americans today. (**Right**) A Bantus Female Slave in **Mogadishu, Somalia**. Mogadishu was a slave trade link for the Arabs in Yemen and the Persian Gulf countries. Many people during the 10th century and beyond saw Mogadishu, Somalia as a "**City of Islam**", called "**Madinat al-Islam**" in Arabic. Over time from 900 A.D. to 1800 A.D. Mogadishu gained a reputation of being a center of trade for Arabian Muslims as well as Emperors in China. By the 1400's the Portuguese would join in with the slave trade business of Bantus Africans. Around the 19th Century, Mogadishu was known as a "**Slavery city**", with as many as two-thirds of the city's population in slavery. Slaves were held at Mogadishu were generally sent to the Slave Port on Zanzibar Island, Tanzania to be shipped off to the Far East (**i.e. Indonesia, China**). Chinese Slave traders often reported different "**dietary customs**" and "**specific days of rest**" that were practiced by the Zanzibar slaves. These customs were in fact "**Hebrew**" **in nature**" but the Chinese didn't know it at the time.

Fact: *Genetic studies done on the Black Akhdam people in Yemen show a high frequency of the "sickle cell trait" which is most commonly seen in West Africans, African-Americans and the native "Vedda" people of Sri Lanka/Southwest India. Genetic Studies have also shown that non-Jewish Yemeni people have more African "Bantus" DNA than Yemeni Jews. Most of the Jews in Yemen were taken to Israel during Operation Magic Carpet between 1949-1950. Meanwhile, slavery for the Black people in Yemen didn't become illegal until 1963.*

GENETIC MUSICAL CHAIRS TO HIDE THE TRUTH!

Prior to 2008, the Ethiopians "E" Haplogroup branch came off the same "**Tree Trunk**" as the "**Bantus Negroes**". Then they did away with the former Ethiopian Y-DNA Haplogroup branch "**E1b1c**", leaving many scientists to label the "**Ethiopians Jew**" or "**non-Jewish Ethiopians**" under the newer branch "**E1b1b**", which is what White Libyans, Egyptians, Algerians, Tunisians and Moroccan Arabs are grouped under. This is called "**Hiding the Truth**" before African-Americans can start researching their DNA to find out the Semitic Ethiopian's DNA is similar to theirs. The reason why this switch doesn't work is because the mtDNA of the Ethiopian woman and Sub-Saharan African woman is totally different than the mtDNA of the North African Arab woman.

- A "woman" had to give birth to all the North African Arabs.
- If this North African Arab woman's father was related to Ethiopians (**as their new "E" Haplogroup suggests**), then the mtDNA of North African Arabs should at least be the same as Ethiopians (Semitic and Hamitic Cushitic). Jewish Rabbis like to sometimes say, "**The only way Jews can turn black is if Jewish women married and had children with native Ethiopian men.**" Some use this as a "theory" to the origin of the Ethiopian Jews while others say that the Ethiopian Jews are simply "converts" to Judaism. But there is a flaw in these "theories" that the Jewish Rabbis didn't pay attention to.
- If White Ashkenazi Jewish women married Black Ethiopian men to create the "**Ethiopian Jews**", then the mtDNA of Ashkenazi women should also be seen in the mtDNA of the Ethiopian Jews. **But it's not!**
- North African Arab men are now grouped into the Y-DNA Haplogroup "**E**" like Ethiopians. So if the Paternal Y-DNA is similar in North African Arabs and Ethiopians we should expect to see the same trend when comparing the mtDNA of both races. Why? Because Maternal **mtDNA** is passed down from a mother to **both her male and female children**. The Ethiopians mtDNA should not be any different than North African Arab mtDNA. **If it is, this would mean that they have different ancestors.** Well it just so turns out that the Ethiopians mtDNA **IS** different than the North African Arabs mtDNA.

- So why are people who call themselves "**Arabs**" so white? Well, the addition of another "**Male Bloodline**" had to have "**entered**" and "**mixed**" itself into the populations of North Africa in order for geneticists to all of a sudden place North African Arabs into the Y-DNA "**E**" Haplogroup. This new "**Male Bloodline**" has to be related to Jacob since the Semitic Ethiopian Jews and Bantus Sub-Saharan Africans all carry the "**E**" Y-DNA Haplogroup. According to the Bible it can only be the **descendants of Edom** (which I will break down later).

However, despite this breakdown of facts, the Ethiopians and Somalians today are classified under the same "**E1b1b**" Haplogroup as white-skinned North African Arabs. The "**A**" Haplogroup is considered to be "**Nubian-Cushite**" in nature, mixed with some Canaanite blood. It is seen mostly in Sudanese Nilotic Africans and Khoi-San South Africans. These are the people on earth today that are genetically the closest to the "**original man**". Haplogroup "**B**" points strongly to the descendants of the **Canaanites**. Most of the pygmy tribes in Africa are Haplogroup "**B**" and occasionally "**A**". The Haplogroup "**T**" is most often seen (>50%) in Somalia and in South India with the "**Yerukala**" Dravidian aboriginal people. The **Yerukala people** pronounce the word father, "**Aava**" like the Hebrew word "**Abba**" for father. They pronounce the word mother, "**Amma**" like the Hebrew word "**Ema/Ima**" for mother.

(**Left**) The **Yerukala people** of Southern India. Their people carry high frequencies of Y DNA Haplogroup "**T**" like Somalians. (**Middle & Right**) The Paliyan people of South India. They live in the Madura district in India. Both the Paliyan people and the Yerukala people speak the Dravidian-Tamil languages of that region. Notice they are brown-skinned people, some appearing more Black than Indian.

(**Left**) Somalian man with reddish-orange hair and beard. It is not uncommon to see Somalians with reddish hair. (**Right**) Ancient Egyptian man with reddish-orange hair. The Y-DNA (Paternal) Haplogroup "**T**" was found in the mummified remains of Egyptians in the Old Kingdom. Haplogroup "**T**" is mostly found in the "**Horn of Africa**" in the Somalian people. The Maternal mtDNA "**M1**" and "**L3**", which is also mainly found in the **Horn of Africa (Eritrea, Djibouti, Ethiopia, Somali, East Africa, West Africa),** was also found in buried bones in Egypt dating to the **Old Kingdom** (2700 B.C. 2000 B.C.) and to the **Middle Kingdom** (2000 B.C. -1650 B.C.). Could this be a subtle clue revealing where the descendants of the Ancient Egyptians are today? Does it also prove that there was a presence of "**Bantus Negroes-Israelites**" in Ancient Egypt? This is a possibility and therefore cannot be totally "**ruled out**".

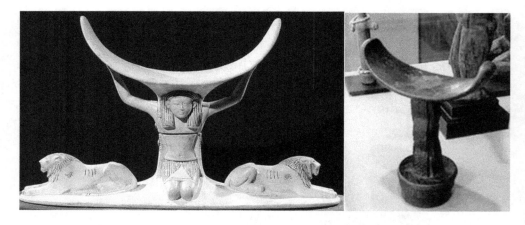

(**Left**) Ancient Egyptian Headrest. (**Right**) Somalian Headrest. This type of headrest is also used in **Kenya** and **Japan**. Japan also has evidence of mtDNA "**M**" being found in some of their people that is the same as those found in Ethiopians and East Africans.

(**Left**) East (Somalian) African man (**Middle**) Ancient Egyptian Braided Wig (**Right**) Ancient bust of Egyptian man with an Afro.

The Ancient Egyptians were Black people with "**wooly hair**", not white-skinned Arabs with straight hair. Modern day White-skinned Arabs in North Africa and the Middle East are descendants of Japhetic peoples from the North who converted to Islam. They are more European genetically than Hamitic or Semitic (like Abraham). The **Ancient Black Egyptians and Black Nubians were the people the Children of Israel mixed with for over 400 years while they were in Egypt before the Exodus.** Knowing this, in the span of 100 years a person can see 4-5 generations born. So at max, 20 generations of Israelites were born while they were in Egypt.

A Pakistani Muslim man once asked me the question:

"**I visited Spain and I didn't see any Blacks but I read that the Black Arabs (Moors) ruled Spain for 800 years until the 1492; so what happened to the descendants of these Black Moors if that was only 500 years ago?**"

The Pakistani Muslim man theorized that if the Black Moors intermarried and had children with other "white" races in Spain, we should see their descendants today in Spain. I explained to him that if a country experiences a "**Mass Deportation or Exile**" of a certain group of Black people (**as in the Spanish Inquisition in 1492**) and this country is repopulated with "**White People**" that after a couple of generations the people will appear to be the same color of the people they are having kids with. Here is another example:

So if a biracial family has children and these children only marry "**white**" from then on, the "**blackness**" contribution in their descendants "**gene pool**" will become less and less after each generation. This is what happened to the "**Black Arabs**" of the Middle East and the "**Black Hebrew Israelites**" of Israel". Exile, slavery, invasion, male castration practices all contributed to the significant disappearance of the Black Arabs/Israelites. But I broke it down for this Pakistani man even more!

Here is an example of how you can get 5 generations of families within 100 years.

- Mr. Samuel Johnson - born 1901 (**Great-Great Grandfather**)
- Mr. James Johnson - born 1927 (**Great-Grandfather**)
- Mr. Tyrone Johnson – born 1951 (**Grandfather**)
- Mr. David Johnson – born 1976 (**Father**)
- Mr. Andre Johnson – born 2000 (**Son**)

The total span here is 99 years and there are 5 generations we see here. So if the Israelites were in Egypt for 400+ years we would assume that **20 generations** of Israelites were born while they were in Egypt mixing with the local Hamitic people of the land. After 20 generations of mixing with Africans, even White people would not be white anymore. This is a known fact.

(**Left**) Somalian Elder "**Hangool staff**". (**Middle**) Egyptian with a "**Was**" staff. **Looks similar doesn't it with the hook at the top and the forked end at the bottom of the staff.** (**Right**) Egyptian goddess **Isis** with a "**Was**" scepter.

The Somalian "**Hangool staff**" seems to be identical to the "**Was staff**" the Egyptian goddess Isis is holding in her right hand. How can this be? The Ethiopians also have a "**Woko**" staff similar to the staff used by the Ancient Egyptians and Somalians. It is a known fact that the Y-DNA types of Hamitic Ethiopians Cushites (**Haplogroup A**) and Somalians (**Haplogroup T**) were found in the skeletal/mummified remains of people in Ancient Egypt (Old, Middle, and New Kingdoms). Somalians call Egypt "**Masar**" which means "**headscarf**" because in Ancient Egypt a lot of the Egyptians wore some kind of headscarf. This name "**Masar**" was also adopted by Arabs for the word "**Egypt**". In the Egyptian hieroglyphics the deity stick is spelled in letters **h-n-g-l** and Somali it is called "**Hangool**". In the Egyptian language the pillow was called "**barshin**" and in Somalian it is called "**barkin**". In the Egyptian language the sun god is called "**Ra/Rah**". In the Somali culture the sun is called "**Qor-rah/Qor-rax-**". **Coincidence?**

55

Many say Somalians (**i.e. Dir Clan**) who carry the "**T**" Haplogroup are the descendants of the Ancient Egyptians. Their style of clothes, their language, their wrestling style, their hair (Afro's, Red Hair), their slim skull patterns (which Europeans labeled "Caucasoid") and more suggest the ancestors of East Africans today ruled the Egyptian Dynasties more than any other Black nation in Africa.

WHO IS SHEMITIC? THE ETHIOPIAN JEW OR THE YEMENI JEW?

The Y DNA Haplogroup "**J1**" is considered to be "**Shemitic/Semitic**". This would make sense, seeing that the Kingdom of Sheba extended also into South Arabia/Yemen and knowing that some of the people in Yemen (? **Joktanites, Keturahites, Ishmaelite's**) passed over the Red Sea to get to the Horn of Africa. We see Y DNA Haplogroup "J1" more frequently in Northern Ethiopians, Sudanese Blacks from Khartoum, Yemeni people, Qataris, Omanis, South Saudi Arabians and the Brown-Black skinned Bedouins living in the Negev Desert.

(**Left**) Yemenite Jew. (**Right**) Ethiopian Jews with the Torah scroll and an Ancient Bible written in Ge'ez script. It is a known fact that the Y-DNA of the Ethiopian Jews is half-Hamitic (**Haplogroup A-Cush**) and half-Shemitic (**Haplogroup E and J**). It is a known fact that regular Muslims in Yemen have more "**African**" ancestral DNA than the Yemeni Jews. This has been tested on the Paternal Side (Y-DNA) and on the Maternal side (mtDNA). So are the Ethiopian Jews and Yemeni Jews related genetically? After all, they should be if they come from an common ancesotr, "Abraham, Isaac and Jacob". Here we go again!

Populations	Mitochondrial Haplogroups
African Origin	L
Native-American Origin	A, B, C or D
Asian Origin	A, B, C, D, F or G
European Origin	H, T, U, V, W, X, I, J or K

(**Above**) The Maternal DNA Haplogroups deemed by Scientists to be "**European**" are **H, HV, I, U, K, W, X, J, V and K**. The Maternal DNA Haplogroups of people in Africa unanimously is "**L**". The Maternal **mtDNA** Haplogroups of Yemenite Jews are: **H, HV, I, J (J2a1a, J1b, J2) K**, M, R2, R0a1, **U, W**, and L3x1. The "**Letters**" in **Bold** are the ones regarded as "**European Haplogroups**". The Maternal Haplogroups of Ethiopian Jews are: Roa1, M1, M1b, **U, W**, L0a1, L0a2, L0f, L2a, L2a1b2, L2b, L3b2, L3h, L32, L3x1, L4g, L5a1, and L6. The only "Eurasian Haplogoups found in some Ethiopian Jewish women were "**U**" and "**W**". The "**Letters**" in **Bold** are the ones regarded as "**European Haplogroups**". As you can see, the Ethiopian Jews and Yemenite Jews really don't have much in common when comparing the Maternal mtDNA of their women.

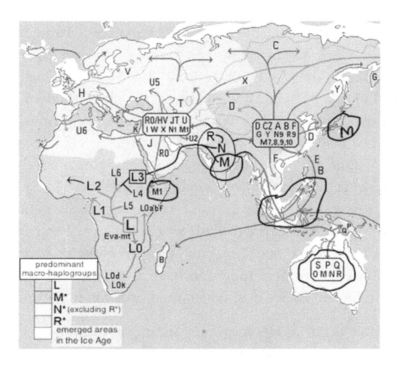

The Ethiopian Jews clearly have a highter percentage of "Black Bantus/African" Blood flowing through their veins. In contrast the women of **"Bnai Israel" in India** and the **"Cochin Jews"** of India share the same **Maternal DNA "M"** which the Yemenite Jews have very small amounts of. Could this mean that the Ethiopian Jews and Indian Jews are **"Israelite Brothers?"** The Ethiopian Jews and the Indian Jews of Cochin **(off the Malabar Coast in Kerala, India who speak Judeo-Hebraic Malayalam)** were both considered to be **"Black"**. Jewish historian **Benjamin Tudela** acknowledged this in his 12th Century (1100 A.D.) book of travels called **"The Itinerary of Benjamin of Tudela**. Benjamin Tudela confirms in his book that the Ethiopian/Indian Jews did not have any knowledge of the Mishnah/Gemara aka…The **Babylonian Talmud**. In order for the **"Real Isrealites"** to have possesion of the **"Babylonian Talmud"** they would've had to still be in Israel or around Israel in A.D. times. Why? Because the **Jerusalem Talmud (Talmud Yerushalmi)** was completed around 300 B.C. to 400 B.C. in Galilee, Israel. The **Babylonian Talmud (Talmud Bavli)** wasn't completed until around 400 A.D. in Babylon,

Iraq. The Ethiopian Jews, the Negro "West African" Israelites and the Indian Jews were already scattered far from Mesopotamia/Levant. For this reason, they did not possess the "demonic" collection of Rabbinical Opinions called the "**Talmud**". Only "**Judaism converts**" have possession of the **Mishnah** and the **Gemara (Talmud)**. This is another "**Red Flag**" proving why the "Yemenite Jews" may not be real "Israelites" after all. The only thing that may connect the Yemenite Jews to Israel is the fact that they share the same mtDNA "**L3, L5 (and some say a newer L6)**", that is also found in Bantus Israelite women. They however **do not** carry in high frequencies the Paternal male Y-DNA "**E1b1a**". Libyan and Tunisian Jews carry the Maternal mtDNA "**X**" while Georgian Jews, Bulagrian Jews and Turkish Jews carry the Maternal mtDNA "**H/HV**"; all which are European in nature.

Proof: "**Mitochondrial DNA reveals distinct evolutionary histories for Jewish populations in Yemen and Ethiopia**", *American Journal of Physical Anthropology doi: 10.1002/ajpa.21360. Amy L*

"**Counting the Founders: The Matrilineal Genetic Ancestry of the Jewish Diaspora**." *PLOS ONE. April 30, 2008 Behar DM, Metspalu E, Kivisild T, Rosset S, Tzur S, Hadid Y, et al.*

The chart on the left shows Y-DNA haplogroup percentages for Ethiopian Jews (44):
- T: 4.7%
- J: 4.7%
- E: 11.5%
- E: 9.0%
- E: 6.7%
- E: 18.0%
- A: 45.3%

Labeled "Ethiopian Jews (44)"

(**Left**) Y-DNA studies prove over and over again that half (45%) of the Ethiopian Jews DNA is Haplogroup "**A**" from Nubia (**Cush**) by way of Ham and (45%) "Haplogroup "**E**" (**Shem**) by way of Isaac/Jacob. The other 10% is Haplogroup "**J**" Semitic. (**Right**) Book "**Rescue: The Exodus of the Ethiopian Jews**" by Ruth Gruber, an American Journalist who was an eyewitness to **Operation Moses** in the 1980's.

The above graph makes sense knowing that Israel's "**Holy Seed**" was merged early with Cush (Nubia) with the Zipporah-Moses union of "Holy Matrimony" in the 15th century B.C. and also the Queen Sheba-King Solomon's relationship which led to their son Menelik being born during the 10th century B.C. Nubia back in Ancient times was the land today known as "Sudan". **Sudan has the most African Tribes that carry the Y-DNA Haplogroup A.** Anyone can google Y-DNA Haplogroup "**A**" and see that the highest percentage of this

Haplogroup is found in the Cushitic Africans living in **Sudan** followed by people in **Namibia** and after that the **Ethiopian Jews**. The **Khoisan** and **Bushmen Pygmy** tribes who are genetically "**Ancient**" also have been known to carry small-moderate frequencies (14-40%) of Haplogroup A.

So what "E" Haplogroup "**specifically**" makes up the other 45% of the Ethiopian Jews? Why have scientists/geneticists made it so difficult? Don't be fooled by modern day searches or studies which show "**E1b1b**" as the answer. Why? It all started in 2008. Before 2008, The Ethiopian Jewish DNA was connected to **E1b1a/E1b1c (see below)**. The Y-DNA Haplogroup "E1b1a" is connected to "African-Americans" as well as other Blacks scattered across the world via the Slave Trades.

Estimated TMRCA of E1b1a UEP dates and distribution of E1b1a component haplogroups in sub-Saharan Africa

| | | | | | | | | Geographic presence (Y/N) | | |
| | | | | | West Africa | | | West-Central Africa | East Africa | South-East Africa |
Haplogroup	Marker	n	ASD (95% CI)	TMRCA (YBP)	Ghana	Nigeria	Cameroon	Congo	Ethiopia	Total
BT*(xDE,KT)	SRY10831	206	1.036(0.939–1.138)	11 731–14 229	Y	Y	Y	Y	Y	Y
A3b2	M13	27	0.556(0.401–0.735)	5015–9182	N	N	Y	Y	Y	Y
E*(E1b1a)	SRY4064	140	0.920(0.816–1.036)	10 193–12 946	Y	Y	Y	Y	Y	Y
E1b1a	sY81	2336	0.510(0.494–0.527)	6175–6588	Y	Y	Y	Y	Y	Y
E1b1a7	M191	1190	0.404(0.384–0.424)	4800–5300	Y	Y	Y	Y	Y	Y
E1b1a8	U175	969	0.161(0.149–0.173)	1863–2163	Y	Y	Y	Y	N	Y
E1b1a8a1	U290	591	0.125(0.113–0.138)	1413–1725	Y	Y	Y	Y	N	Y
E1b1a8a1a	U181	189	0.109(0.088–0.131)	1100–1638	N	Y	N	N	N	Y

(**Above**) "Frequency distribution of NRY Haplogroups in 43 Sub-Saharan African population groups." The chart above shows the presence of the ancestral E1b1a gene labeled "**E*(E1b1a)**", "**E1b1a**", and "**E1b1a7**" in Africa. As you can see the "**E1b1a**" gene is seen in **ALL OVER AFRICA**, including **ETHIOPIA**.

European Journal of Human Genetics, April 2013, 21 (4): pg. 423-429.

CHAPTER 4

PROVING THE "COHEN MODEL HAPLOGROUP" TO BE A "FALSE" ISRAELITE MARKER USING GENETICS AND "CRITICAL THINKING".

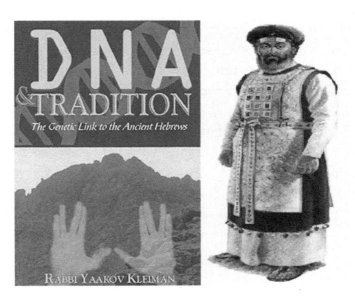

(Above) European Jews believe they have found the "Genetic Signature" that links them to the High Priestly class of the Aaronites (**Levites**). It has sparked a lot of talk with Books by Jewish authors such as **Rabbi Yaakov Kleiman** in his book "*DNA & Tradition: The Genetic Link to the Ancient Hebrews*". Without the physical body of an Aaronite "**High Priest**" they have somehow said that with DNA studies, they believe that the Y-DNA Haplogroup "**J1c**" links them to bloodline of Aaron, the brother of Moses. But have they done all of their research? Is it flawed? Where is the Y-DNA Haplogroup that links them to the Tribe of Judah?

Around the year 2000, at the University of Arizona, geneticists/scientists conducting studies on Y-DNA Haplogroups found out that the Sephardic Jews and Ashkenazi Jews shared a similar

Y-DNA Haplogroup called the "**J1c**" Haplogroup. They called it the "**Cohen Model Haplogroup**" Modern Jewish people who claim to be "**Kohanim/Cohanim**" claim to be descendants to the biblical person named "Aaron", who was the brother of Moses from the Priestly Tribe of Levi. Modern Jewry claims that a person is **NOT** "Jewish" unless their mother is a Jew, however in the Bible the Priestly Cohanite Tribe of "High Priest Status" was always passed down from the father to the son. Somehow without the body of Aaron, the Zadokites, or Ezra the European Jews have come up with the claim that they can link a specific Y-DNA Haplogroup (that was created less than 20 years ago) to a person's lineage that started some 3,500 years ago. There have been no claims by the Jews that state they dug up the skeleton of Aaron or his descendants and even if they dug up a group of skeletons in Israel how could they accurately determine if that skeleton was a descendant of Aaron? Back then did the Israelites have military or Priestly dog tags to identify them at death? Did the Israelites have buildings to house the tombs of the Jewish High Priests? So how can the Jews make this outlandish claim? Easy! **The same way the Jewish-ran Federal Reserve Bank can print money (dollar bills) out of thin air and attach a value to it that the whole world uses without question.** The Jews essentially "made up" this "Cohen Model Haplogroup" gene, linking a Haplogroup letter to the biblical descendants of Aaron. But we don't see them linking any one of the many Y-DNA Haplogroup letters (**A to T**) to any other biblical characters such as **Samson** (Dan), **King David** (Judah), **Joshua** (Ephraim), **King Saul** (Benjamin) and so on.

Fact: *King David's tomb is located at Mount Zion in Jerusalem, Israel. There, per the 12th A.D. century folklore, is the resting place of the body remains of King David from the Tribe of Judah. However, the European Jews have not cracked open the tomb to do DNA testing on the body to see if their DNA matches up with King David's DNA. Most European Jews today will claim to be from the **Tribe of Judah** without providing any proof. So why haven't they cracked open King David's Tomb to confirm a "**Tribe of Judah**" gene? This for sure would be a major scientific blow that would shut up anyone claiming to be from the Tribe of Judah. But the Jews have not done any genetic testing on King David's remains currently held in King David's tomb.*

Perhaps this is because they know they are not the real biblical Israelites and they don't want scientific confirmation.

So have we been "**Bamboozled**" and "**Hoodwinked**" by the Jews to believe their genetic "**Hocus Pocus**" tricks of a created "**Israelite gene**"? Modern Jewry seems to have tricked a lot of people, including Africans (**i.e. Lemba Tribe**), that a single Haplogroup letter can link a person to the "**High Priests**" of Israel. Saying you are an Israelite "High Priest" is one thing, but saying you can prove it with DNA down to the **TRIBE** is going way to far! So that being said, let's investigate this "**J1c**" Haplogroup and the genetic composition of the Ashkenazi Jews Paternal Y-DNA.

In a November 2001 article in the issue of the "**American Journal of Human Genetics**," Ariella Oppenheim of the Hebrew University of Israel wrote that a new study revealed that Europeans Jews are more related to Ottoman Turks, Kurds, Armenians than to the authentic Black Arabs in South Arabia, Yemen, Qatar, Oman or the Bedouins living in South Israel-Jordan. A previous study by Ariella was done in December 2000 showing that 70% of Jewish "**Paternal**" ancestries and 82% of Palestinian Arab "Paternal" ancestries share the same chromosomal pool. What this means is that Ashkenazi Jews and Palestinians are just the descendants of Turks, Kurds, Armenians, Romans (Italy), Greeks, Edomites, and Spaniards who over the last 1,900 years lived in Judea (after the fall of the second temple in 70 A.D.) converting at different times to Judaism or Islam. This is called a "proselyte."

Ashkenazim by Haplogroup

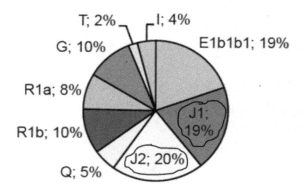

T; 2%   I; 4%
G; 10%   E1b1b1; 19%
R1a; 8%
J1; 19%
R1b; 10%
Q; 5%   J2; 20%

(**Above**) It is believed that only 46% of all Ashkenazi Jews and 56% of all Sephardic Jews carry the Y-DNA "**J1c**" gene. For the ones that do carry this "**J1c**" gene, it still doesn't make up more than 50% of their whole DNA.

Here is the trick, most African-Americans can easily say, "**I am a descendant of Japheth**" and try to prove this by showing using DNA studies that European Haplogroups can be found in our DNA composition. But what we would be leaving out is that the percentage of "**European DNA**" in our **WHOLE DNA COMPOSITION** is **very low** (<10-30% on average). By not acknowledging the "**African**" part of our DNA that makes up the other 70-90% we are essentially trying to "**hide**" the truth about our identity. Or maybe we would just be looking like we are "**ashamed**" of our "real identity". Well, in the Jews case, they don't want the world to know that the majority of their DNA compositon is "**Japhetic-European**" and not Shemitic.

Here are the cold hard facts. The majority of Ashkenazi Jewish DNA is "**Eurasian**", meaning their DNA is from a European and Asia Minor ancestry (Turks, Kurds, Armenians). Above is a pie graph breaking down the Y-DNA composition of the Ashkenazi Jew. **As you can see the Ashkenazi Jews DNA is like a genetic rainbow, with multiple Haplogroups and not one amounting to more than 50% of their**

genome. This is just an average, so on any day someone can randomly test an Ashkenazi Jew in the street and possibly get different Haplogroups that dominant or supercede the other minor Haplogroups. It is a known fact in the science-genetic world Haplogroup G, T, I and R have been associated with Europe. The **Y-**

Note: DNA Haplogroup "R" for the Europeans is the "leftover" mark previous "Black nations" have left after running through Europe (while impregnating white women) and returning back to Africa.

Y-DNA Haplogroup J2 is connected to Asia Minor (i.e Turkey, Armenia, Kurdistan) as all of these three countries have **high frequencies of J2**, just like the Ashkenazi Jews. But why is that? Well, during the Crusades, the Turks and the Kurds possessed Judea longer than anyone else. Over the course of almost 900 years from **Kurdish Leader Saladin** (1174-1193 A.D.) to the end of the **Ottoman "Turkish" Empire** in the 1900's Judea was controlled and populated by the J2-Haplogroup carrying White "Japhetic" Arabs. So what does the Turkish or Kurdish Arabs have to do with the Ashkenazi, Turkeys or Kurdish Jews? To start off, people should find it odd that the Y-DNA of the Arab Turk, Arab Kurd, Turkish Jew, and Ashkenazi Jew are **ALL THE SAME!**

TURKISH JEWISH Y-DNA

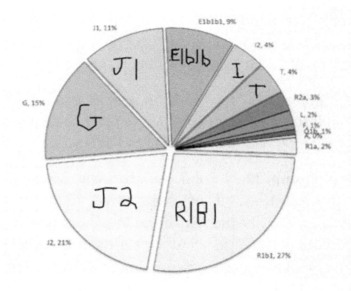

ARAB TURKISH Y-DNA

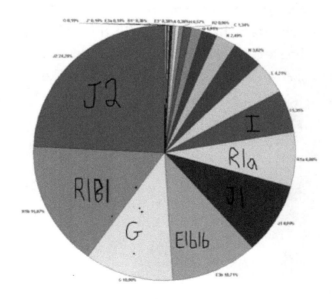

(**Above**) From comparing the Y-DNA of the **Muslim Arab Turk** and the **Jewish Turk** you can see that the main Y-DNA Haplogroups for both of them are **J2, G, R1b, J1 and E1b1b**. How is that possible? How does the DNA of the Turkish Jew "**set him apart**" as being a descendant of Jacob from the Arab Turk (who claims descent from Ishmael)? Why is their DNA the same? Something is not right here. How come their DNA fails to add up to the DNA of Ethiopian Jews? How can the Turkish Jew and Turkish Arab both be white-skinned people with straight black hair? Especially when Ishmael's 12 sons were ¾ Black Egyptian (i.e. Ishmael's mother and wife were Black Egyptian) and ¼ Hebrew. Remember, the Roman "Byzantine Empire" ruled over Turkey for almost a thousand years until the Seljuk Turks settled in parts of Turkey after the "**Battle of Manzikert**" in 1071. Before this time the main languages in Turkey were **Greek** and **Latin**! Who invaded and conrolled Judea from 300 B.C until 600 A.D? The Greeks, Edomites and Romans! Alexander the Great and his Greek Commanders ruled over Judea until the **Maccabean Greek** family took over the land. Then the Romans took control of Judea from the Greeks starting in 70 A.D. after the fall of the Second Temple in Jerusalem. The Byzantine Roman Emperor lost Judea to the Muslim Arabs after 600 A.D. So the Greeks and Romans controlled Judea from 400 B.C. to 600 A.D.. 900 years (300 B.C. to 600 A.D.) is enough time for Romans and Greeks to adopt the religion of Judaism. From 600 A.D. to 1900 A.D. the Black Arabs and the White (non-Ishmaelite Turkish/Kurdish) Arabs ruled over Judea for the most part. 1300 years (600 A.D. to 1900 A.D.) is enough time for the Arabs Turks, Kurds, Romans, Greeks and Edomites to convert to Judaism. It is also enough time for them believe they are descendants of King David. 1300 years of anybody's parents telling them "**We are the Children of Isreal**" is enough time for a lie to believed as truth. **However, if one is a Jew and one is an Muslim Arab (supposedly descended from Ishmael), their DNA cannot be 100% identical**. This is also the case when comparing the Arab Turk's Y-DNA to the Ashkenazi Jews Y-DNA. It is essentially the same! But wait a minute! **Togarmah** is suppsed to be the forefather of the Armenians and **Turkish** people. But hold up! Wasn't **Ashkenaz** the brother of Togarmah in the bible? And was they not both the son of **Gomer**, son of **Japheth**? If they are of the line of Japheth, **they cannot** be of the line of **Shem, Abraham, Isaac, or Jacob**. Neither can they be of the line of Abraham and Ishmael.

Reference – **"Y Chromosome Haplogroup distribution in Turkey". Cengiz Cinnioglu et al. 2004**.

Genesis 10:2-3 "The sons of **Japheth**; Gomer, and Magog, and Madai, and Javan, and Tubal, and Meshech, and Tiras. And the sons of Gomer; **Ashkenaz (Ashkenazi Jews)**, and Riphath, and **Togarmah (Turks, Kurds, and Armenians)**.

White Arabs believe they are descendants of **Ishamel**, Abraham's first Son. Arabs also believe the Real Israelites of the Bible in Ancient times looked like them today. Some Caucasians and even Palestinians believe they are the "**Children of Israel**". How can this be? What does the bible reveal in regards to the color of Abraham, Isaac or Jacob?

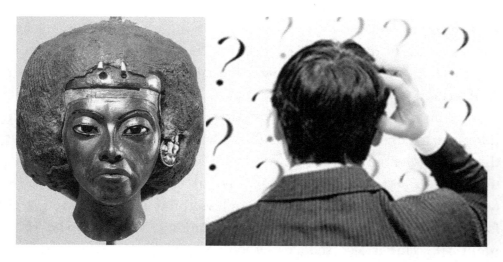

(**Above**) Queen Tiye of Egypt. This is what a "**Real**" Egyptian woman would've looked like in Abraham and Ishmael's time. Queen Tiye lived in around 1300 B.C. For Arabs and Jews, it is very hard to have lived your whole life only to find out your entire heritage is a lie. When the **TRUTH** hits them in the face, it poses a lot of questions and these questions the mind sometimes cannot accept. So they usually deny the

TRUTH and continue to believe a lie. It is easier for them that way. Otherwise, they would have to ask themselves, "**If we are not the original Arab Ishmaelite's or the Original Jews then why are we in the Middle East**" and "**Why are we fighting each other over a land that is not ours?**"

Genesis 16:3-4 "And Sarai Abram's wife took Hagar her maid **THE EGYPTIAN**, after Abram had dwelt ten years in the land of Canaan, and he gave her to her husband Abram to be his wife. And he (**Abraham**) went in unto Hagar, and she conceived: and when she saw that she had conceived, her mistress was despised in her eyes."

Genesis 16:11 "And the angel of the Lord said unto her, Behold, thou art with child and shalt bear a son, and shalt call his name **ISHMAEL**; because the Lord hath heard thy affliction."

Genesis 21:21 "And he (**Ishmael**) dwelt in the wilderness of Paran: and his mother (**Hagar the Egyptian**) took him a wife out of the **LAND OF EGYPT**."

So according to these scriptures and what we know what Egyptian women looked like in Biblical times by looking at Queen Tiye, Ishmael should have been black and his children (by an Egyptian woman) should also be black. So if Ishmael was a son of Abraham and was black wouldn't Isaac, Jacob and the Israelites be "Black" as well? Most biblical scholars would agree that Abraham was born in Mesopotamia (Haran-Syria or Ur-Iraq) according to Genesis Chapters 11, 12, 15, 28, and 29. But we know Abraham was an ancestor of Shem. So was Abraham black? If Abraham was black, this would likely mean that the ancestors of Shem were black as well. Let's examine this closely.

(**Above**) a 300 A.D. Mosaic in the "**Bet Alfa**" Synagogue in Beit She'an, Israel of the "**Binding of Isaac**" by Abraham in which God told Abraham to sacrifice his son **Isaac**. So why would the white Greek "Gentile" Maccabean Jews, the Edomites and the Romans draw a picture or even **ALLOW** a picture of a "**Black-looking**" Abraham with a "**wooly afro**" to exist in Israel if the Hebrew Israelites were never Black to begin with? It doesn't make sense.

Note: In Islam, the story is twisted to fit Muhammad's agenda as "**Ishmael**" is the one that Abraham is told to sacrifice. But we all know the Hebrew Torah, the Hebrew language, and this Mosaic from 300 A.D. **PRE-DATE** the Arabic language, including the Quran, which was written in **ARABIC**. The Arabic language was created and first used shortly after **500 A.D**. The Quran and Islam did not exist until after 600 A.D. If this Mosaic picture of Abraham with a "Black Face" and "Afro", sacrificing his son Isaac **PRE-DATES THE QURAN** by 300 years, this means that the Quran is false in teaching that Ishamel was sacrificed. It also proves that most Arabs are teaching false doctrines when they teach their children that Abraham, Ishmael, Isaac, Jacob, the Hebrew

Israelites and the Arabs were **NOT** originally **BLACK**, like African-Americans today.

As you see in the Mosaic, Abraham has a sword is about to slay his son Isaac and offer him up to the Lord on the Altar. In Hebrew the words for "Abraham" are over the guy with an "Afro". In Hebrew is the word for "Isaac" over the boy child Abraham has held up in the air with his left hand. Though it may be hard to see, in the color version of this picture, Abraham's upper face (from his nose to his Afro) is **BLACK** while the lower part of his face is a faded light brown color (suggesting someone lightening up the original black color of Abraham's skin). Baby Isaac's face is also the same way and if you look closely Isaac's fingertips and hands are brown but not his extremities (arms & legs). This 1500 year old Mosaic picture has been lightened by Europeans as Abraham's hand on the mosaic are significantly lighter than his black face. The same goes for Isaac as "evil people" have completely erased the color of Isaac's arms and legs. This mosaic again is located on the northern panel of the **"Bet Alfa Jewish Synagogue"** located near **Beit She'an, Israel**. It is now part of the **Bet Alfa Synagogue National Park. So there is proof IN ISRAEL, that Abraham, Isaac and Jacob were Black.** But the Jews of today will not admit this. According to many Muslims, Abraham, Ishmael, Isaac and Jacob were not black people with wooly Afros. In the Mosaic ehind Abraham is the Ram in the thicket that Abraham uses instead as a sacrifice.

The Bible states that God told Abraham to sacrifice the "**only son**" that he loved. In other words, Abraham was to sacrifice his only "**begotten-special/unique**" son, and this was Isaac, not Ishmael. Even the Muslim religious book, **the Quran**, explains that the "**covenant**" and "**prophethood**" was only given to Isaac and his descendants. Not Ishamael. Therefore, the Isaac's grandchildren, the "Israelites", would be the people who would speak for God (the Creator) to the nations of the world. They would be a "**set apart**" people who would be "**a light**" and "**example**" to other nations as to what God was to be respected/worshipped.

John 12:36 "While ye have light, believe in the light, that ye may be the **CHILDREN OF LIGHT**. These things **spake Yahusha (Jesus)**, and departed, and did hide himself from them.

Genesis 22:2 "Then He said, "Take now your son, **your only son Isaac, whom you love**, and got to the land of Moriah, and offer him there as a burnt offering on one of the mountains of which I shall tell you."

Hebrews 11:17-19 "By faith Abraham, when he was tried, offered up Isaac: and he that had received the promises **offered up his only begotten son**, Of whom it was said, "**That in Isaac shall thy seed be called (chosen),**" Accounting that God was able to raise him up, even from the dead; from whence also he received him in a figure."

In the New Testament **John 3:16** written in Greek the word "**monogenes**" appears instead of the english word "**begotten**". The definition of "**monogenes**" is:

- Pertaining to being the **ONLY ONE** of its kind within a specific relation ship.
- Pertaining to being the only one of its kind or class, **UNIQUE IN KIND.**

Sahih International (**Noble Quran**)

Sura 29:27 "And We (**Allah**) gave to him **Isaac** and **Jacob** and placed in his descendants (progeny) **PROPHETHOOD AND SCRIPTURE**. And We gave him his reword in this world, and indeed, he is in the Hereafter among the **RIGHTEOUS**."

Nowhere in the Arabic Quran does it mention that Ishmael and his descendants would be given "**Prophethood and Scripture**". Furthermore, there is no proof (Sura) in the Arabic Quran that lists the geneolgy from Ishmael to the Tribe of Muhammad (**Quraysh**). This means that Muhammad cannot be a prophet according to the Older Hebrew Torah and the Newer Arabic Quran.

IS THERE ANY EVIDENCE OF DECEIT IN THE BOOK OF MORMON AND ISLAM?

Fact: *The word "white" is found ONLY "104 times" in ALL Christian religious scripture, including the Book of Mormon/Church of Latter-Day Saints.*

- *40 times in the Old Testament*
- *28 times in the New Testament*
- *24 times in the Book of Mormon*
- *12 times in the Doctrine & Covenants*

Now only 26 times does this word talk about "white" in regards to man and his skin color. Of those 26 times the word "white" is used in reference to man and his "white" skin color, 18 refer to the disease of "Leprosy," which in biblical times was a disorder that made your skin all white or with "White skin patches." Nowadays this can be seen as complete vitiligo or ablinism. This is not a coincedence. So 18 out of 26 times the word white is used for white skn. This leaves us with 8 other times the word white was used in religious texts. These 8 other times are found ALL in the Book of Nephi which is the Book of Mormon. The Mormon Church (like the White Catholic Church) twisted the religious scriptures to hide the fact that the Israelties were BLACK and that the "Mark of Cain" was WHITE SKIN.

- *1 Nephi 11:13*
- *1 Nephi 13:15*
- *2 Nephi 5:21*
- *2 Nephi 26:33*
- *3 Nephi 2:15*
- *3 Nephi 19:25*
- *3 Nephi 19:30*
- *Mormon 9:6*

The Book of Mormon states when the Israelite Native American Indians (termed "**Lamanites**") sinned against God's commandment they were cursed with "**Black Skin**" like the Black Israelites in Africa. The

Nephites were supposedly the White Indians who were "blessed" with white skin because they accepted Christianity and obeyed God. Per Mormon belief, it states that once the Lamanite Indian Hebrew Israelites were converted to Christianity their Black Skin slowly started to "**fade away**" to white skin, like the Nephites.

Book of Mormon, 2 Nephi 5:21 "And he had cursed the cursing to come upon them, yea, even a sore cursing, because of their iniquity. For behold, they had hardened their hearts against him, that they had become like unto a flint; wherefore, as they were white, and exceedingly fair and delightsome, that they might not be enticing unto my people the Lord God did cause a skin of **BLACKNESS** to come upon them."

Book of Mormon, 3 Nephi 3:12-15 "Therefore, all the Lamanites who had **BECOME CONVERTED** unto the Lord did unite with their brethren, the Nephites, and were compelled, for the safety of their lives and their women and their children, to take up arms against those Gadianton robbers, yea, **and also to maintain their rights, and the privileges of their CHURCH and of their worship**, and their freedom and their liberty. And it came to pass that before this thirteen year had passed away the Nephites were threatened with utter destruction because of this war, which had become exceedingly sore. **And it came to pass that those Lamanites who had united with the Nephites were numbered among the Nephites; and THEIR CURSE WAS TAKEN FROM THEM**, and their **SKIN BECAME WHITE LIKE UNTO THE NEPHITES;**"

The Book of Mormon also teaches that the "**Cursed**" **Canaanites** were Black and that the **Seed of Cain** (from the "Mark") were also **BLACK**.

Book of Mormon, Moses 7:22 "And Enoch also beheld the residue of the people which were the Sons of Adam (Seth); and they were a mixture of all the seed of Adam save it was the Seed of Cain, **for the Seed of Cain were BLACK**, and had not place among them."

(Book of Mormon) Moses 7:8 "For behold, the Lord shall curse the land with much heat, and the barrenness thereof shall go forth forever; and there was a **BLACKNESS** came upon all the children of **Canaan,** that they were despised among all people."

So why is there so much decption in regards to the people that's supposed to be teaching the **TRUTH** in the Book of Mormon, the Bible and the Quran? Why must man in each of these religions "**manipulate**" the Books presented to the people to promote a "**Lie**". Satan is a "**deceiver**" and the father of lies! Is there any evidence or clues that we can use to "discern" what religion is right? Many Black Men today are falling by the wayside to African Spirituality by worshipping the pagan gods of Egypt while others are converting to Islam.

مكر *makara u (makr)* to deceive, delude, cheat, dupe, gull, double-cross (ب s.o.) III to try to deceive (ه s.o.)

مكر *makr* cunning, craftiness, slyness, wiliness, double-dealing, deception, trickery

مكرة *makra* ruse, artifice, stratagem, wile, trick, dodge

مكّار *makkār* and مكور *makūr* cunning, sly, crafty, wily, shrewd, artful; sly, crafty person, impostor, swindler

ماكر *mākir* pl. مكرة *makara* sly, cunning, wily

(Above) In the Arabic lexicon the word for **"Deceive" is Makara, Makr, Makra, Makkar and Makir.** So what does the Quran say about "Deception?"

Many people have claimed that there was an Older ARABIC version of the Quran. This Quran had stuff in it that is not seen the Quran today. Perhaps during Umayyad Caliphate (700 A.D.) the Quran had things in it that have since been "**deleted**" to uphold the "**authenticity**" of the Quran as a "**Holy Book**". If Muslims today were to read the Quran during the 7th Century A.D., they might be shocked to see a lot of pagan concepts in the Older Quran vs the Newer Quran.

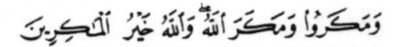

(**Modern**) **Noble Quran Sura 3:54** "But they were deceptive, and **ALLAH** was deceptive, for **ALLAH is the BEST OF DECIEVERS**."

The Quranic Sura here in Arabic even reads "**Khayrul-Makereen**" which means "**Allah is the Greatest of all Deceivers**". This can be verified by looking up the Root Arabic letters for "**Makr**" which is "**Meem/Mim**", "**Kaaf/Kaf**", and "**Rah/Ra**" in the Arabic Dictionary (i.e. Al-Mawrid).

The phrase "**Best of Deceivers**" is from the **ARABIC** word "**Makara/Makr**" which means "**Deceive, Scheme or Plan**". In the **ARABIC BIBLE** used by Christians in Eastern Countries that speak Arabic, **Genesis 3:1** uses the same word "**Makara**" for **Satan**. **WOW!**

(**Left**) The word "**Deceive**" in Arabic. (**Middle**) The beginning of **Genesis 3:1** "**Now the Serpent…**" in Arabic with the word "**The Serpent/Snake**" circled. (**Right**) Al-Makr, means "**Deception**" in Arabic. Is it just me or does the word "**Serpent/Snake**" seem to look identical to the Arabic word for **"deceive or deception"**? We know according to the bible that Satan is the **"Great Deceiver"**.

Revelation 12:9 "And the great dragon was cast out, **THAT OLD SERPENT**, called the **Devil**, and **SATAN**, which **DECEIVEITH THE WHOLE WORLD:**"

Nowhere in the bible does God lie, deceive, plot, or create delusions. God harden hearts (i.e. Pharaoh of Egypt). In the newer versions of the Quran from Arabic writers Yusuf Ali, Sahih International, Pickthall they changed the word from "**Deceive**" to "**Planned**" like Allah is planning a wedding or Allah has to think and plan things out before doing it. This is ridiculous. God does not need to think and "plan" things out. Below is the Arabic and English translation of **Sura 7:99.**

Sura 7:99 says "Are they secure from **Allah's deception** (Makra Allah)? None deemeth himself secure from **Allah's deception** save folk that perish."

What does the Christ say in our Holy Bible about Satan, the Devil, the Serpent and deceiver of the world? Remember according to the Muslim Quran, the Yahusha Mashiach (Jesus Christ) is the one who defeats the dajjal (Muslim Antichrist), not Muhammad or Allah.

John 8:44 "Ye are of your father the devil, and the lusts of your father ye will do. He was a murderer from the beginning, and **ABODE NOT IN THE TRUTH**, because there is no truth in him. When he speaketh a lie, he speaketh of his own: **FOR HE IS A LIAR, AND THE FATHER OF IT.**"

Sura 26:50 "So they schemed a scheme: and **WE** (Allah and the angels) schemed a scheme, while they perceived not."

The ARABIC word here for "**Scheme/Deceive**" is "**Makr or Makara**". According to ARABIC lexicons "Makr" is an act of deception aiming at causing **evil**. In Sura 13:42 it says that "ALLAH is the MASTER OF ALL SCHEMERS." BLACK MAN WAKE UP! Follow the God of ISRAEL, your heritage is ISRAEL, not ISHMAEL. Follow the God of Abraham, Isaac, Jacob and the ISRAELITES. God has a name that is in the Older Torah: **Yahuah (Genesis 4:26, Exodus 3:15).** God's name is not "**The God**" or "**God**" which is what Muslims say as "**Allah**" like Allah's pagan daughters "**Al-Lat**", "**Al-Uzza**", and "**Manat**" in **Sura 53:19-23**. God told Moses and the Sons of Seth his "**Eternal Name**". It is in the Torah!

(**Left**) Exodus 3:14 in Hebrew (**Right**) Genesis 4:26 in Hebrew.

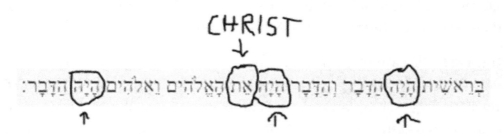

(**Above**) John 1:1 in Hebrew: "In the Beginning was the **WORD**, and the **WORD** was with **GOD**, and the **WORD** was **GOD**."

Notice that the Root "**Hayah**" for the word "**Ahayah-I AM**" appears 3 times in correlation with the English saying "**THE WORD**". Notice that the Hebrew "**Aleph-Tav**" is also in the scripture signifying "**The Alpha and Omega, the Beginning and the End**" as in the Book of Revelation 1:8. So is the scripture saying in **John 1:1**:

"In the beginning **Christ existed**, and **Christ existed with God** (Elohim), and **Christ existed as God** (Elohim).

אֲנִי הָאָלֶף וְהַתָּו רֹאשׁ וָסוֹף נְאֻם יְהֹוָה אֱלֹהִים הַהֹוֶה וְהָיָה וְיָבוֹא אֱלֹהֵי צְבָאוֹת:

Revelations 1:8 "I am the ALPHA AND OMEGA (**circled – The Aleph, The Tav**), the BEGINNING AND THE ENDING, saith the **Lord** (**Yahuah**), which is, and which was, and which is to come, the Almighty."

This is proof that God (Yahuah) is the Christ (Yahusha) and Christ is God!

CHAPTER 5

WHITE MOROCCAN JEWS VS BLACK MOROCCAN JEWS. WHO IS THE REAL JEW AND WHO IS A "CONVERT" TO JUDAISM? WHO WERE THE REAL JEWS WHO WERE BANISHED FROM IBERIA?

(Left)   African Arabic (**Ajami script**). The smaller letters are **Soninke** writing taken from a page of the "**Middle Creed**" by Algerian 1400's Moor **Yusuf al-Sanusi. If you really analyze the Soninke language it kind of resembles the 15th Century Sephardic Hebrew cursive script mixed with Arabic. (Right).** Ancient Soninke Territory in Mali/Senegal. The majority of people of Soninke descent are living in **Mali, Mauritania, Senegal, Gambia, Burkina Faso, Ghana, Ivory Coast and Guinea-Bissau.**   Most of the African Tribes in these countries are related to the Mandingo/Wolof, Mende, Mande family which all are known to carry the **Y-DNA Haplogroup E1b1a.**

(Above) The map of West Africa. Circled is the word "Soninke" which are to the right of the word "Wolof", a tribe commonly seen in Senegal and Gambia. Mali shares its western borders with Mauritania, Senegal, Gambia, Guinea Bissau, and Sierra Leone. All of these countries have high populations of people carrying the same "E1b1a" Y-DNA as African-Americans, South America/Central American blacks and Caribbean blacks. It is a known fact shown by extracts from Hausa records (Northeast Nigeria) that the people of the Ancient Ghana Empire were anciently known to descend from the "Towrood/Taurud" and "Soninke (Sarankaly)" people. The Muslim African Hausa records state both people claim in the past to have come from the territory lying between the **Nile River** and the **Euphrates River** (*Land between two rivers*). This is supported in the Bible to the land given to the Children of Abraham.

Genesis 15:18 "In the same day the Lord made a covenant with Abram, saying, Unto thy seed have I given this land, from the river

On January 28, 2013 in Israel media juggernaut "**Arutz Sheva** www.israelnationalnews.com" it was reported that in **Mali, Timbuktu** Ancient manuscripts were found in a wooden box written in Arabic with some found written in **Hebrew**. The reading portion of the manuscripts was in Arabic but along the border edges written in small print was **Hebrew**. According to Mali Mayor **Ousmane Halle**, the library at the "**Ahmed Baba Institute**" has preserved priceless manuscripts (mostly in Arabic or Ajami script), some dating back to the 1200's A.D. Islamic terrorists tried to burn these Hebrew manuscripts but of course the European Jews in Israel found out about it and took these "**priceless**" Hebrew manuscripts away never to be seen again which obviously proved the "Original Jews" were Black. It is a known fact that records of Jewish history in Mali can still be found in the "**Kati Andalusi library**", where Malian historian "**Ismael Diadie Haidara**" oversees them.

(**Above**) The Book "**Timbuktu, Andalusies in Niger**" by Black Muslim (Mali) philosopher/historian **Ismael Diadie** and politician Spaniard **Manuel Pimentel** talks about the history of Spain beginning from when the Black Moors and Black Hebrew Israelites entered into Europe by way of Spain & Andalusia.

According to Ancient history, Hebrew Israelites who left Spain shortly after the Spanish Inquisition made their way to Mali in Africa, settling in the villages **Kirshamba**, **Haybomo** and **Kongougara** near the city Timbuktu. They belonged to the **Kehath (Ka'ti)** family who were descendants of Ismael Jan Kot Al-yahudi of Morocco. Malian historian **Ismael Diadie Hidara** traced his roots and found out that his ancestors were Moroccan Jewish Traders from the Abana family (Great-grandson of Muhammad Abana) who left Iberia and settled in South Morocco around the 1490's. Malian history reveals that in the 1400's **King Askia Muhammad** rose to power in Timbuktu, Mali. He established Islam as the religion of his kingdom and ordered all the Black Jews in Mali to convert to Islam or face persecution. Back in those days it not safe to reveal to anyone that you were a Jew. Therefore, the history of many Malians Jewish heritage was suppressed and often forgotten throughout the generations. In the 1990's, an emergence of "**Jewish**

awareness" was found in about 1,000 Malians who were no longer hiding the knowledge that they were Black Israelites or had traced their Hebrew ancestry using old records. Because of this Ismael Haidara founded an organization called **"Zakhor"** or **The Timbuktu Association for Friendship with the Jewish World**.

Fact: *The organization "Zakhor" issued a **Manifesto** in 1996, addressing the presidents of Mali and Israel, diplomatic missions in Mali as well as Jewish communities throughout the world. In the Malian newspaper, "**Le Republican**" the Manifesto stated, "**It is incumbent upon us to remember and affirm our Israelite origins, which our fathers and forefathers kept secretly. We are Jews because our ancestors were Jews, whose genes are found in all our families. Our Judaism is based on ethnicity (not religious conversion).**" Zakhor's obligations was to teach their children the Hebrew Language as a second language, to collect and publish oral/written sources of their Jewish history.*

As the bible foretold in Deuteronomy **28:36**, Peace Corps Volunteer **Samatha Klein** in 1996 traveled to Timbuktu, Mali to learn more about the Malians of Jewish descent but was disappointed to find that there were no "**practicing Black Jews**" in Mali because everyone was raised Muslim.

Deuteronomy 28:36 "The Lord shall bring thee, and thy king which thou shalt set over thee, unto a nation which neither thou nor thy fathers have known; **and there shalt you serve other gods**, wood and stone."

Many Malian historians claim that originally these Black Jews settled in North Mali but eventually scattered amongst villages along the Niger River. The Tuareg people are a known group of African people who have most of its population in **Niger, Mali, Southwest Algeria, Burkina Faso, Southwest Libya and Morocco**. 85% of the Tuareg people live in Mali and Niger. The Tuareg people in ancient times were sometimes linked to bringing enslaved people (Israelites?) from the Northern Parts of Africa to West African coastal countries to be sold to

Europeans and Arabs. This is also a practice that was done by the Israelite "Bantus" **Yoruba Oyo Kings** and the Israelite "Bantus" **Kings of Ghana**. What is interesting about the Tuareg people is that their name in Arabic means, "**Abandoned by God**." Were they abandoned by "**Yahuah**" the God of the Israelites for breaking his commandments/laws? Or where they abandoned by "**Allah**"? The Tuareg people follow Islam and pray 5 times a day like Muslims are supposed to do, so why would their god, aka the god of Islam (**Allah**) abandon them? The Tuareg people write from right to left like "**Hebrew**" even though their writing script is unique and different than Hebrew or Arabic. No historian has come up with the "**true origin**" of the Tuareg people, where they came from or when they arrived to Africa. Some say they came from the land between the Nile River and the Euphrates River, while others say that they came from Yemen. To this day, the Tuareg's are reluctant to give away any secrets in regards to their possible Jewish (Israelite) ancestry, or any evidence of extra-marital affairs with the Black Jews (Israelites) in their land.

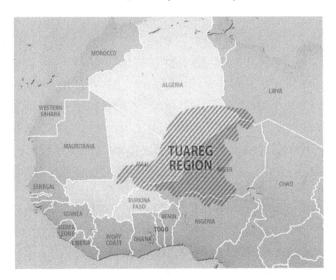

One interesting find is that the Tuareg people **DO NOT** carry the so-called Arab Y-DNA "J" Haplogroup, which is most frequent and potent in **Yemen**. Many geneticists link this "**J1**" Haplogroup to some of the descendants of Shem who were perhaps descendants of Ishmael,

Joktan, Ammon, Lot or Keturah's sons with Abraham. The Tuareg people however **DO CARRY** varying percentages of the "**E1b1a**" Haplogroup like Negroes and the "**E1b1b**" Haplogroup that Ethiopians/Somalians are classified under now. Some (Niger Tuareg's) still carry the Y-DNA Haplogroup "**R1b**" that can still be found in people living in **Spain, Portugal, and North Africa**. Could the Tuareg people be half-Israelite/half-Phuttite? Or could they be a mixture of Israelite, Cushite and Phuttite descent? After all, they don't carry the Y-DNA "**J1**" Haplogroup that is seen in the Black Arabs of South Arabia, Yemen, Oman, Qatar, and the Black Bedouins of Negev, Israel or Jordan.

Population	Nb	A/B	E1b1a	E-M35	E-M78	E-M81	E-M123	F	K-M9	G	I	J1	J2	R1a	R1b
1 Tuaregs from Libya	47	0	42.5%	0	0	48.9%	0	0	0	0	0	0	0	0	6.4%
2 Tuaregs from Mali	11	0	9.1%	0	9.1%	81.8%	0	0	0	0	0	0	0	0	0
3 Tuaregs from Burkina Faso	18	0	16.7%	0	0	77.8%	0	0	5.6%	0	0	0	0	0	0
4 Tuaregs from Niger	18	5.6%	44.4%	0	5.6%	11.1%	0	0	0	0	0	0	0	0	33.3%

(**Above**) Y-DNA studies of the Tuareg people. As you can see in the above chart, the Tuareg people from Libya tested positive for the "**E1b1a**" Haplogroup (42.5%) and also the "**E-M81**" Haplogroup (48.9%) from East Africa. Collectively the Tuareg people from **Niger** are more "**Bantus Negro**" than anything else with their high percentage of "**E1b1a (44.4%)**" compared to "**E-M81 (11.1%)**" and "**R1b (33.3%)**". Here is my "theory" on the Black Tuareg people from Niger.

Theory 1. Could these Tuareg's from Niger be descendants of some of the Hebrew Israelites/Black Moors" who were in Iberia (Spain/Portugal) from 700 A.D. to the late 1400's? This would explain their "**E1b1a**" Y-DNA and their "**R1b**" Y-DNA. After 700 years of rule in Europe the Black Moors (the majority) and the Black Israelites would leave their Y-DNA tattoo on the **Spanish-Portuguese-North African males** in regards to their "**Y**" male sex chromosome. It's possible that while in Iberia, a certain group of Black Israelites (E1b1a) were more likely to intermarry with the Black Moors (R1b) than with white people. Now the big question is if the Black Moors Y-DNA was the result of a mixing of many nations (i.e. Israelites, Egyptians, Ishmaelite's, other Shemites) as is the Y-DNA of the Native Indians (Q).

Theory 2. Did these Tuareg Moors start off in the "**R1b**" Y-DNA Haplogroup but over some generations after being "**exiled**" from Iberia, these Tuareg Moors began to mix with Israelite Muslims from the **Soninke, Mandingo, Mende/Mande, Songhay and Fulani Tribes** of West Africa? From talking to a Gambian man who was half-Wolof/half-Mandingo, he explained to me that the ancient Tribal name of the Mandingo people was the "**Soninke**" people. According to his knowledge the modern term used today was "**Mandingo**", except in Mali where they still kept the old word "**Soninke**" to describe his Mandingo people. In ancient times the Soninke and Towrood people lived in the Senegal, Malia, Gambia, Guinea-Bissau area (Senegal River Valley). They were known are "**Jews**", or "**foreigners**" coming from the land between "**Two Rivers**" when they migrated to Niger and Nigeria. This was quoted by **Muhammed Bello**, the 2nd Sultan of the Nigerian Sokoto Muslim Caliphate in the 1800's.

Muhammed Bello Quoted:

"The **Towrood or Taurud people**, it is said, **were originally Jews**, others say Christians; that they came from the land between the two rivers, **the Nile and the Euphrates**, and established themselves next to the Jews who inhabited the island (**Cape Verde islands**) ; and that whenever they oppressed or encroached upon the Jews, the latter had always recourse to the protection of the officers of the Sehabat (friends of Muhammed), who then ruled over them.- "This is what we found written in our books."

Journal of a Second Expedition into the Interior of Africa, from the Bight of Benin to Sokoto, 1829. London: Forgotten Books. (published 1829).

(**Above**) The Futa (**Fouta Toro**) area was located in **Senegal**, west of Mali. Futa (**Fouta Jallon/Djallon**) was located in **Guinea-Bissau**. Both areas were fed by the Senegal River. These are where the Israelites were. It is a known fact that the Mende and Fulani people in Guinea are mostly "**E1b1a**" carriers, while some are "**R1b-(Fulani)**". It is also a known fact that the majority of the people in Senegal (Wolof) and Gambia (Mandinka/Mandingo-Mande) are "**E1b1a**" Y-DNA carriers. Since we see this strong "predominance" of the "E1b1a" in the Senegal-Gambia-Guinea region let's see what Ancient African records had to say about the people living in the "**Fouta**" territory:

As 2nd Sultan of the Sokoto Caliphate in Nigeria, Muhammad Bello also gave the location and migration of the "**Sarankaly or Soninke people**" as well. He states their origins:

"Near to Bambara (**Timbuktu, Mali**), there is the province of the Towrood, and that of Foota (**Senegal River valley** area traditionally known as **Fouta, Futa Tooro or The Foota**), which are extensive, and inhabited by their own people and by those of **Sarankaly or Soninke** also called "**Ajam**" meaning "**alien or foreigner**".

Fact: *It is a known fact that the "**Soninke/Towrood**" people wrote in an "**Ajami script**" which was similar to Arabic and 13th century Sephardic Hebrew. The word "**Ajami**" was based on the Arabic root word "**Ajam/agami**" for "foreigner". It is also a known fact that the Soninke (Mandingo) people practiced circumcision which they called "**birou**". Despite the fact that most Soninke (Mandingo) today practice Islam, this is proof that prior to the birth of Islam, the people of West Africa living in the Ancient Ghana Empire were Black Hebrew Israelites. Muslims are not obligated to circumcise their boys as the Quran talks against distorting God's creation:*

- *"He created everything in exact measure; he precisely designed everything" - **Sura 25:2***
- *(Satan said:) "I will mislead them, I will entice them, I will command them to mark the ears of livestock, and I will command them to distort the creation of God." – **4:119***
- *"He created the heavens and the earth for a specific purpose, designed you and perfected your design." – **Sura 25:2***

Source: "Deep into the roots of the Libyan Tuareg: a genetic survey of their paternal heritage." *American Journal of Physical Anthropology. (May 2011). Volume 145 (1): pg. 118-124.*

"Y chromosomes and mtDNA of Tuareg nomads from the African Sahel". *(March 2010). European Journal of Human Genetics. Volume 18. pg. 915-923.*

TURKISH JEWS VS MOROCCAN JEWS: ARE THEY SIMPLY "EUROPEAN" OR ARE THEY "AUTHENTIC JEWS"?

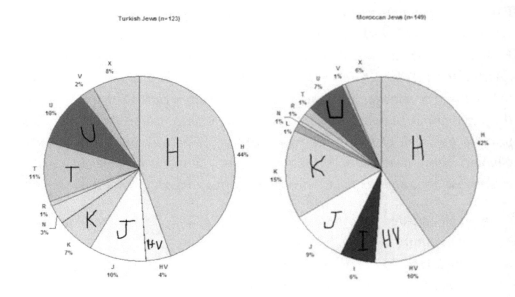

(Left) Turkish Jewish Maternal mtDNA. (Right) Moroccan Jewish Maternal mtDNA. Notice the most common mtDNA Haplogroups for both Jewish groups are **H, HV, J, K, and U.**

Note: They even have a small percentage of the Neanderthal "X" Y-DNA Haplogroup (6-8%) that is primarily seen in Europeans.

European MtDNA commonly has the following Haplogroups: **H, HV, J, K, I, U and X**. These **"European mtDNA"** Haplogroups as you can see makes up the majority of Turkish Jews and Moroccan Jews mtDNA. This essentially means that Moroccan Jews and Turkish Jews are **"genetically"** more European than **"so-called Jewish"**, especially if they are going of the notion, **"you're not a Jew unless your mother is a Jew"**. There is nothing in their DNA that makes them **"different"** than Europeans. Europeans descend from Japheth, not Shem, Abraham, Isaac or Jacob. The Mizrahi-Sephardic-Ashkenazi Jews DNA proves that their **"Jewish"** claim is a lie. This Ashkenazi, Sephardic and Mizrahi Jews are "white" like Europeans, because their DNA shows that they are European.

The Maternal DNA of Africans in **Mali** like historian "**Ismael Diadie Haidara**" falls typically in the "**L**" group, which is totally different than that of North Africans and Middle Easterns (except Yemen, Qatar, Oman).

THE REAL BLACK ISREALITES IN SPAIN/PORTUGAL HAD Y-DNA HAPLOGROUPS FOUND TODAY IN SUB-SAHARAN AFRICA.

According to the study "**Y-chromosomal diversity in the population of Guinea-Bissau: a multiethnic perspective**" by *BioMed Central Evolutionary Biology, (2007) 7:124,* it states that out of 45 Mandinka tribesmen in Guinea, 37 of them carried the Y DNA "**E1b1a**". Out of 59 Fulani (Fulbe) tribesmen in Guinea, 43 carried the Y DNA "**E1b1a**". This means that out of 104 Mandinka's/Fulani's in Guinea tested, **70-80% of them had the "Bantus E1b1a Negro" DNA. The "Mandingo/Mandinka" Tribe is a sub-group of the "Mende" tribe, which makes up the largest tribal group in Mali.** The Fulani Tribe is the largest diverse tribe in Africa with Y DNA Haplogroups ranging from E1b1a to E1b1b to R1b1c. **Some Ancient Arabs in the 16th century believed that some of the Fulani's were Hebrew Israelites mixed with Arab Ishmaelite's and perhaps Phuttite Berbers.** That being said, it is a good possibility that any Black Malian claiming to be descendants of Ancient Moroccan Jewish traders is technically admitting that the Moroccan Jews were the same "**genetically**" as the "**Bantus Negro**". Perhaps this is why the Nigerian "**Bnai Ephraim**" people claim to be descendants of the Jews exiled from Portugal into Morocco following the "**Edict of Expulsion**" by King Manuel I and King John II of Portugal in the late 15th century. Their Torah, which they still preserve in Yorubaland, Nigeria is written in **Moroccan Arabic, Aramaic and Old Yoruba script.** So who is the real "**Moroccan Jew?**" The "**White**" Moroccan Jew or the "**Black**" Moroccan Jew? is a known fact that the major composition of today's Sephardic "Moroccan" Jewish Y DNA consists of **G, J1-J2, R1b, I, and E1b1b**, not "**E1b1a**". The Y-DNA Haplogroups **G, J1-J2, R1b, I and E1b1b** are also found in other Europeans such as those living in the **Balkan Countries**, the area where most White "**convert**" Sephardic Jews fled to following the Spanish Inquisition.

BLACK JEWS WERE HATED BY BLACK MUSLIMS

How do we know that the "Black Jews" were not liked by other Black Muslims? How do we know that these "exiled" Jews from Iberia were not "White Sephardic Jews" instead of "Black Jews?" If there were "White Sephardic Jews" in Mali (Africa), where did they go? Did they travel further south into Burkina Faso and Ghana? Did they travel west to Senegal or East to Niger? Are there any records of there being "White Jews" in the heart of West/Central Africa? Nope. So these "exiled Jews" were Black Jews. The whole reason why these expelled Jews from Iberia (Spain/Portugal) were able to live in Mali (**which is all black**) undetected as "**Crypto-Jews**" is because they were "**Black**" just like everyone around them. This is what the European Sephardic Jews don't want people to know. They have covered the "Real Identity" of the Jews living in North Africa, Morocco, Spain and Portugal prior to the 1500's. This is the same "trick" the European Ashkenazi Jews used to fool the world into believing they were the "Real Israelites" that were returning to Israel in 1948.

While living in Africa, the only thing that would give these "**Black Jews**" away was if they were carrying **Torah Scrolls or Books** written in Hebrew. So instead of doing this and getting killed or caught, they walked around with books written in Arabic with Hebrew written in small fine print along the books borders. That way, if anyone wanted to ask them "**What are you reading?**", they could easily open it up, and at first glance any Arab would see that the writing of the book was in Arabic, not Hebrew. But how can we prove this? Easy.

The King (Askia the Great) is a declared enemy of the Jews. He will not allow any to live in the city (Gao/Timbuktu). If he hears it said that a Berber merchant frequents them or does business with them, he confiscates his goods."
Askia Muhammad – Muslim Emperor of the Songhai Empire from 1493-1528 A.D.

Where these "**White Jews**" that Askia Muhammad despised? No! These were "**Black Jews**"!

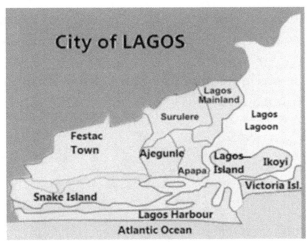

Lagos, Nigeria is a "Port city" situated on a collection of islands. The Yoruba Nigerian name for Lagos is "**Eko**". The Portuguese named the city by its name "**Lagos**" meaning "**Lakes**".

The **Bnai Ephraim** (Children of Ephraim) who live currently in Nigeria amongst the Yoruba's have an oral history that states they came from **Morocco** after they were banished from the **Portuguese** and **Spanish** sometime after **1492 A.D.** This lines up with the "**Spanish Inquisition**" and the "**Edict of Expulsion**" law passed in Iberia in which the Jews in Iberia were banished by the Catholic Church. They possess their own Torah scrolls written in the language from the time period they lived in. This was Moroccan Arabic, Ancient Yoruba, and Western Aramaic (not Eastern Syriac Aramaic). The Yoruba people called them the "**Emo Yo Quaim**" or "**Strange People**". I once talked to a Yoruba preacher

95

about this and he said that it was true. He said that these Yoruba's had different traditions and customs than their Yoruba brothers around them. He said that because of their different religious practices and customs they were seen as different, even if they had the same DNA as the Nigerian Yoruba's they lived amongst. It is known by the **Bnai Ephraim Jews** living in Yorubaland that they came to Nigeria to be with other Jews which they knew scattered via the Portuguese and their "Edict of Expulsion" into the Cape Verde Islands, Guinea Bissau, Sao Tome Island, Principe, Angola and other places. They also knew that some of their Hebrew brethren had settled in Nigeria by traveling from the Eastern direction (**from Ethiopia/Egypt**). Some of the "Black Jews" exiled from Iberia in the late 1400's arrived as slaves, some were fugitives that escaped, and some were blessed enough to be saved on their slave ship voyage from Portugal to the African Portuguese colonies in West Africa (**Note: this I break down the book Hebrews to Negroes 2: Volume 3**).

"In Garura/Ghiryu (Mali, Africa) there were some very rich Jews. The intervention of the preacher (Muhammad al-Maghili) of Tlemcen (Algerian Moorish Kingdom) set up pillage of their goods, and most of them have been killed by the population. This even took place during the same year when the Jews had been expeled (during the Spanish Inquisition along with the Black Moors) from Spain and Sicily by the Catholic King." - Leo Africanus -1526

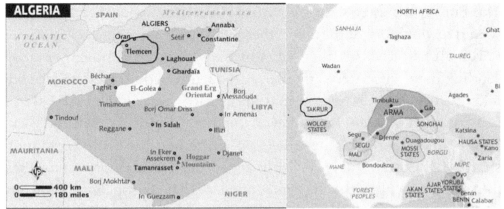

(Left) **Tlemcem** was an ancient Moorish Kingdom in North Algeria that was captured by the white-skinned Algerian Turks in 1559 A.D.
(Right) Note: **Jolof/Wolof** is a Tribe common in **Gambia/Senegal**. **Takrur** is in this area and right below it is Guinea-Bissau, which is southwest of Mali.

As you can see already in Chapter 1, the Europeans, Jews and Arabs did a good job erasing history but not all was lost. The "**Truth**" never remains hidden forever. The truth will always come to the light. Now is the time that knowledge is bringing out the "Truth". But why now? Because we are in the latter days, leading up to the last days. Sexual immorality and confusion is high and evil is all around us. The disciples during the days of Christ talked about these days.

2 Timothy 3:1-5 "This know also, that in the last days perilous times shall come. For men shall be lovers of their own selves, covetous, boasters, proud, blasphemers, disobedient to their parents, unthankful, unholy, without natural affection, trucebreakers, false accusers, incontinent, fierce, despisers of those that are good, traitors, heady, highminded, lovers of pleasure rather than lovers of God, having a form of godliness but the power thereof: from such turn away."

Back in slavery times the slaves outnumbered whites in their states but they still were in bondage. In Ancient Egypt, the Israelites rose in numbers to pretty much outnumber the Egyptians and that is what the Pharaoh's feared the most. So they went into slavery for over 400 years.

The Europeans knew that the "**Black Israelites**" and "**Black Moors**" would eventually outnumber them in Europe so Iberia (Spain & Portugal) had to create the "**Edict of Expulsion**" to get them out. By sending them into Africa, the Bantus Israelites would further expand, taking over all of West, Central and East Soudan. The Arabs and Europeans had a devious plan to further "**divide**", "**confuse**" and "**erase**" the identity of the Israelites. Islam and the Catholic Church strategically used "Religion" to mislead the Black Hebrew Israelites into slavery along with religious conversion. The Europeans and Arabs tricked Hebrew Israelites (**who didn't know they were Israelites**) to sell their own people into slavery for money or goods. The "**Bantus**" Israelites already "**genetically**" outnumbered everyone else in Africa but didn't know it so **Satan** had to use these Gentile races to remove the Israelites far from their borders and with the use of colonization, "**divide**" the people even more from their rich Israelite heritage. But Satan has been at it since the beginning of time, trying to deceive the Sons of Seth, the sons of Ham, the sons of Shem, Terah, Abraham, Ishmael, the sons of Japheth, but most importantly the **Children of Israel. It is a known fact that just in the Country of Nigeria alone (population 170 million), there are more Black Israelites with the "E1b1a" than in America (45 million Blacks in North America).**

CHAPTER 6

THE NAMES CHANGE, BUT THE "FALSE GOD" AKA SATAN, STAYS THE SAME. SATAN'S DECEPTION WAS AROUND BACK THEN AND IT STILL IS AROUND TODAY.

Matthew 24:37-39 "But as the days of Noah were, so shall also be the coming of the Son of man be. For as in the days that were before the flood they were eating and drinking, marrying and giving in marriage, until the day that Noah entered into the ark, And knew not until the flood came, and took them all away; **so shall also the coming of the Son of Man be.**"

In the days of Noah, sexual immorality was high and people were worshipping all types of gods. The pagan gods before the flood were all brought to man by Lucifer/Satan. Over time, from one civilization to the next the names of the pagan gods changed by their overseer (Satan) was still in control doing what he does best, getting mankind to worship everything but the **CREATOR**. Before the Flood, the Fallen Angels enticed mankind to worship the Sun, Moon, Stars, and animals such as the Bull (Apis Bull, Baal) or Fish (Dagon). This was one of the reasons why God created the flood. But the bible says that the Giants survived the flood when it says, "there were giants in the earth in those days; **AND AFTER THAT**".

Some of civilizations earliest pagan gods include **Mu, Nu, Ea, Enki, Marduk, Anu, Ptah, Ra, Osiris, Anubis, Isis, Horus, Zeus, Hermanubis, Serapis, Set, Lucifer, Satan, Baal, Dagon, Chiun, Remphan, Anunnaki, Jupiter, Vishnu, Shiva, Khrisna, and Allah**. The world has seen its fair share of pagan gods. This has been Satan's victory, to get mankind to worship him and fallen angels through "paganism". The Fallen Angels led by Lucifer would do the ultimate "No-No" in God's book. Intermix their "**divine-DNA**" with that of man, then getting man to believe that they were the creators of the world. For this reason, the Sumerians believed in the "**Annunaki**" as their creators, and the people of Sumeria, were in essence "slaves" to their so-called made up creators. Some people believe this is why we have dinosaur bones and relics all over the world, especially near pyramids (South America, India). Some people believe this is why the pig, dolphins, whales and other fish of the ocean "**without scales**" were forbidden for the Israelites to consume (i.e. possible result of ancient pre-flood cross-breeding). Some people also believe that the reason some people have "tails" is because of the fallen angels tampering with the human DNA genome. They believe that some people still have evidence of foreign genes in their DNA carried on from the Fallen Angels mating with humans pre-flood and post-flood. This has been shown on T.V. shows (i.e. **X-Files Season 10, Episode 1, 6) and Movies (Shallow Hal, Star Trek-Into the Darkness, Splice**).

So where do these tails really come from? Many will try to debunk this question as "**normal**" as they say human embryos have a tail remnant before their born, just like tadpoles have tails before becoming frogs. Some say humans with tails has something to do with our DNA and blood type, most notably if someone is **RH positive** or **RH negative**. But why are pregnant women tested to see if they are RH+ or RH-? What does this have to do with the Fallen Angels, the Nephilim Giants, the descendants of Cain, this so-called "**Neanderthal gene**", **Pyramids** all over the world and the "**White race**"?

THE MARK OF CAIN, THE NEPHILIM, THE WHITE INDIANS AND THE NEANDERTHALS.

The DNA of "**really old**" European skeletons called "**Neanderthals**" was analyzed many years ago in search for "**homo neanderthalis**" and "**homo erectus**". The DNA of two "Neanderthal" remains were tested, in particular from **Spain** and **Italy**. They were labeled "**El Sidron 1252**" and "**Monte Lessini**" (**Lalueza-Fox, C. et. al study 2007**). The remains of these two Neanderthals had a mutation on the **Melanocortin 1 receptor (MRC1) gene**. The Neanderthal MRC1 gene was a little different than modern humans but scientists believe that this gene was responsible for "red hair" and "pale skin" in modern humans, just as this specific "trait" was found in the White "**Nivarian**" Guanche Indians in the Canary Islands who were considered "**pre-historic**" by the Spaniards.

Note: *There have been many reports of giants in America with "Red" hair and six fingers. Could the Neanderthal "red-haired" man be a sort of offspring of the Nephilim giants that survived after the flood that didn't get the "Giant gene", thus remaining an average human height?*

The White "**Chepu Tule**" Indians of the Amazon were known by the brown-skinned Amazon Indians to have "**pale skin with red hair**". Three of these Chepu Tule Indians were brought to the U.S. in 1924 and were tested for albinism, however studies confirmed that they were not albino, but a white race. The Mormons called these white-skinned Indians "**Nephites**" similar to the "**Nephilim**" who were the offspring of man and the Fallen Angels in Genesis. However, they believed that

101

the "Mark of Cain" was "Black skin". This was talked about in the book, **"The America before Columbus"** by Deweh Farnsworth.

Book of Mormon-**Moses 7:22** "And Enoch also beheld the residue of the people which were the sons of Adam; and they were a mixture of all the seed of Adam save it was the seed of Cain, for the seed of Cain **WERE BLACK**, and had not place among them."

We know this is false because most Christian Pastors teach that Cain's seed was wiped out during the flood. So if Cain's seed was "Black" and Seth's seed was "White" this would mean that after the flood that Noah's white sons would populate the earth with all white women. The end result would be an earth of "**people without color**". According to the law of the land and the world, "White people cannot have "brown-black babies". We also know that there are more brown-black skinned people of color in the world than white people. Even despite the millions of blacks killed or castrated during the Slave Trades.

But what did others have to say about these "**White Indians**"? Were they the real descendants of Cain? Where they just Guanche Indians from the Canary Island, the Nephilim's white offspring, the descendants of Gehazi (**2 Kings 5:27**) or another race of people that existed with Cain pre-Flood? Why were they considered "**Serpent People?**"

Note: Both Gehazi and Cain are believed to have been "cursed" or "marked" with "white skin", including their seed. If this is the case, are there "two" or perhaps "three" sets of white races on the earth?

 2 Kings 5:27 "The leprosy therefore of Naaman shall cleave unto thee, and unto thy seed **FOREVER**. And he (Gehazi) went out from his presence a leper as **white as snow**."

Genesis 4:15 "And the Lord said unto him, Therefore whosoever slayeth Cain, vengeance shall be taken on him sevenfold. **And the Lord set a mark upon Cain**, lest any finding him should kill him."

Here are some accounts of these White Indians:

- "White-skinned bearded men (**most brown-skinned American Indians don't have enough facial hair to grow beards**) had come over the sea once before, with large parties of **astronomers, architects, priests, musicians, agronomists and magicians (sages)**....and bringing with them many of the "**secrets**" of civilization. **They had mingled with the aboriginal population** and taught them how to build adobe houses, weave, live in town, **ERECT PYRAMIDS**, write on paper and stone, as well as the science of metallurgy (**Metalworkers-Alchemy like Cain's seed**)." - "**The White Indians of Nivaria**" by Gordon Kennedy, p. 68.

  Genesis 4:22 "And Zillah, she also bare **Tubal-Cain, an instructor of every artificer in brass and iron:** and the sister of Tubal-Cain was Naamah."

- "Civilization was brought to them at the dawn of history by white and bearded men, under the leadership of the **SUN KING** Con-Tici Viracocha, who had arrived on reed boats, settled on the Island of the **SUN** in Lake Titicaca (Bolivian-Peruvian border in the Andes Mountains), then later sailed away from there to the south shore and constructed the **SUN PYRAMID**, the massive **megalithic walls** and all the **monoliths** that can still be seen among the ruined city of Tiahuanaco (**Bolivia**)" – "**The White Indians of Nivaria**" by Gordon Kennedy.

- "Legends of the primitive races of Yucatan and portions of Mexico tell of the coming in ships of a "**fair-skinned**" race of men (Europeans?) who became the rulers and the leaders of **DARK-SKINNED ABORIGINES**." – "**People of the Serpent**" by archaeologist Edward H. Thompson. Pg. 75.

- "In Ancient times," said Priest Ah Kin Chan, "my fathers, the Chanes of Nonoual, the **People of the Serpent**, found the **dark skinned savage Mayans** living in damp caves and forests, eating roots and crawling things, more like beasts than men. Then my fathers, the **LIGHT-SKINNED** wise men, took the dark forest people and bound them with fetters of fear and love, raised them to the light of day. Even the Chanes, the wise men of Nonoual, led the Mayans in their advances." – "**People of the Serpent**" – Edward H. Thompson. Pg. 228.

- "Who were these **FAIR-SKINNED** people, tall of stature (giants?) and strangely clad, sailing through unknown seas to an unknown land? The answer to this question has been lost in the passing of the ages and the destruction of the ancient records and now we know only that they came and that until after the arrival of the Spaniards, the place where they landed was known as Tamoanchan, which means, in the native language, the place where the People of the Serpent landed." "**People of the Serpent**" – Edward H. Thompson.

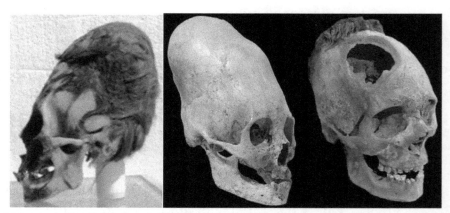

(**Above**) Red Haired-Skulls found in Paracas, Peru. In 1928, Julio Tello found strange looking skulls in a tomb in southern Peru. Many claim because of the shape of the skulls, the appearance of two small holes in the back of the skull, the findings of some skulls without a sagittal suture, and foreign DNA from the skulls that these ancient people in Peru were not human. In Peru it has been said that there are portals/gates that the ancients used to travel-interdimensionally which are found underneath the Pyramids in South America and even in Africa. Some say these gates also connected the "Outer Earth-**where man lives**" to the "Inner Earth-**where the ancient ones live**". Also the practice of "**trepanation**" was used by these long-headed people that was an old barbaric practice of chiseling out "**burr holes**" in the skull in hopes of releasing "**evil spirits**" or curing neurological-mental diseases. The White Guanche Indians of the Canary Islands **ALSO** lived in caves, practiced mummification and built pyramids.

So eventually man got around to testing the Guanche aboriginal women's mtDNA and it came back **H, HV, U, V, and K**, which is most commonly found in European women. Scientists believe the mtDNA to be more accurate and reliable as most aboriginal women retain their mtDNA even if they marry or are raped by foreign invaders/colonizers to the land. This can be seen in Native "Indian" women in South America, Central America, North America and Caribbean. The Guanche men's Y-DNA was tested and it proved to be similar but with more North African Arab and Spanish Influence from the invasion of the Canary Island in the 1500's.

CHAPTER 7

WHERE DOES THE WHITE RACE COME FROM?
DOES ANYBODY KNOW?

(**Left**) The "Big Mystery"! Are these "**White Libyans**" or the
"**Tamahu-Typhonian**" people the Egyptians talked about.
(**Right**) Nubian Cushite.

Some pictures from Egypt depict what seems to have been a race of
white-skinned people in Ancient times (B.C.). Some people have
connected these pictures to the Ancient Libyan Phuttites of the Bible
but we do not know because the Table of Nations in Genesis 10 does
not list Phut (Put) having any sons. But regardless of this, we know
this is not true, because many historians have penned that the Libyans
were some of the darkest people in the world. We also know that the
Libyan Phuttite Pharaoh's (i.e. Iuput, Orsorkon) were black as they
were the sons of Ham. The Phuttite Libyans are mentioned in **Jeremiah
46:9, Ezekiel 30:5 and Ezekiel 27:10**. So who are these "white people"
depicted supposedly on the Egyptian walls? If they are not Libyan's,

then who are they? Who put these pictures there and when did it happen?

In Ancient Egypt, white people were recorded as the **"Tamahu"** which meant **"the created white people"** on the **Tempe of Seti I**. Another name for Satan in the occult world is **"Set"**. There is even a Satanic congregation called the **"Temple of Set"** which is a branch off the **"Church of Satan"**, founded by Anton LaVey. '

The "created white people" theory according to many Egyptologists suggests that "white people" were created or genetically produced by Satan and his Fallen Angels (**not the big-headed black scientist Yakub**). In the Egyptian language, **"Tama"** means **"people"** and **"Hu"** means **"white"**. Egyptians also refer to pale white-skinned people as **"Typhonians"** or the **"People of Set (Seth)"** meaning **"the devils"**.

The **"Starfire"** magazine promotes the **"Typhonian Order"** (**by founder Kenneth Grant**), the **93 Current of Thelema** and it talks about opening the way for the demons of hell. This magazine is the Official magazine of the **O.T.O (Ordo Templi Orientis) Society**. Notice that this Satanic magazine has the Egyptian name of Horus **"Ra-Hoor-**

Khuit" wrapped around the point of the Star in the middle of the magazine. This is because the Egyptian god Horus is affiliated with Satan in the occult. The magazine also has the words "**Nu**" which is the Egyptian water god, father of the Egyptian Sun-God "**Ra**" even though Ptah is supposed to be the father of "**Ra**". "**Nu**" was also worshipped by the Nubians and was believed to be the source of the River Nile. By using the pagan gods "**Ptah-Mu/Nu**", Satan influenced the Nubians Cushites and the Egyptians to build Satanic Pyramids. The motto of the **O.T.O-Thelema society** and Aleister Crowley is "**Do what thou wilt shall be the whole of the law**". The Egyptian god **Typhon** was associated with **evil**, while the Egyptian god "**Set**" was also equivalent of Satan/Lucifer. So why would the Egyptians write that "**white-skinned people**" were "**Typhonians**" if the god **Typhon** was associated with evil?

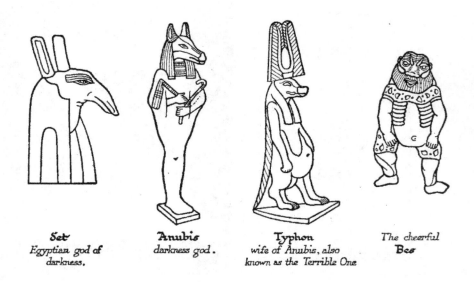

Set	*Anubis*	*Typhon*	*The cheerful*
Egyptian god of darkness.	*darkness god.*	*wife of Anubis, also known as the Terrible One*	*Bes*

The Egyptian god **Set** was believed to have **white skin and red hair** the texture of donkey's hair. In Egyptian hieroglyphics his name uses the words, "**chaos**", "**turmoil**", "**confusion**", "**illness**", "**storm**", and "**rage**". Events like eclipses, thunderstorms and earthquakes were attributed to Set. The Egyptians believed that Set had strange "**sexual** preferences" or **"gay tendencies"** because although he was married, he had no children. They claim he was bisexual and in the Egyptian 20th Egyptian Dynasty literary work the **"Contending's of Horus and Set"**, Set can be caught saying **"How lovely your backside is"** in reference to the back view (behind) of Horus's body. This is why the Egyptian religion and its 200+ pagan gods are rooted in evil. Set had the ability to turn in animals such as the bull which the Egyptians worshipped. Set was also identified with other animals such as the hippopotamus, the pig, and the donkey, which were all animals the Hebrew Israelites were forbidden to eat. These animals however were sacred to **Set. Homosexuality, unclean animals and chaos are all tools that Satan used against the Hebrew Israelites to make them sin against the laws set by God.**

In Ancient Egyptian Mythology Set fell from his high position over the gods to a lower position (just like Lucifer). In Satanism and the **Thelema** occult society founded by Satanist, Jesuit, Freemason and bisexual "**Aleister Crowley**", the Egyptian god "**Set**" is the equivalent of our modern day "**Satan**". It is a known fact that **Anton LaVey**, late founder of the Church of Satan, had a protégé who conjured up evil spirits to find out the infernal name of the "**Wicked One**". This man named **Michael Aquino** claimed that the demons/evil spirits responded to him with the name "**Set**". Michael Aquino then broke from the "**Church of Satan**" and started his own Satanic Church in 1975 called the "**Temple of Set**". Many sources say that the Hyksos people that came into Egypt and ruled also worshipped "**Set**" and had Semitic names.

So the Ancient Egyptians recorded "**white people**" as the "**Tamahu**" or the "**Typhonians**" which meant "**People of Set (Seth)**". For this reason, many people in Ancient times believed that "white skinned" races were associated with the devil. It is believed that back then the Black Hamitic Africans rounded up this "**White Tamahu-Typhonian race**" and exiled them to the caves/hills of the Caucasus Mountains in Europe. Others possibly escaped to the Canary Islands off the coast of

Morocco, Africa where these "**White people**" lived in caves, practiced mummification and erected mound pyramids (learnt possibly in Egypt). Another story says that the Hamitic Africans built walls blocking the "Caucasians" from leaving their habitat in Europe once they were put there. It is here in Europe that they believe these "**white people**" intermixed with the so-called "Neanderthal" white man from Scandinavia and Northern Europe. The "Neanderthal" man was believed to be some "pre-flood/Nephilim" man that somehow survived the "**Great Flood**", possibly using some sort of "Fallen Angel knowledge" to do so. **Scientists have also verified that the Neanderthal Y-DNA "X" Haplogroup is not found in "Pure-Blooded" Africans, Asians or Native Americans (just like the Rh negative factor)**. It is only seen in Europeans or races that have mixed with Europeans.

It is possible that the Black Egyptians (or another Black race) mixed with the "White" Tamahu-Typhonian women, leaving their Y-DNA mark (**Haplogroup R1a, R1b**) on the male children who then populated Western, Eastern and Northern Europe. According to Egyptian sources, the white Tamahu-Typhonian people were causing too much problems among the local Egyptians and threatened their rulership. Once these "White" invaders left they vowed to come back to all "Black" civilizations throughout the Middle East, Asia (China), Africa, and India. **Their mission, to destroy and conquer them**. By looking at the European (i.e. British/Spanish/French) invasion of countries across the world such as **China** (Hong Kong), **India** (British India), the **Middle East** (British Petroleum, British Mandatory Palestine), Australia (British), **Africa** (everybody), **South Africa** (Dutch, British), the **Caribbean** (French, Spanish, British) and the **New World (Americas)** it seems that they kept their promise. God will however "**reset**" things back to the way they should be during the "**End Times**".

(**Left & Middle**) Bes, an Egyptian God from the Old Kingdom, supposedly the son of Ptah, who was a protector of the people. He is seen depicted on the walls in the **Hathor Temple** and **Horus Temple** in Egypt. **Bes** was also worshipped by the Egyptians neighbors, the "**Canaanite people**". The **Twa pygmy** people back then and today worship him as god. The Twa people were believed to be the first inhabitants of Ireland/Scotland. The Europeans thought these "**little black people**" were magical because of their small stature, knowledge of **alchemy**, **metallurgy** and **medicine**. Their pygmy god, "**Bes**" who was fat with a beard became the basis of the "Leprechaun" Irish folklore. (**Right**) The **Twa pygmies** and their relics can be found in Kenya, Tanzania and Uganda. Europeans throughout time have **ALWAYS** been fascinated with the pygmy people all over the world. They included them mostly on display in their "**Human Zoos**" in the 18th, 19th and 20th century.

In ancient times the Twa people were used to perform dances for the gods in front of the Egyptian Royal staff who had rulership of the Land of Canaan (**i.e. see the Egyptian Amarna Tablets**). Today they are still known for their dancing. They are now found in the Congo, Rwanda and the African Great Lakes like other pygmy tribes (i.e. Mbuti, Biaka, San). **The majority of the Twa people's Y-DNA is from Haplogroup "B" while a small percentage (30%) is "E1b1a (E-M2)" which is only seen in the Bantus people of West/East Africa.** The presence of the "E1b1a" Haplogroup in the Twa people is due to intermixing with the "**Stronger**" Bantus "Israelite" people who usually dominated and ruled the land of the Pygmies. Could the "Pygmy" race be the Canaanites? I am led to believe so. The Canaanite people, including their Phoenician language is as about as old as Paleo-Hebrew. It looks like Paleo-Hebrew as well, which many say was the language of Noah and Shem. Some have compared "Paleo Hebrew" to the "Atlantean language" found on the "**Emerald Tablets of Thoth**" which are believed to come from the land known as "Ancient Egypt" prior to the flood.

Pictograph	Pictograph

(Left) Emerald Tablets of **Thoth** (Greek god "Hermes") written in the **Atlantean** "pre-flood" script. (**Right**) **Paleo-Hebrew**, believed to be the writing style of Noah and Shem who both were alive before the "**Great Flood**" when the Fallen Angels/Nephilim existed on the corrupt, evil earth. God created the flood to "**purge**" and "**cleanse**" the earth of the descendants of the Fallen Angels, the Nephilim (Giants), including any "**abominable animals**" that may have been living on the earth during these times. But there is a hidden "sinister" message in these Emerald Tablets that reveal who Thoth is and why his message is purely from the pits of Hell.

The Twa pygmies Y-DNA is almost as old as the Nubian Cushite Y-DNA "**A**" found in the **Oromo Ethiopians, the San Tribe in Namibia, the Nama people in Namibia and the Sudanese people (i.e. Dinka, Shilluk)**. The Pygmy (Twa) people still today live amongst the "**Bantus**" people but they are usually used **for menial work (servant work)**. Hundreds of years ago, Bantus men would often take for them wives from pygmy villages. There is some belief that they are the biblical "**Canaanites**" because wherever they go they are unable to defeat the other Blacks living in Africa (**Nilotes Nubians/Cushites, Egyptians, Libyans and the Bantus Hebrew Israelites**). For this reason, many believe the pygmy tribes left on boats out of Africa to Europe, India (Bay of Bengal), Indonesia, the Pacific Islands and Australia. Along the way, they mixed with other nations, possibly giving rise to other black "**aboriginal**" nations of people. God told the Israelites to **NOT** intermarry with the Canaanites and they did. The Israelites also intermarried with the Egyptians and Nubian Cushites. The culture of the Yoruba/Igbo Nigerians show the Egyptian and Canaanite influence in different aspects of their life (i.e. religion, language, marriage, caste system). Y-DNA (**E1b1a**) and mtDNA (**L**) of the pygmy people also show evidence of a "Bantus" Israelite influence from intermixing. The same can also be said about the Nilotic Cushite East Africans when testing the DNA of different tribes for evidence of the Bantus Y-DNA "**E1b1a**" or mtDNA "**L2/L3**".

(**Left**) **Yoruba "Child of Obatala"**. (**Right**) Egyptian God "**Bes**". See the similarities (i.e. skull necklace, favorite god? Are the Yoruba Nigerians Israelites and the Pygmy tribes like "Twa" are Canaanites? This would make sense seeing that the Bible states that the Children of Israel intermarried for over 1,000 years with the sons of Ham (Canaan,

Phut, Mizraim and Cush). It is a known fact that most of the native "Negro-looking people living in the South Pacific Islands are short in stature whereas the Hebrew Israelites have always been linked to being average height or sligtly taller (i.e. Native Americans taller than Mexicans. Have we been hoodwinked?

Obatala was a sky god in Yoruba religion. In addition to being the King of the Orishas (divine beings of Oludumare/Olurun) he is also the creator of the earth and man in the Yoruba culture. Sometimes Obatala is seen as a sort of "Son of God" figure that comes directly from earth from Heaven. Notice **Obatala's skull necklace** and his chubby-appearance similar to the **Pygmy Twa god '"Bes"** with his **skull necklace**. They both are depicted with their "mouth open" which is usually not the case in statues of Yoruba gods. If the Twa people are descendants of the ancient Canaanites, this would make sense as the Israelites kept many of the religious traditions of the Hamitic peoples they mixed with (i.e. Canaanites, Egyptians, Nubians). The Israelites also picked up some language from the Hamitic people (i.e. "EL", "Ra"). Some even say the Hebrew Language was formed/adopted from the Ancient Canaanite language because it is so similar.

Many Egyptian words can be still seen in the words spoken by Bantus Igbo Nigerians, Somalians, Kenyans, and Bantus Congolese people. The **Congo people** also have a chubby, beer-belly god that has his mouth open with a skull necklace. The **Congo people, Nigerians and Ghananians** all have the highest percentages of people with the "E1b1a" Y DNA Haplogroup. The Pygmy tribal people and the Bantus **"Israelites"** Negroes in West/East Africa both carry the Maternal mtDNA Haplogroup **"L"** from their long history of race mixing as verified in the Holy Bible. But what happened to the languages of the Ancient Hebrew Israelites and the Canaanites (Phoenician)? If they were both the same in B.C. times and the Israelites mixed heavily with the Canaanites forming "Israelite-Canaanite" people, shouldn't the Paleo-Hebrew/Phoenician language dissapear together from the original inhabitants of Israel/Canaan? Well for one group of people, the language of so-called Paleo-Hebrew didn't change.

| Paleo-Hebrew | Samaritan | Phoenician |

(**Above**) The Letter "**Beyt/Bet**" in **Paleo-Hebrew, Samaritan and Phoenician writing styles**. It has been believed that Paleo-Hebrew and Phoenician were the same thing for centuries so much so that people believed that the Canaanites also wrote/spoke Hebrew. The two languages today have been used interchangeably because of their very close similarities. The first major discovery connecting the Phoenician alphabet with Paleo-Hebrew occurred on January 19, 1855 when Turkish workers accidently uncovered an ancient tomb in Sidon/Zidon, a Phoenician city in modern day Lebanon (Tribe of Asher Territory). On the tomb was a lengthy inscription written in the Phoenician alphabet which they found to be identical to Paleo-Hebrew with only a few exceptions. The Samaritan language is also very similar to Paleo-Hebrew as you can see.

The Samaritans claim to be descendants of Jews that were not taken by the Assyrians in 700 B.C. Despite the **Ancient Nimrud Prisim artifacts** and **2 Kings 17:24** in the Bible stating that the people put in Israel after their exile were "**Assyrians**" they still claim to be authentic Jews from Ancient times. They claim to be descendants of the **Tribe of Ephraim, Manasseh and Levi (including Cohenites from Aaron's lineage)**. They claim they have always remained in Israel, mixing possibly only with Arabs and Gentile Jews over the centuries. The Samaritans pass down their lineage through the father, which is different than

Ashkenazi and Sephardic Jews. **They only marry within their people and therefore have 84% of their marriages between first or second cousins.** They are group into four lineages: the **Tsedaka** (Manasseh), **Joshua-Marhiv** (Ephraim), **Danfi** (Ephraim), and the **Cohenite Samaritans** (Levi-Aaron). So what does DNA proof have to say about this? Well, interestingly the **Cohenite Samaritans** had **NO** Semitic Y-DNA "J1" markers found in their DNA. In fact, they had the Y-DNA (**E1b1b-M78**), which is a mixture of the DNA of Turks, Kurds, Romans, Greeks with the **Men of Edom**. The **Danfi** (Ephraim) as well as the **Tsedaka** (Manasseh) Samaritans fell into the Y-DNA "J2" Haplogroup which is seen in Turks, Kurds, Armenians, North African "white" Arabs and Greeks. Only the **Joshua-Marhiv** (Ephraim) Samaritans fell into the "J1" Y-DNA Haplogroup which according to scientists comes from an ancestral "**Semitic**" male forefather. The Maternal mtDNA of these Samaritans (estimated to be about 700 in Holon & Nablus, Israel) came out to be "Europen" as "**U**", "**G**" and "**T**". Scientists concluded that overall, the Jews were more closely related to groups in the north of the Fertile Crescent (Kurds, Turks, Armenians) than to Palestinian Arabs, Yemeni Jews an Bedouins.

Source: "**Genetics and the History of the Samaritans: Y-Chromosomal Microsatellites and Genetic Affinity between Samaritans and Cohanim**", *Human Biology. (December 2013). Volume 85: Issue 6: pg. 825-827.*

So what does all of this mean? In theory if both the Canaanites and the Israelites experienced an "**Out of Israel/Canaan**" event from foreign invasion or exile then these people groups would eventually see a change in their writing styles/language once they started "**mixing with the nations**". So as the Bantus Israelites would "**lose their idenity**", by mixing with the Pygmy tribes (Canaanites?) the Pygmy tribes would also lose their former language by adopting the language style of their surrounding Bantus or Nilotic neighbors. That being said, if the Samaritans today are descendants of the Ancient Assyrians, this would possibly explain how some of them were able to retain the Semitic "J1"

Y-DNA Haplogroup passed on from the father but over time experienced changes in their skin color/hair texture from possible intermarriage with "**white races**". Per Samaritan law, if a Samaritan man has children with a non-Samaritan women, the children are still considered "**Samaritan**". However, the children of Samaritan women who marry outside of their race are "**expelled**" from being called "**Samaritan**". So the possibility of skin color change (**from brown to white**) and hair texture change (**from kinky to straight**) can easily happen with Samaritan male marriage to women from "**white races**".

(**Left**) **Egyptian Pharaoh Rameses II** subduing three men by the hair. According to Ancient History, these are **Canaanites** (Levant men). Nevertheless, either Egyptian Pharaoh Rameses II is a giant or the Canaanite people were really small, like pygmies. (**Right**) The Canaanite people typically wore a headband with their dreadlocks pushed to the back. The Lebanese people today are not descendants of the Black Canaanites from the Sons of Ham. If they were, they would exhibit African Y-DNA Haplogroups and mtDNA Haplogroups.

Fact 1: *The **Pgymy Twa (Batwa)** people also have a creation story in which God **creates man**, a **Garden of Paradise** and a **Sacred tree (i.e. Tree of Knowledge)**. The Pygmy man God creates is deceived by a Pygmy woman to eat of a **certain fruit (i.e. apple)** that God put a ban on. Because of this, God punishes the pygmy people. They also have a ancient story that fits the story of a "**Messiah**" that comes to save mankind. Perhaps the Canaanites from intermarrying with the "**Bantus**" African Israelites for over 1,000 years learned the ways of their God, the Old Testament "Messianic" prophesies and taught this to their children, no matter if they were married to Israelites or not.*

Fact 2: *I talked once to man and a woman from Cameroon. They revealed that in their country the "**pygmy**" people were viewed as a people that were at the "bottom" of society. At one point in history they were numerous but now they are the minority, wherever they go, thanks to the "**Bantus Expansion**" and "**European colonization**". Over centuries the "pygmy" peoples have been subject to a sort of "**servitude**" status in whatever country they happen to dwell in. The Bantus people in these countries typically rule over the pygmy people. The Cameroonians stated that efforts are made by the Government to intergrate them into society, such as offering them school and other resources available to the "majority" Bantus people in the land. However, most of the "pygmy" people declined the offer, choosing to live in the forest/village the way they had been doing for decades/centuries. The stronger Nubian Empire, Egyptian Empire, Libyan Empire and Hebrew Israelite Kingdom in Africa have essentially shrunk the population of the "pygmy" tribes to the small population that we see today in world. This is from centuries of Canaanite people always being "**besieged**" by other "**Black Nations**" with the Canaanite women and children usually taken as "**spoils of war**" to be used as servants or maidservants/sex slaves. Even in Ancient times, the Canaanites were under rulership by the Egyptian Pharaohs, the Hebrew Israelites, the Edomites, the Greeks, the Romans and the Arabs. The African man and woman from Cameroon admitted that "**even today**" the pygmy people were often used by the "**Bantus Africans**" to do "**servitude-type**" of work that no one else would do. This normally happened to the pygmies that ventured to live in the villages instead of the forest. Types of servitude-like tasks include but are not limited to: using the pygmy women to carry large* baskets or using the pygmy men to hunt small animals in the forest which they were able to do with ease because of their ability to navigate through bushes because of their small size. It also includes fishing and manual labor in which the pygmies are paid cigarettes, clothes, a little bit of money or nothing at all. It is a known fact that many Pygmies are born into "**servitude**" to the Bantus people of the Congo. Many Bantus people oversee numerous pygmies, giving pygmy families a hut to live in, food, and in return the pygmies work as slaves-servants for their Bantus masters. Many Bantus masters will say that their pygmies are like "family" but many pygmy people say otherwise. They say that they are tired of being slaves to the Bantus people. Their women complain about being raped by Bantus men, which often results in half-Bantus/half-pygmy babies that carry on their father's Y-DNA "E1b1a" Haplogroup. This mirrors how the Israelites treated the Canaanites throughout the bible and in the famous "**Slaughter of Shechem**" story in **Genesis 34**. Could all of this information be a clue that the real "**Curse of Canaan**" was upon another people, perhaps the Pygmy Tribes of Africa and that maybe we need to re-think what is being taught in Churches.

Genesis 9:26-27 "And he said, **Cursed be Canaan; a servant of servants shall he be unto his brethren**. And he said, Blessed be the Lord God of Shem; and **Canaan shall be his servant.**

HEBREWS AND THE CANAANITES ARE ONE? ARE WE UNDER A DUAL-CURSE FROM THE "CURSES OF ISREAL" AND THE "CURSES OF CANAAN"?

It is a known fact that the Isrealites kept intermarrying with the Canaanites throughout the bible. Judah's first wife was a Canaanite. King David's wife **Bathsheba**, was according to many, a Canaanite (Hittite) woman who birthed King Solomon. King David's son, **Absalom** was the son of a Canaanite woman named "**Maachah**". From the Book of Judges (Chapter 3) until the Book of Ezra (Chapter 9) we see the long duration of race-mixing that occurred between the Israelites and Canaanites. So how does this apply to the people in

Africa today? The "Bantus" people in Africa are "**E1b1a**" Y-DNA Haplogroup carriers, and are thus descendants of the Hebrew Israelites of the Bible. As said before, one of the oldest Black nations in Africa is the "**Pygmy Tribe**" people. The pygmy people in Africa are mainly hunter-gatherers. The mainly live in "Bantus" Sub-Saharan Africa. They are usually classified into two groups, Eastern and Western pygmies. Whether there are a group of pygmies in East Africa or West Africa, they are usually surrounded by the "Bantus" people who are usually farmers or pastoralists (shepards of livestock). The main mtDNA of the Pymgy people can be found in African-Americans, Ethiopians, "Bantus" Africans and even Yemeni people. The maternal mtDNA "**L1c**" is most often seen in pygmies living in "**Western Africa**" while mtDNA "**Loa, L2a, L3e and L5**" are seen in pygmies living in "**Eastern Africa/South Africa**". How did this happen? It happened every time the Bantus men (**or any African nation**) conquered the villages of the pygmies, killing the men and taking the women. These conquered "pygmy women" would birth children to the Bantus men (or other Hamitic Africans) thus mixing and passing along different **haplogroup's** over the span of thousands of years. The Israelites mixed with the Canaanites in "**B.C.**" times and today we see in Africa the mixture of "**Bantus**" and "**Pygmy**" people for the last 2,000 years in "**A.D.**" times. After so much mixing, some scientists believe that many of the pygmy people have undergone a sort of "**metamorphosis**" into the people we call "Bantus" today. All over the world we can see "**Negrito-type**" black people (especially in South Asia/Pacific Islands) who are typically short like the pygmies (Negritos = Little Negroes). On example is the Negrito/Aeta people of the Phillipines. These "Negrito" blacks are also hunter-gatherer people, just like the few pygmy tribes still left in Africa.

Source: "**Insights into the Demographic History of African Pygmies from Complete Mitochondrial Genomes**". *Oxford Journal, Molecular Biology and Evolution, Volume 28, Issue 2. Pg. 1099-1110.*

Abraham gave instructions for his seed to not mix with the Canaanites, amongst whom he dwelled with. This was before 2,000 B.C., before Jacob and the Israelites were born. Ezra lived aroung 400 B.C. during the rebuilding of the Second Temple in Jerusalmen under the Persian Kings as it states Ezra came into Jerusalem "**in the seventh year of Artaxerxes the King**." This would have been around **400 B.C.,** give or take 50 years. So let's put this all together; 2,000 B.C. - 400 B.C. = 1600 years of years that the Israelites were mixing with the **Egyptians, Nubian Cushites and the Canaanites**. Do we have proof of this? We sure do!

Ezra 9:1-2 "Now when these things were done, the princes came to me, saying, The people of Israel, and the **PRIESTS**, and the **LEVITES**, have not separated themselves from the people of the lands, doing according to their abominations, even of the **CANAANITES**, the **HITTITES**, the **PERIZZITES**, the **JEBUSITES**, the Ammonites, the Moabites, the Egyptians, and the Amorites. For they have taken of their daughters for themselves, and for their sons: so that the **HOLY SEED HAVE MINGLED THEMSELVES WITH THE PEOPLE OF THOSE LANDS**: yea, the hand of the princes and rulers hath been chief in this trespass."

(Left) Yakub (Jacob) the Black Big-Headed Scientist who supposedly created the white man 6,000 years ago. **(Right) Unzie the Albino** from New Zealand (late 1800's). He appeared in the Barnum and Bailey Circus Show per some records.

One of the greatest mysteries known to man is the question as to where the **"white man"** came from. People theorize that mankind could not have started with a white **"Adam"** and a white 'Eve" because the majority of people on the earth are **"Melaninated"** people. We know that "white skin" typically turns pink or red when exposed to the sun, instead of brown so it is hard to convince most people that the original people on earth created by God were white. So that leaves us with the question: **"If in the beginning, God created a black man and woman, where do white people come from"**? There are a lot of theories out there including the **"Albino Indian"** theory, the **"Yakub"** theory, the **"Neanderthal"** theory, the **"Mark of Cain"** theory, and the **"Fallen**

Angel" Theory. Ashkenazi Jews that admit the original Jews were Black state that the Black Jews that migrated to Europe turned "white" because of the lack of sunlight in the North. Yet the thousands of Jews in Florida have not turned back "Black" because of the increase in sunlight. So this "Jewish Theory" is false. So where did the white man come from? Here is one theory below.

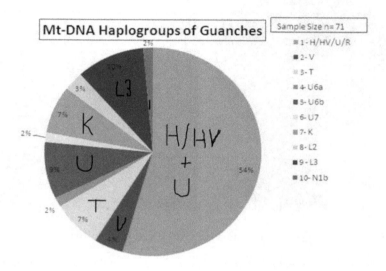

(**Above**) The **Guanche** aboriginal Indians of the Canary Islands were nicknamed the "**White Indians of Nivaria**". The above pie-chart breaks down their maternal mtDNA which is mostly seen today in Europeans and Arabs.

Source: "**The maternal aborigine colonization of La Palma (Canary Islands), Canary Islands Ancient mtDNA**." European Journal of Human Genetics 17, 1314-1324, (October 2009).

Simplified European mtDNA haplogroup chart

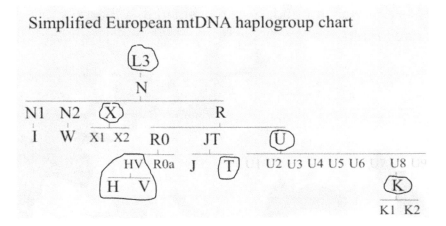

(**Above**) The aboriginal white-skinned, Red-haired Guanche Indians of the Canary Islands exhibit "**maternal DNA Haplogroups**" that match up with those of European women if you compare both their mtDNA and the European mtDNA Haplogroup chart. For the most part, mtDNA Haplogroups **U, H, H/V, K, T, R and X are seen exclusively in Europeans and Arabs**. But these "European" mtDNA Haplogroups are also seen in the aboriginal "**white**" Indians of the Canary Islands. How could this be? Could these ancient aboriginal white-skinned, red-haired Indians living in caves be the progenitor of the white race in Europe from earlier race-mixing? Could they have many years ago mixed with the Black children of Japheth producing a White race? Is part of their DNA "Fallen angel/Giant/Neanderthal" DNA, which has gotten mixed into the bloodline of most White races? Is Esau's seed also in here? Well according to the **Y-DNA** of the Guanche men (**which some say is tainted by the Arabs & Spaniards**), their DNA shows **E1b1b, J1, and R1b1b** which are prime "**Haplogroups**" of the people **Edom** traveled with and mixed with in **North Africa-Middle East** as well as on the other side of the Mediterranean in the **Kingdom of Rome**, Italy (Book of Jasher). The Book of Jasher states Edom lived up in Chittim (which some associate with Cyprus today) but others associate Chittim with Rome, Italy and even Greece. The Book of Jasher states that Edom would live on the **Island of Cyprus,** which before Islam was around, was considered a part of the Roman Byzantine Empire.

(**Above**) The shaded dark gray areas signify the Byzantium Empire back in 475 A.D. At its peak, the "**Roman**" **Byzantine Empire** made up the modern countries of **Algeria, Tunisia, Libya, Turkey, Crete, Spain, Italy, Egypt, Syria, Jordan, Israel, Lebanon, Iraq, Romania, Bulgaria, Serbia, Bosnsi-Herzegovina, Croatia, Macedonia/Greece and almost all of the Balkan Countries**. This is where the Ashkenazi and Sephardic Jews come from. This is also where Edom's playground was at.

(**Above**) The **Paiute Indians** inhabit Arizona, Oregon, California, Southern Utah and Nevada. As you can see they are a brown-skinned race of people. They also have a very "**thick**" grain of hair ranging from straight hair to hair that is akin to African-Americans today with soft-grains of wooly-curly hair. So where did these Indians acquire these traits of brown skin and semi-wooly hair? It had to have come from an "ancestral" **Black** man or woman, not a "**Caucasoid**".

"The **Paiute Indians (Nevada, Utah)** have a legend of **exterminating** a white-skinned red-haired tribe who spoke a different language than themselves. In this area (Nevada-Utah), red haired, Caucasoid mummies have been found in caves. These remains have been determined "**Caucasoid**" by archaeologists and are over 9,000 years old. As you can see these Paiute Indians referred to this different tribe as "white-skinned" with red hair. If the Original Indians were dark-skinned people, then where did these "**white-skinned**" tribal people come from? Surely the Paiute Indians would have known if any of their people were "**Albino family members**". Indians typically fashioned their teepee's all together in a fortress-like fashion so that they could identify "**strangers**" who would enter their village. The "white-skinned" tribe were such a "mystery" to the Paiute Indians that they were afraid to let them live.

Note: *Most Mexicans today will admit the Native Indians who live in Mexico on separate* ***"reservations"*** *are typically* ***darker*** *than they are and are also known to speak a different dialect than Spanish, although some have learned how to speak the language of Spain.*

Red-headed mummified remains also exist in the Paracas region of Peru, and these remains have **HLA-Human Lymphocyte Antigen markers commonly associated with Europeans.** Even more, the Aztec god Quetzalcoatl was considered to have a beard, light hair and white skin. Is it just an inbred trait of the "White Man" to conquer other "Brown Races" throughout the world? Is there some deep animosity or **"Bad Blood"** between the "white races" and the "Black races"? Could it stem from the rival between the descendants of Cain and the descendants of Seth **(Genesis 3:15)**"? What about Esau's and Jacob's rivalry? The Aztecs legends state that their **"white ruler"** came from across the oceans and taught the Aztecs how to farm and build. In South America, the **white-skinned tribe** known as the **Chachapoyas** lived in Peru for thousands of years before being conquered and destroyed by the **Inca people** in the late 1400's, approximately **10 years before the arrival of the Spanish Conquistadors. – "Paleolithic Giants in America"** by Soren Dreier.

The "**White tribe**" called the **Chachapoyas** practiced burial rites similar to the Egyptians and erected large stone statutes that mimic the stone statues of **Easter Island** where there have been found 12-foot giant skeletons. What is also interesting is that Easter Island geographically forms a straight line with the **Great Pyramid** in Egypt, the Nazca lines in Peru, and **Machu Picchu** (Peru). Spanish Conquistador **Pedro Cieza de Leon** in the early 1500's visited the Black Incas in Peru and wrote in his chronicle about these "**Chachapoyas**". Do you see the trend yet? It seems that wherever the "**Children of Israel**" are scattered to on the earth, the "white man" is soon to find them, usually unleashing nothing but slavery, sickness, death and destruction. Perhaps this trait is "**imprinted**" into the DNA of those carrying the bloodline of Edom, Cain or the Fallen Angels who got kicked out of heaven (their first estate).

Jude 1:6 "And the angels which kept not their first estate (home), but left their own habitation, he hath reserved in everlasting chains under darkness unto the judgement of the great day."

Fact: In the Egyptian "**Emerald Tablets of Thoth (Smaragdine tablets)**" it talks about the "**Council of Nine**" or "**The Nine**". It is believed that these "Nine" were "Fallen Angels" changed into deities that were worshiped by the Alanteans (Pre-Flood), the Lemurians (Pre-Flood) and the Egyptians (Post-Flood). These Fallen Angels had "Great Knowledge" that was supposedly buried under the Great Sphinx and

Pyramid of Giza in Egypt. Archaeologists searched for this but found a "Pit" below the below the Pyramid of Giza which was around 60ft x 20ft x 8ft in dimensions. The Emerald Tablets can be seen linking the Pre-flood Atlantean gods to the Egyptian and Sumerian gods. The Sumerians wrote about the "Great Flood" in the Epic of Gilgamesh and they also worshipped the Apis Bull and Half Falcon/Half Man gods called the "Annunaki" similar to the Half Falcon/Half Man god of Egypt "**Horus**" or "**Amen-Ra**". These Animal Faced-Fallen Angels were not unfamiliar to the Bible as Ezekiel's "**Wheel Story**" in the Bible talks about angels with the faces of animals inside of what many believe is a spacecraft:

(**Left**) Egyptian god Horus/Amen-Ra. (**Right**) Sumerian Annunaki god. Both have Falcon heads and the body of a man. Something is fishy here. Satan and his "Fallen demonic Angels" obviously deceived ancient civilizations into worshipping themselves, the Sun, the Moon, and the Stars instead of the "Creator".

Ezekiel 10:14 "And every one (angels) had four faces: the face of the first was the face of a cherub (angel), and the second was the face of a man, and the third was the face of a lion, and the fourth a face of an eagle."

In the Emerald Tablet, it reads "I, **THOTH**, the **Atlantean**, master of mysteries, keeper of records, mighty king, **MAGICIAN**, living from generation to generation, being about to pass into the **HALLS OF AMENTI**, set down for the guidance of those that are to come after, these records of the mighty wisdom of **Great Atlantis**."

(**Above**) Satanist and Grandmaster Freemason, Aleister Crowley wrote the Book called "**The Book of Thoth: Egyptian Tarot**" in the early 1900's. Why would a Satanist have so much love and respect for the Egyptian god **Thoth**? Why are Satanists fascinated with Pyramids, Egyptian spells and sorcery? It's because Ancient Egypt is the "**foundation**" of **ALL** Black magic, sorcery and evil taught to mankind from the Fallen "Demoni" Angels called "**Watchers**". The Book called "**Fallen Angels and the Origins of Evil**" by Elizabeth Clare Prophet talks all about the connection between the Fallen Angels and the beginnings of Evil on the Earth, starting with civilizations like Atlantis......then later Egypt. Black people today are getting caught up in worshipping the evil pagan "fairy tale" gods of Ancient Egypt because they want to connect their whole heritage to Egypt. This is a Satanic Trick! See what the Book of Enoch from the Dead Sea Scrolls has to say about this.

The Enoch Scroll

The **Enoch Scroll** (Dead Sea Scrolls found at **Qumran, Israel-400 B.C.**) Compare to the Book of Enoch 1 (Chapter 7).

"(Enoch speaking)….But you have changed your works, and have not done according to his command, and transgressed against him; and have spoken haughty and harsh words, with your impure mouths, against his majesty, for your heart is hard. You will have no peace…They, the leaders and all…..of them took for themselves wives from all that they chose and they began to cohabit with them and to defile themselves with them; and to teach them **SORCERY** and **SPELLS** and the cutting of roots; and to acquaint them with herbs. And they became pregnant by them and bore great giants three thousand cubits high."

But it gets deeper….

It says in the **Egyptian Emerald Tablets of Thoth (Tahuti)**:

"Now for a time I go from **AMONG THEM** (earthly beings?) into the **DARK HALLS OF AMENTI** (Hell?). **DEEP** (not the direction "up" in heaven) in the halls of the Earth (so we are in the earth but deep), before the Lord of the **POWERS**, face to face once again with the **DWELLER** (SATAN/LUCIFER?). Raised I high over the entrance, a doorway, **A GATEWAY LEADING DOWN** (not up into heaven) to Amenti. Few there would be with courage to dare it (those that try to go here have to have courage?), few pass the **PORTAL TO DARK AMENTI.** Raised over the passage, I, a **MIGHTY PYRAMID (are they pyramids over the passageway to Hell?)**, using the power that overcomes **EARTH FORCE** (magnetic energy of the pyramids overcomes gravity?), Deep and yet Deeper, place I a force-house or chamber; from it carved I a circular passage (CERN-stargate portal?) reaching almost to the great summit… Lie in the **SARCOPHAGUS** (like the Sarcophagus of Osiris below the pyramid) of stone in my chamber. Then reveal I to him the great mysteries. Soon shall he follow to where I shall meet him, even in the **DARKNESS** (not light) of Earth shall I meet him, **I THOTH**, Lord of Wisdom, meet him and hold him, and dwell with him (Satan/Lucifer?) always."

Only a foolish person can read this and think this is the Creator of the Universe who gives LIFE and refers to his followers in the Bible as the "Children of Light". Obviously the Egyptian God is referencing to a sort of "gateway" or "portal" below the Pyramid that leads to HELL! Deep in the Dark Halls of Amenti can only refer to Hell, and nothing else. The Freemasons, Skull and Bones and other occult secret societies are fascinated with the gods of Ancient Egypt and Pyramids. In their rituals they lie naked in a coffin to be baptized-reborn into "death" or "Hell". In Christianity, in the Bible water baptism signifies being reborn into "Christ" who gives us "Eternal Life", not "Eternal Death". Alexander the Great, Napoleon Bonaparte, and Aleister Crowley have all spent the night in pitch-black darkness in the pyramids only to have the "Nightmare" of their lives. Even Adolf Hitler was fascinated with Pyramids (Nuremburg Stadium) and Swastikas because of their connection to the demonic Fallen Angels under Satan. If someone has to have "courage" to go where "Thoth" goes, this is not describing "Heaven" or a "pleasant place". Most people wouldn't think twice if they could board a plane or walk up a staircase that would take them to heaven. Further in the Emerald Tablets it talks about the Abyss, the "Dark Death", casting forth "Order from Chaos" and more. These are all motto's and sayings of the Occult Societies of this evil world we live in. Who did these Fallen Angels infect their "Divine DNA" with?

Genesis 6:2-4 "That the Sons of God (Fallen Angels) saw the daughters of men that they were fair; and they took them wives of all which they chose: And the Lord said, My spirit shall not always strive with man, for that he also is flesh: yet his days shall be a hundred and twenty-years (Physical life limit of man or number of years left preceding the flood?). There were **GIANTS** in the earth in those days; and also after that, when the sons of God came in unto the daughters of men, and they bare **CHILDREN** to them, the same became mighty men which were of old, men of renown."

According to scientists and archaeologists, many Giant skeletons/skulls have been found with "**Red Hair**", just as what was reported by the brown-skinned Indians in the Americas when encountering "**White-skinned Tribes**". These mummified giants were also noted to have Caucasoid white skin.

But what about Noah and his family? Were they infected with Satan's fallen angel DNA or the "**Mark of Cain**"? The Sons of God according to the book of Enoch were White and the Mark of Cain was also believed to be white skin. But was there also an "Albino gene" that caused white skin? Many believe so because it says in the Book of Enoch that Noah had white skin akin to the Sons of God. But Noah was "Perfect" in **ALL HIS GENERATIONS**. So Noah's bloodline (Seth) could not have been infected with Cain or the Fallen Angels. But what about the wives of Noah's sons? That is the "Magic question".

Genesis 6:9 "These are the generations of Noah: Noah was a just man and **PERFECT** in his generations, and Noah walked with God."

So were these "White Indians" found in the Americas and the Canary Islands descendants of Cain or the descendants of the Nephilim without Nephilim traits (six fingers, giant stature). Or were they a Fallen Angel "genetic project" that resulted in humans with "white skin"? There have been reports that some of these "White Indians" were tested for Albinism, but the results showed that they were not "Albino" Indians.

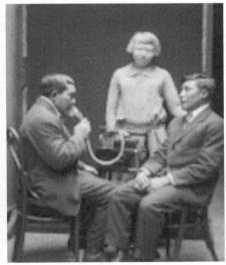

Three leading scientists and linguists in the early 1900's who were experts in the Mayan language recorded 6,000 words spoken by the White-skinned "**Chepu Tule**" people. One of the head priests of the Chepu Tule also gave these scientists a book of their hieroglyphics. They concluded that the Chepe Tule language had a **Sanskrit or Aryan** origin, **not mongloid**, like many of the aboriginal people. They also found that over 60 words recited by these "**White Indians**" were identical to the language of the early **Norse** (North Germanaic/Scandinavian) people, where the Ancient "**Neanderthal**" man/European was said to had its origin. Likewise, the Guanche

Indians of the Canary Islands when they were found were said to be "**white-skinned**" with a "**Nordic/Norse**" appearance.

Fact: The mtDNA of the "**Neanderthal Man**" was tested to be Haplogroup "**X**" stemmed from its ancestral Haplogroup "**N**" which is still mostly found in Europe. The major mtDNA Haplogroups of Native Americans (**A, B, C, D**) and Bantus Sub-Saharan Africans (**L1, L2, L3**) are different than the Nordic people, the ancient Neanderthal people or European people. The **mtDNA Haplogroup "X"** is found in its highest levels in Europe, Eurasians (Asia Minor) and also the people living in current day **Israel, Palestine and Lebanon**. It is also found in the **mtDNA of Turkish Jews, Sephardic Moroccan Jews as well as other Jews**. Haplogroup "X" outside of Europe/Asia/Middle East is only seen in North America/Canada. **It is NOT seen in Africa, India, Asia (i.e. China), Central or South America (message). Could this mtDNA X, be a foreign gene, inserted by Fallen Angels into human beings like many TV shows (i.e. X-Files) often hint on?** Was this gene the "switch" that changed man's skin to white back in Ancient times? If we believe that all of Noah's sons were black in Ancient times but now the land of Japheth is mostly white, this "**X**" gene could explain why the dark races lack this "X" gene (unless they are exposed to admixture with white people via slavery/intermarriage) and why mostly white races have this "X" gene. Or is this gene simply an ancient gene from the "**Seed of Cain**" who intermixed in the bible with the Sons of God (angels).

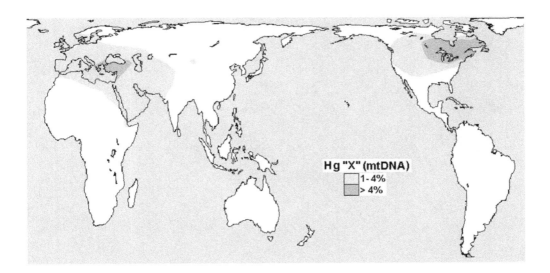

(**Above**) Maternal mtDNA Haplogroup "**X**" distribution around the world. As you can see it is mostly seen in **Europe, Asia Minor, Arab North Africa, the Middle East, Afghanistan, Pakistan and parts of North America**. As you can see, it is **NOT** in Sub-Saharan Africa, Asia, India, the Pacific Islands, Australia, Mexico and South America. Why? If you notice, the "**Colonizers**" and "**Invading**" nations of the **WHOLE WORLD** throughout time come from the same regions we see the mtDNA "X" in. When have you heard of Nigerians, Ethiopians, Australians, Indians, Native Americans or Pacific Islanders invading other countries? What about the Chinese? What other major countries have they invaded and colonized by force? Who are these people that have invaded other countries on the planet earth? The European man and the Arab man, the Slave traders of the Black Israelite man. Coincidentally, mtDNA "X" is seen in the people **ONLY** in their countries.

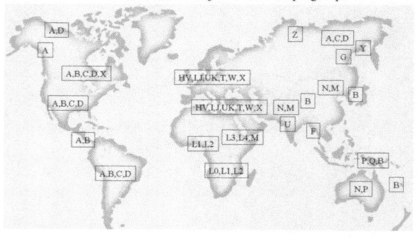

(**Above**) "Maternal" mtDNA Haplogroups of the world. The "**Neanderthal Hypothesis**" claims that the mtDNA Haplogroup X descends from "**Homo Sapiens Neanderthalis**". The skeletons and skulls of Neanderthal most definitely dates back prior to the flood, most likely when giants walked the earth with the fallen angels. The "**Neanderthal Hypothesis**" says that while Haplogroups **I, W, and X** make up only <10% of European Haplogroups, its descendants, **H, V, HV, J, T, U, and K** accounts for over **95%** of the modern European population (including Jews).

Scientists also found the Neanderthal's version of the **skin gene POU2F3** was found in **66% of East Asians**, while the Neanderthal version of **BNC2**, which affects skin color, is found in **70 percent of Europeans**. This means that the "**white man**" in Ancient Times ventured his way into Asia seeking to do business with the local people or to invade the local people. In Africa, the European man did both, and many African Tribal Chiefs succumbed to this trick.

Fact: *Blood type O/Rh negative blood is found in the Oriental Jews in Israel and the Samaritan Jews in Israel. Sometimes people with O/Rh negative blood have an extra tail bone (vertebrae), or an actual tail (like an animal). The Basque people in Spain have the highest percentage of people with Blood Type O/Rh negative blood. Neanderthal Cro-Magnon theorists state in addition to* *living in Spain like the Basque people, the "**Neanderthal Man**" lived in the Atlas Mountains of Morocco and the Canary Islands, who also have been found to have a high incidence of "**Rh negative**" carriers. According to **Juan Bautista de Erro**, author of "**The Primitive World of a Philosophical Examination of Antiquity and Culture of the Basque Nation**" published in 1815, "**Euskera**", the language of the Basque people, is the world's oldest language, having been preserved from the "**Pre-Flood Tower of Babel**" confusion of languages. He believed that the Basque "Rh-negative" people were of the descendant of Tubal-Cain from ancient Basque popular folklore stories stating that the father of the Basque people was a man named "Aitor" that survived the Flood by staying on top of mountains. Others hypothesize that the Basque people are descendants of Tubal, the son of Japheth (**Genesis 10:2**) who inhabited **Iberia (Spain/Portugal)**.*

The incidence of the Neanderthal gene decreases as one goes further east into Asia. The Neanderthal gene was not found in Sub-Saharan Africans or Native Americans. The Neanderthal Gene was also believed to be linked with the **Blood Type O**, the supposed Blood Type of the British Royal Family. Since then many genetic studies have been done using genome sequencing from the remains of Neanderthals (old human fossils) such as **Green et al. 2006, Noonan et al. 2006, Poinar et al 2006, and Miller et al 2008**. Because of this interest a "**Neanderthal genome project**" was initiated in 2005-2006.

NEANDERTHALS, BLOOD TYPE O, AND THE RH FACTOR.

Humans have four possible blood types: **A, B, AB and O**. But there is also a "**Rh factor**" or "**Rhesus Factor**". The RH factor is a protein that is present on the surface of most Red Blood Cells in humans and primates. Most people in the world **have** the RH factor, which means they are **RH positive**. Those that do not have these special proteins on their Red Blood Cells are considered **RH negative**. The RH factor is usually passed down through parent's genes to their children. If a mother is RH negative and the father is RH positive, the chances of baby being one or the other is 50/50. If both parents are RH negative, the baby will be RH negative. The only problem that occurs with this unusual Blood type is when a woman who is **RH negative carries a RH positive fetus**. The body will reject the fetus causing what is called **"Hemolytic disease of the newborn"** which can result in miscarriage. This usually happens when a RH negative woman carrying a RH positive baby for the first time develops **IgM** and **IgG** antibodies as a result of the mixed-blood 1st pregnancy. If this woman gets pregnant again with a RH positive fetus, her antibodies from the previous pregnancy will attack the fetus, that is unless she gets the RH immune globin serum (**Rhogam IgG Anti-D**) shot at **28 weeks during pregnancy, at 34 weeks, and within 48 hours after the delivery of the child**.

Now there has been research linking RH negative people to O blood types. Different theories have linked RH negative people to the descendants of the Nephilim or to the **"mysterious"** creation of the white race **as RH negative people are rarely seen (<1%) in people of pure African, Native American or Asian stock**.

Population	Rh(D) Neg	Rh(D) Pos	Rh(D) Neg alleles
European Basque	approx 35% [citation needed]	65%	approx 60%
other Europeans	16%	84%	40%
African American	approx 7%	93%	approx 26%
Native Americans	approx 1%	99%	approx 10%
African descent	less 1%	over 99%	3%
Asian	less 1%	over 99%	1%

(**Above**) Pure Blooded Africans, **Native Americans and Asians have a <1% frequency rate of being RH negative.** African-Americans have around a 7% frequency of being **Rh-negative**, obviously from **race mixing** with whites during slavery. It is mostly seen in select Europeans. As Europeans intermix with other "RH-positive" races, their chance of passing down RH positive genes to their children get higher. The British Royal Family often practices a form of "**incest**" to keep the "**Blue Bloodline**" pure. Likewise, most of all our American Presidents are related to each other. Could this also be some sort of way of keeping a certain bloodline or "**People**" in the White House as the President of the United States?

RH negative, O blood type carriers also claim to have some odd physical traits which include:

- Extra vertebra/Ribs.
- Higher than average IQ.
- More sensitive vision and other senses.
- Lower body temperature.
- Higher/Lower Blood Pressure.
- Increased occurrences of psychic/intuitive abilities.
- Predominately blue, green or hazel eyes.
- Prone to Red or reddish hair (like the Giants).
- Increased sensitivity to heat and sunlight.
- Increased incidences of "Alien Abduction" and/or other unexplained phenomena.
- Extra vertebrae (tail bone) and/or an actual tail (like an animal).

When it is all said and done, we know that there are tons of conspiracy theories and earthly archaeological finds that man cannot completely explain. Trying to find **ALL** the answer to everything can drive some people mad. Trying to find out if Yahusha (Jesus) Christ existed or if the Piso Family, the Romans or the Greeks made up the New Testament and everyone in it can cause a person to miss "**Salvation**". Man is always trying to explain things with science instead of using some "faith". This is what is happening today as many Blacks in America are researching Ancient Egypt so much that they are tricking themselves out of "**Eternal Life**" and the "**Kingdom of Heaven**". Then you have some who believe that the Black man is "**God**" or that Christianity was made up to control mankind. Sometimes it takes people trying to research "**everything**" to find out that "**all knowledge isn't necessarily good knowledge.**" But sadly, many people get caught up into occultism, gnostism, Cabalism, and eventually Satanism. But when we realize the bible was written by "**Black people**" from their point of view at that particular time we can understand why certain things "**are the way they are**" in the bible. We can see why the "**Elite**" had to "**Whitenize**" the Bible, its characters and even the Messiah. Satan is here to **DECEIVE ALL MANKIND**. The Hebrew Bible **WASN'T** voluntarily given to the Greeks to do their own translation as they please, it was **STOLEN BY THE GREEKS**! The Greeks subdued the Israelites forcing them into captivity and with it took their Hebrew Manuscripts.

Joel 3:6 "The **Children of Judah** and the **children of Jerusalem** have ye sold unto the Grecians, that ye might remove them far from their border."

So the Hebrew Bible was translated to Greek which was later translated to Latin and then Old English which would give rise to the Modern English that we speak today. Despite the Hebrew bible finding its way into the hand of the "**Gentiles**" and certain things being "**added**" or "**removed**", God has still provided us with the means to use our current Bibles to obtain the **TRUTH AND SALVATION**. That being said, in the beginning, all mankind (pre-flood) knew there was **ONE CREATOR AND ONE GOD**. Then came the fallen angels and their leader Lucifer to Earth when they got kicked out of heaven. These Fallen Angels slept with the daughters of men and then started to introduce "paganism" to the world. Mysteriously then we see the appearance of "**Trinity**" religions (Egyptian, Babylon/Sumerian,

Hindu etc.) where different pagan gods had wives and sons, just as the Most High did already in the Book of Genesis. Satan's is a "**great copycat**" and goes against God's natural order of things. Satan brings chaos, destruction and death (Osiris, Shiva, Anubis). God brings life and order to the world. He is the Great Judge.

Fact: *God made Eve out of Adams rib. The ribs are the only organ or structure aside from skin/blood vessels/liver that can regenerate itself and grow back. You can cut a person's rib but if you leave the periosteum it will grow back. It has the DNA building blocks in it to regenerate, aka "**clone itself**". Men have both the "**X**" and "**Y**" sex chromosome to make both sexes (Man-XY and Female-XX). Women **do not** carry the "Y" sex chromosome. So if a woman was the first being that existed in the world with only two "**XX**" sex chromosomes we would not be able get the "**Y**" sex chromosome to have man. Beware of people saying "**we are gods**" and "**the woman**" is our God. The first of the "**Ten commandments**" says we should not worship any gods, including a mortal being. This is Atheistic tendencies. Beware also of people saying **EGYPT** existed before the flood or that Osiris predates the **God of Seth.***

Genesis 4:26 "And to Seth, to him also was born a son; and he called his name Enos: then began men to call upon the name of the Lord (Yahuah)."

Psalms 82:6 "I have said, Ye are **gods**; and all of you are children of the Most High."

Note: In the Bible the big capital "**G**" is used for the creator and the little "**g**" is used for pagan gods. Read what the **1st Commandment** says:

Exodus 20:2 "I am the Lord thy **(G)od**, which have brought thee out of the **land of Egypt**, out of the house of bondage. Thou shalt have no other **(g)ods** before me.

CHAPTER 8

BEWARE OF EGYPTOLOGISTS, KEMETIANS, "NEW AGE" AFRICAN SPIRITUALISTS AND PEOPLE PREACHING "UNIFICATION OF RELIGIONS".

(**Above**) What does the pyramids in South America, **EGYPT** have to do with Satan, Fallen angels (sons of God), Giants, and white skin? What do the pyramids in these different counties have to do with astrology, dinosaurs, Horus, OSIRIS, the Annunaki and the Antichrist? What do they have to do with the **Laws of Ma'at** and the **Code of Hammurabi** (Akkadian-Babylonia) and Satan's deception? What does it have to do with the **ISRAELITES**? Believe it or not, all these Pyramids, different versions of the "10 Commandments" and "Trinity Deities" with their consorts all are Satan's way to deceive mankind from accepting the "**True Messiah**" of the World. Satan has given mankind and all its "civilizations" copycatted versions of what he knows is the "**Real Truth**". Think about it, why would Satan want to tell all these "**Civilizations**" the Truth. Satan is the father of lies. He wants to become like the Most High (the Creator) and he wants mankind to advance in his technology so that he himself will believe that he is God like the Most High. When Mankind believes he is God, then he has no desire to become "**spiritually**" one with God. He has no desire to repent and to ask God for Salvation. He has no desire to worship the Creator. This is what's happening today in the Black "conscious" community. This is Satan's goal, to bring as many souls with him to Hell as possible before **Judgement Day**.

Isaiah 14:13-14 "For thou hast said in thine heart, I will ascend into heaven, I will exalt my throne above the stars of God: I will sit also upon the mount of the congregation, in the sides of the north: **I will ascend above the heights of the clouds; I will be like the Most High.**"

This scripture was talking about "Satan". Don't be deceived.

(**Left**) **Osiris**, the Green-skinned Egyptian god of the Underworld/Dead. (**Right**) **Anubis**, the Half-dog, Half-man Egyptian deity was the god of the Underworld/Dead and Mummification before the title was given to Osiris. Egyptians are always changing the positions of their 2,000+ gods like a Basketball coach switching up his starting five players on the team. At one point **Set** was the God of Egypt along with Horus but that eventually changed. Also depending on who you ask, **Ptah** is the "Creator" of the world and on another day "**Ra**" is the "Creator" of the world.

First consider this about the Ancient Egyptian pagan gods. **OSIRIS** replaced **Anubis** as the god of the dead and mummification during the time (**Middle Kingdom**) the **ISRAELITES** were in **EGYPT** starting with **JOSEPH (2,000 B.C.-1500 B.C.)**. So according to the Bible Noah lived 950 years and died a couple years before **ABRAHAM** was born. There are 4 generations from **ABRAHAM to JOSEPH**. Many scholars believe Noah was born around 3,000 B.C. or 3200 B.C. Now the Epic of Gilgamesh depicting the "**Great Flood**" was dated to **2100 B.C.** during the **Third dynasty of Ur in Mesopotamia** (where many believe Abraham was born). If the Sumerians lived before the Flood because many archaeologists pre-date their existence to **3,000 B.C.-3,300 B.C.** and if someone from their lineage was able **SURVIVE THE FLOOD** in order to pass this knowledge down to the people, could this mean that the Sumerian people were related to the **sons of Seth**? Could the Sumerians be a branch of Shem that were tricked by Satan to believe in pagan Satanic gods, just as Ham, Japheth and their sons were in Biblical times? If Cain and all his descendants died in the flood, per most Christian beliefs, then the only people who could've known about the flood to live to tell the story would have to be Noah and his sons (with wives) who were from the lineage of **Seth**. It is said that the Sumerians (**who called themselves "the black-headed ones"**) spoke a pre-**SHEMITIC** language which some experts in linguistics say is an archaic form of Old Tamil (**South India/Sri Lanka Dravidian-Elamite language**) and Sanskrit (**pre-cursor language for Southwestern India "Malayalam" language and some scripts found in Central Africa/Ethiopia**).

Fact: *The Ancient Dravidian languages of South India are Malayalam and Tamil. Many say South Indians are Elamites (Elam) and Assyrians (Asshur)* *whose Sanskrit-based language is similar to the language of the Ancient Sumerians because all three nations were sons of Shem. If this is so, it would make sense because the Dravidian Indians, Sri Lankans and the Andaman Islanders are "brown-skinned" people just as the Sumerians described themselves 5,000 years ago. They have even found ancient Sanskrit use in Central Africa (Cameroon) and pottery with Sanskrit writings in Ethiopia.*

If the Sumerians knew of things that happened around the time of Noah this would mean that the descendants of the Sumerians lived during the times when the Fallen Angels were sleeping with the daughters of the men creating Giants and influencing mankind to build pyramids or megalithic structures. This would make sense because the Sumerians called these **Fallen Angels** who came from heaven "**Annunaki**" which means in Sanskrit "**Those who from the heavens came**". This is similar to the Biblical story of the "**Sons of Anak**" who were described as "**Giants**" in the bible. So here we have the Sumerian word "**Annunaki**" sounding very similar to "**Anak**" in the younger "Hebrew Semitic" language.

Numbers 13:33 "And there we saw the **GIANTS**, the **SONS OF ANAK**, which come of the giants: and we were in our own sight as grasshoppers, and so we were in their sight."

Notice that **Joshua** said that the Israelites were like "**Grasshoppers**" in the sight of the "**Sons of Anak**". These had to be some "**really big**" giants. Also notice that this peculiar scripture about these "ungodly beings" is in the **13th** Chapter and **33rd** verse of **Numbers** which are special numbers to the occult world/Freemasonry.

(**Above**) Sumerian/Babylonia depiction of the **Annunaki**, along with their reptilian features. Half-animal/Reptilian-looking gods was common in Ancient Sumeria-Babylon and Ancient Egypt. Civilizations with pyramids often used the "**Serpent**" as their symbol of "**Royalty**" or these people were known by their neighbors as "**People of the Serpent**". But are we forgetting that in the Book of Genesis God **cursed the Serpent** out of all the animals on land. So what are ancient civilizations doing paying "**homage**" to the Serpent? This is nothing but a trick of Satan because the "**Serpent**" since the beginning has been a symbol of "**evil**".

Genesis 3:14 "And the Lord God said unto the serpent, Because thou hast done this, **thou art cursed above ALL cattle, and above every beast on the field;** upon thy belly shalt thou go, and dust shalt thou eat all the days of thy life:"

God also makes a distinct difference between the "**Children of the Serpent**" and the "**Children of the Woman (Eve & Seth)**". This was referring to the "**Synagogue of Satan**" with Satan's physical obedient servants on earth being enemies of the **Children of Israel**. This is the ultimate battle between "**Good**" and "**Evil**".

Genesis 3:15 "And I will put enmity between **thee and the woman**, and **between thy seed (Cain) and her seed (Seth)**; it shall bruise thy head, and thou shalt bruise his heel."

Genesis 6:4 "There were **giants** in the earth in those days; and also after that, when the **sons of God (watchers-fallen angels)** came in unto the daughters of men, and they bare children to them, the same became mighty men which were of old, men of renown."

Just like in **Genesis 6:4** the Annunaki were supposedly giants and had wings just as what was reported to be the case of the superhuman people who lived on the land mass known as "**Atlantis**". The **EGYPTIANS (Mizraim)**, the **NUBIANS (Cush)** and the seed of **JAPHETH** (Greeks/Romans) copied from the Sumerians their ancient knowledge of the Flood and came up with their own pagan deity system, including Giant demigods (half-man, half-divine beings) known as the **TITANS**. The also learned how to build Pyramids for pagan Satan worship, the remnants of demonic architecture which survived the "Great Flood" and other remnants that are seen on the bottom of the ocean in places like the Bahamas or India.

GIANTS, PYRAMIDS, LEMURIA AND ATLANTIS (PRE-FLOOD).

Prior to the flood, the earth was one big land mass separated by only rivers, lakes, etc. Two land masses that existed pre-flood that disappeared after the flood were known as "**Lemuria and Atlantis**".

It is believed that prior or after the "**Great Flood**" these land masses (**Lemuria & Atlantis**) disappeared underwater and with it many of the Superhuman Giants-Fallen Angels who were "**Evil**" in the eyes of God. But where did they go? Many historians and occultists (**like Helen Blavatsky**) believed that they knew secret passageways into the "**Inner Earth**" called "**Shamballa**". This was the secret living quarters/hiding places of these Fallen Angels, Giants and so on. In this inner earth, eyewitnesses (like **Admiral Richard E. Byrd** in 1946-1947 during operation "**High-Jump**") found giant trees, plants, animals, people, fallen angels (so-called aliens) and flying aircraft with swastika symbols on it.

THE PATH

The International Official Organ of The Independent Theosophical Society

A Magazine Devoted to the Theosophical Message of H. P. Blavatsky

Annual Subscription (Six Issues), 3/6.   American Subscription, $1.00.   Single Copies, 6d.   Published on Alternate Month
Address: Editor, The Path, 69 Hunter Street, Sydney, New South Wales

Vol. I. No. 1   JANUARY, 1925   Price, Sixpence

Note: "The Path" magazine was developed off the teachings of Luciferianist Helen Blavatsky. **She knew the Satanic Roots of the Swastika, the Hexagram, the Crescent disk/wings (Assyria/Babylon), the Egyptian Ankh and the Serpent. The Swastika is also used by Buddhists who don't believe in a God-head or a "personalized creator".** The largest idol statue in the world is the "**Spring Temple**" Buddha. Buddhism is not an "**Abrahamic**" religion like Christianity, Islam and Judaism. Unbeknownst to some, the Catholic Church is trying to combine all the religions of the world which is Satanic and ungodly. This is called an "**apostasy**" according to the Webster Dictionary and the Bible. **2 Thessalonians 2:3-4** talks about the "**apostate**" showing himself before the Antichrist reveals himself. Could the Catholic Church be the "**Apostate**" that the Bible talks of? In October 1986, Buddhists were invited to **Assisi, Italy** by **Pope John Paul II** to place a golden idol of Buddha above a Tabernacle containing a consecrated Christian host on top of a so-called consecrated altar. The Catholic Church burned incense to it and worshipped the pagan Buddha statue with the heads of the Catholic and Anglican clergy in attendance. 32 Christian organizations, including all of the major denominations were in attendance. Everyone was made to watch this pagan ritual without nobody protesting. What is even worse is the fact that our 112th Pope, Jesuit Francis (**Jorge Mario Bergoglio**) chose his **namesake** after "**Francis of Assisi**", the same place this abomination to God was committed in Italy! **This is a message**. Pope Francis is back at it, trying to merge all religions into "**one**" saying that all religious books are the same and that we are all praying to the same "**God**".

In 2015, **Pope Francis** addressed Rome by saying:

"Jesus Christ, Jehovah, Allah. These are all names employed to describe an entity that is distinctly **THE SAME** across the world. For centuries, blood has been needlessly shed because of the desire to segregate our faiths. This, however, should be the very concept which unites us as a people, as nations, and as a world bound by faith. Together, we can bring about an unprecedented age of peace, all we need to achieve such a state is respect each other's beliefs, **for we are all children of God regardless of the name we choose to address him by. We can accomplish miraculous things in the world by merging our faiths, and the time for such a movement is now**. No longer shall we slaughter our neighbors over differences in reference to their God."

President George W. Bush in 2007 told "**Al Arabiya**", a Saudi Arabia television network:

"I believe there is a universal God. **I believe the God that the Muslim prays to is the same God that I pray to**. After all, we all came from Abraham. I believe in that universality."

In August 2010, the "**Mecca Clock**" started ticking for the first time. It is the biggest clock in the world and can send digital signals anywhere in the world. It has a **large moon** at the top made out of carbon fiber and at night it lights up the sky **green** and shoots out a beam of light almost **19 miles into the sky**! Many believe this clock is a sign that eventually the world's clock system will be in tune with the **Mecca Clock** so that Muslims and people under "**Sharia Law**" everywhere (**including Europe, Africa, U.S.A., Asia, Middle East**) will know what time to face to Mecca to pray. Many theorists believe "**Islam**" is the religion of the "**Beast**" and "**Communism**" is the government of the "Beast" per Freemasonry. Green is the color of "**Islam**" and Red is the color of "**Communism**". The "**Mark**" of the beast is "**Sharia Law**". The Antichrist will arrive to **CHANGE TIMES AND LAWS**! Its is also a known fact that the Aramaic Bible says the word "**Signature**" of the Beast instead of the word "**Mark of the Beast**".

Daniel 7:25 "And he shall speak great words against the Most High, and shall **wear out the saints** of the Most High, and **think to change times and laws:** and they shall be given into his hand until a time and times and the dividing of time.

Swastika symbols were used by Buddhists (China) and Hindus (India) prior to the Nazi's using it. The word "**Swastika**" is derived from the Sanskrit word "**svastika**" – "**Su**" meaning "**good**" united with "**asti**" meaning "**it is**" along with the suffix "**ka**" which means "**All is well**" or "**It is good**". Stories report that in Tibet, Buddhist monks know the secret passageways connecting the "**outer earth**" to the "**inner earth**". They have kept these secret passageways hidden to the inner world in locations purportedly to be at the base of the pyramids in South America, Central America, India, Egypt, the Canary Islands, Tibet and the Solomon Islands. Before the land of "**Lemuria**" and "**Atlantis**" was sunk the people called their God "**Mu/Nu**". Le-**MU**-ria is supposedly derived from the word "**Mu**" which means "**Land of Ancestors-Motherland**". "**Mu-Devi**" is also a Hindu mother goddess whose name in Tamil is "**Jyestha**".

(**Left**) Hindu Goddess "**Mu-Devi**" or "**Jyestha**". (**Middle**) Hindu God Vishnu. (**Right**) Hindu God "**Shiva the Destroyer**" with a snake around his neck who many Indians say is the Christian equivalent of "**Satan**", the Egyptian equivalent of "**Set**" and is in Tamil culture supposedly linked to the Sun per the Tamil word "**sivan**" meaning "**Red One**". A large statue of Shiva sits outside the **CERN** Large Hadron Collider Facility in Switzerland.

In the Tamil literary work "**Silappatikaram**" Shiva is the "**Great Father**" for the Hindu Goddess "**Mu-Devi**". It describes the lost continent of Le-**MU**-ria in the Pacific Ocean-Indian Ocean which they call "**Kumai Nadu**" and "**Kumari Kandam**" as meaning the "**Land of the Dragon Gods Snake**". So what is the coincidence that these submerged lands that supposedly housed the Fallen Angels and Nephilim Giants are still associated today with "**Evil**". The Hindu Goddess "**Mu-Devi**" or "**Jyestha**" was the goddess of evil things, ugliness and misfortune. Her sister, **Lakshmi** was the goddess of beauty and things good. Jyestha was also associated with the sinners, sloth, poverty, sorrow, ugliness and the crow. In the Hindu "**Linga Purana**", the god **Vishnu** divides the world into the good and the bad. Lakshmi being over the good and Jyestha being over the bad. So the continent of Lemuria and the god named "**Mu**" was basically a representative of "**Evil**" like Satan. Temples in South India still exist with her sculptures in it. After 900 A.D. her worship died out.

So per folklore, the descendants of the Fallen Angels, the giants and some believe the descendants of Cain were able to somehow survive the flood by going into the inner earth with the rest of the "**lawless ones**" only to arise to settle in the Americas (South/Central America) and the Canary Islands (off the coast of Morocco). These giants were white with red hair and the people (descended from Cain) were supposedly known as "**White Indians**" or "Nivaria" to the local people they lived amongst most often in caves. Per the Amazon people in South America these "White Indians" were cursed with "white skin" because of something their ancestors did many of years ago in the beginning of time. They had white skin with blonde, reddish or brown hair. Everywhere they lived relics have been found of pyramids, triangles and pagan gods resembling ancient Egypt and ancient Sumeria. The signs are all evident, but are we paying attention.

(**Above**) The remains of the **Lost City of Atlantis** at the bottom of the Atlantic Ocean below the Bahamas. The Lost city of Atlantis and its statues can still be seen at the bottom of the ocean near the Bahamas. This is why Atlantis Paradise Island Resort is located in the Bahamas today. Notice to the right, the Atlanteans/Lemurians worshipped the "**Apis Bull**" figure with the **sun in the middle of the horns** like what was worshipped in Ancient Egypt, often associated with the God of the Dead, Osiris and their Creator God "Ptah".

Image of Apis, the Sacred Bull of Egypt

(**Above**) The "**Apis Bull**" of Ancient Egypt.

(**Above**) Ancient Egypt worshipping the Pagan Satanic-Fallen Angel inspired "**Apis Bull**" aka "**Ptah**" incarnate (**like Atlantis**) in an animal (bull). Even Greek Historian Herodotus was amazed at all the wonders he had seen in Egypt. He could not explain how the pyramids and megalithic structures were built by mortal human hands. This is because the Egyptians, like the people living in Central/South

America, had "outside" non-human help by way of all the knowledge the "Fallen Angels" were able to teach mankind (just like the Book of Enoch).

*"I come there to **Egypt**, about which I shall speak for a long time, because compared with any other country, it is Egypt which contains most wonders and which offers **most works exceeding what we can say about them**."*

Greek Historian Herodotus (lived 484 B.C. to 425 B.C.)

Ptah is **Enki**, and is the Creator God to the Egyptians. He is the builder and creator of all the 2,000 pagan Egyptian gods that the people of Egypt believed in. The name of the people in "Ptah's" position changed but the head designer (Satan) continue to stay the same doing what he does best which is to deceive. The Demi-god Nephilim's, led by Satan-Ptah-Enki-Osiris-Ra had technologies that we in the 21st century do not even have.

Per many beliefs the lands of Lemuria/Atlantis were lost after a major catastrophic event (**volcanoes, flood, comet**s). But per the Bible many of the "Giants" survived the flood.

Fact: The mtDNA of the "**White Indians**" was tested and it matched perfectly with that of Europeans. According to many beliefs (even in the Quran), the people of European descent (Arabs, Jews, Caucasians) who are classified as "**Gog and Magog**" will be the ones who will create "**Chaos**" and "**Corruption**" on the Earth. They will invade everyone's country and will master the power of water (hydrogen-oxygen) to invent weapons of "Mass destruction-**i.e. hydrogen bomb**".

160

WHAT IS TO MAKE OF ALL OF THIS EGYPTIAN CONFUSION THAT IS AFFECTING BLACK PEOPLE TODAY?

OSIRIS (Ausur) is a new God in overall history as his name is first mentioned around 2300 B.C. (**Pyramid Texts**). **He was supposedly 15 feet tall per EGYPTIAN texts (some say 55 feet) with Green skin but his Sarcophagus coffin 95 below the ground is only 6 feet long?** It is said that the **EGYPTIANS** knew that Osiris wasn't real but made a tomb for him anyway with nobody in it. Black Kemetians today need to turn away from the satanic fairy tale pagan gods of EGYPT and come back to the True Creator and Living God of the bible that Satan has been trying to copycat since day one.

REMEMBER! Back in the day Pre-Flood, according to the bible MEN on the Earth knew the name of the Lord. He wasn't called "El", "ELOHIM" etc. Remember God told MOSES his name in **Exodus 3:15** but prior to this **Seth and Enos** (before the flood) knew Gods name. Not the title or word for "**God**".

Genesis 4:26 "And To Seth, to him also there was born a son; and he called his name Enos: then MEN began to call upon **THE NAME OF THE LORD (YAHUAH)**."

(Above) The Nile River in Egypt today. Back in Ancient times, or should I say biblical times Egypt was bountiful with grassland for farms and for grazing. Today this is not the case as most of Egypt is "the Desert". So what does the bible say about the land of Egypt in "Biblical Times"?

(Above) Ancient Egyptian man plowing the field with two cows (kine).

Genesis 41:2 "And behold, there came up out of the river (Nile) well favoured kine (cows) and fat fleshed (fat), and they fed in the grass (meadow)."

(**Above**) Egyptians on boat, ancient artifacts.

Numbers 11:5 "We remember the **fish we ate in Egypt** that cost nothing, the cucumbers, the melons, the leeks, the onions, and the garlic."

Kemetians-Egyptian fanatics on TV like to say the Exodus didn't happen and they want proof that Moses existed. But no one uses "**Critical Thinking**". In Ancient Egypt, the people fished in the Nile River, and they used the plow because they had plenty of grassland and farmland. The Israelites remembered when they had fish to eat, Beef (cows), onions, cucumbers, and melons etc. from Egypt. When was the last time you went to the grocery store and heard that your produce came from Egypt? Never! The Plagues of Egypt orchestrated by Yahuah and Moses proves why the only little vegetation left is along the banks of the River Nile in Egypt. Without the Nile River today (which is 4,000 miles long) the land of Egypt would be an "Inhospitable desert". Don't Believe? Read all of the 10 Plagues and play close attention to Exodus 10:13-15. God's wrath was on Egypt and it shows today. The Egyptian god of grain "**Neper/Nepri**" was quiet when the Plagues hit and after the plagues was done. What did the people of Egypt think about their many gods when their land was destroyed by the "REAL" God of Israel **YAHUAH**? Not Osiris, not Thoth, not even Horus could save them. The Egyptian god of childbirth and crops "**Ermutet**" was quiet during the plagues. So was **Isis, Thermuthis**, and **Seth**. The plague of "**Darkness**" by YAHUAH was an insult and slap in the face to the Egyptian sun god "**Amon-Ra/Horus**". Where was **Ptah**, the Egyptian god that created the sun, moon and earth? **YAHUAH** basically checked All of Egypt by saying in **Exodus 12:12**:

"For I will pass through the land of Egypt on that night, and will strike all the firstborn in the land of Egypt, **BOTH MAN AND BEAST**, and against **ALL the gods of Egypt** (fallen demonic angels) **I WILL EXECUTE JUDGEMENT: I AM YAHUAH (The Lord).**"

If I was an Egyptian in those times and saw the God of Moses kill all the firstborn males, man and animal, I would quickly convert to following the God of Israel. Following the Egyptian gods that didn't do nothing during their time of calamity is utterly **RIDICULOUS**. Why? Because the gods of Egypt are satanic and are as inanimate as rocks. But many Blacks around the world are being deceived into believing in the gods of ancient Egypt. It's almost like we are "**Re-living the Exodus**". The Most High is waking up his "**Children of Israel**" to bring them out of Satan's worldly system of deception. The Most High wants his "**Lost Sheep**" to get back to **Spirituality, Righteousness, and Holiness**. But what do we see? We see black people trying to go back and worship the things that Yahuah brought us up out of! This includes all the "Ungodly" and "Evil" things the Israelites were picking up while in Egypt. Egypt was known for its Magicians, Sorcerers and fascination with death. But no follower of the Egyptian religion today will admit to this. They hate it when everybody links "**Satanism**" to "**Egypt**". But the Truth is the Truth. Kemetian/Egyptian fanatics will try to call "**Christianity**" a plagiarized Religion used to control Blacks but these same Kemetians can never answer the following questions when asked on the spot:

1. Can you show me the disciples, apostles, priests, and prophets of Ancient Egypt and their texts?
2. Which Egyptian god do you pray to and worship each day?
3. How does an "Egyptian" African-American obtain "**Salvation**" into the heavenly "afterlife"? If my heart is weighed against a feather (i.e. Anubis) and I am judged by the **Laws of Maat**, can I be bisexual or homosexual and make it into a good "**afterlife**"?
4. What spells can an Egyptian African-American use to better their chances into a heavenly "afterlife"?
5. When does an African-American have to utter the "spells" to ensure a guaranteed slot in the "afterlife". Does he say the spells right before he dies or when he dies? How does a dead person know if they're doing the spells correctly and how can you prove they can even utter the spells when they are "**dead**"?
6. Is there any "**repentance**" or "**second chances**" allowed in Egyptian theology?
7. What prophesies are listed in the Egyptian texts? And who was the prophet? Where are the tombs of these prophets if there is any?
8. What miracles were performed in the Egyptian texts?
9. Who is the author of the **Book of the Dead**? When was it began and when was it finished? And where is the tomb and body of this author(s)?
10. Who is the author of the **Pyramid Texts**? And where is his tomb or body at?
11. Who is the author of the **Emerald Tablets**? And where is his tomb or body at? Was the Emerald Tablets written in Egyptian Hieroglyphics? And if not, then why?
12. Who is the author of the **Coffin Texts**? And where is his tomb or body at?

13. Who is the author of the **Contending's of Horus and Set**? And where is his tomb or body at?

14. What happened to the once fertile grassland of Egypt? Why is Egypt mostly desert now? This is not how it was in Ancient times? It is a known fact that the Israelites and other nations came to Egypt in times of famine to get food (Genesis Chapter 42)?

15. Where are the people of Ancient Egypt today? Surely, such a "Great" kingdom should show evidence of their "remnant" in the world, just as we see a huge remnant of the Ancient Hebrew Israelites.

16. What "**Tribe**" in Africa still worships **Osiris, Horus, Thoth, Set and Anubis**? Where is their Egyptian texts at? Many Hebrew texts/manuscripts dating to B.C. times have been found all over the world, and not just in Israel. So where is Egypt's stuff at?

17. If **Moses, Jesus and the Israelites** didn't exist according to Egyptian fanatics, then why is there evidence of these biblical person's found in many civilizations across the world? Why is evidence of the "**Great Flood**" accounted by the Sumerians, the Ancient Chinese, the Ancient Native Americans and other civilizations **but not the Egyptians**? Why is there evidence of biblical events found in different countries?

18. Where did Hebrew language/script come from? What about Aramaic? Where did that come from? What language is the father of Greek, Aramaic, Phoenician, Sabaean, Ge'ez, Swahili and Arabic?

19. Why is there evidence on the "**Walls of Egypt**" of the Cities of Israel?

20. Why are there Egyptian artifacts that describe the "Chief of the **Hebrews (Habiru)**" taking over the Egyptian-Canaanite cities?

21. How did the Egyptians make peace treaties with the Hittites? Who created the Hittites? Who was their Ancestral father?

22. How is it that the Libyan Pharaoh "**Iuput**" from the 23rd Egyptian dynasty, carries the root word of his ancestral father "**Put**" from the Bible? Who is "Put's father?

23. If **Amen-Ra or Ptah** is the Egyptian God of all things created, then why was Egypt conquered by just about every major civilization/nation known to man?

24. Where did the Egyptians learn their **Magic** and **Sorcery** from? The bible warns us about Magic and Sorcery in Isaiah **8:19-20, Zechariah 10:2, Revelation 18:23, 2 Chronicles 33:6, 2 Chronicles 33:3-5, Exodus 7:11-12, Exodus 8:16-19, Leviticus 19:26, 2 Kings 21:6, Acts 13:6-8 and Deuteronomy 18:9-12**.

25. Why did **Alexander the Great, Napoleon Bonaparte, and Aleister Crowley** all have terrifying experiences when they spent the night in the Pyramids of Giza in pitch darkness.

26. Who built the Pyramids? And why are their pyramid structures on the ocean floor all over (i.e. below Bahamas, India).

27. Again, why isn't there anything "**forbidding**" Homosexuality in the Laws of Maat?

28. Why do Egyptian texts commonly reference "**Dark**", "**Deep**", "**Evil**", "**Chaos**", and "**Death**".

29. Why do **Jesuits, Freemasons, Satanists, Wicca's, Rosicrucian's, Hermetic Order of the Golden Dawn, O.T.O, Thelema society, the Brotherhood, the Moslem Shriners**, and other occult societies all give praise, worship or reference to Egyptian gods in their texts or religious ceremonies?

30. Why do Black Magicians say the source of their "Power" comes from Egypt?

31. Why did many polytheistic religions of the past worship the **Sun, the Crescent Moon and the Star**, like the Egyptians? These are the "creations" of god. Shouldn't we be worshipping god, not his creations?

32. Why did many polytheistic religions of the past worship gods with "**animal faces**"? Didn't god give man "authority" over all the animals of the earth? If so, why are we worshipping them?

33. Why is the "**snake/serpent**" the symbol for "**Egyptian Royalty**"?

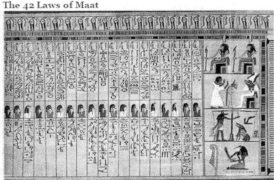

The 42 Laws of Maat

(**Left**) **Ammit/Ammut** is the beast animal that eats the dead that fail to pass the "**Laws of Maat**" test called the "**Weigh-in of the Heart**". (**Right**) **42 Laws of Maat**. The judgement process consists of made up pagan gods: Thoth, Anubis, Ammit/Ammut, Osiris and Isis . So here we have a **Green man** dressed up in white mummy linen, a **dog-faced man**, a **baboon/ibis-faced man**, a **woman** and a **beast that has the head of a Crocodile, the hair of a lion, the front body of a leopard and the hindlegs of a hippopatamus**. How silly is this for a Black Egyptian mad to die, only to wake up to these "**abominable beings**" standing before him judging his "heart"? God is not the author of confusion and fairy-tale/mythical characters. **Wake Up Black man.**

The Egyptian god beast-animal "**Ammit**" or "**Amenti**". Some call this beast "**Ammut**" or "**Ahemait**". In the "**Emerald Tablets**", Thoth takes readers down into the Deep, Dark, Halls of Ammenti/Ammit where death lives. This character was often there to "**devour/eat**" those that didn't pass the "**Weighing of the Heart Ceremony**" facilitated by Anubis, Osiris and Horus. This half-Crocodile. half-leopard, half-hippopotamus beast supposedly guarded the Egyptian version of Hell or "the Lake of Fire". However, there was a "backdoor" side cut method that Egyptians could use to guarantee their way into a heavenly afterlife. Egyptians had to only be able to include the text and illustrations of Chapter 125 of the Book of the Dead in their tomb to have a "pass" into the Afterlife.

Fact: In Northern Iraq there exists a group of Arabs (some say Kurdish Arabs) called the "**Yezidis**" who have been linked by Muslims to "Satanism" or "Devil worship". They worship a fallen angel in the form of a peacock (like NBC) named "**Melek Ta'us**". **Note: CBS is in the form of an "All-Seeing Eye" like the "All-Seeing Eye" of Thoth and Ra from Ancient Egypt.** The Yezidis have two books that they go by, their own "**Book of Revelation** (different from the Bible)" and the "**Black Book**". The Black Book talks about the different Persian, Assyrian, and Babylonian Kings that were Yezidi's. Their text also states that **King Ahab,** the Northern King of Israel who was married to **Jezebel, also** worshipped **Beelzebub** (Satan) along with **Baal** and **Asheroth**. The Yezidi's call him "Pir Bub". According to their "Black Book", The Yezidi's are not allowed to utter their god's name, nor anything that resembles it, such as seitan (Satan), Kaitan (cord), sar (evil), sat (river) and the like. Nor do they pronounce the word mal'un (accursed) or la'anat (curse) or na'al (horseshoe).

So if we fast forward to the 21st century, and we see the same Satan that was in Egypt deceiving the Israelites is back at deceiving us (Israelites) again today. He wants us to go back to worshipping the pagan gods of Egypt (Osiris, Horus, Isis). He wants us to believe we are "**Gods**" or that the "**Woman is God**" like the pagan "**Queen of Heaven**" the Israelites used to worship in Jeremiah 7:18 and Jeremiah 44:19. Satan wants us to convert to Islam, so we can drop Yahusha (Jesus) as our savior and start calling the Creator "**Allah**" instead of **Yahuah**. He wants to keep us in bondage (**Financial Debt and Physical Prison**). He doesn't want the real "Children of Israel" to multiply (**Eugenics, birth control, abortion clinics, infertility, homosexuality**). Satan doesn't want the Real "Children of Israel" to wake up. This is why the population of the indigenous "Indian" and the "Negro" have been diminished or controlled with different types of genocide. This is why we are still oppressed, politically, economically, academically and socially. But this was all part of the "Curses of Israel" listed in Deuteronomy 28:15-68.

CHAPTER 9

HOW MANY DIFFERENT "AGENDAS" HAS SATAN PUT IN PLACE FOR "GOD'S CHOSEN PEOPLE" AKA "THE ISRAELITES"?

In 1680, **four-fifths** of South Carolina's population was white. *However, Black slaves outnumbered white residents **two to one** in 1720, and by 1740, slaves constituted nearly **90% of the population**. Much of the growing slave population came from the West Coast of Africa, a region that had gained notoriety by exporting its large rice surpluses.

1898 Abolition of Slavery in Puerto Rico

AGENDA: KEEP US SLAVES AS LONG AS POSSIBLE

(Left) Walter Hardenburg's book "**The Putumayo, the Devil's Paradise**" talking about the atrocities done to the Peruvian, Columbian, Brazilian, Bolivian, and Amazonian Indians by the Peruvian Amazon Company, a giant rubber making company. As you can see on the cover of the book is three Indians in chains at the Putumayo district who were forced to do slave labor by the Europeans. **(Right)** the Herero people who were forced into slavery by the Germans. **Togoland, East Africa, Samoa and Papua New Guinea** was also hot spots for German Colonialism. The Herero people, under the German Scientist **Eugene Fischer**, had medical experiments performed on them in concentration camps using the full-blooded Herero people and mulatto children of German males as test subjects. They sterilized them, injected them with smallpox, typhus and tuberculosis.

Why would the Germans do this? Well, while the Africans were being persecuted for no reason, the indigenous people in South America were also facing persecution from the "**European Man**".

Here is an account of what the Indians had to go through as told by Hardenburg.

"The agents of the company forced the Pacific Indians of the Putumayo to work day and night....without the slightest remuneration except the food needed to keep them alive. They are robbed of their crops, their women and their children.....They are flogged inhumanly until their bones are laid bare... They are left to die, eaten by maggots, when they serve as food for the dogs.....Their children are grasped by their feet and their heads are dashed against trees and walls (rocks) until their brains fly out... Men, women and children are shot to provide amusement....they are burned with kerosene so that the employees may enjoy their desperate agony."

Walter Hardenburg

The Indian women were used as "**wives**" for the Europeans producing Mulatto children. They were hunted for sport as well and were branded with the name of the company's boss "**Arana**" (i.e. The Arana brothers). A Local publication called "**La Felpa**" would publish the truth about what was going on.

"The chiefs of sections….all impose upon each Indian the task of delivering 5 arrobas (75kg) of rubber every fabric (3 months). When the time comes to deliver the rubber, these unhappy victims appear with their loads upon their backs, accompanied by their women and children, who help them to carry rubber. When they reach the section, the rubber is weighed. They know by experience what the needle of the balance should mark, and when it indicates that they have delivered the full amount required, they leap about and laugh with pleasure. When it does not, they throw themselves face downwards on the ground and, in this attitude, await the lash, the bullet or the machete…They are generally given fifty lashes with scourges, until the flesh drops from their bodies in strips, or else are cut to pieces with machetes. This barbarous spectacle takes place before all the rest, among whom are their women and children."

La Felpa, December 29, 1907.

In the 21st century, since "**physical**" slavery was abolished upon God's people, "mental" slavery had to continue for us or at least some form of slavery where our oppressors could continue to rule over us. So in this sense for poor people in America (Indians/Negroes) who have not benefitted from "**European Colonization & Slavery**" this has changed from the "**Slavemaster**" to the "**Modern-day Boss**".

The Agenda Satan and **Edom** has for God's Children of Israel is to keep us working (slaving) for him, just like in Ancient Egypt. See for yourself the similarities between the "**Slavemaster**" and today's "**Boss**".

AGENDA: KEEP US WORKING FOR THEM

Our Boss or Modern day Slavemaster?

1. Avoids mingling with workers unless he wants to for sexual desires.
2. Carefully monitors profits.
3. Has **COMPLETE** control over workers
4. Not worried about worker turnover.
5. Experiments with moving workers around for better efficiency of profits.
6. Continually demands higher levels of output from the worker.
7. Workers livelihood depends on the Owner, Boss or Master so loyalty is given, even at the expense of selling another co-worker out.

8. Keeps tract of when workers eat, rests, or has to use the bathroom.
9. Tells the worker when he has to work and when he can stop working.
10. Can transfer or send the worker to another location to work (i.e. transfer) without regards of the worker's life.
11. Can punish the worker for disobedience even if the worker didn't do it.
12. Worker depends on his Master/Boss until he is old and gray, but never co-owns or owns anything that his Boss has acquired from having decades of workers making him rich.

So this form of slavery exists at our jobs. But what about when we get off of work and are operating in society as citizens? Post Slavery and even today, Blacks are still in fear of what can happen to us because in America it seems as though "**Blacks Lives Don't Matter**."

Fact: I once overhead two young Middle Eastern Arab men talking at a Tim Horton's coffee shop. Both were in Law school. One was sitting down studying and one was standing up. They talked about how their Fathers and Uncles were business owners in Detroit (i.e. Liquor Stores, Gas Stations, Grocery Stores, Check Cashing/Bill Payment stores, Cell Phone stores, Dollar Stores, Car insurance companies) where 99% of their customers were Black. They said that making money off black people in Detroit had allowed them to buy multiple home properties in Detroit which they were able to get at good deals ($5,000-$20,000) at the auction. These rental properties they used to make money off Black Detroiters needing a place to live. The rent money from Blacks they said was "automatic" every month and that the house would usually pay for itself "**AND SOME**" in the course of a couple years because the house was bought dirt cheap. The two Arab men began to say that even if their relative's businesses didn't do well one year, that all their rental properties where Blacks were paying rent brought in enough money to still support their lavish lifestyle living in the suburbs (**i.e. million dollar homes, multiple luxury cars, private schools, vacations, dining**

at five-star **Restaurants, expensive clothes and jewelry**). They noted that they had relatives who were also established lawyers working for themselves who had made enough money off Blacks to party at the club, vacation, eat a fancy restaurants and frequent with families just about any time that they pleased. Instead of sitting at a Law Office working for a firm they said that they were able "socialize" and enjoy the "nightlife" while still killing two birds with one stone by handing out their business/law cards to just about everybody. This way they were always networking to draw in more clients; Black, Arab, White, Latino, Indian, Asian or whatever. One of the Arab men (standing up) talked about how he was living in Detroit in a duplex so that he could be close to his Law internship with his cousins. The Arab man sitting down immediately asked, "**Your family doesn't live in Detroit do they!**" The Arab man standing up laughed and said, "**No, of course not, they live in the Suburbs like where most of our people live**." The Arab man standing up then said, "**Everybody around me is Black, but I'm not afraid because blacks love me. I can go to the liquor store at night in the ghetto of Detroit in my car and nobody bothers me. When I see Black people that know me they all say, "You gonna be my Lawyer when you get out of school!**" Both the Arab men laughed after that statement, probably because they knew that Black people should never be trying to search for a "**Future Lawyer**". When Black people are in need of a "**Lawyer**", most of the time it is not for a good reason and the outcome is usually not in our favor. The two Arab men knew this. The Arab men then began to talk about how Whites, Jews and Arabs were "**taking back the city of Detroit**" (i.e. "**Gentrification**"). They talked about strategic locations that they had on their "**bulls eye**" as their "**target goals**" for new businesses and homes. These included "**Rivertown**" on Jefferson rd., "Midtown" area, the New Center Area, Wayne State University Campus area, Woodward ave, East Grand Blvd, West Grand Blvd, and the 7 mile & Livernois area/District. The Arab man standing up then said,

"One we get **THOSE PEOPLE (Black people)** out and buy up everything down in that area then we can start putting businesses down there. We can demolish vacant blocks of old Detroit homes and build new luxury condos, lofts, apartments with gated security-police patrol so that it will drive the property value up in that area keeping Blacks out. Then **THOSE PEOPLE** will be forced to leave and go elsewhere and we can be sitting pretty in Downtown Detroit right off the Detroit River with our boats docked, just in time for the **Detroit M-1 Rail System** to be fully operational. It sounds kinda racist though but that's what is happening."

The Arab man sitting down then said,

"Why is it racist? If **THOSE PEOPLE** do not have the money to keep their homes or buy property to open businesses and **WE HAVE THE MONEY** to do so, then they should get out and let someone who does **MOVE IN** (i.e. Gentrification). That's just the way the world operates. That's why **WE** and other races are going to take back **DETROIT CITY** from **THOSE PEOPLE**."

(**Above**) Detroit M-1 Rail System construction in progress and the future "Planned" finished goal for this Rail system in the City of Detroit. Many believe it will not be fully operational until most of the Detroit Black residents in the area are gone or have lost their homes/small businesses, paving the way for non-black races to enjoy the "**New Detroit**". This "gentrification" is happening in Harlem

(New York), Dallas (Texas), Chicago (Illinois), and Baltimore (Maryland).

Sad to say, this is going on in other major cities where black neighborhoods and small black-owned businesses are being displaced by non-black races. Why is this happening? Because we don't **STICK TOGETHER** and pull our **RESOURCES** (i.e. money, connections, skills) to take **FULL OWNERSHIP** of our cities in which we live. This is called "**Gentrification**".

"**Gentrification**" is defined as: A trend in **URBAN NEIGHBORHOODS**, which results in **INCREASED PROPERTY VALUES** and the displacing of lower-income families (Blacks/Latinos) and small businesses (owned by Blacks/Latinos).

(**Above**) African-American couple and Mexican man. Both desire "**equal rights**" in America when America wants to leave the "**Negro**" and "**Latino**" out of the equation. Many Americans want "**Blacks**" to go back to Africa and "**Latinos**" to go back to Mexico or their countries abroad.

Fact: African-Americans are estimated to be around **45 million strong** in America while Hispanic and Latino Americans are estimated to be around **55 million strong** in America. Combined this is a whopping 100 million of "**Negroes**" and "**Latinos**" living in America. We have been here before any Jew, Arab, Indian or Asian arrived to America. This is a known fact. So why is a people "**100 million**" strong working for people 11 million strong? If Blacks and Latinos are the main consumers-workers in the "American Economy", then who really holds the power? A business or corporation cannot survive unless it has "**workers**" to make their product and "**consumers**" to buy their product. If Blacks and Latinos are the main races doing **BOTH** then **WE HOLD THE POWER!** We also have the **NUMBERS (POPULATION)** to create a **POWER SHIFT**. So why haven't we figured this out yet? If the "**Minority races**" in America were to collectively put their monies together and **ONLY SUPPORT THEIR OWN BUSINESSES**, boycotting other businesses we can take back what we deserve. We should be tired of working our lives away for others who really don't care about us. Knowing that we make up 100 million of America, look up the statistics and then ask yourself, "Why are we working for a people less numerous than us?" If we practice **UNITY**, we should be on **TOP**, not the **BOTTOM**. Remember, Haiti figured out this out in their country and drove the French who were oppressing them off the Island.

For those who don't believe what I'm saying, here are the facts:

1. **Arab Americans** are estimated to be around **3.6 million strong** in America living mostly in California, Michigan, New York, Texas, Florida, Illinois and New Jersey.
2. **Jewish Americans** are estimated to be around **8 million strong** in America living mostly in New York City, Miami-Florida, Boston-Massachusetts, Los Angeles-California, Philadelphia-Pennsylvania, Cincinnati-Ohio, Houston-Texas, Chicago-

Illinois, Cleveland-Ohio, Baltimore-Maryland and Detroit-Michigan.

3. **Asian Americans** are estimated to be around **18 million strong** living mainly on the West Coast of America and in Michigan, New York.

4. **Indian Americans** are estimated to be around **3.5 million strong** living mostly in the East Coast of America. Other cities with a large population of Indians are Atlanta, Baltimore, Washington D.C., Boston, Chicago, Dallas, Detroit, Houston, Los Angeles, Philadelphia, New Hampshire, San Francisco, San Jose, and Oakland.

WAKE UP! 100 MILLION (BLACKS & LATINOS) VS 33 MILLION (ARABS, JEWS, ASIANS, & INDIANS) IN AMERICA. WHY ARE BLACKS AND LATINOS ECONOMICALLY AT THE BOTTOM IN AMERICA WHILE EVERYONE ELSE IS ON TOP?

*1935 **Rubin Stacey** lynching, Fort Lauderdale, Florida. Because he supposedly "frightened" a white woman he was lynched. In the same manner, Police officers or regular civilians who are "**threatened/frightened**" by blacks are routinely shot to death with barely no conviction.*

AGENDA: KILL US FOR "BEING BLACK" BECAUSE TO THEM "BLACK LIVES DON'T MATTER".

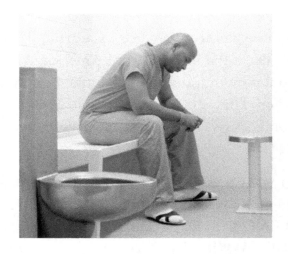

AGENDA: KEEP US INCARCERATED

A new study by **M. Marit Rehavi** of the University of British Columbia and Sonja B. Starr of the University of Michigan Law School shows that **Black Americans receive almost 60% long prison sentences than white Americans who committed the same crime.** The study covered 58,000 federal criminal cases and found that there was a significant difference between the sentences given to Black people to those given to white people.

Black Women in Jail; District of Columbia

AGENDA: EUGENICS

It is fact that Doctors under contract with the California Department of Corrections and Rehabilitation **sterilized nearly 150 female inmates from 2006 to 2010 without required state approvals**, The Center for Investigative Reporting has found at least 148 women received tubal ligations in violation of prison rules during those five years – and there are perhaps 100 more dating back to the late 1990s, according to state documents and interviews. Black women were signed up for the "sterilization" surgery while they were pregnant and housed at either the California Institution for Women in Corona or Valley State Prison for Women in Chowchilla. Former inmates and prisoner advocates maintain that prison medical staff coerced the women, targeting those deemed likely to return to prison in the future.

Genocide for Blacks in the 21 century is real. Planned Parenthood, Plan B, Chemtrails, tainted water, forced vaccinations and unhealthy toxic food is most concentrated in the Inner city where Blacks and Latinos reside.

Since 1973, 13 million black babies have been aborted. This is more than deaths from HIV/AIDS, violent crimes, accidents, cancer and heart disease combined. In 2011 78% of abortions in New York City was done by Blacks and Hispanics/Latinos. In New York City, Blacks and Latinos make up 54% of the population. These statistics is staggering.

Fact: *According to Erma Clardy Craven (Social Worker/Civil Rights Leader), several years ago, when 17,000 aborted babies were found in a dumpster outside a pathology laboratory in Los Angeles, California. 12-15,000 of these babies were black.*

AGENDA: FINANCIAL SLAVERY (BONDAGE)

Blacks are plagued with financial debt and an enormous Wealth Gap in America. Without help from our own people we are forced to borrow. This = **DEBT + INTEREST**. Loans, Loans, loans with **NO OWNERSHIP!**

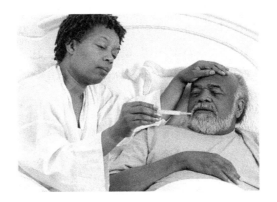

AGENDA: EMPLOYER BONDAGE, "MAKE SURE YOU GET A JOB!" THEN WORK THAT JOB FOR 30+ YEARS UNTIL YOU GET

SICK AND DIE. ARE THESE EXAMPLES OF GENERATIONAL CURSES OR IS THE BLAME ALL ON US?

Most Black Grandparents when asking their grandkids how they are doing are often hit with the response:

> **"Nothing grandpop, just working a lot, paying bills."**

The Grandparents response is:

> **"Thank God you have a job to take care of yourself and your family…..now you make sure you do whatever it takes to keep that job….you need that job…..do not let them fire you."**

Most Black people on the job have to be 100% perfect in order to keep their non-black bosses or non-black co-workers off their back. Still, even being **"perfect"** on the job with perfect attendance, a black person can find himself or herself in the bosses' office getting disciplined, wrote up and maybe even fired. The stress that comes with trying to be in **"perfect"** attendance and performing **"perfect"** on the job in addition to watching **"our back"** can bring on **"physical illnesses"** like high blood pressure, anxiety disorder, cigarette abuse, marijuana abuse and alcohol/substance abuse. Most black parents in the old times were not encouraging their kids to **"create jobs"** by becoming owners of a business. **This has to change**. We must do whatever it takes, even if it means getting together a group of like-minded people to collectively combine resources and money to invest in business ventures that will bring **"Black Economic Freedom"**.

Black Janitor then (1800's) and Black Janitor now (2016). Most black parents do not tell their kids to be Janitors when they grow up, that is unless they can own a Janitorial Service company. No Black Child in High School is going to have "Janitor" on their top Career list at "Career Day". We need to wake up. All over the world, Blacks are looked to "serve" in the country they live in.

We should be asking ourselves these questions:

1. Why must we repeat the same cycle of working 30-40 years like our parents?
2. As long as I continue to work for someone else 5-7 days a week how will I ever become successful?
3. How will I ever get to enjoy my life and experience the world if I'm always working?
4. How will I pass down an "inheritance" or "legacy" to my kids?
5. Is labor work all I'm good for in this life?
6. Why do I still feel broke despite working for 30 years?
7. Why am I in debt in my 60's?
8. Why is my credit messed up still after 20 years and why am I paying double for everything I finance?
9. What do I really own that is of some value?

10. Am I more valuable "dead" to my family than "alive"? My family should not be able to only pay off debts when I die using my Life Insurance.

11. Why are my kids going through the same mistakes I made financially?

With poor credit history, a short job history, and low income, buying a new or used car can be a "**Life Trap**". We often get excited knowing we got approved for a car thinking we are getting a good deal.....that is until they roll in the **finance charge/interest**. Then that new car finance amount seems to almost double, but because we are so used to not having anything new, we sign our life away into repetitive cycle of debt and negative equity. In the Black community, not having "**cash reserves**" or an "**inheritance**" from our parents means we have to borrow money on "**credit**". Our loan applications for different things (Car, house, business, personal) are often rejected, further damaging our hope for positive future. If we are approved for credit or loans (by non-black creditors), it is usually at the highest government allowed "interest-rate". This is like committing "economic suicide", but all over the United States we are doing this on the regular.

(**Above**) For many Blacks, this is a common sight on the kitchen table. Because we lack savings or investments we live "check-to-check", with our bank account only increasing on "**pay-day**" and then decreasing over the course of a week. Other non-black races, continue to build wealth as their "**investments**" from "**working together**" allow their bank accounts to grow while they sitting on the couch, on vacation or sleeping in bed. When we live our lives "**check-to-check**" we are always chasing "**past due bills**" and are forced to ask for "**extensions**", "**promise-to-pay agreements**" and "**post-dated checks**" to keep our "**services**" on. This means that our "future paycheck money" is already accounted for before we even get it. For this reason, many Blacks cannot afford to take a "real vacation" when they actually have vacation time to take off. **WAKE UP!**

So because we are often denied access to "**loans**" or "**credit**", we are subjected to working long hours often at wages that are not enough to take care of the household. Everyone hates to have to worry about making the bills every month, so it's natural for us to think of different solutions to break free from this feeling of "**I'm working but I still feel broke.**" What do we do? What we've been taught to do from our parents. Get another job or go back to school. But is this always the answer? We tend to forget the saying "**We are stronger together**" and we don't thing in the "**Long-term**". Sad to say, that is "Black Americas" pitfall.

For most blacks, especially in the Southern states of America, the only jobs available are jobs in the "Fast Food" industry and "Health Care" jobs. But again, these jobs are not going to build blacks a "bright" future for generations to come. So what about the Negro that goes to school, hoping to land a job in a good Career? What happens when the "Negro" cannot get a job in "White America" after finishing all the required classes in his/her Degree program?

MORE SCHOOL?
THAT MEANS MORE DEBT!
HOW WILL I ENJOY LIFE?

NOW WHAT???

When most blacks graduate from school, they are thinking on a "**me, myself and I**" level. They are most likely to be single, without any kids or any significant financial load. What we don't realize is that this is the perfect time to "**Unify**", pulling our resources together to "invest" in something that is going to make life "financially easier" when it comes time to settle down and have kids. How you ask? Well, imagine a College grad that gets a new job making $60,000-$80,000. He has no new car yet, no 30 year-mortgage on a house, no child support, no alimony, no children to take care of and no real bills. The College grad is young full of energy ready to work and make some money. Many College grads that get jobs find themselves getting exactly what "Satan" wants. That is get a whole bunch of new things……..clothes, new apartments, condos, jewelry, watches, shoes, jackets, cars, furniture, electronics, etc. These College grads travel all over the world because most of them have no real bills. But what if for instance all the extra shifts and overtime this college graduate did went towards a "**greater goal**"?

Case and point.

10 college grads around 23 years old all start working extra-shifts for overtime pay on their jobs. They make a "**pact/agreement**" to bank $1,000 a month into a group bank account. They set up goals for each year as to what they want to do with the money in the "near" future. The word "Near" is very important because with "unity" we can achieve goals faster as a group or collectively as a "Black People". So how much money can these College Grads save from "sticking together?"

10 College Grads x $1,000/month = $10,000. $10,000 x 12 months = $120,000 in 1 year.

So if the College Grads are 23 years old and they do this faithfully for 10 years they would have accumulated 1.2 million dollars by the time they are 33 years old. How many 33-year-old black men have "1.2 million dollars of "**Spending Power**" at their fingerprints. Whatever investment project or idea that they could come up with they would easily have the capital to fund it. This is only using "10" individuals. What about if we had 20? Many Blacks in America have enough brothers, sisters, cousins, nieces, nephews, uncles and aunties to get

"20" people of just family members to start an "investment group". Even the Black Church has the potential to do this, "taking back their community" one business investment at a time. Black Churches have anywhere from 20 members to 10,000 members. Collectively if we use "**Group Economics**" this equates to future "**Economic Power**" as long as we are "**Unified**" in our goals and we remain "**Patient**". This is what we are missing in our equation of "**Being Successful**". We lack "**CAPITAL (money)**", "**Trust**" and "**Patience**". Because we lack capital it makes it harder for blacks to start up their own business. Investing in a business or real estate at certain times can be a "huge win" for blacks. But when the opportunity presents itself or when we see "financial potential" in a certain area, most likely we can't do anything because we don't have the money. So when this happens, who usually steps in to take advantage of these opportunities for "**financial gain?**" Other non-black races (i.e. Chaldeans, Arab Muslims, Indians, Jews, Caucasians, Asians). So, when we don't have an inheritance or the means to acquire "**Real Capital**" we are at the mercies of the "**Lending agencies**" who normally will only lend to us what they want to lend to us, high interest and all. These agencies because of "**Interest-Usury**" always stay ahead and on top of us.

Fact: *The European Jews lend with "**interest**" to all of mankind, except their own people. This is called "**usury**" in the bible and is forbidden for the "**Real Israelites**" to do. **The Federal Reserve, the Bank of London, The World Bank, The International Monetary Fund (IMF), and even the IRS** use the help of "interest" to make "huge financial gains". With these banking institutions shelling out interest to the world, surely some of the "Real Children of Israel" is receiving this "usury". So if the European Jews are "in fact" the Real Jews of the Bible, according to the "**Law of Moses**" from the God of Israel, the Jews should be receiving the "**Curses of Israel**" for breaking God's commandments in regards to "usury" as listed in the Torah. But they are not receiving any "**Curses**". Therefore, they cannot be the Real Jews of the Bible.*

Exodus 22:25 "If thou lend money to any of **MY PEOPLE** that is poor by thee, thou shalt not be to him as an usurer, neither shalt thou lay upon him usury."

Leviticus 25:36-37 "Take thou no usury of him, or increase: but fear thy God; that thy brother may live with thee. Thou shalt not give him thy money upon usury, nor lend him thy victuals (food) for increase."

WORKING TO LIVE OR LIVING TO WORK? IS THE "BLACK RACE" LIVING OR WORKING?

The question most "**Blue Collar**" working Black people should have is: Should I work my entire life to pay for "Things" or "Debt?" or should I enjoy work to enjoy my life? Other non-black races are traveling the world, eating at five-star restaurants, staying at five-star hotels, climbing mountains, snorkeling, scuba diving, sailing the oceans on private yachts, surfing, windsailing, jumping off cliffs into lagoons, walking through exotic waterfalls, jet skiing, outdoor camping, and are buying up prime real estate in Africa or the Caribbean. Many Blacks end up working their whole lives, tirelessly day in and day out, 1-2 jobs, chasing bills with no opportunities to do all the things that the wish they could do. It is time to change our way of doing things and to make our "dreams" a "reality".

Who is living? The Black African slave 1850's with her Arab master? Or what about the Person that was sitting in this folding chair on the beach. Remember, we only live once.

TOP 10 REGRETS OF THE DYING

1. I wish I had the courage to live a life true to myself, not the life others expected of me.
2. I wish I hadn't worked so hard and spent more time with my family.
3. I wish I had the courage to express my feelings.
4. I wish I had stayed in touch with my friends instead of working so much.
5. I wish that I had let myself be happier.
6. I wish I would've paid more attention to my health than my job(s).
7. I wish I would've made better "financial decisions" growing up.
8. I wish I would've paid cash for everything.
9. I wish I would've had a better relationship with my children as they got older.
10. I wish I would've supported my children more in their "dreams" and "visions" or "business" ventures.

True or False: A Black Lady working at a Chase Bank in the Suburbs observes her regular day. She describes one particular day as follows:

A white man comes up to the counter to deposit some money. After making the deposit, he asks the teller, "**What's my balance?**" She says, "$250,000 sir." He smiles and walks off. Then two Mexicans come up to the teller in clothes that you could tell were from their own business or that they were "**independent contractors**". They deposit the money they earned for the day and one of them asks the teller, "**What's OUR balance?**" The teller says, "60,000". The Mexicans seem pleased and walk out the bank. A young Chaldean man dressed in a polo shirt, some casual jeans, designer shoes and a jacket comes in with his black money bag from the business he or his family owns. He makes the deposit and asks the teller, "**What's my balance?**" The Teller says, "$175,000". The Chaldean man nods his head while responding back to a text on his IPhone and walks out the bank. A Middle Aged Jewish man walks into the bank to deposit some money his mother had left in the house before she died. The Jewish man says that his mother played the stocks when she was alive and left him some money in her will. He said he was going to the Dominican Republic after burying his mother to get away. After depositing the money he asks the teller, "**What's my balance?**" She says "798,000". He says, "Thank you" and walks out. A Black man in his 30's comes into the bank talking to his wife on the phone, seeming kind of angry. He tells the teller that he wants to cash

195

a check but first wants to know what his balance is. She asks him, "**Do you want me to tell you or write it down?**" He says, "Write it down." She writes down on the paper his balance and then slides it to him. The paper says -$98.24. The Black man looks even more mad after seeing his balance and says, "Never mind", as he proceeds to walk out the bank.

This is a normal daily occurrence at many banks all across the United States of America. The wealth gap in America is the lowest for Blacks and Latinos. Over the years, the Wealth Gap for Whites is actually increasing. This means they are becoming more wealthy while we stay poor. Wake Up!

Average Family Wealth by Race/Ethnicity, 1963–2013

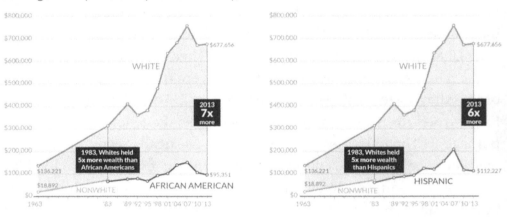

In 1983, Whites had 5 times more wealth than African-Americans and Latinos (Hispanics). By 2013, whites had increased the financial power by having 7 times more wealth than African-Americans and 6 times more wealth than Latinos (Hispanics) respectfully. Blacks and Latinos typically work for "white races", but at the same time we give our hard-earned money back to them. Is that smart? – *Source Urban Institute calculations from Survey of Financial Characteristics of Consumers 1962. Survey of Changes in Family Finances 1963, and Survey of Consumer Finances 1983-2013.*

(Above) Financial bondage affects most Black people in America today. IRS installment agreements, Credit card bills, mortgages, Car payments, Car insurance, Property tax payments, Utility bills, Child support payment, Medical bills, Bill Collection payment arrangements, Wage garnishment, Personal loans, Operating Under the Influence/Driving While Under the Influence infractions, Traffic Tickets fees/Court fines, renewing lapsed Car Insurance and Car repairs can set a Black person or family back into a state of **"financial no-return"**. This causes nothing but **"Stress"** which we all know affects our body and mind.

A survey research of 100 Black men and women indicated that the tendency to embrace mainstream American culture (**i.e. "FIT IN"**) was associated with **higher blood pressure** and **higher heart rates**. This increases the stress and "workload" of the heart, which over time can lead to a Heart Attack or Heart Failure. Trying to "Fit in" to "Corporate White America" was also found to be associated with higher degrees of hostility among blacks. That means that all of that **"butt-kissing"** we're doing at the office or on the job is impacting our health and making us more likely to snap when we step out of the office.

The Division of Population Science at the Fox Chase Cancer Center examined the effects of racial stressors on cardiovascular reactivity. 31 Black males and 31 White males were shown racist videos. Although the racist videos increased blood pressure for both samples, **the Black**

people maintained the high blood pressure after the video was done. So when a White person sees something racist, it affects them at that moment. If a Black person sees something racist or experiences racism, it just keeps affecting them. Black men and women have to deal with this every day.

(Left) Black family under stress. **(Right)** Nuclear family (3 Generations) happy and together. Right after slavery was abolished Blacks were living in "**Nuclear Families**" in "**Black Communities**" where we were forced to look after and depend on one another. Arab, Indian, Jewish, Asian and even some Latino communities still do this today. This helps to build wealth by allowing different people in the house to save money on expenses that they would otherwise be spending if they were living alone with their significant other and kids in a different city/state with no help. Those days have long left us. Maybe it is time we made a change, before it is too late.

Back in the late 1800's after slavery was abolished Black people went back to what they knew from Africa. They lived in tight-nit communities where everyone helped each other. Like the Native Americans, they set up their village so that it was not too many "**entry** points". There was sometimes only "**one way in**", and "**one way out**" of the community. This way the people of the "Village-Community" could identity strangers (i.e. the white man, other tribes). All the Black families knew each other and helped raised the youth. Even though children had their own biological "mother" and "aunt", they still called other older black women or men in their village "aunt" or "uncle". This is still practiced by West Africans still to this day. They operated and survived using the "Barter System". Everyone that had a skill or a trade used what they knew best to help the people in the village. One person was the priest or medicine man (healer), able to use home-made remedies and herbs from the earth to cure illnesses. Someone was skilled at "metal-working", some were skilled at farming, some were skilled at agriculture and tending to livestock used to feed the village. Someone knew how to make clothes and someone had horses with buggies to take people out the village if they needed to venture into the city or the market to sell or buy goods. Someone knew how to fish, and someone knew how to hunt. Someone was good at Astrology and tracking the seasons or changes in the weather. Someone was an "educator", which was important for the freed-slaves that needed to know how to read or write. The "elders" had knowledge of the "ancestors" and were able to give "words of wisdom" to the people so that they wouldn't forget who they were as a people. Someone was good with their hands at fixing things or building things (i.e. houses, sheds, tools). Someone was good at training the young boys and men for "warfare" using training methods like what is used today (i.e. wrestling, shooting bows & arrows, shooting a gun, laying traps for the enemy, scouting). So every day, the people in the village had everything they needed to survive. They had each other: food, shelter, medicine from the earth, water, transportation, education, security and their God. On a typical day, the older men and young men were responsible for hunting animals and catching fish. The women of the village gathered the vegetables, bread and water for the evening meal. Once the men came back with the meat and fish, dinner was prepared. The men ate first, then the women and children. At night the people in

199

the village celebrated with dance, stories and more. It gave the young men and women in the village a chance to develop crushes, socialize and develop pre-relationships leading up to marriage. Families "Home Schooled" their children and there was no concern for "I want my kid to learn how to be social around other kids" because the community had plenty of kids to play with. There was no need for money, bills, health insurance, car payments, loan payments, child support payments, IRS payments, EBT cards, Social Security, SSI disability checks, Tax Refund Checks, WIC, or house payments/rent. No stress, no confusion, and the "**Nuclear Family**" was together. People married within their race/tribe and there was "**preservation**" of the people. Therefore, there was no outside "corruption".

In today's society, we have our Grandparents in nursing homes that often do not meet "our standards of care". But because the modern-day black family has both parents working, there is no one at home during the day to watch grandma or grandpa. This is not the case in Africa as there are no nursing homes there. In today's black family, when people get married or finish school, most people end up leaving the city or state where their family is. This results in us being scattered all throughout the United States with no close help at hand. Because we are scattered we cannot "**effectively**" support each other in different things (**i.e. businesses, raising children**). Our "**Nuclear Black Family Model**" is essentially lost. While we live our lives in different cities/states our kids end up being raised by the T.V, the radio, the internet, their friends at school, their teachers and people in the neighborhood (good or bad). This is where we went wrong.

AGENDA: DESTROY THE NUCLEAR BLACK FAMILY

How was the Black Family in the 1960's. Most Blacks born in the 1960's-1970's grew up with both parents in the house. We all ate dinner at the table, like other families still do and there was no beef with the "in-laws". Everyone got along, and helped raise the family. The black father was in the house with his black wife raising the kids. He was the head of the household, he brought home the paycheck and provided the food while mom dukes raised the kids. He was there to discipline the kids and teach his boys how to be men. Homosexuality was taboo in those days and not to many men were on Child support with the standard "8 days a month of parenting time". Why? Because the Black father was home. Even though "White America" limited blacks to rentership in the projects we still made it work. **WHITE AMERICA** hated it. Then **Crack** and **Heroin** hit the streets supplied by them. Laws changed and Black men were thrown away for long term sentences. With no Black man in the house, **THEY** could infiltrate homosexuality and disease into the black communities. Add some **vaccination programs, toxic Gentically Modified food and poisoned water** to help speed things along and now we have increasing HIV, Autism, ADHD along with a host of other problems plaguing the black community. Destroy our values, morals with T.V/Music and you create an **immoral** generation of black people. Take away our jobs, close down our children's schools, give us welfare benefits (**EBT, Obamacare, Obamaphones, WIC, Section 8**) and now you have the Black Inner City dependent on the Government. Elimate the Black man and bogg down the Grandparents with bills to disrupt the Strong "Black Family Unit". Now the black woman has to worry about everything: school, her job, her fatherless kids, her life and her sanity. The main factor in this picture is the **BLACK MAN**. Destroy the black man and you will destroy the **BLACK RACE**. It shouldn't be no wonder that 65% of black children are living in single parent homes and >60% of black women are not married.

AGENDA: CREATE CONFUSION, LOSS OF HOPE AND UNCERTAINTY. CREATE AN UNSTABLE MIND AND THE BODY WILL FOLLOW

For many Blacks in America, there is a feeling of "**uncertainty**" that lingers in our mind about the future as we see things getting worse for our people. Satan's government has got people busy, busy, busy. Busy paying bills, debts, traffic fines and court fees/costs. Busy working, but trying to fit in a social life so that we can find a mate suitable for marriage. Busy trying to keep our house and children in order. Busy trying to figure out what religion to follow and what is God's purpose in our lives. The stressors of all of this is wearing Black America down. Mental illness (i.e. Schizoaffective, Depression, Bipolar, Anxiety disorder) is on the rise in Black America and it is now slowing down. Substance abuse (Alcohol, Promethazine with Codeine cough syrup, bath salts, Cocaine, Heroin, Marijuana) is also on the rise not only in the young but also in middle-aged and elderly blacks. When people are confused on how to handle different aspects of their lives (**domestic, social, financial, education, religious**) it leaves a sense of uncertainty, loss of hope and low morale. We lose that "pep in our step" and "skip in our walk". We stop smiling and instead of having joy or happiness throughout the day, we tend to feel a little angry inside. Especially when you look around and it appears that other non-black races are prospering day after day eating "all of the pie" while we can't even get a slice. You start to wonder and ask God, "**Why?**"

Satan wants to **steal, kill** and **destroy** the "**Joy**" of "God's People". He wants to confuse and mess with our minds because he knows that the mind affects our body, which in turn affects what we "**physically do**" or how we "**physically act**" during the day. This is all part of the "**Deception**". Satan is for "**Chaos**" while God is for "**Order**". In these days, "**deception**" and "**confusion**" is high and people don't even see it. But the Bible told us this was going to happen.

Mark 13:3-6 "And as he sat upon the Mount of Olives over against the temple, Peter and James and John and Andrew asked him privately, Tell us, when shall these things be? And what shall be the sign when all these things shall be fulfilled? And Jesus answering them began to say, **TAKE HEED LEST ANY MAN DECEIVE YOU:**"

Yahusha (Jesus) knew many people would come saying they were the Christ and many would come preaching other doctrines.

So the Bible teaches us not to "**fall**" to Satan's game of deception. We must have strong minds, not easily led to doubt or confusion for the bible says in James 1:8 that "**A double minded man is unstable in all his ways.**" So in in these days we must stay "**mind-strong**" to not sway even in the midst of a chaotic, stressful life. If we stay rooted in the "**Word of God**" we cannot be easily misled.

So the Black person in America tries his best to stay rooted in God's word. He/she goes to Church on the Sabbath or Sunday (per their religious preference), paying tithes faithfully and praying. But outside of church, when the service ends, we realize that the situation around us has not changed. The Big Question is WHY? It seems that everything is becoming more expensive but in the same instance money is becoming more harder and harder to come by. So that leaves most people to acquiring a second job, or working more hours. Of course this takes away from everything else that God wants us to focus on such as our marriage, kids, school, hobbies, vacation, and HIM! Constant "**working**" eventually puts stress on the home (spouse and kids) so that the black person at some point has to **"re-visit"** the drawing board.

The Black Person is thinking: **"I have an unhappy stressed marriage"**. "I have to figure something out. I can't just work my whole life and then get sick and die. That's what my parents did. Why am I repeating the mistakes that they made? Why is this happening to me? What did I do wrong? Have I disobeyed God?

Satan: "You have no solutions; you are just going to have to work more. You need the money."

But there ARE SOLUTIONS! We just have been taught to **"fend for our own"** by our parents. We are given the **"pull yourselves up from your bootstraps"** mentality. Our parents didn't' stress the importance of **"unity"** or the concept of a business. We were not encouraged to ask questions or to **"think out of the box"**. We were thought how not to **"Trust Each"** other.

AGENDA: DISCOURAGE BLACKS FROM GOING AND SUPPORTING BACK BUSINESSES.

The burning question for a lot of blacks in America are:

1. What's the solution? Why can't blacks have an "**Economy within an Economy**" like other races have?
2. Why can't we have our own banks, grocery stores, schools, affordable/green housing, businesses and restaurants in our own communities.
3. Aren't there rich blacks out there in America willing to help?

There is an entire industry built upon the exploitation of African-Americans, particularly in the area of financial services. Many black people can't get bank accounts and are trying to survive day-to-day financially. This is how payday lenders get over on us, asking us to pay insane interest rates on modest loans.

Not having money isn't something we can always control. But there is no excuse to not have financial literacy. **Dr. Claude Anderson** stressed this importance in this quote:

"Only 2% of all the black folks in America work for their own community, for their own people. You have not moved one Iota in 140 years in terms of employment. Our people still do not understand that you can **NOT** enrich yourself working a job. A job is **NOT** designed to enrich you. A job is designed to maintain you....to keep you one week away from welfare, unemployment, and the food stamp lines. If you want to get rich you **MUST** move into a business and business ownership. Business will transfer and redistribute wealth 6 to 8 times faster than working a job. The only way you're gonna get rich working a job is if you steal."

Dr. Claude Anderson

(**Above**) This is a Black-Owned Tire/Rim and Auto Detailing shop in Detroit, Michigan. Most African-Americans are shocked when arriving into a shop for business to see a black man as the owner. The New and Used Tires here at this **"Black-owned Tire Shop & Detail business"** are priced cheaper than anyone else around but still when we visit **"Black-owned businesses"** we tend to still ask for a discount as if the price is not low enough. However, when most African-Americans visit non-black businesses they **ALWAYS** pay full price, no questions asked. They are led to believe that they are getting a good deal from the "Arab man, the Indian man, the Jewish man or the White man" but when buying from our own we wonder if we're being scammed. It is almost as if we have built-in **"trust issues with our people"** and built-in **"phobias"** about supporting our own people; as if we don't want to see anybody else Black doing better than us. This is one of the reasons why Black Businesses are slim-to-none in Black inner cities.

Fact: There **ARE** Black Owned Banks in the United States of America. People just don't know where they are. Here is a list of some to check out and visit if they are in your state.

- Alamerica Bank-Birmingham, AL
- Commonwealth National Bank-Mobile, AL
- First Tuskegee Bank, Tuskegee, AL
- Broadway Federal Bank (FSB)-Los Angeles, CA
- Industrial Bank-Washington, D.C
- Capital City Bank & Trust-Atlanta, GA
- Citizens Trust Bank-Atlanta, GA
- Carver State Bank-Savannah, GA
- Covenant Bank-Chicago, IL
- Highland Community Bank-Chicago, IL
- Illinois Service Federal Savings & Loan-Chicago, IL
- Seaway Bank & Trust-Chicago, IL
- Liberty Bank & Trust-Louisiana
- One United Bank-Boston, MA
- First Independence Bank-Detroit, MI
- City National Bank of New Jersey-Newark, NJ
- Mechanics and Farmer Bank-Durham, NC
- United Bank of Philadelphia-Philadelphia, PA
- University National Bank of Houston-Houston, TX
- First State Bank-Virginia
- North Milwaukee State Bank-Milwaukee, WI

Fact 2: Donald Sterling was the owner of the NBA Los Angeles Clippers from 1981 to 2014. His net worth is around 3 billion dollars. This is what he had to say about blacks:

Sterling says that while successful Jews often reach back to help their own to climb the ladder, many wealthy blacks do not do the same.

**"Jews, when they get successful, they will help their people,"
Sterling said. "Some of the African-Americans, they don't want to
help anyone."**

Basically Sterling is saying that while successful Jews often give back
to help other Jews climb the ladder, many wealthy blacks do not do the
same. Does he have a point? Is he right on this or partially right?

If our famous Black Leaders in the 1960's would've told us to donate
$20 in church every Sunday to a **Black Central Bank** or **Black Fund**
designed to help fund other Black Local/State Banks bringing back
jobs, money and opportunities back to black people, would we have
done it? Let's do the math.

There are **45 million** African-Americans in America today. There are
52 Sundays in a year. From 1960 to 2016 is **56 years**. **$20 dollars** is
not much money for an average Black Christian to give on Sundays.

- 52 Sundays x 56 years = 2,912 potential Sundays to donate $20
- 45 million Blacks in America x $20 dollars = 900 Million.

So if every black person in America gave $20 **JUST ONCE** to a Black
Fund, that is a total of 800 million. So if we multiply this **ONE TIME**

donation of $900 million dollars by the assumed 2,912 Sundays in a 56 year span we get a whopping **2.6 TRILLION DOLLARS! To put this in perspective, the United States National debt amount in 2016 is around 19.2 Trillion dollars.**

Now we would all agree that **2.6 Trillion dollars** is enough money for Blacks to have their own **"Economy within an Economy"**. With this kind of money, we wouldn't have to work for other races or spend our money on other races unless we chose to. Wake up Black America. This can easily be done today with the cooperation of the Black Church, Certified Public Accountants, Business companies and like-minded Black people seeking change. This can be done by groups of blacks all over the USA. Whether it is 10, 20 or 50 black people putting their money into a "pot", the financial reward if we are patient (**i.e. 5-year plan, 10-year plan**) is enormous. Imagine owning rental properties, vacation properties, small franchises (Jimmy Johns, Jersey Mike's subs, Tim Hortons, Subway) at the age of 30 or 40. It "**takes money to make money**" so if we don't have it in abundance than we need to put our heads together to get it "**collectively**". There lies our "**economic freedom**", but not without "**Unity**".

So in today's Black Society, why do we still not have more Black Independent Communities that are financial independent from other races and self-sufficient? Where is all the Wealthy Blacks at? What are they doing?

FORBES
2013

Black Billionaires

Here are the stats on these Black Billionaires (from 2013) including their age, country of origin and net worth.

#1 Aliko Dangote, $16.1 billion *55, Nigerian.*

#2 Mohammed Al-Amoudi, $13.5 billion *68, Saudi Arabian.*

#3 Mike Adenuga, $4.7 billion *59, Nigerian.*

#4 Patrice Motsepe, $2.9 billion *51, South African.*

#5 Oprah Winfrey, $2.8 billion *59, African-American.*

#6 Isabel Dos Santos, $2 billion *40, Angolan.*

#7 Mohammed Ibrahim, $1.1 billion *66, British. Sudan*

The Jewish Community Center of Metro Detroit

All over the United States of America, there are **State of the Art-Jewish Community Centers**, some so big that they are called "**Campuses**", like **the Jewish Community Center of Metro Detroit in West Bloomfield**. In Detroit, there are small Community Centers scattered here and there but nothing big enough or equipped enough to support the city of Detroit. When any Jewish person has to re-locate to another U.S. city, all they have to do is call the Jewish Community Center and they will use their massive network to find them housing, transportation and a job. Any help that a Jewish person needs is quickly answered by the Jewish Community Center. **This is why we rarely see a homeless or unemployed Jewish man or woman in America**. For Blacks in America we do not have that luxury. Black men find it very hard to land good-paying jobs, even if he is qualified. Black families that are looking to relocate but are scared because of uncertainties in regards to "housing" or "jobs" could essentially be a "thing of the past" if we had our own network of "**African-American Community Centers**" all throughout the United States of America. However, because of our "**Lack of Unity**", there is no one to help, no one to call. He is essentially all alone, frustrated, not knowing what to do next.

Has anything changed? According to the Bureau of Labor Statistics, the national unemployment rate for white Americans was 5.3% in 2014. The unemployment rate for African-Americans was more than twice that number at 12.0%. The unemployment rate for white teens was 17% but for black teens this number was 33% in 2014. Many Black Americans cried when Obama got into office as if he was the "**Saviour of Black America**" but after years in the office and things getting worse in regards to issues such as the shutting down of black inner-city schools, the building of more prisons and rising unemployment for blacks, many Blacks have been wondering when is Obama going to keep his promises. Many Blacks say Obama made a promise to create more job opportunities for them and for this reason they still have been waiting patiently for change. However, this change ain't coming.

President Barack Obama sat down with the people at Black Enterprise Magazine during his term and quoted about the issues "**Black America**" had with him. Here is what he said to Black Enterprise Magazine:

"My general view has been consistent throughout, which is that I want all businesses to succeed. I want all Americans to have opportunity. **I'M NOT THE PRESIDENT OF BLACK AMERICA.** I'm the president of the United States of America, but the programs we have put in place have been directed at **those folks** who are least able to get financing through conventional means, who have been in the past locked out of opportunities that were available to everybody. So, I'll put my track record up against anybody in terms of us putting in place broad-based programs that ultimately had a **HUGE BENEFIT FOR AFRICAN AMERICAN BUSINESSES**."

Fact: Black owned businesses only get **2%** of Black Dollars. If Black customers spent 10% more of their income in Black Businesses, it would generate 1 million jobs for "**Black Americans**". After the government, small black businesses are the biggest employer for African-Americans.

(Left) Black Business owners in Detroit are being "**ran out**" by increased "**rent rates**", meanwhile slick tactics are being used by the

Mayor to bring in non-black businesses to cater to a **"New non-black Detroit". (Right)** The **Oriental Market** in the **Detroit Metropolitan Suburb** area that cells *African, Caribbean and Asian food*. If you look closely at the sign on the window it says **"Asian, African and Caribbean food"**. Also in Oak Park, Michigan which is majority **"African-American"**, the **"K & F International Market"** is an Arab-owned Grocery store that sells African and Caribbean food. It is the most popular food market in Michigan that Africans and Caribbean Blacks go to for their groceries. The money going to this store is making Arab-Americans have a better future, **not Africans or Caribbean's**.

In **2015**, in Downtown Detroit, Michigan, Activists marched from Hart Plaza to City Hall to raise awareness about the extinction of Detroit's black businesses. Many Black businesses had their rent or property taxes increase as a way to force them out of Downtown Detroit, where new projects were beginning to be done, paving the way for the return of non-blacks to Detroit. Downtown Detroit is now also known as **"Midtown"**, which is the new name of the **"Re-juvenated"**, and **"Re-modeled"** Detroit. During the Economic Stock Market Crash of 2008 and worsening economy, many Detroit Businesses closed down. Schools were shut down, people left their houses and Detroit was left with a lot of vacant buildings and vacant homes. This meant that Real Estate property would be at its lowest in years. Rich non-black investors had a plan. They bought up all the Prime-Real estate in Detroit for pennies on the dollar waiting for the right time to use property to make some money. All they needed was a new non-Black Mayor and the **"Green-light"**. Once this happened with the election of Mayor Mike Duggan, all types of monies, projects and plans started to flow in to **"Upgrade"** Detroit. Detroit has seen the building of a new stadium for the Detroit Lions, Detroit Tigers and a projected plan for a new Red Wings stadium. The kicker is that the majority of the initial startup costs for the Detroit Red Wings Hockey stadium was to be funded by Black Detroit Taxpayers **(who don't really watch hockey)** while the smaller half was to be **"privately funded"**. Meanwhile just outside of "**Midtown**", Black people are in poverty and many families have left their homes, paving the way for Group homes, Halfway houses or Transitional homes. Nobody cares about Detroit city when poor black people are living in it. But when Black families and Black businesses leave the opportunity is prime to displace the poor black people living in Detroit City with non-black races.

Re-gentrification is defined as: "**The restoration of run-down urban areas by the middle class resulting in the displacement of Black/Latino low income residents.**"

Fact: *Detroit's population during the Auto Boom in the 1950's peaked to a population of 1.86 Billion residents. Black families were employed, with good jobs and health care. They had jobs and traveled. The children had schools to go to. Then things changed. So now the population of Detroit is now at 700,000 people. 38% of the Black residents live UNDER the poverty line, and the cities mean income is less than $27,00. At least 70,000 homes or 20% of Detroit's housing stock are considered to be abandoned beyond reasonable repair. This allows non-black people (Jews, Chaldeans, Indians, Asians, Greeks, Italians) with **CASH and CREDIT** to buy up the cities Real Estate for dirt cheap and then sell it to Blacks for double the price they paid for it or use the Real Estate to have black tenants move in and pay rent. This means the more Real Estate they can buy to entice blacks into purchasing or paying rent, it increases their chance of retiring early or being able to travel and not work.*

AGENDA: WE WANT SAMBO AND BOJANGLES BACK! WE DON'T WANT THE EDUCATED "MILITANT" NEGRO.

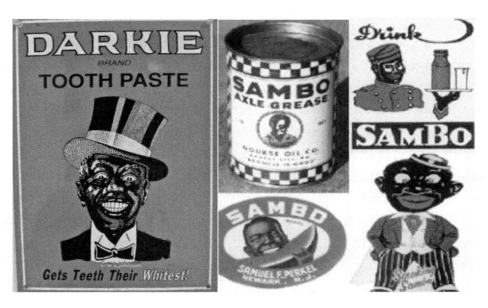

Just like "Sambo", many of our favorite Black Actors and Black Singers/Rappers have "**Sold their Soul**" to the devil for money, fame and "**White-Acceptance**". For this reason, they have to do anything and everything they are told in order to keep riding the wave of success. Many call this being "**Bought and Paid for**". This often means blacks have to accept roles where they are wearing a dress, dancing around cracking jokes, kissing a man, playing typical "**Niggafied**" movie roles or agreeing to promote whatever the "agenda" is at the time.

PLAY THE GAME BLACK MAN

The "Elite" will always allow Rich Blacks to give scholarships, give away free bikes, food, give away cars, give free tickets, etc. but will **NEVER** allow them to use their money, their "**STAR POWER**", and connections with other powerful rich blacks to start buying property in Black communities, opening up black schools/academies (which control the curriculum), black grocery stores, black farmland, black hospitals, black small businesses, affordable clean new housing for blacks, black banks, or Car dealerships to name a few. Just look at what happened to "**Black Wall Street**" in 1921 in Tulsa, Oklahoma. It's not hard to do. We just need "UNITY". There seems to be a "**Hindering Force**" that is preventing all the "Rich blacks of America" to bring their money together to build something that will help blacks be in better control of their own future and also promote "Self-independence". Oprah has 2.8 billion dollars but she obviously didn't' help save the inner-schools for low-income blacks in Chicago, her hometown. Why is that? Oprah can do all the black movies she wants to and fund it herself but she and other influential rich black men/women know they have to "**Play the Game**". Monique was on the Wendy Williams show in 2015 and exposed how Blacks in Hollywood have to "**Play the Game**", thus being the reason why we haven't seen her in any TV projects lately. Of course, "Wendy Williams" quickly changed the subject because the "**Wendy Williams Show**" is controlled by a non-Black Television company.

**"Yassuh...
it's *Genu-wine* Hires"**

(**Above**) Most non-Black races in America have been **"taught"** by various tactics (**one being the Media**) that a Black persons prime position in life is to **"serve"**. This goes for the Black man as well as the Black women. Whether we are cleaning office buildings, cleaning tables, cleaning cars, cleaning houses or serving food, it's the same scenario. Often times I hear stories of Black housekeepers and Black food service workers in different hospitals complaining of how they are still looked upon as like "slaves" to everyone in America. Some of the comments these workers get are:

- "You are supposed to clean my urine and feces from inside the toilet as well as clean my room....where is your supervisor, I'm filing a complaint."
- "You better come back here back here before I call your master and report you."
- "Hey girl, you better come back here when I'm talking to you."

After a while black women and men get tired of doing "servitude work" aka "Menial Jobs". They want to do better for themselves. So they enroll in college. But what are the pitfalls in this? Does every Black person with a degree have an "Equal" chance at employment in America? Can a Black person use a College Degree to start a business? A black man can graduate from college with a Degree but then what? Will he eventually own his own business? Will he ever be hired? Who will give him the money and training to start and run a business? Black men are not at the top of the priority list for jobs in America. Until we start owning something we will always be saying **"Yes Boss"** to someone else. Our kids will see that too and emulate us. But yet we are given the "illusion" by the Media that everything is ok and this is where black people are supposed to be in society. **Working a job to make someone else rich**. Meanwhile we all sing **"I'm so Happy"** alongside with Hip Hop artist Pharrell in the car on our way to work for 30-40 years. Wake Up Black America.

CHAPTER 10

IT'S IN OUR BIBLE! THE CURSES OF ISRAEL IS ABOUT US!

THE RECAP: THEY KNOW WHO WE ARE, DO WE?

The "**Negro**" and the indigenous "**Indian**" both were victims of slavery, rape, death from disease and from brutal murder by the Europeans/Arabs. One group (**House of Israel**) for the most part reached the "New World" and "Africa" after being "**Outcasted/Exiled**" from Israel while another group (**House of Judah**) reached the New World by being "**Dispersed**" via slavery.

Isaiah 11:12 "And he shall set up an ensign for the nations, and shall assemble the **OUTCASTS OF ISRAEL**, and gather together the **DISPERSED OF JUDAH** from the four corners of the earth."

So what proof is out there that proves, the Europeans and Arabs knew who the "**Indians**" and "**Negroes**" where. The words "**Indian**" and "**Negro**" are "bywords" for two groups of people. The "indigenous" people of the "New World" did not call themselves "**Indians**" and the people in West Africa did not call themselves "**Negroes**". This was a term given to them. So why not call them by who they said they were? The Bible talks about Greeks, Chaldeans, Romans, Babylonians, Assyrians, Cush/Ethiopians, Edomites, Persians and Canaanites but nowhere do we see the term "**Negroes**" or "**Indians**" in our Old Testament or New Testament. Prior to the Europeans venturing to the "New World" they read the Bible and suspected that the Lost Tribes were "West" of Africa and Europe. They just never traveled that far west. They were afraid they would fall off the edge of the earth.

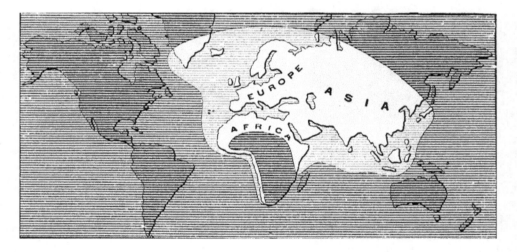

(**Above**) The world as Christopher Columbus knew it before 1492. The Spaniards world did not yet have confirmation that there was land to the "west" as in the "Americas". Christopher Columbus wished there was a faster way to get to the Orient (specifically Indonesia/Philippines) to get Spices. Many of his peers believed at the time that the world was flat (except the Greeks) so Columbus believed that if they sailed westward they would fall of the edge of the earth. Columbus was convinced however to try. The King and Queen of

Spain believed in him and trusted him with a fleet to search the west waters. Others around that time also were looking for a faster way to get to Asia instead of going around the west part of Africa.

Title page of a 17th cent. book claiming that Native Americans are of Jewish origin.

(Above) This book is dated to 1650 A.D., by Thomas Thorowgood. 400 years ago they believed that the so called "Indians" were descendants of the Lost 10 Tribes of Israel.

In the Book "**Iewes in America, Or, Probabilities That the Americans are of that Race**" written in 1650 by Thomas Thorowgood, it says: "**For the Iewes (Jews) did Indianize, or the Indians did Iudeaize (Jews), for surely they are alike in many, very many remarkable particulars, and if they be Iewes, they must not for that be neglected.**

Many believed that the Indians were descended from the **ISRAELITES** who were displaced by the Assyrian King Shalmaneser. They note that

223

in addition to the Americas, they scattered into other countries. The Indians during "close observation" by European Jews, said they hoped to return to two provinces in the world to meet with the rest of the ISRAELITES: **Assyria and Egypt**. The Indians said when this happened they would have one Prince, **The Messiah the Son of David**.

The European Jewish travelers in those times believed the Indians were Lost Karaite Jews, different from their heritage, which was a "Sect of the Ancient Pharisees". The Europeans noticed vast differences but some similarities. They noted that the Karaite Lost "Indian" Jews did not take up no doctrines but what the Scriptures taught in the Old Testament. by comparing one text with another and the Pharisees have wild beliefs about the Messiah and his reign. **The Europeans documented the Natives language, their rites and customs, their man-devouring ways, and the fact they hadn't been "Gospelized" with the New Testament**. They noted that when the Indians talked about their ancestors it was basically what the Europeans read about the Israelites-Jews in the Bible. The Europeans said that the Indians talked about a "**Great Prince**" that a long time ago brought them in a fleet. The Indians described that God made one man and one woman, commanding them to live together and multiply, and how in a famine he rained bread (Manna) for them from Heaven. They also said that during a time of drought and thirst that God gave them water out of a **rock ("Horeb Rock"-Exodus 17:6**).

Exodus 17:6 "Behold, I will stand before thee there upon the rock in **Horeb**, and thou shalt smite the rock, and there shall come water out of it, that the people may drink. And Moses did so in the sight of the elders of Israel."

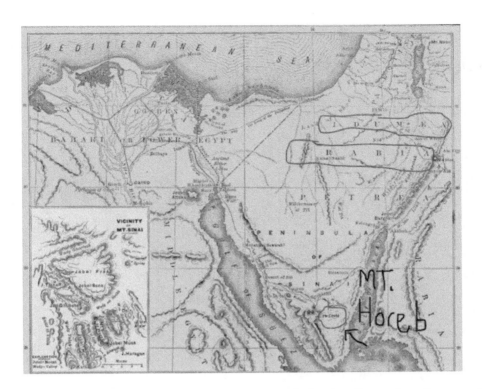

(**Above**) 1st Century A.D. Jewish historian "**Flavius Josephus**" states in his works: "Moses went up to a mountain that lay between **EGYPT** and **ARABIA**, which was called **SINAI**." Greek Egyptologist **Apion** (20 B.C.-40 A.D.) also confirmed this in his works to be true. Many Pro-Arabic scholars will try to place Mt. Sinai in Arabia saying that there lies "**stone rock altars**" that Moses erected as instructed by God. But this is false according to the Torah. The altar God commanded Moses to make was to be of "**Earth**" not "**Stone**".

Exodus 20:24-25 "And altar of **EARTH** thou shalt make unto me, and shalt sacrifice thereon thy burnt offerings, and thy peace offerings, thy sheep, and thine oxen: in all places where I record my name I will come unto thee, and I will bless thee. And if thou wilt make me an altar of **STONE**, thou shalt not build it of hewn (cut or shapen) stone: for if thou lift up thy tool upon it, thou hast polluted it."

WHERE DID THE EGYPTIANS GO?

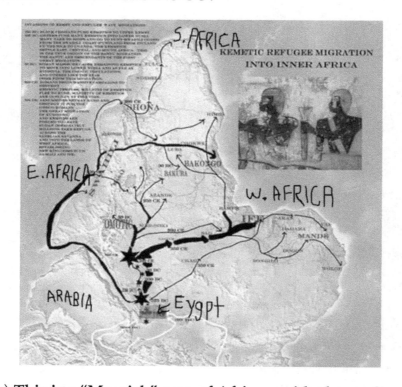

(**Above**) **This is a "Moorish" map of Africa upside down**. It portrays the possible route Black Egyptian refugees migrated into the heart of Africa during its numerous power shifts with different Egyptian Dynasty Rulers (**Libyan, Nubian, Hyksos, Greeks, Romans, and 10 plagues by the God of Israel**). It is proposed that the Egyptians scattered into Africa mixing with the people of the land (**Canaanites, Israelites who were exiled, Nubian Cushites etc.**). This map shows the Kemetian (Egyptian) people scattering into West Africa, East Africa, the African Great Lakes region and South Africa. So do we have any evidence of this genetically? Some people believe so, although many believe that "**pure-breed Egyptians**" are very hard to find with all the race mixing that has happened in Africa. This is very true, seeing that Egypt was invaded and conquered by almost every major civilization known to man at that time.

Population	Region	Size	E-M75+	M41+	M54+
Alur[1]	East Africa	9	66.67%	66.67%	0.00%
Hema[1]	East Africa	18	38.89%	38.89%	0.00%
Xhosa[1]	South Africa	80	27.50%	0.00%	27.50%
Rimaibe[2]	Western Africa	37	27.03%	?	27.03%
Mbuti Pygmies[2]	Central Africa	12	25.00%	?	25.00%
Daba[2]	Central Western Africa	18	22.22%	?	22.22%
Eviya[3]	Central Western Africa	24	20.83%	?	?
Zulu[1]	South Africa	29	20.69%	0.00%	20.69%
Bantu (Kenya)[4]	East Africa	29	17.24%	3.45%	13.79%
Ethiopia[5]	East Africa	88	17.05%	17.05%	0.00%
Ganda[1]	East Africa	26	15.38%	7.69%	3.85%
S.Africa[5]	South Africa	53	15.09%	0.00%	15.09%

(**Above**) In the above graph the "Size" column represents the total number of people tested in that particular study from that tribe. The percentages (**i.e. Alur Tribe-66.67%**) show that out of the 9 people tested from the Alur Tribe, 66.67% of the subjects tested positive for the **E-M75 Y DNA Haplogroup**. Based on the Travel pattern of the Egyptians down the Nile River, many Egyptologists and historians have theorized that the descendants of the Ancient Egyptians lie in the **Luo group** which consists of the **Alur Tribe** which we see above with the highest percentages of **Y-DNA E-M75**. The Luo group can be seen in Ethiopia, Kenya, Tanzania, South Sudan, North Uganda and the Congo. The Luo group supposedly was not affected by Slavery or "European Colonization" because of their powerful 10 "**Chiefdoms**" that held the fort down during the expansion of Europeans and Arabs into East Africa. The **Alur Tribe** in South Sudan and North Ugandan per some have linguistic evidence that links them to the Ancient Egypt (i.e. Acholi language). In addition, the Alur Tribe, including those living in East Africa, South Africa and the African Great Lakes region have higher MLI (**Match Likelihood**) index scores when their

Autosomal chromosome alleles (i.e. markers) are compared to those of Ancient Egyptian mummies. So despite traces of some Egyptian words in the Ewe Tribe (Ghana) and Igbo Tribe (Nigeria) language, the MLI index scores for these two tribes were very low compared to the Alur (Luo) Tribe and the previously mention areas of Africa. In fact, there are more Hebrew than Egyptian words found in the Ewe (Ghana) and Igbo (Nigeria) language. In addition, the traditions and customs of West Africans are more "Hebrew" than "Egyptian". This is also the case for certain Tribes in East and South Africa. The African tribes we see the most "**Hebrewisms**" in (**i.e. language, customs, oral history**) all fall into the "**Bantus**" group, testing positive for the Y-DNA "**E1b1a**" rather than the "proposed" Egyptian Haplogroup "**E-M75**". The **Alur Tribe** was one of the only Luo Tribes tested that mysteriously had an overwhelming high frequency of **Y-DNA E-M75**. We all know that the Egyptians from around 2,000 B.C. to 1450 B.C. mixed heavily with the Israelites so much so that when they left Egypt, the bible says they left a "**Mixed Multitude**". This means the Exodus consisted of Israelites and also Egyptians (**with Israelite blood perhaps**) that wanted to go with Moses to the Land of Canaan.

Exodus 12:37-38 "And the Children of Israel journeyed from Rameses to Succoth, about **SIX HUNDREN THOUSAND ON FOOT** that were men, beside children. And a **MIXED MULTITUDE** went up also with them; and flocks, and herds, even very much cattle."

Need more proof?

Leviticus 24:10 "And the son of an **ISRAELITISH WOMAN, WHOSE FATHER WAS AN EGYPTIAN**, went out among the Children of Israel: and this son of the Israelitish woman and a man of Israel strove together in the camp;"

So if the Egyptians and Israelites intermixed with each other for almost 5 centuries (500 years), the generations that would follow are enormous! 20 generations would be a fair guess. When our ancestors were first brought to the Americas by way of the Atlantic Ocean during the 1500-1600's they numbered less than 100 slaves. Fast forward 400-500 years later, and African-Americans now number 45 million strong! So the DNA of the Egyptians and the Israelites would eventually "merge" into **ONE**.

Scientists and Geneticists can only trace man's ancestry back so far. The Y-DNA Haplogroups of Sub-Saharan Africa are mainly "**A**", "**B**", and "**E**". We all know that Ham had 4 sons (Mizraim, Phut, Canaan and Cush). **So theoretically if "Israel" spent a lot of time mixing with the Sons of Ham (Canaanites, Egyptians, Cushites) we could possibly see a "merger" of DNA's, in what today would be known as Y-DNA Haplogroup "E".**

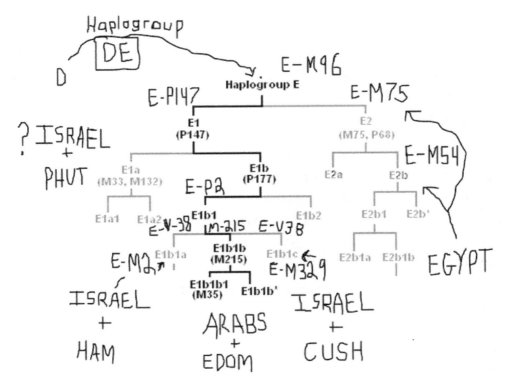

(Above) The "Hebrews to Negroes" estimated Y-DNA "E" Haplogroup chart.

Initially around 2,000 B.C.-1800 B.C. **Egypt** was a country that was connected to **Phut** (Libya) on the Western Border, to **Canaan** on the Northeastern border and **Cush** (Ethiopia/Sudan) on the Southeastern border. When the Israelites spent almost 500 years in Egypt they had access and communication with all of these sons of Ham. In theory, once all these different nations started to "**MIX**" the beginnings of the earliest "**E**" Haplogroups (subgroups) could've been formed. The earliest "**E**" Haplogroup, "**E-96**" would've been the start of the "**E**" **haplogroup family tree,** branching from its ancestor Y-Haplogroup "**DE**". Scientists are still somewhat confused to the "**true origin**" of the **E Haplogroup Tree** but they do narrow their possible answers to Northeast Africa (**i.e. Canaan/Syria where the 12 sons of Jacob were born**) or Asia (**Middle East-Land of Shem**)? After all, in ancient times, the people living in the most busiest area of Africa (**which is Northeast Africa**) consisted of the **Phut Libyans, Mizraim Egyptians, Canaanites, Cushites and Israelites**. As more Israelite generations passed, there would be Israelite family trees that would have more Canaanite/Egyptian blood vs Cushite blood vs Phuttite blood. This is where we see the development of "**E**" subgroups/subclades like **E-P147** and **E-M75**.

Here is where it gets interesting. Over time **E-P147** transitioned into **E-P177**. Then over some more time **E-P177** transitioned to **E-P2**, which then was followed by another transition to "**E-V38**". **E-V38** would give rise to "**Two branch groups**" that would identify the Semitic Israelite Bantus Negroes (**E-M2/E1b1a**) and the Semite Ethiopians (**E-M329/E1b1c**). True Hamitic Ethiopians carry the Y-DNA Haplogroup "**A**" like the Dinka Tribe and other Nilotic Tribes who are known for their "above-normal" height.

So then back in Ancient times there were Egyptians, Phuttites, Canaanites and Cushites that had **little to no ties to the Israelites**. The majority of their family tree was lacking a significant "Israelite" influence but nevertheless was still considered under the "E" Haplogroup. We also have to remember that the Israelites spent the most time around the Egyptians and the Canaanites. **To confirm this, scientists have found out that the maternal DNA of many "non-Bantus" Africans is in fact Bantus mtDNA (L2, L3).** This means that in Ancient times, Hamitic men, married Bantus "Israelite" women. It shows in the DNA too!

(**Left**). In the Book, "**The African Origin of Civilization: Myth or Reality**" by *Cheikh Anta Diop*, it explains how the culture and language of the Alur people who are a part of the larger "Luo" Tribe, gives clues that led him to believe that these people were descendants of the Ancient Egyptians. (**Right**) The Book, "**Kingship and the Gods**" by *Henri Frankfort*, also talks about Ancient Egyptian practices being done by certain Tribes in Africa.

The Alur people were strong Africans who lived in South Sudan, Northern Uganda and the Congo. Their tribe was broken up into ten chiefdoms. Their people did not experience slavery because they were a powerful "united" kingdom. The "Bantus" people in West Africa and East Africa were the main Africans that were sold into slavery, even sometimes even by their own kinfolk. How do we know this? DNA and slave ship records have proven that that the majority of Slaves taken from West Africa carried the "**E1b1a**" Haplogroup. The Alur people carry the **E-M75 Y-DNA Haplogroup**, whereas the "Bantus" people stem from their ancestral "**E-P147 Y-DNA Haplogroup branch.** So many people might think, "Well, does one group of people have more Israelite blood than the other?" Possibly, but the actual "**Letter**" **of the Haplogroup** isn't the "**sole**" determining factor of who is an Israelite (which I will explain later). Author Cheikh Anta Diop, researched the language of the Alur people and the Luo people. What he probably didn't expect was the findings that he would get later after learning the script language (hieroglyphics) of the Ancient Egyptians. He found out that larger "**Luo**" tribe and "**Alur** people" had many similarities to the Ancient Egyptians when comparing the spelling, pronunciation and meaning of certain words. Luo history states that their people originated in South Egypt and later moved to South Sudan in 970 A.D, near the "**Bahr el Ghazal**" River. Their history states they had to flee further south to Sudan because of the rise of Islam and the invasions of Egypt by the Muslim Arabs. According to Cheikh Anta Diop they were in Sudan from 990 A.D. to 1125 A.D. After 1225 A.D. they moved to North Uganda, led by their leader **Rwoth Olei**.

In the **DNA Tribes Digest** January 1, 2012, the DNA analysis of mummies from **Amarna, Egypt** was performed using STR markers (Short-Tandem Repeats) on numerous tested positions on the human genome. These mummies were descendants of the line of King Tut (i.e. Amenhotep III, Akhenaten). They used their DNA database of all the nations of the world to see if they could find anybody who was a match to the Ancient Egyptian mummies. Using the MLI (**Match Likelihood Index**) score they were able to pinpoint the region in Africa where the remnant DNA of the Ancient Egyptians could be found in. So let me explain the **Match Likelihood Index**. Say for instance an African-American male named **Malcom** wants to know if he is more related to Nigerians than Ghanaians. So he gets a DNA test using STR markers and he gets his MLI scores in the mail. The results explain that "MLI scores" **can locate the ethnic groups and regions where his DNA**

profile is most common. So let's say Malcom has a MLI score of **734.50** for Nigeria and a MLI score of **222.45** for Ghana. The score of 734.50 would indicate that Malcom's total combination of alleles (specific STR markers) are 734.50 times more common to be seen in Nigerians compared to the rest of the world. A North African Arab might have a score of 0.21. This basically means that North African Arab is not related to Nigerians. So in order for Malcom to know if he is more Nigerian than Ghanaian he would simply divide the bigger number from the smaller number. Thus, 734.50/222.45 = 3.30, so Malcom is basically 3.30 times as likely to be Nigerian than Ghanaian. Or Malcom could say that he is more "Nigerian" than "Ghanaian". But of course if Malcom digs deeper into his Y-DNA he might find that both Ghanaians and Nigerians are descendants of common single ancestor because they both carry the Y-DNA Haplogroup "**E1b1a**".

(**Above**) **Amarna, Egypt** was the capital city of **Pharaoh Akhenaten** during the Egyptian Eighteenth Dynasty around 1300 B.C. It was dedicated to the monotheistic worship of the pagan god "**Aten**".

So what were the results of the Ancient Egyptians MLI index scores compared to African MLI index scores? The MLI scores of the **Amarna mummies** (King Tut lineage) showed that people living in South Africa and the African Great Lakes area had a higher MLI index scores than those people living in West Africa or the Horn of Africa. The MLI average scores of the region of **South Africa** were **326.94** while the MLI average scores of the region of the **African Great Lakes** (Burundi, Congo, Kenya, Rwanda, Tanzania, and Uganda) were **323.76**. The Egyptian "Amarna" DNA study of King Tut's family presented on www.DNAtribes.com also found out that **Egyptian STR markers** and higher-than-normal MLI scores could be seen in some Native American Tribal territories from the West part of North America. It was not seen in the indigenous "Indians" of Central America or South America.

According to www.DNAtribes.com, their results do not necessarily indicate an "**EXCLUSIVE**" **South African, African Great Lakes and Native American North America** ancestry with the Amarna "**King Tut**" Pharaoh family but it does indicate that there are people in these regions that inherited some of the DNA of Ancient Egypt more frequent than in other parts of the world based on their DNA database collection of the world.

So here is the big question that I know people want to know, "**What Tribes in Africa have inherited some of the DNA of Ancient Egypt and do they also have Israelite ancestry?**" Here we go!

1. **Alur Tribe** (more than 50% of their DNA is Egyptian). Most Alur people speak Alur, which is a language related to Acholi. Others speak Lendu. The Acholi language has striking similarities to the Ancient Egyptian language. This was researched by Author Dr. Cheikh Anta Diop in his Book, "**The African Origin of Civilization: Myth or Reality**". Senegalese **Dr. Cheikh Anta Diop** and Author **Henri Frankfort** believe there are people alive today in Africa who speak the very same language or one very close to the language spoken in Ancient Egypt. They believed

these "Egyptian" Africans can be found in the large **Luo Tribe** which consists of mostly Nilotic Hamites and lesser Bantus Africans. **Dr. Terrence Okello Paito** also presented this argument that the Nilotic people known as Luo (Lwoo) were descendants of the Ancient Egyptians and the Acholi language bore witness to it.

2. **Kenya** (15-20% of their DNA is Egyptian).
3. **Tanzania** (15-20% of their DNA is Egyptian).
4. **East Congo** (20% of their DNA is Egyptian).
5. **Hema Tribe** in Congo, Rwanda and Uganda (40% of their DNA is Egyptian). The Hema Tribe in the north speaks Lendu and the Hemas in the south speak Hema, a Bantus language.
6. **Zulu Nation**-South Africa (28% of their DNA is Egyptian while >50% of their DNA is Israelite).
7. **Xhosa**-South African (21-27% of their DNA is Egyptian while >50% of their DNA is Israelite).
8. **Mbuti Pygmies** of Central Africa (25% of their DNA is Egyptian while the rest is a mixture of Hamitic Y-DNA "B" Canaanite blood).
9. **Mbuti Pygmies of East Africa** (>60% of their DNA as Y-DNA "B" which has been considered by some the Canaanite Haplogroup while 30% of their DNA can be seen to be "Bantus" Israelite Y-DNA "E1b1a"). This of course is due to the race mixing of the Pygmies and the Bantus people.
10. **Rimaibe Tribe** of Mali, Mauritania, Burkina Faso, Guinea-Bissau are the slaves of the Fulani/Fulbe Black Muslims. (27% of their DNA is Egyptian while >50% of their DNA is Israelite). The slaves of the Tuareg Black Muslims are called "**Bella**".
11. **Daba Tribe** of Chad (22% of their DNA is Egyptian).
12. **Ethiopians** (17% of their DNA is Egyptian).
13. **Muganda** Bantus people of Uganda (15% of their DNA is Egyptian while >50% of their DNA is Israelite). In their **Lugandan language** the word for "**Angel**" is "**Malayika**". In

Hebrew (Strong's Lexicon #4398) the word for **"Angel"** is **"Malak"**.

14. **Akele Tribe** of Gabon (12% of their DNA is Egyptian).

15. **And there are others like Somalia (Iraqw people + other tribes).**

Note: *The Majority of these African Tribes live within Central Africa, East Africa, but mostly in the African Great Lakes region and South Africa. They all have been found to have the **Y-DNA E-M75 Haplogroup** in their people. E-M75 is one of two branches that come off the older E-M96 Haplogroup tree trunk. The E-M75 Haplogroup is present throughout Sub-Saharan Africa, in **East Africa, South Africa, and Central Africa. It also has been found in Burkina Faso, Cameroon, Gabon, Rwanda (Hutu/Tutsi), Madagascar, Benin (Fon Tribe), Tanzania (Iraqw people), Qatar, Oman, and Somalia.** This can be easily researched on* www.familytreeDNA.com, www.DNA.ancestry.com, www.DNA-explained.com, www.23andMe.com, and www.eupedia.com.

So according to Senegalese Dr. Cheikh Anta Diop, we have Africans like the Luo (i.e. Alur) Tribe that have traces of Egyptian culture, language and DNA. These Africans never experienced their ancestors going into slavery. They **DO NOT** have **"Hebrewisms"** in their customs/traditions, nor do they have **"Hebrew"** mixed within their language. However, according to author Joseph Williams in his book, *"Hebrewisms of West Africa"*, many West Africans (i.e. Nigerians, Ghana) do. But in addition to having strong evidence of "Hebrewisms" in their culture, West Africans also have traces of the **"Egyptian language"** in their language mixed with **"Hebrew language"**. In my Book, "Hebrews to Negroes 2: Volume 1" I show how the Nigerian Igbo Tribe has Hebrew all up in their language. I also show small examples of **"Hebrewisms"** in the people of Ghana and other **"Bantus"** African countries. So this brings me to the question, "Who were the only people that knew of the Egyptian Culture and Hebrew Culture"? The Hebrew Israelites! Here are some examples.

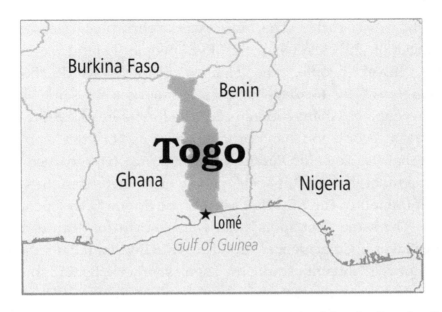

(**Above**) In 2015, I once met a Togo man in Myrtle Beach, South Carolina who was the owner of a souvenir shop. I asked him did he know that the African Slaves taken from Benin, Togo, Ghana and Nigeria were **Hebrew Israelites**. He said "Yes" and that he had heard this from among his people about the "**Real Jews**" being Black. I asked him what tribe was he from. He said "**Ewe**". I also talked to an African-American man who went on a trip to North Africa to tour Egypt. He said the local Arab people in Egypt knew the African-Americans walking around were tourists and that they kept saying the words "**Ibn Yakub (Yaqub)**" in Arabic. "**Ibn**" in Arabic means "**Son**" and "**Yakub/Yaqub**" in Arabic means "**Jacob**". Together they mean "**Son of Jacob**". Jacob is the father of the **12 Tribes of Israel**, aka the "**Children of Israel**". It seems as though a lot of people know that African-Americans are the "**Real Jews**" of the Bible except us. It's time to wake up.

GHANAIAN "EWE" TRIBE

Note: Originally, when the Europeans arrived to the coast of West Africa some of the people they encountered in modern day Togo/Ghana described "**themselves**" with the sound pronunciation of

"Er-vreh" or "Ibri". The Europeans corrupted this African pronunciation and called them the "Eve" people. Later it was changed to the "Ewe" people. The Hebrew Strong's word #5680 for "Eber/Hebrew" is "Ibri/Ivri" and it's pronounced the same way that the Ewe people in Ghana pronounced who they were to the Europeans. The African people in Ghana pronounced it as "Er-vreh". It is also known that the nomadic **Fulani Tribe** in Africa (who owned slaves) confirmed that that the "Er-vreh" people originated from the **Land of Canaan (Israel) in the Middle East**. Where do the "Ewe" people live today? The same "**hot spots**" that were known for "**capturing and selling slaves**". Coincidence? No. The **Anlo Ewe (smaller sub-sect of Ewe's)** people inhabit, southern Togo, southern Benin, southwest Nigeria, and the south-eastern parts of the Volta Region of Ghana. The other Ewe people inhabit the southern part of Togo and southern Benin (**Door of No Return**). Like the Israelites, they still worship deities that mimic the deities the Israelites worshipped while living amongst the Canaanites. For instance, they worship "**Yewe**", which is the god of thunder and lightning. The Yoruba's worship "**Shango**" as the god of thunder and lightning. **Baal** was the Canaanite god of thunder and lightning. The Ewe people also worship a goddess called "**Mami Water**" like most West Africans and Caribbean Blacks. Mami Water is equivalent to the "**Queen of Heaven**" the Israelites worshipped. The Ewe people also celebrate many of the feast holidays the Jews do including the Passover. Many of the Ewe/Akan people in Ghana today will even admit that they are the "**Real Jews**" of the Bible and that this was told to them from their elders, generation after generation. Aside from having Hebrewisms in their customs, they also have bits and pieces of Egypt in their language. We know that Moses and Joseph was well learnt in the ways of the Egyptians, including their language. It is also a known fact that the Egyptian language and Hebrew language is similar. Many historians say there is proof that the Ancient Hebrews also knew how to write Egyptian after spending 400 years (20 generations) there. It is said that some ancient texts from Egypt/Israel are a mixture of both languages called "**Egyptian Hieratic**".

Acts 7:22 "And Moses was learned in all the wisdom of the Egyptians, and was mighty in words and in deeds."

Now Joseph (the father of Ephraim/Manasseh) spoke to his brothers in Egypt by way of an "**interpreter**". This means that some of the Egyptians knew how to speak and understand Hebrew. Ancient Hebrew and Ancient Egyptian language must have been similar.

Genesis 42:23 "And they knew not that Joseph understood them; for he spake unto them by an interpreter."

According to the Book of Mormon, which some say is really African Hebrew Israelite manuscripts stolen by Joseph Smith, it attests that the Hebrews knew the language of the Egyptians.

1 Nephi 1:2 "Yea, I make record in the language of my father, which consists of the learning of the Jews and the **language of the Egyptians.**"

In the text "**Mormon 9:32-34**" this language/script is called "**reformed Egyptian**".

Mormon 9:32-34 "And now, behold, we have written this record according to our knowledge, in the characters which are called among us the **reformed Egyptian**, being handed down and altered by us, according to our manner of speech. And if our **plates** had been sufficiently large we should have written in Hebrew; but the Hebrew hath been altered by us also; and if we could have written in Hebrew, behold, ye would have had no imperfection in our record. But the Lord knoweth the things which we have written, and also that **none other people knoweth our language;** and because that none other people knoweth our language, therefore he hath prepared means for the interpretation thereof."

Egyptian Hieratic is Egyptian cursive writing with Hebrew Influences. The Hebrew Israelite "**Soninke/Manding**" people in the Senegal-Gambia-Mali area also wrote in Arabic with a Sephardic Hebrew cursive writing influence which some same is their "**Ajami script**".

It is a known fact that over 200 samples of Hieratic script was found in the regions of Israel and Judah. Latter-Day Saint scholars John A. Tvedtnes and Stephen D. Ricks in their book **"Jewish and Other Semitic Texts Written in Egyptian Characters"**, (*Journal of Book of Mormon Studies 5/2, 1996: pg. 156-163, re-printed as "Semitic Texts Written in Egyptian Characters"*) describe how archaeologists found texts written in a Hebrew-related language which was transcribed in Hieratic Egyptian dating back to the times of Samson and King Saul (1300-1200 B.C.). They also found examples of Psalms 20:2-6 written in Aramaic using Egyptian characters dating around 300-200 B.C. Archaeologists also found Egyptian hieratic writing on broken pottery from cities in Israel. They noted that the writings were a combination of Egyptian writing and Hebrew characters but could be read entirely as Egyptian.

(**Above**) Egyptian Hieratic script and below Paleo-Hebrew. The "**Real Israelites**" of the Bible knew how to **read/write/speak** both Egyptian and Hebrew. This can only be seen in Sub-Saharan Africans (i.e. Nigerian Igbo, Ghanaian Ewe) and the Native Americans (i.e. Mi'kmaq or Micmac Tribe). Ironically, these two people groups also have "**Hebrewisms**" in their traditions/customs as well as believe in a "**Supreme Creator**". The "**Brass Plates**" that Joseph Smith found in Africa were supposedly written in **Egyptian Hieratic with Hebrew influences**. This type of writing style could be seen in the Native Indian Algonquian language (i.e. Mi'kmaq Indians).

Fact: *A number of Northwest Semitic texts are included in Egyptian Papyrus. These are the **London Magical Papyrus** (1300 B.C.), the **Harris Magical Papyrus** (1200 B.C.), **Papyrus Anastasi I** (1200 B.C.), and **Ostracon** (1000 B.C.) during the time of the Book of Judges-King Saul-King David. On the Ostracon papyrus, a Semitic Hebrew text appears on one side and on the other side it is pure Egyptian. On **the Papyrus Amherst 63** text, the language is Hebrew-Aramaic, but is written in Egyptian demotic script (100 B.C.). Egyptologists struggled to make sense of this text as they could not make any insensible words out of it in Egyptian. It wasn't until 1944, that Raymond Bowman of the University of Chicago realized that the script was Egyptian, but the underlying language was Aramaic. ("**An Aramaic Religious Text in Demotic Script**", **Journal of Near Eastern Studies 3**, 1944: pg. 219-231.) Also in 1965, during excavations at Tel-Arad, in South Israel a number of ancient texts were found dating back to 600 B.C. One was written in Egyptian Hieratic. Since then many Ancient texts have been found written in a mix of Hebrew and Egyptian language.*

So knowing all of this we should be able to find Egyptian influences in the language of some Sub-Saharan Africans who openly confess they are Israelites and still practice Hebrew Customs. Some of these Sub-Saharan African tribes still possess the Torah written in Aramaic-Hebrew, Arabic/Ajami or their African dialect. They **DO NOT** possess the Babylonian Talmud or the Jerusalem Talmud as these non-biblical works were made around the time of Roman Emperor Constantine the Great in the 4th century A.D., which would have been centuries after Yahusha's (Jesus) death. The Sub-Saharan Africans didn't have the New Testament either. Why? Because they were the "**Scattered Lost**

Tribes of Israel". So let's look at the language of the Ghanaian "**Ewe**" people.

GHANAIAN "EWE" TRIBE

Word: Stability/Stable/Solid

Egypt-Djed, **Ewe**-Dje/Djeti

Word: White

Egypt-Hedj/He dj, **Ewe**-He

Word: Land

Egypt-Ta/To, **Ewe**-Ta/To

Word: Soul

Egypt-Ba, **Ewe**-Ba

Word: Spirit

Egypt-Ka, **Ewe**-Ka

Word: Sky Goddess

Egypt-Nou/Nouou, **Ewe**-Nou/Nouou

Word: Dead/Spirit of Dead/Death

Egypt-Akhou/Khou, **Ewe**-Ekhou/Khou/Kou

Word: Sound

Egypt-Hou/Hu, **Ewe**-Hou/Hu/Houn

Word: Perception, Imagination

Egypt-Sia, **Ewe**-Sia

Word: Home

Egypt-P/Per, **Ewe**-Pe

Word: Deity

Egypt: Sokar, **Ewe**-Soka

Word: Black

Egypt-Kam/Kem, **Ewe**-Ka/Kami

Word: Much, Infinite, Great

Egypt-Wur, **Ewe**-Wu

Haplogroup E: E1B1A

Ethnic Group or Tribe	Country	%
Bamileke	Cameroon	100
Nande	DR Congo	100
Ga	Ghana	97
Ewe	Ghana, Togo	97
Fon	Benin	95
Yoruba	Nigeria, Benin	93
Cameroon South	Cameroon	93.3
Akan/Kwa	Ghana, Ivory Coast	92
Mossi	Burkina Faso	90
Igbo	Nigeria	89.3
Cross River	Nigeria	87
Ovambo	Angola	82
Wolof	Senegal, Gambia	81.3
Bantus	Gabon, Equatorial Guinea	79.4
Mandinka	Mali, Senegal, Liberia, SL	79
Fula	Niger, Nigeria, Mali, Senegal	73

(**Above**) It is a known fact that the most heavily populated African countries with the "**E1b1a**" Black Israelite marker is **Cameroon, the Congo, Ghana, Togo, Benin, Nigeria, Senegal, Gambia, Angola and Rwanda**. These countries were the main "**hot spots**" for the Transatlantic Slave Trade (Americas/Caribbean) by the European Jews and Anglo-Saxon Caucasians. Even the Fulani's are known to carry the "E1b1a" Y-DNA Haplogroup (in addition to R1b).

(**Above**) Many Igbo's in their 60's and 70's today were told as little children by their Elders in Nigeria that they are descendants of the "**Children of Israel**". If this is true, who are the people today living in the Land of Israel? The Nigerian Igbo people also have Hebrew mixed with Egyptian seen in their language, **just as was practiced by the Ancient Hebrew Israelites in B.C. times**. They like African-Americans and Caribbean blacks, fall into the Y-DNA "E1b1a" Haplogroup. Black People, **WE NEED TO WAKE UP! WE ARE THE "REAL" CHILDREN OF ISREAL. THE PEOPLE IN ISRAEL ARE IMPOSTERS WHO HAVE STOLEN OUR IDENTITY.**

NIGERIAN "IGBO" TRIBE

Word: Greater, Superior

Egypt-Ka, **Igbo**-Kaa

Word: To die, To kill

Egypt-Khu, **Igbo**-Nwu, Gbu

Word: Smell

Egypt: Em, **Igbo**-Imi/Emi

Word: To become

Egypt-Bi, **Igbo**-Bu

Word: Living being, Life

Egypt-Un, **Igbo**-Ndu

Word: To go away/to fly away

Egypt-Feh, **Igbo**-Fee/Feh

Word: Dwelling place

Egypt: Budo, **Igbo**-Obodo/Ubudo

Word: Living area, house

Egypt: Un, **Igbo**-Ulo/Uno

Word: Pray, confess, to plead

Egypt-Beka, **Igbo**-Biko/Beko

Word: Mouth

Egypt-Aru, **Igbo**-Onu

Word: Settle, Settlement

Egypt-Dor, **Igbo**-Dor Nor/Du-No

Word: Water Mother

Egypt: Nen, **Igbo**-Nne (Mother), **Nnem** (My mother)

Word: Rise, Up

Egypt-Aru, **Igbo**-Anu/Enu/Elu

Word: Children

Egypt-Amu, **Igbo**-Umu, **Yoruba**-Omo, **Hebrew**-Amo

Word: Land of

Egypt: Ala, **Igbo**-Ala

Word: Land below

Egypt-Ani, **Igbo**-Ani

Word: Inside, Among

Egypt-Mm, **Igbo**-Imme

Word: Beast (like Egyptian crocodile beast Ammit/Ammut)

Egypt-Au-nu, **Igbo**-Anu-ma-nu

Word: Leader, The Head

Egypt-Isi, **Igbo**-Isi

Word: They, Them

Egypt: W, **Igbo**-Uwe

Word: Sixth

Hebrew-Shishi, **Igbo**-Isii

Word: Tenth, Ten

Hebrew-Asiri, **Igbo**-Iri

Note: *Evidence of the Ancient Egyptian language can also be seen in the language of* **Senegal**. *Senegalese men for the most part have the same Y-DNA Haplogroup as Nigerian Igbo men* (**E1b1a**). *Senegal and Gambia were major areas where the slavetraders took from, sending to the East Coast of America.*

SO HOW CAN AN AFRICAN TRIBE HAVE BOTH "EGYPTIAN" AND "HEBREW" IN THEIR LANGUAGE UNLESS THEY ARE HEBREW ISRAELITES?   THE ISRAELITES ARE THE ONLY PEOPLE WHO SPENT ENOUGH TIME IN EGYPT TO KNOW THE EGYPTIAN LANGUAGE BUT YET, STILL SPEAK THEIR "MOTHER HEBREW TONGUE".

Again, the Nigerian Igbo's have the same "E1b1a" as other West Africans including the Ewe and Akan Tribe in Ghana. The Igbo's Y-DNA is different however from the Luo Tribe such as in the Alur Tribe of South Sudan/Northern Uganda. Both have "**Egyptian Influences**" in their language but only **ONE HAS HEBREW** in their language and practices **HEBREW** customs! Do you get the hint? **THE BANTUS PEOPLE ARE NOT EYGPTIANS! THEY ARE HEBREW ISRAELITES**. What about the Ashkenazi, Sephardic and Mizrahi Jews in Israel? Who are they? **THEY ARE IMPOSTERS**, converts to Judaism. The definition for this is a **proselyte**.

Matthew 23:15 "Woe to you, scribes and Pharisees, hypocrites, because you travel around on sea and land to make one **PROSELYTE**; and when he becomes one, you make him twice as much a son of hell as yourselves."

MORE HEBREW IN THE IGBO LANGAUGE? WHAT IS GOING ON HERE?

The **Hebrew** word for the letter "O" or "Eye" is "Ayin". In **Igbo** "Anya" represents round objects including the eye. The Sun is "Anyanwu". The **Hebrew** word for "Stranger" is "Zar". In Aramaic "Zur" means "to hide". In **Igbo** "Zere/zeru/Zor" means "dodge, refrain from or hide". In **Hebrew** the word for the wall gecko or Lizards is "Anaquah" derived from the Hebrew "Anak" which means "Long necked". In **Igbo**, lizard or Lizard-like is "Anika/alika". In **Hebrew** "Natan" means "God has given or I have received from God". In **Igbo** "Nata" means "received". In **Hebrew** the name "Nebat" comes from the verb "nabat" which means "Looked at". In **Igbo** the word "Neba/nebe" means "looked at".

Let's look at some more examples of the Hebrew language in the Igbo language:

In Modern Hebrew the word "**Bayit**" means "**house**". In Igbo the Hebrew word "**Bayit**" is hidden but not gone. "**Bayi**" is hidden in the Igbo word "**Ebe ayi**", meaning "**our home**" or "**our house**". "**Ulo**" also means "**home**" or "**house**" in Igbo but it can be transcribed as "**Ulo ayi**". "**Ebe**" doesn't mean "**house**" because "**Ebe**" in Igbo refers to a place, a place which can be transitioned from a place to house, or home, assuming we put "**Ebe ayi**". "**Ebe ayi**" which sort of sounds like "Bayi" in the Igbo language is similar to the Hebrew word "Bayit" if you drop out the "**t**" from the Hebrew word "**Bayit**". The name for "**House**" in Hebrew and Igbo then becomes very strikingly similar to "**Bayi/Ebe ayi**". Likewise, "**Emet**" in Hebrew, refers to the "**act of doing**" but in Igbo "**Eme**" also means "**the act of doing**" or something that is "**happening**", but notice the only difference is that the "**t**" is lost. The last demonstrable example is "**Husot**" in Modern Hebrew which is derived from the Ancient Hebrew word "**Usot**" meaning "**street**", "road" or "**roadway**" which is pronounced "**Uzo**" in Igbo. You see "**Uzo**" in Igbo refers to "**street**", "road" or "**roadway**" just like "**Usot**" refers to "**street**" or "**roadway**" in Ancient Hebrew. They are both pronounced the same despite the different languages. However, in Igbo version of the word for "**street/roadway**", the letter T is lost and the letter "**z**" replaces the letter "**s**". In Hebrew, "**Sixth**" is called "**Shishi**" and in Igbo "**Six**" is pronounced "**Isii**". In Hebrew "**Amo Israel/Y'srael**" is the name for "**Children of Israel**" because "**Amo**" means "**children of**". Some Igbos call themselves "**Umu Israel**" because "**Umu**" means "**children of**". Now "**Amo**" and "**Umu**" sounds kinda similar and both words in these different languages mean "**Children of**" or "**Children**".

HEBREW WORD: "ANI" is a Hebrew that means "I". ANYI is an Igbo word that means "US/WE". For example, ANYI na-abia (WE are coming), ANYI na ebe akwa (WE are crying), ha na Anyi biara (They came with US).

HEBREW WORD "AGUR" (compiler, brave one and one who pursuit wisdom) AND THE IGBO WORD "AGU" (lion, crave for food) in the Igbo language Agu means lion and it's also a title given to a brave individual. For example, Agu (odum) biara ani (ana/ala) Igbo (means the brave one who came to Igbo nation/land). Also, agu means craving for food (agur crave for wisdom), hunger.

HEBREW WORD "HA" (meaning "the").   "HA" in Igbo language means THEY e.x. Hana- abia (they are coming) or HA bere akwa (THEY cried).

HEBREW WORD "AHA YAH" (meaning "I AM"). THE IGBO WORD "AHA YA" (meaning "HIS NAME"). AHA in Igbo language means name. YA sometimes refers to "HIM". For example, AHA YA BU TOCHUKWU (his name is Tochukwu) or AHA YA BU CHUKWU ABIAMA (HIS name is God of Abraham).

HEBREW WORD "CHAI"(life/living). THE IGBO WORD "CHI" (God-source of all life) is the Igbo word for God. UKWU means mighty in the Igbo language. Hence, CHI UKWU means MIGHTY GOD OR GOD ALMIGHTY. The original form for TO-CHUKWU is TO-CHI UKWU but the "I" was removed because in writing, Igbo's avoid placing two verbs side by side. For example, HA NA ABIA (they are coming) is written as HA N'ABIA or you separate it with dash HA NA-ABIA.

HEBREW WORD "URI"(meaning fire/light). THE IGBO WORD "URI" is a traditional Igbo fire lantern made from the extract of palm fruits. It is damped with palm oil and ignited with fire. Its light is used in the night. In traditional Igbo society without electricity URI is still in use as a source of light.   FIRE LANTERN in the Igbo language is also known as URI MMU.

HEBREW WORD "AMI" (my people). THE IGBO WORD "ANI" symbolizes the land, nation and the people. Grave sin against the people is called NSO ANI meaning what the land forbids.

HEBREW WORD "ASA"(to heal or healer). THE IGBO WORD "ASA" (meaning seven and a number of perfection).

HEBREW WORD "TOVIYAH" (meaning "Yah-GOD is good"). The Igbo word "TOVIYA" (praise him). In some Igbo dialect TOVIYA can be pronounced and written as TOBEYA or TOBEYA(H) when singing to God.

HEBREW WORD "AMARIAH" (God has said or promised by God). The Igbo word AMARACHI (grace of God). "Amara" in Igbo language means GRACE, whereas "CHI" means GOD. AMARACHI then means GRACE OF GOD

HEBREW WORD, "BETH"(house). The Igbo word "BE" (home)

HEBREW WORD "Y" (HE). The Igbo word "YA" (HIM). The components of YHWH-Tetragrammaton, are Y, meaning roughly HE and the consonants root HWH which is connected with the "acts of creation". There appears to be two main line of reasoning to explain the origin of the name. The first suggests that it is the shortened form of a sentence "**HE CAUSES TO BE or HE CREATES**".

Chineke is the Igbo word for "**God of Life**." Chileke is the Hebrew word meaning, "**To Create Life**."

SO LET'S BREAK DOWN THIS Y-DNA "E" HAPLOGROUP!

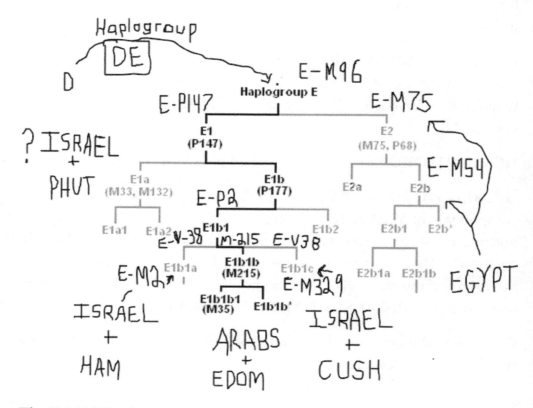

The **E-M96** Haplogroup starts from the **Haplogroup DE**. So essentially the Haplogroup E-M96 **IS** the start of the **E-Haplogroup**. In Genetics, the E-M96 splits into **TWO MAIN BRANCHES**. One split goes into the E-P147-E-P177 branch (**which before 2008 lead to the "African Bantus Branch" and the "African Ethiopian Branch"**). The other split goes into the **E-M75** branch which holds the "**missing link**" to the Ancient Egyptians.

It is possible that the "Ancient" E branches were **E-M75 (Egypt), E-M33 (Libyan/Phuttite Berbers +/- mixed with Israel)** and **E-P177-E-P2 (Early descendants of Eber the Hebrews)**.

Note: *The **Dogon Tribe** of Mali tested around 50/50 for the Haplogroups E1b1a (E-P2) and E-M33.*

E-P2 would eventually lead to the Bantus Semitic people and Ethiopian Semitic people. The Y-DNA Haplogroup "**E1b1b**" would be a "**New Haplogroup-subgroup**" formed from the mixing of "**Edom's Seed**" with the Hamitic people of North Africa, the Semitic Black Arabs and the Japhetic European people living along the Mediterranean Sea.

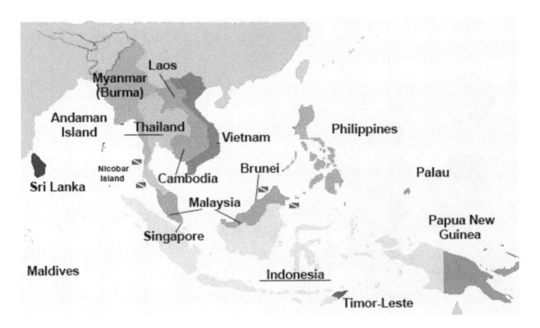

(**Above**) **Southeast Asia**. The people living in Southeast Asia are for the most part, "**Brown-skinned**" people. Many indigenous "Negritos" live in Southeast Asia (**i.e. Indochina**). Many African "Bantus" slaves were taken from East Africa during the Arab Slave Trade (i.e. Indian Ocean Slave Trade) and dropped off in Southeast Asia. This has been documented by the Ancient (South) Chinese Dynasties who used to receive Bantus "**Zanj** (Zanzibar)" slaves from Africa.

The Y-DNA Haplogroup "**D**" is not found in Africa. Neither is the Y-DNA Haplogroup "**C**". It is possible that the **Haplogroup "D" branch** represents a sub-sect of possible Israelites that never intermarried extensively with the Sons of Ham. Could these be Israelites that intermarried with the Sons of Shem (**Moab, Ammon, Aram, Asshur,**

Lud, Joktan, Ishmael etc.). The Andaman Islanders that live in the Bay of Bengal south of **India/Burma** carry the "**oldest**" form of the Haplogroup "**D (M-174)**" which is the root of all the "D" Haplogroup "subgroups" like **D1** and **D2**. **Haplogroup D1 (M15)** is found mainly in Tibeto-Burman speakers near Tibet (Asia) and in some Southeast Asians (**Indonesia, Malaysia, Singapore, Philippines, East Timor, Brunei, Christmas Island, Cambodia, Laos, Myanmar-Burma, Thailand, and Vietnam**).

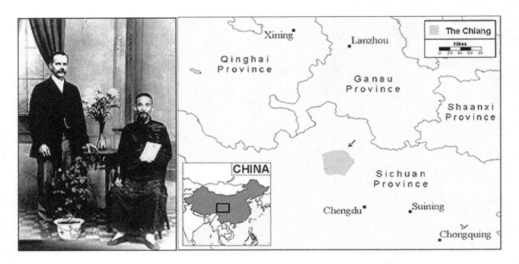

(**Above**) Scottish Christian Missionary **Thomas Torrance** (1871-1959 A.D.) did extensive research and ministering to the people in the Sichuan (Szechuan) Province in China, near Tibet. He strongly believed that the "**Chi-Ang/Qiang**" people came from the Middle East and that these so-called Asians were descendants of the "**Ancient Hebrew Israelites**". Thomas believed that Buddhism had corrupted the Chinese so much that God had sent a Tribe of Israel to try and awaken the Chinese to the True God of the Universe. He believed that this tribe was the "Qiang" people. While living in Southwest China, Thomas paid close attention to the Qiang people and found pottery in the Sichuan province that resembled "**Israelite-Levant**" pottery, he believed that he had found a "**Lost Tribe of Israel**". Reverend Thomas

Torrance would write a book in 1937 called "**China's First Missionaries: Ancient Israelites**". The Qiang people have been found to carry the Haplogroup "**D**" (a branch of the larger "**DE**" Haplogroup) which has the same genetic YAP+ marker (**Y-Chromosome Alu Polymorphism**) that is seen in Igbo Nigerians and other Bantus Africans. This would make the Qiang people a relative of Bantus Sub-Saharan Africans, and thus Israelites.

Fact: *The "Chi-Ang" people, aka the "Qiang people" in Southwest China have also been found to carry the Y-DNA **Haplogroup D1 (M15)** which is an ancestor of the Y-DNA "**E1b1a**" Haplogroup. They erected large white stones in their land to remind them of the pathway their people took when they left their homeland (Israel?) in the ancient past for the "**Orient-China**". They are also believed to be descendants of the Black Chinese **Shang** and **Zhou** Dynasty people. In the 1920's, a British Missionary named **Thomas Torrance** visited the Qiang region to spread the Gospel and was surprised to see certain practices among the Qiang people that resembled Ancient Israelite customs. The Qiang people lived in stone houses (like Israelites), they wore white robes, and sacrificed sheep or goats on stone altars. Although there were other historians stating that the Qiang people were polytheists, Terrance believed that the Ancient Qiang people worshipped only one god called "**Abamubi**". Other records show the name "**Abachi**" or "**Mabichu**", meaning "**father in Heaven**". "**Abba or Ab**" in Hebrew Strong's Lexicon (#1) means **Father** and "**Achi**" in Hebrew Strong's Lexicon (#277) means "**brother of Yah**". In Nigerian Igbo, "**Chi**" means "God" as "**Chineke**" means "God the Creator" in the Igbo language. Reverend Thomas Torrance noted that in times of trouble the Qiang people called upon God as "**Yawei**" similar to "**Yahweh**" or "**Yahuah**". The stated that their ancestor was Abraham and his seed who had 12 sons (Jacob). Because of pressure from Buddhism and Christianity they worship many gods now in different villages but still worship their "Main God" at the "**top of the mountain**" which was a common meeting place for the Israelite prophets and God (Mount Sinai-Moses, Mount Hermon-Transfiguration of Christ with Moses & Elijah). In the "**Journal of the West China Border Research Society**", other Western scholars and Christian missionaries attested to similar discoveries. They believed that many ethnic* groups (like the Israelites) migrated eastward into China and South Asia. Another interesting find is that in the Sichuan province in Qiang territory, researchers found **Tall "Caucasoid" white mummies** (i.e. **Tarim mummies**) who had elongated bones, blonde-brown-reddish hair and abnormally positioned teeth. In Southern Xinjian, China they uncovered bones from a tomb that measured 7 feet, 6 inches. Like the other giant skeletons, the teeth arrangement was not the same as normal human teeth. This appearance of **"White Red-haired Giants"** is also a story told by the Ancient Native Americans, which mimics the Bible account of Giants living amongst the Israelites. Could it be that wherever the Israelites (seed of Seth) "migrated to" the Giants (seed of Satan/Cain) would not be far away? There are also Giants reported by the natives to be found in Southeast Asia (i.e. Solomon Islands). The Nephilim Giants that lived before and after the flood were essentially the seed of Satan, the Fallen "demonic" angels and man (Cain). Why? Because the Bible says that Noah was "perfect" in **ALL** his generations (**Genesis 6:9**).

Genesis 3:15 "And I will put enmity between thee and the woman, and between thy seed (**Seed of Satan/Cain**) and her seed (**Seed of Seth**); it shall bruise thy head, and thou shalt bruise his heel."

Haplogroup D2 (M55) is found in the Black Japanese Ainu/Jomon people and the Japanese Rykyuan people. It is a known fact in Asia, there are select populations that use **"Shamans-Spiritual Priests"** like the Ancient Israelites used the Aaronite High Priests to be their connection to the God of Israel. The men in Asia (Russia/Siberia/China/Japan) found with **"Shamans"** in their community often carry the **Y-Haplogroup "D" and "Q"** which can be traced back to the **"E" Y-DNA Haplogroup**. Native Americans also use **"Shamans"** in their communities, but their Y-DNA (**Q**) and mtDNA (**A, B, C, D**) can also be traced back to the Bantus/Ethiopian people by mtDNA Haplogroups "**L2, L3, M**" or Y-DNA Haplogroup "**E**".

Note: *Remember, in the Hebrew Books of Jubilees/Jasher, it states that the wife of Eber was "Azurad" the daughter of Cush. This would explain why some Ethiopians fall into the "E Haplogroup" and some fall into the "A" Nilotic/Cushitic Haplogroup. Over time as Jacob would have children with different women and the **12 sons of Jacob** would have children with the Sons of Ham, "Israel" would be thrust into the "E" Y-DNA Haplogroup. But this would change after the exile of the Israelites by the Assyrians in 700 B.C. The "**Out of Africa (Israel)-Stay Out of Africa (Israel)**" movement vs the "**Out of Africa (Israel)-Partial Return to Africa/Arabia**" movement would determine if some Israelites would fall into the Y-DNA Haplogroups "**D", "E", "R", or "Q"**. Some Israelites would also pick up the "**J**" Haplogroup from mixing with the Semitic peoples in the Middle East or Arabia/Yemen (i.e. Lemba Tribe, North Ethiopians, Eritreans). But remember, the "**Haplogroup Letter**" is only a "**Mark**" that is put on the "**Y-Sex Chromosome**" that only makes up **1/23rd** of our DNA (Mankind has 23 total Chromosomes). Thus a white person cannot help it if his "**Ancestral Father**" 20 generations (500 years) back in the past (i.e. Black Moor) happened to impregnate their white "**Ancestral Mother**" and from that point the family tree has been "**essentially white**" but they still carry a Y-DNA Haplogroup (**R**) that is seen mostly in people of "**color**" (Africans, Indians, Pakistanis, Sri Lankans). Likewise, a Latino person or a Black person cannot help it if his "**Ancestral Father**" 20 generations (500 years) back in the past was a White man who happened to impregnate their "**Black or Native Indian Ancestral Mother**" but from that point the family tree has been "**essentially Melaninated**" with the Blacks/Native Indians. Thus the "Y Haplogroup" letter only gives us 1/23rd of the genetic information about our heritage.*

(**Left**) Eritrean man. (**Right**) Sudanese Nilotic Cush/Nubian Shilluki men.

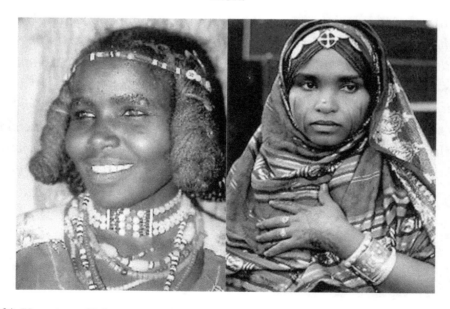

(**Left**) **Kunama** Eritrean woman. (**Right**) **Nara** Eritrean woman. It is a known fact that the 80% of the Black Kunama people live in Eritrea but they only make up 2% of Eritrea. The Black Nara people of Eritrea only make up 1% of the total population of Eritrea. The rest live in Ethiopia and Sudan. These Eritrean Tribes are "**E1b1a**" carriers.

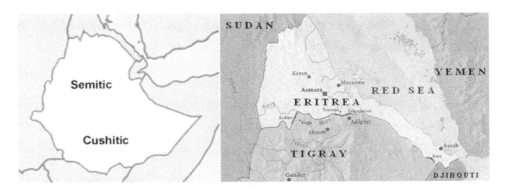

(**Left**) The Northern part of Ethiopia is a mixture of **Semitic** and **Cushitic** blood. The Southern part of Ethiopia has more Cushitic blood. (**Right**). **Eritrea** is a country that lies north of Ethiopia. Some of the people there have Semitic Blood from the **Sons of Joktan, the Black Arab Ishmaelite's and the Israelites**. The Ethiopian Jews, the people in Eritrea and North Ethiopians (**Tigray/Amharic area**) are all genetically "**verified**" to have Semitic Blood from Arabia (**Haplogroup J1-Sons of Joktan, Ishmael, Keturahites**). They also harbor Hebrew Israelite Blood (**E1b1a + Haplogroup E1b1c and the creation of E1b1b after 2008**), and Cushitic Blood (**Haplogroup A**). Around 800 B.C., it is said that the Sabaeans crossed over the Red Sea into modern day Northern Ethiopia setting up their kingdom before the Aksumite Kingdom existed. The Old Sabaean South Arabian language is similar to the Ethiopian language of **Ge'ez, Tigray, Amhara, including Hebrew**. They eventually established the **D'MT kingdom** in North Ethiopia (Tigray area) where the **Yeha Temple** is located at. Many historians are somewhat confused to the Biblical origin of the Sabaean people from South Arabia/Yemen. In the Bible there lists three different people who could be the progenitor of the Sabaean people. Either way it goes, genetically scientists have proven that the "**J1**" gene is not only a "**claim**" that European Jews can boast, but is a claim that **mostly Black-looking people** in East Africa, Yemen, Oman, Qatar, the

United Arab Emirates, South Africa (Lemba Jews) can attest to have thus proving that the "Biblical descendants of Shem" were Black.

Genesis 10:7 "And the **sons of Cush**; **Seba**, and Havilah, and Sabtah, and Raamah, and Sabtecha: and the sons of Raamah; **Sheba**, and Dedan."

Genesis 10:26-28 "And Joktan begat Almodad, and Sheleph, and Hazarmaveth, and Jerah, and Hadoram, and Uzal, and Diklah, and Obal, and Abimael, and **Sheba**.."

The people in Africa that remained genetically the **purest** and **oldest** would be the **Cushite/Nubians** (Y-DNA Haplogroup A) or **Pygmy tribes/Canaanites** (Haplogroup A & B) that didn't intermarry that much with the Israelites. Y-DNA Haplogroup A is **NOT** defined by any Mutations. This means that they essentially have **NO ANCESTOR** that they evolved from as far back as human genetic testing goes.

Haplogroup A is seen in different amounts in the DNA of the Bushmen-Tsumkwe San Tribe (Namibia), the Nama Tribe (Namibia), Khoisan people (South Africa, Botswana, Namibia), Ethiopians (Ethiopian Jews, Amhara, Tigray, Oromo), Sudanese people (Nuer, Dinka, Shilluk, Fur, Nuba), Kenyans and Eritreans.

Per **Eritrean history**, by some, it is said that their people left Israel around 600 B.C. (around the Babylonian Invasion) and migrated south to West Arabia/Yemen where they crossed over the Red Sea into the land/area that is now "**Eritrea**". They said that initially while in "**Nubian territory**" they fought with the Nubian **Nilotic** people, but eventually establishing a homeland. They are known today as "Habesha" people, perhaps stemming from their mixture with the 8th-6th Century B.C. Sabaeans in Arabia who wrote "**Habashat**" as "**HBST**" which then was changed to "**HBS**" in the younger "**Ge'ez**" language. If the Sabaeans were descendants of Joktan, son of Eber (Father of the

Hebrews) like Peleg (forefather of Abraham) than this would explain the moderate amount of "**J1**" Y-DNA in the bloodline of the Northern Ethiopians/Eritreans. Because the Israelites started out around 2,000 B.C. mixing with the Egyptians and Nubians this would thrust most of the Israelites into the **Y-DNA "E" Haplogroup**. This mixing with the "**Sons of Ham**" continued around **1300 B.C.** (Canaanites in Judges 3:5-6), **1000 B.C.** (Queen Sheba-Solomon in 1 Kings 10:1) to **400 B.C.** (Canaanites/Egyptians in Ezra 9:1-2). So as we can see Israelites DNA merged with the Nubian Cushites in East Africa and the Egyptians-Canaanites. This is where I believe the Israelite Y-DNA subgroups "E1b1a" and "E1b1c" started in Northeast Africa. **BUT SOMETHING HUGE HAPPENED IN THE SCIENTIFIC WORLD OF GENETICS!** Pay close attention because there are many people saying that the Ethiopian Jews are simply "**converts to Judaism**".

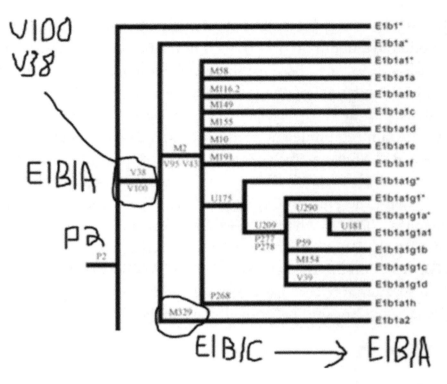

(**Above**) Most Y-DNA maps and studies will show Eritreans and North Ethiopians (Amharas) as belonging to Y-DNA "**E1b1b**", just like the classification of the North Africa white-skinned Arabs. But prior to **2008**, Ethiopians and Eritreans were both brothers with the "Bantus Negro Africans" from the same Haplogroup "**E-P2**" branch. E-P2, prior to 2008 had **ONLY 2 BRANCHES**. **E-M329** (Ethiopians/Eritreans) and **E-M2** (Bantus Sub-Saharan Negro Africans). Here is what happened:

Before there was the "**E1b1a**" Haplogroup-subgroup there was an ancestor Haplogroup called "**E1b1**", defined by the SNP marker "**P2**". Then in 2008, there was an "unanimous decision" in the scientific world of genetic studies. Scientists found two new SNP (Single Nucleotide Polymorphism) mutations (markers) that required a new position on the "E" Haplogroup Tree. These mutations/SNP's were called "V38" and "V100". Because of these two mutations, the E subgroups "E1b1a (E-M2)" and "E1b1c (E-M329)" were united together into one branch. Scientific studies will say that the Ethiopian "E1b1c (M329)" branch was merged with the "E1b1a (M2)" but most genetic studies today will list the Ethiopians/Eritreans as having mainly the "E1b1b" and "J1" Y-DNA Haplogroup in their DNA. This confuses the avid researcher who is trying to figure out the origin or heritage of the Northern Ethiopians, Eritreans, and Ethiopian Jews in regards to the Bible. With the disappearance of the Ethiopian "E1b1c (E-M329)" Haplogroup, scientists inserted a new branch called "**E1b1b**" or "E-M215", which is now assigned to **ALL** the white-skinned Arabs and European Jews we see today. Where is this "E1b1b" Haplogroup found in the world? In Mediterranean (Southern) Europe, North Africa and East Africa. If you're wondering what "New" countries were added, it's Morocco, Algeria, Tunisia, Libya, Egypt, Israel, Lebanon, Italy (Rome), the Balkan countries, Turkey, Cyrus, Greece, Spain, and Portugal. **Ironically, these are the same countries Edom's descendants lived in, mixing amongst the people of the land throughout various time periods**. Is it a coincidence that "Edom" is now grouped into the same "E" Haplogroup as his brother "Jacob/Israelites"? Nope.

Chart Source and Reference: "**A New Topology of the Human Y Chromosome Haplogroup E1b1 (E-P2) Revealed through the Use of Newly Characterized Binary Polymorphisms**". *Benjamin Trombetta, Fulvio Cruciani, Daniele Sellitto, Rosaria Scozzari*. **Public Library of Science PLoS One**. January 6, 2011.

(Left) **Archibald Forder** was an American "Caucasian" Missionary born in 1863 who worked for 13 years "**undercover**" in the Middle East (mainly in Al-Karak, Ottoman Turkish Palestine). He wrote about his travels and what he observed in his Book (published in 1909) called **"Ventures among the Arabs in Desert, Tent, and Town: Thirteen Years of Pioneer Missionary Life with the Ishmaelite's of Moab, Edom, and Arabia."** Archibald was able to dress up in Arab clothes and go "**undetected**" in the Middle East because he was white-skinned, like the Arabs. **This is part of Edom's "camouflage" amongst the nations. (Right)** Book **"Who is Esau-Edom?"** by Charles A. Weisman. As you can see, many people want to know "**Who is Esau**" today. Esau mixed himself with the white-skinned non-Ishmaelite North African/Middle Eastern Arabs (Turks/Kurds) and the Caucasian (South) European nations off the Mediterranean Sea. Many of the "**White**" Arabs during the "**Barbary Slave**" Trade (1400's-1800's A.D.) also had children with their European female sex slaves. This is why the maternal DNA (mtDNA) of the Arabs and Jews is mostly "European" but yet the Y-DNA of these nations have traces of the "E1b1b" Haplogroup. The rest of their Y-DNA is a mixture of Semitic (**J1**), Turkish/Kurdish/Grecian/Italian (**J2**), Ham-Shem mix (**R1b**), and European (**N/I**).

It is also probable that **Edom**, the brother of Jacob, in the beginning also started intermixing with the people that he lived among (Egyptians, Canaanites). Edom is mentioned mixing with the Canaanites and Ishmaelite's Arabs in the Bible but is also mentioned on a list of the Egyptian Pharaoh Seti I from 1215 B.C. Edom is also mentioned in the chronicle of a campaign by Ramses III (1100's B.C.). Edom would mix with the Arab Nabateans and then would mix would the Greeks (Ptolemaic, Seleucid Empire) when they conquered Judea prior to the birth of **Yahusha HaMashiach**. During the Greek and Roman rule over Judea the Edomite (Herodian's) would intermarry with the different sons of Japheth.

(**Above**) The name "**ydwma**" (**Aduma**) is found on Egyptian Hieroglyphs as our English name "**Edom**" in the King James Bible. According to Archaeologists, the Assyrians listed "**Edom**" on their cuneiform inscriptions as "**Udumi**" or "**Udumu**". **Note:** The "**Assyrians**" would also write the name "**Yah-u**" for the name "**Jehu**" in the name King Jehu from the Black Obelisk tribute to Assyrian King Shalmaneser. This proves the "**u**" was used before "**w**" was used in Ancient Semitic script (i.e. Yahuah vs Yahawah). The Greeks and Romans during the 1st Century A.D. named the Edomite territory as "**Idumaea**" or "**Idumea**"

After the "**Zealot Temple Seige**"in 68 A.D. (by 20,000 Edomites) and the destruction of the Second Temple in Jerusalem in 70 A.D., **Edom** would scatter into North Africa.

Fact: *Egypt and the Land of Edom have been completely arid desert land since Biblical times because of what they did to the Children of Israel. This is supported in the Bible in Joel 3:19 "Egypt shall be a desolation, and Edom shall be a desolate wilderness, for the violence against the Children of Judah, because they have shed innocent blood in their land. "*

Here are some more **Y-DNA** facts:

1. **Haplogroup DE** split into two separate Haplogroups a very long time ago. These two Haplogroups were "**D**" and "**E**". Haplogroup "**E**" makes up the majority of Africa. In the beginning it is possible that Haplogroup **A** and **B** were the majority Haplogroups in Africa prior to race mixing. But then something "**Big**" happened. The Children of Israel entered into Egypt numbering less than 70 people but after spending 430 years in Egypt they left about 1-2 million strong. This mixture of the DNA of Israel, Moab (**Ruth-King David**), Ammon (**Ezra 9:1-2**), Edom (**Deut 23:7-8**), Egypt (**Ezra 9:1-2**), Cush (**Moses-Zipporah, Solomon-Queen Sheba**), Canaan (**Judges 3:5-6**), and Phut would create in my opinion the Haplogroup "**DE**" or "**E**". Haplogroup "**D**" in theory could represent Israelites who after "**leaving Israel**" never came back to the Middle East or Africa. This is the reason why Haplogroup "**D**" is not found in Africa. These "Haplogroup D" Israelites would stay in Asia. The proof is the fact that all persons falling into the **Y-DNA Haplogroup D (M-174)** exhibit the **SNP (Single Nucleotide Polymorphism) M168** as well as the **Y-Chromosome Alu-Polymorphism (YAP+)** which is **ONLY** found in the "**E1b1a**" Bantus people (**i.e. Nigerians, Kenyans, Guinea-Bissau**). Haplogroup D is found in select populations in Asia (**India, Tibet, China, Japan, Siberia**). Some Geneticists argue that the **YAP+ positive** people

266

(i.e. **Potential Israelites**) falling into the Y-DNA "**DE**" Haplogroup that "**returned back to Africa**" after mixing with other nations in Asia/Asia Minor, came back under a new Haplogroup (**Y-DNA R1b1**). The Y-DNA **R1b1** is seen in mostly in Latinos, some Africans, and the people who conquered Iberia-Spain/Portugal (**i.e. Black Moors & Israelites**) for 700 years and then left.

2. So the **Israelites** would leave Egypt around **1450 B.C.** during the time of Pharaoh Thutmoses III but would return after numerous invasions to their land (which the bible prophesies). It is my belief that those Israelites that "**re-entered**" Africa "**immediately**" would fall into the "**E**" Haplogroup. The Israelites that left Israel, mixing with "**other nations**" would eventually form other Haplogroups (**i.e. Q, R, P,**). Upon entering Africa, the Israelites moved through Egypt settling in **East Africa** (Sudan, Ethiopia, Kenya, Tanzania, Uganda, Rwanda), **Central Africa** (Rwanda, Angola, Gabon, Congo, Cameroon), **South Africa** (Zulu, Xhosa, Shona countries), **West Africa** (Nigeria, Benin, Togo, Ghana, Ivory Coast, Sierra Leone, Liberia, Guinea-Bissau, Gambia, Senegal, Niger, Burkina Faso, Mali) and **North Africa** (Egypt, Libya, Tunisia, Algeria, Morocco). These "Bantus" Israelites took over and dominated most of Africa in what historians called the "**Bantus Expansion**". What seemed like "overnight" in history, the "Bantus People" became more numerous than the Phuttite Berbers, the Cushites, the Egyptians and the Canaanites. Just like in the bible in Exodus 1:9 the Bantus Israelites were becoming "**too numerous**" in the continent of Africa.

Exodus 1:8-19 "Now there arose up a new king over Egypt, which knew not **Joseph**. And he said unto his people, Behold, the people of the **Children of Israel** are **MORE** and **MIGHTIER** than we are:"

Note: After the 7th Century A.D., foreign colonization, slavery and the appearance of Islam would cause the Bantus people to lose their heritage. This was prophesied in the Bible.

ARE THERE OTHER DESCENDANTS OF "EBER (HEBREWS)" OUT THERE IN THE WORLD? ARE THERE ANY OTHER HEBREW ISREALITES SCATTERED INTO OTHER NATIONS?

We know according to the Bible that all the Descendants of **Eber** were considered to be **Hebrews**. Thus the Children of Eber would have spoken the "**Hebrew language**". This is verified by looking at the language of the "**Moabite Stone/Meshe Stele**". It is Paleo-Hebrew!

(Above) Moabite Stone written in Paleo-Hebrew. The 4 Hebrew letters (**Tetragrammaton**) circled are the letters that spell out the name of the God of Israel, **Yahuah (Yod-Hey-Uau-Hey)**.

The Genealogy of Shem

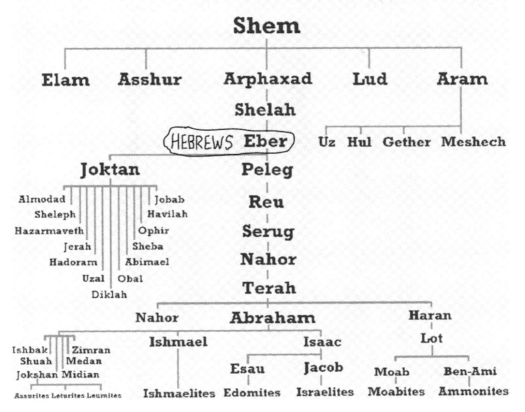

Shem

Elam   Asshur   Arphaxad   Lud   Aram

Shelah

(HEBREWS) **Eber**   Uz Hul Gether Meshech

Joktan   **Peleg**

Almodad   Jobab   **Reu**
Sheleph   Havilah
Hazarmaveth   Ophir   **Serug**
Jerah   Sheba
Hadoram   Abimael   **Nahor**
Uzal   Obal
Diklah   **Terah**

Nahor   **Abraham**   Haran

Ishbak   Zimran   **Ishmael**   Isaac   Lot
Shuah   Medan
Jokshan Midian   Esau   **Jacob**   Moab   Ben-Ami

Assurites Leturites Leumites   Ishmaelites Edomites   Israelites Moabites Ammonites

(**Above**) The Family Tree of Noah. As you can see "**Eber**" fathered many nations: The **sons of Joktan**, the **sons of Nahor**, the **sons of Ishmael**, the **sons of Isaac**, and the **sons of Haran/Lot**. Most people talk about the Moabites, Ammonites, Ishmaelite's, Israelites, Edomites but nobody talks about the **Joktanites**. Where are they at today? Have they been absorbed into the Arab people today? Is there any clues or evidence pointing to their whereabouts in history?

COULD THE HYKSOS INVADERS OF EGYPT BE THE DESCENDANTS OF THE JOKTANITES OR OTHER SHEMITES?

(Left) **Hyksos** woman with child. **(Right)** Defaced statues from Egyptian 15th Dynasty (1660-1550 B.C.) believed to be the **Hyksos "Shepard King"** Pharaohs found at Avaris (Tanis) in the Nile Delta, capital of the small short-lived Hyksos kingdom. If these Hyksos people were the descendants of the Joktanites, you can see clearly that they were "**Negroid**" in appearance. Therefore, it would be correct to say that the other "**early**" descendants of **Eber** (father of the Hebrews) were also "**Negroid**" in appearance.

The interesting thing is that according to the "**Book of Abraham**" from the **Book of Mormon,** it states the "**Hadoramites**" during the time of Abraham took over the land of Egypt, driving the Hamite Egyptians to the South of Africa. **Could these people have been the Hyksos "Semitic" invaders that had Semitic names?** Hadoram was one of the sons of **Joktan,** who also was a Hebrew from their grandfather "**Eber**", the progenitor of the Hebrews and "**Abraham**".

Genesis 10:25 "And unto Eber (**Hebrew Strong's #5680-Ivri/Ibri**) were born two sons: the name of one was **PELEG**; for in his days was the earth divided; and his brother's name was **JOKTAN**."

Genesis 10:26-29 "And Joktan begat Almodad, and Sheleph, and Hazarmaveth, and Jerah, and **HADORAM**, and Uzal, and Diklah, and Obal, and Abimael, and **SHEBA (Sabaeans?),** and Ophir, and Havilah, and Jobab: **all these were the sons of Joktan**."

Fact: *It is a known fact that there have been found plenty of Y-DNA consisting of **E-M2, E-M96, E-M75, E-M78, and E-M41** found in Ancient Egypt in addition to Y-DNA groups "A", "B", "R", "J" and "T".* All of these Y-DNA Haplogroups can be found in Africa/Arabia as seen below:

- **E Haplogroup** – (Sub-Saharan Bantus Africans, Ethiopians, Eritreans and Non-Bantus Arab Africans.)
- **A Haplogroup** – Nilotic Cushite Africans, Khoi-San tribe, Bushmen Pygmy Tribe.
- **B Haplogroup** – Nilotic Cushite Africans, Khoi-San tribe and Pygmy Tribes.
- **R Haplogroup** – Fulani (only some in Sudan/North Nigeria), Hausa (only some in Sudan/North Nigeria), Ouldeme (Cameroon), North Cameroon, Chadic peoples, and Tuareg (only some in Niger/Mali). It is also seen in some Iranians, Pashtun Pakistanis, Sri Lankans, and North Indians.
- **J Haplogroup** – Seen in **High Percentages** in Sudanese Copts, Black Sudanese from Khartoum, South Dravidian Indians, Yemenis, Omanis, Qataris, Northwest/Northeast Ethiopians (Tigray, Amharic), Eritreans and Middle Eastern Arabs/North African Arabs. Also seen in **Small Percentages** in Ashkenazi, Sephardic and Mizrahi Jews.
- **T Haplogroup** – Somalians (**highest**), South Egyptians, Fulani (Cameroon), Ethiopians, Tanzanians, and Kenyans. Also seen in select groups in India.

THEY Y-DNA "E" AND "D" GETS EVEN DEEPER!

The Haplogroup "**D**" seen in Tibet-Burmese speakers along the India/China border could be a "**Israelite**" Haplogroup that eventually experienced "Mutations" after mixing occurred with "**other nations**". Haplogroup D is also seen in Japan and the Andaman Island Negritos in the Bay of Bengal.

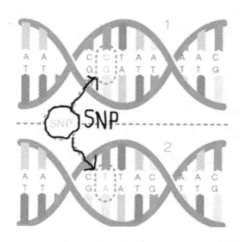

Haplogroup DE is an "**Ancient**" Paternal Y-DNA Haplogroup that is very unique. It is defined by certain mutations or "**SNP's**" which stand for "**Single Nucleotide Polymorphisms**". These "**SNP's**" are also called "**UEP's**" or "**Unique Event Polymorphism's**". This Haplogroup DE is defined by the Y-Chromosome **ALU** Polymorphism, otherwise known as **YAP.** A Y-Chromosome that has the YAP mutation is called **YAP-positive (YAP+)** while a Y Chromosome that **DOES NOT** have the YAP mutation is labeled **YAP-negative (YAP-)**.

Here are some facts about this YAP mutation.

- Africa has the highest frequency of the YAP mutation in Nigeria, Guinea Bissau, Kenya and Tanzania. These areas all reflect the different locations where the slave trades hit over the last 2,000 years (i.e. Arab Slave Trade and Transatlantic Slave Trade).

(**Left**) Australia Aborigines. (**Middle**) Andaman Island Aboriginal man (**Right**) Ainu/Jomon natives of Japan. These men are still believed to be not be pure-blooded "Ainu/Jomon" people per the Japanese. If this is the case, are they implying that the original Ainu/Jomon Japanese people were more "Black" in appearance? After all, Haplogroup **D** is significantly older and less "mutated" than Haplogroup "**Q**" or "**O**".

- Y DNA Haplogroup "**C**" and "**D**" are not found in Africa but seemed to originate in Asia around the same time era that Haplogroup **E** were formed. The carriers of Y-DNA Haplogroup "**C**" (**i.e. Indians in North America, Samoans, Hawaiians, and Australian Aborigines**) never went back to Africa. Likewise, the Black Andaman Island aborigines (**carriers of Y DNA Haplogroup "D"**) never went back to Africa. These Black Andaman Island aborigines share the same Y-DNA Haplogroup (**D**) as the Black Japanese Jomon/Ainu people who are said to be the progenitors of the **Japanese Shinto Jews**. The Andaman Islanders, the Australian Aborigines and the Jomon/Ainu people have all had their land invaded by foreigners. Geneticists state that the Australian Aborigines are

273

related to the people in South India, including the Black Andaman Islanders.

THE "MISSING LINK" TO THE "LOST ISRAELITES" MAY BE IN THE MATERNAL DNA!

Relationship to You	Approximate % Of Their DNA You Inherited
Parents	Exactly 50%
Grandparents	About 25%
Great-grandparents	About 12.5%
Great-great-grandparents	About 6.25%
Great-great-great-grandparents	About 3.125%
Great-great-great-great-grandparents	About 1.5625%

When a "**Foreign (i.e. Spaniards)**" group of men invade another country, the native men (**i.e. Black or Native Indian**) are usually captured as prisoners, killed or sent away. The women become the "**spoils of war**". These foreign men will often have children with the native women, thus producing "**Mulatto**" children. Because Y-DNA is based **SOLELY** on the Male "Y" Sex Chromosome, this foreign man's **Y-DNA** is "marked" onto any male child that is born throughout the generations.........that is unless there is a "**break**" in this process. When a "**native man** (i.e. Black or Indian-blooded man)" comes into the picture and happens to marry a "mulatto (**i.e. mixed**)" woman **HIS Y-DNA (i.e. E1b1a, Q)** is now passed along each "paternal" male born from generation to generation. Based on the chart above, by the 7th-8th Generation if no other white man enters the paternal line, his "huge white DNA" contribution is essentially weeded out. So in essence, if Latinos had a pure-blooded "**Caucasian**" in their family tree from 100-200 years ago but never married a White person afterwards you could possibly start to see Latinos turning more "**Indian-Black**" in appearance than "**White**" in appearance. For example, in Miami, Florida there are many Latinos from Cuba, Dominican Republic, Puerto Rico, Venezuela, Columbia and other South American Countries who recently have "**Black**" parents in their family tree. Since Blacks and Latinos live in close proximity to each other (like in the old days pre-Columbus), they are naturally going to intermix with each other. Because the days of "**Spaniard invasions**" is over in America, we are seeing more Latinos in New York and Miami, Florida becoming "**less-white**" and "**more-brown/black**" despite if the Y-DNA Haplogroup of Latinos remains as **R1b, C, E1b1b or Q**. This is due to a Black Father vs a Black Mother "**insertion**" into the family tree.

It is a known fact that the Maternal mtDNA **L2**, and **L3** are the most common maternal haplogroups found in African-Americans and West Africans. In East Africa (i.e. Ethiopia) we see the "**L3**" mtDNA Haplogroup in addition to mtDNA Haplogroup "**M**". This "**M**" Haplogroup is also seen in Yemen, India, South Asia and Australia.

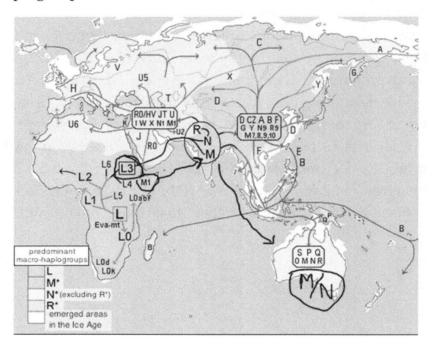

(**Above**) The maternal DNA "**L3**" originated in East Africa and the Horn of Africa (Ethiopia/Nubia/Somalia/Eritrea). Different West African tribes (i.e. **Yoruba Nigerians, Igbo Nigerians, Ghanaians**) have different varying percentages of (maternal) mtDNA L3, L2 and L1 in their blood straight from their mother. It is from this "**L3**" **Bantus African** mtDNA Haplogroup that the mtDNA Haplogroup "**M**" comes from. Who are the women outside of Africa that pass this mtDNA Haplogroup "**M**" down to their children? The women living in South India (**Kerala, Tamil Nadu**), Sri Lanka, the Andaman Islands, South Asia and the Australian Aborigines! Does this mean that these people a **Hebrew Israelites** too, or does it link them to **Shem** and thus the **Semite people**? This deserves much consideration when we talk about who is really a "**Semite**" in the world.

276

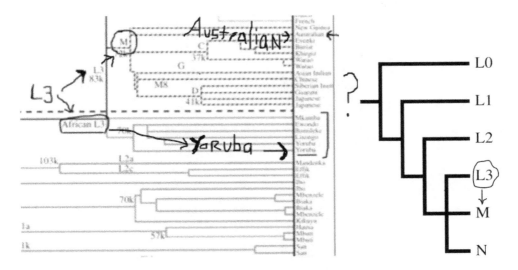

(**Above**) If the Maternal mtDNA "**L3**" is the progenitor of mtDNA "**M**" does this mean that all people bearing the mtDNA "**M**" are descendants of the "**L3**" carriers who left "**Out of Africa**" many centuries ago? It would appear so! If West/East Africans (Bantus Negroes) are the main carriers of mtDNA "**L2**" and "**L3**" this would mean that they are the forefathers of the "**Out of Africa**" nations carrying the mtDNA haplogroup (**M/N**). As you can see in the chart above, the African L3 (circled) branch turns into the "M" branch which leads to some select populations (i.e. Japanese, Siberians, American Indian, Australian Aborigines, Papua New Guineans). How is this possible? Because mtDNA "**C & D**" is the descendant of mtDNA "**M**", which is the descendant of Bantus mtDNA "**L3**"! The most common mtDNA seen in Caribbean Latinos is mtDNA "**A, C and D**". The Most Common

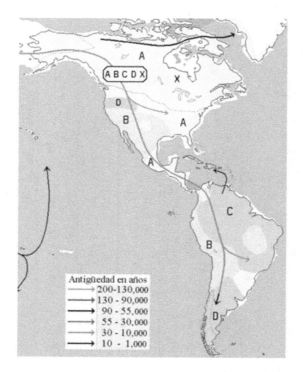

(**Above**) For **Native Americans Indians**, the most common mtDNA in North America is **A and B.** The most common mtDNA in South America is **C and D**, followed by a small percentage of indigenous people that carry "**B**". In Mexico and Central America these mtDNA Haplogroups vary. In the Amazon Rainforest, the indigenous Indian Tribes carry mtDNA Haplogroup "**C**". Keep in mind, if a child's mother is "Black" or "White" the mtDNA results will change. But "mtDNA testing" only takes into account 1/23rd of our Genetic make-up. **The other 22 Autosomal Chromosomes that we have are not tested in Y-DNA and mtDNA testing**.

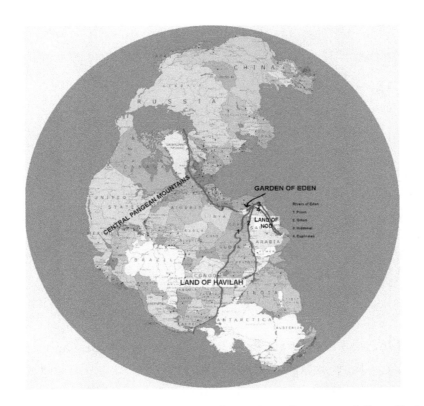

(**Above**) Pangea. If you notice, **Turkey, Iraq/Iran, and Saudi Arabia** are attached to **Northeast Africa** in the single land mass known by many as "**Pangea**". With the "Pangea" model there is no "**Middle East**", especially if you eliminate the Mediterranean Sea. In addition, the **Tigris**, **Euphrates** and **Nile River** are all "near" each other. In Hebrew, the word "**Pelag** (Strong's #6385-6386)" means "**to split**", "**to divide**" or "**divided**". Hebrew Strong's word "**Peleg** (Strong's #6388)" means "**channel, canal**". Could it be than when Pangea split, it caused the formation of many "**channels**" which we call today "**Seas**", "**Oceans**" or "**Straits**"?

Genesis 10:25 "And unto Eber was born two sons: the name of one was **Peleg**; for in his days was the **EARTH DIVIDED**; and his brother's name was Joktan."

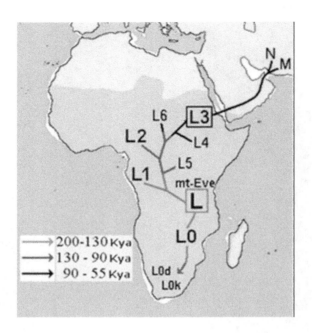

In the bible, we know that Noah had three sons, who each had a wife. Considering they were all from the lineage of Seth and Eve, they should've all had the same Maternal DNA from their mother **Eve**. Well, scientists believe that mtDNA "**L(1)**" arose as the Mitochondrial "**Eve**" DNA of the first woman. **L1** eventually evolved into **L2**, **L3**, **L4**, and **L5** which is seen entirely in Africa. The newer "**L6**" is only seen in Yemen. The "**L**" mtDNA as a whole is "Native" to Africa only, thus supporting the belief that the first man and woman started in Africa. **L2** is a native to Sub-Saharan Africa and is present in almost 1/3rd of all the people in the world (**if you dissect everyone's mtDNA to the core**). L3, which is also confined to Africa (East mainly), is the mtDNA haplogroup from which the larger "**M**" and "**N**" mtDNA haplogroups are believed to have arisen. Could this be the "**Out of Africa**" settlement of Japheth (Europe) and Shem (Middle East/Asia)? Possibly so. The Hebrew Israelites of "old" stayed close to Africa mixing their bloodline with the Egyptians starting around 2000 B.C. They continued their stay in Africa mixing with the Cushite Nubians and Canaanites. This is probably why the Hebrew Israelite maternal mtDNA stayed in the same "**L**" group as other Hamitic Africans. Once the families of Ham, Shem and Japheth left "Out of Africa", mtDNA Haplogroups changed. This can also be seen in Y-DNA Haplogroups and their evolution. Therefore, "**Migration**" patterns "**Out of Africa**" plays a "**big part**" for the different Y-DNA haplogroups and mtDNA Haplogroups we see today.

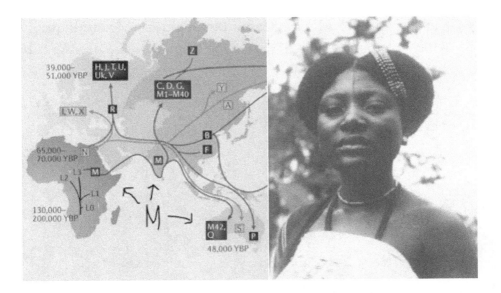

The Maternal mtDNA "**L3**" haplogroup which gives rise to the mtDNA "**M**" haplogroup is seen in the "**Bantus**" peoples like Yoruba Nigerians (**above**) and the majority of African-Americans/Caribbean Blacks. The mtDNA "**M**" is seen in South Indians, the Andaman Island Aborigines, Polynesians and the Australian Aborigines. Maternal DNA "**N**" is also believed to arise from Haplogroup **L3** and is seen in high frequencies in the North Africa, the Middle East, Asia and South Asia. Maternal mtDNA "**N**" is also seen in India and some of the Australian Aborigines. Scientists "**theorize**" that mutations happened within the "**mtDNA N**" which gave rise to the "**European mtDNA haplogroups**". **Some mtDNA charts link mtDNA "N" to Native American mtDNA Haplogroups "A & B" while some don't.**

Maternal mtDNA "**L3**" is seen in the following groups of people:

- Bantus East Africans/Bantus West Africans

- Chad Basin, Central Africans
- Ethiopian Jews (L3c),
- Yemenite Jews (L3c).
- Fulani's, Chadians, Ethiopians, Akan's, Yemenis, and some scattered forgotten Black Egyptians (L3d).
- Afro-Brazilians, Caribbean Blacks (L3e)
- Certain parts of Algeria, Cameroon, Angola, Mozambique, Kikuyu tribe the Kenya, Kisii tribe from Kenya, Sukuma tribe from Tanzania. (**L3e1**)

(**Above**) The **Shompen** people live in the south region of the "**Great Nicobar Islands**" off the coast of India, right below the Andaman Islands. The Shompen people's ancestry stems back to Africa. Their mtDNA is mostly mtDNA "**N**". Notice they are Brown-skinned "**Afro-Mongloid**" looking people.

(**Left**) Shompen people. (**Right**) Apache Indian leader "**Geronimo**" from present day "**Arizona**". Because of the scattering of the Hebrew Israelite people into Africa, Arabia and Assyria it is difficult to assess the changes that occurred with the Hebrew Israelite "**Maternal**" seed when they mixed with men of different nations. Starting around 300 B.C. the Gentile Greek nations entered into Africa conquering Egypt, Judea and the Middle East from the Persians. From then on the majority of ruling nations in North Africa and the Middle East were descendants of Japheth. So where were the Hebrew Israelites during this time? Many suspect they were already in Africa, South Arabia, Asia and perhaps the Americas. We do know that there were other foreign nations the Israelites had to have encountered if they traveled East into Asia. We also know that Japheth and his seed also traveled on the "**Silk Roads**" East as they have evidence of "**white mummies**" with **blonde to reddish hair** found in Asia. These "foreign men" over time would contribute some of their DNA with the "Israelite women's DNA" to make a daughter, or a son. Over time, new haplogroups would form. Some people in the East (i.e. China, South Asia) would appear more white-skinned with "mongloid Asian features" like the Siberians/Eskimos while others would appear more brown-skinned with "mongloid Asian features (i.e. Negritos, Australia Aborigines, South Asians)".

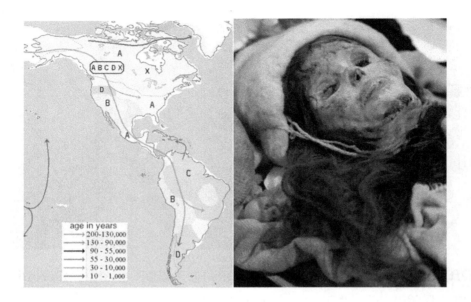

(Left) mtDNA map of the Americas. Notice the distribution of Maternal mtDNA Haplogroups **A, B, C, and D**. Haplogroup "**X**" has been often linked to the "**Neanderthal Ancient European gene**". The "X" mtDNA haplogroup found in Canada proves that "**Caucasoid races**" also made their way with the "**Indians**" into the New World. Like the Red-Haired Guanche White Indians from the Canary Islands, the Red-haired Neanderthal and the Paracas elongated skulls with "**Red Hair**", they also found the mummified remains of "**Caucasoid**" people with red hair as far east as China. **(Right)** Tarim red-haired white mummy found in **Xinjian, China**. Xinjian China is right along the Silk Road area near Tibet, Pakistan and Afghanistan.

Fact: *The **Tarim mummies** in the Xiaohe tombs in China were placed in coffins made of wood that were shaped like boats. This was similar to what the Egyptians did and their concept of a boat that would take the "**Pharaoh's**" to the "**Afterlife**". These white mummies had clothes and jewelry buried with them in small baskets as if they were going to have them in the afterlife similar to what the Ancient Egyptians believed. The bodies were wrapped in wool garments and cowhide was used to wrap the coffins so nothing could get inside. The "Tarim" Caucasoids preserved or "mummified" their people like the Guanche White Indians used to do.*

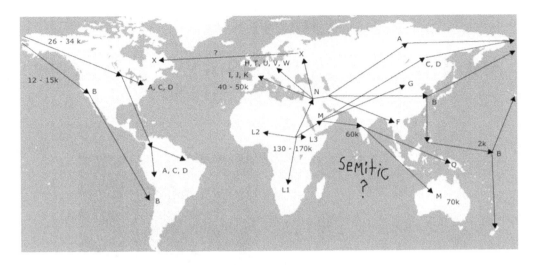

The travelers migrating East across the Bering Strait would enter into the "**Americas**", dispersing all throughout the land from North America to South America. They would be grouped "**Maternally**" under **mtDNA Haplogroups A, B, C, and D**. Haplogroup "**A**" would be more Northwest Canada/Alaska and parts of North America while Haplogroup "**B**" would be more Southwest America and Mexico. Haplogroups "**C**" and "**D**" would make up the majority of South America. "**Paternally**" the Indians would be classified under **Y-DNA Haplogroups** "**Q**", "**C**" and "**R1b**". The "**Big Question**" is, how can we trace the Paternal DNA of the "**Native Americans**" to the Hebrew Israelites? This is very hard seeing that you have so many different "**Paternal**" and "**Maternal**" haplogroups within the "Indians". We see African-Americans, Caribbean Blacks and "Bantus Africans" with the same Y-DNA "Paternal Haplogroup" "**E1b1a**". We also see that these groups of blacks also carry the same **L2/L3** Maternal mtDNA Haplogroup. However, when talking about the Native Americans we have mtDNA Haplogroups **A, B, C, D** and Paternal Y-DNA Haplogroups **Q, R, and C**. In this case, we have to look at the "indigenous Natives" language, traditions/customs and eye-witness testimonies. Using "**Critical Thinking**" we can then draw our own conclusions.

CHAPTER 11

ARE THE INDIGENOUS "INDIANS" HAMITES?
IF NOT, ARE THEY SHEMITES?

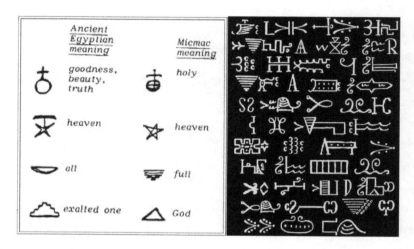

(**Above**) The Mi'kmaq Indians live primarily in Canada and parts of Maine. They have an ancient writing style that was similar to Ancient Egyptian hieratic (aka "reformed Egyptian). But something was also "peculiar" about these Mi'kmaq Indians.

(**Above**) Jesuit Missionaries in the 1800's trying to baptize and convert the "**Mi'kmaq Indians**" to Christianity.

When the Jesuits and the Mormons came into Canada, Northeast America (Maine) they noticed that the Mi'kmaq tribe was writing in what looked to be Egyptian Hieratic script from **right-to-left** like Hebrew. It is said that there are over 200 samples of Egyptian hieratic with "**Hebrew influences**" found in the regions of Northern Israel (House of Israel) and Southern Israel (House of Judah). Mormon-Latter Day Saint scholars John A. Tvedtnes and Stephen D. Ricks collected samples of these texts which they attributed were written in a Hebrew-related language. They also had in their possession an example of Psalms 20:2-6 written in Aramaic translation using Egyptian characters. In Israel, there have been found texts written in both Egyptian hieratic/Hebrew but can be read as Egyptian. Also at the Sinai Peninsula they found evidence for the commingling of Hebrew and Egyptian scripts dating back during the time of the Babylonian Invasion (7th and 6th Century B.C.) at which time some of the Israelites went into Egypt despite the warning Jeremiah the Prophet gave them from the Lord in Jeremiah Chapter 42-44.

Jeremiah 43:7 "So they came into the **land of Egypt**: for they obeyed **NOT** the voice of the Lord: thus came they even to Tahpanhes.

(**Above**) The similarities between Ancient Egyptian writing style (**E**), Ancient Semitic Hebrew (**S**), Ancient Phoenician-Canaanite (**P**), Ancient Greek (**G**), and the Roman writing style (**R**). As you can see Ancient Egyptian, Paleo-Hebrew and Phoenician script are similar.

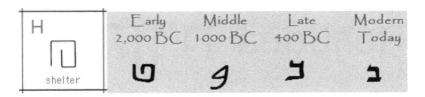

(**Left**) is the Egyptian letter/hieroglyphic for "**House/Shelter**". (**Right**) This picture shows the "time" transition for the Semitic Hebrew word "**Bet/Beth**" which means "**House**" as in Mount Sinai **Beth Israel** Hospital in New York City which means "**Mount Sinai House of Israel**".

As you can see the Ancient Hebrew language has strong influences/similarities from the Egyptian writing style most likely adopted from their almost half-century stay in the land of Egypt. 20 generations of Israelites were born in Egypt. Joseph and the Israelites walked into Egypt all together less than 100 strong and left with Moses almost 1-2 million strong. It shouldn't be no surprise that the Israelites knew how to speak or write Hebrew/Egyptian mix in their day-to-day life. Likewise, we see this evidence of "**Egyptian Influence**" in the Akan-Ewe Ghanaians, Wolof Senegalese, Igbo Nigerians, East Africans (Ethiopians, Somalians, Kenyans) and also Native Americans. We have to remember the nation of Israel also had a lot of "**Egyptian DNA**" in their bloodline/family tree from mixing with the people they lived amongst. This is why we have two Tribes (**Ephraim & Manasseh**) that sprouted from an Egyptian woman.

to judea ליהודה

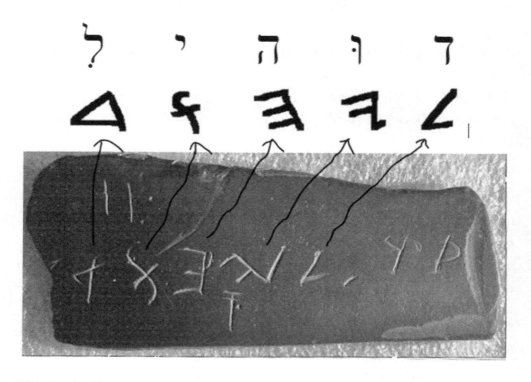

This is the "**Bat Creek Stone**" found in Tennessee in 1889. This stone dates back to Paleo-Hebrew script times (**Assyrian Invasion, Babylonian Invasion**). Tennessee was the territory of the **Cherokee and Chickasaw Indians**. This is strong evidence that the Hebrew Israelites made it to America during the time after their Exile from Assyria and/or Babylon.

(**Top**) The words "**To Judea**" in Modern Hebrew read from **Right-to-Left**. (**Middle**) Some of the Hebrew Characters that make up "**To Judea**". (**Bottom**) Corresponding Paleo-Hebrew Characters from the middle row lining up with the **Tennessee Bat Creek Stone**.

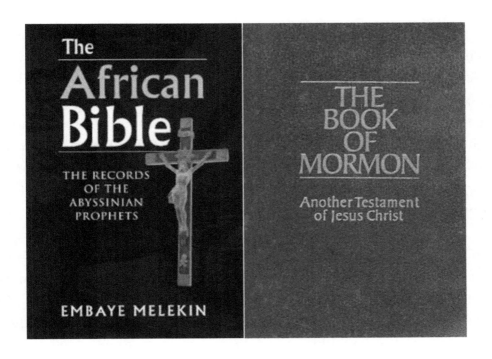

The African Bible is supposedly the record of the **Abyssinian (Eritrean/Ethiopian) prophets** who came to Africa from Jerusalem in around 600 B.C. The Sabaeans-**Eritreans/Tigray's** (so-called **Nephites**) and the Agazians-**Amhara Ethiopians** (so-called **Lamanites**) according to the **Book of Mormon (interpreted by Eritrean Embaye Melekin)** were descendants of the Hebrew Israelites during the 7th Century B.C. that left during the time there was Invasions in Judea.   According to Embaye Melekin's Book *"The African Bible: The Records of the Abyssinian Prophets"*, the different tribes discussed in the Mormon Bible and its history are in actuality Hebrew Israelite tribes.   The **Eritreans** are what Mormon history lists as the **Nephites, Jacobites, Yosephites, Zoramites, and Almadas**.   The **Mulekites** are the Beta Israel "Falasha" **Ethiopian Jews**.   The **Lemanites/Lamanites** are the **Amhara Ethiopians**.   According to the **Book of Mormon** (aka **"The African Bible"**), the prophecies of the Bible have been fulfilled upon the Israelites and the Gentiles. The Black African Hebrew Israelites were prophesied to decrease in number (**i.e. from the death toll from slavery/invasion**) as was apparent in the history of the continent.   In the **Book of Mormon,** it was prophesied that Black (Israelite) people living in Africa would be enslaved and scattered by the Gentiles. It was said that knowledge of the identity of the "**Real Israelites**" would be known by the "**Gentiles**" but not known by the "**Israelites**" until the "**Last Days**" when "**knowledge would increase**". The Mormons believed that when all the "**Real Israelites**" found out who they were (**in regards to their heritage**) it would reveal that the 2nd coming of Christ was near. Initially the Mormons didn't allow Blacks into their congregation. Were they trying to keep their "**secret knowledge**" of the Israelites hidden for a good reason or a bad reason? Did Joseph Smith purposely alter the Mormon Bible so that Blacks wouldn't figure out their "True Identity"? Why was the Mormon Church so against letting Blacks into their church? Maybe they didn't want "Blacks" to know that the Holy Bible was actually talking about them and they were in fact the Israelites of the Bible. Here is some of what was revealed in the "African Bible" of the Abyssinian Israelites, which many say has been incorporated in today's "**Book of Mormon**".

- Blacks shall be shielded from the outside world until Africa is "**liberated**" again by the descendants of the Hebrew Israelites that first migrated to Africa starting around the 8th-6th century A.D.
- Yahusha HaMashiach (Jesus Christ) would introduce the Christian faith using his disciples/apostles to the descendants of the Hebrew Israelites starting with Ethiopia/Egypt.
- The descendants of the Hebrew Israelites would stray away from the "**Path of God**" and shall worship idols.
- The dwelling place of the Hebrew Israelites would be invaded by Gentiles (**i.e. the "white races (Europeans-Arabs)"** and shall be enslaved, taken to a far off land **foreign** to them.
- In this "**foreign land**" they shall be "**trampled upon**" and shall have "**no power**".
- The Hebrew Israelites scattered in "**foreign lands**" would not completely die off, but they would continue to "**multiply**".

- The Hebrew Israelites would "**re-find**" their "**Lost Identity**" in the "**Last Days**" when "**Knowledge**" would increase among mankind. (**this is happening now with the Internet**).
- The Hebrew Israelites would eventually "**rise up**" despite all the obstacles placed in front of them by the powers of Satan.

Liberated means: "**being freed from imprisonment, slavery, and enemy occupation.**"

Fact: Until June 8, 1978, the Church of Latter Day Saints (Mormon Church) officially barred Black men of African descent from its priesthood. It was taught in the Mormon Church that Blacks couldn't be in the "**Priesthood**" because they were from the lineage of Cain, who was cursed with "**Black skin**" after killing his brother "**Abel**." This story in the Book of Nephi is said to have been altered in order to disconnect Blacks from the Seed of Seth and therefore **ISRAEL**.

Here are some quotes showing the Mormons attitude towards blacks in its early years:

"Having learned with extreme regret, that an article entitled, 'Free People of color,' in the last number of the Star has been misunderstood, we fell in duty bound to state, in this Extra, that our intention was not only to stop free people of color from emigrating to this state (Utah), but to prevent them from being admitted as members of the Church."

Joseph Smith, founder of the Church of Mormon

There is more!

"Shall I tell you the law of God in regard to the African race? If the white man who belongs to the "**Chosen Seed**" mixes his blood with the "**Seed of Cain**", the penalty under the law of God, is death on the spot. This will always be so."

Brigham Young, 2nd President of the Mormon Church

Now in the Book of Mormon the story of "**Nephi**" and "**Lehi**" sort of parallels the story of the prophet "**Jeremiah**" and King Jehoiakim of Judah. Nephi's father "**Lehi**" is described as a sort-of-prophet like "Jeremiah" who warns the people of Judah about the coming Babylonian invasion. Nephi describes his father making this prophecy about "Babylon invading" during the first year of "Zedekiah King of Judah". However, according to the bible during King Zedekiah's reign the deportation of all the people in the Southern Kingdom of Judah had already happened. For this reason, many believe that the person Nephi was referring to was King Jehoiakim of Judah. Different explanations for this name mix up has baffled Bible Historians. They believe that Zedekiah might have been another name for Jehoiakim (**who also had a brother named Zedekiah and a son named Zedekiah in 1 Chronicles 3:15-16**). So it's possible that the confusion between "Jehoaikim" and "Zedekiah" is simply from the fact that they were all kinfolk to each other!

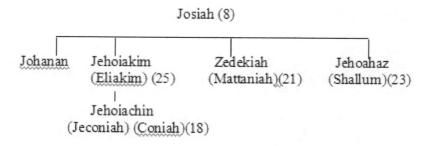

1 Chronicles 3:15-16 "And the sons of Josiah were, the firstborn Johanan, **the second Jehoaikim**, the **third Zedekiah**, the fourth Shallum. And the sons of Jehoaikim: Jeconiah his son, **Zedekiah his son.**"

Other explanations are how in the Bible, the name "**Zedekiah**" is used interchangeably with the name "**Jehoaikim**" in Jeremiah 27:1-3.

Jeremiah 27:1-3 "In the beginning of the reign of **Jehoiakim the son of Josiah King of Judah** came this word unto Jeremiah from the Lord, saying, Thus saith the Lord to me; Make thee bonds and yokes, and put them upon thy neck, And send them to the King of Edom, and to the King of Moab, and to the King of the Ammonites, and to the King of Tyre, and to the King of Zidon, by the hand of the messengers which come to Jerusalem unto **Zedekiah King of Judah**;"

We know that there cannot be **two "Kings of Judah"** at the same time so is it possible that Jehoaikim was referred to as "**Zedekiah**"?

Other possibilities include the fact that King Nebuchadnezzar could've changed **Jehoiakim's** name to **Zedekiah** for it was common for ruling nations to change the names of their captors as they saw fit, plus Zedekiah was Jehoaikim's younger brother (**1 Chronicles 3:15-18**).

So after the invasion of Southern Israel by Babylon it is said according to the Book of Mormon that the descendants of **Nephi (Nephites)** including the **Lamanites, Jaredites, and Mulekites** made their escape across the oceans to the Americas. **The Church of Jesus Christ of Latter-day Saints (LDS Church)** state it is historical fact that the "**Nephites**" existed but archaeologists and historians say there is no prove to back this claim up.

Nephite	Mi'kmaq		Nephite	Mi'kmaq

(Above) The **Mi'kmaq Indians** writing style according to the Jesuits and the Mormon Church match up to the writing style used on the "**Nephite**" metal plates supposedly written by the Israelite "**Nephi**" himself. These metal plates are what Mormon Church founder "**Joseph Smith**" used to start the following of his church. Egyptian hieratic was like "reformed cursive Egyptian hieroglyphs".

(**Top Row**) A comparison of the Old **Sabaean script (left)** to Ethiopian Ge'ez script (**right**). The Tigray, Amharic and Ge'ez script of Abyssinia is similar to the Sabaean script. (**Bottom Row**) More Ancient Sabaean Scripts, which can be found in the Yeha Temple in Ancient Abyssinia (Eritrea/Ethiopia). The Sabaeans were believed to be either the descendants of Joktan or the people of the Kingdom of Sheba of Ethiopia which back in the day ruled Ethiopia and the territory now encompassing South Saudi Arabia, including Yemen. The **Sabaean** "South Arabian" script, the Ethiopian **Ge'ez** script (writing style of the Ethiopian Orthodox church and Ethiopian Jews) all are "Semitic" languages that are very similar to "**Hebrew**". The South Arabian "Semitic" people brought with them the **Sabaean language** into Ethiopia sometime around 1,000 B.C., the same time King Solomon lived. Believed to be brought by "Aguezat" settlers (aka-who the Mormons call "Lamanites") this Sabaean (Hebrew-like) language influenced the "Cushitic speaking" people in Ethiopia. There are still stone inscriptions in Ethiopia bearing the Old Sabaean script. This is even more proof that Israel merged with Ethiopia back in B.C. times when King Solomon sent the firstborn sons of the 12 Tribes (including

297

the priests) down to Ethiopia with Menelik to teach the way to worship the God of Israel.

(**Left**) The Kingdom of Sheba/Sheva which encompasses Ethiopia, the land of Punt, South Arabia and Yemen. (**Right**) "**King Ezana's Steel**" which is a 1700-year-old 70 feet tall stone Obelisk in Axum, Ethiopia. This obelisk was built in around 300 A.D. before the Arabic language existed (500 A.D.) and even before Islam existed (600 A.D.). On the smaller "**King Ezana Stone**", written in Greek, Sabaean, and Ethiopian Ge'ez it describes King Ezana's conversion to Christianity.

Fact: The Sabaeans are mentioned in the **Book of Job, Joel, Ezekiel, and Isaiah.** They are also mentioned in the Quran.

The Mi'kmaq are a part of the "**Algonquian Indian**" family but what about the rest of the Indians? What "**Hebrewisms**" did they exhibit in the "**New World**?"

The **Native Indians** told the Europeans many other things that God had done for their ancestors, exactly as the scriptures stated concerning the Israelites and their coming out of Egypt. They knew about the "Great Flood" and the "crossing over the Red Sea". The Indians talked about the Oracles (i.e. Words of God-Torah) they received, the Tabernacle of the Ark of the Covenant carried by four Priests and how they pitched the Tent facing East. They were told that no one could come near the tabernacle except those appointed. For this reason and more the Europeans wrote in their books that the "**Mexicans/Indians**" were Jews/Israelites. Here is more of what the European noticed of the Indians.

- They called their Uncles and Aunts, Fathers or Mothers. This is also done in Africa.
- They marry into their own Tribe and Kindred.
- They really mourn when someone dies and they have garments that are to be used during funerals.

299

- They speak and write an Archaic form of Hebrew.
- They separate women who are on their period in separate huts called "Wigwams" or "Wikiup" until they are off their cycle.
- They believe that ONE GOD, created the Heavens and the Earth.
- They wore one coat and a square/rectangle sized cloak (**i.e. Jewish Tallit**).

Apache Indian Wick-i-up, Arizona, 1880.

(**Above**) These are Apache Women in 1880 A.D. separated during their menstruation (periods) in huts called "**Wigwams**" or "**Wikiups**". They could not return back to the rest of the people in the tribe until they were off their periods. This is also practiced as a tradition/custom in West/East Africa and with the Ethiopian **Falasha** Jews. Prior to being visited by **Europeans**, the Indians, West Africans, and Ethiopian Jews had no knowledge of the "**Gospels-New Testament**". For this reason, they were called by the European "**convert**" Jews from Portugal/Spain/Holland "**Karaite Jews**" and not Pharisee Jews. Remember, many of the Pharisees of Yahusha's (Jesus) time were

Edomites, Greeks and people of other nations who had converted to Judaism. They were not real Israelites. Many of the "Real Israelites" during the time of Christ were already scattered or exiled into the **NATIONS**. For this reason, they didn't know about Yahusha Hamashiach. The did know however know from the Old Testament that the Messiah would be a Prince from the **Line of David (Judah)**.

(**Left**) This is a painting of a Spanish man and his Mestizo (mixed) child with an Indigenous Peruvian women in 1770. The Spanish Mestizaje Agenda was designed to "erase" the brown-blackness of North America, Central America and South America. They promoted the re-settling of Spanish and Portuguese people in the "**New World**". Once there, they were instructed to have children with the "native women". The men that fought back to protect their territory were barbarically killed by the white **Spanish Conquistadors**. Those native Indian men that were able to get away fled into the mountains and forests.

(**Left**) **Francisco Pizarro** arrived in Peru in the 1500's and in this picture he is executing the last of the **Inca Kings of Peru**. Pizarro enslaved the Incas living in the Andes Mountains. This was prime "**Israelite**" territory per Sephardic Portuguese Jewish traveler **Antonio de Montezinos**, aka "**Aaron Levi**" when he visited the Andes mountain area and told Menasseh Ben Israel (Rabbi of Amsterdam) in 1644 that he had found one of the Lost Tribes of Israel. Cortes conquered the Aztecs and their leader Moctezuma in the city of **Tenochtitlan in 1519**. Many scientists/archeologists believe that the Mayan, Inca, Aztec and Olmec's were Israelites who came to the "New World" many centuries prior to the Europeans. (**Right**) The Inca (YNGA) kings were "people of color", not white.

(**Above**) The Spanish Conquistadors used the Indian "**Israelites**" in "**New Spain-America**" to work as **SLAVES** on the large plantations to grow food, tobacco and sugar just as they did the Negro "Israelites" in the Americas/Caribbean. The Europeans came to other people's lands stealing Gold (**i.e. Queen of England and all their stolen treasures**), enforcing "**Whitenized Christianity**" and enslaving the people. This law was called "**Incomienda**". The Spanish brought "Negro" Israelites they had taken from Iberia (Spain/Portugal) and placed them in the Caribbean Island during the late 1400's/early 1500's to help with labor when they needed more slaves. They also took "Negro" Israelites from West Africa to help out wherever they need slave labor. At the top of the hierarchy class system in the new world were different groups:

1. **Nobles** – People born in Spain
2. **Creoles** – Spanish people born in the New World (Americas)
3. **Mestizos** – People of Spanish and Native American parents
4. **Indians/Africans/Mulattoes** - (Black and Indian mixed people).

The Indians and Negroes did not know about the New Testament or the Gospels. So the Europeans converted them to Catholicism (Catholic Church). Bartolome de las Casas and Father Junipero Serra were Europeans who helped force-convert the Indians to their Catholic Church sect. There was a Pueblo Indian named "Pope" who in 1680 helped stage a revolt against the Spanish, driving them out of Santa Fe, New Mexico area.

Fact: The Europeans brought diseases to the Indians in the New World which they had no immunity to. Just as many of these diseases inflicted those living in West Africa, the Indians felt the wrath of the Europeans and their diseases.

1. Smallpox
2. Malaria
3. Chicken Pox
4. Measles
5. Yellow Fever
6. Bubonic Plague
7. Typhus
8. Diphtheria
9. HIV
10. Syphilis and a host of other STD's.

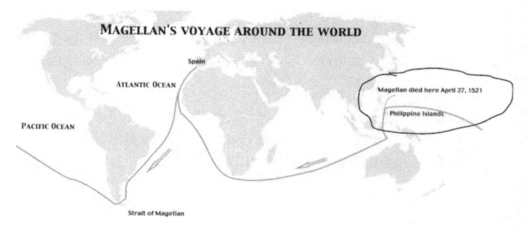

Fact: Around the same time Spanish Christopher Columbus was traveling in the late 1400's/early 1500's, Portuguese explorer **Ferdinand Magellan** set out from Spain with a fleet of five ships to discover a different route to the Spice Islands in Asia. On the way he found a waterway through Argentina and Chile which he named the "**Strait of Magellan**". This Strait led him to the Pacific Ocean and on his way to the Orient (Asia) as he desired to accomplish. While in the Orient, he traded with the Chinese for spices, silk and small toys which he would bring back to Europe to sell for huge profits. He also traded with **Rajah Humabon**, the King of the Philippines after collecting their goods. While in the Philippines they got into a fight with a rival Filipino leader and Magellan was killed (**Filipinos actually know this**). His crew sailed west without their leader to the Spice Island of Indonesia arriving in 1521 and then set sail west past India and around South Africa to get into the Atlantic Ocean to get to Portugal. It took from 1519 to 1522 to navigate across the world going in a westward direction, proving that the world was round, just as the Greeks had documented. They did not encounter an ice wall as it is commonly believed in the "Flat Earth Theory".

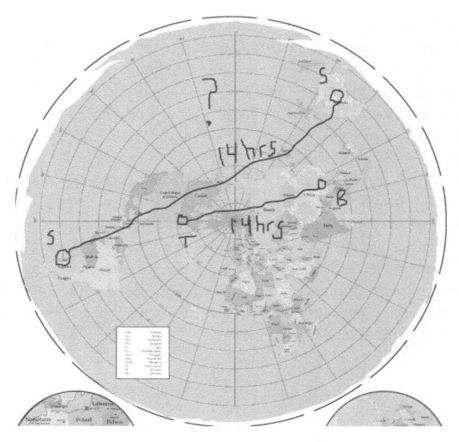

(**Above-Flat Earth Map**) Even today comparing 14 hour Non-Stop flights from Santiago, Chile (**S**) to Sydney, Australia (**S**) (**using Qantas Airlines**) a vs 14 hour Non-Stop flights from Toronto, Canada (**T**) to Beijing, China (**B**) (**using Hainan Airlines**) debunks the Flat Earth Map Theory. Magellan did it also 500 years ago. How can a non-stop flight from Toronto, Canada to Beijing, China be 14 hours when it takes 14 hours to fly non-stop from almost the tip of South America (**S**) to Sydney, Australia (**S**)? Something is not adding up with this "**Flat Earth Theory**". Unless one plane is flying "**Supersonic speeds**" and one is flying super slow.

Moving Forward, the hardships the Hebrews experienced over many centuries parallel the hardships people of African descent have gone through since the beginning of the Common Era (C.E. or A.D). Is this a coincidence........NO!

Deuteronomy 28:45-46 **"Moreover all these curses shall come upon thee, and shall pursue thee, and overtake thee, till thou hearkenedst not unto the voice of the LORD thy God, to keep his commandments and his statutes which he commanded thee: <u>And they shall be upon thee for a sign and for a wonder, and upon thy seed FOREVER."</u>**

Did the Children of Israel (Our Forefathers) disobey the commandments? Are these curses justified upon us **FOREVER**?

Daniel 9:9-14 "To the Lord our God belong mercies and forgivenesses, though we have rebelled against him; **NEITHER HAVE WE OBEYED THE VOICE OF THE LORD OUR GOD**, to walk in his laws, which he set before us by his servants the prophets. Yea, **ALL ISRAEL** have transgressed the law, even by departing, that they might not obey thy voice; **THEREFORE THE CURSE IS UPON US**, and the oath that is written in the law of Moses the servant of God, because **WE HAVE SINNED AGAINST HIM**. And he hath confirmed his words, which he spake against us, and against our judges that judged us, by bringing upon us a **GREAT EVIL**: for under the whole heaven hath not been done as hath been done upon Jerusalem.

CHAPTER 12

WHO ARE THE REAL HEBREWS? WHICH ONE OF THESE RACES/NATIONS ARE GOING THROUGH THE CURSES OF ISRAEL AS LISTED IN DEUTERONOMY 28:15-68?

DO THE JEWS TODAY EVEN LOOK LIKE THE ANCIENT ISRAELITES?

(**Left**) Real Israelites with kinky hair and kinky beards from the Tribe of Judah, taken from the city of Lachish, Israel in 700 B.C. by the Assyrians. This "slab" stone relief taken from the Palace of Sennacherib, King of Assyria in Nineveh, Iraq is currently in a British Museum. Why? Because they don't want Black People to know the Truth! (**Right**) Former Prime Minister of Israel, Ariel Sharon with white straight hair. **Who is an authentic Jew and who is fake Jew? You be the Judge.**

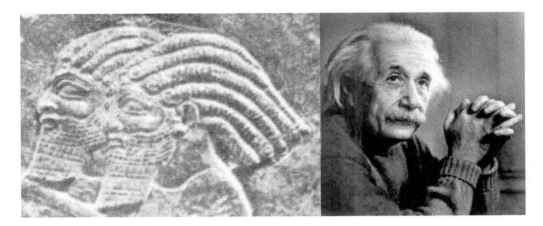

(**Left**) Ancient Hebrew Israelites with thick Dreadlocks/Cornrows in B.C. times. On one side of the hair you can see distinctly 6 rows of dreads/braids. This is not a "common" hairstyle of Europeans, let alone white Ashkenazi Jews. It is a common hairstyle among "Black people". (**Right**) Ashkenazi Jew, Albert Einstein (No locks). **Who is an authentic Jew and who is a fake Jew? You be the Judge.**

In 2015, I had the pleasure of talking to Ashkenazi Jewish lady in her 60's. She told me that her mother always talked about the horrors of the Holocaust. So I asked the lady, "**Where is your mother from?**" She said, "**She is from Poland which is in Europe.**". She explained to me that before the European Jews came to Israel in 1948, the Jewish people in Europe had to go to "**Hebrew School**". I asked her why did they have to go to "**Hebrew School**" if they were descendants of the "**Hebrew-Speaking**" 12 tribes of Israel who had simply left their homeland (Israel) for Europe. I expressed to her that "**True Israelites**" should be born learning how to speak Hebrew, like children in America are taught how to speak English as early as 2 years old. She said that the European Jews spoke their forefather's language which was **Germanaic, Slavic or Turkish (this proves who they really are)**. She said that they fused this language with their **learnt** "Hebrew" language to form "**Yiddish**". She said that "**Yiddish**" and "**Hebrew**" were two different languages and were **NOT THE SAME** because "Yiddish" had a lot of German words in it. So I started naming off some Hebrew words and she was impressed. She said, "How do you know Hebrew?". I said, "I don't, I just memorized some Hebrew words during my research." She told me the "**Yiddish**" version of every Hebrew word that I said to her and indeed it was very different. This was a "**Red Flag**" sign that the Ashkenazi Jews were not the real Jews of the Bible. But don't take my word for it, see what the "Jewish" NY Times magazine said about the Jews "**Yiddish**" language and their identity.

The October 29, 1996 N.Y. Times, in an article entitled, "Scholars Debate Origins of Yiddish and the Migrations of Jews," states:

"Arching over these questions is the central mystery of just where the Jews of Eastern Europe came from. Many historians believe that there were not nearly enough Jews in Western Europe to account for the huge population that later flourished in Poland, Lithuania, Ukraine and nearby areas. By reconstructing the Yiddish mother tongue, linguists hope to plot the migration of the Jews and their language with a precision never possible before."

"It has even been suggested, on the basis of linguistic evidence, that the Jews of Eastern Europe were not predominantly part of the diaspora from the Middle East, but were members of another ethnic group that adopted Judaism.

"One linguist has recently argued that Yiddish began as a Slavic language that was 'relexified,' with most of its vocabulary replaced with German words. Even more troublesome are demographic studies indicating that during the Middle Ages there were no more than 25,000 to 35,000 Jews in Western Europe. These figures are hard to reconcile with other studies showing that by the 17th century there were hundreds of thousands of Jews in Eastern Europe"

(**Left**) Ashkenazi Jews (1800's). (**Right**) Negro Civil War Troops (1800's).

"Many assert that the Hebrews are a RACE OF ETHIOPIAN (Black) ORIGINS"

Cornelius Tacitus 56 A.D.-117 A.D.

So which group fits this statement?

(**Left**) Menelik II, Emperor of Ethiopia (1844-1913 A.D.). Menelik's wife Empress Taytu Betoul named the capital of Ethiopia, "**Addis Ababa (New Flower)**". Under his rule, Ethiopia defeated the Italians in the "**Battle of Adwa**" in 1896. (**Right**) Hamitic Cushite Nubian Warrior (Archers). The Egyptians called the Nubians "**Ta-Seti**" or "**Land of the Bow**" as they were good with the bow and arrow.

311

(**Bottom**) Hamite Cushite Nubian man in B.C. times. Before the 4th Century B.C., Nubia was known as "**Kush**". During B.C. times Greeks and Romans (**Cornelius Tacitus**) believed the Hebrew Israelites were from "Ethiopia". When the Greeks conquered Egypt in around 300 B.C. (4th Century) they called the land "Aithiopia/Ethiopia" which means "**Burnt Black**". Could this be because around 1,000 B.C., Israel merged with the Cushites with the relationship between Queen Sheba of Ethiopia and Tribe of Judah King Solomon? Menelik was sent back to Ethiopia with Israelites from each of the 12 Tribes, including the Levites and Aaronites. The Children of Moses (A Levite) were also half-Israelite/half-Cushite. Aaron (Cohenites) was the brother of Moses. This means that the descendants of Moses (Israel-Cush Ethiopia) and the descendants of Aaron **WERE COUSINS**, just like Mary (mother of Jesus) and Elizabeth (mother of John the Baptist) **WERE COUSINS**! If Elizabeth's father was an "**Aaronite**", could this mean that Mary, the mother of Jesus could perhaps be of **Levite-Ethiopian descent?** This would make sense even more that the Gentile Romans and Greeks would refer to the Israelites as sort of "Ethiopian-like Israelites". The Ethiopians and Jamaicans often refer to themselves as the "**Lion of Judah**". Jesus (Yahusha's) earthly father was "**Joseph**" from the Tribe of Judah. His Genealogy traced back to Zerubbabel is found in the New Testament in Matthew 1:2-16 and Luke 3:23-38. These scriptures cannot be talking about Mary because both list Salathiel, and Zerubbabel, all son of the Tribe of Judah, not Levi.

Luke 3:27 "Which was the son of Joanna, which was the son of Rhesa, which was the son of **Zorobabel**, which was the son of **Salathiel,** which was the son of Neri.

Matthew 1:12-13 "And after they were brought to Babylon, Jechonias begat **Salathiel**; and Salathiel begat **Zorobabel**;"

Luke 1:5 "There was in the days of Herod, the King of Judea, a certain priest named Zacharias, of the course of Abia: and his wife was of the daughters of **AARON**, and her name was **ELISABETH**."

When you are Cousins you typically have the same Grandfather. If **Zacharias (John the Baptist's father)** was a **PRIEST**, he had to be a Levite/Aaronite. Therefore, if Mary was a cousin of Elisabeth (**Mother of John the Baptist**), she would've also had to have a Grandfather and Father who was of the **Tribe of Levi (Aaronite).**

Luke 1:34-36 "Then said Mary unto the angel, How shall this be, seeing I know not a man? And the angel answered and said unto her, The Holy Ghost shall come upon thee, and the power of the Highest shall overshadow thee: therefore also that holy thing which shall be born of thee shall be called the **SON OF GOD**. And behold, **THY COUSIN ELISABETH**, she hath also conceived a son in her old age: and this is the sixth month with her, who was called barren."

THE PROOF IS IN THE BIBLE! Yahusha (Jesus) was born of a Levite/Aaronite (Cohenite) woman, and possibly Ethiopian woman (via Moses wife Zipporah or Queen Sheba). Wow!

(**Left**) St. George Church, a monolithic church carved out of solid rock underground in the shape of a cross in **Lalibela, Northern Ethiopia**. (**Right**) The Church of Our Lady Mary of Zion in Axum (Aksum), Ethiopia. It is here that many say the "**Ark of the Covenant**" is kept, underground a network of tunnels and rooms in a room called the "**Holy of Holies**".

Amos 9:7 "ARE YE NOT AS **CHILDREN OF THE ETHIOPIANS** UNTO ME, **O CHILDREN OF ISRAEL**."

The Bible also proves that among the people the Assyrians took captive in addition to the Israelites during their invasions were the Ethiopians and Egyptians.

ISAIAH 20:4 "So shall the King of Assyria lead away the **Egyptians** as prisoners and the **Ethiopians** as captives, young, old, naked and barefoot."

(Left) Ancient Nubian Cushite men with no girdle, no bonnet, no fringes, no tassels. **(Middle)** Possible Israelite man with Bonnet **(arrow)**, Golden Earring, Girdle and Fringes **(circled)**. **(Right)** King Jehu Obelisk. King Jehu was the 10th King of Israel around 800 B.C. Notice the circled Girdle, Tassels and Fringes (circled and arrow).

Definition "Girdle": A belt, cord or sash worn about the waist.

Most of the pictures of the Ancient Cushite Nubians show them to have their shirts off with their hair in a braided fashion. They have golden Earrings just like the Egyptians of Royalty (King Tut). They are never wearing Bonnets, Girdles, coats, sashes or fringes. **This was the fashion/dress attire of the Israelites.** Looking at the picture of the dark skinned man in the middle, it would appear that this man more fits the description of an Israelite vs a Nubian Cushite. **You be the judge.**

Exodus 28:40 "And for **Aaron's sons** thou shalt make coats, and thou shalt make them **girdles, and bonnets** shalt thou make for them, for glory and for beauty."

Exodus 29:9 "And thou shalt gird them with **girdles**, Aaron and his sons, and put the **bonnets** on them: and the priest's office shall be theirs for a perpetual statute: and thou shalt consecrate **Aarons and his sons**."

Leviticus 8:13 "And Moses bought Aaron's sons and put coats upon them, and then with girdles, and put **BONNETS** upon them; as the LORD commanded Moses.

Exodus 32:2 "And Aaron said unto them, break off the **GOLDEN EARRINGS**, which are in the ears of your wives, **OF YOUR SONS**, and if your daughters, and bring them to me?

The only people that wore earrings were the EGYPTIANS and Cushite NUBIANS (Ethiopians). Where the EGYPTIANS and Ethiopians led away from their countries with the ISRAELITES by the Assyrians? YES!

ISAIAH 20:4 "So shall the King of Assyria **lead away the Egyptians as prisoners and the Ethiopians as captives,** young, old, naked and barefoot."

(**Left**) Nubian (**"A" Y-DNA Haplogroup**) or an Israelite B.C. times (**Middle**) East African (**E1b1a Y-DNA Haplogroup**) (**Right**) West African (**E1b1a Y-DNA Haplogroup**). It is a known fact that half of the Ethiopian Jews DNA is "**A" Y-DNA Haplogroup** while the other half is the "E1b1c (P2 Ancestor of E1b1a) Haplogroup". Didn't Cush (**Nubia-Ethiopia**) mix their seed with **Israel** in the Bible? Yep! There is your proof.

Isaiah 3:17-21 "Therefore the Lord will smite with a scab the crown of the head of the **DAUGHTERS OF ZION**, and the Lord will discover their secret parts. In that day the Lord will take away the bravery of their tinkling ornaments about their feet, and their cauls, and their round tires like the moon, the chains, and the bracelets, and the mufflers, the **bonnets**, and the **ornaments of the legs**, and the **headbands**, and the tablets, and the **earrings**, the **rings**, and **nose jewels**."

LET'S DO A RECAP!

How do we know that the Israelite Tribes were scattered all across the Earth? The Ashkenazi Jews and Sephardic Jews **were not** scattered all across the earth. So if they are not the Israelites of the Bible then why are they calling themselves "**Jews**" or "**God's Chosen People**".

"**Scatter**" in the Merriam-Webster Dictionary means: To cause (**things or people**) to **SEPARATE** and go into different directions.

- **Deuteronomy 32:26** "I said, I would scatter them (Israelites) into the corners (of the earth), I would make the remembrance of them to cease among men".

- **Psalms 83:4** "They have said, Come, and let us cut them off from being a nation; that the name of Israel may be no more in remembrance".

- Jeremiah 17:4 "And thou, even thyself, shalt discontinue from thine heritage that I gave thee; and I will cause thee to SERVE THINE ENEMIES in the land which thou knowest not: for ye

317

have kindled a fire in mine anger, which shall burn **FOREVER**".

Who is the Synagogue of Satan? Who was Jesus referring to? What is a "Jew"?

- Revelation 2:9 **"I know thy works, and tribulation, and poverty (but thou art rich) and I know the blasphemy of them which say they are Jews, and are not, but are the synagogue of Satan."**

- Revelation 3:9 **"Behold, I will make them of the synagogue of Satan, which say they are Jews, and are not,"**

What race or nation of people would knowingly call themselves Jews when they are not? Blacks, Arabs, Asian, Latinos, Indians? I don't think so..

CHAPTER 13

THE PUNISHMENT MUST FIT THE CRIME! IT IS WRITTEN IN THE TORAH!

(**Above**) European Children attending Torah School (**Hebrew School**) in the late 1800's. Prior to the Holocaust the European Ashkenazi/Sephardic Children growing up had to go to Hebrew School to learn Hebrew. Because the European Ashkenazi Jews were Germanaic, Slavic and Turkish they mixed Modern Hebrew with their native tongue creating the language called "**Yiddish**". Yiddish was spoken by the Ashkenazi Jews who were born before the Holocaust and the State of Israel creation. If they were real Hebrew Israelites all they would have known would've have been "**Hebrew**" as their first language. They would be speaking "Yiddish" using "**Western Aramaic (which was spoken in Israel)**" and not "**Eastern Aramaic (spoken by Arameans-Syrians and Iraqis)**". They wouldn't have children learning how to speak Hebrew in Elementary School. They would've learnt it as soon as they were able to form sounds to talk.

But let's get down to the "**nitty gritty**" with this claim of the "**Chosen People**" being strictly "**European-looking**" while any Black Jews are considered "**converts**" to Judaism. If the European Jews and Sephardic Jews are truly Israelites, the "**Covenant**" God made with them should still apply today. Thus, according to **Deuteronomy 28:1-14**, if they obeyed the covenant they would receive blessings. If they disobeyed the covenant that God gave them they would receive curses listed in **Deuteronomy 28:15-68**. Let's see if the Ashkenazi/Sephardic Jews have been keeping God's Commandments. After all, God hasn't given his "**Children of Israel**" a "**Second Covenant**" yet. This is a "**future**" prophecy by Jeremiah in Chapter 31 of the Book of Jeremiah.

- Judaism **rejects** Yahusha Hamashiach (Jesus Christ) is the **Messiah** and **God**. **Commandment 1 DISOBEYED**. -Exodus 20:3.

- The European Jews **killed/murdered** thousands of Black slaves in addition to Native Americans during the Exploration of the "New World" and during the Transatlantic Slave trade. **Commandment 6 DISOBEYED**. - Exodus 20:13.

- The European Jews committed **adultery** with the African/Native American female slaves both young and old. **Commandment 7 DISOBEYED**. - Exodus 20:14.

- The European Jews did in fact **steal** Africans/Native Americans from their land to be forced into inhumane slavery. **Commandment 8 DISOBEYED**. – Exodus 20:15

- The European Jewish Slavemasters did in fact **bear false witness (lie)** against the Black slaves and Native Americans repeatedly. **Commandment 9 DISOBEYED**. – Exodus 20:16

- The European Jewish Slavemaster did in fact **covet** the Black male slaves wives. **Commandment 10 DISOBEYED**. – Exodus 20:17

- The European Jews helped manipulate the words of the bible which goes against Deut 4:2, Rev 22:19 and Proverbs 30:5-6. **(Replaced God's name with "Lord", labeled Jesus the "King of the Jews", and added/hid different books from different bible canon's of different nationalities**).

- The European Jews inserted the word "**Jew**" into the Old Testament (54-74 times in the Book of Esther). There is no Letter "**J**" in the Hebrew or Greek language.

- The European Jews adorn the Hexagram "**graven**" star as the symbol for Israel. This is not commanded in the Torah anywhere. The hexagram does not appear naturally in life except in (maybe) snowflakes and nowhere in the Bible does God say to carry a "**snowflake**" image as the symbol of Israel. Therefore, a "hexagram" has to fashioned or made in order to exist as a symbol. **Commandment 4 DISOBEYED.** – Exodus 20:4

TRADITION VS BLOOD

THE PROSELTYE CALLS HIMSELF "**JEW**" AND THE BIRTHRIGHT MAN CALLS HIMSELF "**AFRICAN-AMERICAN.**" THIS IS CALLED "**IDENTITY HIJACKING**"

THESE ARE SOME QUESTIONS THAT NEED TO BE ANSWERED. THE PEOPLE NEED TO KNOW THE TRUTH.

1. If the European Jews are God's "Chosen People" then why aren't all the 12 tribes of Israel in the Holy Land right now? Why does **Lebanon** possess the **Territory of Asher**? Why does **Palestine** still possess part of the **Territory of Judah**? Why does **Jordan** still possess the **Territory of Reuben, Gad, and East Manasseh**?

2. How come they don't possess the "**Ark of the Covenant**".

3. How come God allows Israel and the Jews to have Gay pride parades every year for the last 15 years in Jerusalem without punishment?

4. How come God allows 3 major religions to worship their Gods in Temple Mount, Jerusalem? (**Catholic Church, Islam, and Judaism**).

5. The land and borders that modern day Israel possesses is much smaller than the biblical borders that were promised to Moses by God in Numbers 34:1-3. It is also smaller than the territory occupied by King David and King Solomon. God does not do things halfway.

6. Shouldn't there be more Black "Israelites" in Israel knowing that the Israelites who many attest were Black themselves intermarried with the Ancient Egyptians, Ethiopians, Canaanites and Libyans for thousands of years?

7. Who are they preparing to build the Third Temple for in Jerusalem when in Revelation 21:1-2 it says that a "**New Jerusalem**" is seen coming out of heaven for God to sit on the throne? Who is going to sit on the throne in this man made Jewish Temple? **THE ANTICHRIST!** So the Jews are building a Third Temple for Satan? That doesn't seem right according to the Bible. You be the Judge.

(**Left**) Ashkenazi Jews late 1800's – **Job 30:30** says "**My skin is BLACK upon me, and my bones are burned with heat**." The Hebrew Strong's #7838 for Black is "**Shachor**". It is an adjective describing a color as in of hair (**Song of Solomon 5:11**), skin (**Song of Solomon 1:5**) and horses (**Zechariah 6:2**). (**Right**) Lebanese family late 1800's – occupying the territory of **Asher**.

(**Left**) Jordanian woman late 1800's - The Jordanians are occupying the territory of the **East Manasseh, Gad and Reuben** right now. Where are Samaritans in Israel who claim to be from the Tribe of Manasseh? (**Right**) Palestinian man in late 1800's. The Palestinians occupy a portion of the territory of **Judah**. Over the last 2,000 years Gentiles such as the Persians, Greeks, Romans (Byzantine), Kurds (Saladin) and Turks (Suleiman the Magnificent) have been occupying Israel. Their descendants along with the European Gentile Jews are right now as we speak in the Holy Land of Israel.

(Above) Samaritan High Priest 1905 A.D. The Israelite High Priests were supposed to not intermarry with Gentiles. The Samaritans men today are discouraged from intermarrying with other nations. The Cohenite Samaritan Family had their Y-DNA tested and it was **E1b1b (E-M78)**, the same Y-DNA found in North African Arabs. So does this mean that every Arab in North Africa is a Aaronite High Priest? NO! In Ezra 9:1-2 around 400 B.C. it states that the High Priests were intermixing with the Canaanites and the Egyptians. But these Samaritan High Priests do not look like the Ancient Black Egyptians or Canaanites. The **Tsedakah** Samaritan clan claim descent from Manasseh yet they do not look Black like the Egyptians of old. The **Joshua-Marhiv** Samaritan clan claim descent from Ephraim yet they also do not look Black like the Egyptians of old. What is going on? Yahusha (Jesus) said that Israel would be infiltrated with Gentiles during the 1st Century A.D. He said the "Gentiles" would possess Jerusalem and Israel until his Second Coming. Are we missing something here?

Luke 21:24 "And they (Israelites) shall fall by the edge of the sword, and shall be led away captive into <u>all nations</u>: **and Jerusalem shall be**

trodden down of the GENTILES (those who are not Israelites), until the times of the Gentiles be fulfilled."

Has the world been tricked to believe that the White Europeans are "Jews" and thus God's chosen people?

Deuteronomy 28:68 **"And the Lord will bring thee into Egypt (meaning bondage) again with ships."**

What does this mean? Were the Israelites brought into Egypt for a second run of slavery? Who would waste the time and resources to bring the Israelites from Israel right next door to Egypt when all throughout the bible people crossed over Israel into Egypt on foot? Did the Romans, Greeks or Persians take the Israelites to Egypt in Huge Sail Boats or Trading Ships? Where is this recorded? And how many Israelites did they take? What Tribes were they from? How many Israelites were on each ship? What year did this happen? All of these questions are unanswered because Deuteronomy 28:68 is talking about future prophecy.

The only thing that separates Egypt from Israel today is a Giant Fence created by the Israeli Government. Prior to this, anyone could walk from Egypt into Israel just as the Children of Israel did thousands of years ago. Surely having Israelites walk from Israel to Egypt would be most cheaper than spending money on a fleet of ships to take Israelites only a couple of miles on boats. I'm also sure the Romans boats were not the size of Carnival Cruise Ships today. **The average occupancy of a standard Cruise ship is 2,000-3,000 passengers**. The population of the city **Tel Aviv** in Israel boasts a whopping **411,000 people**. This is only one city, so if even if the Israelites were all hiding in one city it would take over 100 Cruise-type Ships to transport 400,000 Israelites on ships from Israel to Egypt. I doubt the Romans or Greeks had 100 ships the size of modern day Cruise Ships to transport the Black Israelites back to Egypt.

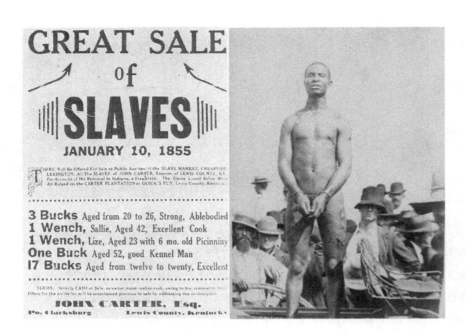

Deuteronomy 28:68 **"Thou shalt see it no more again: and there ye shall be sold unto your enemies for bondmen and bond women, and no man shall buy you."**

If you pay close attention to end of this verse it doesn't make any sense but yet it is in our King James Bible. Why would a slave be sold unto his enemies only to have no one buy him/her? A slave is bought by his slavemaster. That's what makes him/her a slave. This is because the word "**buy**" in this verse is really in "Old English" meant to say "**save**" or "**redeem**".

- **Redeem =** to buy or pay off; buy back, clear by payment, recover, or save.

It is evident that the Black Hebrew Israelites that were sold into slavery were not saved, nor did they have their freedom bought back (**i.e. redeemed**). This was part of the punishments/curses of Israel that God set on them for not obeying his commandments for thousands of years.

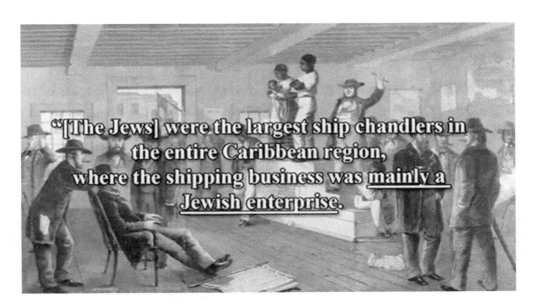

"[The Jews] were the largest ship chandlers in the entire Caribbean region, where the shipping business was mainly a Jewish enterprise.

It is essential to comprehend the Seaport "**Slave Port**" of Newport, Rhode Island. It is important in order to recognize the Jewish involvement in the Slave commerce. There was a period when it was commonly referred to as **'The Jewish Newport-World Center of Slave Commerce**.' At this time, there were in North America **Six Jewish Slave-Trading communities: Newport, Charleston, New York, Philadelphia, Richmond, and Savannah**. There were also many other Jews, scattered over the entire East Coast (**many took on Gentile last names like Johnson, Smith, Rivers**). New York held first place and Newport, Rhode Island held second place.

Here is a quote:

"In an 80-year period, people in Rhode Island got rich" from the slave trade. Jamestown was home to the last known slave in Rhode Island. "No one would ever think that,"

Ray Rickman, former President of the Rhode Island Black Heritage Society.

Slavery was everywhere in Rhode Island, Rickman says. Slaves worked on South County farms and in the mansions in Newport. But it was the slave trade that was the "**number one financial source**" for Rhode Island from 1720 to 1807.

The slave trade started in Rhode Island with the trade of spirits (Liquor): Rhode Islanders would manufacture rum, which they would ship to Africa and sell or trade for slaves. "Rhode Islanders were really good at making rum," he says.

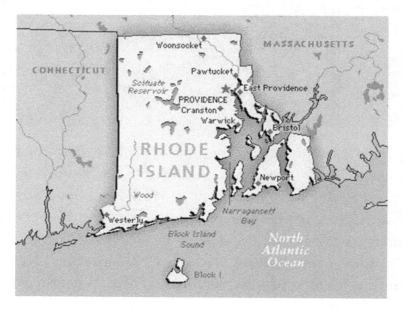

Rhode Islanders would also transport the slaves in the Caribbean and the southern colonies, which later became states, where the slaves would be sold or traded for sugar cane. "They would fill the boat with sugar" that was brought home to the Ocean State to make the rum, Rickman says. It was a trading triangle, he says. Slaves were packed below decks on the ships and many became sick and died. Their treatment was brutal and inhuman. All for some Liquor.

Many Rhode Island residents were involved in the slave trade. There were "16 or 17 rum factories" in the state. "Newport had six".

Fact 1: In American cities with a strong "**Black community**", non-black business owners typically set up liquor stores because they know that poverty typically goes hand in hand with "**substance abuse**". In this case "**Liquor**" is the substance. After the liquor store is established a "**Wing Shack**" or a "**Bar**" is next. The new trend in Black communities is for "Arabs or Whites" to open up a "**Chicken Wings establishment**". During the day, these **Wing Shacks** sells "**Chicken Wings**", other types of snack foods, beverages and liquor. Throw in some flat screen T. V's with sports channels playing 24/7 and the business owner is guaranteed to sell enough wings to pay the rent for the building in one day, at best a week. But they have figured out another way to make **MORE** money off Blacks **WITH CHICKEN WINGS AND LIQUOR.** At 9:30pm many of these "Chicken Shacks" are clearing out the dining room area and are turning their "Chicken Shacks" into a "**Night Club**". To capitalize off of Blacks and our "consumerism habits" they charge a $5 cover charge to get in, they offer "all-night" wings with an upcharge from 79 cents/wing to $1.00/wing from 10 pm-2am, over-priced liquor shots, Hip-Hop/Jamaican music and now the non-black business owner is at home with his family making more money while Blacks party the night away, spending more money on his liquor or wings.......till 2am! These "Chicken Shack-turned Clubs" can rake in an easy $450 an hour on wings alone! So imagine how much these businesses are making if they charge $10-$12 for shots of liquor which they buy at wholesale for cheap.

Fact 2: New York was also the main source of Kosher meat, supplying the North American settlements, then the West Indies and also South America. Newport also became the great trade harbor of the East Coast of North America. There, vessels from other ports met, to exchange commodities. Newport, as previously mentioned, represented the foremost place in the commerce of rum, whiskey, and liquor dealings. **And to conclude, it finally became the Main Center of Slave dealings.** It was from this port that the ships left on their way across the ocean, to gather their Black human (Israelite) cargo and then derive great sums of money in exchange for them.

An authentic, contemporary report, based on authority, indicates that of 128 Slave ships that unloaded in Charleston, within one year, 120 of these were undersigned by Jews from Newport and Charleston by their own name. About the rest of them, one can surmise, although they were entered as Boston, Norfolk, Baltimore, their real owners were similarly the Jewish slave dealers from Newport and Charleston.

The simple question is, "**How can the European Jews and Sephardic Jews be scattered into all nations as captives if they were the actual "Slavemasters/Captors?"** This proves that they are not the descendants of the Biblical Israelites. When will we wake up?

CHAPTER 14

KNOW THYSELF AND ALSO YOUR SWORN ENEMIES (CAIN & EDOM). WHERE ARE THEY AT?

"To be ignorant of what occurred before you were born is to remain always a child. For what is the worth of human life, unless it is woven into the life of our ancestors by the records of history?"

Marcus Tullius Cicero (Roman Statesman, orator 106 B.C.-43 B.C.)

Since releasing the Books "**Hebrews to Negroes**" and "**Hebrews to Negroes 2: Volume 1**", many Christians have been "**awakened**" to the truth. Satan desires mankind to be in darkness, believing a "lie" that will work towards his goal. Unfortunately, the Bible foretold that we would be deceived by Satan, but that we would eventually receive the Truth. The bible says that "**Knowledge will increase in the last days**" and that people of all ages would start having visions/dreams from God in regards to what is to come upon the world. One of the biggest lies of history, was orchestrated by the "Children of the Tares" (aka. The Wicked One) and Edom. The Gentiles of this world driven by Satan used the words of Black Israelite Prophets to their advantage to sway mankind from the **TRUTH**, using false religions (**Islam, Kemetism-Egyptian Religion**) and "Man-made" doctrines (**Modern Judaism-Talmud/Kaballah**). The Covenant of God with man was given to Isaac and his seed only (**Jacob-Children of Israel**). This is supported in the Torah (Bible) and the Quran.

Genesis 17:19 "And God said, Sarah thy wife shall bear thee a son indeed; and thou shalt call his name **ISAAC**: and I will establish my **COVENANT** with him for an **EVERLASTING** covenant, and with his seed after him."

The Muslim Quran even states this! So why are the Arabs constantly fighting and warring with the European/Sephardic Jews? If they were

333

obedient to Allah you would think they would embrace the descendants of Isaac and Jacob. Maybe they are not "embracing" them because they too know that the people in Israel are just "**imposters**" posing to be "**God's Chosen People.**"

Sura 29:27 (Quran) "And We gave him **ISAAC** and **JACOB** and placed in his descendants **PROPHETHOOD AND SCRIPTURE**. And We gave him his reward in this world, and indeed, he is in the Hereafter among the righteous."

Deuteronomy 18:15-16 "I will raise them up a Prophet from among their brethren, like unto thee, and will put my words in his mouth; and he shall speak unto them all that I shall command him. And it shall come to pass that whosoever will not hearken unto my words which he shall speak in my name, I will require it of him."

Muslims like to say that this scripture is about Muhammad, but we already saw from the Bible and their Quran that Muhammad, a supposed descendant of Ishmael, cannot be a prophet because prophethood was not given to Ishmael's seed. **Nowhere in the Arabic Quranic Sura 29:27 does it list the name of Ishmael. It doesn't matter what version of the Quran you read....Ishmael is not listed. Prophethood was given to Isaac's seed**. The Covenant God made with Isaac was destined for Jacob and the Israelite prophets to come. In the verse, "**Brethren**" means kinfolk or "**brothers**" which in this case is someone along the Israelite lineage. This person ultimately was **Yahusha (Jesus)** even though many other prophets came in-between paving the way from the Son of God. Yahusha (Jesus) combined the office of prophet, High Priest of God, leader, and deliverer. Both Moses and Yahusha (Jesus) were prophets in their own right. The both were delivered from death as an infant. They both performed miracles. The both were leaders and both were willing to die for the sins of others. Moses offered to die, if necessary, to forgive the sins of the Israelites he was leading. God however, refused Moses offer because Yahusha was the one that was going to die for the sins of all mankind, so that we can get to the father through him.

Exodus 32:31-33 "And Moses returned unto the Lord, and said, Oh, this people have sinned a great sin, and have made them gods of gold. Yet now, if thou wilt forgive their sin-; and if not, **BLOT ME**, I pray thee, out of thy book which thou hast written. And the Lord said unto Moses, Whosoever hath sinned against me, him will I blot out of my book (Book of Life)".

As natural enemies of Seth and Israel, the descendants of Cain and Edom are going to do everything they can to destroy the Children of Israel, including distorting the teachings which were revealed to them by God. They started by infiltrating the Temple and Levitical Priesthood (**Jeremiah 35:1-19**). These people were called the Rechabites, the sons of the Kenites (**many say Cainites**). They took up the "**Nazarite Vow**" which helped them gain admission into taking over some of the duties of the Levities. Jeremiah was impressed by their customs and commandments given to them by their father Jonadab (Jeremiah 35:1-19). After the invasion of Israel by King Nebuchadnezzar and his Babylonian army these Rechabites took over the duty of being "**scribes**", which was an occupation carried out by only the Levites. This allowed an "**unholy**" seed to change or delete things in the scriptures as if it was allowed by God. But this was all in accordance with "**God's Perfect Plan**" for the Israelites.

1 Chronicles 2:55 "And the families of the scribes which dwelt at Jabez; the Tirathites, the Shimeathites, and Suchathites. These are the Kenites that came of Hemath, the father of the house of Rechab."

Fact 1: European Convert-Jew Benjamin of Tudela, who lived during the 1100's spoke about 100,000 people calling themselves Rechabites living in Babylon (Iraq) whose tradition includes abstaining from wine and meat. Could these be the "Mizrahi Jews" of today?

Fact 2: Benjamin Tudela visited Kollam (Quilon) on the Malabar Coast and wrote "Throughout the island, including all the towns thereof, live several thousand Israelites. The inhabitants are all black, and the Jews also. The latter are good and benevolent. They know the law of Moses and the prophets, and to a small extent the Talmud (Gemara/Mishnah) and Halacha. Benjamin Tudela described them as being black like the Black Jews living in Portugal/Spain with the Moors. Today, these Indian Jews are known as the descendants of Cochin Jews/Bene Israel Jews of India. The supposedly had their DNA studied which showed them in the same cluster as the Ethiopian Jews although they were believed to be closer to Yemenite Jews.

The Rechabites belonged to the Kenite clan and according to the bible they were eventually absorbed into Israel in 900 B.C. during the time of King Solomon/King David. Some researchers say that these Rechabites intermarried with the Levites since the Bible states that Jethro, Moses father-in-law was a Kenite. The Rechabites tagged along with the Israelites during their journey from Egypt into Canaan and even shared in the spoil that the Kings of Israel (David) would get from defeating different nations (Canaanites/Edomites).

1 Samuel 15:6 "And Saul said unto the Kenites, Go, depart, get you down from among the Amalekites (Grandson of Esau), lest I destroy you with them: for ye shewed kindness to all the children of Israel, when they came up out of Egypt. So the Kenites departed from among the Amalekites."

Fact 1: In 1839 the Reverend Joseph Wolff, found in **Yemen**, near **Sana'a**, a tribe claiming to be the descendants of **Jehonadab** (The father of the Rechabites). Also in the late 1800's a Bedouin tribe was found near the Dead Sea (**Israel/Jordan**) who professed to be descendants of Jehonadab. The Rechabites were considered to be "**Children of Cain**" as their descendants, the "**Kenites**" were believed to be named after Cain. 19th century German Lutheran Bible critic Heinrich Friedrich Wilhelm Gesenius believed this because the Hebrew name for Kenite,

"Qeni/Qini" (Strong's #7017) is derived from Hebrew Strong's #7014 "Qayin".   British Assyirologist and linguist Reverend Archibald Henry Sayce also believed the Kenites were descendants of Cain because the word "**Kenite**" or "**Qeni**" is identical to the Aramaic meaning of "**smith**" which the Cainite children of Tubal-Cain were known to be good at (**Metal-workers in iron, bronze, and gold**). Also in the Bible (Judges 4:11) it states that the Kenites went to live in Northern Canaan.

Fact 2: There seem, in fact to have been two branches of the Kenites – one having **Edomitish**, the other **Israelitish**, affinities. Records of the former (**Edomitish**) **Kenites** still exist in inscriptions found in the Sinai Peninsula, and in the Arabian histories. There is still a tribe called **Benu-l-Qain** (often contracted into Belqein) in the Belqa (the ancient land of Ammon-now Jordan); and it would seem that there is an Arab tribe in the Arabia Petraea (Jordan, Southern Canaan, Sinai Peninsula, North Arabia), eastward of Kerak, which traces itself to **Heber the Kenite**, and goes by the name of **Yehud Chebr**, though it now denies any connection with the Jews.

So the big question is, "**Where did the Rechabites/Kenites go?**" The Kenites lived in Edomite mountain territory with the Amalekites for a long time until they left them and linked up with the Israelites. **So was the Kenites half the seed of Cain and half the seed of Esau?** If we assume that Edom and Cain's seed is still alive we must also assume that the physical descendants of Children of Israel are still alive. We know this because Revelations 7:4-8 tells us that 12,000 Israelites from each tribe are sealed to be included in the 144,000 during the Tribulation period.

Revelation 7:4 "And I heard the number of them which were sealed: and there were sealed **an hundred and forty and four thousand** of all the tribes of the children of Israel."

But who are the people living today amongst the "Real Israelites/Jews" who call themselves Jews and they are not?

Revelation 2:9 "I know thy works, and tribulation, and poverty, (but thou art rich) and I know the blasphemy of them which say they are Jews, and are not, but are the Synagogue of Satan."

So who are the people out in the world who are the fake Jews? Where are these Rechabites/Kenites. Even more, where are the Nethinims and where is Edom?

God has a plan for Edom and it fits into the persecution-identity hijack of the Israelites. The **Book of Malachi** (1:1-5), the **Book of Jeremiah** (49:7-22), the **Book of Ezekiel** (25:12-14) and the entire **Book of Obadiah** tells the final fate of Edom. The sins of Esau per the bible were passed down to his children and children's children.

Ezekiel 25:12-14 "Thus saith the Lord God; **Because that Edom hath dealt against the house of Judah by taking vengeance, and hath greatly offended, and revenged himself upon them; Therefore thus saith the Lord God; I will stretch out mine hand upon Edom, and will cut off man and beast from it;** and I will make it desolate from Teman; and they of Dedan shall fall by the sword. And I will lay my vengeance upon Edom by the hand of my people Israel: and they shall do in Edom according to mine anger and according to my fury; and they shall know my vengeance, saith the Lord God."

So we know that the Kenites/Rechabites were not of Israel but managed to finesse their way into the Israelites camp. **But what about the Nethinims?** Who were these guys? The "**Nethinims**" appear mysteriously after the Babylonian captivity of the Israelites. These "Nethinims" could not show their fathers house or their seed; nor could they prove that they were Israelites.

Ezra 2:58-59 "**All the Nethinims**, and the children of Solomon's servants, were three hundred ninety and two. And these were they which went up from Tel-melah, Tel-harsha, Cherub, Addan, and Immer: **BUT THEY COULD NOT SHEW THEIR FATHER'S HOUSE, AND THEIR SEED, WHETER THEY WERE OF ISRAEL:"**

When Ezra led the Southern Israelite tribes exiled in Babylon to Jerusalem there were no Levites to be found. But these Nethinim people were mysteriously on the scene, without their Levite masters.

Ezra 8:15 "And I gathered them together to the river that runneth to Ahava; and there abode we in tents three days: and I viewed the people, and the priests, **AND FOUND NONE OF THE SONS OF LEVI.**"

So Ezra had the "**Nethinims**" go back to Babylon (Iraq) to look for some of the lost Levite men.

Ezra 8:17-18 "And I sent them with commandment unto Iddo the chief at the place Casiphia, and I told them what they should say unto iddo, and to his brethren the **Nethinims, at the place Casiphia, that they should bring unto us ministers for the house of God.** And by the good hand of our God upon us they brought us a man of understanding, of the sons of Mahli, the son of Levi, the son of Israel, and Sherebiah, with his sons and his brethren, eighteen;"

The Mystery behind the Kenites and the Nethinims could be in fact a hidden message. Similar to the message of the **parable of the wheat and the tares** (Matthew 13:24-30). The Tares were of the "**Wicked One**" in reference to Cain and Satan. The Wheat was "**God's Children**". God told the Israelites not to intermarry with any foreign nations that were in the land of Canaan. This included the Kenites, Edomites and Canaanites. Wheat and Tares look almost identical when they grow together, but the tares have to be separated from the wheat during the harvest once they are full grown. If the Kenites and Nethinims were in fact descendants of the sons of Cain then this would explain why they stayed close to and wanted to infiltrate the different tribes of Israel, including the priestly Levite tribe. This would explain why they would work their way to being the scribes of the Israelites and servants of the Levites. They could then institute and change the **doctrines of the Most High God** to the Kenite (Cainite) **doctrines of men**. They would do exactly what they needed to do to (**not drink wine**) in order to fit in. But this was all bible prophecy. Just as Cain named his sons similar names to the sons of Seth, the Kenites would also adopt similar Israelite names (**Enoch-Enoch, Lamech-Lamech, Methushael-Methuselah**), thus blending in with the Israelites. The Israelites would also intermarry with these Kenites, Nethinims, Canaanites, Egyptians, and Ethiopians that they dwelled with. During the time Jesus walked the earth, the face of Judea and the face of the people in the Temple had changed. Many of the Children of Israel were scattered, leaving only a remnant of Israelites left. Other Gentile nations living in Judea calling themselves "**Jews**" because of their religious conversion to Judaism had adopted new laws and religious practices that went against the commandments/laws of the Most High. These nations included the Greeks, Assyrians, Romans, Edomites, Kenites, Nethinims, Babylonians, and so on. The Gentile Kenite scribes, the Gentile Nethinim Levite servants and the other Gentile peoples in Israel changed things according to their ways, which was that of Satan. The new laws and religious practices would be a combination of all the pagan religious practices learned in Babylon as well as other pagan religions from other nations such as Greece (**ex. Hellenistic Judaism**).

Fact: **Antiochus IV "Epiphanes" (Above)** was a **Greek King** of the Hellenistic Seleucid Empire. He died in 164 B.C. Mattathias the Hasmonean during the time Antiochus IV started the revolt against the Greek "Hellenistic" Seleucid Empire. Mattathias's Greek son, **Judas Maccabee** would be the one who would win the battle defeating the Seleucids. Shortly after the Hasmonean-Maccabean rule, less than 100 years before the birth of "Christ", Herod the Great and his Edomite family were declared the "**Kings of Israel/Judea**" or "**King of the Jews**". The Book of Maccabees was not written in Hebrew because it was not a "**God Inspired Book**". There were no "real" Hebrew Israelite Prophets around to write the Book of Maccabees. So how could the people in Judea during 150 A.D. be witnessed to correctly if they didn't have a Prophet that was an Israelite to witness to them? Thus the Book of Maccabees by many was just a "**historical book**", especially to **Protestant Martin Luther**. The Book of Maccabees is mostly a book about Greek Jewish converts who had enough zeal to fight their Greek and Roman governments in defense of their religion, "Judaism". When the Edomites were in power in around 50 B.C., nothing bad was bestowed on them. They did not experience any of the "**Curses of Israel**". They didn't have the "**Ark of the Covenant**" and they didn't even have real Israelite Aaronite "**High Priests**". Edom at this time was known strictly as "**Jews**" and not **Edom**. They followed Judaism to a tee. Antiochus IV made the **Greek Gentiles** and the Greeks who converted to Judaism (**called Jews**) worship Greek gods, stop circumcision and even abolish the Sabbath.

This is why Paul states "**Neither Jew nor Greek**" and not "**Neither Jew nor Arabian**" or "**Neither Jew nor Elamite**" when talking about Salvation in regards to being "one" in Christ Jesus. All the people he was talking to were mostly Greeks or proselyte Jews. **Paul knew very well that a Greek or a Roman (Flavius Josephus) were not of the "physical bloodline" of Abraham.** Judea at the time consisted of pagan Greeks (**still loving Zeus and the family**) and converted Jews (**Greeks/Edomites**).

Galatians 3:28-29 "There is **neither Jew nor Greek**, there is neither bond nor free, there is neither male nor female: for ye are all one in Christ Jesus. And if ye be Christ's, then are ye Abraham's seed, and heirs according to the promise."

They Gentile Greeks sacrificed unclean meet (pig) in the God-less Temple without the Ark of the Covenant. During the time of the Apostle Paul and the Christ, they knew these pagan practices were still going on. Paul knew that ever since 300 B.C. the Greeks had settled into Israel, keeping their former Greek religions. They were called "**Gentiles**". Paul also knew that there were "**Jews**" in Judea, but that they were proselytes and not "**REAL ISRAELITES.**" Paul and the 1st Century Apostles knew according to the Tanakh, the Samaritans had long been occupying the land of the Northern 10 Tribes of Israel since 700 B.C. This is the reason why Yahusha (Jesus) told his disciples to not go into Samaria, **BUT GO INTO THE LOST HOUSE OF ISRAEL**.

Matthew 10:5-6 "These twelve Jesus sent forth, and commanded them, saying, Go not into the way of the Gentiles, and into any city **OF THE SAMARITANS ENTER YE NOT**: but go rather to the **LOST SHEEP OF THE HOUSE OF ISRAEL.**"

This was during the 1st century A.D. But there is more. See for yourself:

*"That country is also called Judea, and the people **Jews**; and **this name** is given also to as many as embrace **THEIR RELIGION** (Judaism), though of **OTHER NATIONS**. But then upon what foundation so good a governor as Hyrcanus (grandson of Matthias patriarch of the Maccabees, a family of Judahite patriots of 2nd and 1st centuries B.C). Took upon himself to compel these Idumeans (Edomites) either to become Jews (**BY RELIGION**) or to leave their country, deserves great consideration. I suppose it was because they had long ago been driven out of the land of Edom, and had seized on and possessed the Tribe of Simeon (the land not the people), and all the southern part of the land of the Tribe of Judah, which was the peculiar inheritance of the worshippers of the **True God** without idolatry....."*

Flavius Josephus

*(**Note**: Proof that the Jews in that time were simply Judaism converts from other nations like Greece or Rome).*

Anybody that practiced the religion of the Gentile Pharisees (Judaism) were considered "**Jews**"! This means that the term "**Jew**" was not associated with the Hebrew Israelites or 12 tribes of Israel!

Let's look at this "**Neither Jew nor Greek**" scripture again that Christians typically give in response to why does it matter if Blacks are the Real Hebrew Israelites of the bible. I usually ask people the question:

"If you were given up for adoption by your parents at an early age, wouldn't you as you got older feel a "void" in your life until you actually met them face to face?

I also pose this question:

"If a child slave is separated from his mother and father during slavery but finds out from someone newly brought to that child's plantation that his/her parents are at a plantation nearby, wouldn't that child as he got older try to escape to find his parents?

343

But the bigger questions is, "Since when does the **TRUTH** not matter"? When is a **"Lie"** important but the **"Truth"** not important?

For **"African-Americans"**, **"Afro-Latinos (those claiming African ancestry"**, **"Caribbean Blacks"** and those who are the product of slavery/invasion it does matter who we are as a people. Our history does not stop at 1619 A.D. with slavery in Africa or when the Europeans invaded our country.

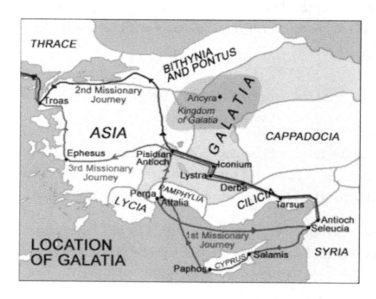

Galatians 3:28 "There is neither **Jew nor Greek**, there is neither bond nor free, there is neither male nor female: for ye are all one in Christ Jesus." Galatia was a Kingdom in Turkey, the Land of the Romans, Greeks and Turks. Many of the people in Galatia, Greece and Roman converted to "Judaism" during this time. Prior to Christ, other nations in close vicinity to Israel had people decided to leave their pagan religions to convert to Judaism. The Pharisees were good for converting others to their man-made form of "Judaism". Prime example is the **Greek** Maccabean Jews (who converted the Edomites to Judaism), **Roman**-Jewish Historian Flavius Josephus and the many Gentiles

(from different countries) who were described as proselytes in the Pauline Book of Acts.

Matthew 23:15 "Woe unto you, scribes and Pharisees, hypocrites! **For ye compass sea and land to make one proselyte**, and when he is made, ye make him twofold more the child of hell than yourselves."

Acts 21:27 "And when the seven days were almost ended, the **Jews which were of Asia (Minor)**, when they saw him in the temple, stirred up all the people, and laid hands on him."

Acts 2:10 "Phrygia, and Pamphylia, in Egypt, and in the parts of Libya about Cyrene, and **STRANGERS OF ROME (ITALY)**, **Jews** and **proselytes**.

*Fact: Books of Paul - Pauline Epistles (**letters**) to the Gentiles in Asia Minor (Greeks, Turks, Romans, Syrians).*

- *Thessalonians (Greece)*
- *Corinthians (Greece)*
- *Galatians (Turkey)*
- *Romans (Rome, Italy)*
- *Ephesians (Turkey)*
- *Philippians (Greece)*
- *Colossians (Greece)*
- *Philemon*
- *Timothy*
- *Titus*
- *+/- Hebrews (some say Paul wrote the Book of Hebrews).*

In the Hebrew Bible, in Daniel 11:2 and Daniel 8:21-22 the Hebrew Strong's word #3120 "**Yavan**" is used for today's country of Greece. **Javan was the son of Japheth, the son of Noah**. Kittim (Chittim) was always associated with Rome, and the Italians in ancient Hebrew texts (**Book of Jasher and Jubilees**). Togarmah was associated with Armenia, the Turks, Kurds and so on. Togarmah was the son of Gomer, who was the son of Japheth. Paul could've went anywhere else in the world but he was chosen to preach the Gospel of Christ to the "**Isles of the Gentiles**." Who was chosen to go preach the Gospel of Christ to the Egyptians? St. Mark was. Mark was not listed as an "**Apostle of the Gentiles**". St. Thomas was the one who brought the Gospel of Christ to the Hebrew Israelites in South India (Kerala, India). He was not known as a "**Saint to the Gentiles**."

Alexander the Great   **Seleucus I Nicator**

At this time the Jewish converts to Judaism were plentiful as well as those regular Greeks who were just "**new**" residents of Judea. After all, Greek **Alexander the Great** (Ptolemaic empire) and the Greek **Seleucus I Nicator** (Seleucid Empire) did control a wide area of land, including Israel. So Paul wasn't referring to an "**Israelite**" in **Galatians 3:28** when he made this comment to the Kingdom of Galatia because the majority of Israel was already scattered into the **FOUR CORNERS**.

Corinthians, Thessalonians, Colossians, Ephesians, Romans, Galatians, Timothy and Philippian, Titus, Philemon, Titus and Hebrews were all written mainly to the people in the "**Gentile Lands**" described in Genesis 10:1-5.

Galatia was a Kingdom in Modern turkey. Paul wrote the Book of Galatians to them as he was the designated "**Apostle to the Gentiles**". The Greeks lived in Turkey and also thought of themselves to be what the "**people of the lands**" were called. For this reason, the Greeks in Israel called themselves "**Judeans**". If they converted to Judaism, they called themselves "**Jews**". If they lived in Turkey/Syria they called themselves "**Syrians**". Greece (Thrace) was not too far from Turkey so it was easy for them to call themselves another name, simply based on their new home and new religion. The Ottoman Turks also stemmed from Turkey, the land of Togarmah, son of Gomer, **son of Japheth**. This is why their skin is white. It is also a known fact that the Samaritans that live in Northern Israel today are believed to be descendants of Semitic Arabs, Edom and the sons of Japheth (Turks/Kurds/Grecians) who converted to Judaism a long time ago and did not "fold" to Islamic conversion when the Ottoman Empire establish Muslim rule in Judea/Samaria. The Muslim Palestinians today are believed to be descendants of these Samaritans that did in fact fold to the pressure of "Muslim Rule" by converting from Judaism to Islam.

347

(**Left**) Syrian Noblemen 150 A.D. This is what the "Real" Syrians (Arameans-Sons of Aram) looked like. Notice the thick locks of the hair. (**Middle**) Ancient Syrian. This head bust in real life is depicted with **dark chocolate brown skin**. Why would any Syrian depict the people of Syria to have chocolate brown skin if they were originally white-skinned people? **It doesn't make sense!** Also notice the thick locks of the hair on his head and beard. (**Right**) President of Syria Bashar al-Assad who we all know does not have brown-black skin.

The Gentile and the Samaritans who were in Israel prior to Yahusha (Jesus Christ) had been living their whole life as "Jews" by conversion. How? They got their teaching from other Gentile Jews and learning from possible "Real Israelites" way back in the past (Assyrian invasion 700 B.C).

2 Kings 17:27 "Then the King of Assyria commanded, saying, Carry thither "**ONE**" of the **PREISTS** (Aaronite/Levite priests) whom ye brought from thence; and let them go and dwell there, and let him teach them the manner of the God of the land."

Fact: Even the Book of Maccabees admits the people of Israel were mostly Gentiles.

1 Maccabees 41:41-43 "Then the King (Antiochus) wrote to his **WHOLE KINGDOM** that all should be **ONE PEOPLE**, and that should give up their particular customs. **ALL THE GENTILES ACCEPTED THE COMMAND OF THE KING**. Many even from Israel gladly adopted his religion; they sacrificed to idols and profaned the Sabbath."

(**Above**) Bronze coin from 1st Century A.D. of Edomite "Herod Agrippa I". Herod Agrippa I in the Book of Acts imprisons Peter the Apostle and kills James, the son of Zebedee. The distinct feature of the Edomites were the typical "Long Nose" that some people associate with the Jews of today and Arabs. African-Americans and Africans typically do not have "Long pointy noses". The Hebrew Israelites mainly intermarried with the Black Sons of Ham in Africa. The Edomites intermarried with the Greeks, Romans, Turks, Kurds, and Arabs. According to the **Bible**, the **Apocrypha Books** and the Hebrew **Book of Jasher**, Edom (descendants of Esau) mixed his seed with the Arabs Ishmaelite's in addition to the European "White" nations of the Gentiles (i.e. Rome, Italy, Greece, Turkey, Kurdistan, Syria, and so on). For this reason, many Biblical scholars believe that the "Blood of Edom" flows through the veins of Ashkenazi Jews, Sephardic Jews,

Mizrahi Jews, Europeans and Modern Day Arabs. These are the same nations that participated in the "oppression" of the Bantus "Hebrew Israelites" in Africa and Arabia (i.e. Arab Slave Trade, Transatlantic Slave Trade). Edom has always been the sworn enemy of the Israelites and in the **Book of Obadiah** it states that Edom would inhabit the Land of the Israelites. So in essence, the Heathen and the Gentiles are the ones fully occupying the "Holy Land". Japheth and Edom have fully occupied the "Land of Shem" as told in the Bible. What is the Land of Shem? The Middle East, Asia Minor and Arabia.

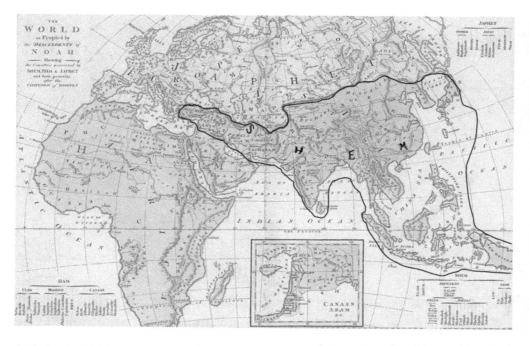

(**Above**) 1823 Map of the World according to Cartographer **Robert Wilkinson**. The Descendants of Shem was believed by the Ancients to be living in Turkey, Arabia, the Middle East, South Asia and the Pacific Islands. If you research the **Book of Jasher** and the **Book of Jubilees,** it will list the boundaries given unto Shem and his descendants. The Sons of Japheth and Edom are now living in the Lands of Shem as Kings-Rulers while the "**Brown indigenous people**" are usually at the bottom.

Genesis 9:27 "God shall **ENLARGE JAPHETH**, and he shall dwell in the tents of Shem; and let Canaan be their servant."

(Left) Herod Agrippa I, was the grandson of **"Herod the Great"**, son of **Antipater the Idumean** & his Arab wife **Cypros the Nabataean (Jordanian)**. Herod Agrippa's father was **"Aristobulus IV"**, the son of **Herod the Great** and his second wife, a Greek woman named **"Mariamne I"**. Mariamne I was a descendant of the Greek Maccabean Hasmonean Dynasty via her father **"Alexandros (Alexander of Judea)"**. **(Right)** An old depiction of **"Herod Agrippa II"**, the son of **Herod Agrippa I**. He is mentioned in Acts 25:13 and Acts 26:32. This depiction of Herod Agrippa II looks like your modern day **"Arab, Chaldean or Turkish Jew"**. The mixing of Edom with Japheth's seed is why the DNA (**Y-DNA, mtDNA**) of Arabs, Chaldeans and Jews point to a "Eurasian ancestry". **These people are essentially Europeans by stock (blood) who converted to Islam or Judaism over the last 1400-2300 years, which initially was the religion of the Black Arabs and Black Hebrew Israelites respectfully.** Wake Up People.

So the verses in **1 Maccabees 41:41-43** could imply that some of the remaining Israelites were also tricked into adopting the religion of the Greeks. We know that Yahusha's Disciples were Israelites (**i.e. Paul, Mark**) and they were in and around Israel during the time period of

Herod Agrippa (10 B.C.-44 A.D.). But the Bible says eventually the Gentiles would take full possession of Israel until the time of the Son of Man was at hand. The Bible describes it as their "**Day of Fulfillment**".

The word "**Fulfilled**" means "**to bring to an end**" or "**the achievement of something desired, promised, or predicted.**"

So if the bible says the Gentiles would rule until the "**Times of the Gentiles be Fulfilled**", this means that the Gentiles reign would come to an end eventually. So then the question becomes, "If the Jews in Israel are **Gentiles**, then were are the **Real Jews** at?" But the bible reveals another "**Piece of Information**" about the Israelites as to where they would be removed to.

Luke 21:24 "And they (Israelites) shall fall by the edge of the sword, and shall be **led away captive** into **ALL NATIONS**; and Jerusalem shall be trodden down (taken over) of the **GENTILES**, until the times of the Gentiles be fulfilled."

The message Yahusha Hamashiach made in Luke 21:24 is very clear. It means the white skinned Jews (Ashkenazi/Sephardic/Mizrahi) in Israel are the "**Gentiles**". This is the definition of an "**Imposter**". The real "Israelites" are **scattered into the four corners of the earth** by way of their ancestors being used as human cargo in the Slave Trades.

So for years the bible has had the truth about who the "**Real Israelites**" are and who the Gentiles are but we were blind to this mystery. However, the Jews themselves have been revealing this information to each other.

CHAPTER 15

MODERN DAY ISLAM AND MODERN DAY TALMUDIC JUDAISM: HOW IS IT DECEIVING BLACKS? WHAT IS THE TRUTH?

(Above) Medina is the 2nd most holiest site of Islam and is where Muhammad's house and burial place is located at (**Mosque of the Prophet**). It used to be called "**Yathrib**" before Muhammad's days and is located in West Saudi Arabia. Edomite Herod the Great's mother, Cypros was a Nabataean from Arabia (Modern day Jordan and North Arabia). Nabataean and Roman artifacts can still be found in Medina as these two groups of people occupied the area of Medina in ancient times. Edom in the Book of Jasher infused his bloodline with the people of Rome (Italy), even at one point being their leader over the Roman Empire. According to Arab theology scholar **Alfred Guillaume** (1888-1965 A.D.), the Arabs we see today are descendants of Greeks, Romans and Edomites by the history of the conquering nations who ruled Arabia prior to the birth of Muhammad. Alfred was well schooled

from the University of Oxford, the American University of Beirut, Lebanon and the University of Istanbul, Turkey. **He quotes:**

"At the dawn of Islam the Jews dominated the economic life of the Hijaz (Arabia). They held all the best land....at Medina they must have formed at least half the population. There was also a Jewish Settlement to the north of the Gulf of Aqaba...What is important is to note that the Jews of the Hijaz made many **PROSELYTES (OR CONVERTS)** among the Arab Tribesmen."

Alfred Guillaume, 19th Century Arab-Muslim Theologian

In the last half of the fifth century (450 A.D.), many Jewish converts (descendants of Greeks, Persians, Turks, Kurds, Romans, Edomites) fled from "religious" persecution to Arabia, swelling the Arab population there. But around the sixth century (500 A.D.), Christian writers report of the continuing importance of the Jewish community (Gentile converts according to Luke 21:24) **that remained in the Holy Land**. For the dispersed Arabian Jewish settlers, Tiberias in Judea was central. In the **Kingdom of Himyar (Yemen)** on the Red Sea's east coast in Arabia, "**conversion to Judaism of influential circles" was POPULAR**, and the Kingdom's rule stretched across "**considerable portions of South Arabia**." This was all prior to "Islam" even being a "religion". Once Islam was introduced to Arabia, Muhammad and his Muslim Arabs would clash with the Gentile Jews, including the Real Black Jews (Lemba Jews, certain Yemeni Jews). Many of the real Gentile Jews would convert to Islam, while many of the "Real Black Jews" with Black Semitic Blood would migrate to Yemen or cross over into Africa from Arabia (Eritreans/Amhara people) or Yemen (Lemba Jews).

Note: The reason why we see the highest proportion of the so called **"Semitic" Y-DNA J1 Haplogroup gene"** in Arabs with Brown-Black skin is because the original descendants of Shem and Eber were "Black-looking people". **Yemenite people, Black Palestinians, Brown-**

skinned Iraqis, Qataris, Omanis, (Khartoum) Sudanese and the Negev Bedouins of South Israel are for the most part "brown-skinned" people that exhibit this "J1c" gene in HIGH PERCENTAGES (more than Sephardic, Ashkenazi and Mizrahi Jews). But these people are not calling themselves "Jews". The descendants of Joktan (son of Eber), the Moabites, Ammonites, Ishmaelite's, and the Keturahites were all "Hebrews" by classification (sons of Eber). Therefore, they were "Black" in the appearance of their skin color, like the Hebrew Israelites who did most of their intermixing with the very dark-skinned Sons of Ham. We know that the Jews in Arabia were Black because the Lemba Jews came from Arabia and Yemen (Sana'a). They came into Africa already practicing all the Jewish customs and claiming to be Jews who left Israel in B.C. times. They admitted to their migration from Arabia to Yemen (Arabia Felix/Himyar) once Islam started and the Arabs started to persecute them. They eventually got pressured so much from the Arabs that they had to leave Yemen for Africa. But these Lemba Jews look like AFRICANS AND NOT YOUR TYPICAL ARAB! Correction, they don't look like your typical white-skinned Arab in Saudi Arabia or the Middle East. The Lemba Jews carry a higher percentage of the Y-DNA "J1c" Haplogroup gene than most Arabs in the Middle East or Arabia. They also carry on half of their genome the Bantus Y-DNA "E1b1a" like Nigerians, Ghanaians, African-Americans and Caribbean Blacks. If you research the Y-DNA of Yemenite people today using the "Family Tree DNA-Yemen Project" you will still see the "E1b1a/E-M2" Y-DNA Haplogroup found in Yemen men living in the cities of Hadramout, Shabwah, Al Bayda, Marib, Ibb, Dhamar, Sa'dah, Sana'a, and Dhofar. But what is "Negro" E1b1a Y-DNA doing in Arabia and Yemen? What's the cause for this? Well, these are descendants of the Hebrew Israelites that were scattered into Arabia/Yemen.

HISHĀM IBN-AL-KALBI
TRANSLATED BY NABITH AMIN FARIS

The Book of Idols

Being a Translation from the Arabic of
the Kitāb Al-Aṣnām

(**Left**) Arabic Goddess "**Al-Uzza**", who was worshipped in Arabia before Muhammad was born. Somehow she and her sisters found their way into the Early Quran, probably read by the Umayyad Muslim Caliphate Arabs (661 A.D.-750 A.D.). She was known as the "**Mighty One**" and shrines to her can still be seen in North Arabia and Jordan. (**Right**) **The Book of Idols** (Arabic called "Kitab al-Asnam"), written by 7th century Arab Scholar Hisham Ibn Al-Kalbi (737 A.D.-819 A.D.), describes the many pagan gods and rituals of the Arabs (**pre-Muhammad**) which influenced Islam. It describes how paganism created the Kaaba stone in Mecca, not Abraham.

Noble Quran Sura An-Najm (The Star) 53:19-22

(**53:19-20**) "So have you considered **al-Lat and al-Uzza**? And **Manat**, the third- the other one?

Removed Satanic Verses- "These (al-Lat, al-Uzza and Manat) are the exalted cranes (intermediaries-mediators) whose intercession (worship) is to be hoped for."

(**53:21-22**) Is the male for you and for him the female? That, then is an unjust division.

It is a known fact that before Muhammad was born, the moon god "**Hubal**" or some would like to say "**al-Ilah**" had three goddess daughters: **al-Uzza, al-Lat and Manat**. Each of these goddesses had shrines near Mecca. According to the Quran in **Sura 17:73-75 and Sura 22:52-53** Satan tricked Muhammad into adding a verse in the Quran that told Muslim Arabs to worship these three pagan goddesses. However, Muhammad claimed later that he got a revelation from "**Allah**" or the **angel Gabriel** to remove the Satanic verses. Making revisions to religious scripture supposedly given from God or his angels for "**after-the-fact**" revelations was common with Muhammad as it was with Mormon Church founder **Joseph Smith**. It is said that over the course of 20+ years Muhammad would claim to have "**revelations**" that his scribe would write down (**since Muhammad was supposed to be illiterate**). Muslims does not teach this as do Muslims do not explain which one of Noah's 3 sons **dies** in the "Great Flood" in Sura 11:42-43 (**despite mentioning Alexander the Great (Japheth), Egyptians (Ham) and Abraham (Shem) in the Quran**). Despite worldwide history proving that Yahusha HaMashiach (Jesus Christ) was crucified, Muslims claim and promote the lie that it was a case of mistaken identity. Muslims don't explain how they teach that Abraham was told to sacrifice Ishmael when Ethiopian Jews (**whose Sabaean/Ge'ez language and culture pre-date the Arabic language**) all know in their "sacred texts" that Isaac was the one who Abraham was supposed to sacrifice at **Mount Moriah (Temple Mount)**. Even Mosaic pictures in Israel dating to 300 B.C. (**prior to the Arabic language and foundation of Islam**) depict Abraham about to sacrifice Isaac before he uses the "**Ram in the thicket**" as the alternative. Ishmael is **NOW WHERE** to be found.

Here in the Quran it shows that Satan tricked Muhammad (or the angel Gabriel) when Muslims claim their book is "**untampered**" and "**pure**".

Sura Al-haj (The Pilgrimage) 22:52-53 – Sahih International

"And We did not send before you any messenger or prophet except that when he spoke (or recited), **SATAN** threw into it (some misunderstanding). But Allah abolishes that which Satan throws in; then Allah makes precise his verses. **And Allah is knowing and Wise**.

357

That is so He may make what Satan throws in a trial for those within whose hearts is disease and those hard of heart. And indeed, the wrongdoers are in extreme dissension."

If Allah is **ALL-KNOWING AND WISE**, how did he allow Satan to trick Muhammad or Gabriel into reciting the wrong thing which would be placed in a Holy Book (Quran) for Muslims? Why did the Quran have to go through a "**revision**", deleting the Satanic verses, so that future Muslims couldn't see the mistake that Allah made when Satan got the best of him?

Fact: The **Kaaba stone** was used to serve as a shelter or containment unit for the pre-Islamic pagan idols prior to the birth of Muhammad. Muslims say that it is the first altar that Abraham build for God, but this is nowhere in the Hebrew Torah or the Hebrew Dead Sea Scrolls which pre-date the Quran by over thousands of years. Destroying Idols but leaving the "cuboid" stone allowed another way for pagans to worship their idols. There is also evidence in the history of Black Arab pagans that on the Kaaba stone was engraved the names of all the hundreds of pre-Islamic idols. It is said that for this reason that the "original" Kaaba was destroyed and it was only after the death of Muhammad that another cuboid stone was erected in its placed (**which follows pagan practices**). It is also said that for a while there was a cuboid structure without the "black stone" that the Muslims kiss. Over the years it is said that the "Black stone" was kidnapped and held for ransom or that many tried to destroy the stone because it represented pagan gods. Different stories state the stone was brought down to earth by Angels during the time of Adam and Eve while other stories say Abraham found it when building the Kaaba with his son Ishmael. Both stories are not supported in the old Hebrew Torah which predates the Quran for thousands of years. The question is, "If Allah is Master of the Universe, All-Knowing, Wise and his presence is EVERYWHERE then how can he be contained in pieces of stones? Even in the Quran it states not to pray or bow towards the East or the West. Even the place that Abraham was told to sacrifice Isaac (Temple Mount), and where

Muhammad was supposed to ascend to heaven, the Muslims bow and pray **AWAY FROM IT**. So in essence, they are praying to a black cube for no reason according to their Quran and the **BOOK** (Torah/Tanakh) of the Israelite Prophets whom according to the Quran are the **ONLY PROPHETS OF THE WORLD.**

Sura 29:27 (Al-Ankabut-The Spider)

"And We Gave to Him **ISAAC AND JACOB** and placed in his descendants **PROPHETHOOD** and **SCRIPTURE**. And We gave him his reward in this world, and indeed, he is in the Hereafter among the righteous."

THE BIBLE IS AGAINST STONE WORSHIP!

Deuteronomy 4:28 "And there ye shall serve gods, the work of **MEN'S HANDS, WOOD AND STONE**, which neither see, nor hear, nor eat, nor smell."

Deuteronomy 28:64 "And the Lord shall scatter thee among all people, from one end of the earth even unto the other; and there thou shalt serve other gods, which neither thou nor thy fathers have known, **EVEN WOOD AND STONE.**"

Ezekiel 20:32 "And that which cometh into your mind shall not be at all, that ye say, We will be as the **HEATHEN**, as the families of the countries, **TO SERVE WOOD AND STONE.**"

Habakkuk 2:19 "Woe unto him that saith to the wood, Awake; **TO THE DUMB STONE**, Arise, it shall teach! Behold, it is laid over with gold and silver, and there is no breath at all in the midst of it."

THE QURAN IS EVEN AGAINST BOWING AND PRAYING IN DIFFERENT DIRECTIONS (I.E. TO A STONE)!

Sura 2:177 Al-Baqarah (The Cow) Sahih International

"Righteousness is **NOT** that you turn your faces toward the **EAST OR THE WEST**, but true righteousness is in one who believes in Allah, the Last Day, the angels, the Book (Bible), and the prophets (Israelites) and gives wealth, in spite of love for it, to relatives, orphans, the needy, the traveler, those who ask for help, and for **FREEING SLAVES**; and who establishes prayer and gives zakah; those who fulfill their promise when they promise; and those who are patient in poverty and hardship and during battle. Those are the ones who have been true, and it is those who are the righteous."

PAGAN ARABIC GODDESSES: AL-UZZA, AL-LAT AND MANAT

So the goddess **Al-Uzza** was a major god to the Arabians and Nabataeans. They equated her with the older Greek goddess Aphrodite and the ancient Egyptian god "ISIS". A stone cube (like the Kaa'ba stone) in the city of **Ta'if** near Mecca was a sacred place for her worshippers. This proves Abraham and Ishmael did not build a black cuboid stone for the worship of God. This Black cuboid stone was to worship pagan false gods. Al-Uzza was called upon by the **Quraysh Tribe clan (SAME TRIBE AS MUHAMMAD)** for help and protection. The Qurayshites war cry often was:

"O people of Uzza, people of Hubal!"

According to the "**Book of Idols**" written by Hisham ibn al-Kalbi, the Quraysh tribe prior to Muhammad's birth used to circumambulate in a counterclockwise direction (like Muslims do) around the Kaa'ba back during the 6th-7th century and say:

"By al-Lat and al-Uzza, And al-Manat, the third idol besides. Verily they are al-gharaniq Whose intercession (worship) is to be sought."

Fact: In Judaism folklore, **Al-Uzza** was also used as a name associated with the angel of the "**All-seeing eye**" named **Metatron**, who is associated with **Satan** in the Occult world. In the **Books of Enoch** (3rd Book), the fallen demonic angel "**Semyaza**" was also named "**Ouza**", "**Azza**" and "**Uzza**". This angel was one of the angels that fell from heaven along with **Azazel** and **Lucifer**. They later (along with other fallen angels) breeded with the women of the earth. **Al-Uzza** has also been linked with the **Orion belt**, after which the Great Pyramids in Egypt are aligned with. The Orion Belt constellation is also the birthplace for **Osiris and Horus**. Wake Up Folks!

(**Left**) Bulls in Sudan (Ancient Nubia). (**Right**) Apis Bull worshipped in Atlantis and Egypt.

Ancient Nubia (**Sudan**) loved the Bull/Ox and the Nile River. It was the basis for the Egyptian **Hathor Cult** and Cattle burial rituals. Hathor was often depicted wearing cow horns and was believed to be the **Mother of Ra**, but in some stories was the daughter of Ra. But all of this surrounded with the Earth and the Cosmos (Stars/Planets) which was introduced to man by the Fallen Angels. The origin of this type of Planetary/Earth or so called "**Creation-worship**" came from no other person than Satan, the "Serpent". For this reason, the Nubian and Egyptian Pharaoh's wore crowns with serpents on the top. In Chapter 17 of the Book of the Dead it opens:

"I am Tem in rising. I am the only ONE. I came into being in NU. I am Ra who rose in the beginning (After Nu gave birth to Ra)."

The Le-MU-rians/Atlanteans prior to the "Great Flood" worshipped "MU" and the Apis Bull. The NU-BIANS worshipped "NU" and the Apis Bull. The Sumerians worshipped "A-NU" and the "A-NU-NAKKI" falcon gods. The Egyptians worshipped Hawthor, the apis bull (Crescent Moon and Sun) and the Falcon God Horus. The Muslims worship Allah and adorn the Crescent Moon and Star.

*Fact: The Nile was the beginning of all civilization. The **Basin Nabta Playa** in Nubia have stone Megaliths that pre-date Egypt. It is from the Nubians and the Sumerians that the Egyptians adopted their religion which would be the most Satanic religions of its time.*

Satan convinced the Egyptians and other civilizations to worship the **Apis Bull, the Sun, the Moon, the Stars, the Serpent and so on**. The Atlanteans who were Giants and Fallen Angels before the "**Great Flood**" worshipped the **Apis Bull** and the Sun like **PTAH**, the Creator God of Egypt. They did "**Abominable things**" and taught man to build Pyramids which influenced the people living in Central America, South America, Egypt, Canary Islands, India and so on. The Nubians also wore Pharaoh Egyptian crowns with the serpent on the front like Egypt. In Ancient Nubia (Sudan/Ethiopia) it was common to worship the **SUN, MOON AND THE STARS**. Per Deuteronomy 4:19, the Israelites were not supposed to worship or adorn any of these planetary bodies (Host of Heaven). When Menelik was born to King Solomon and Ethiopian Queen Sheba around 950 B.C. he sent Israelites back with Menelik to Ethiopia to teach them how to worship the **God of Israel** instead of his "**Creations**". This is why Israelites don't have that stuff. But Muslims have the "**Crescent Moon and Star**" at the top of every Mosque. The **Crescent Moon** is even on the "**Mecca Clock**" so when Muslims pray towards Mecca they are praying towards a **Crescent Moon**. But how long has Arabia and Africa been worshipping pagan stuff? The **Yeha Temple** in Northern Ethiopia/Eritrea (Abyssinia) is super old (700 B.C-400 B.C.). It is called the "**Great Temple of the Moon**". Built in **Sabaean** Style with Sabaean script (**which is similar to Eritrean Tigray, Ethiopian Amharic, Ethiopian Jewish Ge'ez**) it proves that before Christ and after, people were worshipping pagan gods. According to the history of the Yeha Temple, the people in Arabia and the Kingdom of Seba/Saba (Yemen) worshipped pagan gods with the **Crescent Moon and a Star** as their symbol, just like Muslims do today. So basically Satan changed the names of his pagan gods all the way from Mu, Nu, Ptah, Ra, Osiris, Horus, Zeus, Baal, Moloch, Jupiter, Shiva, Vishna, Khrisna to Allah. It's a shame how Blacks are deceived into believing in Horus and Allah in today's society. We are Israelites with a **LIVING GOD** and he has a **NAME** that was given to man in **Exodus 3:14-15** and **Genesis 4:26** (Pre-Flood). Not a title, like "Allah" or "HaShem". This is a trick of Islam and modern Judaism (Phariseeism). Think about it! Why would Satan ever give man a religion and tell man to worship the **TRUE GOD AND HIS NAME?** Because he is a deceiver and the Father of lies. Wake Up!

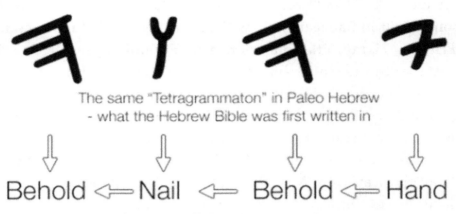

The same "Tetragrammaton" in Paleo Hebrew
- what the Hebrew Bible was first written in

Behold ⇐ Nail ⇐ Behold ⇐ Hand

Meaning of Paleo Hebrew symbols

(**Above**) The Name of God appears over 7,000 times in the Old Testament. In Ancient Hebrew it means: Behold the Hand, Behold the Nail! Who is that referring to? Yahusha Mashiach (Jesus Christ). Yahusha is God the Creator of all things.

Exodus 3:16 "And **GOD SAID** moreover unto Moses, Thus shalt thou say unto the Children of Israel, **YAHUAH** (i.e. The Lord) **ELOHIM OF YOUR FATHERS**, the **GOD OF ABRAHAM**, the **GOD OF ISAAC**, and the **GOD OF JACOB**, hath sent me unto you: **THIS IS MY SHEM** (name) **FOREVER**, and this is my **MEMORIAL UNTO ALL GENERATIONS**."

"**Memorial**" is defined as: something designed to **PRESERVE THE MEMORY OF A PERSON** as a monument or a holiday. In the content of this scripture, it is pertaining to the Creator.

Rabbinic Judaism prefers to use the word "**HaShem**" meaning "**The Name**" instead of the Creators real name. But according to the Torah, God's name is a "**Memorial**" and should be "**preserved throughout all generations**".

Do not fall for pagan worship like the Ancient Israelites did. Worship and Serve the Creator. The name of the Creator (Yahuah) was a Paleo-

Hebrew pictograph meaning that reveals that Christ is God. When read from Right-to-Left the Hebrew letters read "Yod-Hey-Uau-Hey" which means "**BEHOLD THE HAND, BEHOLD THE NAIL**". Was Allah nailed to the Cross/Tree? Was Horus? I rest my case. Did Horus perform any miracles that have been documented by other historians from other nations? Did Muhammad perform any miracles that were documented? Where is the tomb and dead body of Horus or Muhammad? Where are their bodies. Where are the tombs of the Egyptian writers of the Emerald Tablets, Book of the Dead, Pyramid Texts, Coffin Texts and The Contending's of Horus and Set? If Egypt had prophets, where are their prophecies? If Muhammad was a greater prophet than Jesus than why is Yahusha (Jesus) in the Quran coming back from heaven to defeat the Antichrist? If Muhammad ascended into heaven like Jesus and according to Muslims Yahusha (Jesus) is a "lesser prophet" why not the "**bigger prophet**" defeat the Antichrist (dajjal)? It's all based on lies and confusion, which Satan is good at.

CHAPTER 16

ARE TODAY'S JEWS AND ARABS SIMPLY EUROPEANS WHO CONVERTED TO JUDAISM OR ISLAM? THERE CAN ONLY BE ONE TRUE ARAB AND ONE TRUE JEW (ISRAELITE).

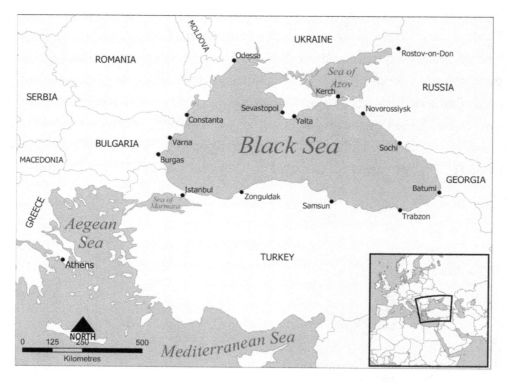

The European Ashkenazi Jews all come from Eastern Europe, Russia, Germany, Turkey and the Slavic countries. The Slavic countries are Russia, Belarus, Ukraine, Poland, Czech Republic, Slovakia, Slovenia, Croatia, Serbia, Bosnia, Macedonia and Bulgaria. Yiddish, is a "combo" language mixed with the language of the Gentile Jews European ancestry and Modern Hebrew.

Many of the Ashkenazi Jews who claim to be from the tribal bloodline of Judah, Benjamin or Levi are actually descendants of the ancient people of Khazaria in addition to the Caucasian races of Eurasia (i.e. Turkey, Greece, Italy/Rome, Eastern/Western Europe). The Khazarian people were a Turkish people. This is why the DNA of Turkish Jews, Turkish Muslims and Ashkenazi Jews are the same. Russian Bolshevik dictator "**Josef Stalin**" prohibited any research done in Russia to expose the "Khazar Empire" to be true. However, in 2008 "**Atil/Itil**", the capital city of the Khazarian Empire (750 A.D. to 969 A.D.) was found. Russian archaeologist "**Dmitri Vasiliev**" and his team found the lost Khazarian city including a Khazarian fortress at Samosdelka in Southern Russia. The fortress was **triangular-shaped** and had remnants of yurt-like huts which resembled the yurts made by **Turks**. They found evidence that the fortress was burned down, which they believed happened in the 10th Century by **Kievan Rus' prince Svyatoslav**. The people of Belarus, Ukraine and Russia all claim the Kievan Rus' as their ancestors.

Read **Vasiliev's** Russian article "Itil'-mechta (Na raskopkax drevnego tsentra Xazarskogo kaganata)" in Lekhaim, 10 (174), October 2006.

The Khazarian were also a heathen nation (like the Edomites) that adopted the religion of Judaism, thus taking on the name "**Jews**".

Here are some excerpts from the **Jewish Encyclopedia** and **Encyclopedia Britannica**:

1. "A people of **Turkish origin** whose life and history are interwoven with the very beginnings of the history of the Jews of Russia. The kingdom of the Chazars (Khazars) was firmly established in most of South Russia long before the foundation of the Russian monarchy by the Varangians (855 A.D.).

2. "Jews have lived on the shores of the Black and Caspian Seas since the first centuries of the common era. Historical evidence points to the region of the Ural as the home of the Chazars (Khazars). Among the classical writers of the Middle Ages they

367

were known as the "Chozars," "Khazirs," "Akatzir," "Akatirs," and in the Russian chronicles as "Khwalisses" and "Ugry Byelyye."

3. "The Chaghan (the king) of the Chazars and his grandees, together with a large number of his heathen people, embraced the Jewish religion."

4. "The most striking characteristic of the Khazars was the apparent adoption of Judaism by the khagan and the greater part of the ruling class in about 740 A.D. The circumstances of the conversion remain obscure, the death of their adoption of Judaism difficult to assess; but the fact itself is undisputed and unparalleled in central Eurasian history. A few scholars have even asserted that the Judaized Khazars were the remote ancestors of many European and Russian Jews."

(**Right**) Ancient Babylon (Iraq) man compared to former President of Iraq **Saddam Hussein (Left)**. As you can see by looking at the Ancient Babylonians of Iraq this guy looks more like a Black man than a white Arab. This Ancient Babylonian statue has **full lips and a wide nose**, typical of a "**Negro**". Why? Because the Babylonians, Sumerians and Chaldeans who all lived in Iraq were Semitic Black people with a mixture of also Cush. It's in the bible in regards to Nimrod (**founding cities Babel, Shinar, Erech (Uruk), Akkad, Calneh**) and is also in the Hebrew Book of Jasher which **JOSHUA** references in the Bible and the Ethiopic/Hebrew book of Jubilees. Nimrod was called the King of Shinar (**Sumer-Babylon**) and Assyria (Syria/Iraq/Turkey) was labeled in the bible as the "**Land of Nimrod**". Therefore, it was a synonym for the area known as Mesopotamia. Nimrod's (Cushite) seed was also grafted into the Hebrews. In the Book of Jubilees, Nimrod's daughter (Greek-Nebrod) "**Azurad**" was the wife of Eber and the mother of Peleg (also Joktan) from wince the Hebrew Israelites would come from. The Ethiopians compromised the Ancient Nubian empire of South Egypt and the land of Joktan in South Arabia/Yemen. This is why the Ethiopian Ge'ez language is similar to Ancient Semitic South Arabian language. Therefore, back in Ancient times the people of Mesopotamia and the Middle East were brown-black skinned people. The original Arab Ishmaelite's and Semites (Sons of Shem) were people of color. Not the color of the Modern Arabs we see today in the Middle East. The Iraqis, Iranians, Syrians, Jordanians and Saudi Arabians of today genetically are mostly Y-Haplogroup "J1" or "J2". Why is this? In Muslim culture the Muslim Arab man could have many women of other nations (i.e. marriage, slavery or polygamy). The offspring of the Black Arabs and "White women" would by default obtain half of each parent's DNA. This would attribute to the change in the skin color of the Arabs. It would also "Europeanize" their look. Because the Black Arabs Y-DNA was passed directly onto every son's "Y Sex Chromosome" the Arabs of today would still show their "J1" Y-DNA Haplogroup on genetic testing no matter how many generations forward would pass with not "1" Black Arab ancestor. However, because Muslim women were expected to be virgins before marriage and "strict" marriage rules enforced Muslim women to marry Muslim men, it is not surprising to see the Maternal "mtDNA" of Arabs today being linked to "Europeans". Therefore, as the "Black Arab" was faded out of Arabia and the Middle East, the "J1" gene would still be present in Arab men despite their "white appearance". However, the "J1" Y-DNA Haplogroup would only make up 1/4th of the total Genetic Make-Up of the Arab. They also carry the Y-DNA of Japheth (I, G, J2,) and Edom.

J2 is mostly connected to Turkey and the Mediterranean European countries (Greece, Italy,) that invaded Judea and the Middle East 2,000 years ago.

J1 is mostly connected to the Black Arabs living in Khartoum, Sudan, the Negev Desert, Yemen, Qatar, United Arab Emirates, South Iraq (Basra) and South Saudi Arabia. It is also seen in high percentages in the Black Lemba/Remba Jews of Zimbabwe and South Africa. Some Tribes in South India have also been found to carry the "J1" Haplogroup.

So how do we know that the "**J2**" Haplogroup DNA is partly the result of Ottoman Turks, Kurds and Mediterranean Europeans? The White Ottoman **TURKS/KURDS** conquered Iraq, Syria, Jordan, ISRAEL, Turkey, the Caucasus, Greece, Egypt, Libya, Tunisia and parts of Yemen, Arabia and North Sudan where the Y-Haplogroup J DNA can be found in high numbers. But who **ALSO** conquered many of these places prior? The Greeks! Under the **Ptolemaic** and **Seleucid empire**.

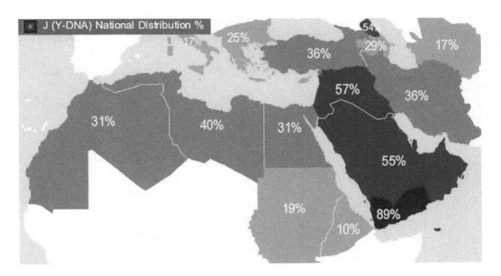

(**Above**) The Total "J" distribution (**J1 & J2**) is seen highest in the Ancient territory of the Ethiopian **Kingdom of Sheba** (Saba, Seba, Sheva-**Sabaeans**). This area is today known as Yemen. Don't worry, I will break down who has the J1 and the J2 gene since the Jews like to say "**J1c**" **Cohen Model Haplogroup** makes them direct descendants of Levi/Aaron.

The Y-DNA Haplogroup J is found in North Africa, Egypt, Greece, Israel, Lebanon, Palestine, Jordan, Syria, Iraq, Iran, Saudi Arabia, and Yemen. It is also found in in Italy (Rome), Sudan and North Ethiopia. Remember, the Italians were present in Ethiopia for only a short time under Italian Dictator Mussolini. So who is carrying the highest percentages of the Y-DNA "J1" Haplogroup gene. We will soon find out. But first we need to understand who has been living and breathing in the Middle East (including Israel) for the last 2,300 years starting with the Greek Emperor "**Alexander the Great**" in 330 B.C. This will be a "**Huge Factor**" in the DNA of the people we call "**Arabs**" and "**Jews**" today.

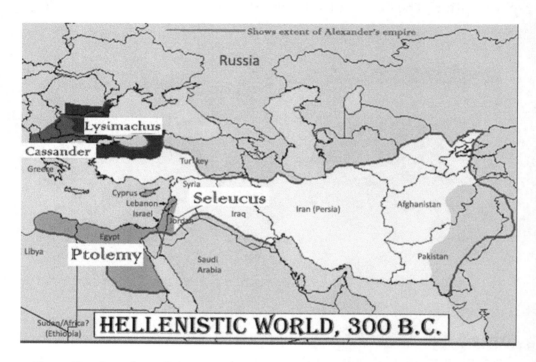

Fact: During the **4th Century B.C.** the Greeks ruled and dominated Egypt, parts of Libya, Israel, Palestine, Lebanon, Jordan, Turkey, Macedonia, Iraq, Iran, Turkmenistan, Afghanistan, Pakistan, and Northwest India (Indus River).

The Mauryan Empire in India led by **Chandragupta Mauryan (above)** around 300 B.C. was able to defeat the Greek Seleucid Empire leader "**Seleucus I Nicator**" and claim ownership of India. It is said that **Chandragupta** had 100,000 Indian soldiers and 9,000 fighting elephants. He supposedly married Seleucus's Greek daughter **Durdhara**. Per Strabo, the Greek Leader agreed to break bread and declare peace as long as the Indian Leader Chandragupta was ok with intermarriage between the Greeks and the Indians. This could be when the "**Aryan**" light skinned Indians were born.

> "The Indians occupy some of the countries situated along the Indus, which formerly belonged to the Persians: Alexander deprived the Ariani of them, and established there settlements of his own. But **Seleucus Nicator gave them to Sandrocottus in consequence of a marriage contract**, and received in return five hundred elephants."

> *Strabo, Geographica*

"The geographical position of the tribes is as follows: along the Indus are the Paropamisadae, above whom lies the Paropamisus mountain: then, towards the south, the Arachoti: then next, towards the south, the Gedroseni, with the other tribes that occupy the seaboard; and the Indus lies, latitudinally, along all these places; and of these places, in part, some that lie along the Indus are held by Indians, although they formerly belonged to the Persians. Alexander the Great took these away from the Arians and established settlements of his own, but **Seleucus Nicator gave them to Sandrocottus (aka. Chandragupta), upon terms of intermarriage** and of receiving in exchange five hundred elephants."

Strabo 15.2.9.

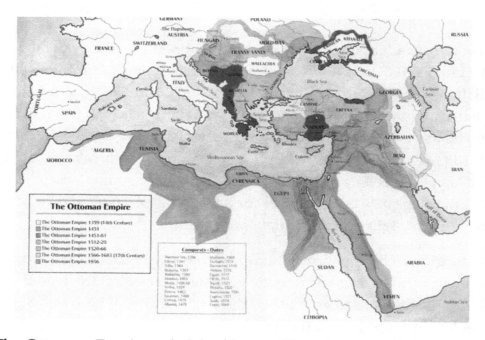

The **Ottoman Empire** ruled for almost 700 years controlling, Tunisia, coastal Algeria, Libya, Egypt, North Sudan, Western Arabia, Yemen, Turkey, Greece, Lebanon, Palestine, Israel, Syria, Jordan and Iraq. These are all hotspots for the Y-DNA Haplogroup J gene.

Population	No.	% Tot. J	M172 J2	M267 J/J1
Arab Morocco (49)	20	20.4	10.2	10.2
Arab Morocco (44)	7	15.9	2.3	13.6
Berber Morocco (64)	4	6.3		6.3
Berber Morocco (103)	11	10.7	2.9	7.8

Population	No.	% Tot. J	M172 J2	M267 J/J1
Saharan (North Africa)	5	17.2		17.2
Algerian	7	35.0		35.0
Tunisian	25	34.2	4.1	30.1
Ethiopia Oromo	3	3.8	1.3	2.6
Ethiopia Amhara	17	34.5	2.1	33.3
Iraqi	79	50.6	22.4	28.2
Lebanese	15	37.5	25.0	10.0
Muslim Kurd	38	40.0	28.4	11.6
Palestinian Arab	79	59.2	16.8	38.4
Bedouin	21	65.6	3.1	62.5
Ashkenazi Jewish	51	37.8	23.2	14.6
Sephardi Jewish	17	40.5	28.6	11.9
Turkish-Istanbul	18	24.7	17.8	5.5
Turkish Konya	41	31.8	27.9	3.1
Georgian	15	33.3	26.7	4.4
Balkarian (so. Caucasus)	4	25.0	25.0	
Northern Greek (Macedonia)	8	14.3	12.5	1.8
Greek	21	22.8	20.6	2.2
Italian North Central	14	26.9	26.9	

(Above) The Population frequencies of J2 and J/J1 in Selected Populations – Semino 2004. If you look closely at this chart you can see that the percentage of the Total "J" gene seen in Iraqis, Lebanese, Kurdish Muslims, Palestinian Arabs, Bedouins, Turkish Muslims, Algerians, Tunisians, Georgians, Greeks and Italians is similar (and if not higher) to the total "J" gene seen in Ashkenazi/Sephardic Jews. But since the Jews like to focus on the "J1" gene as being a Jewish "Levite-Aaronite" marker, we need focus on the "J1-M267" results of this study. By looking at the above chart you can see the Arabs (Algerians, Tunisians, Palestinians, Iraqis, Bedouins) and Ethiopians (Amhara) have MORE of the "J1-M267" Y-DNA Haplogroup than the Jews (Ashkenazi/Sephardic). So does this mean that all these other

375

nation groups are "**Jews**" too?   Of course not! But according to the European Jewish "**Cohen Model Haplogroup**" Theory, they do! This is ridiculous. Once again, their "**Lie**" has been **EXPOSED!**

Note: *According to multiple genetic studies, the **Northern Amharic/Tigray Ethiopians**, **Eritreans**, Khartoum **Sudanese Arabs**, some **Algerians**, some **Tunisians**, the **Bedouins** in Negev, South Israel, the Bedouins of Jordan, and some **Iraqis** have higher percentages of the "J1" gene than Ashkenazi-Sephardic Jews but do we see these people all calling themselves "**Jews**"? Nope!*

The Y-DNA J2 gene is connected to Europeans living in around the Mediterranean Sea (**Greece, Italy, Algeria, Tunisia, Morocco**) and Asia Minor (**Turkey, Kurdistan, Armenia etc.**). Remember for the last 2,300 years the people living in the Mediterranean European countries and Asia Minor have been the people who "**invaded**" the Levant (Judea, Jordan, Iraq), displacing the "**Original people**". These are your Greeks (**Hasmonean Maccabees, Alexander the Great, Seleucus Nicator**), your Edomites (**Antipater the Idumean, Herod the Great**), your Romans (**Pompey, Julius Caesar, Augustus, Titus, Nero, Septimius Severus**), your Kurds (**Saladin-Ayyubid Dynasty**), your Turks (**Ottoman Suleiman the Magnificent**), the French and the British (**Mandatory Palestine**).   During this time, "white-races" of people from North of the Mediterranean Sea came down to North Africa and the Middle East to "conquer". After they conquered these lands they displaced the "indigenous black races" of the land and colonized it with their people.

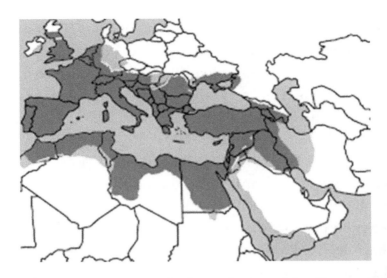

(**Above**) The shaded areas are the boundaries of the **Byzantine Roman Empire** from 70 A.D. to around 697 A.D. The accomplished this by winning the "**Punic Wars**" along with other battles. As you can see the Romans ruled (or were present) in **Morocco, Algeria, Tunisia, Libya, Egypt, Palestine (Israel), Syria, Iraq, Turkey, Spain, Portugal, France, Italy, Greece** and other **European countries**.

The Romans under **Julius Caesar** and **Augustus** (aka **Gauis Octavius**) extended their empire in North Africa as far west as **Algeria** which Roman emperor Septimius Severus kept under control. It wasn't until the late 7th Century (697 A.D.) after Islam was born that the Roman Byzantine Empire fell to the **Black Arabs** and later the "**White Arabs**" from Asia Minor (Turkey, Kurdistan).

- From **300 B.C. to 600 A.D. (total 900 years) the Greeks and Romans (including Edom) populated** the Middle East, the Levant (Israel/Palestine) and North Africa leaving their "phenotypic" mark on the land. A persons' "**phenotype**" is their individual "**observable traits**", such as their height, eye color, hair color and skin color. These Japhetic nations also left their "**Genotype (genetic makeup)**" on the people of the land.

- From 600 A.D. to 1000 A.D. the White "**Phenotype**" and "**Genotype**" of the Middle East/North Africa got an infusion of the Semitic Black Arab Blood with the rise of Islam. The Black Arab Ishmaelite's and the Black Saracens/Moors would dominate this area under the religion of Islam. The Black Moors would rule Europe up until 1500 A.D.

- From 1000 A.D. to today (**1,000 years**) the "**White Arabs**" from Asia Minor (Ottomans) infused their bloodline into the people of North Africa/Middle East/Levant. They left their "**Phenotype**" on the land but the Y-DNA slightly changed. Their DNA now consists of Y-DNA "**J1/J2**" and Y-DNA "**E1b1b**". The maternal DNA of these people stayed "**European**" because normally men would sleep around passing down their Y-DNA to their sons but the women would keep their mtDNA "**purer**" because in the Arabic culture a Muslim woman was to be a "**virgin**" before marriage. So the woman's mtDNA was a "**True Indicator**" of the ancestry of the people in the region. Therefore, the DNA of Greeks, Italians, North African Arabs, Turks, Kurds, Iraqis, Palestinians, Lebanese, and European Jews are all mixed with the same Haplogroups, each in varying percentages.

So by analyzing the data in this chart (Y-DNA J1 and J2) from different populations we can see the White European/Asia Minor influence in the DNA heritage of the Ashkenazi/Sephardic Jews and Arabs of today in relation to their surrounding neighbors. The Jews and Arabs are all basically descendants of Japheth, with a splash of Edomite DNA mixed in with their seed. The Y-Haplogroup J gene is not "specific" to claiming Ancient Israelite Ancestry. **The gig is up**!

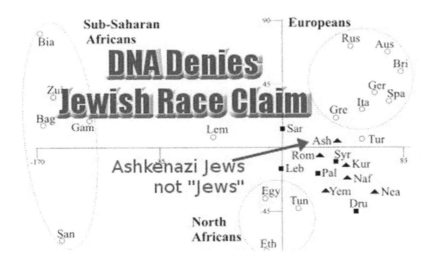

Fact: Geneticist **Michael Hammer** and countless others have proven that the Ashkenazi Jews are genetically brothers to the Europeans and the White-skinned Arabs. In the "**Science World Report**", posted on October 9, 2013, researchers at the University of Hudderfield, headed by **Professor Martin Richards** proved that the Ashkenazi female line (maternal DNA or "mtDNA") descended from Southern and Western Europe, not the Middle East. Mr. Richards is co-author of the new article called "**A substantial prehistoric European ancestry amongst Ashkenazi maternal lineages.**" Professor Martin explains that "Ashkenaz/Ashkenazi" in Hebrew means "**Germans**" and is used for Jews of Eastern European origin who historically spoke Yiddish or Judeo-German/Slavic/Turkish language. **Dr. Harry Ostrer**, pathology pediatrics and genetics professor at the Albert Einstein College of Medicine in New York, stated based on his research that on an average **ALL** Ashkenazi Jews are genetically as closely related to each other as fourth and fifth cousins.

Here is Biblical proof that the Genetics composition of the Ashkenazi Jews claiming Cohenite (Priestly) heritage should contain African DNA as well, which is not found in substantial amounts in European and Ashkenazi/Sephardic Jews.

Ezra 9:1-2 "Now when these things were done, the princes came to me saying, The people of Israel, **AND THE PRIESTS, AND THE LEVITES**, have not separated themselves from the people of the lands, doing according to their abominations, even of the **CANAANITES**, the Hittites, the Perizzites, the Jebusites, the Ammonites, the Moabites, **THE EGYPTIANS**, and the Amorites. For they have taken of their daughters for themselves, and for their sons: so that the holy seed have mingled themselves with the peoples of those lands: yea, the hand of the princes and rulers hath been chief in this trespass.

Judges 3:5-6 "And the Children of Israel dwelt among the Canaanites, Hittites, and Amorites, and Perizzites, and Hivites, and Jebusites: **AND THEY TOOK THEIR DAUGHTERS TO BE THEIR WIVES, AND GAVE THEIR DAUGHTERS TO THEIR SONS** and served their gods."

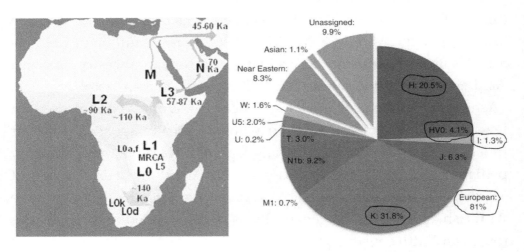

(**Left**) mtDNA of Africa. Most of the Bantus in "Sub-Saharan" Africa fall under the "L" maternal haplogroup. Bantus East Africans fall under the "L" and "M" maternal haplogroup. (**Right**) The Maternal Haplogroup of Ashkenazi Jews is a "mixture" of different Maternal Haplogroups with mtDNA "K" being the most significant followed by "H". Haplogroup "K" is found in Northwest Europe and Haplogroup

"H" is the most common mtDNA Haplogroup found in **ALL OF EUROPE**, especially Western Europe, Eastern Europe and the Caucasus region. There is **NO** "L" maternal DNA found in Ashkenazi Jews despite 800 years of the Biblical Jews intermarrying with the Canaanites, Egyptians and Nubian Cushites from the Sons of Ham (Africa). If look closely the maternal DNA of Ashkenazi Jews is about 80% European. Genetically, there is nothing that ties the "Jewish" maternal blood to the Middle East or Africa. How can this be so, if the whole Old Testament (Tanakh) takes place in Middle East and Africa? This proves that the Ashkenazi Jews **ARE NOT** the descendants of the Biblical 12 Tribes of Israel. So the saying "You're only a Jew, unless your mother was a Jew "is flawed because "genetically" the mothers of most Jews are "European", not Semitic.

Based on the Maternal lineage (which Jews claim that make them Jewish) and based off the Bible from 1200 B.C. times before King Solomon, during the Book of Judges (Judges 3:5-6) and 500 B.C. times when Ezra (Levite/Aaronite) lived, we should see **African maternal DNA** in **the Jews mtDNA studies** of today but this is not the case. The Jews claiming "Cohenite-High Priest" heritage should show substantial amounts of African **L1, L2, and L3 mtDNA** (Maternal), and at least also Y-Haplogroup DNA that sets them apart from normal European or white-skinned Arabs. This is not the case.

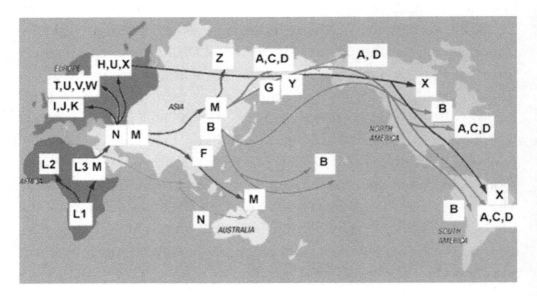

Maternal DNA of Africa is mostly **L1, L2, L3**. As you can see in Europe the **Maternal DNA** (mtDNA) is **I, J, K, H, U, X, T, U, V, W and N (Asia Minor).** Ashkenazi and Sephardic Jews claiming to be Cohenite Priests or Levites today according to their own Old Testament (Tanakh) bible should have Hamitic Canaanite, Nubian (Zipporah) and Egyptian blood.

Ashkenazi Jewish mtDNA haplogroup distribution varies among distinct subpopulations: lessons of population substructure in a closed group – Feder J, Ovadia O, Glaser B, and Mishmar D.

Haplogroup	Polish Jews N=192	%	Polish non-Jews N=436	%	Russian and Ukrainian (RU) Jews N=150	%	Russian non-Jews N=201	%
U (non K)	12	6.3	70	16.1	11	7.3	36	17.9
K	72	37.5	15	3.4	25	16.7	6	3
HV*	20	10.4	25	5.7	19	12.7	15	7.5
H	27	14.6	197	45.2	41	27.3	85	42.3
J	18	9.4	34	7.8	15	10	16	8
T	9	4.7	50	11.5	11	7.3	22	10.9
N1	12	6.3	2	0.5	11	7.3	0	0
I	3	1.6	8	1.8	0	0	5	2.5
W	6	3.1	16	3.7	4	2.7	4	2
X	1	0.5	8	1.8	0	0	7	3.5
L1 and L2	6	3.1	0	0	2	1.3	0	0
L3	0	0	1	0.2	0	0	0	0
R*	0	0	2	0.5	0	0	1	0.5
M	2	1	8	1.8	0	0	3	1.5
Pre-HV	2	1	0	0	6	4	1	0.5
Others	2	1	0	0	5	3.3	0	0

Here is the maternal lineage represented by mitochondrial DNA (mtDNA) variation in one of the most commonly studied populations, the Ashkenazi Jews whom most come from Poland, Russia, Ukraine and Prussia. Based on the Hebrew Old Testament (called the Tanakh), the Book of Ezra (500 B.C.) in Ezra 9:1-2 states that the maternal lineage of the High Priests (Cohenite) and Levites should consist of Hamitic (African) blood. The Maternal (mother) mtDNA most common in Africa is L1, L2 and L3. **However, in the Ashkenazi Jews, the 2 most common Maternal DNA (mtDNA) haplogroups are K and H.** These mtDNA haplogroups are not found in Africa. Maternal DNA Haplogroup "K" and "H" is found **exclusively** in Europe. As you can see on the chart the African mtDNA haplogroups are barely detected in the European Jews. The Gig is up again folks. A lie cannot live forever. – *source - European Journal of Human Genetics, 2007 Apr;15(4):498-500. Epub 2007 Jan 24./PubMed Abstract.*

Iranian Jews 1800's

Iranian Jews 1800's

Fact: Persian white-skinned Jews look nothing like the original Hebrew Israelites or the original Persians depicted on the walls of the Palace of Susa (Shushan) during the reign of King Cyrus and King Darius in 500-400 B.C. Are they telling the truth about who they are? Are they truly "Hebrew Israelites" or are they descendants of "Foreign Invaders (i.e. Turks, Greeks) who conquered and then colonized the land of Persia many centuries ago? What does the Bible and Historical fact have to say about the Persian Jews in Persia?

(**Above**) Depiction of the "**Real**" Persians from the "**Palace of Susa (Shushan)**" in the 6th Century B.C. Taken from the walls of the Palace of King Darius and King Cyrus. These Ancient Persians were "**people of color**". Todays Persian Jew and regular Persians are the same skin complexion as European Caucasians. How can that be? They had Kinky tight curled hair and beards like that of a "Negro/African". Most Persians today have straight hair and will even admit that they are more European than Arab. So what did the Israelites hair look like back then during the times of Ezra and Mordecai?

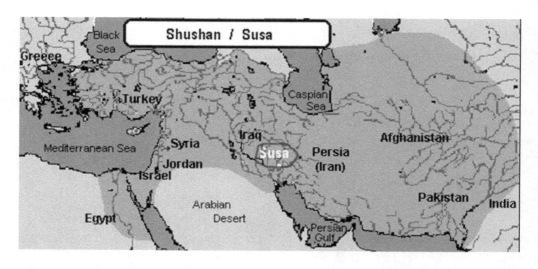

The city of Susa (Shushan) was right in Elamite Territory. It was basically in West Persia (Iran) not to far from the East Babylonian (Iraqi) border. The Persian Jews justify themselves from the Book of Esther. But what were Jews still doing all the way in Persia, if the bible (Ezra) says the Tribe of Judah and Benjamin came back to Israel with Ezra/Zerubabbel. Why would any Jews stay in Persia if the King of Persia allowed them to come back to Israel to rebuild the "Second Temple"? Let's see what the Book of Esther says about how the Persians Jew came on the scene because we know that nowhere in the Old Testament does it say the word **"Persian Jew"** or **"Medes Jew"**. When when did the Persians "Become" Jews?

Esther 8:15-17 "And Mordecai went out from the presence of the king in royal apparel of blue and white, and with a great crown of gold, and with a garment of fine linen and purple: and the city of **Shushan** rejoiced and was glad. The Jews had light, and gladness, and joy, and honour. And in every province, and in every city, whitersoever the king's commandment (Not God's) and his decree came, the Jews had joy and gladness, a feast and a good day. **AND MANY OF THE PEOPLE OF THE LAND (PERSIA and perhaps Babylon-Iraq) BECAME JEWS**; for the fear of the Jew fell upon them."

NOTE: YOU CANNOT BECOME A "JEW" ONCE YOU ARE BORN. IT IS A BIRTHRIGHT, YOU HAVE TO BE BORN A JEW. A PERSON CANNOT BECOME A KENNEDY, A BUSH, A BIN LADEN, A ROTHSCHILD, AN OPPENHEIMER, A ROCKEFELLAR, A DISNEY.

Note: The Book of Esther was not written by any Israelite prophets and it is questionable if it was really written by any Israelites period. Esther's lineage cannot be accurately traced to any Tribe and Mordecai's lineage cannot be traced accurately without error and time gaps to Benjamin, not even King Saul. The Book of Esther says Modecai is related to Kish (Saul) but if that's the case the Old Testament should line up the lineage perfectly like it does the high priests. If Esther was part of the Old Testament it should have the genealogies of Benjamin in it for anybody to follow using the timeline from King Saul (A Benjaminite) in II Samuel to Mordecai, the person in the Book of Esther who is supposed to be from the Tribe of Benjamin. The word "**Jew**" is in the Tanakh a total of 74 times but it "magically" appears in the Book of Esther over 50 times! Wow! The word "Jew" is nowhere in the TORAH but it happens to be slammed down bible readers throats till no end in the Book of Esther. But what does the Book of Esther say about the Persian Jews and who they are? Let's read it again!

Esther 8:17 "And in every province, and in every city, whitersoever the King's commandments (Not God) and his decree came (Not God), the Jews had joy and gladness, a feast and a good day. **AND MANY OF THE PEOPLE OF THE LAND BECAME JEWS**; for the fear of the Jews fell upon them."

Surely this scripture wasn't referring to them becoming "Judahites" aka "people of the Tribe of Judah". Or was it referring to them becoming Judeans? Both are not the answer because you cannot just "**make yourself**" into the Tribe of Judah and you cannot make yourself a "Judean" living in Persia. So we have to assume it means a follower of the religion of Judaism which today is known as "**Jews**". So these people were Judaism converts or proselytes and not the biblical Hebrew Israelites. Just to clear things up.....You cannot become a Israelite when you are already alive. It is a **BIRTHRIGHT**. A Black man cannot become "Chinese" or "Indian". The Persian Jews are "**GENTILES**" and so are the "**Mizrahi**" Middle Eastern Jews. It is a known fact also that the Book of Esther was not found in the 400 B.C. Dead Sea Scrolls found in Qumran, Israel in 1948. All the other Books of the Old Testament were found in the Dead Sea Scrolls except the Book of Esther. Also there is hardly any mention of "**worship**" in the Book of Esther and there is no "**Thus saith the Lord**" or "**The Lord came unto me saying**". If the Essenes, who were said to be descendants of Zadok (High Priest) lived in the 1st Century A.D., how come they didn't have the Book of Esther in their possession? Surely they had 400 years to have gotten it and deem it "Biblical". The Book of Esther is the only Book that justifies the existence of the Iranian Jews and in Islamic prophecy the Iranian Jews play a huge part in the arrival of the Antichrist figure (Dajjal).

So what does history and the bible have to say about the Children of Judah?

Genesis 49:9-10 "Judah is a lion's whelp: from the prey, my son, thou are gone up: he stooped down, he crouched as a lion, and as an **OLD LION**; who shall **ROUSE HIM UP?**" The sceptre **SHALL NOT** depart from Judah, nor a lawgiver from between his feet, until Shiloh (**the Messiah**) come; and unto him shall the gathering of the people be."

(**Above**) These two men are **Hebrew Israelites** from the **Tribe of Judah** take as captives from the city of **Lachish, Israel**. Lachish was a fortress city outside of Jerusalem. It was a city designed to be a "**first responder**" to any outside threat to the city of Jerusalem where the Solomon's Temple stood. This relief is from 700 B.C., 200 years prior to the Jews return to Israel under the Persian Rule where the Book of Esther leaves off. Surely the Israelites/Jews hair texture couldn't have changed that quick from wooly, tight-curled hair to straight. From the 1600's to 2015, Black peoples hair in America is still considerd "**wooly**" and "**Kinky**". How can the Persians Jews be truly the "Israelites" of the Bible if their hair is straight and the original Hebrew Israelites hair was "Kinky?". You can find proof of the Seige of Lachish in the Hebrew Bible (**2 Kings 18, 2 Chronicles 32, Micah 1:13, Isaiah 36:1-2**) and Sennacheribs Annals taken from his palace in Nineveh (Northern Iraq, Ancient Capital of Assyria). These pictures are on display at the British Musuem.

Do the Jews today wear their hair in cornrows and dreadlocks like the Ancient Israelites wore in Biblical times? No, but African-Americans do. This is clearly a case of **"Stolen Identity"**.

Hebrew Israelites singing, playing the Cymbals and Harp (lyre) as they were led away captive by their enemies. Singing and playing instruments (blowing trumpets, cymbals) ws often done by the Levites.

Notice these Israelites (perhaps Levites) hair, which is similar to black dreadlock and cornrow hairstyles today. Notic the thickness of each lock or strand of hair as noted by the separation between the lines. On just one side of his head we see 6 rows. Notice the Fringes at the bottom of their garment. They are definetely Hebrew Israelites, but their hair doesn't match what the European Jews hair looks like today. What happened?

Psalms 137:3 "For there they that carried us away captive required us of a song; and they that wasted us required of us mirth, saying, Sing us one of the songs of Zion. How shall we sing the LORD'S son in a **STRANGE LAND**?"

CHAPTER 17

SYNAGOGUE OF SATAN: MASTERS OF DECEPTION! THERE IS MORE THAN MEETS THE "EYE".

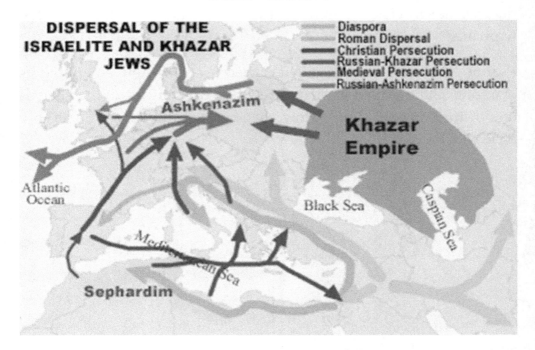

(**Above**) The migration patterns of the **Sephardic** and **Ashkenazi Jews**. After the 1400's, the word "**Sephardic Jew**" started to appear in vast numbers. When the Black Moors along with the Black Hebrew Israelites were kicked out of **Iberia** in the 15th century thanks to the "**Spanish-Portuguese Inquisition**", many of them returned back to Africa (Morocco) and (Libya). Others were exiled to the West African Islands of **Principe**, **Sao Tome** and **Equatorial Guinea**.

There has been however some "confusion" as to whether or not these exiled Jews from Iberia were "**Black Jews**" or "**White Jews**". The European Sephardic Jews, like the former late Israeli Ambassador **Tamar Galon** all like to make up the story which involves the White Portuguese Jews being banished to West African Islands where they would mix with Black Africans creating a new "mixed-breed" people. The Portuguese Jews would be nicknamed the "**Lancados**", which means "**Thrown Out Ones**".   But the question is, history likes to say that the Portuguese Jewish "Lancados" were known for purposely kidnapping and raping African women back in the 16th Century on the Islands of **Sao Tome**, **Principe** and **Equatorial Guinea**, creating mulatto-blacks that would help the Portuguese capture full-breed Africans during the Slave Trades. These mulatto blacks per history would supposedly be trained by their Portuguese Jewish fathers to be "**undercover slavetraders**". However, "**mysteriously**" when you type in the word "**Lancados**" in Google or Yahoo you get **NO** pictures of white Portuguese Jews or mulatto blacks. You don't even get pictures of ancient manuscripts or books written about these "**Lancados**" people. **Not a single piece of evidence!** In addition, when you check the Y-DNA of the people living in the Portuguese territorial African Island of Sao Tome, Principe and Equatorial Guinea you find **NO EVIDENCE** of Sephardic Jewish Y-DNA. If the Male Portuguese Jews slept with African women creating "mixed-children" you would see their Y-DNA (J1/J2) spewing through the men of these Islands. But you don't. The majority of the Y-DNA in these Islands and inland in Angola is the Bantus Sub-Saharan Y-DNA "**E1b1a**". The "**maternal**" mtDNA of the women on these Islands also falls in the "**L**" Haplogroup, which lines up to their Hebrew Israelite "**Bantus**" Heritage. Even in the Cape Verde Islands where the Portuguese Jews were supposed to inhabit, their Y-DNA J1/J2 is not found. Only Y-DNA R1b and E1b1a were found, which is also found in Africa.

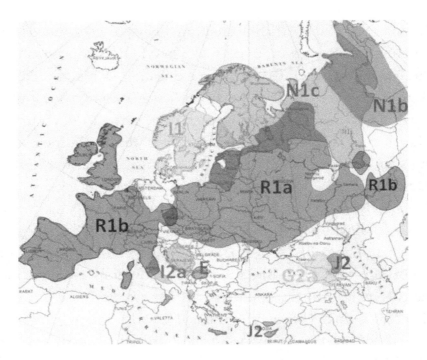

The Y-DNA Haplogroup "**R1b**" is not "**Jewish specific**" to the Sephardic Jews as people in **Scotland, Ireland, Spain, Portugal, Western Wales, France and Russia also carry this Haplogroup (specifically R1b1a, which is different than the R1b1b/R1b1c that Latinos and Africans carry).**

Many tribes in Africa also carry this "**R1b**" Haplogroup (**which is the secret link to the people known as the Black Moors who were a mix of Black Arabs and Black Jews**). **The Jews claim the J1c Haplogroup gene is "Jewish Specific".** But here is where the Jews are "stuck". Admitting that the Y-DNA R1b is also "**Jewish specific**" would mean that way more countries could start claiming "**Jewishness**" thus requesting to come to Israel under the "Law of Return". So what does this mean? It means that the Jews that were "**exiled**" from Spain and Portugal during the 16th Century were "**Black Jews**"! It was these same Black Jews living in Angola, Gabon, the Congo, Equatorial Guinea, Mozambique, Nigeria, Cameroon that were taken by the Portuguese to Bahia, Brazil to be their slaves working on Portuguese owned slave plantations.

Other Black Hebrew Israelites during this time were sent as slaves to the Spanish Colonies in the Caribbean (**Jamaica, Cuba, Puerto Rico, Hispaniola-Haiti/Dominican Republic**). These "**tag-along**" European converted Sephardic Jews were the ones that would end up becoming the Slavemasters of the Black Jews brought to the Caribbean. Those that were fortunate escaped back into Africa (Morocco) following the trade routes south to Mali.

So we know that the Ashkenazi/Sephardic/Mizrahi Jews were never slaves in Egypt, nor were they exiled from Israel during the Assyrian and Babylonian invasions. Therefore, their descendants **as a whole** never stepped foot into the Holy Land until they came to Israel in 1948. **Yahusha (Jesus) would make mention about a people who worshipped in synagogues calling themselves Jews and were not**. Thus, we know that to find these "fake Jews" we would have to look for people who worship in synagogues. This is not Blacks, Latinos or Native Americans.

Revelations 2:8-9 "And unto the angel of the church in **Smyrna** write; These things saith the first and the last, which was dead, and is alive; I know thy works, and tribulation, and poverty, (but thou art rich) **and I know the blasphemy of them which say they are Jews and are not, but are of the Synagogue of Satan.**"

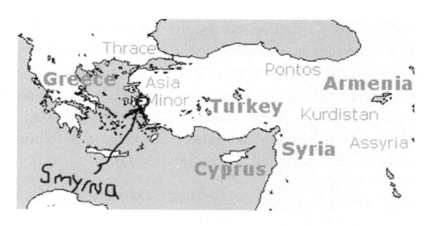

In the **Book of Revelation** 2:8-9, **Smyrna** was an ancient **GREEK CITY** located on the Aegean coast of Anatolia (Turkey). Today this place is known as Izmir, Turkey. Since 300 B.C. with the conquest of Judea by the Greeks under Alexander the Great and his generals (i.e. the Diadochi) the face of Judea changed from Black to White. The Southern House of Judah was allowed to come back to Israel during the Persian Rule (King Cyrus) in the 6th Century B.C. When the Greeks defeated the Persians many of the Israelites from the Tribe of Judah and in Jerusalem were "deported" as slaves according to Joel 3:6.

Joel 3:6 "The Children also of Judah and the children of Jerusalem have ye sold unto the Grecians, that ye might remove them far from their border."

The **Book of Revelation** in Chapter 2, verse 9 details the letters of Yahusha (Jesus) to the Church in Smyrna which was involved in "Emperor Worship (**i.e. Julius Caesar**) and persecuting the followers of Christ. Yahusha's disciples were mostly Israelites (**except Simon was a Canaanite**) and also followers of Christ they were persecuted (**thrown in Jail**) and some were even executed (**i.e. John the Baptist, James**). Revelations also reveals that Yahusha (Jesus) knew that there were people in the Greek city of Smyrna (**most likely Greeks or Syrians**) who said they were "**Jews**" but were not. He attributed them to the "**Synagogue of Satan**", like the Pharisees who most likely at the time consisted of Greek converts, Samaritan converts (from Assyria) and Edomite Jews by conversion. Yahusha (Jesus) in Revelation Chapter 2 also reveals to us his title as "**The First and the Last**", which is a title only belonging to **God the Creator**, aka "the **Most High**" according to **Isaiah 41:4, Isaiah 44:6, and Isaiah 48:12** in the Hebrew Dead Scrolls dating back to before the Maccabean Era.

Revelations 2:8 "And unto the angel of the church in Smyrna write; These things saith **THE FIRST AND THE LAST, WHICH WAS DEAD, AND IS ALIVE.**"

Isaiah 41:4 "Who hath wrought and done it, calling the generations from the beginning? I the Lord, **THE FIRST, AND WITH THE LAST; I AM HE.**"

Isaiah 44:6 "Thus saith the Lord the King of Israel, and his redeemer the Lord of hosts; **I AM THE FIRST, AND I AM THE LAST**; and beside me there is no God."

Isaiah 48:12 "Hearken unto me, O Jacob and Israel, my called; **I AM HE; I AM THE FIRST, I ALSO AM THE LAST.**"

So because of this "Gentile" occupation of Israel, Jesus told his disciples to not go into the Gentiles or Samaritans, but to instead go looking for the "Lost Sheep in Israel". How do we know the 12 disciples were "**True Black Israelites**" and not "**converts to Judaism**?"

Matthew 10:5 "These **TWELVE** Jesus sent forth, and commanded them, saying, Go **NOT** into the way of the **GENTILES**, and into any city of the **SAMARITANS** enter ye not: **BUT GO RATHER TO THE LOST SHEEP OF THE HOUSE OF ISRAEL**.

Jesus knew which people to send his disciples to and which people he wanted them to avoid. If the Israelites were the majority in Israel and if those Maccabeans Greeks or Samaritans were truly "**Israelites**" he wouldn't have said this statement. The fact that he attached the word "**Lost**" to the House of Israel signifies that the Israelites were in few in number. For example, I'm not going to tell a black person to look for the "Lost Black people in Detroit" if the majority of Detroit is Black. That doesn't make sense.

Let's look at some of the 12 disciples to see if they were Israelites.

Matthew 10:2 "Now the names of the twelve apostles are these; The first, Simon, who is called Peter, and Andrew his brother; James the son of Zebedee, and John his brother; Philip and Bartholomew; Thomas, and Matthew the publican; James the son of Alphaeus, and Lebbaeus; who surname was Thaddaeus; Simon the Canaanite, and Judas Iscariot, who also betrayed him."

John 1:47 "Jesus saw Nathanael (Bartholomew) coming to him, and saith of him, **Behold an Israelite** indeed, in whom is no guile.

Romans 3:4 "For I could wish that myself were accursed from Christ for my brethren, my kinsmen according to the flesh: **Who are Israelites**; to whom pertaineth the adoption, and the glory, and the covenants, and the giving of the law, and the service of God, and the promises."

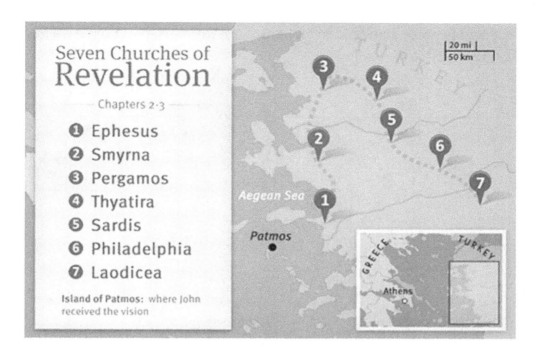

Seven Churches of
Revelation
— Chapters 2-3 —

❶ Ephesus
❷ Smyrna
❸ Pergamos
❹ Thyatira
❺ Sardis
❻ Philadelphia
❼ Laodicea

Island of Patmos: where John received the vision

Back during the time that the "**Messiah**" walked the earth the same people in Turkey (Greeks) were the same people that ruled over Judea during the reign of Greek 4 kingdoms (Ptolemy, Seleucid etc.) until the Edomite/Byzantine (Roman) period.

Note: around 100 B.C. the people living in/around Syrian started to become known as "**Syrians**".

Most Jews associate themselves with people called the "**Maccabees/Hasmoneans**" but in reality they were simply zealous "Greeks" who had converted to Judaism back in the 2nd Century B.C. Saint Ignatius of Antioch visited the Smyrna Church and wrote letters to its **Bishop, S. Polycarpus** who was born in 80 A.D. and died in 167 A.D. It was recorded by Irenaeus and Tertullian that they heard Bishop Polycarpus speak and that he was a disciple of John the Apostle (author of Revelations) before he was burned at the stake. Polycarpus, Irenaeus and many Greeks in that time had the "**ous**" or "**us**" on the end of their name. Back then in those days when the Greek Empire under Alexander the Great ruled over Judaea, there was a power struggle. The

Seleucid Empire managed to Hellenize the Gentiles living in Judea and also the Gentile Greek Jews.

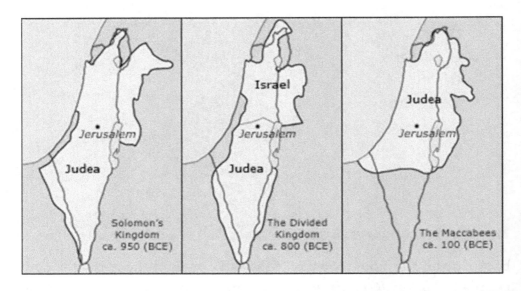

(**Above**) This is the map of the extent of King Solomon's undivided kingdom, the dived kingdom (after the split into both nations), and the Maccabean kingdom in 100 B.C. Judas Maccabees (Hasmonean) around 160 B.C. defeated the Greeks Seleucid Empire (**Antiochus IV Epiphanes**) and re-claim Judea from the "Hellenizing Greek rulers" of the time. History says that Judas Maccabees was a Cohenite (descendant of Aaron, Moses' brother) and thus was an Israelite. However, his Hebrew Israelite ancestry cannot be traced back to any of the High Priests recorded in the Tanakh/Torah (Old Testament) and Flavius Josephus even admitted that there was a time for about 8 years prior to Judas Maccabees where the people did not have a Jewish High Priest. This raises a big "**Red Flag**" in regards to this claim of being a "**Jew**". Many of the Hasmoneans/Maccabees were supposedly **High Priests** but were also somehow signing treaties with the Edomites, Romans and were also fighting in battle. The High Priests were instructed to do the daily "**Temple Duties**", not "physical work" or let alone lead an army into battle. This is another "**Red Flag**". The Real

Israelites mortal enemy was the Edomites but these Maccabean wanna-be High Priests were allowing every and anybody into Israel. This was forbidden and shunned by God (**Obadiah 1**). These Maccabean Gentiles were converting other Gentile-Heathen nations into the "**Nation of Israel**" which was unheard of in the Old Testament. To put this into perspective, Ezra, an Aaronite High Priest, got mad and started pulling out his hair when he saw that the Israelites had intermarried with "**strange women**" who were by heritage "**Gentiles**".

Ezra 9:2-3 "For they (the Israelites) have taken of their daughters for themselves, and for their sons: so that the holy seed have mingled themselves with the people of those lands: yea, the hand of the princes and rulers hath been chief in this trespass. And when I (Ezra) heard this thing, I rent (tore) my garment and my mantle, and **plucked off the hair of my head and of my beard**, and sat down astonished."

The Aaronite High Priest were commanded not to have contact with dead people so how could the Maccabeans lead people into battle? The High Priest were also commanded to keep their hair neat and their clothes from being tore. So how could the Maccabean High Priests keep these laws fighting in battle against enemy forces? We all know that in "War" there are a lot of people who die. There is a lot of torn clothes and wounds that result from battle. This means the High Priests would be exposed to dead bodies and their clothes/hair would be "out of order". The Aaronites were commanded by God not to be defiled with dead bodies. This is another "**Red Flag**" the Maccabees were "Jewish High Priest Imposters".

Leviticus 21:1 "And the Lord said unto Moses, Speak unto the priests the sons of Aaron, and say unto them, There shall none be defiled for the dead among his people."

Leviticus 21:10-11 "And he that is the High Priest among his brethren, upon whose head the anointing oil was poured, and that is consecrated to put on the garments, shall not uncover his head, **nor rend his**

clothes; Neither shall he go in to any dead body, nor defile himself for his father, or his mother;

To sum things up, after 300 B.C. the people in Judea who were called **"Syrians"**, **"Greeks"**, **"Jews"** and **Edomites** were all **GENTILES** in Revelation 2-8-9. They were not Israelites. The 10 lost tribes were exiled. They never all came back. Then you have the Khazar history which eventually is the foundation history of the Ashkenazi Jew. Most Ashkenazi and Sephardic Jews today will claim they are from the Tribe of Judah, Benjamin, Levi or (Cohenite) without really knowing the bible in regards to how it proves their claims to be false. But lately, the Jews are reverting to Science and DNA to prove they are Jews and that they are genetically related to the Cohenite Sons of Aaron. Because of this, it is necessary to address how DNA testing STILL proves that the Ashkenazi/Sephardic Jews are not the descendants of the Biblical 12 Tribes of Israel.

CHAPTER 18

THE NORTHERN HOUSE OF ISRAEL: WHERE DID THEY GO? DID SOME MAKE IT TO THE "NEW WORLD" AND THE "CARIBBEAN"?

Since the days of Joshua (Joshua Chapter 9) **"Gentile nations"** have infiltrated the camp of the Israelites. By allowing the Canaanites, Egyptians, Nethinims, Rechabites and other nations into the Israelite camp the Children of Israel continued to follow the customs of the heathen such as worshipping false idols. This disobedience eventually broke the "Nation of Israel" into the **"House of Israel"** and the **"House of Judah"** after the reign of King Solomon. King Solomon's son **"Rehoboam"** took over the Southern **"House of Judah"** while **"Jeroboam"** the son of a Nebat (Tribe of Ephraim) took over the **"House of Israel"**. Centuries later, the Assyrians exiled the 10 Northern Tribes in stages, which was followed the Babylonians capturing the Southern Tribes under King Nebuchadnezzar. Then later the remnant of Judah was sold to the Grecians (**Joel 3:6**) followed by any other remaining Tribes (Benjamin, Judah and some of the 10 tribes) that happened to be in hiding in Judea/Samaria when the Romans sacked Israel in 70 A.D. How do we know this? 2 Chronicles records many times how the members of the Northern Tribes immigrated to the Territory of Judah after the Northern and Southern Kingdom division.

2 Chronicles 10:16-17 "And when all Israel saw the king would not hearken unto them, the people answered the king saying, What portion have we in David? and we have none inheritance in the son of Jesse: every man to your tents, O Israel: and now, David, see thine own house, So all Israel went to their tents. But as for the children of Israel that dwelt in the cities of Judah, Rehoboam reigned over them."

In fact, in **2 Chronicles 11:3, 16, 17, 2 Chronicles 15:9, 24:5, 25, 30:10-21, 31:6 and 34:9** it describes how there were remnants from all the Northern Tribes who came down and settled in Jerusalem.

Fact: *The Northern 10 Tribes of Israel were essentially "exiled" from their land while the Southern Tribes were dispersed. The House of Joseph/Ephraim would also spread throughout the world and mix among the nations they dwelt in. This change of scenery, climate and change of wives/husbands over time would amount to a change in their Y (Paternal) DNA Haplogroup. Perhaps this is why the Y Paternal Haplogroup "Q" is only specific to the Indians that live in South America, Central America and North America while the Maternal mtDNA haplogroup A, B, C, D of the Amerindians can be traced back to Africa.*

Jacob blessed Ephraim and Manasseh giving them predictions of their future.

Genesis 48:13-14 "And Joseph took them both, Ephraim in his right hand toward Israel's left hand, and Manasseh in his left hand toward Israel's right hand, and brought them near unto him. And Israel stretched out his right hand, and laid it upon Ephraim's head, *who was the younger,* and his left hand upon Manasseh's head, guiding his hands wittingly; or Manasseh **was his firstborn.**"

Jacob was set to bless Ephraim first although he wasn't the firstborn and Joseph tried to stop him, but Jacob knew what he was doing.

Genesis 48:18-19 "And Joseph saw that his father laid his right hand upon the head of Ephraim, it displeased him; and he held up his father's hand, to remove it from Ephraim's head unto Manasseh's head. And Joseph said unto his father, Not so, my father: for this is the firstborn; put thy right hand upon his head. And his father refused, and said, I know it, my son, I know it: he also shall **A PEOPLE (Nation)**, and he (**Manasseh**) also shall be great: but truly his younger brother (**Ephraim**) shall be greater than he, and his seed shall **BECOME A MULITITUDE OF NATIONS.**" Now according to some Biblical

Scholars like Eritrean-born **Embaye Melekin**, author of the Book *"The African Bible: The Record of the Abyssinian Prophets"*, this particular scripture in Genesis 48:18-19 could hint to the fact that perhaps the "Bantus" people in Africa that were taken as slaves into **ALL NATIONS** were a part of **ONE PEOPLE/ONE NATION**, that being of the **Tribe of Manasseh**. The Tribe of Ephraim would become **MULTITUDE OF NATIONS**, meaning that perhaps the indigenous "Indian" people in the Caribbean and the Americas who belonged to many tribes would fall under the Tribe of Ephraim. Could this possibly be true, if in fact the Maternal mtDNA of some Native Americans is traceable to the mtDNA of Bantus West and East Africans. After all, Ephraim and Manasseh both had the same mother and father. Ephraim and Manasseh both should have evidence of "Egyptian language/customs" learned from their Egyptian mother. Usually in African customs people speak the "**working language**" of the land (i.e. Swahili) and also their "**Mother Tongue**". It is a known fact that "Egyptian influences" can be seen in the language of the Wolof Tribe (Senegal), Ewe Tribe (Ghana) and the Igbo Tribe (Nigeria). Egyptian influences have also been suspected in the "Algonquian" Indian language. Ephraim and Manasseh were both the product of an "Egyptian" **mother** and a Hebrew **father**. It is a known fact that many Native Americas today have "**Hebrewisms**" and "**Egyptisms**" in their ancient customs that they could've only got if they were Israelites to begin with. Read for yourself:

*"**Aaron Levi, a Portuguese Jew**, had been at Honduras, from whence he proceeded to Papuan, perhaps Popayan, that is, he says, to Quito, where he hired mules of a Spaniard to go into the country, and took with him a guide, who was called Francisco. With him he proceeded towards the Cordilleras. Falling into conversation with his guide, he found him to be one of the original natives of America, who had much violence and injustice to charge the Spaniards with. He complained bitterly of their cruelties, and expressed not only a hope, but even his persuasion, that his country-men would one day have the satisfaction of a revenge through the means of a people that were then*

concealed. Aaron's curiosity was much excited to know more of these people; and, learning from his guide that some of them wore very long beards, other short ones, and they observed the rite of circumcision, his anxiety greatly increased to see them, and he begged his guide to accompany him to the place where they resided. His guide consented, and he gave him three dollars to buy provisions, with a part of which money he purchased canvas shoes, and they began their journey. As they proceeded, Francisco made many enquiries."

Single Story of the Pretended Aborigines of America

"*The Indian guide named who was called* **"Francisco"** *asked Aaron Levi about his origin, to which Aaron said his ancestor was Abraham. Francisco took Aaron Levi through the woods and climbing up mountains with ropes fashioned with iron spikes. On the Sabbath day Francisco rested and after two days they arrived at a large river. Francisco told Aaron Levi,* **"Here you will see your brethren."** *Francisco did not know the Spaniard was a Gentile Jew. Francisco made a flag with two pieces of cloth and waved it back and forward, when a great smoke arose on the other side of the river. The smoke sign was a sign letting Francisco know that the Indian Israelites knew they were there. Francisco gave another sign and three men and a woman come over in a little boat. Aaron, although being a Portuguese Jew, fluent in Hebrew did not understand the language in which the Indians spoke, but Francisco understood it. They hugged and kissed Francisco and said to him in their language which Francisco translated* **"The Lord is our God, the Lord is One"**. *This is the Daily Shema prayer the Israelites spoke in Deuteronomy 6:4. The Indians used signs which Francisco explained as the Indians also knowing that Francisco was a Jew. They told Francisco in their language that the Tribe of Joseph dwelled in the midst of the sea (Caribbean); and they held up two fingers, first joined together and then held apart, to reveal that they were two families descending from one head....* **Manasseh and Ephraim**. *The Indians added that they believed that one day they would all meet their Israelite brethren. Over the course of three days, Aaron met more Indians that were living across the river and he described them as their skin complexion was reddish-brown from the sun. Aaron described them as being tall,* **with beards and often wearing a type of turban on their heads**. *After their stay, Francisco and Aaron Levi returned to Quito, Ecuador (South America).*

Aaron Levi was so happy of his encounter that he asked Francisco to tell him more about the Indians he had just met. Francisco told Aaron that what he was told was handed down to them by tradition. He said that the Most High brought the Children of Israel into the New World, by great miracles and wonderful works. He said that when they got to the land they had great battles with the people that had been living there before them. He said there were wizards who advised them to do battle with them which they said always ended up in their defeat.

During this trip Aaron Levi was asked by the indigenous "Indian" how did he know he was a Hebrew. The Europeans Jews today stutter or don't know the answer to "What Tribe are you from" or they cannot prove that they are from a certain tribe of Israel, **but Levi said the following words**:

"I am a Hebrew of the Tribe of Levi, my God is Adonay, and all the rest are nothing but mistakes and deceits." The Indian Israelite asked him the name of his ancestor and Aaron Levi replied, "Abraham, Isaac, Jacob and Israel." The Indian asked Levi if he had a father and Levi said, "**Lodwick of Montezinos**". The Indian was not satisfied and said these words to the fake Jew, "On the one side I did rejoice at that which thou hast said unto me, and on the other **I AM RESOLVING TO DISBELIEVE THEE**, because thou cannot tell me who were thy fathers (ancestors)." Aaron Levi told the Indian that he was telling the truth.

In other words, the Indian was saying "**I am finding it hard to believe you.**" Even the indigenous Indian from the 1500's didn't believe that Aaron Levi was a real Israelite. Why? His first guess was right. God gave that Indian "discernment" in what was Truth and what was a Lie.

Fact: It is a known truth that the "indigenous" Indians (Tainos, Caribs, Mayans, Incas) claim to have come from the "**East**". As in the "Atlantic Ocean" East. Blacks from West Africa also came from the "East" to the Caribbean Island prior to getting to South America, per the report the Taino Indians that told this to the Spaniards (Christopher Columbus). If these "**Indians**" or "**Blacks**" would've came from the "West-Pacific

Ocean" they would've said so. So why would the Israelite Indian that Levi met say that "**Manasseh and Ephraim (Tribe of Joseph)"** lived to the East (Caribbean Islands)? Many of the Taino Indians and Carib Indians had ventured into South America prior to the Europeans arrival. The Caribbean Islands were closer to South America than North America. The mtDNA of Cubans, Puerto Ricans, Dominicans, and South American Latinos (**mtDNA A, C, D**) are mostly connected to mtDNA of Bantus Africans-Ethiopians/East Africans (**mtDNA L3, M**). Hmmmm.........the plot thickens.

Aaron Levi is also sometimes known as **Antonio Montezinos**, a Portuguese traveler and a Marrano Sephardic Jew who in 1644 persuaded **Menasseh Ben Israel**, a rabbi of Amsterdam, that he had found one of the Ten Lost Tribes of Israel living in the jungles of the "**Quito Province**" (that is, the Pichincha Province) of Ecuador. This supposed discovery gave new light to Menasseh's Messianic hopes. Menasseh wrote a book about this narrative called "**The Hope of Israel**". In it Menasseh argued, and tried to give learned support to the theory that the Native inhabitants of America at the time of the European discovery were actually descendants of the Lost Ten Tribes of Israel. The book was originally written in Hebrew (Mikveh Israel) and in Latin (Spes Israelis) around 1648, but its publication in English in 1650 in London caused great controversy and polemics in England.

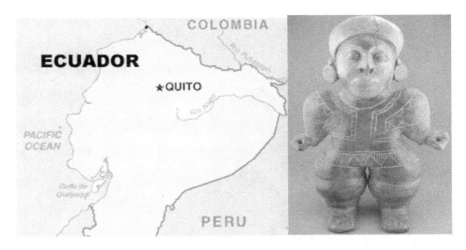

(**Left**) Quito, Ecuador. (**Right**) Chorrera people from Ecuador, 300 B.C.

Francisco and Aaron Levi traveled through the Andes Mountains and into Quito, Ecuador. The Andes Mountains extend through Venezuela, Columbia, Ecuador, Peru, Bolivia, Chile and Argentina

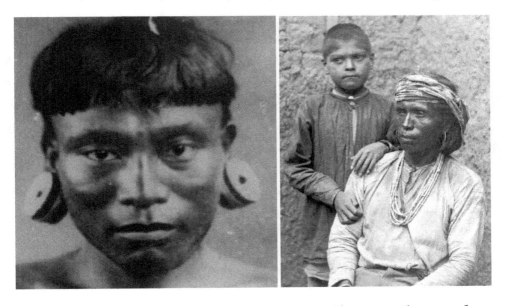

Hosea 7:8 "Ephraim, he hath mixed himself among the people; Ephraim is a cake not turned."

(**Left**) Brazilian Indian from the "**Botocudo**" Tribe. (**Right**) **Zuni** Indian man and his son (New Mexico) 1800's.

(**Above**) Polynesian Men with Afros.   They man to the left has a "**Asian-Mongloid**" appearance. Where did he get it from? Polynesia consists of Samoa, Fiji, Tonga, Easter Island and is west of South America/Central America.   The Polynesian Paternal **Y-DNA** falls under the "**C**" Haplogroup like the Australian Aborigines and some Native Indians in the Americas.   The Polynesians Maternal **mtDNA** falls under the "**B**" Haplogroup which is also seen in American Native Indians.   **Maternal mtDNA B** is also found in the Philippines, Japan, China, Indonesia, Thailand and Madagascar.   But here is where it gets deep!

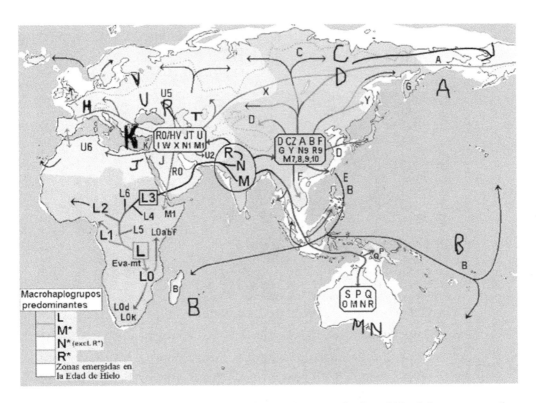

(**Above**) Maternal DNA (mtDNA) chart of the World except the Americas/Caribbean. **Note: This requires very close attention! Please refer back to this graph as a reference.**

1. It is a known fact that the "**European mtDNA Haplogroups**" are defined as **R, J, T, H, V, U and K**. These mtDNA Haplogroups are all found in North Africa, Europe, and the Middle East up until India (**keep this in mind because the Greeks couldn't invade any further than the northwest part of India**). The mtDNA "**Macro-haplogroups**" of the world are **L, M, N and R**. Maternal Haplogroup "**L**" is seen primarily in Sub-Saharan "**Non-Arab**" Africa/Yemen where the people are essentially "**Brown-skinned**". Who inhabited Africa mainly throughout time? **The Sons of Ham and the Hebrew Israelites. RESULT: (SKIN COLOR BROWN).**

2. The Maternal mtDNA Haplogroup "**M**" is seen in East Africa/Horn of Africa (i.e. Kenyans, Ethiopians/Eritreans),

411

Yemen, South India, the Andaman Islands and Australia (Australian Aborigines).

(**Above**) Andaman "**Negrito**" Islanders. The Andaman people have genetic similarities to Bantus Sub-Saharan Africans (Igbo, Yoruba's), Ethiopians (Amharas, Afar, Beja), Dravidian South Indians (Kerala, Tamil Nadu), and Australian Aborigines. They like pure-blooded Asians, Africans and Native Americans do not have any evidence of the "**Neanderthal gene mtDNA X**". The Neanderthal man was busy in Europe mixing with modern "**white races**" as the **Neanderthal mtDNA "X"** is seen in today's **Caucasians, European/Mizrahi Jews and White-skinned Arabs**. However, the "Neanderthal Man" also made his way to South Asia (**i.e. Australia, Melanesia**) and Siberia, eventually crossing over to Canada. Geneticists often use the term "**Denisovans**" when referring to Neanderthals. A Denisovan "Neanderthal" Cave was found in Russia/Siberia in the Altai Mountains near the border of China and Mongolia.

Genetic analysis of the Y-DNA "**D**" and the mtDNA "**M**" of the Andaman Islanders provides proof that some of the Hebrew Israelites left East to Asia while some trickled back into Africa. Geneticists have concluded that Y-DNA Haplogroups "D" and "E" originated in Northeast Africa (Egypt/Israel) because they are so similar genetically but are not seen in the same continents (Africa/Asia). They believe Y-DNA Haplogroup "**DE**" split into **TWO** Haplogroups (D & E) when there was a mixing of this Haplogroup "DE" with different regions. One group of people went to Africa and stayed there. One group of people went east to Asia and primarily stayed there. Some of these people prior to settling for good in their new habit, mixed with other nations (Shemitic tribes including Shemitic Arab Ishmaelite's) and re-entered North and East Africa. This brought the mtDNA "**M**" and "**N**" into Africa.

Note: Some people also believe it brought the Y-DNA "R1b" into Africa (i.e. Fulani of Cameroon/Nigeria, Hausa, Tuaregs, Black Moors?). **They believed the "R1b" carriers were half Arab/half Israelite**.

Maternal mtDNA "**M**" is seen in the Andaman "Negrito" Islanders, South Indians, and the Australian Aborigines but is also seen in Eritreans, and Ethiopian (**Amharas, Tigray, Beja, Afar**). So how is this "**M**" mtDNA seen in the men and women of the Andaman Islands but is also seen in **Africa/Yemen**? The Andaman Negritos are similar to Africans in terms of "**craniology/craniometry**" but are genetically closer to East Asians (**Indians, Malaysians, Australian Aborigines, Melanesians, Polynesians, Papua New Guineans, Japanese**) because of their **Y-DNA "D"**. They also have similar dental morphology to people living in South Asia. So in essence, these Black Andaman Islanders have a genetic connection to Africa, the Middle East and Asia. Their Y-DNA "D" also has the same YAP+ (**Y-Chromosome Alu-Polymorphism**) marker that Bantus Nigerian Igbo's have. Their Y-DNA haplogroup "D" is also found in Tibet, Japan (Ainu/Jomon) and Southwest China (i.e. Pumi people, Qiang people) but these people have straight hair and look "**Mongloid/Asian**". This is amazing. However,

413

for the most part "**mtDNA M carriers**" in these regions have different textures of hair from black straight hair to soft, bushy, curly hair to tight-curled kinky hair. They are able to grow for the most part an Afro (most of them). They also are "Brown-skinned" people. Who inhabited these "M" regions? **The sons of Ham, the Hebrew Israelites, and the Sons of Shem (Elam, Arphaxad, Asshur). RESULT: (SKIN COLOR BROWN).**

3. **SO WE HAVE CONCLUDED THUS FAR MACROHAPLOGROUPS "L" AND "M" ARE FOUND IN SUB-SAHARAN AFRICA AND SOUTH ASIA!**

4. The Maternal mtDNA Haplogroup "N" is found primarily in the Middle East (i.e. **Turkey, Syria, Lebanon, Palestine, Israel, Iraq, Iran, North Saudi Arabia near the Persian Gulf**). It is also found in **Western Europe, Eastern Europe, North Africa, Central Asia, China, the Philippines, India, Australia, Southeast Asia, and Japan**. Materna mtDNA "**N1b**" has been identified as one of four **Ashkenazi Jewish founder lineages**. It is a known fact that the Ashkenazi Jews, Turkish Jews, Moroccan Jews, Polish Jews, Russian Jews, Ukraine Jews, and Romanian Jews all carry the "**mtDNA N**" in small frequencies up to **11%**. So who used to occupy these mentioned areas very early in biblical history (**2,000 B.C. to 300 B.C.**)? **The descendants of Shem, including Edom!**

Shem's sons: **Arphaxad, Asshur, Aram, Elam and Lud** occupied most of the Middle East and Asia Minor. It is believed that the descendants of Shem occupied the "**Orient**", meaning the East, while Ham occupied the West, and Japheth occupied the North. **But then something happened!** The **descendants of Japheth** came down from the North in 300 B.C. starting first with the Greeks (**Alexander the Great, Seleucus I Nicator**) who invaded North Africa, the Middle East, and West Asia.   Later the descendants of Japheth invaded the lands further east by following the **Silk Trade Routes** into China! **RESULT: (SKIN COLOR BROWN TO LIGHT BROWN TO WHITE).**

5. After 1000 A.D., more "**Japhethites**" came from the North to the Middle East, Africa and West Asia (**i.e. Afghanistan, Pakistan, Turkmenistan**). The "**invasion**" of and "**mixing**" of the Middle East by the Greeks, Romans, Turks, Kurds, Armenians, and the Balkan countries could've been the "**main trigger**" that shifted the "**N**" mtDNA macrohaplogroup into the "**R**" mtDNA macrohaplogroup. The R mtDNA macrohaplogroup would be the ancestor of the "**Japhetic/European**" **mtDNA Haplogroups**, including those nations who had an infusion of "**Japhetic**" blood by invasion or migration (i.e. India, Hong Kong-China).   The "**Movement**" of Japheth's seed into the Middle East, Africa, and

415

Asia would be the reason why the "White" **Arabs-Jews-Asians** of today can be found to have the mtDNA of European-Caucasoids **(i.e. mtDNA J, T, H, V, U and K). RESULT: (SKIN COLOR WHITE).**

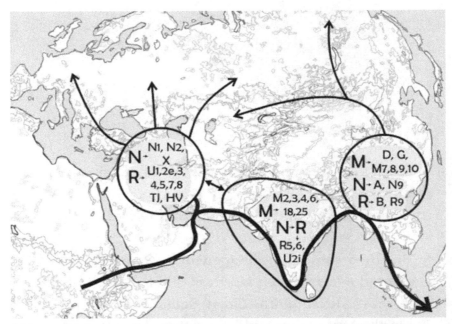

(Above) Maternal mtDNA macrohaplogroups M, N and R. As you can see mtDNA M, N and R is clearly seen in India-South Asia. Maternal mtDNA "M" which is the descendant of **L3** (most common mtDNA in African-Americans/Bantus African) is **NOT** seen in West Eurasia, but it is seen in **East Africa, India, Australia** and **South Asia**.......all places where the people are "melaninated". **Note: their skin color is not due to the Sun. So what could this possibly mean?**

(Above) "Real" Native Americans. Notice their brown skin complexion compared to the two white children in the photo at the bottom left. How did the "**Indians**" get this dark? Some of these Indians are darker than African-Americans. Surely they didn't get it from Japheth. If they did, they should share the same mtDNA and Y-DNA as Europeans. But they don't.

6. So were the descendants of **Shem** very early on strictly "**Negroid**" to begin with? Perhaps some were "**Negroid**" and some were "**Less Negroid**". Were some of the Shemites "**Brown Mongloids**" while others were "**Brown Negroes**"? After all, **Azurad** (the daughter of Nimrod, son of Cush) married Eber (father of the Hebrews). **We also know Nimrod, a Nubian Cushite started his Kingdom in Africa, Arabia and the Middle East according to the Bible.**

*Genesis 10:8-10 "And **Cush begat Nimrod**: he began to be a mighty one in the earth. He was a mighty hunter before the Lord: wherefore it is said, Even as Nimrod the mighty hunter before the Lord. **And the beginning of his kingdom was Babel (Babylon), and Erech***

(Uruk), and Accad (i.e. Akkadian), and Calneh, in the land of Shinar (Iraq/Iran)."

Scientists also say there are 3 major races of humankind: **Negroid** (Ham), **Caucasoid** (Japheth) and **Mongloid** (Shem?). These are considerations we must keep in mind. Were the Hebrews a brown-skinned people with variations in hair textures and facial features, not typical of an African or a European? We know the dark-skinned Australian Aboriginal race has softer hair textures and dark skin. We all have seen at some point in our life a dark Skinned Dravidian Indian who has semi-straight hair or dark-skin. What about the South Asians? Maternal mtDNA Haplogroups "M/N" are both seen in India, South Asia and Australian (Aborigines) as we saw earlier. The mtDNA Haplogroups of the indigenous Indians (**A, B, C, D**) in the Americas **comes straight off the branch** of macrohaplogroup mtDNA "**M/N**" and not macrohaplogroup mtDNA "**R**". Those peoples carrying mtDNA "**A**" typically are "lighter" in appearance than those carrying mtDNA "**B, C**, and **D**". Could mtDNA A & B carriers have more "**Shemitic-Japhetic**" Blood while mtDNA C & D carriers have more "**Shemitic-Hamitic**" Blood? This is a good question we need to ask ourselves in regards to the True Origins of the **Native Americans** and the "**Lost Children of Israel**"!

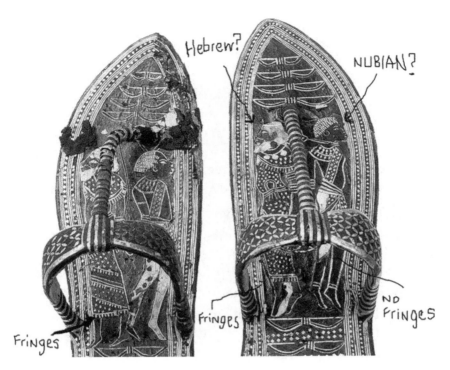

(**Above**) This is an actual sandal of the Ancient Egyptian Pharaoh's. They typically had pictures of Egyptian slaves on their sandals as a symbol of power. Therefore, the Pharaoh's would always have his "**enemies/captured slaves**" underneath his feet (**figuratively** and **literally**). As you can see the man on the left with the **fringed garment** is brown-skinned with what looks to be different type of "**hair texture**" and "**skin tone**" compared to the **non-fringed** Nubian man. During the Egyptian "Dynastic" period the Egyptians conquered the Nubians and the Nubians would also conquer the Egyptians. One man has "**fringes**" and one man has "**no fringes**". Could this be a Hebrew Israelite man and a Nubian Cushite man we are seeing here? Could some of the Israelites after mixing with the Sons of Ham for centuries, turned into a "Negroid" people themselves? Do all African-Americans look like Africans, or do some look like Black Pacific Islanders from South Asia or Native Americans?

419

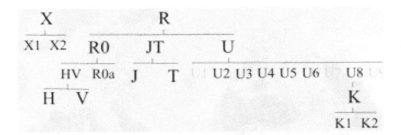

(**Above**) The mtDNA of all "**European**", "**White Jewish**", and "**White Arab**" peoples come off the mtDNA "**R**" macrohaplogroup which is "**Caucasoid/European**" genetically. This means that European Jews and modern-day Arabs today are mostly "**European**" by genetic stock.

The Maternal mtDNA Haplogroup "**A**" and "**B**" is a descendant of mtDNA "**M & N**", not mtDNA macrohaplogroup "**R**" which has been proven to be the ancestor of all European/Arab mtDNA Haplogroups. Maternal mtDNA Haplogroups A, B, C, or D are **NOT SEEN IN AFRICA**. This could possibly suggest that early on (**700 B.C. – 400 B.C.**) "**Israelite-Hamite**" people left Israel and the Middle East for a "**New Home**" to the East (**ASIA**). Over time the descendants of Japheth would catch up to Shem's seed and encroach its way into Asia. This "**insertion**" of Japheth's seed into Asia would begin the "**lightening up**" process of the brown skin color in Asia. After sprouting from mtDNA Haplogroup "**M-N**", maternal mtDNA "**A, B, C, and D**" would then only be found in Asia and the Americas.

Note: Maternal mtDNA "**A, C and D**" are the most common maternal haplogroups seen in Caribbean Latinos. Trace these mtDNA Haplogroups backwards and you get to "**Black**" mtDNA Haplogroups such as "**L3 or M**". This means that there is common ancestor way back for the Native American, the Polynesian, the Melanesian, the Australian Aborigine, the South Indian, the Sri Lankan and Blacks living on the Andaman Islands. Could this common ancestor be Abraham or Jacob?

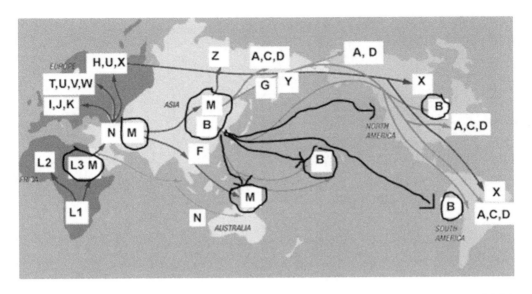

(**Above**) Notice how mtDNA Haplogroup "**L3**" gives rise to mtDNA "**M**" which then gives rise to mtDNA Haplogroups **A, B, C, and D**.

- **L3c** – Ethiopian Jews and Yemeni Jews
- **L3f3** – Chad Basin
- **L3d** – Some Fulani, Ethiopians, Akan, Mozambique, Akan people (Ghana/Ivory Coast),
- **L3j** – Some Sudanese
- **L3e** – Most common L3 subgroup seen in the "**Bantus**" **people**", African-Americans, Afro-Brazilians, and Caribbean's. The Bantus people includes Kenya, Tanzania, Zimbabwe, Ghana, Congo, Rwanda, Gabon, Cameroon, Angola, Nigeria, Burkina Faso, Benin/Togo, Liberia, Sierra Leone, Guinea Bissau, Gambia, Senegal and others.

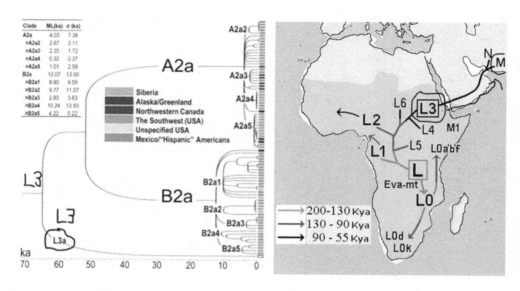

(Above) **mtDNA sequences belonging to mtDNA A2a and B2a.** Notice **mtDNA L3** is an ancestor of mtDNA "**A**" and "**B**". Southwest USA and Mexican "Hispanic" Americans are liked to mtDNA "B". Siberians and Alaskan Inuit's are lined to mtDNA "**A**". So is the brown-skinned Algonquian "**Mi'kmaq**" Indian Tribe in Northeast Canada and Maine. Their mtDNA "A" all stem from the older "**L3**" mtDNA Haplogroup. But we must keep in mind, that there are many people living in Latin America that have European Spanish mothers and European Spanish fathers. Their mtDNA will not show any "Indian DNA". It will show "European" DNA. It is a known fact that many Europeans came to South America in the early days.

Graph Reference:

Reconciling migration models to the Americas with the variation of North American native mitogenomes *Alessandro Achillia,1, Ugo A. Peregob,c, Hovirag Lancionia, Anna Olivierib, Francesca Gandinib, Baharak Hooshiar Kashanib, Vincenza Battagliab, Viola Grugnib, Norman Angerhoferc, Mary P. Rogersd, Rene J. Herrerae, Scott R. Woodwardc,f, Damian Labudag, David Glenn Smithh, Jerome S. Cybulskii, Ornella Seminob, Ripan S. Malhid,j, and Antonio Torronib*, **- Proceedings of the National Academy of Sciences, August 27th, 2013. Vol 110. #35**

The Expansion of mtDNA Haplogroup L3 within and out of Africa, *Soares P, Alshamali F, Pereira JB, Fernandes V, Silva NM, Afonso C, Costa MD, Musilová E, Macaulay V, Richards MB, Cerny V, Pereira L.* **Molecular Biology and Evolution, March 2012, 29(3): page 915-927**

Keeping on the subject, "**Native Americas**" and the "**Negro**" make up **2/3** of the races in the heritage of "**Latinos/Hispanics**". Many avid Bible readers are still not convinced that the "Native Americans" could be descendants of the "Lost Tribes of Israel". So let's take a look at the Native Americans and their documented "Hebrewisms" by Europeans in the 16th Century. In the Book "**Jews in America or Probabilities That the Americans Are of That Race**" by *Thomas Thorowgood* (1595 A.D.-1669 A.D.) the "Indians" living in **Mexico, Peru, Ecuador, Yucatan, Brazil** amonst other places were known to exhibit the following customs:

- Some of the Indians wrote from **Right-to-Left** (like Hebrew and Egyptian) while others wrote from Left-to-Right.
- The Indians held 2-3 wheat harvest festivals annually. (Similar to the Israelites). The **Pentecost (Pesach)**, the **Feast of Weeks (Shavuot)** and the **Feast of Ingathering/Tabernacles/Booths (Sukkot)** are 3 required festivals/holidays that God gave to the Israelites. The "**firstfruit**" offerings given at these 3 festivals were to be made as a way of expressing thanks to God. The Feast of Firstfruits included the **barley harvest**. The Feast of Weeks was the **wheat harvest** and the Feast of Tabernacles was sometimes **olive or grape harvests.** (Exodus 34:22).
- Indians wore forbidden to swear oaths.
- Indians performed circumcision with stone knives.
- Indians worship **the God** that created the sun, moon and the stars. They **DID NOT** worship the sun, moon and stars like the Egyptians, Sumerians, Ethiopian Nubians, Canaanites and Babylonians used to do.

- They knew of the "**Great Flood**" that drowned the world because of the "**sin of man**" and unlawful lust. They knew from their ancestors that there would never be another "Great Flood" again as promised by God.
- They were told from their ancestors that after many years, "Fire" would come down and consume the earth.
- The Indians in some areas have a **King, a Priest and a Prophet**.
- The Indians believe in immortality of the soul and Hell, which they call "**Popoguffo**".
- Indians have "**Temple Robes**" like the Cohenite Aaronite "**High Priests**". They also have certain "**Chambers**" that only the priest can enter. This was seen in the village of Tamazulapan, in the state of Oaxaca, Mexico. **Note: this was 400+ years ago.**
- The temples in Mexico where the Indians worshipped, sung, pray and made their offering was built "foursquare" **(i.e. hundred cubits long and 100 cubits wide like Ezekiel 40:47)**.
- The Indians in Mexico in the temple burned incense, performed drink offerings and had cake offerings like in **Jeremiah 7:18.**

  Jeremiah 7:18 "The children gather wood, and the fathers kindle the fire, and the women knead their dough, to make cakes to the **Queen of Heaven**, and to pour out drink offerings unto other gods, that they may provoke me to anger."

- The "**Firstfruits**" of the Indians corn (maize), bread and what they gathered by hunting or fishing was offered up to God at a certain time of the year.
- In Peru, there was "**One Temple**" and other smaller sort-of places were the Indians would congregate (i.e. like synagogues).
- The Indians observed a "**Year of Jubilee**" like the Israelites in Leviticus 25:10.

Leviticus 25:10 "And you shall sanctify the fiftieth year, and proclaim freedom throughout the land for all who live on it. It shall be a **Jubilee** for you, and you shall return, each man to his property, and you shall return, each man to his family."

- Indians were forbidden to drink (i.e. wine, liquor, beer).
- Indians believed in "**resurrection**" after death.
- Indians believed that the world would have an "end", but not until a "**great drought**" came, as if it was a "**burning of the air**", when the Sun and the Moon shall "fail", and lose their shining. They believed this would herald an eclipse of the Sun and the Moon would happen. (**i.e. Blood Moons, Solar Eclipse in 2014-2015**).

Joel 2:31 "The **Sun shall be turned into darkness**, and the **moon into blood**, before the great and the terrible day of the Lord come."

- Indians were forbidden to commit adultery.
- Indians were heard speaking the word "**Hallelu-Yah**" perfectly which they didn't learn from European Christians. The Spaniards also digged up some grave stones in the **Azores Islands**, Northwest of the Canary Islands which had Hebrew Letters on them saying "**Why is God gone away**". They also found the writing of **Yod-Hey-Uau-Hey** which they pronounced as "**Yo-He-Wah**".
- Some of the Indians practiced Cannibalism like some people living in the Congo or Papua New Guinea. This is like what is read in **Ezekiel 5:9-10**.
- Indians in America called their Kings/Chiefs "**Caciques**" like what the Taino Indians in the Caribbean called their **Chiefs**.
- Indians claimed that during the reign of Hoshea King of Israel (8th Century B.C.) they were carried out of Samaria (Northern

Israel) by the King of Assyria Salmanasser (**Shalmaneser V**) and displaced into Assyria and Medes/Persia.

- Indians claimed their Journey took under 2 years (1 ½ years).
- Indians claimed when they first came to America they kept the Torah.
- Indians claimed that prophecy states that they will eventually re-gather with other Israelites to two places in the world, namely **"Egypt-Nile"** and **"Assyria-Euphrates"**, which is the land promised to Abraham's seed, aka **"The Greater Israel"**. This is what the Jews today are striving for (**i.e. Greater Israel Project**).

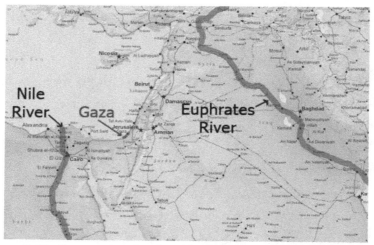

The Land God promised Abraham and Isaac's seed is listed in **Genesis 15:18.** It was reiterated again to the Israelites in Joshua **1:4.** It is basically the land from the **Nile River** (Egypt) to the **Euphrates River** (Syria/Iraq-Persian Gulf). The North Border is the **Mediterranean Sea.** If you can imagine what the South border is you can safely say that the land given to Abraham is **VERY LARGE!**

- During the **"regathering"** of the Israelites in the **"Last Days"**, the Indians say they will be **"no more divided"** and they shall have **one Prince, the Messiah**, the **Son of David.** Egyptians and Arabs don't believe in this. The Indians did not have the New

426

Testament, so they did not know about the name "**Jesus**" or the Gospels.

- Indians said their King, Moctezuma of Mexico and their forefathers told them how they would be "**strangers in the land**" that they would come to, they would be eventually led by a "**great prince**" and that they would be "**preferred by God**."

- The Indians never heard of the name "**Jesus**" and had not been "**gospelized**". Therefore, the Spaniards and Portuguese felt it was their "**Godly**" duty to "**Gospelize**" the Indians. The Gentile Japhetic Europeans believed that before end of the world the "**Israelites**" would be converted to their Catholic Church Christianity. The Spaniards had a saying:

"From the Jews our faith began, To the Gentiles then it ran, To the Jews returned it shall, Before the dreadful end of all."

- The Indians in America had a tradition that the "**White**" and "**bearded nations**" would subdue their countries, abolish all their rites and ceremonies, and introduce a new religion. The Spanish brought "strange diseases", rape, murder, and in 3 months 7,000 infants were reported dead secondary to lack of milk from their mothers. Millions of "Indians" died in Cuba, Puerto Rico, Haiti, the Dominican Republic and Jamaica. The Inca King of Peru, **Attabaliba** in the 1533's was conquered by Spaniard **Francis Pizarro** and killed despite his payment of gold/silver vessels for the ransom on his life. **The Spaniards documented "woeful" servitude and captivity for the male, female and child Indian**. Spanish dogs attacked and ate the native "**Indians**" and the Spanish made bets as to who could dig the deepest with their sword into the body of an Indian or who could cut an Indians head off with one single blow. The Europeans also dashed Indian babies against the rocks, dismembered limbs of Indians with the sword and scattered their "**remnant**" amongst the people.

Hosea 13:16 "**Samaria** (Northern House of Israel) shall become desolate (700 B.C.); for she hath rebelled against her God: they shall fall by the sword: **their infants shall be dashed into pieces, and their women with child shall be ripped up**."

- They were told by their forefathers the story of their people by explaining that **God** (singular) made **one man** and **one woman**. **Note: Egyptians don't believe in this story**. He told them to be fruitful and multiply. They told of the story of Moses being placed in a "**Ark of Bulrush**", during a famine "**bread (i.e. manna) rained from heaven**", afterwards they received "**water from a rock (i.e. Mount Horeb)**". The Indians stated that when they came out of Egypt, God gave them the Oracles (**Covenant**). The Ark/Tabernacle was carried by four of their priests. They pitched tents facing the east. The Indians believed in Angels and that the Sun, Moon and Stars were living creatures (**Egyptian learnt behavior**).
- The Indians were required to marry into their own tribe/kindred.
- They called their uncles and aunties "**mother and father**" like many Africans do today (**i.e. Igbo Nigerians**).
- During Funerals the Indians mourned a great deal.
- During women's monthly cycle (menses) they separate the women in "**wigwam**" huts.
- The Indians wear a "**single-coat**" garment and a square cloak like the Jewish "**Tallit Katan/Tallit Gadol**".
- The Indians wear nose earrings and ear earrings.
- The Indians bath frequently and dance after victories.
- The Indians didn't eat pork.
- The Indians washed stranger's feet.
- The Indians tell time by the night.

- The Indians followed the "**Lunar Moon**". Egyptians didn't practice this and the Native Indians were in the Americas/Caribbean way before Islam began in 600 A.D.
- An Indian man's widow has to marry/befriend the brother of the deceased husband. This is called a "Levirate Marriage" and was an old Israelite Tradition mandated in Deuteronomy 25:5-6. This practice is seen in Yoruba, Igbo, Hausa, and Fulani Nigerians.
- Dowries given during marriage.
- They punish by whippings/lashes (**Deuteronomy 25:3**).

After the **10 Northern Tribes of Israel** were exiled from their land by the Assyrians in 700 B.C. the **Southern Tribes of Judah** were led away into captivity by the Babylonians around 597 A.D. The Return of the Israelites (Southern Kingdom of the Tribe of Judah & Benjamin) would later come under the rule of Persian King Cyrus led by **Ezra (Levite/Aaronite)** and **Zerubbabel (Judah/Davidic Line)**.

Ezra 1:5 "Then rose up the chief of the father of Judah and Benjamin, and the priests, and the Levites, with all them whose spirit God had raised, to go up to build the house of the Lord which is in Jerusalem."

Ezra 4:1 "Now when the adversaries of Judah and Benjamin heard that the children of the captivity builded the temple unto the Lord God of Israel."

However, God promised that he would bring his **Children of Israel** back and that the Scepter of Judah would never depart. So who was left? Who would restore the Line of King David (Judah)? King David had many children: **Solomon, Nathan, Absalom, Adonijah, Ammon, Daniel/Chileab, Shephatiah, Ithream, Shammua, Shobab, Ibhar, Elishua, Eliphelet, Nogah, Nepheg, Japhia, Elishama, Eliada, Amnon,** his daughter **Tamar** and many others born to him by concubines.

The name "**Ephraim**" was used often synonymously with "**Israel**" or the **Northern Kingdom of Israel**. Per the Bible Ephraim was to father a multitude/commonwealth of nations while Manasseh was to be one single nation. **Hosea**, an 8th Century B.C. Minor prophet was known for his prophecy/warning directed towards the Northern Kingdom led by Ephraim. The Northern Kingdom led by Ephraim was deep into idolatry and Hosea was warning them to repent. Some believe the Book of Hosea foretold the migration of Ephraim to the West (New World) via an East Wind.

Hosea 12:1 "Ephraim feeds on the wind, and pursues (chases) the east wind."

But what about what Jeremiah prophesied about the Nation of Israel?

Greek Septuagint Jeremiah 3:18 "In those days the **House of Judah**, shall come together to the **House of Israel**, and they shall come, together, from the **Land of the North**, and from all the countries, to the land, which I caused their fathers to inherit."

So what did Jeremiah mean by the "**Land of the North**?" Is this referring to the Israelites entering into "**North America**?"

Where is the Lost 10 Tribes of Israel? What about the Southern 2 Tribes (Judah and Benjamin)?" Where are they at? We know according to the Bible, the Ashkenazi, Sephardic and Mizrahi Jews **ARE NOT** the biblical Israelites. Their possession of Israel does not fit Bible prophecy. The Bible says that when ALL the Israelites return to Israel there will be peace and none shall make them afraid.

Jeremiah 30:10 "Therefore fear thou not, O my servant Jacob, saith the Lord; neither be dismayed, O Israel: for lo, I will save thee from afar, and thy seed from the land of their captivity; and Jacob shall return, and shall be in **rest**, and be **quiet**, and **none shall make him afraid**."

Well, to find this out we should look to who has been or is going through the "**Curses of Israel**" in Deuteronomy 28:15-68. We also have to see who has been the "target" of destruction by the **Children of Edom** and the **Gentile Children of Japheth**. This will help point to where the Children of Israel are. Using DNA and the "migration history of the Israelites" we can bring together pieces of information that can reveal were most of the 12 Tribes are at. There is one big question that many people have asked. This question is, "**Are the Latinos/Hispanics in the "New World" also descendants of the Children of Israel like the Native American Indian and the Negro?**" Well, the "**missing link**" may lie in the DNA of the **Moors who were Black Arabs in** Ancient times.

CHAPTER 19

THE NORTH AFRICAN, MOORISH, ISRAELITE AND LATINO CONNECTION.

(**Left**) A Black Moor and his Wife 1800's in Morocco. (**Right**) Depiction of a Black Moor in France. The Moors dominated Western Europe and parts of Eastern Europe for about 700 years (**longer than the time period of the Transatlantic Slave Trade to today's time**). Many speculate that they left their Y-DNA "**R1b**" mark in Western Europe. But who actually were these "**Moors**"? Noah did not have a son named "**Moor**" and there is no Tribe called "**Moor**" in history. Many ancient Arab historians say the Fulani Tribe in Cameroon, Nigeria, Burkina Faso are **half Arab/half Israelite**. They say they came from the Middle East and Arabia into Africa bringing the **Y-DNA "R1b" Haplogroup**, which is also seen in Spaniards, Latinos and other Africans. **But is the Latinos and Moors "R1b" Y-DNA different than that of Western Europeans?**

(**Left**) **Moorish Berber man** from Tunisia. Most pictures on T.V. of Tunisia show white-skinned Arabs (i.e. Arab Spring). His religion is **Islam**. (Right) Tunisian Jewish man and woman. Their religion is Judaism. Only one can be "**authentic**". Perhaps this Jewish couple is a descendant of the Edomites, Romans, Grecians, Turks and Kurds who over time decided to convert to the religion of the land of Israel. Notice how this man looks like a typical Muslim Arab and a Jew (Ashkenazi/Sephardic/Mizrahi) all at the same time. The "deception" is very real!

The Moors were Black Muslims that ruled North Africa, Iberia (Spain/Portugal), France, Sicily, and Malta starting from 711 B.C. to the late 1400's. It is common knowledge that the Moors were black as in most languages the word "Moor" has its root in the meaning "**Black**" like the Spanish word "**Moreno**". Many people believe that the Moors left their Y-DNA "**mark**" in the lands that they conquered and ruled over for 700 years. This "mark" would only be on the male "Y" sex chromosome and therefore would only be seen in males from Western Europe. The mtDNA of men and women in Western Europe would be show "strictly" European mtDNA. During the 8th century the Moors were ruling mostly in Western Europe while the Muslim Umayyad Caliphate was ruling from the Middle East to Spain. So the big question is, "**Was the Moors a mixture of Semitic peoples, Ishmaelite's, Black**

Egyptians, Black Libyans and Israelites?" Also, "Was the Black "Umayyad Caliphate filled with Black Ishmaelite Arabs?" According to Geneticists and Scientists, the major Y-DNA Haplogroups in Western Europe is "**R1b**". This "R1b" Haplogroup is also seen in Spain, Portugal, France, Southern Italy, Sicily, Malta. It is also seen in Israel, Lebanon (Druze), the Egypt, the Egypt-Libyan Border, the Sudanese Copts, the Hausas (Sudan/Nigeria), the Fulani, Chad, and Northern Cameroon. The people in Chad, North Cameroon and the Fulani have the highest percentages of **R1b (V88)** in the world. So how did this R1b Haplogroup get from the Levant to North Africa to Spain/Portugal and to Central Africa?

(**Above**) The **Fulani Tribe** are known to have first accepted Islam out of all the people in Africa. The have been attributed with setting up the **Tekrur/Takrur Empire** aka the "**Futa Toro**". Some say the Fulani are descendants of Jacob through Joseph's Children. Others say they are a people who are half-Black Semitic (Ishmael, or the Sons of Shem) and half-Israelite. Many believe the Fulani have a Judeo-Syriac origin and that they migrated from Israel/Assyria-Syria into Egypt making their way into West, Central and East Africa. **This story would in a way link them to the Israelites exiled to Assyria (Modern Syria) who returned back to Africa instead of heading towards Asia.** The Fulani people are just about "**everywhere**" the Hebrew Israelite "**E1b1a**"

carriers are: **Ethiopia, Sudan, Chad, Niger, Senegal, Gambia, Mali, Sierra Leone, Benin, Cameroon, Ivory Coast, Central African Republic, Ghana, Liberia, Mauritania, Burkina Faso, Guinea Bissau, and Nigeria** but they are usually the majority. The Fulani Tribe have always been amongst Israelites because half of their Large "Diverse" Tribe consists of men that test positive for the "**E1b1a**". So who are these "Fulani" people and what is this "R1b" gene that they carry. The "Ancient Moors" must've carried this "**Y-DNA R1b gene**" because it is prevalent in the countries they ruled in Western Europe. But why is there such a strong presence of "**R1b**" carriers in Chad, Niger, Nigeria and Sudan? Are they the "modern-day" descendants of the Moors? Let's put it together:

1. The "**R1b**" Haplogroup is found primarily in the countries the Moors ruled over for 700+ years.

2. The "**R1b**" Haplogroup is also found in West and Central Africa. In Sudan, the "R1b" Haplogroup is found in the same hot spots where the "**J1 Semitic Haplogroup**" is found (**Khartoum, Sudan, Egypt**). *Note: We know that J1c gene originated from Black Semitic people because the people with the highest percentages are usually Black-appearing Arabs (i.e. Meheri/Mahra people in Yemen, Bedouins of South Israel/Jordan, Khartoum, Sudan, Qatar, Oman and the Lemba Jews).*

3. Noah didn't have a son named "Moor". Neither did Shem or Ham. So we can't be sure that the Moors are all Libyan, Egyptian or Ethiopian Hamites. They could also be a mixture of Shemitic blood (i.e. Ishmael, Israelite).

4. According to Genetics the Y-DNA "**R**" Haplogroup and the Native American Indian "**Specific**" Haplogroup "**Q**" belong to the larger Haplogroup "**P**". The "R" Haplogroup is also found in the people of India, the Pathan/Pasthun Jews in Afghanistan and Sri Lankans. Sri Lankans call themselves "**Elam**" or "**Eelam**". The people living in Kerala, South Indian speak a

435

Hebrew-inspired language called "**Malayalam**" which many state makes up the combo words "**Malay**" + "**Elam**". Benjamin Tudela in the 12th Century A.D. visited these people in South India and said they were "**Black Israelites**".

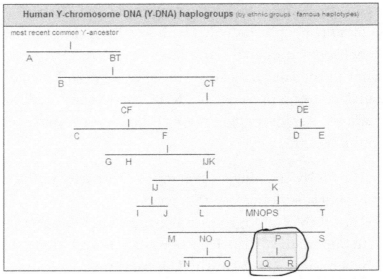

(**Above**) As you can see the "**P**" Haplogroup branches into the "**Q**" and the "**R**" Haplogroup.

5. The women in South India and Sri Lanka carry the "**M**" mtDNA Haplogroup which his seen in Ethiopian Jews, Yemeni Jews. The "**M**" mtDNA haplogroup comes from the Bantus "**L3**" mtDNA Haplogroup.

6. The Moors wore Turbans on their heads and the Israelite Native Americans that Aaron Levi encountered in the 16th Century A.D. in Quito, Ecuador also wore Turbans on their heads.

7. Technically, the Y-DNA Haplogroups "**R**" and "**Q**" are related.

8. If the **Paternal** "Y" DNA is passed down from Grandfather to father to son and so on…. this "**R**" Haplogroup should be older than the "Moors". The Moors have lived, intermarried and fathered biracial babies with the European women they lived amongst for 700 years until 1492 (when they were exiled). It has

only been 500 years that Western Europe has been mostly "White". Since a "Y" DNA Haplogroup takes thousands of years to change (from multiple mutations) into another Haplogroup we would still expect to see this "Black" R1b gene transferred to the DNA of every son born in the Western Europe unless there is an "interruption" in the family tree with a man with a whole different haplogroup (**i.e. Haplgroup I, G,**). No matter how "light" or "black" the Moors "Male offspring" would be from getting white European women pregnant, the "**R1b**" Y-DNA would always be passed down. The "R1b" subgroups would change though (**ex. R1b1a, R1b1b, R1b1c**). So when the Moors were banished back to Africa in 1492, many of them simply migrated into the heart of West and Central Africa. So when the Spaniards and Portuguese came to the "New World" raping the Native women or taking them as wives, they still were unaware that they were passing down a "Black gene". But we know that in Genetics, one can look outwardly "white" but carry Black genes (**former KKK Grand Dragon Craig Cobb**) and one can look "black" and carry half "white genes" (**i.e. Henry Louis Gates Jr., 66th Secretary of State of America, Condoleezza Rice**). But this is based off the "Y" sex chromosome which makes up 1 of our 23 total chromosomes. So the Haplogroup letter by itself and skin color really has no meaning.

9. If the Native Americans mtDNA is a descendant of Bantus Israelite mtDNA and if their DNA is different than Europeans mtDNA as well as Hamitic Africans DNA then the Native Americans cannot be straight "**Hamites**" or straight "**Japhethites**". This leaves Shem, with mix of Ham or Japheth.

10. If the Y DNA Haplogroup "R1b" is a cousin/brother of Y-DNA "**Q**" then the "**R1b**" Haplogroup has to be "Semitic" in nature. So perhaps the Moors were Part-**Israelite**, Part-**North African** (**which the Children of Israel were with their mixing with the**

Egyptians) and Part-**Arab-Semite**. This would explain why the Fulani were believed to be half-Israelite and half-Arab.

(**Above**) Yemen men from Lahij, South Yemen 1800's. You can also find many Black Yemenite people in **Socotra, Yemen** and **Sana'a, Yemen** (Lemba Jews home). Note that these men appear "**Black**" and not Arab. It is a known fact that the **E-M2/E1b1a Y-DNA Haplogroup** of the "**Bantus Negro**" can be still found in some of the people of Yemen. It is also found to compromise half of the DNA of the Lemba Jews who came from Israel. How did this Israelite gene get in Arabia or Yemen? How did the Lemba Tribe get this "**E1b1a**" gene if they passed this Y-DNA down through their paternal lineage from Israel? If the Lemba Jews claim they left Israel around 600 B.C. into Arabia, later settling in Sana'a, Yemen where did the "**E1b1a**" gene come into play? If the Lemba Jews believe that the Bantus people are just "**Hamitic Africans**" then what happened? Did some Bantus African men manage to rape or marry the Lemba women in their Tribe while in Israel, Arabia or Yemen? How else could they pass down this **E1b1a "Paternal Y DNA"**? If the E1b1a Haplogroup carriers were native Arabians or Yemenites, then we should see high frequencies of their DNA in the people of Arabia and Yemen. **But we don't!** If these E1b1a carriers were Ancient Assyrians or Babylonians, then how come we don't see this "**E1b1a**" Haplogroup to be a common haplogroup found in the Middle

East. It's because these "**E1b1a**" carriers were the "**Real Israelites**." Some Israelites escaped into Egypt traveling through North Africa while some Israelites scattered into Arabia, eventually moving further south, after which they could easily cross over the Gulf of Aden into the Horn of Africa (Somalia, Ethiopia, Eritrea). The "**E1b1a, E1b1c and E*(xE1b1a)**" Haplogroups" are seen in many different Tribes in **Eritrea, Ethiopia, Somalia** and even **Mali**. This was the same route that the founder of the 4th Century A.D. Hebrew "**Songhai**" Empire, "**Za el-Yemeni**" (i.e. meaning **he comes from Yemen**) took when crossing over from Yemen into East Africa (**Ethiopia/Eritrea**), eventually making his way to **Mali**.

Need facts?

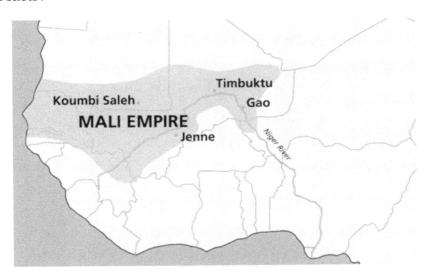

In 1853 a German Scholar/Explorer by the name of **Heinrich Barth** visited Timbuktu, Mali on behalf of the British government. While there he looked at a copy of the **Tarikh al-Sudan** and **Tarikh al-fattash** manuscripts depicting the "**Songhai Hebrew Israelite Empire**" in Mali, West Africa (Gao). Both of these manuscripts were written in Arabic around the 1600's. It verified the existence of the Hebrew Kingdom called "**Songhai**" from the reign of "**Za el Yemeni** (also known as **Alayaman**), the first ruler in 300 A.D. to the last Hebrew ruler "**Sonni Ali** in 1492 A.D.". According to the Tarikh al-Sudan, the 15th ruler, **Za Kusoy** converted to Islam around the 11th Century A.D. but **Sonni Ali refused to convert to Islam**.

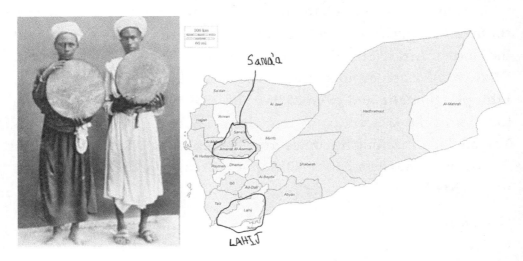

(**Left**) Black Yemen men from Lahij, Yemen.   (**Right**) Lahij, Yemen (circled) where many Black Arabs are at. Sana'a, Yemem (circled) is where the "Negro-looking" Lemba Jews are from.

They most common Paternal Y-DNA haplogroup in Yemen and Saudi Arabia is "**J1**". It is also common in Sudan, South Israel, South Jordan, Southern Iraq (Basra), Oman, Qatar and the United Arab Emirates. Just about everyone in this region carry it. So, we know that the Lemba Jews state they came from Israel and migrated into Arabia, finally settling in Yemen, while other Israelites over time settled with them in in the town called **Sana'a**. If we know that the whole land of Arabia, Yemen, Qatar and Oman wasn't full of Israelites back then we should assume that the **Y-Haplogroup J1** is not associated with the "**Israelites**".   The Israelites were not the "**majority**" when they migrated into Arabia escaping exile and persecution. Many Arabs (pre & post Islam) however did convert to Judaism during the Medieval period.   So in theory, the **remnant minority** "Haplogroup" in these areas should be the potential Haplogroup that indicates "**Hebrew Israelite ancestry**". What is this Y-DNA Haplogroup? **Haplogroup "E"**. But here is where it gets interesting. Esau/Edom also intermixed his seed with the daughter of Ishamael. This is in the Bible in Genesis 28:9.

Genesis 28:9 "Then went Esau unto Ishmael, and **took unto the wives which he had Mahalath the daughter of Ishmael** Abraham's son, the sister of Nebaioth, to be his wife."

So lets break down the facts:

1. In Yemen the majority DNA Haplogroup is **J1-M267** which has been link to the Black Semitic people (**i.e. Arabs, possibly sons of Joktan, Moab, Ammon, Keturah**).

2. In Yemen the second majority Haplogroup is **J2-M172** which is associated with the **Japthetic Turks and Kurds** by way of Gomers son "**Togarmah**". J2 orginates in **Asia Minor/Turkey/Greece area**. Back in the day the Roman Byzantine Empire ruled over Turkey as Latin and Greek were the main languages instead of Arabic.

3. Esau was the twin brother of Jacob. They had the same father, Isaac. **Therefore we would assume that Jacobs children and Esau's children would fall under the same Y-DNA Haplogroup**. Edom's seed mostly intermarried with white nations from 300 B.C. and afterwards. The Edomites mixed with the Romans, the Greeks, the Turks, the Kurds, the Arabs and other European countries according to the Book of Jasher. After the fall of the 2nd Temple in Jerusalem, the Edomite Jews fought hard to keep their place in Israel. Instead they were forced to leave into Europe and into North Africa where the Romans had limited control. The peoples in these lands would aquire the bloodline of "**Esau**" in addition to the bloodline of Black Arabs and White Europeans. These are your "North African light-skinned Arabs". They have within their blood the Y-DNA Haplogroups "**R1b, R1a, E1b1b, J1, and J2**". The bloodline of Esau sparked a "**New**" subgroup within the already "E" Haplogroups (**E1b1a-Negroes and E1b1c-Ethiopians**). This

new Haplogroup is called today the Y-DNA "E1b1b" Haplogroup. Under this "**Daddy Esau**" haplogroup there would be other "**E haplogroup extensions**" that are primarily seen in **North Africa (white arabs), Russia, Belarus, Ukraine, Poland, Hungary, Germany, France, Spain, Romania, Lithuania, England, Italy, Greece, Israel, Lebanon, Syria, Iraq, Saudi Arabia, Palestine, and Yemen**. These "E" extensions are E-L117 (**most common in Europe, Saudi Arabia, Yemen**), E-M34 (**2nd most common**), E-L677, E-M35, E-M84, E-V12, E-V13, E-M78, E-V22 and E-V36.

4. In Yemen and Arabia the top 3 Haplogroups are **J1 (J-M267), J2 (J-M172)and E1b1b (E-L117).**

5. At the very bottom of the Y-DNA Haplogroup list in Yemen is the "**E1b1a-E1b1c**" Haplogroup, which is linked to the **Lemba Jews**, the **Ethiopian Jews** (by way of Haplogroup P2), the Tutsi Jews, the Jews of Nigeria, the Jews of Uganda and the Bantus "Negroes" of West-East Africa.

Note: All of this can be verified on the "Jewish DNA Project" on www.familytreedna.com.

So basically we would expect Yemen and Arabia to have little to no "**E1b1**" DNA in their people because the Hebrews there had to flee into East Africa or risk being raped/killed (**See: "Battle of Khaybar in 629 A.D."**). The Black Arabs (**J1-M267**), the Edomites (**E1b1b**) and the Japhetic "White Arabs" from Turkey/Kurdistan (**J2-M172**) drove the "Israelites" out of the land and made sure that they would "**sexually**" enslave only the "**Israelite women**", castrating the male slaves so that **THEIR MALE BLOODLINE** (full of Ishamel, Edom and Japheth) would be preserved. By castrating the Black Male Hebrew Israelite Slaves captured during the "**Arab Slave Trade**" from East Africa it would ensure that little to no "Hebrew Israelite Y DNA" would be passed along in Yemen, Arabia or the Middle East. For one to detect a "**Hebrew Israelite DNA presence**" in the land of Arabia or Yemen, they would have to collect mtDNA samples of all the women in the land and see who comes up positive for the "L" or "M" mtDNA Haplogroup markers, for these are associated with the Black "Bantus" Jews in Africa. But this was all predicted and predestined to happen.

(**Above**) A Slave Market in Yemen of Black Hebrew Israelites. These Yemen men are not the "**Original Black Arabs**". They are "**watered-down**" Arabs from the seed of Japheth and Edom in Asia Minor (Turkey, Kurdistan). The Turks/Kurds "**J2-M172**" Haplogroup gene is seen all up in Yemen if you do the research. Controlling the "**Black Races**" in Yemen from having children with the local Arab women and "**promoting**" the mixing of the Black Arab women (and possibly Israelites) with white-skinned "**Eurasian Arabs**" eventually would change the "**phenotype**" of the people in Yemen. For this reason we see Yemeni people with white skin and straight hair and we also see dark-skinned more "Negro" looking Yemeni people with "wooly" hair.

(**Above**) All these men are from Yemen, but **who is the "Original Arab"?** The people in Yemen call themselves **"The Arab of Arabs"** indicating they are the "Original Arab" since they know the "Black Arab" was the "Original Arab". There are 3 major Haplogroups in Yemen (**J1, J2, E**), so there are 3 distinct sets of people in Yemen with 3 distinct backrounds. We must know the difference as it will help us decide who is a **"Real Israelite"** and who is not. The Jews lived also amongst these people in Arabia and Arabia Felix (Yemen).

Here is an account of what an Italian traveler named "**Ludovico di Varthema**" aka "**Barthema or Vertomannus**" said about the Jews living in Arabia during the 1500's in his book called, "**Itinerario de Ludovico de Varthema Bolognese**".

*"At the end of eight days we found a mountain which appeared to be ten or twelve miles in circumference, in which mountain there dwell **four or five thousand Jews**, who go naked, and are in height 5 or 6 spans, and have a feminine voice, **AND ARE MORE BLACK THAN ANY COLOUR**. They live entirely on the flesh of sheep, and eat nothing else. They are **circumcised,** and confess that they are Jews; and if they can get a **MOOR (Muslim)** into their hand, they skin him alive."*

Notice that the "**eye-witness**" here expressed that the Jews were "**More Black than any other color**". This would imply that these Jews were

444

straight black and not mixed-breed Jews. The eye-witness also states that the Jews are enemies of the Moors. The Moors were in those days (Medieval times) were always known to be "**BLACK**" and **NEVER WHITE!**

(**Above**) Dr. Christian Snouck Hurgronje was a Dutch scholar of Oriental languages and culture. He wrote his dissertation for his Doctorate of Philosophy on "**The Festivities of Mecca**". He was fluent in Arabic and through mediation with the Ottoman governor in Jeddah, Saudi Arabia he completed a "**Muslim examination**" and was allowed to make a pilgrimage to Mecca in 1885, after which he converted to Islam. He quoted the following in the 1880's in regards to Arab slavery in Saudi Arabia and Yemen.

"There is a preference for Abyssinians (Ethiopians/Eritreans), who have many good qualities, and abound, of **all shades from light yellow to dark brown**. Circassians (white people) … are little valued on account of their enormous pretensions. More important, as workers, are the African (**Israelite**) Slaves. They come mostly from **the Soudan** (Negroland/So Yuda-West Africa to East Africa) and are set to the heavier tasks of building, quarrying, etc."

This fate of slavery for the Children of Israel was prophesied in the Bible.

Psalms 83:4-8 "They have said, Come, and let us wipe them out as a nation, That the name of Israel **BE NO MORE IN REMEMBERANCE**. For THEY have consulted together with ONE **CONSENT**: they are confederate against thee: **THE TABERNACLES OF EDOM, AND THE ISHMAELITES; OF MOAB, AND THE HAGARENES, BYBLOS, AMMON, AND AMALEK, PHILISTIA, WITH THE PEOPLE OF TYRE. EVEN ASSYRIA HAS JOINED THEM TO REINFORCE LOT'S DESCENDANTS.**"

Fact or Fiction?: The region of India was known to the Ancient Hebrews as "**Hodu**", and was identified as "**Hindostan**". **Hind-o-Stan** was a word of Persian origin as its root "**Hindu**" was believed to mean "**Blacks**" and "**Stan**" was another word for "**land**". So in essence saying "Hindostan" was like saying "**Negroland**" or "**Soudan**".

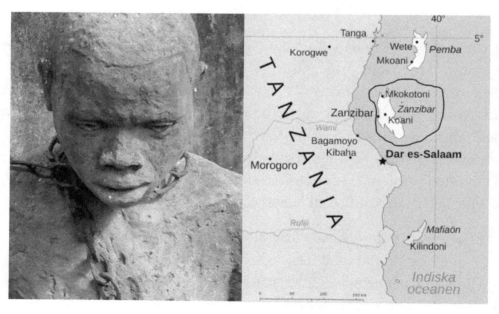

(**Left**) Stone Town in Zanzibar near the Anglican Cathedral Church of Christ is a stone monument of Zanzibar "**Israelite**" Slaves in the Slave Pits that were used to grease the slaves before they were put on the auction blocks to be sold to the highest bidder (**i.e. Neighboring Arab Tribes or Europeans**). These slaves were sold East as far as China and West to places like Madagascar, Brazil and the Caribbean. During the 1600's, 1700's and 1800's while the Transatlantic Slave Trade was going in Bantus **West Africa**, the Arab Slave Trade was going on in Bantus **East Africa**. (**Right**) Zanzibar Island off the coast of Tanzania.

(**Left**) The Zanzibar slaves were chained to these stone pillars and beat before they were sold into slavery. (**Right**) The Altar at the Anglican Cathedral Church in Zanzibar now sits where the Zanzibar slaves were whipped. The Cross you see is next to the former whipping tree marked by the altar by a white marble circle surrounded by red to symbolise the blood of the slaves.

The Black Arabs got Israelite slaves from Malawi, Kenya, Abyssinia (Ethiopia/Eritrea), Sudan (Khartoum), Mozambique, Somalia, the Congo and Uganda. There was a huge Slave Trading Market in **Khartoum, Sudan** where Israelites were sold to other Arabs. This is the reason why there is such a strong presence of **Y-DNA "J1" Haplogroup carriers** in Khartoum, Sudan compared to the whole Middle East.

Fact: Ancient Chinese Texts mention ambassadors from the Kingdom of Sri Vijaya in Java (Indonesia) presenting the Chinese Emperor with two "**Seng Chi-Zanji**" slaves as gifts. **Zanj** slaves were Bantus East African Israelite slaves taken and brought to the Tanzanian Zanzibar

Island Port for shipment across the Indian Ocean. The Tang Dynasty and the Song Dynasty were known for doing business with Black Arab Slavetraders who brought East African Slaves across the Indian Ocean to China.

(**Above**) Black Arabs from **Yemen, Arabia, Oman, and Qatar** who **ALL** participated in the slave trade of Black Hebrew Israelites. **The Bible is TRUE!** Remember, Edom's blood was also mixed with the Arab Ishamaelites! This is why Bible Prophecy holds true then and today. No other book on the planet has "**Prophecies**" for a select group of "**Set Apart**" people. The **HEBREW ISRAELITES**!

Here are some personal accounts of the horrific sights of slavery in East Africa:

- "We saw several poor sickly skeletons lying on the deck, evidently dying and much disfigured.....the others were all covered with craw-craw (**filarial worm skin disease-Ocnocerciasis**) and itch (**Deuteronomy 28:27**), and were scratching large sores all over them and howling like maniacs for water."

- "Those taken out of the country are but a very small section of the sufferers. We never realized the atrocious nature of the traffic until we saw it at the fountainhead. There truly 'Satan has

448

his Seat.' Besides those actually captured thousands are killed and die of their wounds and famine, driven from their villages by the internecine war waged for slaves with their own clansmen and neighbors, slain by the lust of gain, which is stimulated be it remembered always, by the slave purchasers of Cuba and elsewhere."- (**19th Century Missionary David Livingstone's**).

- "Two of the women had been shot the day before for attempting to untie the thongs. One woman had her infants brains knocked out because she could not carry her load and it (baby); and a man was dispatched with an axe because he had broken down with fatigue."

The Chinese described their Israelite Black slaves (circled) under different names such as "**Kunlun**" or "**gulun**". They believed there were many types of them such as the "**Zanj (Zanzibar, Tanzania)**", the

449

"**turmi**", the "**kurdang**" and the "**Khmer**". They believed that they were all related. The Chinese described their black slaves as "**Devils**", "**theives**", "**Cannibals**" and "**Good-swimmers**". Accounts of Arabs bringing black slaves go back as far as the late 600's A.D.

Boys. — Zanzibar

(**Above**) **Zanzibar** (Tanzania) boy slaves. Arabs called them the "**Zanj**" and typically castrated all their male slaves by the age of 11 years old. This ensured that they would not procreate and have any children in the Middle East or Asia. When the Arabs sold the Bantus "Zanj" people to Asia the Japanese called them "**Tsengu**" and the Chinese called them "**Tsengpat**".

Fact: Al-Jahiz was a 8th century Arab scholar. He was born in Basra, Iraq around 776 A.D. In his Book he wrote that he was from the "**Banu Kinanah**" tribe. Other reports from his relatives state he was the grandson of a Black African. Back in the 8th Century A.D. the majority of Arabs were black. Today they are not. **Al-Jahiz quoted that the people living in the Islands beween African and China were inhabited by Black people.** Here is what he said:

"The Blacks are more numerous than the whites. The whites mostly consist of the people in Persia, Jibal (Iran/Iraq border), and Khurasan (North Persia/Iran), the Greeks, Slavs, Franks (German/France), and Avars (Caucasus), and some few others, not very numerous: **the Blacks include** the Zanj, Ethiopians, the people of Fazzan (Libya), the Berbers, the Copts (Egypt/Sudan), and Nubians, the people of Zaghawa (East Chad/West Sudan), Marw, Sind and India, Qamar and Dabila, **CHINA, AND MASIN (PHILIPPINES)**.... the Islands in the seas between China and Africa are full of blacks, such as Ceylon, Kalah, Amal, Zabij, and their islands, as far as India, China, Kabul, and those shores."

Al-Fakhar al-Sudan min al-Abyadh (the prides of blacks over whites) by 8th Century Arab history Al-Jahiz

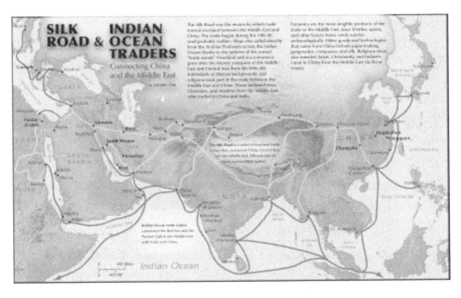

Silk Road and Indian Ocean were key routes for trade with the Chinese, even in Slave Trading.

The Old Testament states that the Children of Israel would be regathered from the **North, South, East and West**. The New Testament says that the Israelites would be "**Scattered into ALL NATIONS.**" It is a known fact that the "**Silk Roads**" and the Indian Ocean was various travel routes the Arabs used to do "**business**" with the Chinese. This included the "**Slave Trade**" business of the Black Hebrew Israelites in East Africa. One of the earliest Chinese sources describing Africans along the East Coast involves the testimony of "**Du Huan**" in his book "**Jing xing ji**", which means "**Record of My Travels**". Du Huan was supposedly captured by the **Abbasid Caliphate** Arabs near the city "**Samarkand**" (present day **Uzbekistan**) during the "**Battle of Talas**" during the 8th Century A.D. This was a Battle between the Abbassid Caliphate, the Tibetan Empire against the Chinese Tang Dynasty. . Samarkand was a "**bridge city**" along the "**Silk Roads**" between the Middle East and China. Du Huan was able to escape, and in 762 A.D. **Du Huan** wrote his literary work, which appeared in the "**Tong Dian**", compiled by his relative **"Du You"** in 812 A.D. Some people debate the authenticity of his testimony, believing he simply recorded what he heard the Arabs say about the East African Slaves. Du Huan's work described his alleged visit to present day **Kenya**. Here is what he said:

"**The people are Black**, and their customs uncouth. There is little rice or wheat, and no grass or trees; the horses eat dried fish and the people eat gumang. **Epidemics and plagues are particularly severe in this kingdom (Deuteronomy 28:21-24).** Traveling by land, the mountain Hu whom one encounters are of only one type. But they have different kinds of law: they have Dashi (Arab) law, Daqin law, and Xunxun law. These Xunxun exceed all the Yi and Di in their sexual depravity. They do not talk during meals. Those who follow the Dashi law rely on their relatives to dispense justice, and even if the fault is slight others are not involved. **They do not eat the meat of pigs, dogs, donkeys, horses and the like (Leviticus 11).** They do not revere their country's king or respect their fathers and mothers. **They are great believers in ghosts and spirits (ancestoral worship still practiced in Africa) and make** offerings only to heaven (Mami Wata-Queen of Heaven, Jeremiah 44:19, 7:18). As for their customs, **EVERY SEVENTH DAY IS A DAY OF REST (Israelites keep Sabbath, Muslims don't-Exodus 20:8); they do not do business or collect loans (Leviticus 25:36-37, Deuteronomy 15:1-3, Exodus 22:25), they only drink wine and rejoice all day (Muslims don't drink wine or alcohol, Hebrews do)**. Those of Daqin excel in the treatment of eye illnesses and dysentery. Some can even detect illness before the patient falls ill and some open the brain to remove bugs.

Note: This is **Undeniable Proof** that these East Africans were Hebrew Israelites with a possible influence in Arab culture from the Arabs who came enslaving them. This infusion of Arabic culture (including the people) into Kenya, Tanzania, Zanzibar, Mozambique and Oman is how the "Swahili" language emerged in East Africa. "**Swahili**" is a language comprised of the "**Bantus Israelite language**" and "**Arabic**". Swahili people speak it as their "native tongue" while Bantus East Africans all have their "original" mother tongue, which is derived from a Hebrew-Hamitic dialect mix.

Do we need any more proof that these East African "**Bantus**" Slaves from Kenya (**Kikuyu Tribe**) and Tanzania (**Sukuma Tribe**) were "Hebrew Israelties?" The Bantus people in Kenya and Tanzania (**Zanzibar**) have the same Y DNA "**E1b1a**" Haplogrouop gene as "African-Americans", "Caribbean Blacks", and Bantus West Africans. It is not a coincidence that people with the same Y-DNA (E1b1a) were going through slavery at the same time (17th century to 20th century) but were all located within the "**Soudan-So Yuda(h)**" area of West, Central and East Africa!

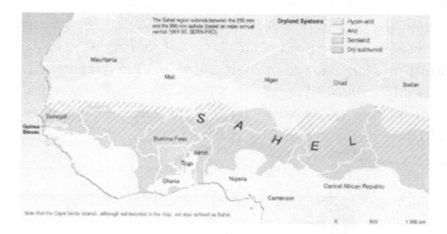

(**Above**) The area known as the "**Sahel**" was also known in Ancient times as "**So Yuda**" which later was renamed "**Soudan**" by the Arabs. **Sahel** in Hebrew (Strong's #6214) means "**God-made**" from the Hebrew Strong's #6213 word "**Asah**" meaning "**made, accomplish**" and Hebrew Strong's word #410 "**El**" which means "**God**". So did Yahuah make this "**Sahel**" region a "**Land of Punishment**" for the disobedient "**Children of Israel**"? Let's take a look. Like the "**Soudan**", the "**Sahel**" extends from the Senegal-Gambia region and Mauritania straight across into East Africa. This area basically encompasses the land known as "**Negroland**", **Central Africa** and **East Africa**. The Sahel receives 4-8 inches of rainfall each year secondary to constant drought. In the Sahel (**Soudan**) there is also destruction of grasslands, food shortages, malnution, disease (to humans/animals), destruction of crops from locusts, animal die-offs from multiple factors and slavery. If I didn't know any better, the **Curses of Israel** listed in **Deuteronomy 28:15-68** and the "**Sahel/Soudan**" were "**designed**" for the "**future inhabitants**" of Africa......the Hebrew Israelites! It is not a coincidence that the area (Sahel/Soudan) with the highest concentration of "Israelites" were the locations for the two biggest Slave Trades in history (Transatlantic, Arab Slave Trade).

(**Above**) During the 1800's the "**Black**" indigenous Arabs of **Muscat, Oman** held three slave markets every week selling "**Bantus**" people from East Africa. Some of the captured "**Bantus**" people were transferred to Turkey, Iraq, Iran, Arabia, and India.

(**Above**) Black Arab Muslims of Muscat, Oman. Their frequency rates of men carrying the Y-DNA "**J1**" Haplogroup gene is **3 times more** than that of the Ashkenazi Jews and Sephardic Jews. The Jews "**Cohen Model Haplogroup**" theory states that those males carrying the Y-DNA "**J1**" Haplogroup are descendants of **Aaron** (the brother of Moses **a Levite**). The Aaronite family were commanded by God to be the "High Priests" of Israel. Are these Black Arab Muslims and every Muslim man in the Middle East calling themselves "Jewish High Priests" or "Jews" period? The answer is **NO**! Do we really think that the Jews are the only people that can do or interpret Genetic Studies? I hope not.

CHAPTER 20

EXPLAINING HAPLOGROUPS ALL OVER AGAIN. WHAT CAN DNA TELL US?

The Beginning

Haplogroups correspond to a single line of descent usually dating back thousands of years. In the 1980's and 1990's different academic researc groups had their own system of naming Y-DNA Haplogroups. This created a sort of "**Tower of Babel - confusion**" in terms of genetic information communication and how other scientists were able to interact with other in regards to their genetic finds. In 2002, the **Y-Chromosome Consortium (YCC)** proposed a new "**standard**" of naming all the Y-Chromosome Haplogroups. In 2008, the new YCC Y-DNA Tree was introduced by scientist Tatiana Karafet, but comprehensive re-testing had to be done. Before everything was complete, Haplogroups were assigned letters of the alphabet. This meant that the letter assignment system did not have any correlation as to who came first or who is was the oldest. What the research did do, using these Haplogroups, was to find out the "**migration patterns**" of different people groups. This is very important in understanding "Y-DNA and mtDNA Haplogroups"

Mutations

Mutations can occur on both the "Paternal" Y-DNA and the "Maternal" mtDNA at the chromosome level. When they happen, they remain "fixed" in place in the DNA. If a man has "Mutation A" and has a child, he will pass that "Mutation A" down to his child. The father of this child could have a long family tree history of his parents having this "mutation A". Now over time, Scienitists say more "Mutations" happen. Mutations can happen for a lot of reasons.

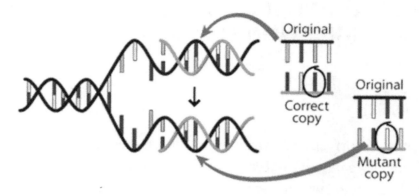

Mutations happen when our DNA fails to copy itself correctly or when external forces (**i.e. changes in environment, radiation**) causes changes to our DNA on a cellular level. Mutations can have small changes on the way we look or they can have big changes on the way you look. Mutations can also lead to diseases (i.e. Sickle Cell from Malaria exposure). External mutations can be from the Sun, radiation, changes in the composition of the air people breath, the food we ingest, the water we drink and so on. Of course when races mix with each other, half of the father's DNA and half of the mothers's DNA is distributed to the children. Of course whatever "**Mutation**" your parents had, you will likely have. Now when people do DNA tests on their brothers and sisters in addition to themselves (from the same parents), their results can come back with varying percentages of African, White and Native American DNA. One sibling can be 80% black/15% white/5% Native Indian and another sibling can be 55% Black/30% White/15% Native Indian. So even though both siblings have the same birth parents, one simply received more genetic copies from the more recent White or Native Indian regions on one of their parents genome. This also explains how some Black people can be born lighter than their parents while olthers can be born darker than their parents.

Haplogroup E-V38/ E3a/ E1b1a

Possible time of origin	approx 25,000-30,000 years BP[1]
Possible place of origin	East Africa [2]
Ancestor	E-P2
Descendants	E-M2, E-M329
Defining mutations	L222.1, V38, V100

So in applying this to Genetics we see that different groups of Africans belong to different Haplogroups. Bantus Nigerians, Ghanaians and Kenyas belong to the Haplogroup "E". Ethiopians also belong to the Y-DNA Haplogroup "E". Bantus Sub-Saharan Africans and Ethiopians/Eritreans all are descendants of the "Ancient" Y-DNA Haplogroup "**E-P2**". Everyone else in Africa belong to "other" Haplogroups, some within the "E" family and some outside of it. Remember, all of these Haplogroups are unique because of their "Migration Patterns". What is "unique" about the African people in "E-P2" or "E-M2/E-M329"? They all claim to have arrived to Africa from "another place". What is this place if you ask them? **Israel, aka Northeast Africa!** Scientists also agree that E-P2 came from "Northeast Africa" because they won't dare say that E-P2 came from **ISRAEL!** This would be like telling the scientific world that "**Black people are the Real Jews**".

So here is how it works. All the African people carrying the mutation "**E**" form the single Haplogroup "**E**". Then over time there is another Mutation. This Mutation forms a "Subgroup or Subclade". So now instead of "E" we have **E-P2** or let's say (**E1b1**). So from this "**E-P2**" there are more generations born and at some point there is a slight split from **E-P2 (E1b1)** into **E-M2 (E1b1a)** and **E-M329 (E1b1c)**. So we know that **E1b1a** and **E1b1c** are related to each other because they have the

459

same ancestor **E-P2**. In the genetic world today, the carriers of the "**E1b1a**" gene are Bantus Africans or Black people of "**Bantus**" Descent. The carriers of the "**E1b1c**" gene are **Ethiopians, Eritreans and some Somalians.**

Note: E1b1a carriers are: **African-Americans, Caribbean Blacks, Blacks in South America, Blacks in Central America, Blacks in West India, Blacks in the Middle East, Blacks in Europe, Blacks in Turkey, Blacks in Yemen, Blacks in West Africa, some Blacks in Madagascar, some Blacks in East Africa and some Blacks in South Africa.**

Reference: "**A New Topology of the Human Y Chromosome Haplogroup E1b1 (E-P2) Revealed through the Use of Newly Characterized Binary Polymorphisms,**" *Beniamino Trombetta, Fulvio Cruciani, Daniele Sellitto, Rosaria Scozzari*. PLOS-Public Library of Science, January 6, 2011,

(**Above**) The "**Genetic-Scientific**" world do not want Black people, Latinos or Native Americans to know the Truth about their "**Real Identity**". But "**Knowledge has increased**" in today's world.....all according to Bible prophecy". Not Egyptian Book of the Dead prophecy, not Muslim Quranic prophecy but **BIBLE PROPHECY**.

Daniel 12:4 "But thou, O Daniel, shut up the words, and seal the **BOOK (Bible)**, even to the **TIME OF THE END**: many shall run to and fro, **AND KNOWLEDGE SHALL BE INCREASED**."

During the course of time (during the Biblical era) there was a mutation called "**V38**" and "**V100**" that would change the former **E-P2 (E-M2, E-M329) E-Haplogroup "subgroup"**. This mutation happened when the Gentiles and Edom came into the **Levant** (i.e. Modern day Syria, Lebanon, Israel, Palestine, Iraq) and **North Africa**. In the religious world it happened in the **Old Testament, the New Testament and the Apocrypha Book of Maccabees**. This is where the "**deception of the scientific-genetic world**" tries to take us for a twist. Maybe they were trying to throw a "**Do Not Enter**" sign in the road to prevent people for digging too deep into the truth about the Hebrew Israelites using genetics. Here is what happened. In 2008, the Haplogroups of "Negroes-**E1b1a**" and "Ethiopians/Abyssinians-**E1b1c**" merged into one Haplogroup "**E1b1a**" from the genetic mutations (SNP's) V38 and V100. But the scientific world was not done! They then added a "New" branch to this old existing "E" Haplogroup model. This branch was called the "**E215-E1b1b**" Haplogroup. Where did this branch come from and who was it's descendants? This branch came from the mixing of Edomites, Greeks, Romans (Italians), Scythians, Balkans, Turks (Anatolia), Kurds (Anatolia) and other Europeans. During time time frame from 300 B.C. starting with the Greeks under Alexander the Great until now "**white-skinned**" nations from Japheth have lived in Africa, the Levant and the Middle East. Edom and his people we know intermarried with Canaanites, Black Arabs, Greeks, Romans and Turkish people. According to www.Eupedia.com which specializes in discussing genetics it reads:

"Haplogroup **E1b1b** represents the **LAST MAJOR DIRECT MIGRATION FROM AFRICA INTO EUROPE**."

CHAPTER 21

FINDING EDOM AND HIS Y-DNA....REQUIRES DIGGING DEEP INTO HIS HISTORY. "THIS IS YOUR LIFE EDOM!"

So what is the connection? Edom and his seed did a lot of living and mixing with the people in Southern Europe off the Mediterranean Sea.

The "**Land of Chittim**" has been linked to Rome and the Island of Cyprus by 1st century A.D. Roman-Jewish Gentile historian **Josephus Flavius** and others. Italy and Cyprus today are countries that were apart of the initial "**European Union**". Cyprus is an Island south of Turkey. So no matter if we go with Italy or the Island of Cyprus we still know that Edom lived amongst the "**Seed of Japheth**". Here is what it says in the Book of Jasher about Edom and Chittim. This was during the time that Joshua lived if you read the whole chapter.

Jasher 90:8-9 "And the children of **Chittim** ruled over **Edom**, and Edom became under the hand of the children of Chittim and **BECAME ONE KINGDOM FROM THAT DAY**. And from that time they could no more lift up their heads, and **THEIR KINGDOM BECAME ONE WITH THE CHILDREN OF CHITTIM**."

So before the Assyrian Invasion and the Babylonian Invasion of Israel, Edom was already becoming "**Whitened**" by mixing with the Children of Japheth. So, if the Israelites carried the "E" Haplogrouop in the ancient times and their uncle was "**Esau**" from their father "Isaac" we would expect the Edomites to also fall under the "E" Haplogroup. Thus the "E" Haplogroup would be spread to any offspring of an Edomite man and a "Japhetic" woman. This would continue on until the Edomites would have high positions under Rome/Greece over the Land of Judea starting with "**Antipater the Idumean**". Jewish historians even document that "Romulus" the first King of Rome was from the line of "Esau".

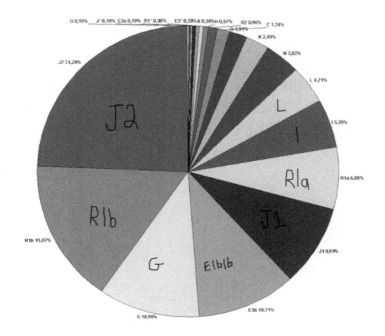

O 0,19% J' 0,19% E3a 0,19% R1' 0,38% E3' 0,38% A 0,38% H 0,57% R2 0,96% C 1,34%
Q 4,91%
K 2,49%
N 3,82%
L 4,21%
I 5,35%
R1a 6,88%
J2 24,28%
R1b 15,87%
J1 8,99%
E3b 10,71%
G 10,90%

J2

L

I

R1a

J1

R1b

G

E1b1b

(**Above**) Y-DNA Haplogroup Breakdown of Turkish People (Turkey). The top 3 major Y-DNA Haplogroups seen in Turks is: 1. **J2** 2. **R1b** 3. **G & E1b1b** (Edom bloodline?). The Kurds (**General Saladin**) and Turks (**Ottoman Empire**) ruled over Israel for almost 1,000 years. Edom and the Gentiles continued in Judea/Israel even after the Romans left.

Fact: There are people living in Turkey in the Taurus Mountains that are called the "**Isaurians**". If you replace the first letter "**I**" with an "**E**" the name changes to "**ESAU-rians**". It is a known fact that Y-DNA haplogroup "**G**" and "**E1b1b**" are tied in 3rd place for the top three major Y-DNA Haplogrouops in Turkey. Number 1 is "**J2**" and Number 2 is "**R1b**". The phrase "**Edom is in modern Jewry**" is recorded in the **Jewish Encyclopedia, 1925th edition, Volume 5, page 41.** But why? Well, before the Jewish in Europe learned "**Hebrew**", they were speaking a **Turkish**, Slavic and Germanaic tongue. Mixing these tongues with Hebrew would form "**Yiddish**".

Fact 2" The Roman Byzantine Empire ruled large territories of land in North Africa and the Levant from the time of Christ until the rise of the

463

Black Arab Ishmaelites united under the religion of Islam. Back then the Roman Byzantine Empire made up the countries of **Algeria, Tunisia, Libya, Spain, Italy, Egypt, Syria, Jordan, Israel, Lebanon, Iraq, Romania, Bulgaria, Serbia (Slavic), Turkey (Turkish), Greece/Macedonia, Bosnia-Herzegovina (Slavic), Croatia (Slavic) and almost all othe Balkan Countries.**

So how can we tie **Rome, Edom** and the "**White**" nations of North Africa/Mediterranean Sea to genetics? Well the Haplogroup "**E1b1b**" is **more common in the Southern Balkan countries (Greece-Southern Italy) than anywhere in the Middle East, except in Egypt.** Now according to the Hebrew Bible Edom's territory stretched from the Sinai Peninsula in Egypt to Kadesh Barnea (Canaan/Israel).

Fact: Some people identify the "**Shashu**" people as Edomites who worshipped Yahuah after being "**crushed**" by the "traveling" Israelites who were being brought by Moses from Egypt around "**Edomite Territory**" to Israel. Egyptian records that the "**Shashu**" people were nomadic raiders. The "Shashu" people were thought to be Edomites or Israelites because the Egyptians gave the generic name "**Shashu**" to

Bedouin nomadic tribes that lived beyond the Eastern border of Egypt and the Sinai Peninsula. It is said in Egypt/Nubia on the **Temple of Soleb** (Nubia-Sudan) the first three letters of the "Tetragrammaton" **YHU, YHV** or **YHW** is clearly seen which scholars say is the Hebrew name "**Yahu**". Scholars say the inscription seen in Soleb, Egypt/Nubia on the temple built by Pharaoh Amenhotep III to the Egyptian god Amun-Ra identifies "**the wandering area of the clan of the worshippers of Yahu, the God of Israel.**"

Strabo (63 B.C.-24 A.D.), who wrote around the time of Christ the Messiah, quoted that the Idumeans (Edomites) were of "**Nabataean**" Arab origin. He stated that that they made up most of Western Judea at the time and mixed in with the other people living in Judea (**i.e. Greeks Jewish converts called the "Hasmonean Maccabees"**), adopting their religious customs. Both the Maccabean family, the Edomite family and the relatives of Muhammad (founder of Islam) were involved with Nabataean "**Arab**" women. So it appears here that we would have "**two sets**" of Edomites: Those Edomites that were mixed in with "**White Nations** (Greece, Italy, Turkey)" and those Edomites that were mixed in with "**Black Nations** (Egypt, Canaanites, Black Arab Ishmaelite's). Later the Edomites would mix with the "**White Arabs**".

(**Above**) The name of Edom in Egyptian Hieroglyphs. It is a known fact that around 1000 B.C.-900 B.C. that the Edomites were hanging around in Egypt. In the Bible, an Edomite prince named "**Hadad**" escaped and fled into Egypt with his family during the reign of King David. After King David died, he returned back to Israel and tried to start a rebellion but failed. Hadad and his Edomite brethren miserably had to then retreat to Syria/Turkey. This is when these guys also got a "piece of Edom", which the "E1b1b" gene shows in their Y-DNA.

1 Kings 11:15-18 "For it came to pass, when David was in Edom, and Joab the captain of the host was gone up to bury the slain, after he had smitten every male in Edom; For six months did Joab remain there with all Israel, until he had cut off every male in Edom: **That Hadad (the Edomite) fled, he and certain Edomites of his father's servants with him, to go into Egypt; Hadad being yet a little child.** And they arose out of Midian, and came to Paran (Sinai Peninsula, Egypt): and they took men with them out of Paran, and they came to Egypt, unto Pharaoh king of Egypt; which gave him a house, and appointed him victuals, and gave him land."

So the Egyptians took in the Edomites and gave them land. Perhaps some of the Edomite men took Egyptian wives and had children. This is proof that Edom also "**infused**" his seed into North Africa, the first place the Arabs conquered with Muhammad's army when Islam began in 7th century A.D.

(**Left**) The Kingdom of Edom was in the Southern Levant (South Israel) region, west of the Nabataean Tribes (North Saudi Arabia). The Nabataean Tribe was a prominent Arab culture that was believed to have sprung from the south part of the Sinai Peninsula in Egypt, which was Edom's territory according to the Bible.   They had a close relationship with the Edomites as they both claimed a female line of the descent of Ishmael through **Bashemath**, one of the three wives of Esau. Bashemath was the daughter of Ishmael and the sister of the firstborn son of Ishmael, **Nabaioth**.   Arabs say the Nabataean people were an Arab people from the line of Ishmael from his firstborn son **"Nebayoth/Nabaioth" which his tribe was nicknamed "Nabatu"**. It was said that the Nabataeans referred to themselves as the "**Nabatu**", meaning "**People who draw water**." Arab literature states that there were a group of Nabataeans from **Iraq** known as the "**Nabat al-Irak**" and also a group from **Damascus, Syria** known as "**Nabat al-Sham. Hmmmm......it seems we are uncovering all the "secret sites" of the Edomites.   (Right)** The 13th Emperor of the Roman Empire "**Traja**" (Marcus Ulpius Traianus) conquered the Nabataeans in the 1st Century A.D, giving this land to the Romans.   **Petra** was a city that the Nabataeans shared with the Edomites. Many of the Arab Nabataeans were **forcefully converted** to Judaism by **Hasmonean Maccabean King Alexander Jannaeus**. The city of Petra was basically a city carved and made out of **mountainous rock** in the middle of the desert. Just as the bible describes the "**dwelling place of Cain**".

CAIN
QAYIN

כִּי אִם-יִהְיֶה, לְבָעֵר קַיִן -עַד-מָה, אַשּׁוּר תִּשְׁבֶּךָ.

(**Above**) **Numbers 24:22** in Hebrew with the word for Cain "**Qayin**", Hebrew Strong's #7014 in plain view. In verse 21, the word "Kenite" is Hebrew Strong's 7017 "**Qeni/Qini**" which is from the root word "**Qayin**" or **Cain**. So according to the Hebrew bible and Numbers **24:21-22**, the Kenites are descendants of Cain and their home was set in rock (Petra). The word "**Petra**" in Greek means "**Rock**".

Numbers 24:21-22 "And he looked on the **Kenite**, and took up his parable, and said: Though firm be thy dwelling-place, and though thy nest be **SET IN ROCK**; Nevertheless, Kain shall be wasted; How long? Asshur shall carry thee away captive."

(**Above**) The city of Petra, in modern day Jordan is **SET IN ROCK (MOUNTAINS).**"

(Left) Picture of Al-Uzza, the pre-Islamic pagan satanic goddess the Arabs and Edomites used to worship. She can be seen surrounded **by Moon deities, Sun deities, and the Eagle (like Edom in the Book of Obadiah)**. She can also be seen inside of a zodiac circle carrying a "**Moon Staff**". She was likened after by the Egyptian goddess "**Isis**", the Greek goddess "**Aphrodite**" and the Roman goddess "**Venus**". Satan is very "**deceptive**". She was worshipped at the "**Al-Ta'if**" Stone **Cube** near Mecca. Notice the constant use of the "**Cube**" in pagan religions. The cube represents "**Saturn**" which represents also "**Satan**" in the occult Satanic/Witchcraft world. You can find the pagan god "**Al-Uzza**" in **the Quran in Sura 53:19** as a part of the "**Satanic Verses**". According to the "Satanic Verses" story and why certain verses were "removed", it is said that Satan deceived Muhammad into writing stuff in the Quran for Muslims to read instead of the angel Gabriel or "Allah". Part of these "**Satanic Verses**" were deleted from earlier Qurans (Umayyad/Abbasid dynasty time period?) so that in today's Quran you will not found these "Satanic Verses".

(**Above**) Prior to Islam being founded, in Petra (Jordan) a stele was found dedicated to **Qos-Allah**" or "**Qos is Allah**", otherwise saying "**Qos is the god**". Many people today still believe the word "**Allah**" means "**the god**" and not "**God**". Qos is identified with "**Quash/Kaush**", the God of the Ancient Edomites". This stele is known as the "**Qosmilk stele**" or the "**Dus shara Stele**"and displays a **STAR AND A CRESCENT, BOTH CONSISTENT WITH A MOON DEITY**. The "Crescent Moon and Star" is still used today by Muslims as their symbol for Islam, just as it was used hundreds of years ago as a pagan symbol of worship. Just look at the "**Mecca Clock**" and every Muslim Mosque. Muslims use the Lunar Calendar and the Crescent Moon to know when to start "**Ramadan**". Also found during the Nabatean/Edomite Era before the beginning of Islam was the worship of the goddesses Al-Uzza, Manat and Al-Lat. (**Right**) **Dushara** was the "**Lord of the Mountain**" and was an ancient pagan satanic deity worshipped by the Edomites and the Arab Nabataeans. He was frequently associated with his wife **Al-lat** who many claim is one of the daughters of the pagan deity **Al-Lah** or "Allah". Dushara was frequently worshipped as an "**uncut stone cube**" or the "**Kaaba cube**" in Mecca. In Greek times (whose language predates the Arabic language the Quran was written in), Dushara was associated with Zeus and also Dionysus. **So does this mean that the Kaaba Cube in Mecca is a shrine to the Greek gods Zeus and Dionysus but under a different name and religion**? Dushara had a sanctuary/temple in which a large cuboid stone (like the Muslim Kaaba) was the main attraction for his worshippers. This shows that Satan has tricked man into worshipping false gods and shrines (cubes, obelisks, bulls, falcons, owls, hexagrams, stars) since way back and has continued to deceive man even up to the most "newest" religion on the planet, **Islam** which is full of "**Pagan**" history.

The Mystery behind the Nabataeans, the Edomites and the Seed of Cain gets deeper! 1 century B.C. Greek Historian, **Diodorus Siculus (60 B.C.-30 B.C.)** in his book "**Bibliotheca Historica**" wrote this about the **Arab Nabataeans**:

*"Here it is worthwhile to recount the institutions of these **ARABS**, by the practice of which they seem to project their liberty. Their country has neither rivers nor copious springs from which it is possible for a hostile army to get water (because they lived in mountainous rock areas). **THEY HAVE A LAW NEITHER TO SOW CORN (SEED) NOR TO PLANT ANY FRUIT-BEARING PLANT (SEED), NOR TO USE WINE, NOR TO BUILD A HOUSE.** This law they hold because they judge that those who possess these things will be easily compelled by powerful men to do what is ordered them because of their enjoyment of these things. Some of them keep camels, other sheep, pasturing them over the desert. Of the Arabian there are not a few who graze the desert and these are much superior to the others in the amenities of life, being in number not much more than 10,000. For not a few of them are want to bring down to the sea frankincense and myrrh and the most costly of spices, receiving them from those who convey them from what is called Arabia Felix (Yemen). They are conspicuously lovers of freedom, and flee into the desert, using this as a stronghold. They fill cisterns and caves with rain water, making them flush with the rest of the land, they leave signals there, which are known to themselves, but not understood by anyone else. They water their herds every third day so that they do not constantly need water in waterless regions if they have to flee."*

So if these Nabataeans originally lived in North Arabia and Moab (Jordan) territory in biblical "B.C." times but then were found in Assyria (Iraq and Syria) in "A.D." times, this could possibly mean that some of these Arabs were descendants of the occupiers of Israel after they were exiled by the Assyrians in 700 B.C. If these Arabs were **restricted to sowing seed, drinking wine or building a house**, they could possibly be descendants of the Kenites (Rechabites) who some believe were the **Children of Cain** (Tares and Wheat). The Kenites were nomadic people who were known to live and mix with the Children of Edom in the Desert land east of the Sinai Peninsula (1 Samuel 15:6). The Kenites in the Hebrew Bible (Numbers 24:21-22) is listed as "**Cainites**", which the Hebrew word used is "**Cain**". When the Children of Israel were removed from Israel, the Kenites, Edomites, and neighboring peoples would eventually make their new home in Judea. They would become known as Samaritans or Jews. But centuries later around the time of Christ, the Japhetic Greeks, Romans, Turks, Kurds and Khazars would join the scene of "**Imposters**" in Israel. Like Cain, and his descendants, the Jews today have been "**vagabonds**" of the earth, always being kicked out of every country they are in until they settled in Israel in 1948.

Genesis 4:11-12 "And now art thou cursed from the earth, which hath opened her mouth to receive thy brother's blood from thy hand: When thou tillest the ground, it shall not henceforth yield unto thee her strength; **a fugitive** and a **vagabond** shalt thou be in the earth."

The Jews also do not toil the land as "farming" is an occupation that they are not encouraged to do. This is in the Talmud where it says: "**The occupation of farming is the LEAST of all occupations.**" – **Yebamoth 63a**. This sounds like the "**Traits of Cain**" or the "**Kenites**". Yahusha said by their **FRUITS** we will know the Children of Cain. The first "**Impostor Jews**" on the scene would've been the Sephardic Jews because they evolved from the mixing of the Canaanites, Kenites, Edomites and the children of Japheth. These "bastard" children also intermarried with the local Arabs (i.e. Nabataeans). It is said that these Black Arab Nabataeans also dwelt as far South as Yemen. Because the Black Arabs mixed their bloodline with the "Blood of Edom", **and by default the Kenites (Cain)**, they would be the ones that would commit

472

atrocities against the Black Hebrew Israelites during the "East African Arab Slave Trade". Based on all of this, it would seem that the Bible is showing the connection on why the Edomite-Kenite family were used throughout the bible to "**Oppress the Israelites**", taking on their "**identity**", enslaving them and also being crucial in pushing for the "Crucifixion" of **Yahusha HaMashiach** (Jesus Christ).

So Arab literature states that there were a group of Arab Nabataeans from **Iraq** known as the "**Nabat al-Irak**" and also a group from **Damascus, Syria** known as "**Nabat al-Sham. Ancient Babylon is "Iraq". Ancient North Assyria is modern day "Syria".** Per Muslim Palestinians, the clan called the "**Kenites**" still live in the region of **South Israel (Negev Desert), Jordan, Saudi Arabia and Iraq**.

So were the Kenites driven from Iraq, Edom territory (South Israel), Jordan, North Arabia and Syria into **Jerusalem** (Israel) back in Biblical times? YES! And if they were driven to Jerusalem wouldn't they also settle in Jerusalem, Israel and have kids? Their offspring would thus be a part of the "**Jewish People**" that we see today. Let's look at what the Book of Jeremiah says about this. Jeremiah was the Israelite prophet who warned the Israelites that the army of Babylon was coming to conquer their land, led by Babylonian King Nebuchadnezzar around 600 B.C.

Jeremiah 35:1-11 "The word which came unto Jeremiah from the LORD in the days of Jehoiakim the son of Josiah king of Judah, saying, Go unto the house of the Rechabites, and speak unto them, and bring them into the house of the LORD, into one of the chambers, and give them wine to drink. Then I took Jaazaniah the son of Jeremiah (not the prophet), the son of Habaziniah, and his brethren, and all his sons, and the whole house of the Rechabites; And I brought them into the house of the LORD, into the chamber of the sons of Hanan, the son of Igdaliah, a man of God, which was by the chamber of Maaseiah the son of Shallum, the keeper of the door: And I set before the sons of the house of the Rechabites pots full of wine, and cups, and I said unto them,

Drink ye wine. But they said, We will drink no wine: for Jonadab the son of Rechab our father commanded us, saying, **YE SHALL DRINK NO WINE, NEITHER YE, NOR YOUR SONS FOR EVER: <u>NEITHER SHALL YE BUILD A HOUSE</u>, <u>NOR SOW SEED</u>, NOR PLANT VINEYARD, NOR HAVE ANY: BUT ALL OF YOUR DAYS YE SHALL <u>DWELL IN TENTS</u>; THAT YE MAY LIVE MANY DAYS IN THE LAND <u>WHERE YE BE STRANGERS</u>.** Thus we have obeyed the voice of Jehonadab the son of Rechab our father in all that he hath charged us, to drink no wine all our days, we, our wives, our sons, nor our daughters; Nor to build houses for us to dwell in: neither have we vineyard, nor field, nor seed: **But we have dwelt in tents, and have obeyed**, and done according to all that Jonadab our father commanded us. But it came to pass, when **Nebuchadnezzar king of Babylon came up into the land**, that we said, Come, and let us go to Jerusalem for **fear of the army of the Chaldeans**, and for **fear of the army of the Syrians**: **SO WE DWELL AT JERUSALEM.**

So obviously from Biblical times to the end of the Old Testament we see a "**Transition Point**" of when the "**Face of Israel**" started changing. The Arab peoples living in countries around Israel did not experience this change (**whitening of skin color**) until the Japhetic Greeks and Romans started invading the Levant, Middle East and North Africa.

Note: *Some of the Old "**Bedouin**" Arabs living today will still admit that the "**Original Jews/Israelites**" were "Black" like their ancestors back in Ancient times.*

(**Left**) **Bedouin Arab,** 20th century. Does he look like President Assad of Syria or Sadam Hussein? Does he look like a Chaldean or Iranian? Or does he look like a Black man you know? (**Middle**) Bedouin woman 1860 A.D. Does she look more Black or Arab to you? (**Right**) Early 1900's Bedouin man from **Jordan**, the place where "**Petra**" was, where the Nabataean Arabs lived, and where many of the Edomites dwelled. These people carry the Y-DNA "**J1**" Haplogroup gene. If Jews claim to also have this "**J1**" Haplogroup gene, did the "Original" J1 Haplogroup carriers start off "White" or "Black"? Ask yourself, "Can white people living in Africa, Australia or Israel get darker without mixing with Black people?" No they cannot. So the Ashkenazi Jews and the Original Shemitic (Semitic) people of the Bible **COULD NOT HAVE BEEN WHITE TO START OFF!**

(**Above**) Bedouins in Jerusalem 1800's. If you look closely, they do not look like Ashkenazi or Sephardic Jews. They do not even look Arab. They look more like "**Asians**" and your typical "**Mongloid**" type peoples, whose ancestors are the basis of today's Native Indians. The little boy's hair circled is curly and not straight like most European Jews and most white-skinned Arabs. **Stephen Pidgeon**, author of the "**Cepher Bible**" stated that while in the Northern part of the Sea of Galilee, he met an Iroquois Indian woman of "**Algonquian**" descent who claimed that her people knew the name of the God as "**Yahuah**". She sung a song for Mr. Pidgeon in her native Algonquian tongue which is the "mother tongue" of the **Blackfoot, Chippewa, Mi'mkaq, Ojibwe and Shawnee Indian Tribes**.

So to conclude things, the Edomites, Kenites and the Arabs all lived amongst each other. As we expect, they all intermixed with one another. Therefore, their "**destiny**" is to "Persecute" the **REAL CHILDREN OF ISRAEL**. We all should know by now that the Arab Slave Trade existed for over 1,000 years and its effects are still evident in East Africans, especially those Siddis who are trapped in generational surgery in West India. By reading the Book of Jasher we can find out that **Edom** fused his seed with **Ancient Rome,** which is now the **British Royal family**, which is **England**, which is the **Vatican**, which is **America**. All of these "peoples" were key players in the enslavement of blacks. Therefore, the oppression of the "**Bantus**" people in Africa and the "**Indians**" in the New World was "**destined**" to happen, set forth by the hand of God because of our forefather's disobedience to the Covenant that was given to us by the Creator.

MORE IMPORTANT THINGS TO KNOW IN REGARDS TO DNA

So now when we go searching for **Edom**, we want to be searching for people with evidence of the Haplogroup "**E**" in their DNA, either primary, secondary, tertiary. This means that the Haplogroup "**E**" can be detected in this certain individual or group of people, even at low percentages (i.e. 20%). This Haplogroup "**E**" should match up perfectly with the "**E**" Haplogroup found in Europeans and Arabs, since we know that these two mixed with Edom's seed. It is also possible that Edom mixed with the Israelites back in Biblical times because of **Deuteronomy 23:7-8** where it says,

"Thou shalt not abhor an Edomite; for he is thy brother: thou shalt not abhor an Egyptian; because thou wast a stranger in his land. The children that are begotten of them shall enter into the congregation of the Lord in their third generation."

We must also be careful, because scientists have caused a lot of confusion when they eliminated the Ethiopian/Somalian "**E1b1c**" Haplogroup and created the "**E1b1b**" branch. Looking at many DNA graphs/maps, including scientific studies, it mostly appears that some scientists have "infused" the Ethiopians/Somalians into the "**E1b1b**" branch. So this new branch called the "**E1b1b**" consists now of Europeans, Arabs, and Africans. Nevertheless, we know that the "Gentiles" are supposed to possess and control Israel until the Second

Coming of Christ. So if we look at the genetic makeup of the people living in the land of Israel, we can find out who is Israel, and who is not. Roughly 50% of the Ashkenazi Jews Y-DNA comes from **Europeans** (J2, I, T, G, R1a, Q), 20% comes from **Edom** (E1b1b), 20% comes from the **Arabs** (J1), and the other 10 percent comes from a mixture of **Semitic/Hamitic** DNA (R1b). The Ashkenazi Jews make up about 80-85% of the Jews recognized worldwide. As you see, their DNA is mostly "**Gentile**" in nature.

This is why Yahusha (Jesus) said these words prior to the Roman invasion of Judaea and their destruction of the Second Temple in Jerusalem.

Luke 21:24 "And they (Israel) shall fall by the edge of the sword, and shall be ***led away captive into all nations:*** *and Jerusalem shall be* ***TRODDEN*** *down of the* ***Gentiles,*** **UNTIL** *the times of the Gentiles be fulfilled."*

The word "**Trodden**" means "**subdued**". The word "**Until**" is used to indicate the time when something will happen, become true etc. So what is the "**Until**" about? When will we know when the "**Gentiles**" control of Jerusalem will come to an end? When will the Gentiles complete their "**fulfillment**" according to the Bible? If you read the next verses, you will see.

Luke 21:25-27 "And there shall be ***signs*** *in the* ***Sun,*** *and in the* ***moon,*** *and in the* ***stars;*** *and upon the earth* ***distress of nations,*** *with perplexity; the* ***sea and the waves roaring;*** *Mens hearts failing them for* ***fear,*** *and for looking after those things which are coming on the earth: for the power of heaven shall be shaken. And then they shall see the* **SON OF MAN COMING IN A CLOUD WITH POWER AND GREAT GLORY."**

The key words are "**Signs**", "**Sun**", "**Moon**", "**Stars** (meteors)", "**distress of nations**", "**sea/waves roaring**", and "**fear**".

Does this sound like we are gearing up for the "End of the Gentiles" and the return of "Christ"?

So with all the mixing of Edom's seed with the children of Kittim (**Book of Jasher**) in Rome, Greece, Turkey, and Cyprus, this might explain why the **E1b1b** gene is seen in the **Balkan countries** on the same level that it is seen in Egypt. The most dominant form of the "**E1b1b**" Haplogroup in **Southeast Europe**, is called "**E-V13**". Geneticists state there is a high frequency of the "**E1b1b**" in Southern Europe (**Balkan Countries**). The Balkan countries were known to be heavily populated by the Sephardic Jews after the Spanish Inquisition in 1492. But what happened to the Greek and Edomite Jews living in Judea that were exiled by the Romans in 70 A.D. after the "Jewish-Roman Wars"? Did the First "**migration-shift**" happen when the 2nd temple of Jerusalem was destroyed by the Romans in 70 A.D. and the Edomite/Greek Jews/Samaritan Arabs were kicked out of Judea into Europe and North Africa? This is a strong possibility when looking at the Y-DNA of North Africa and South Europe today.

UNLOCKING THE Y-DNA "R" HAPLOGROUP MYSTERY!

Essentially one must look at both the **Maternal DNA, Paternal Y-DNA** and the **Autosomal DNA** to see what ancestry they are made of. Since the Paternal-Y DNA carries only from the **father to son**, we are still missing a huge piece of information. Many scientists will label the Y-DNA "**R**" as an "**European Haplogroup**", but what they won't tell people is that the Y-DNA carries on no matter what women come into the picture, almost like a permanent tattoo. It doesn't matter if the woman is White, Black or Arab. Here is an example:

*A Black man named **James** (R1b carrier) moves to Spain with his brothers and has a son named "Cameron" with a Black woman in Spain who is friends of the family. Cameron's Y-DNA will be "R1b", like that of his father. James and his brothers get into some trouble with the law in Spain and have to flee back to Africa, to avoid going to jail. James's brothers have also fathered kids with Spanish women but they have to leave. Cameron stays in Spain with his mother and grows up becoming a successful businessman. While in his 30's he marries a white woman and has a son named "Blake". Blake is biracial so* *he looks half-black and half-white. Blake's Y-DNA will also be "R1b". Blake grows up marries a white woman and has a son named "**Alex**". Alex is 3/4th white and 1/4th Black. Alex looks almost white except for his curly hair but his Y-DNA is still going to show "R1b". So Alex grows up and marries a white "Spanish" woman". They eventually have 3 boys and 3 girls. All three of Alex's boys will carry the "R1b" Y-DNA Haplogroup but they will look "white" in their appearance to the average person after 3 generations of marrying "white".*

Stop for a minute and imagine 500,000 men like James who ventured into Spain, had children with the local women in Spain and then had to leave after some time. This is what happened to the Black Moors and Black Hebrew Israelites during the Spanish Inquisition in 1492. For 700 years, Black races ruled Western Europe, leaving their Y-DNA mark in the land. When these Black men all had to go in 1492 A.D., it left an opportunity for the land to become "white" again. From 1492 to 2016 (500+years) whites have dominated and reproduced but the "R1b" Y-DNA Haplogroup still is preserved in most of the people. But the "R1b" Haplgroup is now also in Africa. This is a prime example why the **Y-DNA "R" Haplogroup** is seen in Africans, Arab North Africans, Ancient Egyptians, Indians, Afghanis, Pakistanis, Western Europeans, Eastern European, some Middle Eastern peoples and Latinos. But how can this be? How can the Y-DNA Haplogroup "R" be seen in all these people? Easy, there had to be some serious "**migration**" going on. What we do know is that this single man labeled "R" or "R1" most likely had an origin in Northeast Africa. Over time his descendants would've migrated into South Europe and Asia.

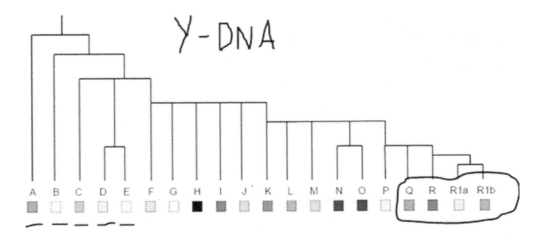

The Egyptians and the Black Moors were mixed with a lot of different peoples very far back. These were initially mostly "**Black nations**". The Egyptians mixed with the Israelites, the Cushite Nubians, the Phuttites, the Canaanites, the Hyksos and the Arab Ishmaelite's. When the Greeks and the Japhetic Gentile Arabs invaded Egypt they also mixed with some of the Egyptians. The Moors also were a combination of Black Muslims of Arab Ishmaelite descent, Hebrew Israelite descent, Phuttite descent, Egyptian descent and Nubian descent. Therefore, the people carrying the Y-DNA "**R**" Haplogroup are situated further down the Alphabet like the Native American Y-DNA Haplogroup "**Q**" is. The "**Haplogroups**" that are "**diverse**" because of the mixing of many "**people groups**" just happens to fit on the end of the "**Haplogroup Alphabetical list**". This is partly for a reason. The Haplogroups "**A**", "**B**", "**C**" and "**DE**" are very old Haplogroups that haven't had much of any "race mixing". They have had little to no Mutations. The Dark-Skinned "**Dinka Tribe**" Nubians of Sudan and the Khoisan people in South Africa are in the **Y-DNA "A" Haplogroup which has NO MUTATIONS**. They are both known to have the oldest DNA known to man. The African Pygmy tribes (**Twa, Mbuti, Biaka**) and some Khoisan people carry the **Y-DNA Haplogroup "B"**. The Pygmy tribes and the Nubians were believed to inhabit most of Africa before the "Bantus" Hebrew Israelites would enter into Africa in large numbers causing what is called in science/genetics the "**BANTUS**

481

EXPANSION". The Egyptians were also an Ancient people group but their people (including DNA) merged very early in the beginning with the Semitic Hebrew Israelites. Almost 500 years of Egyptian-Israelite mixing, and then many off the offspring leaving with Moses left the Egyptians in a state of "**mulatto-ness**". From then, many other nations would conquer Egypt becoming the "Pharaoh's" of the land. This included the Libyans, the Hyksos, the Copts, the Nubians, the Assyrians/Babylonians, the Greeks, the Persians and the Romans. This is why the **Y-DNA Haplogroups "A", "B", "E", "R", "T" and "J"** can be seen in mummies of Ancient Egypt (**Old Kingdom/Middle Kingdom/New Kingdom**). In the Native American Indian's case, the Y-DNA Haplogroup "**Q**" is a mixture of "**Many Nations**" as the bible foretold would happen with Ephraim, the son of Joseph.

Genesis 48:19 "And his father (Jacob) refused, and said, I know it, my son (Joseph), I know it: he (Manasseh) also shall become **A PEOPLE**, and he (Manasseh) shall be great: but truly his younger brother (Ephraim) shall be greater than he, and his seed shall be come a **MULTITUDE OF NATIONS**."

Haplogroup "**Q**" and "**R**" are brothers on the Y-DNA Haplogroup Tree, descendants of the ancestral Y-DNA Haplogroup "**P**". Maternally, the mtDNA of the Native American Indian woman (**A, B, C, D**) can be traced back to Africa (**L, M**). The Native America Indian "**Maternal DNA**" is not seen in European or the Middle East because the Native American Indian women did not leave the Americas to go have children with these races. If they did, their offspring carrying mtDNA A, B, C, and D would be seen in these countries or the people of the land. In history, it was the European man or the Arabic man that came invading countries and having children with the local native women. This "act" would only pass on the Y-DNA to the mulatto sons. In history, it is the "**Man**" that invades a foreign country and then rapes the "**indigenous**" women of the land. Remember, the "**Man's**" Y-DNA is passed down through the bloodline of **EACH SON** his male seed bears.

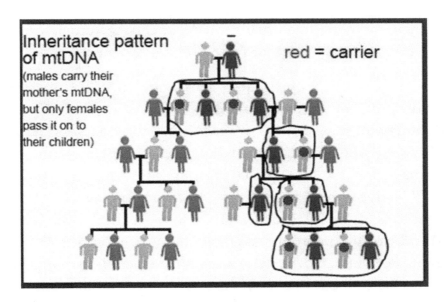

(Above) Mothers (women) pass down their mtDNA Haplogroup to both their sons and daughters but only daughters can pass it on to their children. No matter who these women marry, the mtDNA of their mother gets passed down generation after generation. With that being said, the maternal mtDNA of Native Americans is totally different than that of Europeans. Only the Y-DNA is passed only from father to son. A woman **CANNOT** test for her Y-DNA Haplogroup becaue she only has two "X's" for her sex chromosome "XX" which makes her a female. Boys have both the "X" and the "Y" sex chromosome which makes them males. Scientists estimate that the total amount of Y-DNA a man has is less than 1% and the total mtDNA a man or woman has is also less than 1%. The majority of our DNA ancestry history lies in our "Autosomal" Chromosomes. Autosomal testing estimates what percentage of a person is European, African, Asian, Middle Eastern etc. It is usually more costly than testing your Y-DNA or mtDNA.

The "**Maternal**" mtDNA of "**Males**" carrying the **Y-DNA "R"** **Haplogroup** however varies. Now I know this sounds confusing but remember there is a "Paternal Y-DNA" Haplogroup labeled "R". The men on planet earth that fall into this Y-DNA "R" Haplogroup **ALSO** carry their mothers "maternal" mtDNA. This maternal mtDNA is however **different** for many of these **Y-DNA "R" men!**

For example, **Spanish, Portuguese, Italian and Greek** women always pass European mtDNA Haplogroups (**H, HV, U, K, J, T**) to their children (boy or girl). Their boys may carry the Y-DNA Haplogroup "R1b" but the woman that birthed them was straight European. Latino males may carry the Y-DNA Haplogroup "R1b" but their mtDNA is usually "Native Indian" (**A, B, C, D**). Women in **India** pass the mtDNA Haplogroups **M, N and R** to their children while the African women in **Chad and North Cameroon** pass the mtDNA Haplogroup "**L**" to their children. Both Indian men (**R1a**) and African men (**R1b**) carry the "**R**" Y-DNA Haplogroup but they can have totally different mtDNA Haplogroups. Why? A lot of race mixing from more than two races happened in Western Europe (Iberia), India, the Americas and in certain parts of Africa. So who was the forerunner of the Y-DNA Haplogroup "R"? Surely I can tell you it wasn't the European Caucasian man.

Generation	%DNA
Parents	50
Grandparents	25
Great grandparents	12.5
Great great grandparents	6.25
Great great great grandparents	3.125

(**Above**) Many people get their DNA tested and they are shocked to see **NO EVIDENCE** of Native American Tribal ancestry. Some may say, "**My Great-Great-grandmother was Part-Cherokee**". But when we look at the percentage of the DNA contribution of a relative that lived many generations far back it can be less than 3-6 percent. When the

"**Percentage**" of Native American blood is that small it may be "**too small**" to detect. For the most part the DNA of your previous 3 generations makes up most of who a person is, with the parents of course making up at least **50%** of your DNA as a whole. This is why many white Japhetic Arabs wrote in their manuscripts that if Black men were allowed to procreate with the women of the Middle East and Arabia, that within "**3 GENERATIONS**" their land would turn back "**BLACK**". The white-skinned, straight-haired Arabs we see today know that the original land of the Middle East was filled with "Black Arabs" with wooly hair. This is why Bantus slave boys had to have their testicles removed before the age of 11 by the Arabs to ensure they could not "impregnate" any Arab women while they were in the Middle East or Arabia.

CHAPTER 22

ARE LATINOS/HISPANICS ISRAELITES? HOW CAN ALL THE ISRAELITES BE "AFRICAN-LOOKING" PEOPLE WHEN THE BIBLE SAYS THE ISRAELTES "MIXED" WITH MANY NATIONS?

Hosea 7:8 "Ephraim, he hath **MIXED HIMSELF AMONG THE PEOPLE**; Ephraim is a cake not turned."

A big question circulating throughout the "Hebrew Israelite Community" is, "**Are Latinos/Hispanics also ISRAEL**"? We have to come at this question using "Critical Thinking". How can "Israel" all look like "Negroes" if it is a known fact that Ephraim would become a father of "**MANY NATIONS**". Also if Ephraim mixed himself with the nations his descendants would have to have different looks. We can see this in people today. **Kimora Lee Simmons**, the founder of the "**Baby Phat**" women's clothing line has a Black father and a Japanese mother but looks more Asian than black. The Rapper and music producer "**Pharrell**" is also half Black/half Asian, as is the Female Rapper "**Foxy Brown Afro-Trinidadian/Chinese-Trinidadian**". In Ancient times, it was believed that "Shem's" descendants lived in Asia. Well, Asia is very large! Today, people like to call the physical characteristics of "Asians" as "Mongloid". But we know that Noah didn't have a son name "Mongloid" or "Asia". We also know that the only people that have been known to exhibit the "Mongloid" Asian eye trait (single upper epicanthal fold) are Asians, South Asians and Africans (San Tribe). This trait is not seen in Europeans. It is also a known fact that out of all the "Straight-haired races" the Chinese, have the thickest/heaviest hair. It has also been proven by science (American scientists and Chinese Scientists) that Chinese people descend from "Africans/People of Color" and not Europeans. So who are "Asians" according to the bible? Are they Moabites, Ammonites or

486

Canaanites who eventually mixed with Israelites? Are the indigenous "Indians" of the Americas and the Caribbean, descendants of Hebrew Israelites who migrated in the "**Eastward**" direction after being exiled from Israel? Did they mix with some of the "**Semitic**" and "**Hamitic**" people in Asia during their travels to the "New World-Caribbean"? This would explain the Indians "**Brown**" skin tones, which the Caucasian man does not have. But what gives the indigenous "Indian" his look? I once talked to a woman worked at my neighborhood grocery store who looked Indian but talked like a black person. I had to ask her what was her "**racial background**". So one day I asked her the question, "Are you mixed?" She responded, "Yes, I'm Black and White". I asked her did people mistake her for an East Indian, Native American or Latino and she said, "Many Indians and Latinos come up to me talking in Spanish or Hindi". She told me that her dad was Black and that her mom was White. I told her that when Black people mix with other people we can come out looking like every race on the planet. I said to her, "Biracial Blacks can be mistaken for Arabs, Latinos, Asians, and Indians." She agreed. When talking to other people who say, "Only Negroes are Israelites", I usually give them an example of King Solomon's many wives. I usually ask them, "If King Solomon had children with a Chinese woman, an Indian woman, an Arab woman, or a White woman, wouldn't these children be considered Israelites?" These people usually have nothing to say or they sadly admit and say "Yes". So then I start giving them examples of people today who are "Biracial", yet they do not look white, but instead look like people we would consider "South Asian" or "Indian". For example, these are some well-known celebrities who have "mixed" racial backgrounds, but DO NOT look like White Ashkenazi Jews or regular White people but they are still considered "Black"? Would they be considered "Israelite" under the "All Israelites are Negroes" Rule? Let's take a look:

- Rapper Pharrell (Black father/Filipino mother).
- Model Chanel Iman (Black/Asian-Korean).

- R&B singer Cassie (Father is Filipino, Mother is half Black/half Mexican).
- Singer Kelis (Father is Black, Mother is half Chinese/half Puerto Rican).
- Model Tyson Beckford (Jamaican, Panamanian and Chinese ancestry).
- WWE wrestler/Movie Actor Dwayne Johnson, aka "The Rock" (Black/Asian).
- Tiger Woods (Father is half Black/quarter Chinese, Mother is half Thai, quarter Chinese, quarter Dutch).
- R&B singer Amerie (Father Black, Mother Korean).
- NFL football safety Henry William Demps (Father is Black, Mother is Korean).
- Actress Karrecuhe Tran (Jamaican and Vietnamese ancestry).
- Singer Jhene Aiko (Black and Japanese ancestry).
- Actress Denyce Lawton (Black and Filipino ancestry).
- Reggae artist Sean Paul (Jamaican, Portuguese, Chinese and White ancestry).
- Actress Lisa Wu (Black and Chinese ancestry).
- Actress Sharon Leal (Filipino and Black ancestry).
- R&B singer Neyo (Father is Black, Mother is half Black/half Chinese).
- Model La'Shontae Heckard (Black and Korean ancestry).
- Clothing CEO (Baby Phat) Kimora Lee Simmons (Father is Black, Mother is Japanese).
- Rapper Foxy Brown (Trinidadian and Chinese ancestry).
- Model/Actress Naomi Campbell (Father half Chinese, mother Jamaican).

All of these people have "**Asian**" DNA in their blood in some form or fashion but still are "**melaninated**" people like the Native Americans. They all have some "Mongloid" features in their appearance like the Native Americans. The Native Americans could not have been Europeans or the Children of Japheth because indigenous "Indian"

DNA traces back to ancestors who are "**People of Color**". Since we know that the "**White Race**" cannot make the "**Brown/Black Race**", the white man (**Japheth**) cannot be the ancestor of the Native Americans. That leaves us with two other roots from Noah's lineage, "**Shem and Ham**", which we know according to the bible are the ancestors of the Hebrew Israelites that came out of Egypt.

(**Left**) **Philip II of Macedon** (Greek-Macedonia). He was the Father of Alexander the Great. (**Right**) **Alexander the Great**, Emperor of Greece during 4th century B.C. Most Scholars believe Ezra the Israelite Aaronite lived during the 5th century B.C. during the reign of the Persian King Artaxerxes I. It is a known fact that the Persian Empire ruled Judea before it was taken from them by the Greeks under Alexander the Great. It is easy to understand that Ezra and the Israelites were not "**white**", nor did "**Children of Shem**" all migrate into Europe. It they did we would see a high frequencies of the Y-DNA "**E1b1a**", "**J1**", and "**Q**" in Europe.

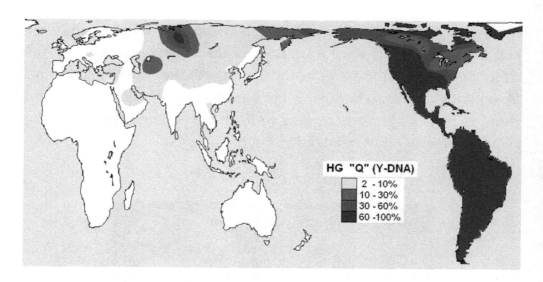

HG "Q" (Y-DNA)

	2 - 10%
	10 - 30%
	30 - 60%
	60 -100%

(**Above**) **Haplogroup Q** (Y-DNA) Distribution by *Mauricio Lucioni Maristany.* As you can see the Haplogroup "Q" is mostly seen in the **Americas, Tibet, Siberia,** and less seen in **Turkey, Arabia, Iraq, Iran, North Asia** and **Mongolia.** So we know that the Native Indians were **NOT Japhetic Europeans** from dissecting this theory earlier. How do we know they are not **African Hamites**? Well, the most common "Y-DNA of the Native Americans, labeled "**Q**" is **NOT** found in Africa. This explains the "Hebrew Israelite" migration to the East called the "**Out of Africa**" expansion. These Hebrew Israelites **NEVER** came back to Africa after being exiled from Israel. If they did leave Israel, eventually coming back after hundreds of years we would expect to see the "Q" Haplogroup in Africa. The maternal DNA of the Native Americans traces back to Africa (L3, M) but does the Y-DNA "Q" trace back to the Middle East or Africa? This we will explore later. The third most common haplogroup seen in Native Americans, **Haplogroup "C"** is also **NOT** found in Africa. Haplogroup C is also seen in the indigenous Australian Aborigines and some of the people on the Pacific (South Asian) Island of Samoa. **So if the Native Americans are not African Hamites, then who are they?**

Let's take this approach since people like to group Asians and Native Americans under the term "**Mongloid People**". Who are the people

490

we call "**Asians**"? Are they Shemites, perhaps the children of Moab and Ammon? Well, what does the bible say about the mixing of the Israelites with the Moabites or Ammonites? Did the Israelites mix with these descendants of Lot?

Ezra 9:1-2 "Now when these things were done, the princes came to me, saying, The people of Israel, and the priests (Aaronites), and the Levites, have note separated themselves from the people of the lands, doing according to their abominations, even of the Canaanites, the Hittites, the Perizzites, the Jebusites, the **AMMONITES**, the **MOABITES**, the Egyptians, and the Amorites. For they have taken of their daughters for themselves, and for their sons: so that the **HOLY SEED HAVE MINGLED THEMSELVES WITH THE PEOPLE OF THOSE LANDS:**"

(**Above**) Moabite statues (B.C. times) with a sort of **Asian-like** appearance. Did the Moabites and Ammonites have "**Asian**" features? The Moabites and Ammonites lived in close proximity with the Canaanites so it is possible that they mixed their bloodline with that of the Canaanites. So who had this "Asian-eye" trait first? Did a certain Canaanite tribe give it to the Moabites/Ammonites or vice-versa? Some say the "Asian-eye" trait comes from Africa (i.e. San People in South Africa) and not Asia. It is believed that the Canaanites migrated to the

East into China amongst other places. The Asian eye (**single epicanthal fold**) feature is seen remarkably in the **San Tribe of South Africa**. Their Y-DNA Haplogroup "**B**" is older that the Y-DNA Haplogroup "**O**" of most Asian people. This means that Chinese/Japanese people got their classic "Asian Eye" look from Africa. For this to happen, the people with this "Asian Eye" trait had to have left Northeast Africa (Land Canaan-Mo to the East.

(**Above**) Where did the "Asian-eye" trait come from? Some say it came from the Canaanites (i.e. San Tribe in South Africa) and some say the Asians are the Moabites/Ammonites. All of these nations lived basically on opposite sides of the **Jordan River** in the **Levant region**. But we have to look at what direction the "Native Americans" went to get to the Americas and what direction the "Asian-Eye" carriers went.

It obvious the "Asian-Eye" carriers traveled "East" from looking at all the people in Asia with their distinct "Eyelid" trait. So if the Native American Indians have this trait, they had to have gotten it from the Land of Canaan, Moab or Ammon. Did the Israelites mix with the Canaanites, Moabites or Ammonites? Yes they did**! Read Ezra 9:1-2. Look at Ruth (Moabite), the Great-Grandmother of King David.** Either way it goes, this "Asian-Eye" trait would linger in the Israelites depending on who they did more "**mixing**" with when they left Israel. The Israelites that went into Africa probably mixed more with other Hamites (with typical eye-traits) and the Israelites that left Israel for the East probably mixed more with the Ammonites, Moabites and the Canaanites (with the "Asian-Eye" trait) who happened to also migrate East to Asia. After all, if the "**Asian-Eye**" trait came from a Canaanite Tribe or the Moabites/Ammonites, they would've had to travel East to bring this unique "eye trait" to Asia. So it doesn't matter if the "Asian-Eye" trait came from the Canaanites, the Moabites or the Ammonites. The "Asian-Eye" carriers had to have traveled East in order to pass it along to the Chinese, Japanese and South Asian population. The Israelites that left East just happened to pick up this trait either early on in Israel or during their travels to the China before crossing the Bering Strait into the Americas.

The Israelite men covered a lot of ground having babies with other nations: The Canaanites (Ham), the Egyptians (Ham), the Cushites (Ham), the Moabites (Shem), and the Ammonites (Shem). So how could the Israelites **ALL LOOK THE SAME**? How could they all look like Black "Negroes"? We all know Somalians, Ethiopians, Fulani's, West Africans, East Africans and South Africans (Xhosa, Zulu, Khoisan) all have different "**Looks**". It is impossible for all the 12 Tribes of Israel to look the same. All it takes is a couple Israelite men to marry women with lighter-skin tones, different hair textures or facial features to "change-up" the appearance of the Israelites.

(**Left**) San Tribe African. (**Middle**) Tibetan Chinese woman. (**Right**) Modern day Chinese woman. All have the "Asian Eye" trait as you can see which is the single upper "**epicanthal fold**" trait. If the DNA of the San Tribe woman is older than the Chinese woman then the "Asian Eye" trait came from Africa and thus is an "Ancient" Black Trait.

(**Above**) Ancient China, (Manchu Area) 1800's. Notice the Brown Color of their skin.

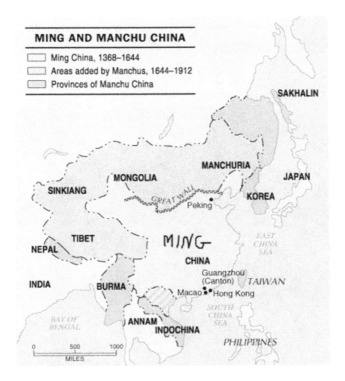

MING AND MANCHU CHINA

- Ming China, 1368–1644
- Areas added by Manchus, 1644–1912
- Provinces of Manchu China

(**Above**) The "**Great Wall**" of China separated **Manchu and Ming China**. During the Tang Dynasty of China (618 A.D.-907 A.D.), Negro "Bantus" Slaves from East Africa (Kenya, Ethiopia, Tanzania, Congo) were taken by the Arabs to South Asian and China. The Manchu Dynasty shows the "Negro-influence" in the people. The last Emperor of China (Qing Dynasty), **Emperor Pu-yi**, was of "**Manchu descent**". Looking at the lower part of his face from the nose down you can see the "Negro" influence in his appearance.

Fact: *In 2005, Chinese DNA geneticist **Jin li**, collected and analyzed over 10,000 DNA samples from 165 different ethnic groups in Asia and found stunning similarities between Southeast Asians and Africans. He concluded that the ancestors of Asians came from Africa. Southeast Asia consists of* **Burma, Thailand, Taiwan, the Philippines, Myanmar, Cambodia, Laos, Indonesia and Malaysia**. *Hong Kong in China is also situated in Southeast Asia. Back in the day, and even today you will find that the majority of "Mongloid" people living in South Asia are in fact "Brown-skinned" people,*

495

some even darker than "African-Americans" who are anywhere from 70-98%
"African-Israelite" by DNA.

(**Above**) Ancient Japanese men (1800's A.D.). As you can see they are "Brown-skinned" individuals, not like the typical Japanese people we see today. Can you see the now the Hebrews developed their "Asian-look"?

So by looking at the possible "theory" that Asians or "Mongloid-looking" people came from Africa (**i.e. Canaanites, Moabites, Ammonites mixed with perhaps Japhethites, Israelites and other Shemites**), we have to take that into consideration when determining if the indigenous Indians of the New World/Caribbean were in fact Hebrew Israelites. We know that by reading the bible the Hebrew Israelites mixed with the Canaanites, Egyptians, Nubian Cushites, the Moabites and the Ammonites. We also know that these non-Israelite nations also likely mixed with the Japhetic nations and Edom. (via Silk Trade Routes).

WHAT CAN WE LEARN ABOUT CARIBBEAN LATINOS FROM THEIR DNA?

(**Above**) Spaniards buying **slaves** in Havana, Cuba (1837).

When Columbus arrived in Cuba in 1492, he found three different indigenous people living there: **Tainos**, **Ciboneys** (Tainos in Cuba) and **Guanajatabeyes/Guanahatabeyes** (non-Taino Indians with a different language). After 700 years most of the indigenous were reported to have been killed off due to epidemic diseases (small pox), physical abuse from slave labor, or mass killings by the Europeans. The first Spanish settlement in Cuba was in 1511 A.D. by **Diego Valazquez**, who was Governor until 1524. During that time the population was mixed consisting of 7,000 people in 1544, of whom 600 were Spaniards, 800 were African slaves and the rest indigenous people (5,600). The Negro Slaves and indigenous "Indians" were used for shipbuilding, cattle ranching, tending to tobacco fields and sugarcane fields. The population of Cuba was disrupted in 1762 when the British attacked Havana. However, by this time The Negro Slave population grew to about 45,000 by 1774 and by 1791 the population was 84,000. That same year a slave rebellion on the Island of Haiti (St. Dominique) caused many French Sugar Planters to flee to Cuba.

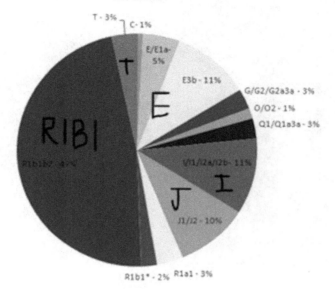

Y-DNA Haplogroups Cuban DNA Project Sample Size n=142

According to the Cuban DNA project at Family Tree DNA, the **Y-DNA R1b1 Haplogroup** is the most prevalent Haplogroup found in Cuban Latinos. It is also the most prevalent Haplogroup found in the Family Tree DNA Puerto Rico project. The "**R1b1**" Haplogroup in Caribbean Latinos is higher than those found in the Azore and Canary Island off the west coast of Morocco. In a Study done by Beatriz Marcheco-Teruel it was found that the European, African, and Indian contribution to 1,019 Cubans tested were 72%, 20% and 8% respectfully. **But this is based off European Scientists believing that the Y-DNA Haplogroup "R" is primarily "European", despite the fact that other races (i.e. Chadic peoples in Africa, North Cameroon, Sri Lankans, Indians) also fall into the Y-DNA "R" Haplogroup but are very "dark" compared to Western Europeans (Spaniards/Portuguese).** So this "European" claim is false!

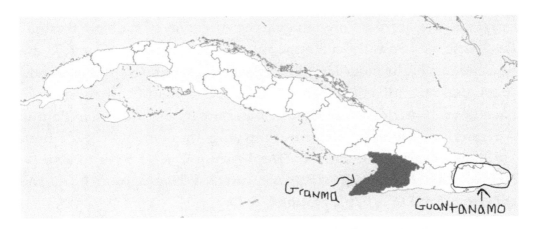

(**Above**) The Eastern part of Cuba which has highest percentage of Native Tainio blood and Africa blood. These areas are **Granma** and **Guantanamo** in Cuba. The **Guanajatabey/Guanahatabey** Indians lived on the Western part of Cuba. Their language was different than the Taino Indians as Christopher Columbus's Taino interpreters could not communicate with these Indians. The Taino (**Ciboney**) people mainly lived on the East part of Cuba. The highest place of African ancestry in the population of Cuba was in the Eastern provinces of **Guantanamo and Santiago de Cuba**. For Indians it was **Granma, Holguin, and Las Tunas**. In Cuba, the most common maternal mtDNA Haplogroups were "**A**", "**C**" and "**D**". Maternal mtDNA Haplogroups "**C**" and "**D**" are most commonly seen in Mexico, Central America and South America. Maternal mtDNA Haplogroup "**A**" is found in Native Indian tribes **Cherokee, Choctaw, Navajo, Apache, Na-Dene and Chippewa**, amongst others tribes.

Fact: In 2001, 27 Pre-Columbian "**Taino**" bone samples from La Caleta, **Dominican Republic** were dug up an analyzed for their mtDNA. 75% of the Bone samples fell into the mtDNA "**C**" Haplogroup while 25% of the Bone samples fell into the mtDNA "**D**" Haplogroup. East Cherokee Indians are also known to fall in the mtDNA "**C**" Haplogroup category. Another interesting find is that the **Botocudos (Aimores) Indians of Brazil** also were found to belong to the mtDNA "**C**" Haplogroup. These South American Indians were believed to have arrived to Brazil from Polynesia via the Arab Slave Trade of "**Bantus**" East Africans. So if the maternal mtDNA Haplogroups C and D are descendants of the older mtDNA macrohaplogroup L3/M, this would prove that the indigenous people in the "New World" are most likely Israelites. **If African-Americans, Nigerian Igbos and other Bantus Africans are Hebrew Israelites carrying the mtDNA "L3", then "Indians" bearing the mtDNA Haplogroup C & D have to also be Hebrew Israelites. Why? Because mtDNA Haplogroup L3 is the ancestor of mtDNA haplogroups C & D**.

(**Left**) **Botocudos Indian** with ear plate from the Amazon in Brazil. Many of the Botocudos also have lip plates, like Africans. (**Right**) **East African with Ear ornament. Ear and Lip plates are most common in East Africa** (i.e. Mursi Tribe). The mtDNA "**C**" and "**D**" and be traced back to the mtDNA of East/West Africans (**L3, M**). Based on these results the Botocudos Indians in Brazil have ancient ancestors from Africa.

In Puerto Rico there were more than 20 chiefs (**Caciques**) at the time when Christopher Columbus arrived on his second voyage to the "New World". The Taino Indian "**Agueybana**" was the "**Head Chief**" of the Tainos who ruled the southwestern part of Puerto Rico in what is now Guanica. Chief "**Guarionex**" ruled the island of Quisqueya (Santa Domingo). From the Genetic studies of the Taino Indians fossil remains in Puerto Rico, the Taino people there were known to belong to the Maternal mtDNA Haplogroups "**A**" and "**C**". Haplogroup "A" is seen in the Mi'kmaq, Cherokee, Apache, Dogrib, Inuit/Aleut Eskimos, Na-Dene, Mexicans and Central Americans. The majority of mtDNA Haplogroup "A" carriers are found in the indigenous Indian tribes of Alaska, Canada, North America, Central America and Siberia. For this reason, it is believed that "mtDNA Haplogroup A" was brought into the Americas via Siberia and the Bering Strait. Haplogroup "B" on the other hand is found primarily in the indigenous people of Southeast Asia, China, Japan, Melanesia, Polynesia and South America. Japanese and Chinese scientists have also theorized that mtDNA Haplogroup "**B**" came from the people that escaped the destruction of the lost continent/Island called "**Mu**" or "**Lemuria**" dating back per some, before the "**Great Flood**". They believe this might explain why most of the worlds "**Pyramid Structures**" are also built in South America.

Source: MtDNA from extinct Tainos and the peopling of the Caribbean. *Lalueza-Fox, F.Luna-Calderon, F. Calafell, B Morera and J.Bertranpetit*. **Annals of Human Genetics**. (March 2001), Volume 65, Issue 2, pg. 137-151.

Mitochondrial DNA from Pre-Columbian Ciboneys From Cuba and the Prehistoric Colonization of the Caribbean. *C.Lalueza-Fox, M.T.P. Gilbert, A.J.Martiínez-Fuentes, F.Calafell, and J.Bertranpetit*. **American Journal of Physical Anthropology**. Volume 121. Issue 2, pg. 97–108 (June 2003).

Fact: *The **Top Three** Paternal Y-DNA Haplogroups in Latinos are: **R1b1b, Q, and C.** Other Haplogroups found include: **B, D, R1a, T, E1b1a, E1b1b, T, I, J2, J1, and G.***

CHAPTER 23

WHO ELSE FALLS INTO THE Y-DNA "R1B" HAPLOGROUP THAT SCIENTISTS SAY IS PROOF THAT LATINOS ARE MOSTLY EUROPEAN?

In the Y-DNA Haplogroup "R" we have the R1b1a, R1b1b and the R1b1c. Most of all "R1b" Haplogroup carriers fall into the subgroups "**R1b1c/R-V88**" and "**R1b1a/R-P297**". The Majority of Europeans DNA started out from the **R1b1a/R-P297** subgroup, which over time turned into the **R1b1a/R-M269** subgroup. For this reason, most Europeans today are mainly from the **R1b1a/R-M269** subgroup (**i.e. Wales, Spain, Portugal, Ireland, France, England, Italy**). Latinos fall into the Y-DNA haplogroup "**R1b1a**" or "**R1b1b**". In the African Fulbe/Fulani people of Niger there was a recorded **14.3%** frequency of the **R1b1c** gene. The **Berbers of Siwa** (South Egypt) exhibited a **27%** frequency rate. The **Hausa Tribe** of North Nigeria exhibited **20%-45%** frequency rates but frequencies of **60-95%** were found in the African country of Chad and Cameroon. The African country of Cameroon also has one of the highest frequencies of the "**E1b1a**" Haplogroup. Scientists have proven that the **R1b1c (V88)** "R" subgroup found in Africans is genetically more closer to the root "R1b" than the "R-M269" subgroup found in many Europeans. This means the "R1b" Haplogroup most likely originated from Black people.

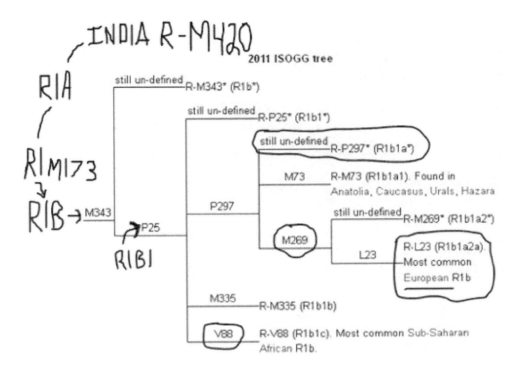

The handwritten and printed tree contains:

INDIA R-M420
2011 ISOGG tree

R1A

R1 M173
↓
R1B → M343

R1B1

still un-defined — R-M343* (R1b*)

still un-defined — R-P25* (R1b1*)

still un-defined — R-P297* (R1b1a*)

M73 — R-M73 (R1b1a1). Found in Anatolia, Caucasus, Urals, Hazara

P297

still un-defined — R-M269* (R1b1a2*)

M269

L23 — R-L23 (R1b1a2a). Most common European R1b

M335 — R-M335 (R1b1b)

V88 — R-V88 (R1b1c). Most common Sub-Saharan African R1b.

(Above) The 2011 **International Society of Genetic Genealogy** (ISOGG) "R" Haplogroup Tree. The Haplogroup "R1-M173" has been proven to have its origin in Africa. According to Clyde Winters, the "R-M173" Haplogroup was brought to the Americas from Blacks that came from West Africa. Haplogroup "**R1-M173**" would give rise to Haplogroup "**R1a**-M420", "**R1b**-M343", "**R1b1**-P25", "**R1b1a**", "**R1b1b**" and "**R1b1c**". It is interesting to note that the Native American Indian Tribes that intermixed with Blacks the most also carry the highest frequency of the Haplogroup "R1b" (**Ojibwa-79%, Seminole-50%, Cherokee-47%**).

Source: "**Is Native American R Y-Chromosome of African *Origin*".** Clyde Winters. *Current Research Journal of Biological Sciences*. 2011. (3)6: pg.: 555-558.

(**Above**) South Dravidian Indians often carry the Y-Haplogroup "**R1a1**" and "**R2a**" amongst Y Haplogroup "**H**". If the Y-DNA "**R**" Haplogroup is European, why is it seen in mostly people of color?

The Y-DNA Haplogroup "**R1b**-M343", "**R1b1**-P25" and "**R1b1a**-P297" are essentially listed as "**still un-defined**" because scientists have not found enough people going back thousands of years that have tested positive for these "**Ancient**" branches of the Paternal Y-DNA Haplogroup "**R**". The **TWO** oldest branches (sub-group) of the Y-DNA "**R**" Haplogroup are Blacks living in Central Africa (**R1b1c**) and men in India (**R1a1**). Many of the men carrying high percentages of "**R1a**" and "**R1a1**" are **Indian Brahmin men**. Brahmins are the "**priestly**" class in India. These two subgroups are "older" than the "R" subgroup seen in Europeans, "R1b1a2a". One way to tell that they are older is "R1a" or "R1a1" which is seen in **India** is shorter than "R1b1a2a" or "R1a1a1b" which is seen in **Europe**. Who came first? The Brown man came first!

(**Above**) Brahmin men in India (1800's). Notice they are brown-skinned. The carry the Y-DNA **Q5** (like Native Indians), the Y-DNA Haplogroup **R1a*** and **R1a1**.

The men carrying the "**R1a*/R1a1**" Haplogroup are the **Andhra Pradesh Brahmins, Uttar Pradesh Brahmins, Bihar Brahmins, West Bengal Brahmins, Himachal Brahmins and J&K Kashmir Gujars**. These two "R" Haplogroups are higher up on the "R" Haplogroup Tree and are thus older than the European "R" Branch "**R-M269**" or "**R1b1a2a**".

(Above) Sri Lankans and South Dravidian Indians also carry the Y-DNA Haplogroup **R2a**, which is also older than the "R" Haplogroups seen in Europe.

Source: **"The Indian origin of paternal haplogroup R1a1* substantiates the autochthonous origin of Brahmins and the caste system."** *Journal of Human Genetics/The Japan Society of Human Genetics* (2009). 54, pg. 47-55.

Most Blacks in Africa that carry the Y-DNA R1b1c are Muslim. Where did they learn Islam? In the Middle East or Africa? These are questions that could help find out the true "root" of the "R" Y-DNA Haplogroup ancestry. Could these Central Africans bearing the "R1b1c-V88" Y-DNA Haplogroup be descendants of **Hebrew Israelites, Ishmaelite's or Hamites** that mixed with each other while sharing the same religious customs/traditions in Islam?

Here are some African Tribes in Central Africa/West Africa and their R1b1c (V88) frequencies:

- Ouldeme Tribe (Cameroon) 95.5%

- Mada Tribe (Cameroon) 82.4%
- Mafa Tribe (Cameroon) 87.5%
- Guiziga Tribe (Cameroon) 77.8%
- Daba Tribe (Cameroon) 42.1%
- Guidar Tribe (Cameroon) 66.7%
- Massa Tribe (Cameroon) 28.6%
- Shuwa Arabs (Cameroon) 40%

Fact: A slave narrative written down in the 1850's found in **Sierra Leone** revealed that Blacks around the **Lake Chad area** were also transported to the Bight of Biafra to be sold as slaves, although they were in small number in proportion to the Bantus slaves (Igbo, Yoruba, Ewe, Akan, Ga). This discovery came from a slave named **Ali Eisami**, born near Bornu, Northeast Nigeria (Hausaland). In 1815 the Slave Register of Saint Lucia shows one slave being from Bornu amongst almost 3,500 slaves who were mostly of Nigerian Igbo descent. Many records from the Bight of Biafra show that many Hausa slaves were shipped from Benin to Brazil. The majority of the slaves shipped to Brazil however were listed as "**Eboe, Ibo, Ibibio or Moco**". There are historians that state the "Negro" slaves were given these names as a new "identity". The frequency of the Y-DNA Haplogroup "R1b" was also found in Jamaica and Haiti at low frequencies (<4%).

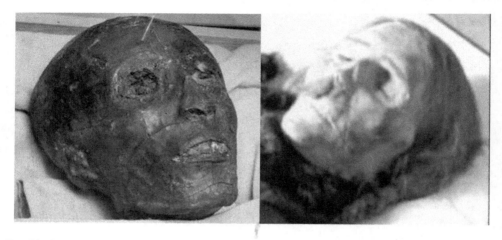

(**Left**) Mummy head of King Tut (Tutankhamun). (**Right**) Mummy head of a Caucasoid.

King Tut was the grandson of Pharaoh Amenhotep III and the son of Pharaoh Akhenaten. Scientists proved that King Tut died most likely from Malaria at the age of 19. Today, Malaria most often afflicts Sub-Saharan Africa, with a high prevalence being centered in West Africa. For this reason, the highest rates of Sickle Cell Disease are found in West Africa, the place most Negro Slaves were taken from to America. Sickle Cell Disease is the body's natural adaptive way to fight Malaria. Why? Because a person with Sickle Cell Anemia cannot get Malaria. This is the same way Scientists try to figure out how Black Tribes such as the Andaman people can live and survive hundreds of years isolated on an island without modern medicine. Well, it just so happens that when they supposedly tested King Tut's DNA, it came back as **R1b1b2**. This would connect King Tut's DNA with Central Africans. Others say King Tut's DNA came back as "**R1b1a2**", which is a common Y-DNA Haplogroup for Western Europeans. It is clear by this Mummy head that King Tut was Black as Blacks remain black in death and Whites remain White in death. So how is the R1b1 gene a "**European Gene**" if

King Tut was black? People, we have to wake up and see that "History" and "Science" will always be "whitenized" to cover up the Truth about the original people of Planet Earth.

So who else falls into this Y-DNA "R1b" Haplogroup? We have talked about Puerto Rico, Dominican Republic, Cuba, Western Europe, Central Africa (Chad, Cameroon, Nigeria). What about Mexico?

Fact: The Top 5 Y-DNA Haplogroup in Mexico are:

1. **R1b**
2. J2
3. E1b1
4. **Q1a3**
5. G2

So the question is, how can the R1b gene be a European gene if Mexicans, Central Africans and North Africans carry it? Scientists state the Y-Chromosome Haplogroups Q and C are acknowledged as the only two authentic Native-American Haplogroups, but state the R Haplogroup is the result of European admixture. Once again, the "Whitenization" of history is evident even until today. Even DNA companies are falling in with the "lie" that Y-DNA Haplogroup "R" lineages are strictly "**European**".

Fact: *Native-American Testing of Genele Health and DNA, Accredited DNA Testing Pioneer Since 1987 stated: "Three major haplogroups account for 96% of Native-American Male Y-Chromosomes. The Haplogroups are called Q, C and R. Haplogroups Q and C represent early Native-American founding male lineages. Haplogroup R lineages present in Native-Americans are believed by scientists to most likely have come from recent admixtures with Europeans."*

So let's explore continue to explore this "European" Theory closely.

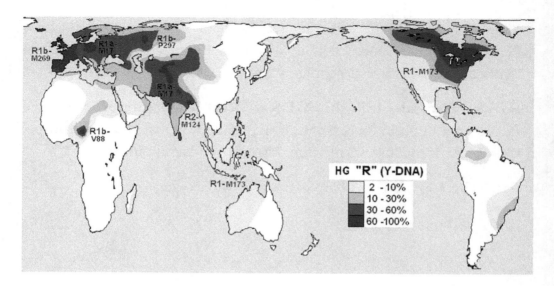

(**Above**) **Haplogroup R** (Y-DNA) Distribution in native populations by *Mauricio Lucioni*.

If you notice, the Y-DNA Haplogroup R is seen in North America, India, Sri Lanka, Central Africa, West Asia, and Western/Eastern Europe. It is heavily concentrated in North America where there was less race mixing with the White man compared to South America. It is also heavily concentrated in Scotland and Ireland. So in order to find out the "**Root**" of the Y-DNA Haplogroup R, we have to see who was there first in these areas.

(**Above**) Aztec Couple in 1800's. How do they have "Wooly Hair?" Is that a "European thing?" Does this couple carry the Y-DNA "**Q**", "**R**" or "**C**"?

The Ancient Aztecs, Mayans and Incas were "**People of Color**". The Europeans had to "**Erase**" this history by killing them off because if they were still around it would reveal the Truth about everything and the Children of Israel. In the Early 1400's, the Aztec capital city of "**Tenochtitlan**" was the center of the Aztec Empire. It was built on an island in a lake, the current site of **Mexico City**. It had pyramids and everything. It was conquered by Spaniard **Hernando Cortez**.

(**Above**) Amazon Indians in Brazil. Notice they are not white, but are brown-skinned people. Are they the Sons of Ham, Shem or Japheth?

(**Above**) Mexican Immigrant 1800's. How can this man's Y-DNA test results say he is "**European**" when the white man only did his damage for 200-300 years? Mexican history is older than that.

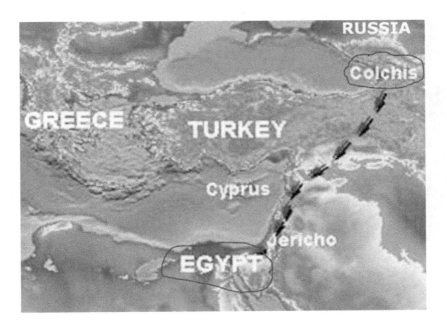

In Book II, Chapter 104, of the 400 B.C. Greek book **"Histories"** Herodotus says: '**I believe the Colchians are the same as the Egyptians, because like them they have black skin and wooly hair.**" Colchis is now the modern day Asia Minor country Georgia. During this time **Egyptian Pharaoh Sesostris III** (Senusret III) lead his army into that area in Asia Minor. Pharaoh **Sesostris** ruled around 1878 B.C., probably around the time when Joseph, and his brother's families were already in Egypt.

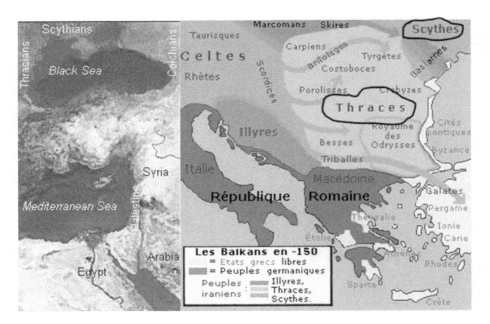

(**Above**) Thrace and Scythia today are modern day Bulgaria, Romania and Ukraine. Paul mentions the "convert" Jews in Greece and Scythia in **Colossians 3:11**. in The Erythraian Sea is the Indian Ocean and the Arabian Gulf is the Persian Gulf. Below are the words of Greek Historian Herodotus from 400 B.C. He writes how it is possible that the Egyptians spread themselves into Europe.

"Therefore passing these by I will make mention of the king who came after these, whose name is **Sesostris**. He (the priests said) first of all set out with ships of war from the **Arabian Gulf** and subdued those who dwelt by the **shores of the Erythraian Sea (Indian Ocean)**, until as he sailed he came to a sea which could no further be navigated by reason of shoals (large group of fish or submerged ridge/bank): then secondly, after he had returned to Egypt, according to the report of the priests he took a great army and marched over the continent, subduing every nation which stood in his way: and those of them whom he found valiant and fighting desperately for their freedom, in their lands he set up pillars which told by inscriptions his own name and the name of his country, and how he had subdued them by his power; but as to those of whose cities he obtained possession without fighting or with ease, on their pillars he inscribed words after the same tenor as he did for the nations which had shown themselves courageous, and in addition he drew upon them the hidden parts of a woman, desiring to signify by this that the people were cowards and effeminate (female acting). Thus doing he traversed the continent, until at last he passed over to Europe from Asia (Asia Minor?) and **subdued the Scythians** and also the **Thracians**. These, I am of opinion, were the furthest people to which the Egyptian army came, for in their country the pillars are found to have been set up, but in the land beyond this they are no longer found."

Herodotus (5th Century B.C.)

(Above) Pashtun people of South Afghanistan/North Pakistan. It is believed by some that they have "Israelite ancestry".

Fact: The Y-DNA Haplogroup "**R1a**" is seen in the people of Scythia and Thrace today. Thrace is Greece/Macedonia. Scythian territory was confined to the Ukraine, Southwestern Russia, Eastern Poland, Northeastern Balkans, **Southern Afghanistan**, Eastern Iran, **Southwest Pakistan**, Romania and Bulgaria.

515

(**Above**) The Pasthun people are one of the most numerous tribes in Afghanistan and Pakistan. The Pashtun Jews claim to be from the **Tribe of Benjamin**. As you can see from this 1800's picture, these Pakistani/Afghani people are a "**people of color**" So how can **Scythians** and **Eastern Europeans** also carry the Y-DNA Haplogroup "**R1a**". So is the original "**R1a**" carrier? Who is the original "**R1b**" carrier? It is not the "**European man**".

Fact: *The **Pashtun "Bani Israel" Jews** in Pakistan/Afghanistan also carry the "**R1a**" Y-DNA Haplogroup. They claim to be from the Tribe of Benjamin and state they have medieval documents from Persian texts that say they are descended from "Kish" or "Qais", the father of **King Saul**. They say originally they lived for hundreds of years in India before moving to Afghanistan and Pakistan. The 7th century book, "**Taaqati-Nasiri**" records the historical traces of the Pashtun people. The book "**Makhzan-al-Afghani**" written in the 17th century supposedly contains a printed table of descent from Abraham to the Pashtun Tribes through the **Tribe of Benjamin**.*

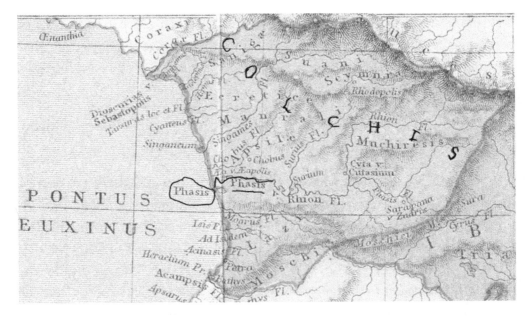

(**Above**) Greek historians wrote stories about people who they thought were "**Egyptians**" entering into the land of "**Colchis**" which is between the **Black Sea** and the **Caspian Sea**. Were these really Egyptians or were they "**Hebrew Israelites**" who back in those times were often mistaken for Egyptians except for maybe their **Israelite customs** and **attire**?

Herodotus also states, "From this point he (Sestrosis III) turned and began to go back; and when he came to the **River Phasis**, what happened then **I cannot say for certain**, whether the king Sesostris himself divided off a certain portion of his army **and left the men there as settlers in the land**, or whether some of his soldiers were wearied by his distant marches and remained by the River Phasis (**river in Georgia that dumps into the Black Sea**). "

Perhaps Black people (Shemites/Hamites) were in Europe first and not the other way around. It is believed that "Lud" the son of Shem, lived in what is now Western Turkey or Turkey period. Would this explain the introduction of the "**R**" Haplogroup in Europe? But was the Y-DNA "**R**" Haplogroup a Shemitic, Hamitic or Mixed Marker (Ham & Shem). **POSSIBLY!** The people Herodotus describes in Colchis; were they

517

Egyptians also mixed with "Hebrew blood" from almost 500 years of mixing with the 12 Tribes of Israel? Let's investigate if the people that invaded the land called "**Colchis**" were Egyptians or perhaps Hebrews with Egyptian influences?

Read Below? Pay close attention to the words in parentheses (italics). This might be a hidden clue to the "R1" branch.

"For the people of Colchis are evidently Egyptian, and this **I perceived** (*interpreted*) for myself before **I heard it from others** (*second-hand story*). So when I had come to consider the matter I asked them both; and the **COLCHIANS HAD REMEMBRANCE OF THE EGYPTIANS MORE THAN THE EGYPTIANS OF THE COLCHIANS** (*why would the Colchians know about the Egyptians but the Egyptians didn't know about the Colchians?*); but the Egyptians said '**they believed**' that the Colchians were a portion of the army of Sesostris. That this was so I conjectured myself not only because they are dark-skinned and have curly hair (*this of itself amounts to nothing, for there are other races which are so*), but also still more because the **Colchians**, **Egyptians**, and **Ethiopians** alone of all the races of men have practiced circumcision from the first (*were they influenced by the Hebrews?*). The Phoenicians and the Syrians who dwell in Palestine confess themselves that they have learnt it from the Egyptians, and the Syrians about the river Thermodon and the river Parthenios, and the Macronians, who are their neighbors, say that they have learned it lately from the Colchians. They are the only races of men who practice circumcision, and these evidently practice it in the same manner as the Egyptians. Of the Egyptians themselves however and the Ethiopians, I am not able to say which learnt from the other, for undoubtedly it is a most ancient custom; **but that the other nations learnt it by intercourse with the Egyptians** (*the Hebrews also intermixed with the Egyptians around that time*), this among others is to me a strong proof, namely that those of the Phoenicians who have intercourse with Hellas (Greeks) cease to follow the example of the Egyptians in this matter, and do not circumcise their children. Now let me tell another thing about the Colchians to show how they resemble the Egyptians: they alone work flax in the same fashion as the Egyptians, and the two nations are like one another in their whole manner of living and also in their language (*the Hebrews in Pre-Kingdom days wrote Egyptian-Hebrew mix and knew the language*): **not the linen of Colchis is called by the Hellenes Sardonic (funny)**, whereas that from Egypt is called Egyptian. (*the Hebrews attire was different than the Egyptians and could be seen as funny to outsiders*)."

Where these Colchians "**Hebrew Israelites**"? All of these certain "peculiar" statements by Herodotus seems to suggest that these people were not "**Egyptian**" but were "**Egyptian-like**". This could only be the "**Hebrew Israelites**" as the Nubians were definitely different than the Egyptians in language and clothing. The Hebrew Israelites were the only ones who traveled into the Levant and settled there. The Levant was right below the area of Colchis. Herodotus died around 425 B.C. The "**Sestrosis**" Pharaoh's lived around the time that Joseph and the Israelites would've first been living in Egypt under good favor with the Egyptians while Joseph was still Governor of all of Egypt.

Here is more of what Herodotus said:

"The pillars which Sesostris king of Egypt set up in the various countries are for the most part no longer to be seen extant; but in Syria Palestine I myself saw them existing with the inscription upon them which I have mentions and the emblem. Moreover, in Ionia (Westernmost part of Turkey) there are two figures of this man carved upon rocks, one on the road by which one goes from the land of Ephesos to Phocaia, and the other on the road from Sardis to Smyrna (Turkey). In each place there is a figure of a man cut in the rock of four cubits and a span in height, holding in his right hand a spear and in his left a bow and arrows, and the other equipment which he has similar to this, for it is both **EGYPTIAN AND ETHIOPIAN** (*the Israelites also* *intermixed with the Ethiopian Nubians*): and from one should to the other across the breast runs an inscription carved in sacred Egyptian characters, saying thus, **"This land with my shoulders I won for myself**. *(why would an Egyptian win land for himself and not his kingdom, unless this man didn't have his own kingdom?)* But who is he and from whence, he does not declare in these places, though in other places he had declared this. Some of those who have seen these carvings conjecture that the figure is that of Memnon (Ancient Ethiopian King), but herein they are very far from the truth."

Herodotus, 5th Century B.C.

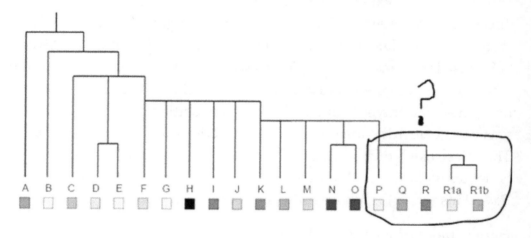

(**Above**) Y-DNA Haplogroup Tree from A-R. Notice how Haplogroup **Q** and **R** are closely related with their ancestor Haplogroup "**P**", which is commonly found in the Indigenous **Black Negritos** of the Philippines Island. The Y-DNA Haplogroup "**Q**" is primarily found in the indigenous Indians of the Americas and the Caribbean Islands. This "Q" Haplogroup is not found in Europe, which is one of the places where the "R" Haplogroup is found. **So how can Y-DNA Haplogroup "Q" and "R" carriers be so closely related, and also carry Maternal mtDNA Haplogroups that are the descendants of mtDNA male carriers of the Y-DNA Haplogroup "D" and "E"?** Well let's consider this:

1. The Hebrew Israelites were also known to be in **West/Central Africa** where the Y-DNA Haplogroup "**R1b**" can be found.

2. The Hebrew Israelites were also in **Iberia (Spain/Portugal)**, which is **Western Europe**, where the Y-DNA Haplogroup "**R1a**" and "**R1b**" is found. The Hebrew Israelites were "kicked" out of Spain and Portugal towards the end of the 1400's with the Black Moors. This was called the "**Spanish Inquisition**" or the "**Edict of Expulsion**".

3. The Hebrew Israelites in the Bible were exiled to **Medes-Persia (Iran)** which is right next door to **Afghanistan, Pakistan and India**, the place were the Y-DNA Haplogroup "**R1a**" and "**R1b**" is found.

Fact: Benjamin Tudela in the 1100's witnessed some Hebrew Israelites in South India (**Kerala**) and said they were "**Black**". Again, we know according to the Bible the 10 Lost Tribes of Israel were scattered into Assyria and as far as Medes (Persia-Iran). It took the Assyrian Kings **YEARS** to get rid of all of the 10 Northern Tribes of Israel out of their allotted territories in Israel.

2 Kings 17:5-6 "Then the **King of Assyria** came up throughout all the land, and went up to Samaria, and besieged it **THREE YEARS**. In the ninth year of **Hoshea** the King of Assyria took **SAMARIA**, and carried Israel away into **Assyria** (Syria, Iraq), and placed them in Halah and in Habor by the river Gozan, and in the cities of the **MEDES (Iran).**"

What is the coincidence that the Y-DNA "R" Haplogroup would be found in Europe, Africa, the Middle East? It is a known fact the oldest forms of the "R" Y-DNA Haplogroup are found in Africa and the Middle East, with the very oldest form of "R" being seen in the **Indo-Persian region**. The newest Y-DNA "R" subgroups are seen in Europe. This could mean the Y-DNA "R" Haplogroup started outside of Africa in the Indo-Persian region and did a "**Back-Migration**" into Africa after which the next stop was Europe. How do we know this might be true?

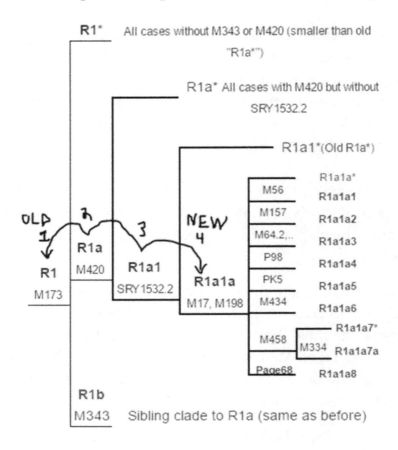

(**Above**) Y-DNA Haplogroup "R". **R1** is older than **R1a** and **R1b**. **R1a** is older than **R1a1**. **R1al** is older than **R1a1a**. **R1a1a** is older than **R1a1a1**. It is a known fact that **Y-DNA R1a1a1 (M417)** is the "base" R subgroup for **ALL** Europeans. Also **R1a** (India), **R2a** (India/Sri Lanka/Iran) and **R1a1** (India) are older than **R1b1c** (Central Africa).

Could this "**Back-Migration**" from the **Medes-Persia/India** area to Africa and then to Iberia (Western Europe-Spain/Portugal) be the "Back-Migration" pattern of the **Hebrew Israelites**? The word "**Omoros/Amoros**" which many say was the Ancient Yoruba word for "**Children of Light**" was also used as another name for the "**Moors**".

Were these "**Black Moors**" Hebrew Israelites that converted to Islam? The Hebrew word **Amo-Or-Os** is derived from the Hebrew word "**Amo**" which is "**Children of**" and the Hebrew word "**light**" which is "**Or**". The Yoruba word for Children is "**Omo**".

This "**Back-Migration Pattern**" of the "R" Y-DNA Haplogroup in Africa could easily have been some of the Northern Tribe Israelites. **So what Y-DNA "R" Haplogroups can be found in Iran (Persia)?**

- R2a-M124 (Azeri Iranians)
- R-L584
- R-M512
- R-M17
- R-M434
- And there are many more.

These Haplogroups are similar to "**R1a1**". **R2a** is found in Iran and Indian (West Bengal, Uttar Pradesh, Gujarat, and Mumbai-Bombay). **R-M434** is found in Pakistan and Oman.

Note: *Almost **40%** of Iranian Y-DNA is within the "R" Haplogroup (**R1a +R1b**). The most common "**single**" major Y-DNA Iranian Haplogroup is J2-M172. This Haplogroup comes from Asia Minor countries like "**Turkey**".*

Black Afro-Iranian (20th century) with an Afro. Most Iranians we see in America cannot grow their hair like this. Is this man a descendant of the Original Black Persians, a descendant of the Bantus Israelite Africans taken in the Arab Slave trade, or is he simply a "foreigner" who came to Iran looking for work? The Bible says the Children of Israel were scattered in the cities of Medes (Persia/Iran).

This is what Jewish Convert Benjamin Tudela had to say about the Jews he found living in **Medes (Persia-Iran)** in the 12th Century A.D.:

"There are men of Israel in the land of **Persia (Medes)** who say that in the mountains dwell four of the tribes of Israel, namely, the tribe of **Dan**, the tribe of **Zevulun (Zebulon)**, the tribe of **Asher**, and the tribe of **Naphtali**. "They are governed by their own prince, Joseph the Levite. Among them are learned scholars. They sow and reap and go forth to war as far as the land of Cush (Ethiopia or India?), by way of the desert. They are in league with the **Kofar-al-Turak**, pagan tribesmen who **worship the wind** and live in the wilderness."

Benjamin Tudela 12ᵗʰ Century A.D. "The Itinerary of Benjamin of Tudela-Book of Travels"

Fact" In the documentary "**Afro-Iranian Lives**", by Behnaz Mirzai, it reveals Afro-Iranian people living in the Iranian community in **Qeshm** (an Island in the Strait of Hormuz-Persian Gulf). It talks about their practice of a 1700's religious practice called "**Zar**", which is a belief that people can be **possessed by up to seventy-two different types of winds or female spirits**. This "Zar" belief is also found in the ancient indigenous people of **Egypt, Sudan, Somalia and Ethiopia**. The Ethiopian "Beta Israel" Jews are also known to have "**Zar beliefs**" mixed in with their **Jewish beliefs** and that to cure this possession of what they consider an "**evil spirit**", one has to sacrifice a goat or a hen. In Ramla, Israel "Za" practices can still be seen practiced by Ethiopian Jews with of course their "base" religious practice of Judaism.

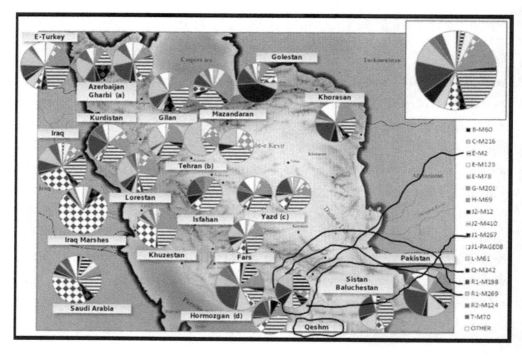

Fact: In South Iran (where the Afro-Iranians are), in the cities of **Qeshm** (circled) and **Hormozgan** (bottom middle of map) you will find that these Black Iranians carry the Y-DNA Haplogroup **Q-M242**. This Haplogroup is carried exclusively by the indigenous **Native American Indians**. These "Black" Iranians in the South also carry the Y-DNA Haplogroups R1-M269 (**East North Indian/Eastern Europe**), R1b-M269 (**Latinos/Western Europe/Central Africa**), R2-M124 (**Sri-Lanka-Elam**), L-M61 (**South India**), J1-M267 (**Yemen, Lemba, Sudan, Black Bedouin Arabs, Oman**), E-M78 (**North Africa**) and E-M2 (**Bantus Negroes**). If you notice, all of these different Y-DNA Haplogroups are affiliated with "**People of Color**" and not the "**White Race**". So this tells us something about the Afro-Iranian people that we possibly would've never known. These Y-DNA Haplogroups reveal who the **10 Northern Tribes of Israel** might have mixed with during their travels "**Eastward**" after their "exile" from Israel in 700 B.C.

The Top 4 Haplogroups seen in these Afro-Iranians in order are:

1. **E-M2** (Negroes/Bantus West and East Africans).
2. **R1b/R1a** (Latinos, Europeans, Pakistanis, Afghanis, Indians, Sri Lankans and Central Africans).
3. **Q-M242** (Native Americans)
4. **J1-M267** (people of Black Ishmaelite Arab descent and/or Shem).

Reference: "**Ancient Migratory Events in the Middle East: New Clues from the Y-Chromosome Variation of Modern Iranian**" by *Viola Grugni*, Public Library of Science (PLOS ONE), Published July 18, 2012. Volume 7 (7).

As the Israelites traveled further "**East**" towards China-Japan, the "**E-M2**" and "**J1-M267**" Haplogroups would no longer be seen. Y-DNA Haplogroups "**Q**" and "**R**" would mainly be found in Asia or Americas. This should tell us something. Some of the Hebrew Israelites that were exiled but stayed in the Middle East for a while did one of two things: Some did a "**Back Migration**" into North Africa, and perhaps Iberia (Spain/Portugal) while some traveled "**East**" past Afghanistan/Pakistan/India territory into Asia, eventually making their way across the Bering Strait into the Americas. Think about it. The Hausas, the Fulani's and other Tribes in Africa carry the Y-DNA "**R**" Haplogroup. They cannot be solely "pure" Black Arabs because if they were they would carry the Shemitic "**J1**" Y-DNA Haplogroup. They can't be pure "**Libyans**" because the Y-DNA "**R**" Haplogroup is a product of numerous mutations (**i.e. ancestors**). For this reason, the Y-DNA "**R**" Haplogroup represents a people who have had a long history of "**Mass Migration**" with some "**Mixing**" along the way. For instance, Y-DNA Haplogroup "**R**" is the descendant of Haplogroup "**P**", which is the descendant of Haplogroup "**K**", which is the descendant of Haplogroup "**IJK**". Notice this "combo" Y-DNA "**IJK**" Haplogroup has the Shemitic Haplogroup "**J**" in it. "Original" carriers of the Bantus "**E-M2**" Haplogroup look like Africans. For this reason, it is possible that the Black Moors were a people of "mixed heritage". This heritage had to include the Shemites (Ishmaelite Arabs, Joktanites, Israelites) and some Hamites (Cushites, Phuttites, Egyptians). Remember, the Black Moors had contact with **Europeans** (i.e. Spain/Portugal), **Hamites** (i.e. Phuttites, Egyptians, Cushites), **Shemites** (Arab Ishmaelite's, Joktanites), and the **Israelites** living in North Africa.

Y-DNA HAPLOGROUP R AND THE "MONGLOID CONNECTION".

(**Left**) **Tippu Tip** 1800's. He was a Black Arab that helped sell Black Bantus "Israelite" slaves from East Africa to all nations. (**Right**) **White Arab** from the Levant (Palestine, Israel, Syria, Lebanon). Who is the Original Arab? Who came first? Can a white couple birth black children? Someone is lying. Ishmael's mother and wife were Black Egyptians therefore the Arab Ishmaelite Tribes in the Middle East should be Black.

(**Left**) Captured Arab Slave Trader on a British Ship. Slavery was abolished for the British in 1807 so they figured if they couldn't do it anymore the Arabs shouldn't be able to do it. (**Right**) These Bantus "Israelite" African slaves were on an Arab Dhow slave ship in chains. The British Royal Navy West African Squadron intercepted the Arab Slave ship off the coast of Zanzibar, Tanzania and Mozambique. They took the chains off the men and gave them clothes. These Bantus East African men were either headed to Brazil, the Middle East, China, Japan or the Pacific Islands in Asia (i.e. Indonesia-Java, Papua New Guinea, Philippines). The Bible "**Curses of Israel**" foretells which way the Israelites have been scattered upon the Earth. We have just been focused on Africa for the time being. Now we need to find our brethren to the East!

(**Above**) Descendants of "**Israelite slaves**" in America "**Stolen from Africa**".

Deuteronomy 28:32 "Thy sons and daughters shall be given unto another people, and thine eyes shall look and fail with longing for them all the day long: and there shall be no might in thine hand."

Deuteronomy 28:36 "The Lord shall bring thee, and thy king which thou shalt set over thee, unto a nation which neither thou nor thy fathers have known; and there shalt thou serve other gods, wood and stone.

(**Above**) The Moros Muslims of the Philippines 1800's. Notice that they look Black with a sort of "**Mongloid-Asian**" look. Prior to the 1200 A.D. the indigenous "**Black People**" of the Philippines had their own religious beliefs. But the Arab Slave Traders and Persians came bringing "Bantus" East African Israelites. Because of this and also the occupation of their island by Chinese Muslims, their religion today is Sunni Islam. But were these people descendants of the Bantus Israelite slaves from East Africa? Scientists will like to say some of the "indigenous" Black people living in the Pacific Islands have been there for 50,000 years. This is possibly a "cover-up" to prevent people from using "critical thinking" to find out the true story of these people. The bible says that the Children of Israel would be brought to a land that their forefathers wouldn't know and that they would worship other gods there. Is this a clue?

(**Above**) The **Moros "Black" Muslims of Mindanao** (South Philippines). Pictured here are the Sultans in the front. As you can see they are Black with Asian-Mongloid features. Some of these people have mixed with the local Asians (i.e. Filipinos, Japanese, Chinese). Islam arrived to the Island of Mindanao around the 1300's A.D.

The people of **Mindanao** are called "**Maranao**" people. Their mtDNA showed two Haplogroups: mtDNA Haplogroup "**M**" and "**D**". Maternal mtDNA "**M**" is seen in East Africa (Ethiopia/Eritrea), South Arabia, Yemen, Australia (aborigines), Asia and India. The highest frequencies of mtDNA "**M**" in Asia are seen in **Tibet** and **Japan** which are the same locations known to carry people with the **Paternal Y-DNA YAP+ Haplogroup "D"**. Y-DNA **YAP+** "D" Haplogroup carriers share a common genetic ancestry to **Y-DNA YAP+ "E"** Haplogroup "**Israelite**" carriers (i.e. Igbo Nigerians, Kikuyu Kenyans, Sukuma Tanzanians, Muganda Ugandans). Maternal mtDNA "D" is seen in the indigenous Indians of South America and is a direct descendant of the mtDNA "**L3**" (i.e. African-Americans/Bantus Africans) and "**M**" (East Africans, Abyssinians). This suggests that these "Black Moro Muslims" living in the Philippines are of "**Israelite**" stock, in addition to possibly other "**select**" people groups living in Tibet, Japan, India, Australia, Yemen and other parts of Asia. **Remember, the Maternal DNA that is passed down to both male and female children is not affected by "Rape" or "Marriage" from a Foreign man (i.e. White man). Only the Y-DNA is affected when a foreign man bears children with an "indigenous" woman by rape or marriage (i.e. Spaniards raping Indians and Negroes). The Y-DNA in this case is passed down from father to son ONLY.** Therefore, the maternal DNA aka "**mtDNA**" is a good genetic tool in determining "**who is who**" in regards to the descendants of the Hebrew Israelites. So where did these "Black Filipinos" get their Black and Mongloid features from? Europe, Japheth? No way. They got it from Shem and Ham, just as the Israelites in Africa were of Shemitic-Hamitic heritage.

Source: "**Complete mtDNA genomes of Filipino ethnolinguistic groups: a melting pot of recent and ancient lineages in the Asia-Pacific region**". *European Journal of Human Genetics*. (February 2014), 22(2). Pg. 228-237.

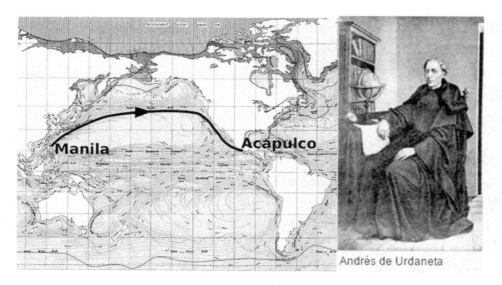

Andrés de Urdaneta

(**Above**) The Slave Trade route from Manila, Philippines to Acapulco, Mexico (**1500's-1800's**). Spanish friar "**Andres de Urdaneta**" was an interpreter and the so-called "**protector of the South Asian Indians**". Did he mean to call them something else other than "**Indians**"?

Manila, the capital of the Philippines and Acapulco, Mexico were big trading centers centuries ago. They often did trade with one another thanks to **Spaniard King Phillip II** (1554 A.D.) and his brethren. The Spanish got involved in the Slave Trade in Asia, but not primarily with stealing Black people from Africa (**like they normally did**), but now with stealing Black people from **India, Burma, Indonesia, Papua New Guinea), Guam, the Mariana Islands, Malaysia, the Island of Mindanao in the Philippines**. The used large ships called "**Galleons**" to transport goods from China, Japan, Indian **and slaves** from South Asia to Mexico. Some of these Galleons were named "**Trinidad, San Pedro and San Juan**". Why these areas? Historians say because they needed to fill up the "**labor shortage**" caused by the widespread death of the indigenous Mexican Indians at the hands of the Spanish. This was also done by the Spanish with the "**Negroes**" in the Caribbean Islands when there was a "slave" shortage on the Spanish Plantations from the death of the Taino Indians in the Caribbean. So why did the Spaniards selectively choose these "**Black Asian-looking**" people in

534

South Asia? Why didn't they select other races? Perhaps they knew these Black, "mongloid-looking" people were also **Israelites**. It's a known fact that the Spanish and Portuguese went snooping in the **Land of Taina (Puerto Rico)** and the "**New World-Americas**" with Hebrew interpreters looking for "**Israelites**". So did the Spanish have knowledge of where the rest of the Hebrew Israelites were? The Spanish claimed according to 2 Esdras 40-45 that the Israelites went into another country to follow their laws, commandments and statutes? Perhaps they had some other information revealing where other Israelites were scattered.

The Moros Muslims of the Philippines hated American Governor Taft and General Sumner. The would rather die as Muslims than have Christianity and "Americanism" shoved onto their people. But the Europeans of course tried to "**woo**" them with all types of material things (i.e. guns, ammo) and treaties to work their way into eventually controlling the Philippines with help from the Catholic Church. When Mexico had finally gained its independence from Spain in 1821, all ties of Mexico to the Philippines were cut off.

(**Above**) General **Vicente Guerrero** fought against Spain for Mexico's Independence in 1821 A.D., later becoming the **2nd President of Mexico** in 1829 A.D. **He was of Afro-Mestizo descent**. After Mexico's victory, General Vicente Guerrero stepped in and said:

535

"Now that we Mexicans have obtained our independence by revolution against Spanish rule. It is our solemn duty to help the less fortunate countries...Especially the Philippines, with whom our country had the most intimate relations during the last two centuries and a half. We should send secret agents...with a message to their inhabitants to rise in revolution against Spain and that we shall give them financial and military assistance to win their freedom. In the eventuality of the separation of Philippines from Spain we must take utmost efforts to revive the former Acapulco-Manila trade which had been the most contributory factors to Mexico's economic prosperity. As revived, this trade shall not be a government monopoly, as Spain made it, but shall be free enterprise which all merchants are welcome to be engaged in. The restrictive measures that Spain previously imposed must all be abolished."

(**Above**) The East African "**Arab Slave Trade**" took Bantus Israelite Africans and Abyssinians (Ethiopians/Eritreans) across the Indian Ocean into Asia (Pacific Islands, China, Japan) and the Middle East.

It's a known fact that the "**Original**" carriers of the Black Arab "**J1-M267**" Haplogroup looked "Negroid" like Africans. Take a look at some 19th century pictures of the Black Arab Muslims of Oman, Qatar, Yemen, Jordan, and Sudan (Khartoum). The "**Original**" carriers of the "**Q**" and "**R**" Haplogroup (India/Afghanistan/Pakistan/Native America) are more "**Mongloid**" in appearance. If you don't believe it, look at some pictures of the people that carry the Ancestral Y-DNA "**P**" Haplogroup to the Haplogroup "**Q & R**". The people that carry the "**P**" Y-DNA Haplogroup in South Asia look like "**Brown-skin Mongloid-Negritos**".

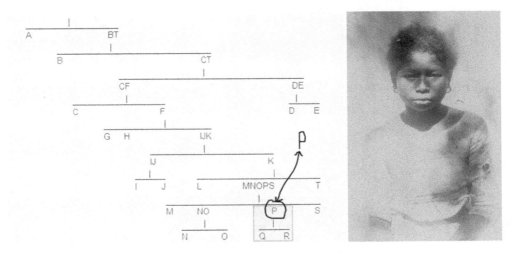

(**Left**) Y-DNA Haplogroup Tree. As you can see, Haplogroup "**P**" evolved into Haplogroup "**Q**" and "**R**", which are both seen in Asia, and the "**Indigenous**" Native Americans (North/Central/South). (**Right**) The Y-DNA Haplogroup "**P**" is commonly seen in the mongloid "**Aeta**" negritos of the Philippines. It is also found in the Black natives of "**Papua New Guinea**".

(**Above**) Aeta women. They carry the Ancestor "**P**" Haplogroup of the Native American Haplogroup "**Q**".

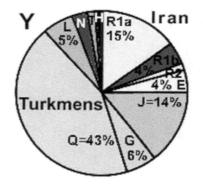

(**Above**) 43% of the Turkmen people's Y-DNA consists of Y-DNA **Haplogroup Q**, the same Haplogroup primarily seen in the "**indigenous**" Indians of the Americas. But the Turkmen people live in Iran. How do we explain this? The Turkmen people do not look like the Original "**Native American Indians**".

So here is the kicker! The highest rates of the Y-DNA "**Q-M242**" Haplogroup is seen in the indigenous "**Indians**" of the Americas. We all know that **African slaves, Indians, Asians** and **Europeans** make pretty much the genetic makeup of "Latinos". This is also true for the

"**Negro**" in America. Well, outside of the Afro-Iranians living in Qeshm, Iran (South Iran) the only other Iranians with a "higher" frequency of the "Q-M242"Y-DNA Haplogroup is Iranian people living in **Golestan, Iran**. Golestan, Iran is near the country called "**Turkmenistan**". The "**Turkmen**" people look like Turkish-Asian people. So what is giving them their "Arab" look and what is giving them their "**Asian**" look? Well according to the pie graph above, less than half of the men (43%) in Turkmenistan test positive for a "primary Q-M242" Haplogroup ancestry. The other 57% tested positive for Y-DNA Haplogroups that are commonly seen in **light-skinned/white-skinned races (J2, R1a, G, N, E1b1b)**. So in theory, the "light-skinned" phenotype (appearance) should dominate in the country of Turkmenistan. If you Google pictures of Turkmenistan people you will find this to be true as the "Turkmens" are a white-skinned people. So we see a suppressed "Asian" look in the Turkmenistan people although it is sometimes subtly seen in the people there. But we know that the Native Americans hundreds of years ago (pre-Columbus) were brown-skinned people. They **ALL** for the most part carried the "**Q-M242**" Y DNA Haplogroup (Males). So what is suppressing the "**Brown skin color trait**" in the Turkmenistan people who have this "Q-M242" Y DNA Haplogroup in moderate amounts compared to the rest of the world? Perhaps we have to look at the what the Maternal (Mother) mtDNA of these Turkmenistan people has to do with the skin color and why it is not "Brown" like the Indians in the Americas.

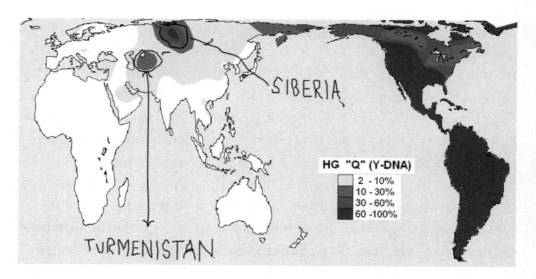

(**Above**) The Paternal Y-DNA "Q" Haplogroup distribution in the world.   Notice the highest "Q" Haplogroup carriers are in Turkmenistan, West Siberia (**Selkups**), and the Americas (Indians). The Turkmenistan people in **Northern Iran** (South of Russia and West of Asia) have on average 10% to maybe at best 40% of their Paternal Y-DNA coming from the "Q-M242" Haplogroup. These "**Turkmen**" people have a slight Asian appearance their look. Does the Turkmens subtle "Asian look" come from the Y-DNA Q-M242? To find this out let's compare notes with other people in the world that carry this "Q" Haplogroup.

(**Above**) Y-DNA Haplogroup Breakdown of the Selkup West Siberian people. **They also live in Teepee's like the Indians and Eskimos.** As you can see most of their people fall into the Y DNA "**Q**" Haplogroup.

The Siberian "**Selkup**" people have over **60%** of their people carrying the "**Q-M242**" Y DNA Haplogroup. This is more than the "Turkmen" people who had a **43%** frequency rate of the Haplogroup "**Q-M242**". Strikingly, the Selkup people have more Haplogroup "Q" in their blood and they also have a more distinct Mongloid "**Asian**" appearance to them than the Turkmen people. But here is what keeps both these races of people "**white**" in skin complexion, despite both groups having a moderate amount of the Native American Y-DNA Haplogroup "Q". About 70% of the **Turkmen and Selkup** people's maternal mtDNA is dominated by **European Haplogroups** such as **H, HV, J, T, U, N, X and R** (Ottoni 2011 study). Only 30% of their mtDNA is linked to the mtDNA "**M**", that is linked to "**Brown-skinned**" people (**India, Andaman Island, Ethiopia, Nigeria, Yemen, Kenya etc.**). This means that European women at some point in time traveled to West Siberia (Selkup) and Central Asia (Turkmenistan). They most likely settled there, set up communities and started having children. Men carrying the Paternal "Y" Haplogroup "Q" traveled through these areas of Central Asia/West Siberia having sons with these women. Obviously, the "Q" men had more sons with the local "white" women of Selkup than of Turkmenistan. This is reflected in the Selkup's Y-DNA.

Note: The small presence of the Maternal "**M**" mtDNA in the Turkmen women and men means "Black-melaninated" women traveled (of course with their men) all the way to Turkmenistan, which is not too far from Asia (China). These women had some children in this area for a while and then kept moving to the East. So who were these "Black People" that left their DNA mark in this land of "whites"? Where they descendants of East African slaves? Where they Black people looking to conquer Asia or where they a group of Black People who were exiled from their lands and was hoping to find a place they could eventually find home? The later scenario sounds like the **Hebrew Israelites**.

The Selkup's mtDNA mostly falls in the "**U**" mtDNA Haplogroup category (**about 70% of it**). This is the reason we see a whopping "**European**" influence to the skin color of the Selkup Siberian people in the 21st century. This means that obviously in the past, "Brown-skinned, Mongloid" looking men came into Russia/Siberia area before crossing over the Bering Strait into the Americas. The left their Y-DNA behind when they had children with the local "Europe-White Arab" blooded people that were also living in this area. Who were these "**Brown-skinned**" looking "**Mongloid**" people? Well, the mtDNA of the Native Indians can be traced back to the mtDNA of **Nigerians, Kenyans, and Ethiopians,** however the Native Indians Y-DNA "**Q**" is **NOT** found in Africa or Arabia. This means that these people originated from the same racial "**stock**" as Nigerians, Kenyans and Ethiopians, but at some point in time they left their original land (**Israel**) and never came back. If they did we would see the "Q" Y-DNA Haplogroup in Africa and Israel. Instead they mixed with the "**Nations**" around them causing their "look" to change to what people today would call "**Mongloid**". People like to claim there are 3 races of man: **Negroid, Caucasoid and Mongloid**. The problem with this is, who according to Noah's family is the "father" of the "**Mongloid** race? Noah did not have any children of grandchildren named "**Mongloid**".

Reference: **Mitochondrial analysis of a Byzantine population reveals the differential impact of multipole historical events in South**

Anatolia. Claudio Ottoni, Francois-X Ricaut, Nancy Vanderheyden, Nicolas Brucato, Marc Waelkens and Ronny Decorte. *European Journal of Human Genetics.* (May 2011). Volume 19, pg. 571-576.

So let's finish talking about the Black Iranians (Persians) and explaining what this all means.

(**Above**) Blacks in Persia (Iran) late 1800's/early 1900's. Now some historians say Benjamin Tudela's account of finding Israelites in Persia is in error, mainly because they believe he uses the story of "**Eldad the Danite**" to come up with his story. Persia (Iran) in older times did have a significant number of Blacks that look like every day Africans or African-Americans. Mainstream TV and the Media will not show us this side of "**Black Iran**". Cities like **Bandar Abbas** and **Persepolis** in South Iran show a significant "**Black presence**". Because of the Arab Slave trade of East "**Bantus**" Israelites for over 1,000 years and the abolishment of slavery in Iran in 1929, many historians say that **ALL** Afro-Iranians in the country of Iran are descendants of slaves. The Persian Gulf was a hot spot for dumping off Black "**Israelite**" Slaves so it is not uncommon to see **Afro-Iraqis, Afro-Pakistanis, Afro-Omanis, and Afro-Saudis.** It is a known fact that Iran sold slaves to slave owners in South Asia (i.e. Philippines) and also had a history of getting Black slaves from **South Russia** and the **Caucasus regions** just past the Black Sea.

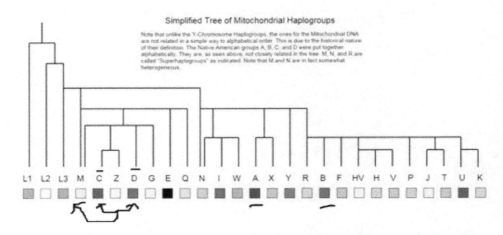

Fact: The Most Common mtDNA Haplogroups of Puerto Ricans, Cubans and Mexicans is A, C, and D. The mtDNA Haplogroups closely associated with Nigerians, Ethiopians and Kenyans is "C" and "D". Why? **The most common mtDNA of African-Americans, Nigerians, Kenyans and Ethiopians is "L3" and "M", which is a direct ancestor of mtDNA Haplogroups "C" and "D".** These Haplogroups (C & D) are mostly seen in Central and South America. If you follow the mtDNA Haplogroup Tree you will see how the mtDNA of Latinos and Native Americans is linked to the "Negro" race in Africa. Maternal mtDNA Haplogroup "**B**" is mostly seen in China, Taiwan, the Philippines, Laos, Thailand, Japan and Indonesia.

CHAPTER 24

DID THE ANCIENT EGYPTIANS-HEBREWS ALSO OCCUPY WESTERN EUROPE? DID THEY LEAVE THEIR GENETIC "MARK" THERE?

The History of Scotland can be traced to a Black presence. **King Kenneth III** was the King of Scotland from 997 A.D. to 1005 A.D. He was known as **"Kenneth the Niger"** or **"Kenneth Dubh"**, a surname which means **"The Black Man"**. Some say King James was a descendant of "Kenneth the Niger". It was a known fact that many seafaring warriors were North African. Many would travel to via Iberia (Spain/Portugal) into Europe, joining in many cultures and holding power positions. Kenneth lived and reigned over certain black divisions in Scotland, and some historians state that a race known as the **"Sons of the Blacks"** succeeded him (JA Rogers, Sex and Race). Kenneth was the last king of Scotland to succeed to the throne through the tanistry system (alternating rulership within a clan). This clan rivalry for rulership of the throne would ultimately lead to his death in 1005.

So I know you are wondering, so when did whites come onto the scene to become rulers over the land of Japheth again?

(**Above**) Black Moorish Knights. Many sources say the word "Knight" comes from the word "**Night**" because back in the day the Knights "**skin color**" were as dark as the nigh. This was especially seen with the Moors, who many believe were a mix of Black North Africans (**Hamitic**), Black Arab Ishmaelite's (**Shem**) and Black Hebrew Israelites.

Fact: When you study the symbol of the Moor from The Renaissance Period (1500's) you will see no Black servants. If you look up the Drake Jewel (1575 A.D.), it shows the profile of a Black King dominating the profile of a White woman. Inside the Drake Jewel is a miniature of **Queen Elizabeth I**. Her father's sister Mary Tudor was the grandmother of Mary of Scots. Mary of Scots' son was James I who married Anne of Denmark. They were the grandparents of Charles II Stuart who was named "**The Black Boy.**" This symbolizes Africa dominating Europe and Black superiority in Europe.

The symbol of the Moor shows a Blue man which is a Black man and means "**Blue Blood**". Back then, the Blacks in Europe were referred to as "**Blue men**". But now we associate "**Blue Blood**" with Nobility. After the French Revolution in 1789 A.D. everything began to be whitewashed. Even the noses of the Pharaoh's of Egypt started to become mysteriously blown off. It was even the Black people from North Africa, like the Hebrew Israelite disciples of Christ who introduced Christianity to Europe. For this reason, the Roman catacombs, Russian Churches and French Monasteries still depict images of a Black Mary with a Black Jesus. They also portray all of the disciples/apostles of Christ to be Black. The Europeans then flipped the script and brought their "**Whitewashed**" version of the Bible to West Africa and the New World where most of the Israelites had already been scattered into centuries before.

James 1:1 "James, a servant of God and of the Lord Jesus Christ, to the **TWELVE TRIBES WHICH ARE SCATTERED ABROAD**, greeting."

Fact: *In the bible there was **James the son of Zebedee, James the son of Alphaeus and James the brother of Christ**. Regardless of who wrote the Book of James, the scriptures say, "**the 12 Tribes of Israel scattered "abroad"**. Not the 12 Tribes of Israel scattered in **Europe**, in **Rome**, in **Antioch** or **Scythia**, but "abroad". If the author of the Book of James knew Hebrew Israelite history he would have known if all the Israelites were scattered into Europe. Obviously the Israelites were scattered abroad. Now the Ashkenazi Jews claim that the original Jews were not Black like African-Americans. But around the 1st century A.D. were the European white Jews scattered into Africa, India, South Asia, Australia, Arabia, the Middle East, the Americas or the Caribbean? No, **ALL** the Ashkenazi Jews come from one place, "Europe". There is no "scattered abroad" in their history.*

His Most Sacred Majesty George III, King of Great Britain

(**Above**) Who is the "Real" **King George III** (reign 25 October 1760 – 29 January 1820) of the United Kingdom/Great Britain? Does anybody know?

These are the great-great-great grandparents of the present **Queen Elizabeth II**. All the nobility of Europe intermarried across different countries. Beware of the white fantasy paintings of George III. The French Revolution was a revolution against the ruling Black Nobility. So who is the real "**King George III**".

(**Above**) Which is the real "**Black**" face of **Charles I of England**, House of Stuart, who was executed in 1649. He was Ruler of the three kingdoms of England, Scotland and Ireland at the time. This is the original Front cover of the Book "**Leviathan**" written by Thomas Hobbes in 1651. The Black Stuarts were also called "**Jacobite's**". Hmmm.......I wonder why? History says the Jacobites were members of a political movement to return the Stuart Kings back to the thrones of England, Scotland and Ireland.

OK, NOW WE ARE GETTING SOMEWHERE INTO THIS Y-DNA HAPLOGROUP R1B? SOMEBODY HAS TO CRACK THE PUZZLE!

So we know the Black Moors ruled Europe starting with Iberia (Spain/Portugal) from 711 all the way till 1492. Spain and Portugal is hot markers for the Y-DNA Haplogroup **R1b** gene. The Black Moors were the Muslim inhabitants of Maghreb (North Africa), the Iberian Peninsula, Sicily (Island South of Italy), and Malta (Island south of Sicily) during the Middle Ages. It is also a known fact that the Black Moors often had White European women as concubines.

(**Above**) "**The Bath**"-1800's **Jean-Leon Gerome**. Notice how the Black Moors were also "**fond**" of the white woman. Back in Ancient times the Moors could take the wife of any man to be the Sultan's "**sex slave**" in his luxurious palace. Even women in Europe. The Y-DNA of Arab North Africans is mostly **E1b1b (E-M81), J1, R1b and Ra**. "E1b1b" is a mix of Edom along with the invading nations that invaded North Africa and the Levant from 300 B.C. to present. "**J1**" is the original marker for the Black Shemitic people. "**R1b**" is believed to be a Haplogroup of the (Shemitic-Hamitic) people that like the "**E-M2**" Haplogroup left Africa to Israel (Moses/Joshua) and over some time came back, but not after mixing with other types of Shemitic people. Some came back to Africa because we see the "**R1b**" Y-DNA Haplogroup in Iberia (Spain/Portugal) and Africa. But for those that decided not to come back? These people left their Y-DNA "**R1b**" mark in the **Middle East, Central Asia, India and South Asia**.

The Black Moors during the Roman Period A.D.

Black King of Thrace (Greece) and White Queen fresco?

(Above) Princess Meritaten, Princess Scotia of Ireland.

This is the sculpture of **Princess Meritaten**, daughter of **Pharaoh Akhenaten and Queen Nefertiti,** who sailed away in political exile, to Ireland sometime between 1400 B.C. to 1350 BC to become "**Princess Scotia**", after whom Scotland (Ireland) is named. Did Princes Meritaten and the Egyptian men leave their "DNA Mark" on the people? Or did the Hebrews-Egyptians leave their mark later after populating Iberia and Western Europe during the medieval times? Remember if the Black Egyptian men in Ireland/Wales messed around with the white women of the land having "**illegitimate**" children, the Y-DNA of the Egyptian men would be passed down to EVERY MALE for generations regardless if the Egyptians decided to leave Europe never to return back like the Black Moors/Black Israelites did after 1492 A.D. after the "**Edict of Expulsion**" by Spain and Portugal. Even if these "illegitimate" children started only marrying "white" instead of "black" as they got older, the Y-DNA would still remain, but the skin color and hair texture of the people would obviously change after about

3-4 generations of straight "**white-mixing**". Does this mean that everyone in Western Europe is "**Egyptian**" or "**Israelite**" by blood? The answer is no. The "Y" chromosome is unique to males in that it is only passed down from father to son. Thus, this Y-DNA marker can change when invading nations "**conquer and colonize**" other people's lands. Y-DNA also only makes up 1% of our total Genetic Make-up. Therefore, our Y-DNA is only a "small" indicator of who we actually are. Just because Blacks or Latinos may have a "White-European" Great-great grandfather in their family tree, that doesn't make them strictly "**European**". The percentage of "actual" DNA that Blacks and Latinos inherit from their Great-great grandfathers or even Great-great-great grandfathers is less than 10%.

Relationship to You	Approximate % Of Their DNA You Inherited
Parents	Exactly 50%
Grandparents	About 25%
Great-grandparents	About 12.5%
Great-great-grandparents	About 6.25%
Great-great-great-grandparents	About 3.125%
Great-great-great-great-grandparents	About 1.5625%

(**Above**) Native American and African-American in the 1800's A.D. The DNA of our Parents and Grandparents make up 75% of who we are. No matter if there is a "**White man**" or "**White Women**" in your Family Tree at the **Great-great-great grandparent level**, if both your parents are **Black** (i.e. African, African-American, Caribbean) in addition to your Grandparents, it is safe to say that the "**White**" DNA contribution to your DNA is very slim. Most Black people in America today have Black Parents and Black Grandparents. Most Latinos today have Latino Parents and Latino Grandparents. After about 7 generations of **NO race mixing** the "European DNA" in Blacks and Latinos is slim to none. This is why we must not be so tied up on the "Y-DNA" Haplogroup letter; instead we must look at the "**Big Picture**". This includes:

1. Taking into account "**Migration Patterns**" and comparing the areas where certain Y-Haplogroups and mtDNA Haplogroups are found in regards to where slaves were "**taken from**" or "**taken to**".

2. Using **Bible history** and **Post-Bible history** (beyond 1st Century A.D.) we can tell who invaded Israel, the Middle East, Africa, Europe and Asia. We can find out the time frame that these invasions happened and correlate it with the different "majority" or "minority" haplogroups in different particular areas.

3. Using our knowledge of "**skin color**" in regards to certain "**Haplogroups**" we can trace different "**brown-black**" Haplogroups and their "**travel pattern**" to other countries "**Outside of Africa**". This would correlate strongly with a "**nomadic, wandering people with no true home**". The 12 Tribes of Israel haven't had a "**true home**" since the time of Christ and according to the Bible, the Israelites are still in other people's countries as "**strangers**" to the land. This should be recorded in the "histories" of these lands. Who are the "**newcomers**" or "**strangers**" to the land, when did they come and where did they come from? What are the religious customs of these "strangers"?

4. We must keep in mind that other DNA tests like "**Autosomal DNA**" and "**Maternal DNA**" tests can give more clues into your ancestry because a woman's mtDNA that is passed down to her

children is not affected by intermarriage or forced rape. Therefore, invasions by Arabs or Europeans would not change a person mtDNA. The mtDNA can be a huge tool in finding out what it is you are made of because most men throughout history have married people of the same race; either for cultural or religious reasons or simply because they live in close proximity to a certain people (who usually have the same physical characteristics).

CAN OTHER "NATIONS" BE GRAFTED IN TO THE "PHYSICAL" 12 TRIBES OF ISRAEL? WHY HAS THE "CHURCH" REPLACED THE ORIGINAL "ISRAELITES"?

Many Israelites today hold fast to the Biblical scriptures that state that after "**Three Generations**" any children born to Israelite men of "**other nations**" can be grafted into the House of Yahuah (Israel). However according to the scriptures this "**Three Generations**" **DOES NOT** to apply to full-blooded Moabite/Ammonite people that happen to be in the camp of the Israelites and desire to be grafted into the "**Physical Israel**". For them, they can enter into what many call now a "**Spiritual Israel**" but in essence they are those who bear the testimony and gospel of **Yahusha HaMashiach**. They can be saved and have "**everlasting life**" without the need of a title such as "**Spiritual Israel**". Gentiles shouldn't feel the need to attach themselves to the word "**Israel**" because at the end of the day, Israel and Gentiles together should be striving to "**Enter the Kingdom of Heaven**" by doing what Yahusha taught us in the New Testament. However, according to the **Old Testament** it was the "**SEPARATION**" of Israel from the nations that God would use in order to bring salvation to those nations via "**prophethood and scripture**". Isaiah wrote this and even Muhammad understood this when reading the bible.

Isaiah 61:6 "But ye shall be named the **Priests of the Lord**: men shall call you the *Ministers of our God*: ye shall eat the riches of the Gentiles, and in their glory shall ye boast yourselves."

Noble Quran, Sura 29:27

"And We gave to Him Isaac and Jacob and **placed in his descendants prophethood and scripture**. And We gave him his reward in this world, and indeed, he is in the Hereafter among the righteous."

Noble Quran, Sura 2:122 and 2:47

"O Children of Israel, call to mind My favour which I bestowed on you and **how I preferred you to all creatures**."

Noble Quran, Sura 17:104

"And We said unto the Children of Israel after him: Dwell in the land; but when the promise of the Hereafter cometh to pass **We shall bring you as a crowd gathered out of various nations**."

Romans 2:28-29 and Galatians 3:28:29 is one of the popular scriptures used to teach that the "**Physical Israel**" is not important anymore. This type of interpretation refers to the "**Church**" as Israel. But how can we just "**write off**" the Blood descendants of the Children of Israel? Are they all dead and have been wiped off the face of the earth? **NO!** The prophecy of **Jeremiah Chapter 31** would be "**Null and Void**" if this were the case. Or what about **Isaiah 11:11-13**? Even the Book of Revelation and the **144,000** clearly is talking about a "**Physical Israel**" (12,000 from each Tribe) who have never been with a woman. **So Israel has to exist in the "Physical" Flesh**.

Revelation 14:3-4 "And they sung as it were a new song before the throne, and before the four beasts, and the elders: and no man could learn that song but the hundred and forty and four thousand, which were redeemed (saved) from the earth. These are they which **WERE NOT DEFILED WITH WOMEN**; for they are **VIRGINS**. These are they which follow the Lamb whithersoever he goeth. These were redeemed among men, being the firstfruits unto God and to the Lamb."

It is often a "**trick**" in some Churches to disregard the Old Testament and teach strictly "**Pauline Gospels**". We know that the Old Testament is a Book of Prophecy which foretells the future of Israel and the coming of the "**Messiah**". These two prophecies cannot be ignored because they play a role in the "**End Times**". We must not forget one and strictly teach whatever we want. The last "**continuation**" book of the Bible (**i.e. The New Testament**) talks all about "**Salvation**". This is what God (Yahuah) sent Yahusha to do as that is the meaning of the "Messiah's" name. **Yah** (Strong's #3050) + **Yasha** (Strong's #3467) = **Yahusha** or "**Yah is Salvation**". Yahusha talked about how to achieve "Salvation" and how to get to the Father (Creator) by coming through him. Followers of the Bible must not reject the Old Testament and what the Lord (Yahuah) says about the "**Flesh and Blood**" Children of Israel. This is partly why we do not understand Luke 21:24-28 when it talks about "**Jerusalem being trodden down of the Gentiles**". We must understand who are the "**Chosen People of God**" and who are the "**Gentiles**". Only then will Bible Prophecy truly make sense.

Deuteronomy 7:6 "For thou are an **HOLY PEOPLE** unto the **LORD (YAHUAH)** thy God: the **LORD (YAHUAH)** thy God hath **CHOSEN THEE TO BE A SPECIAL PEOPLE UNTO HIMSELF**, above **ALL PEOPLE THAT ARE ON THE FACE OF THE EARTH.**"

Right there this should be enough for people to know that the "**Israelites**" are a "**set apart**" people unto God. But that doesn't mean the Israelites have the "**golden ticket**" to get into heaven.

Galatians 3:7 "Know ye therefore that they which are of faith, the same are the children of Abraham."

Romans 9:6-8 "For they are not all Israel which are of Israel; neither because they are the seed of Abraham are they all children....but the children of promise are counted for the seed".

HEBREW ISREALITES ON "RACE MIXING". CAN WE GET AN EXAMPLE?

The Egyptians and Edomites for many **"Israelites"** can be seen as **"the enemy"** of Israel. Why, because in their involvement of the "Israelites" suffering for many of years. But the children born to Israelite men from women of other nations were to be shown love too according to the Bible. Favor was to be shown to the **half-Israelite/half-Egyptian** children and the **half-Israelite/half-Edomite** children. We all know the Israelites sprouted out as a **"Nation of People"** out of Egypt. Joseph, his brothers and their wives walked into Egypt by themselves and after 430 years they left Egypt **"A NATION"**. Egypt was the place where the **"Nation of Israel"** really had its first beginnings. We all know **Edom** was the brother of Jacob. The Edomites would thus be cousins of the Israelites. Some of the Egyptians showed the Israelites "hospitality" during their time in Egypt (**Exodus 12:36**), plus the Tribe of Ephraim and Manasseh were half-Egyptian. For the Moabites/Ammonites things were a little bit different. In **Deuteronomy 23:1-8** Moabites and Ammonites **ARE NOT** to be accepted into the Nation of Israel, even after 10 generations (200-250 years). However, the children of a Moabite woman or Ammonite woman with an Israelite man can be grafted into Israel after **"Three Generations"**. According to the above **"DNA percentage contribution chart"** this would mean that the DNA contribution of a sole **"Moabite"** or **"Ammonite" mother** inserted into an Israelite Family Tree by way of marriage would only be around **12.5%** by the **"Third Generation"**. This means that if a Child has an Israelite Great-grandfather and a Moabite Great-grandmother, that child would be **"grafted"** into the Nation of Israel, of course after circumcision and denouncing their former Moabite-Ammonite idolatry worship. A perfect example of this is King David's **Moabite** Great-grandmother, **"Ruth"** who married **Boaz from the Tribe of Judah**. Boaz is mentioned in the Book of Matthew as the ancestor of Joseph, the earthly father of Jesus.

Deuteronomy 23:3 "An Ammonite or Moabite **SHALL NOT ENTER** into the congregation of the Lord; even until their tenth generation shall they not enter into the congregation of the Lord forever: "

Back in Biblical Times different Nations wanted to "**hang**" with the Israelites. They wanted to be "**absorbed**" into the camp of the Israelites, thus learning their culture and religion.

But God saw this as a potential way for "**bad things**" to enter into the Nation of Israel, corrupting everything he had commanded them not to do. Also, not all the time did other nations have the best interest for the Children of Israel.

Deuteronomy 23:4 "Because they (Moabites/Ammonites) met you not with bread and with water in the way, when ye came forth out of Egypt; and because they hired against thee Baalam the son of Beor of Pethor of Mesopotamia, to curse thee.

So because the Moabites/Ammonites were "**hostile**" against the Israelites during the Exodus and because Balak, the King of Moab in Numbers 22 tried to get Baalam to curse the Israelites God's anger towards the Moabites is shown in the last book of the Torah after Numbers (Deuteronomy). Baalam came up with the scheme to get the Israelites to "**self-curse**" themselves by enticing them with prostitutes and by getting them sacrifice unclean food to God. Because of this God sent a deadly plague to the Israelites in Numbers 31:16.

Numbers 31:16 "Behold, these caused the Children of Israel, through the counsel of Balaam, to commit trespass against the Lord in the matter of Peor, and **there was a plague among the congregation of the Lord**."

Deuteronomy 23:7-8 "Thou shalt not abhor (hate/despise) an Edomite; for he is thy brother: thou shalt not abhor an Egyptian; because thou wast a stranger in his land. **THE CHILDREN THAT ARE BEGOTTEN OF THEM** (Moabites, Ammonites, Egyptians, Edomites etc.) **SHALL ENTER** into the congregation of the Lord in their **THIRD GENERATION."**

Therefore, the Israelites can **ONLY** graft in the child of a Moabite-Ammonite according to **Deuteronomy 23:7-8** and **Ruth 4:19-22** after **THREE GENERATIONS!**

See for yourselves this **"Three Generations"** with **King David, the Great-grandson of Ruth, the Moabitess.**

Ruth 4:19-22 "Now these are the generations of Pharez (**Son of Judah**): Pharez begat Hezron, and Hezron begat Ram, and Ram begat Amminadab, and Amminadab begat Nahshon, and Nahshon begat Salmon, and Salmon begat **Boaz**, and Boaz begat Obed (**1st generation after Ruth**), And Obed begat Jesse (**2nd generation after Ruth**), and Jesse begat David (**3rd generation after Ruth**)."

Relationship to You	Approximate % Of Their DNA You Inherited
Parents	Exactly 50%
Grandparents	About 25%
Great-grandparents	About 12.5%
Great-great-grandparents	About 6.25%
Great-great-great-grandparents	About 3.125%
Great-great-great-great-grandparents	About 1.5625%

(**Above**) Chinese man and African-American man in 1800's. Was the Lord basing **"Three Generations"** on the way DNA works in regards to the contribution of Moabite blood/Ammonite vs Israelite Blood?

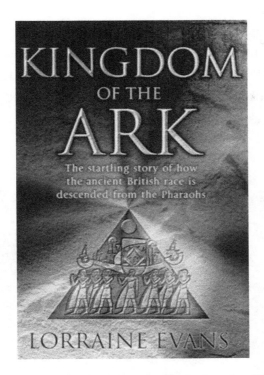

Author **Lorraine Evans** in her compelling book, "**Kingdom of the Ark**", reveals archaeological connections between Egypt, Scotland/Ireland and Britain. Evans argues that the connections between the two distant lands were plausible and there is archaeological evidence to support the theory. In 1937 in North Ferriby, Yorkshire, the remains of an ancient boat were discovered. While thought to be a Viking longship at first, continued excavation produced additional ships, wrecked in a storm. Further investigation showed that the boats were much older than Viking ships and were of a type found in the Mediterranean. It was concluded that these boats originated from 2000 years before the Viking age and were radiocarbon dated to around 1400 to 1350 BC. Evans then made connections to argue that these boats could have originated from Egypt, as the time frame fits the dating of the faience (ceramic) beads. While investigating the origins of the people of Scotland in the **Bower manuscript**, the **Scotichronicon**, she discovers the story of "Scotia", the Egyptian princess and daughter of a pharaoh who fled from Egypt with her husband **Gaythelos** with a large following of people who arrive in a fleet of ships. They settled in **Scotland** for a while amongst the natives, until they were forced to leave and landed in **Ireland**, where they formed the "**Scotti**", and their kings became the Kings of Ireland. In later centuries, they returned to Scotland, defeating the Picts, and giving Scotland its name.

(**Left**) Queen Tiye (Grandmother), (**Middle**) Queen Nefertiti (Daughter), (**Right**) Queen Meritaten (Granddaughter).

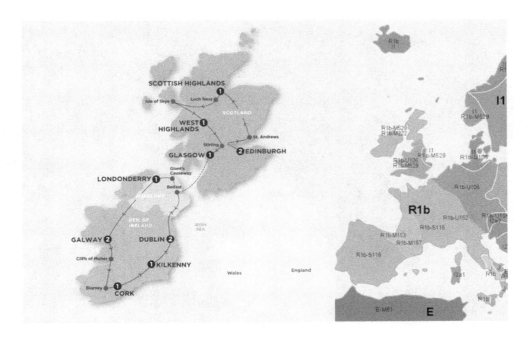

(Left) Scotland and Ireland. To the East is Wales and England.
(Right) Y-DNA Haplogroup "**R1b**" is frequently seen in
Spain/Portugal, Scotland, Wales, and Ireland although there are
multiple "**R1b**" subgroups for each island. These "**R1b**" carriers in
Europe are "**fairly new**" compared to the "**R1b**" carriers in Africans
(**R1b1c-V88**). The "**R1b**" subgroups in Western Europe can consist of
R1b1a2a1a2c (M529) or **R1b1a2a1a2b** (U152). Notice the African
"R1b" subgroup has **5 characters** while the European "R1b" subgroup
has **11 characters**! Who came first and dominated Europe? The Black
man! The European man is new to that area. These are the same areas
that the Egyptians and then the Black Moors conquered leading up to
the 1500's.

(**Left**) This is **Melqart**, the equivalent of "**Hercules**" to the **Phoenicians**. Notice he is wearing the same crown as Egyptian Osiris. (**Right**) The Egyptian God **Osiris** who is in the middle of **Horus** and **Isis.** The "**Greeks**" after occupying Canaan/Lebanon would call themselves "**Phoenicians**" like Lebanese people today refer to themselves as "Phoenicians" when we know the Black Canaanites were there first. But why would the Greeks from Europe fashion a pagan god named "**Melqart**" copied after the pagan god of Egypt? This artifact was found in Spain, where there are carriers of the Y-DNA Haplogroup **R1b** like the Ancient Egyptians, the Ancient Moors, Latinos, Central Africans, Indians and possibly the Ancient Israelites that were living in Iberia (Spain/Portugal) with the Moors from 700 A.D. to 1500 A.D. Remember, although a white race, many Spaniards, Portuguese and Italians have the ability to "tan better" compared other European Caucasians. Could this be because of some "**lingering**" ancient Hamitic/Semitic DNA from the Egyptians and Black Moors (Phut/Ishmaelite Arabs) showing forth in miniscule amounts?

KEEP THIS IN MIND

DNA mutations are changes in the DNA sequence of a cell. They are defined as sudden and spontaneous changes in the cell. Mutations can be caused by radiation, viruses, transposons (**aka "jumping genes" that create multi-colored Indian corn**), mutagenic chemicals in our food (inserted or caused by broiling, grilling, or frying), as well as errors that occur during meiosis or DNA replication. They can also be induced by the organism itself, by cellular processes.

Here are some examples of "**mutagenic chemicals**" that are injected into our food. "**Mutagenic**" reactions occur when certain foods are mixed with certain bacteria's/viruses.

- Tryptophan.
- Flavonoids.
- Coffee, Black tea, Green tea and roasted tea has been found in certain studies to be mutagenic to Salmonella (Typhimurium strain TA100) whether it is brewed, instant, or decaffeinated.
- Nitrosamines (Nitrites/Nitrates).
- Aflatoxins.
- Hydrazine's.
- Alcohol.
- Estrogenic Substances or by-products.
- Quercetin.
- Food additives.
- Ingredients in Cigarettes.
- Heavy metals (mercury, aluminum).
- Radioactive isotopes (in water).
- Antibiotic residues in meat, poultry and dairy products.
- Pyrolzed Proteins and Amino Acids from (broiled fish and beef).
- Polycyclic aromatic hydrocarbons from frying and grilling meat using gas.

(**Above**) Seedless Oranges vs. Oranges with seeds. Just like "**Seedless**" watermelons and grapes. But what does the bible say?
"

Genesis 1:29 "And God said, Behold, I have given you every herb bearing seed, which is upon the face of all the earth, and every tree, in the which is the fruit of a tree **YIELDING SEED**; to you it shall be for meat."

Facts: Mutation using "**atomic radiation**" called "**mutation breeding**" has produced a huge amount of the worlds crops. Different types of wheat, pastas, vegetables, fruit, rice, and herbs have been altered or enhanced with gamma rays (**like the Hulk or Spider-man**). They are also sometimes soaked in toxic chemicals in hopes of achieving man's desirable traits. Scientists found out that by exposing plants to different types of radiation it damages the plants DNA and causes new mutations. The radiation allows them to create mutations at a faster rate, which increases their likelihood of finding the trait they have been looking for (**i.e. seedless watermelons, grapes and oranges**). These crops are sold in our supermarkets without labels or without us knowing the long-term effects of these manipulated crops full of radiation. The long-term result which scientists know, is increasing cancer rates in America and child development syndromes such as

Autism. Don't believe? Ask some people from Africa how many people in their country get cancer, dementia, heart disease, high cholesterol or diabetes. Then ask them how often do they see kids diagnosed with Autism in their country. If they say "**we don't see these kinds of things in our country**", it's because their food, air and water is still "**pure**". Their children are also not forced to take all the vaccines the CDC pushes on parents today in America. But Monsanto and other GMO companies are now trying to break their way into Africa so they can do the same thing that they are doing in America.

Mutations that are negative are most often automatically eliminated by nature. Other mutations that help survival tend to stick around in dominant races (**i.e. Malaria causing Sickle Cell adaptation in Blacks**). But this is not always the case. Mutations lead to a loss of DNA information or they lead to changes in SNPs. SNPs (Single-nucleotide polymorphism) are "**changing points**" in the DNA sequence. So the "R1b1c" for Chadic/North Cameroonian Africans, the changing SNP that created the "R1b1c" was **SNP V88**. Differences in the SNPs (i.e. appearance of new ones) are used in sections of Y-DNA to classify different haplogroups or subgroups within that Haplogroup (i.e. E1b1a/E1b1c). So the Y-DNA Haplogroup "R1b1c" (seen in Central Africa) has went through less mutations than "**R1b1a2a1a2b**" (seen in Europeans). It's a known fact that DNA mutations increase with a rise in climatic temperature. That is, the hotter it is, the more mutations take place. Like moving a Tribe from a hot, dry climate to a hot, tropical climate or even a cold climate. This leads to both an increase in variation amongst existing DNA types and also to a simplification of those types through loss of DNA information. The 10 Northern Tribes of Israel were scattered amongst the nations in different weather conditions (hot vs cold) and then they "**mixed**" with these nations (**Hosea 7:8**).

Hosea 7:8 "Ephraim, he hath **MIXED HIMSELF AMONG THE PEOPLE (NATIONS)**, Ephraim is a cake not turned. **STRANGERS**

have devoured his strength, and he knoweth it not: yea, gray hairs are here and there upon him, yet he knoweth not."

In the case of Ephraim and the 10 Tribes, the environment had an influence on them. Man was created with adaptation abilities and changes take place in response to environmental influences. Once these changes are set in place they will continue through heredity until new changes occur. This is often explained by Lee M. Spetner **("Not by Chance," 1996**). He stated that Genes (i.e. DNA sequences that determine specific functions in our body) switch on and off. Once the switch is on the change is inherited until the switch is flicked on/off again. These changes on the whole take place quickly in one or sometimes a few generations.

Fact 2: 1st A.D. Century Roman Historian **Cornelius Tacitus** wrote that when the Germanaic people were moving from Eastern Europe into Western Europe, the Black people living in Europe before them **were killing German males and taking their females as the "spoils of war"**. This allowed their offspring (that married again white) to gain the ability to produce some "melanin" in their skin. The German females that bore children to the Black men in Europe were not often taken as wives, but instead were sent back to return to their white descendants and relatives. The Y-DNA of the Black Europeans that had "illegitimate" children with these Germanaic women "stuck" to the European men, no matter how many years, decades or centuries had passed. When these "biracial" Germanaic males had children with their white females the resulting offspring would be (1/4) black, but the Y-DNA of their **Black Great-great-great grandfather** would live on in the Y-DNA of their sons forever. This doesn't mean that European people with "Black" Haplogroups are to be considered "Black" or a part of a Biblical Black Nations (i.e. Black Israelites, Black Ishmaelite Arabs, Black Egyptians). It also **DOESN'T** mean that "melaninated" people (like Latinos) with so-called "White Haplogroups" are to be considered "**White**". **Note: A Spaniard from Spain is different than a Latino man from Peru.** When dealing with "Y-DNA Haplogroups" we have to look at the "**Big Picture**" (i.e. history, travel patterns, mother's mtDNA, autosomal DNA, critical thinking).

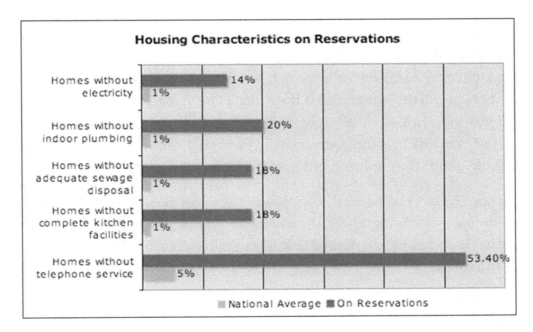

(**Above**) The disparity between the Native Americans and their surrounding non-Indian neighbors are still manifesting today. Many of us have seen "**fake $5 dollar White Indians**" but have never seen a real indigenous "**Brown-skinned Indian**". There are many Native American reservations which do no not have electricity. Others Indian reservations are known to be without sinks, adequate sewage disposals, kitchen cookware (pots/pans/utensils') and even telephone service. This mimics how many Black families are living in the rural south and in the crowded inner-city Ghettos/Projects in the North. **Curses of Israel** perhaps?

Still think that we should not be looking at "**Negroes**", "**Native Indians**" and their descendants when searching for the "Real Israelites?"

Keep this in mind. A large number of Black people were "**Dispersed**" into **ALL NATIONS** by way of "**Slave Ships**". A large number of so-called Brown-skinned "**Mongloid**" people were "**Exiled**" from their land (Africa/Asia) never to return but somehow ended finding land that is essentially surrounded by water (**The Americans, Caribbean**). Where the "**Indians**" brought to the "New World" by way of slave ships? Or did they migrate there over time? This fits the scriptures talking about the Children of Israel perfectly.

Isaiah 11:12 "And he shall set up an ensign for the nations, and shall assemble (bring together) the **outcasts** (exiled ones) of Israel, and gather together the **dispersed** (scattered) of Judah from the four corners of the earth."

Fact: The first known use of the word "**Mongloid**" was in **1868**. Individuals classified to be Mongloid are those with certain traits such as **distinct epicanthic (eyelid) folds** or **sinodonty** (study of tooth records) that differs from Caucasian white races. In the study of teeth. **Sinodonty** and **Sundadonty** are used to describe the teeth of the people in Asia (North/South). "**Sino**" refers to old name for China "**Sina**" and "**Sunda**" refers to South Asia/Indonesia/Australia. "**M**" is the single most common mtDNA haplogroup in Asia, according to Kivisild et al. (**"The Emerging Limbs and Twigs of the East Asian mtDNA Tree"**). It peaks in Japan and Tibet, where it represents about **70%** of the maternal lineages and is pervasive in India, where it has approximately **60%** frequency. Among the Chinese, haplogroup **M** accounts for approximately 50% of all people. The root word "**Dont**" refers to teeth, like an Ortho-**DONT**-ist. People with **Sinodonty** type-teeth patterns are seen in China. People with Sundadonty teeth patterns (**who are also mostly mtDNA "M" carriers**) are seen in **South Asia, India,** the indigenous **Black Japanese Ainu/Jomon people** and people in **Tibet (China)**.

Note: There have been genetic studies that link the Ainu people to the Native Indians.

Ironically, the mtDNA "**M**" of the people in India, Japan, the Andaman Islands, Tibet and Australia can be traced back to the Bantus people in Africa/Ethiopians (Nigerian Igbo's, Kenyan Kikuyus, Tanzania Sukumas). **AGAIN**, the mtDNA "**M**" peaks in Japan/Tibet where it represents almost 70% of maternal lineages. In India it can be found with 60% frequency among the people. The mtDNA Haplogroup "D", which his common in South Americans, can be seen also in some Japanese people. **The Y-DNA Haplogroup "DE" gave rise to Haplogroups "D" and "E". African-Americans, Caribbean Blacks and Bantus Africans belong to Haplogroup "E".** Haplogroup "D" and "E" share a common "denominator". However, only Bantus Africans, Caribbean Blacks, Black Siddis of India, and African-Americans share an even more deeper common denominator with Y-DNA Haplogroup "D" carriers. This again is the **YAP-positive element** that is seen in Chinese Tibetans, some Indians, some Japanese people, and certain populations in India/Andaman Island. These "core groups" of people could be the founding fathers (i.e. building blocks) of "Modern-Day Israelites" today. Meaning, their descendants found across the world could also be Israelites.

Many people believe the early indigenous Japanese people were descendants from Sub-Saharan Africa/Israel. Could this be where the Japanese "**Shinto Jews**" get their Jewish heritage from? *Note: I break this down in Volume 3).* It is said that their ancestors were the Black Ainu/Jomon people. In addition, the Y-DNA of the indigenous Ainu/Jomon people of Japan, the Andaman Island natives and some of the people in Tibet can be linked to the DNA of the Bantus people (Nigerian Igbo's) by way of the **Y-Chromosome Alu Polymorphism (YAP+ Marker)**. Dental records of the "**Kennewick Man**" found in the

USA state of Washington in 1996 showed that the skeletal remains/dental records of this man linked him to the **Ainu/Jomon Japanese people** and **sundadonty teeth traits**. It is believed that his mtDNA was from Haplogroup "**D**", which is found in South Americans/Central Americans (Mayans) and can be traced back to the mtDNA "**M**" which is related to mtDNA "**L3**", the most common mtDNA in African Americans.

ISAIAH 11:12 "And he shall set up an ensign for the nations, and shall assemble the **outcasts (exiled) of Israel**, and gather together the **dispersed of Judah** from the four corners of the earth.

Please Wake Up. All of the Children of Israel cannot be Negro-looking people. We must explore everything. All of the Children of Israel did not end up in Africa and all of the Israelites didn't arrive to their current locations by way of slave ships. Isaiah 11:12 and other scriptures in the Bible proves this to be a false theory.

CHAPTER 25

WHERE DO THE MACCABEES COME FROM? WHEN DID THE "GENTILES" INSERT THEMSELVES INTO BIBLE HISTORY?

Before we dive into where the "**Maccabees Jew**" comes from and get explanation as to why the "**Apocrypha**" is simply a "**Historical Book**" that fills in the gaps of the time frame between the Persian Rule of Judea and the Birth of Christ during the Edomite Rule of Judea we have to complete the investigation of the Persian Empire. According to the Old Testament in our King James Bible these are some of the Persian Kings listed:

1. **King Cyrus** (2 Chronicles 36:22-23, Ezra 1:4-11, Ezra 6:4-5, Daniel 10:1).
2. **King Darius the Great** aka "**Darius the Mede**" (Daniel Chapter 5-9, Ezra 6:14-15).
3. **King Artaxerxes I** (Ezra 4:7, 7:13-28, Nehemiah 2:1, 3:2-8)
4. **Xerxes I /Hebrew-Ahasuerus** (Daniel, Ezra).

Understanding the Kings of Persia in relation to the bible is very tricky because of small "**errors**" seen when the Hebrew Old Testament was translated to Greek, then Latin, then Old English and then to Modern English but here is a timeline that historians believes is accurate.

Note: The Persians defeated the Nubian Pharaoh of Egypt before gaining all their territory.

- 538 B.C. – **Cyrus the Great** conquers Babylon with Darius the Great (538 B.C.)
- 529 B.C – **Cambyses II**
- 522 B.C. – **Bardiya** (Smerdis)
- 521 B.C. - **Darius King of Persia** (? = Ahasuerus of Esther)
- 485 B.C. - **Xerxes I** (Ahasuerus in Book of Esther 1:1)

- 474-465 B.C. - **Artaxerxes I** (Longemanus)
- 425 B.C. - **Xerxes II**
- 423 B.C. – **Darius II**
- 404 B.C. – **Artaxerxes II** Memnon
- 361 B.C. – **Artaxerxes III** Ochus
- 338 B.C. – **Arsaces** (Arses)
- 336 B.C. – **Darius III**
- 331 B.C. – **Greek King Alexander the Great** conquers the Persian (Achaemenid Dynasty)

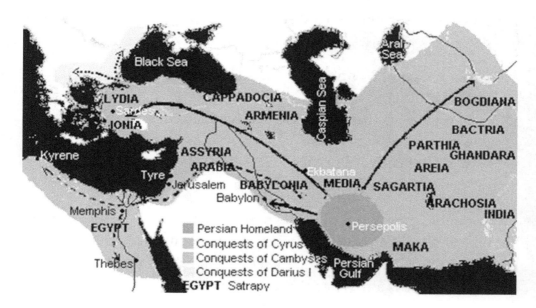

PERSIAN RULE 525 B.C – 404 B.C. Before the Greeks arrived on the scene in the Egypt, the Middle East and Judea **the Persians ruled this area.** With the conquest of Egypt, the Black Persian kings became Pharaohs, constituting the 27th and 31st dynasties. **Cyrus the Great** conquered the former territory of the Babylonians and ruled over Israel, Turkey, Syria, Armenia, Babylon, and modern day Pakistan. He appointed his son **Cambyses** to rule Egypt (Thebes, Memphis). King Darius I ruled over parts of Greece, Macedonia and Thrace.

(**Left**) Nubian Pharaoh **Amose II**. (**Right**) Amose II son **Psamtik III.**

Before the Persians came on the scene in Egypt, Judea and the Middle East, the Cushite Nubians were ruling as Pharaoh's in Egypt. The last Nubian Pharaoh was **Psamtik III**. Most of what is known about Psamtik III reign and life was documented by the Greek historian Herodotus in the 5th century BC. Herodotus states that **Nubian Pharaoh Psamtik III** ruled Egypt for only six months before he was confronted by a **Persian invasion** of his country led by **King Cambyses II of Persia**. Cambyses II would reign as the first Persian Pharaoh in the 27th Dynasty. **Cambyses I** was the father of the Persian King **Cyrus the Great** that allowed the Southern Tribes of Israel (House of Judah) to come back to rebuild the 2nd Temple. King Cyrus did not try to go to Egypt because he was too busy fighting the Scythians/Huns to the East. King Cyrus would die fighting in battle in 530 B.C. **King Cyrus** was succeeded by his son **Cambyses II** who would manage to add to the Persian Empire the nations of **Egypt, Nubia and Libya (Cyrenaica)**.

Fact: Were the Egyptian 10 Plagues unleashed by Yahuah and Moses real? In the early 19th Century an ancient papyrus was found in Egypt. It was taken to the Leiden Museum in Holland and interpreted by A.H. Gardiner in 1909. The papyrus described violent upheavals in Egypt, starvation, drought, escape of slaves (with the wealth of the Egyptians), and death throughout the land. The papyrus was written by an Egyptian named **Ipuwer** (which was a common name in Egypt during 1850 B.C. and 1450 A.D.). **According to many biblical scholars it is believed that the Israelites left in the Exodus around 1500-1450 A.D**. This work was translated by Alan Gardner in 1906 titled "**Admonitions of an Egyptian Sage from a Hieratic Papyrus in Leiden**". Alan Gardner believed he had found an Egyptian manuscript to be an eyewitness account of the effects of the Exodus plagues. Dr. Lange attested that the literary work of the Papyrus dated to the Middle Kingdom which is the same time the Israelites were in Egypt. It also talks about "**foreign invaders**" by Asiatics (i.e. Hyksos). Read the comparison of the Egyptian Papyrus to the scripture down below in the Book of Exodus and see for yourself. You be the Judge.

IPUWER PAPYRUS – LEIDEN 344. EGYPTIAN HISTORY MEETS BIBLICAL HISTORY!

River turns to blood in Egypt!

Papyrus 2:5-5 & 2:10 "Plague is throughout the land. Blood is everywhere." "The river is blood. Men shrink from tasting, human beings, and thirst after water."

Papyrus 3:10-13 "That is our water! That is our happiness! What shall we do in respect thereof? All is ruin."

Exodus 7:20 "...all the waters that were in the river were turned to blood." **Exodus 7:21** "...there was blood throughout all the land of Egypt and the river stank. **Exodus 7:21** "And all the Egyptians dug around the river for water to drink; for they could not drink of the water of the river."

Fire consumes Egypt and kills off the crops/food!

Papyrus 2:10 "Forsooth, gates, columns and walls are consumed by fire.

Papyrus 10:3-6 "Lower Egypt weeps....The entire palace is without its revenues. To it belong by right wheat and barley, geese and fish."

Papyrus 4:14, 6:1 "Trees are destroyed. No fruit nor herbs are found."

Papyrus 6:3 "Forsooth, grain has perished on every side."

Papyrus 5:12 "Forsooth, that has perished which was yesterday seen. The land is left over to its weariness like the cutting of flax."

Exodus 9:23-24 "….And the fire ran along the ground….there was hail, and fire mingled with the hail, very grievous. "

Exodus 9:25 "…and the hail smote every herb of the field, and broke every tree of the field."

Exodus 9:31-32 "…and the flax and the barley was smitten; for the barley was in season, and flax was ripe."

Exodus 10:15 "….there remained no green things in the trees, or in the herbs of the fields, through all the land of Egypt."

All the Cattle in Egypt are sick and in distress!

Papyrus 5:4 "All animals, their hearts weep. Cattle moan…"

Papyrus 9:2-3 "Behold, cattle are left to stray, and there is none to gather them together."

Exodus 9:3 "…the hand of the Lord is upon the cattle which is in the field….and there shall be a very grievous sickness."

Exodus 9:19 "Send therefore now, and gather thy cattle, and all thou hast in the field; for upon every man and beast which shall be found in the field, and shall not be brought home, the hail shall come down upon them, and they shall die. He that feared the word of the Lord among the servants of Pharaoh made his servants and his cattle flee into the houses: and he that regarded NOT the word of the Lord left his servants and his cattle in the field."

There is no light in Egypt!

Papyrus 9:11 "The land is not light."

Exodus 10:22 "And Moses stretched forth his hand toward heaven; and there was a thick darkness in all the Land of Egypt three days."

Massive death in Egypt!

Papyrus 4:3 (5:6) "Forsooth, the children of princes are dashed against the walls."

Papyrus 6:12 "Forsooth, the children of princes are cast out into the streets."

Papyrus 6:3 "The prison is ruined."

Papyrus 2:13 "He who places his brother in the ground is everywhere."

Papyrus 3:14 "It is groaning throughout the land, mingled with lamentations."

Exodus 12:29 "And it came to pass, that at midnight the Lord smote ALL THE FIRSTBORN in the land of Egypt, from the firstborn of Pharaoh that sat on his throne to the firstborn of the captive that was in PRISON.

Exodus 12:30 "And Pharaoh rose up in the night, he, and all his servants, and all the Egyptians; and there was a great cry in Egypt; for there was not a house where there was not one dead."

The Egyptians give the Israelite slaves all their gold and silver!

Papyrus 3:2 "Gold and lapis lazuli, silver and malachite, carnelian and bronze…are fastened on the neck of female (Israelite) slaves."

Exodus 12:35 "And the children of Israel did according to the word of Moses; and they borrowed of the Egyptians jewels of silver, and jewels of gold, and raiment (clothes): And the Lord gave the people favour in the sight of the Egyptians, so that they lent unto them such things as they required. And they spoiled the Egyptians."

Papyrus 9:11 - The land is not light....

Exodus 10:22 - ...and there was a thick darkness in all the land of Egypt.

Note: It is a known fact that in the Brooklyn Papyrus in the Brooklyn Museum, from the 13th Dynasty reign of Egyptian **Pharaoh Sobekhotep III** (1740 B.C.) there were recorded household "slave names" of which 45 of them would be considered today "Semitic". (Israel).

(**Above**) **A relief of King Cyrus** who allowed the Jews to come back to rebuild the 2nd Temple. As you can see by the circles (**signifying tight curled hair**) in the beard and hair of Persian King Cyrus, the Ancient Persians did not have straight hair like the Iranians we see today in society.

(**Left**) The only antelope whose back is lower than the front is the "**Nilgai/Nilgau**", which is the most commonly found in Pakistan, Central India, and Northern India; all areas that used to belong to the **Persian Empire**. The Nilgai has thin legs and a husky body that slopes down from the shoulder. (**Right**) An Ancient Persian man during the 6th Century, the time of the Jews return to Israel under the Persian rule of Cyrus the Great. In the original picture you can see this man with the Nilgai/Nilgau animal. **The exiled Northern 10 Tribes of Israel lived amongst these Black Persians/Assyrians who had kinky, wooly hair just like the Nubians and Egyptians.** According to the Hebrew Book of Jasher/Jubilees the Persians (Medes) started out half Semitic and half Japhetic. Cush also mixed in with the Ancient Persians.

THE PROOF IS IN THE PICTURE! ARE THESE **ANCIENT IRANIANS (INDO-PERSIAN)** OR **ANCIENT CUSHITES**? HISTORY IS AMAZING!

2 Kings 17:6 "In the ninth year of Hoshea the King of Assyria took Samaria, and carried Israel away unto Assyria, and placed them in Halah, and on the Habor, the river of Gozan, and **IN THE CITIES OF THE MEDES.**"

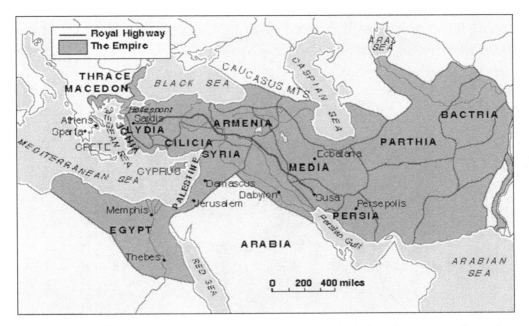

Note: The "Medes" were an ancient Persian-Iranian people who lived in Iran in an area known as "Media" and spoke a northwestern Iranian language referred to as the Median language.

In **525 B.C**. Persia, Cambyses defeated **Egyptian Pharaoh Psamtik III** at the "**Battle of Pelusium**" and ruled Egypt. This took part during the reign of the **Kushite King Amani-natake-lebte** (538-519 BC). Various historical records mention military frictions between **Kush** and **Persia**. **Herodotus**, the B.C. Greek historian and geographer, reported that Cambyses wanted to conquer Kush so he sent to the King of Kush "**spies**" as **messengers** bearing gifts. The King of Kush, as Herodotus explains, was aware of the fact that the Persian messengers were spies. However, the King of Nubia made a ridicule of Cambyses' "undercover" gifts. The King of Nubia insulted the Persian King Cambyses back by sending him a bow back with the messengers telling him "**when the Persians draw their bows (of equal size as mine) as easily as I do this, then he should march against the long lived Ethiopians**," (**Herodotus iii. 21**). According to Herodotus, Kush did not pay tribute to Persia but instead constantly sent the Persian King precious gifts including gold, ebony and elephant tusks. We also know from Herodotus as well as from other Greek reporters that part of the Persian army of King Xerxes (486-465 BC) was composed of Kushite archers (Herodotus vii.69-70)

(**Left**) Pharaoh 30th Non-Persian Egyptian Dynasty. (**Right**) Pharaoh 27th Persian Dynasty. Does that Persian King look kind of "**Asian**" or "**Mongloid**" in appearance? Could this be a clue how some of the Israelites "**physical look**" changed? Some say the descendants of the Ancient Persians, Elamites, Assyrians and perhaps Babylonians are in the area known as India, Pakistan, Afghanistan and South Asia. Maybe some of the lighter peoples in this area are simply "**watered**" down from mixing with the **white Japhetic Turks** and **white Japhetic Europeans.**

CHAPTER 26

WHAT HAPPENED NEXT IN BIBLICAL HISTORY LEADING UP TO THE FINAL "GENTILE" EXPANSION OF ISRAEL BY THE GREEKS?

 VS

(Left) The Greek Ptolemaic Empire under "Alexander the Great" did battle with the Mighty "10,000" immortals of the Persian Empire (Right).

THE PTOLEMY (GREEKS) AND THE SELEUCID (GREEKS).

After the death of Alexander the Great of Macedonia in 323 B.C., the territories he had conquered were divided between his Greek generals, the so-called **Diadochi**.

Note: The Wars of the Diadochi marked the beginning of the Hellenistic period and the infusion of Greek culture/religion into Judaism.

Bust of **Seleucus Nicator** ("Victor"; 358 B.C. – 281 B.C.), the last of the original **Diadochi**. The **Diadochi successors** were the first generation of military and political leaders after the death of the Macedonian king and conqueror **Alexander the Great** in 323 B.C. To settle the question whether his empire should disintegrate or survive as a unity, and, if so, under whose rule, they fought **FOUR** full-scale wars. The result, reached by 300 B.C., was a division into **THREE LARGE PARTS**, which more or less coincided with Alexander's possessions in Europe, Asia, and Egypt.

Alexander's friend **Seleucus Nicator** (312–280 B.C.) became king of the Eastern provinces—approximately modern day **Pakistan/Afghanistan, Iran, Iraq, Syria, Israel and Lebanon, together with parts of Turkey, Armenia, Turkmenistan, Uzbekistan, and Tajikistan**. His kingdom would be called the "**Seleucid Empire**" The huge kingdom had two capitals, which Seleucus founded in around 300 B.C.: **Antioch** in Syria and **Seleucia** in Mesopotamia (Iraq). Seleucus established a dynasty that lasted for two centuries, during which time Hellenistic art, a fusion of Greek and Near Eastern artistic traditions, developed and flourished.

LET'S RE-ITERATE THIS "NEITHER GENTILE, NOR GREEK" THING AGAIN!

Galatians 3:28 "There is neither **Jew** nor **Greek** (**sometimes replaced with "Gentile"**), slave or free, male or female; for you are all one in Christ Jesus."

During the entering of "**The Gentiles**" into Judea with the **Greeks**, most of the people in Judea, **Idumeans** and **Samaritans** were also Gentiles from way back (600 B.C.). Around 600 B.C. the Edomites were in Jerusalem watching with "**We Got Next**" signs as the Babylonians under King Nebuchadnezzar destroyed Solomon's Temple. Once the Temple was destroyed and the House of Judah was taken prisoner, the Edomites set up shop in the Land of Judea, below Samaria. This had to be Solomon's Temple because the Second Temple in Jerusalem would not be destroyed until 70 A.D., which is after Yahusha (Jesus) ascended into Heaven. The Edomites would be later "**converted**" to Judaism by the Gentile Greek Maccabean crew, led by **John Hyrcanus I, King of Judea (175 B.C.)**. John was also a fake **High Priest**. Real "**Aaronite-Cohenite**" High Priests were not supposed to allow full-blooded Edomites to be grafted into "**Israel**". Likewise, no Edomite was supposed to do any of the Temple duties. This was supposed to be done by the Levites.   After John Hyrcanus I converted these

"Heathen", that day forth the Edomites were no longer called "**Edomites**", but "**Jews**".

Psalms 137:7-8 "Remember, LORD, what the Edomites said that day at Jerusalem: '**Rase it (destroy it), rase it (destroy it), even to the foundation (ground) thereof'**. O daughter Babylon, doomed to destruction, happy is the one who pays you back what you have done to us."

Those that wanted to worship the God of the Land of Israel had to convert to Judaism. If a Gentile, Samaritan or Edomite did this, they became known thus forth as a "Jew". Remember though, "**ONE CANNOT BECOME AN ISRAELITE FROM THE TRIBE OF JUDAH IF HE IS ALREADY BORN AND ALIVE**".

Here is an example of how Gentile people "**became**" Jews while already being a full-grown adult with a family and children. If a white person is of the **Roman Flavius Dynasty Bloodline**, how can this person "**become**" a **Levite** from the **Tribe of Levi**? Notice below that the Book of Esther is the only book not found in the Hebrew Dead Scrolls.

Esther 8:17 "And in every province, and in every city, whithersoever the King's commandment and his decree came, the Jews had gladness and joy, a feast and a good day. And **MANY FROM AMONG THE PEOPLE OF THE LAND BECAME JEWS**; for the fear of the Jews was fallen upon them."

Note: Being from the Tribe of Judah or Levi is strictly a **BIRTHRIGHT**, meaning one has to be born of parents whose descendants are linked to Judah or Levi the son of Jacob. But in the New Testament there is constant talks about "**Jews**" and "**Gentiles**" when the Old Testament primarily uses the word "**Israel**". What is going on? Did someone insert the word "**Jew**" into the Old Testament to confuse us? Here is what these two words meant in the New Testament:

1. "Jew" – **any Gentile who converted to "Pharisee-ism" or "Judaism"**.
2. "Greek" – **descendants of the son of Japheth, "Javan" from Genesis 10:2,4.** Flavius Josephus believed the Greeks were also descendants of **Javan (Ionians)**.

"**Samaritan**" – descendants of the people brought in by the Assyrians (Sennacherib, Tiglath-Pileser I, Shalmaneser V, Sargon etc.). These "**Gentile People**" people were brought to Samaria (Northern Israel) in 2 Kings 18. **Sargon II** was an Assyrian King who became the ruler of the Assyrian Empire in 722 B.C. after the death of Shalmaneser V. He took the Israelite city of **Ashdod**. Sargon II was the son of Tiglath-Pileser II. Sargon's son King Sennacherib helped capture the Israelites, exiling them from their land and replaced the empty land of Israel with the people of Assyria/Babylon. The **Samaritans** today claim to be descendants of the Original inhabitants of Northern Israel but the Bible states they are descendants from "**foreigners**" imported into the land of Israel by Sennacherib after he had destroyed the Northern Israelites Kingdom, exiling the people from the land but bringing back **ONE** Levite priest to teach them the ways of the Torah. Ezra and Nehemiah also considered these people to be "**foreign**" and not allow them to help in the building of the temple or worship with them.

2 Kings 17:24 "And the King of Assyria brought men from Babylon, and from Cuthah, and from Ava, and from Hamath and Sepharvaim, and placed them in the cities of Samaria **INSTEAD OF THE CHILDREN OF ISRAEL;** and they possessed **SAMARIA**, and dwelt in the cities thereof."

Isaiah 20:1 "In the year that Tartan came unto Ashdod, when **Sargon the King of Assyria** sent him, and he fought against Ashdod and took it."

2 Kings 18:9 "And it came to pass in the fourth year of King Hezekiah, which was the seventh year of Hoshea son of Elah King of Israel, that

Shalmaneser King of Assyria came up against Samaria, and besieged it."

2 Kings 18:13 "Now in the fourteenth year of King Hezekiah did **Sennacherib King of Assyria** come up against all the fortified cities of Judah, and took them."

What about Biblical proof that the Samaritans today are definitely not the Israelites of Ancient times. **Let's do a double-rule out!** First we will prove that the "**Ancient Samaritans**" were not Israelites and then we will prove the **Samaritans** today are not "**Israelites**".

Sargon II Inscriptions, COS 2.119A, p. 293

"The Samaritans who agreed with a hostile king…..I fought with them and decisively defeated them….carried off as spoil "**Assyrians**"). 50 chariots for my royal force…the rest of them I settled in the midst of Assyria….The Talmudi, Ibadidi, Marsimani and Hayappa, who live in distant **Arabia**, in the desert, who knew neither overseer nor commander, who never brought tribute to any king-with the help of Ashshur my lord, I defeated them. **I DEPORTED** (send out) the rest of them. **I settled them in Samaria/Samerina (Northern Israel)."**

(Above) Nimrud Prisms, COS 2. 118D, pg. 295-296. Assyrian **King Sargon II** wrote of his **Above** conquest of Samaria (Northern House of Israel), the deportation of the Israelites and the re-population of Samaria by the **"foreign peoples"** of Assyria and Babylon. It dates to 720 B.C. On it he writes:

"The inhabitants of **Sameria/Samerina (Sumeria)**, who agreed and plotted with a king hostile to me, not to do service and not to bring tribute to Ashshur (**Asshur-Assyria**) and who did battle, I fought against them with the power of the great gods, my lords. I counted as spoil **27,280 people**, together with their chariots, and gods, in which they trusted. I formed a unit with **200 of their chariots** for my royal force. **I settled the rest of them in the midst of Assyria. I REPOPULATED Sameria/Samerina (Northern Israel) more than before.** I brought into it people from countries conquered by my hands. I appointed my eunuch as governor over them. And I counted them as **Assyrians**.

Note: *This is proof that the King of Assyria captured all those living in Babylon, Elam, Persian, and Assyria. He eventually settled these people in the midst of Assyria and Israel.*

Fact: Today's Samaritans look either Caucasian/European or Arabic. There are **FOUR** main lineages of White Samaritan Jews (**estimated 900 total in Israel**) that claim to be Israelites:

- The **Tsedakah** lineage – claim descent from the Tribe of Manasseh. They tested positive for the Y-Haplogroup **J2 (Turks, Kurds, Armenians, Greeks, Italians). This Haplogroup is from Japheth.**

- The **Joshua-Marhiv** lineage – claim descent from the Tribe of Ephraim. They tested positive for the Y-Haplogroup **J1. J1 is seen mainly in Black Arabs and some "watered down" light skinned Arabs. This is a Semitic Haplogroup, but not an Israelite Haplogroup.**

- The **Danfi lineage** – claim descent from the Tribe of Ephraim. They tested positive for the Y-Haplogroup **J2 (Turks, Kurds, Armenians, Greeks, Italians). This Haplogroup is from Japheth.**

- The **Cohen lineage** – claim descent from the Tribe of Levi. They tested positive for the Y-Haplogroup **E1b1b-M78 (Edomite Blood). This is a Haplogroup sprung from the mixing of the Edomites with the sons of Japheth.**

CHAPTER 27

IS THERE ANY MORE DNA PROOF TO PROVE THAT THE EUROPEAN JEWS ARE NOT THE DESCENDANTS OF THE BIBLICAL HEBREW ISRAELITES?

When Italian geneticist and biologist **F. Cruciani** tested the Y-DNA of some of the Samaritan population he found out that 83% of the 12 Samaritan males tested belonged to **Y-DNA Haplogroup J**, which included three of the four Samaritan families. The Joshua-Marhiv family belonged to Haplogroup J1, while the Danfi and Tsedakah families belonged to Haplogroup J2. **Haplogroup J1** is seen in the Arab countries including Saudi Arabia, Yemen, Egypt, Nubia/Sudan and along North Africa, Europe/Asia Minor in smaller numbers. However, it is seen **mostly** in very high numbers in "**Melaninated Brown/Black Arabs**", meaning nonwhite-skinned Arabs. But first let me give you an example.

African-Americans have mixture of African, European and Native Indian heritage in their DNA. If a Nuclear War destroyed everyone on the planet Earth except two people, the world would have to re-populate using the DNA of these people. Say these two people are a Pure un-mixed African man from Sudan and a Pure un-mixed White woman from Scandinavia. Each person has a specific gene. If this African man and White woman have children, we would expect their DNA to be half-African and half-White (50/50). Well, in African-Americans the Average percentage of "African DNA" can range from 60% to 95%. Let's call the African gene "**E1b1a**". This means that for most African-Americans their DNA comprises of mostly 65%-95% the "E1b1a" gene that links them to "Bantus" Africa. Keeping this in mind let's turn our attention to the **Y-DNA "J1"** gene which scientists and the Jews say is the "**Aaronite-Israelite gene**". If they don't fess up and say the "J1" Haplogroup is the gene that links them to the Aaronite Israelite High Priests by way of the Tribe of Levi they definitely claim that it is a "**Semitic/Shemitic**" marker. That being said, how much of this Y-DNA "**J1c**" gene is actually seen in Ashkenazi/Sephardic Jews compared to other nations that also carry the "J1c" gene? **Is it 15%, 25%, 50% or 75%?** Surely if the Ashkenazi/Sephardic Jews "J1c" gene only makes up 15% of their total DNA while the remaining 85% is European DNA, they cannot claim that they are "Jewish" by blood. If this is the case, they can only claim that they are mostly "**European**" by Blood. Let's use some "**critical thinking**". Does an African-American man who gets his DNA test done which shows his DNA is **10% European** and **90% West African** go around saying to people he is "European". NO! So what are the facts about the European Jews DNA? We know they are not going to openly admit they are "European" from Japheth. So "**Hebrews to Negroes**" will make them admit. The Truth doesn't have to prove itself to **NOBODY**. The **Truth is the Truth!** Example: We all know that if someone jumps off a 50 story building without a parachute they will most likely die, no matter if they believe they can fly. The Truth is the Truth. It doesn't have to prove itself. The Facts prove itself without anyone's opinion or believe (i.e. in this case **Gravity** is the fact).

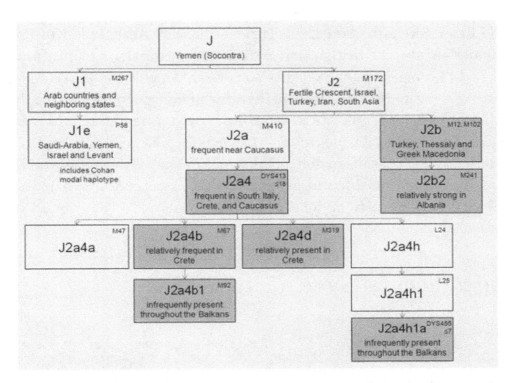

(**Above**) the **Y-DNA J1 Haplogroup** is seen primarily in Arab countries (**Middle East, Israel, North Africa**). However, it is seen at frequencies of less than 50% in most of these countries, especially with fair-skinned White Arabs. It is seen in frequencies of >50% in the Brown-skinned Arabs in **Yemen, South Saudi Arabia, South Iraq, Oman, Qatar, North Sudan, and the Black Bedouin Arabs of South Israel/Jordan**. The **Y-DNA Haplogroup J2** is seen frequently in the countries off the coast of the Mediterranean Sea (**Italy, Crete, Balkan countries, Greece, Macedonia, Crete, the Caucasus mountain area, Turkey, Israel, Palestine, Lebanon, Syria, Egypt, Libya, Algeria, Morocco, Tunisia etc.**). It is also seen in Middle Eastern countries like Jordan, Iraq, Iran, and Saudi Arabia. This is just some to name a few. But there is something that people are forgetting. Y-DNA and mtDNA Haplogroups can tell us "**Migratory patterns**" of certain groups of people. It can also tell us "**Invasion patterns**" of certain groups of people. Wow! The countries that the **J1 and J2 Haplogroup** are seen in today in the countries (Judea, Middle East, North Africa) that were invaded for over 2,000 years by the **Greeks**, the **Romans**, the **Edomites**,

595

the **Black Shemitic Arabs**, the **Turkish "white" Arabs**, the **Kurdish "white" Arabs**, the **British**, and the **French**.   So if the Y Haplogroup **J1** and **J2** is a genetic marker that you are an Israelite (or an Aaronite) does this mean that all of the **Mediterranean European** people and the **Middle Eastern** people are all Israelites? According to the Ashkenazi Jews, the Y-DNA Haplogroup **"J1c"** makes you an Aaronite High Priest. So does this mean that all the Arabs in North Africa, the Middle East, including Mediterranean people would be considered Jewish High Priests by way of the Tribe of Levi/Aaron?   That would be ridiculous.

WHAT ABOUT THIS Y-DNA "Q" HAPLOGROUP?

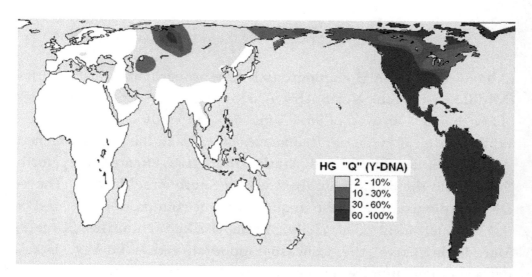

(**Above**) Y-DNA "Q" Haplogroup distribution throughout the Earth by *Mauricio Lucion*. The dark shaded areas represent where the most concentrated amount of "Q" Haplogroup carriers are in that region. If you notice on the map above, there is a gap in **Syria** and **Iraq** which shows no "Q" Haplogroup Carriers. But it mysteriously picks back up in Medes-Persia (Iran), Afghanistan, Pakistan and Turkmenistan. Is this because the 10 Northern Tribes of Israel were taken out of Israel and placed into Medes-Persia after 700 B.C.?

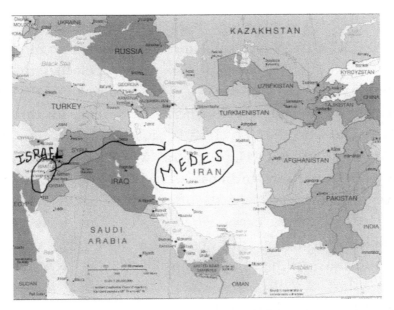

2 Kings 18:11 "And the King of Assyria did carry away Israel unto Assyria, and put them in Halah and in Habor by the river of Gozan, and in the cities of the **MEDES (PERSIA-IRAN).**"

Did the scriptures say the Northern Tribes of Israel were placed in **Jordan (Moab)**, in **Iraq (Babylon)** or in **Turkey**? No!

Is it possible that some of these Israelites followed the **Euphrates River** South to the Persian Gulf (East Arabia) after which they were able to travel on water to other lands via the **Arabian Sea** and **Indian Ocean**? What about the other Israelites? Did they travel "eastward" into Asia spending some time in **Tibet** and in **Siberia**? Based on the "Q" Haplogroup pattern above, it would seem that the "Q" Haplogroup carriers spent a lot of time in **Tibet** and **Siberia (perhaps picking up some Asian-traits)** before traveling to the Americas. Many historical documents list "**Semitic/Asian-like**" people in Tibet (**Sichuan province**) who claimed to be Israelites (**i.e. Qiang people**). They had a high percentage of the **Y-DNA Haplogroup "Q"**, just as some Mongloid Tribes in Siberia. Only one of two things can explain why we see a very **SMALL** (<5%) percentage of the "Q" Haplogroup in **Israel, Turkey, Palestine and Lebanon** but yet see (>90%) of the "Q" Haplogroup re-emerged in the **Americas**. Here it is:

- **Theory 1:** The Northern Tribe of Israel underwent a **MASS DEPORTATION** out Israel and was dumped off on the border of the Middle East/Central Asia after which they migrated all the way to the Americas. The resulting Y-DNA "**Q**" in Israel/Turkey after the Northern Tribes "exile" is different and "**younger**" on the "**Q**" Tree because of a mutation from the "**original**" older **Q Haplogroup, which is primarily seen in Native American Indians.** It is a known fact that the Amerindians carry oldest subgroups of Y-DNA Haplogroup "Q" than Asians, Turks, Siberians, Tibetans, Jews (Sephardic, Ashkenazi, Moroccan and Yemenite). Therefore, the "**evolution**" of the original root Paternal Y-DNA Haplogroup "Q" started with the so-called "indigenous" people in the Americas. Based on the Maternal mtDNA of Amerindians, we see that they originated in Northeast Africa- Israel (like Bantus-Negro Africans) and migrated to the Americas. This "**Theory 1**" makes the most sense logically. Whatever "Q" Haplogroup subgroups that are detected in non-Amerindian people are just the "Y-DNA left overs" of when the Amerindian Israelites were in Middle East and West/Central Asia.

Note: Many Scientists also connect Y-DNA Haplogroup "Q" to the Ancient Assyrian peoples. The Assyrian people lived in the land intersecting between Turkey, Syria, Iran (**Medes-Persia**) and Iraq. Assyrians who spoke Aramaic in later times practiced endogamous relationships because of their religious faiths (**Islam, Christianity, Judaism, Zoroastrianism**). Just as in Yemenite Jews, Ashkenazi Jews, Sephardic Jews, Moroccan Jews, Afghans and Pakistanis, trace amounts of the Y-DNA "Q" subgroup "**Q-M378/Q-M323**" can be seen in some Assyrian people today. Because trace amounts of these **Y-DNA "Q" subgroups** can be seen in Mesopotamia and Afghanistan/Pakistan (**Ancient Gandhara Empire**) many Scientists believe Haplogroup "Q" began in this area. This is the same area that the 10 Northern Tribes of Israel were exiled to in **2 Kings 18:11**.

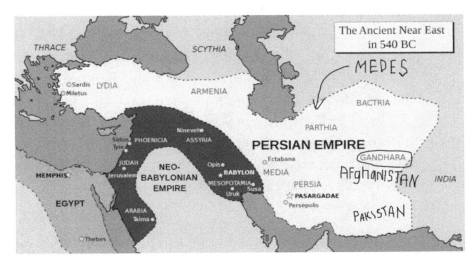

Fact: The Israelites from the 10 Northern Tribes were taken out of Israel in 700 B.C. and placed into Assyria and the towns of the Medes (**Persian Empire**) territory. The **Median (Medes-Persian) Empire** back in those days consisted of Modern day **Turkey, Syria, Iran, Afghanistan** (Gandhara Empire) and **Pakistan** (Gandhara Empire). This is why some Pakistanis and Afghans that carry the Y-DNA "**Q**" Haplogroup (10% frequency) look like Turks mixed with Indian blood. It is obvious that the Native American Indians retained their "**brown skin**" Israelite trait while mixing with "**Mongloid**" nations on the way to the Americas.

- **Theory 2:** Some Native Americans left the Americas and traveled into Asia via the Bering Strait, after which the migrated "**westward**" all the way to Iran. Then somehow they managed to bypass settling in Iraq and Syria to finally arrive in Israel. The only problem is the maternal mtDNA of the Native Indians (**A, B, C, D**) is not found in Israel or Africa, neither is their specific Y-DNA "**Q-M242**" Haplogroup. How can this be? Outside of the Americas the mtDNA **A, B, C, and D is found only in**

Asia/Middle East. How can it be missing in Israel if the Native American women traveled from the Americas to Israel? Native Indian MtDNA Haplogroups "**A, B, C, D**" are descendants of **mtDNA M and N**. Maternal mtDNA Haplogroups "**M**" and "**N**" are descendants of mtDNA Haplogroup "**L3**" which originates in Northeast Africa (i.e. Bantus Africans, Abyssinians). So based on **Genetics** and **Science** in regards to the "**evolution**" of the Native Indian mtDNA (**A, B, C, D**) from "**L3**" and "**M**", **it only makes sense that the Native American Indians were the descendants of the 10 Tribes of Northern Israel who were deported by the Assyrians 2,700 years ago.** Theory 2 is not logically sound.

Fact: The highest concentration of Y-DNA Haplogroup "**Q**" outside of the Americas is found in the **Kets people** (Russia), the **Selkup people** (Siberia), **Golestan/Gorgan people** (Northern Iran), **Han people** (China), the **Tuvan people** (Siberia), and the **Akha Tribe** (North Thailand).

CHAPTER 28

THE "GENTILE HEIST" OF ISRAEL

So now that we have established a little bit of what happened during the Persian rule of Judea (also Middle East) we can transition to when **Alexander the Great** defeated **King Darius III** in 331 B.C., taking over Judea into "**Gentile Hands**". Alexander the Great while in his 20's defeated the Persians in the **Battle of Granicus** (334 B.C.), the **Battle of Issus** (333 B.C.) and the **Battle of Gaugamela** (331 B.C.). Alexander the Great and his Greek Generals would later conquer more nations, creating the largest empire in the Ancient World, stretching from Egypt (West of Israel) to the border of present day Pakistan/India (East of Iran). The "**When did the Gentiles insert themselves into Judea**" question is very easy to answer if we pay attention to what Flavius Josephus said himself in his literary work. Josephus was born in the 1st Century A.D. before the Romans destroyed the Second Temple in Jerusalem in 70 A.D. His grandparents and relatives lived during the times of the Maccabean rule in Judea. Take heed to what he says here very closely. Sometimes we need to read things over and over again before we really get what is being said.

Per Gentile Jewish Flavius Josephus:

"That country is also called **Judea**, and the people **Jews**; and this name is given also to as many as embrace **THEIR RELIGION** (Judaism), though of **OTHER NATIONS**.

Note: This is Proof that the Jews in that time were simply Judaism converts from other nations like Greece or Rome.

Read further what he says,

"But then upon what foundation so good a governor as Hyrcanus (grandson of Matthias patriarch of the Maccabees, a family of Judahite patriots of 2nd and 1st centuries B.C). Took upon himself to compel these Idumeans (Edomites) either to become Jews (**BY RELIGION**) or to leave their country, deserves great consideration. I suppose it was because they had long ago been driven out of the land of Edom, and had seized on and possessed the **Tribe of Simeon** (the land not the people), and all the southern part of the land of the **Tribe of Judah**, which was the peculiar inheritance of the worshippers of the **True God** without idolatry...."

Flavius Josephus 1st Century A.D.

Anybody that practiced the religion of the Gentile Pharisees (Judaism) were considered "**Jews**" including the **Edomites**! This means that the term "**Jew**" was not associated with the Hebrew Israelites or 12 tribes of Israel during the times of the Greek Gentile Jewish Maccabeans! It isn't until the Book of Malachi, Nehemiah and Esther do we see the common practice of the word "**Jew**". In the Book of Esther (which was not found in the Paleo-Hebrew Dead Sea Scrolls) the word "**Jew**" appears more than any Book in the Old Testament.

Matthew 10:5 **"These twelve Jesus sent forth, and commanded them, saying, Go not into the way of the Gentiles, AND into any city of the Samaritans enter ye not: But go rather to the LOST SHEEP OF THE HOUSE OF ISRAEL."**

Yahusha HaMashiach (Jesus Christ) knew during his time in the 1st century A.D that those people living in Israel (Judea/Samaria) were Gentiles and that the true Children of Israel (descendants of the 12 tribes) were LOST. **Yahusha (Jesus) made a distinction here**: he said don't go **the Gentiles** (Judea) **AND** into any city of **the Samaritans** (North Israel). He obviously knew the Samaritans were not Israelites and the Gentiles in Judea at this time also consisted of mostly Edomites, Greeks, Nubians, Romans and other foreign peoples.

Prior to Yahusha's (Jesus) birth, the Greeks Gentiles were all up in Judea, some as Greeks practicing Judaism called "**Jews**" and other Greeks who were simply referred to as "**Gentiles**" because they continued to follow their pagan ways worshipping the gods of Greece. **King Antiochus Epiphanes IV** of Judea issued a decree to "**Hellenize**" Judea (i.e. building Coliseums-Arenas for different games). In addition, the Greeks even destroyed the surrounding walls of the City of David and erected new ones.

1 Maccabees 1:31-33" He plundered the city and set fire to it, demolished its houses and its surrounding walls. And they took captive the women and children, and seized the animals. Then they built up the City of David with a high, strong wall and strong tower, and it became their citadel."

1 Maccabees 1:41-44 "Then the king wrote to his whole kingdom that all should be one people, and abandon their particular customs (Judaic customs). All the **Gentiles conformed to the command of the king,** and many Israelites (some versions say "Jews") delighted in his religion; they sacrificed to idols and profaned the Sabbath. The King sent letters by messenger to Jerusalem and the cities of Judah, ordering them to follow customs foreign to the land:"

THE SELEUCID EMPIRE AND THE HELLENIZATION OF THE SO-CALLED JEWS.

Greek King Antiochus III

BEFORE THE MACCABEANS ARRIVED ON THE SCENE, around 246 B.C., the **Seleucids Greeks** lost substantial territory in the east, as a nomadic group called the "**Parni**" settled in the **satrapy** (administrative district) of Parthia in **Northern Iran**. In the same period, the satrapy of Bactria (**Afghanistan**) claimed independence. However, the **Seleucid king Antiochus III "the Great"** reconquered much of these regions between 209 B.C. and 204 B.C. when he campaigned in the east as far as India. In the west, the Seleucid king fought several wars with his fellow **Macedonians, the "Ptolemaic dynasty of Egypt"**. The **Greek-Egyptian** forces were crushed in 200 B.C. by the Seleucids and the Ptolemy's were forced to give up Palestine to Antiochus III, who was proclaimed conqueror of the East. Most of the Black Israelites were already scattered and Islam wasn't even a religion yet.

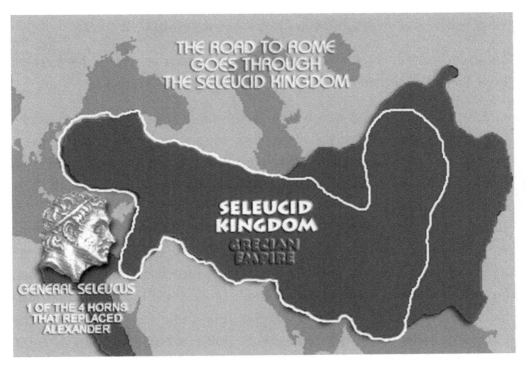

(**Above**) The whole territory of the **Greek Seleucid Empire** which in Ancient times included **Israel, Turkey, Armenia, Syria, Jordan, Iraq, Iran (Medes/Persia), Afghanistan, Pakistan**.

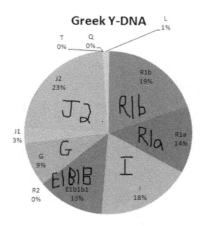

Greek Y-DNA

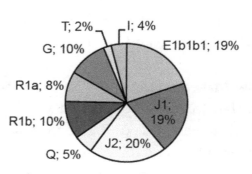

Ashkenazim by Haplogroup

(**Above**) The main Y-DNA Haplogroups for **Greeks** are **J2, R1b, R1a, E1b1b and G.** Now compare and look at the 5 major Y-DNA Haplogroups of the **Ashkenazi Jews**. Seems similar doesn't it?

Note: *Notice the Y-Haplogroup "Q" is not seen in Greece because 10 Lost Tribes of Northern Israel were not exiled to Greece.*)

These "**five**" Haplogroups above alone make up **78%** of the Greeks DNA. The **Children of Israel** are supposed to be a "**set apart**" special people but yet the Ashkenazi Jews main Y-DNA Haplogroups also consist of **J2, E1b1b, R1a, R1b and G**, making up almost **70%** of their DNA. How can this be? Does this mean that the Jews we see today are simply "**European converts**" to Judaism? **YES!** Where the Maccabeans who called themselves "**Jews**" and "**High Priests**" Greek by blood? **YES!** They simply converted to Judaism and lived in Judea after Greek Emperor **Alexander the Great** cleared the way for the Greek Gentiles to occupy the land of the Israelites. For both the Greeks and the European Jews, these 5 Haplogroups make up at least **70%** of their Total DNA heritage. This means that the Ashkenazi Jews today are genetically Greek with a mixture of other Japhetic races (i.e. Romans) with also a small to moderate percentage of Edomite Blood. If you notice, the Ashkenazi Jew is a mixture of many different bloodlines/populations. The Hebrew Strong's #4464 word for this is "**Mamzer**" which means "**bastard**".

"**Bastard**" is defined as a "**child of incest**", a **mongrel race**, a person of "**mixed**" population.

Knowing this, it is not a coincidence that the Y-DNA **J2** Haplogroup gene that Mediterranean peoples, Arabs and Jews have is also found in the areas that the **Greek Seleucid Empire** conquered. Why? Because the European Jews today are nothing more than Hebrew-speaking Gentile Greek Europeans, like the Greek Maccabean "convert" Jews that lived 2,000 years ago in Judea. Another common Y-DNA Haplogroup found in the Mediterranean peoples (i.e. Greeks), Arabs and Jews is the Haplogroup "**R**". Haplogroup "**R**" however is a "**genetic mark**" that has been passed down from an "**earlier**" group of people who happened to invade Southern Europe. Don't get it twisted. The Y-DNA "**J2**" Haplogroup, which is most concentrated in **Asia Minor** (Turkey, Kurdistan, Armenia), **Greece** and **Rome** (Italy) confirms that the Jews today are also descendants of **Turkish/Kurdish** Crusaders that invaded Judea hundreds of years ago. If anybody researches the "**Crusades**" in Israel they will see that starting from 1187 A.D., the white-skinned Arabs (Kurds/Turks) ruled over the land known as Judea/Palestina. These people are the forefathers of the Ashkenazi, Sephardic and Mizrahi Jews today.

Fact: *The Letter written to the **Church in Smyrna** (Revelation 2:8) to which the scripture in Revelation 2:9 states "I know thy works, tribulation, and poverty (but thou art rich) and I know the blasphemy of them which say they are Jews, and are not, but are the Synagogue of Satan" is an actual Ancient **GREEK CITY** off the coast of **Turkey** on the Aegean Sea. The written language at the time was Greek. These Greeks were the ones who invaded Judea in the 4th Century B.C., controlling Judea with the Edomites all the way up until the time of Christ and the later fall of the Second Temple in Jerusalem in 70 A.D. (**foretold by Yahusha HaMashiach in Luke 21:24**). This is proof that back then, 2000 years ago, the Greek Jews in Smyrna were recognized as the "**Synagogue of Satan**" and per the bible were "**Fake Jews**". The DNA of the Greeks, Italians (**Rome**) and Turks (**Turkey**) today is also found in "**High Frequencies**" in the Ashkenazi/Sephardic Jews living all* *throughout the world, including Israel. This means genetically, their heritage has not changed, and they are still like the people back then….. "**people who say they are Jews AND ARE NOT.**"*

In 196 B.C., Greek leader **Antiochus III** crossed the Hellespont **(Dardanelles strait which links Aegean Sea to Black Sea)** and in just two years he had added the region of **Thrace** (Eastern tip of Greece) to his empire. This brought the Seleucid empire into direct contact with the dominant Mediterranean power of Rome, Italy. In 190 B.C., Roman soldiers for the first time set foot in Asia and the following year a Seleucid army of 75,000 met Roman forces numbering only 30,000 at the **Battle of Magnesia**. Despite the odds, Antiochus was completely defeated by the Romans and the Seleucid empire lost its possessions in Anatolia (Turkey).

Fact: *The terms, "**Asia Minor**" and the "**Middle East**" are just made up words to confuse people as to the geographical position of Israel on the map. Israel shares the same tectonic plate (land mass) as Egypt, therefore Israel **IS Northeast Africa**. There is no "**Middle West**", "**Middle South**" or "**Middle North**". Likewise, where is "**Asia Major**" and why don't they call Iran, Afghanistan, and Pakistan "**Asia Minor**" since these countries are closer to Asia than Turkey.*

In the 2nd century BCE, Judea lay between the Greek **Ptolemaic Kingdom** based in Egypt and the Greek **Seleucid Empire** based in Ancient Assyria (Syria/Iraq), kingdoms formed after the death of Alexander the Great (356–323 BCE). Judea had been under Greek Ptolemaic rule, but fell to the Greek Seleucids around 200 BCE. Judea at that time had been affected by the Hellenization begun by Alexander. Some Jews, mainly those of the urban upper class, notably the **"Tobiad family"**, wished to get rid of Jewish law and to adopt a Greek lifestyle. According to the historian **Victor Tcherikover**, the main motive for the Tobiads' Hellenism was economic and political. The Hellenizing Jews **(Jews that encouraged Greek religion/culture mixed with Jewish religion/culture)** built a gymnasium in Jerusalem, competed in international Greek games, **"removed their marks of circumcision and repudiated the holy covenant"**. In 168 BCE, the ruler of the **SELUCID (GREEK)** kingdom, **Antiochus Epiphanes IV**, stepped up his campaign to squash Judaism, so that all subjects in his vast empire–which included the Land of Israel–would share the same culture and worship the same Greek gods (**i.e. Zeus, Pegasus**). He marched into Jerusalem, vandalized the Temple, erected an idol on the altar, and desecrated its holiness with the blood of swine. **Decreeing that studying Torah, observing the Sabbath, and circumcising Jewish boys were punishable by death, he sent Greek overseers and soldiers to villages throughout Judea to enforce the edicts and force Jews to engage in idol worship.**

When the Greek soldiers reached Modin, Israel aka **"Modi'in Maccabim-Re-ut"** (about 12 miles northwest of the Jerusalem), they demanded that the local Gentile Jew leader, **Mattathias** the fake *Kohenite* (**Gentile Greek member of their priestly class**), be an example to his people by sacrificing a pig on a portable pagan altar. Mattathias refused and killed not only the Hellenistic Jew who stepped forward to do the Greeks bidding, but also the king's representative. With the rallying cry **"Whoever is for God, follow me!"** Mattathias and his five Hasmonean Maccabean sons (**Jonathan, Simon, Judah, Eleazar, and Yohanan**) fled to the hills and caves of the wooded Judean wilderness.

Joined by a ragtag army of others like them, simple farmers dedicated to the Laws of Moses, armed only with spears, bows, arrows, and rocks from the terrain, the Maccabees, as Mattathias' sons, particularly Judah, came to be known, fought a guerilla war against the well-trained, well-equipped, seemingly endless forces of the mercenary Greek army. In three years, the Greek "convert" Maccabees cleared the way back to the Temple Mount, which they reclaimed. They cleaned the Temple and dismantled the defiled altar and constructed a new one in its place. Three years to the day after Antiochus' mad rampage (*Kislev* **25, 165 BCE**), the Greek Gentile "convert" Maccabees held a dedication *(Hanukkah)* of the Temple with proper sacrifice, rekindling of the **Golden Menorah,** and eight days of celebration and praise to God. After that proper Jewish worship according to them had been reestablished.

WHO MADE HANUKKAH LAW? MAN OR GOD?

Greek Jewish "convert" **Mattathias** killed a Hellenistic Jew who stepped forward to offer a sacrifice to an idol in Mattathias' place. He and his five sons fled to the wilderness of Judah. After Mattathias' death about one year later in 165 B.C., his son Judah Maccabee led an army of Jewish dissidents to victory over the Greek Seleucid dynasty in guerrilla warfare, which at first was directed against Hellenized Jews, of whom there were many. The Maccabees destroyed pagan altars in the villages, circumcised boys and forced Jews into outlawry. The term Maccabees as used to describe the Jewish army is taken from the Hebrew word for "**hammer**".

Fact: *On **March 22, 2016**, the Jews in Israel performed animal sacrifices and blew trumpets in Israel. **Rabbi Yosef Berger** wrote a **special Torah Scroll** for their awaited Messiah (the biblical Antichrist). After writing this "**Special Torah Scroll**", the Jews walked it to King David's Tomb in Jerusalem's Old City. Rabbi Berger's dream was to write a Torah scroll to present to their **Messiah (Christian Antichrist)** upon his arrival. Berger believes that by writing this "Torah Scroll" and keeping the scroll on Mount Zion, it will fulfill the requirements to usher in the Messiah-Antichrist. Now the "Convert" Jews, aka the "**Synagogue of Satan**" are waiting to possess Temple Mount so they can start rebuilding the "**Third Temple**" in Jerusalem for the Biblical Antichrist. Some people are saying however, that the Temple Mount has no connection to Jewish History, thus possibly giving Jews a possible "**alternate location**" to try and build the "Third Temple" for the Christian Antichrist.*

1 Maccabees 4:59 "Judas, with his brothers and the whole assembly of Israel, MADE IT LAW that the days of the dedication of the altar should be celebrated yearly at the proper season, for eight days beginning on the twenty-fifth of the month of Chislev (December), with rejoicing and gladness."

In the Book of Maccabees there is no "**Israelite Prophet**", no "**Thus Saith the Lord**" and no "**The Lord came unto me saying**" in this scripture so how is this an additional Jewish Holiday that the Israelites or Jews should keep in addition to the original Three Feast Holidays God gave Israel in the Torah? Is the Book of Maccabees even a part of the Hebrew Tanakh (Old Testament)? The answer is **NO!** Was the Book of Maccabees found in the Hebrew Dead Sea Scrolls? The answer is **NO!** Is Hanukkah "God's Law"? The answer is **NO**.

Many people say that Yahusha (Jesus) celebrated Hanukkah because he happened to be walking in the temple around that time but in John 10:22-23 it doesn't say that he celebrated it.

John 10:22-23 "And it was at Jerusalem the feast of dedication, and it was winter. And Jesus walked in the temple in Solomon's porch."

Yahusha (Jesus) had no choice that Hanukkah was going on in Jerusalem because they had already commanded it to be a national holiday prior to his birth (**165 B.C.**). The Greek Maccabean brothers told the Gentile Jews that they should follow the **Feast of Dedication** like the Feast of Booths (Shelters)/Tabernacle which is the "**Sukkot**". They set **December** as the date in the month of **Kislev**. There was no prophet for 397 years after the Book of Malachi and even Josephus Flavius attested to this. So no prophet and surely no God ordained this man-made Jewish holiday. In addition, **Hanukkah replaced the 7-candle stick Menorah with 9 candle sticks which is what the Egyptians used to worship Amen-Ra.** Nowhere in the Torah does it command the Israelites to light 9 candles for a holiday called "Hanukkah". **This pagan practice is from the Greeks believing in a false miracle that their oil lasted 8 days.** Hanukkah was the celebration of Gentile Greek Jews who stole the Throne of David, replaced the High Priesthood of Zadok with **Gentile men** and made military action permissible on the Sabbath. This alone is a **Commandment Violation**. The Greek Jews under John Hyrcanus I also allowed the Edomites to rule over Judea and join the Sanhedrin/Sadducees club.

Amen-Ra was often depicted as a Ram. Notice the **9 candles** or Serpents on his horns. Each of the **9 Serpents** on Amen-Ra's horns has a "**Sun**" on top of its head which symbolizes "**Light**". Why would a people follow a religion with the "**snake/serpent**" as a National symbol? God cursed the snake in Genesis prior to Noah and Mizraim (Egypt) being born but yet Satan slides his way into civilizations to deceive and lead man astray. Hanukkah was placed into Modern Jewry today in error out of "**The Doctrines of Man**". It shows in their work.

2 Maccabees 1:9 "**We (not God)** are now reminding you to celebrate the feast of Booths in the month of Kislev."

This scripture says "**We**" are now reminding you, not "**Thus saith the Lord**"!

2 Maccabees 1:18 "Since we shall be celebrating the purification of the temple on the twenty-fifth day of the month Kislev, we thought it right to inform you, that you too may celebrate the feast of Booths and of the fire that appeared when Nehemiah, the rebuilder of the temple and altar, offered sacrifices."

Note: The **Feast of Booths (Ingathering)** or Sukkot in Hebrew is celebrated on the fifteenth of Tishri (**Sept-Oct**) and marks the end of the year and harvest time. Why? **Because people don't gather the harvest in December**. However, this newly appointed man-man feast/holiday is on December 25th. This further violates the "**Feast of Booths/Ingathering**".

2 Maccabees 10:5-8 "They rededicated the Temple on the **twenty-fifth** day of the month of Kislev (**December 25th like Christmas**), the same day of the same month on which the Temple had been desecrated by the Gentiles. The happy celebration lasted eight days, like the Festival of Shelters (Booths), and the people remembered how only a short time before, they had spent the Festival of Shelters wandering like wild animals in the mountains and living in caves. But now, carrying green palm branches and sticks decorated with ivy, they paraded around, singing grateful praises to him who had brought about the purification of his own Temple. **Everyone agreed (but God didn't agree)** that the entire Jewish nation should celebrate the festival each year."

It wasn't until the Greeks arrived in the 4th Century B.C. that the face of Judea/Samaria started changing. As the Greeks, Edomites and Romans came to Judea, things got "**lighter**" in Israel, meaning the "**skin complexion**" of the people. Once the Black Israelites were exiled and led away captive from Israel, they never came back. Only the "**Gentile**" calling themselves "Jews" and not "Israelites" would come back. The Old Testament leaves us with the Persian Empire in control of Judea allowing the Israelites (Zerubbabel, Ezra, Nehemiah, Jeshua) the task of restoring the Temple and its practices. It wouldn't be until the mid-300 B.C. that the Prophethood of Israel ends, paving the way for the Messiah to come. The Book of Maccabees itself even attests that the prophets were **NOWHERE TO BE FOUND** during the Greek occupation of Judea. **Here it is folks:**

- **1 Maccabees 4:45-46** "So they tore down the altar, and stored the stones in a convenient place on the temple hill **UNTIL THERE**

614

SHOULD COME A PROPHET TO TELL WHAT TO DO WITH THEM."

- **1 Maccabees 9:27** "Thus there was great distress in Israel, such as **HAD NOT BEEN SINCE THE TIME OF THE PROPHETS CEASED TO APPEAR AMONG THEM.**"

- **1 Maccabees 14:41** "And the Jews and their priests **DECIDED** that Simon should be their leader **AND** High Priest **FOREVER, until a trustworthy prophet** should arise."

So the question is, "**If there was no prophet in the land during the Maccabean era then how is the Book of Maccabees a God-breathed book?**" How can the Greek Jews decide that a mortal man can be their leader and High Priest forever? **This is blasphemy.** Only Christ can be the "**High Priest**" **forever** in the Order of **Melchizedek.** The role of the High Priest was usually passed down from Father to Son. Thus it was a matter of birthright, and we all know that humans at some point will die. This is not "**Forever**".

Psalms 110:4 "The Lord has sworn and will not change his mind: You are a priest forever in the **order of Melchizedek.**"

Hebrews 5:6 "And he says in another place, You are a priest forever, in the **order of Melchizedek.**"

Hebrews 6:20 "Where our forerunner, Yahusha (Jesus), has entered on our behalf. **He has become a high priest forever, in the order of Melchizedek.**"

In the Gentile Book of Maccabees there is:

- No Prophet.
- No Ark of the Covenant.
- No supernatural confirmation.
- No predictive prophecy.

- No Messianic truth revealed.
- No **"Thus Saith the Lord"** or the **"Spirit of the Lord came unto me saying"**.
- No **"Authentic"** Israelites or Israelite **"High Priest"**.
- No **"Amen"** at the end of 1 Maccabees or 2 Maccabees.
- NO "Hebrew" **Tetragrammaton** (The name of God-Yahuah). Instead the word used is "Adonai/Adonay".

The Book of Maccabees is just a **"Historical Book"**, detailing the Gentile takeover of Judea, nothing more.

CHAPTER 29

THE IDENTITY HIJACK OF ISRAEL'S HIGH PRIESTHOOD. WITHOUT A "TRUE" LEGITIMATE PRIESTHOOD ANY BUILDING OF ANOTHER JEWISH TEMPLE IS A SHAM.

Many European Jewish people today with the last names: **Levi, Levy, Levinson, Levine, and Cohen** claim to be descendants of the **Tribe of Levi**, the Israelite family of Priests/High Priests. But how can a Jewish "**convert**" honestly believe that they are descendants of Israelite High Priest when a Jewish convert is not related to a "**Blood**" descendant of Jacobs 12 sons? This is called "**Delusions of Grandeur**", which is basically having "**delusions**" that you are something you are not. So how could the Maccabees be Jewish High Priests? Is this supported in the Tanakh? After all, we should be able to accurately trace the High Priests with the Bible.

LIST OF ISREAL'S HIGH PRIESTS (FROM THE RETURN FROM BABYLON TO THE GENTILE POSSESSION OF JUDEA)

Old Testament.	Josephus.
31. Jeshua (Hag. i. 1)	Jesus ("Ant." xi. 3, § 10)
32. Joiakim (Neh. xii. 10)	Joiakim ("B. J." xi. 5, § 1)
33. Eliashib (Neh. iii. 1)	Eliashib ("B. J." xi. 5, § 5)
34. Joiada (Neh. xii. 10, 22)	Judas ("Ant." xi. 7, § 1)
35. Johanan (Neh. xii. 22)	Joannes ("Ant." xi. 7., § 1)
36. Jaddua (Neh. xii. 22)	Jaddus ("Ant." xi. 7, § 2)
37............................	Onias I. ("Ant." xii. 2, § 5)
Apocrypha.	*Josephus* ("Antiquities").
38. Simon I. (Ecclus. [Sirach] 4, 1)	Simon the Just (xii. 2, § 5)
39............................	Eleazar (xii. 2, § 5)
40............................	Manasseh (xii. 4, § 1)
41............................	Onias II. (xii. 4, § 1)
42............................	Simon II. (xii. 4, § 10)
43. Onias (I Macc. xii. 7)	Onias III. (xii. 4, § 10)
44. Jason (II Macc. iv. 7)	Jesus (xii. 5, § 1)
45. Menelaus (II Macc. iv. 27)	Onias, called Menelaus (xii. 5, § 1)
46. Alcimus (I Macc. vii. 5)	Alcimus (xii. 9, § 7)
47. Jonathan (I Macc. ix. 28)	Jonathan (xiii. 2, § 2)
48. Simon (the Prince) (I Macc. xiv. 46)	Simon (xiii. 6, § 7)
49. John (I Macc. xvi. 23)	John Hyrcanus (xiii. 8, § 1)
50............................	Aristobulus I. (xiii. 9, § 1)
51............................	Alexander Jannæus (xiii. 12, § 1)
52............................	Hyrcanus II. (xiii. 16, § 2)
53............................	Aristobulus II. (xv. 1, § 2)
54............................	Hyrcanus II. (restored) (xiv. 4, 4)
55............................	Antigone (xiv. 14, § 3)
56............................	Hananeel (xv. 2, § 4)

(**Above**) The list of the Israelite High Priests according to the **Bible**, the **Apocrypha** and **Gentile Jewish Historian Flavius Josephus** (1st Century A.D.). Notice that the Old Testament (Tanakh) stops at the Aaronite "**Jaddua**" in the Book of **Nehemiah 12:22**. But does "Jaddua" serve as the High Priest in the Book of Nehemiah? The Apocrypha "poorly" tries to pick up where the Old Testament left off but the Apocrypha has many gaps where no "**High Priest**" seems to have existed during the Greek control of Judea. Mysteriously though, Josephus seems to have **ALL** the High Priests listed. So the question is, "**What scrolls or manuscripts is he using to get this information?**"

Before and after the Babylonian exile of the Israelites the succession of the Cohenite High Priests was from father to son. **King Zedekiah**, (Last

King of Judah) during the Babylon invasion died in jail and when the Princes of Judah were killed off, **Shealtiel**, the son of Zedekiah's nephew "**Jeconiah**" became the heir to the line of **Judah** from which **Zerubbabel** would come. From Zerubbabel would eventually come **Joseph** the earthly father of Yahusha (Jesus). After the Greeks came selling most of the Children of Judah (**Joel 3:6**) into slavery we see a disappearance in the Israelite prophets and Israelite High Priests. There is no longer a record kept of these bloodlines. The Maccabees and Edomites gave themselves (from 164 B.C. to 64 A.D.) the right to appoint their own "**High Priests**". This is a "**Red Flag**" because "**Man**" cannot appoint his own "**High Priest**". Greek Seleucid Leader **Antiochus IV** removed **Onias III** from the priesthood in favor of **Jason**, who was followed by **Menelaus**. Josephus chalks this in his Books as bonified Israelite "High Priests" but this is not the way Aaronite High Priests are selected. But the Apocrypha doesn't have any written mention of the prior "High Priests" of Israel. The only "High Priest" they list prior to this "gap" is **Simon the Just**. Prior to this the Hebrew Old Testament stops at either Joiada or his son Johanan. There is no evidence proving that Juddua served as the last High Priest of Israel. Nehemiah supposedly drove out and chastised many of the High Priests during that time for violating their Covenant with God as "Levites/Priests".

Nehemiah 13:28-31 "And one of the sons of Joiada, the son of Eliashib the high priest, was son in law to Sanballat the Horonite: therefore I **chased him** from me. Remember them, O God, because **THEY HAVE DEFILED THE PRIESTHOOD**, and the **covenant of the Priesthood, and of the Levites**. Thus cleansed I them from all foreigners, and appointed charges for the priests and for the Levites, **EVERY ONE** in his work; and for the wood-offering, at times appointed, and for the first-fruits. Remember me, O my God, for good."

Fact: The Horonites and Ammonites were two of the people groups God had driven from the Promised Land for the Israelites. **Sanballat, Tobiah, and Geshem** were governors serving under the King of Persia.

Sanballat, called a Horonite, was believed to be from **Horonaim**, a city of **Moab (Jordan)** and thus would have been a Moabite. The Bible forbade the Children of Israel to have children with Moabites or Ammonites but if they did they could not be grafted into Israel until after "Three" Generations. Tobiah was an **Ammonite (descendant of Lot)**. Geshem was believed to be an **Arab Ishmaelite**. These three men attempted to disrupt the Israelites and Nehemiah from rebuilding the 2nd Temple. This was going against Nehemiah and the instructions of God. They tried to harm him (**Nehemiah 6:2**), intimidate him with false reports (**Nehemiah 6:5-6**), deceive him with false prophets (**Nehemiah 6:7-13**), and influence the prominent men of Judah (**Nehemiah 6:17-19**). In the verse above Nehemiah exposes that the Priesthood was "**tainted**" in Eliashib and his grandson (son of Joiada). Therefore, Nehemiah (Tribe of Judah) drove out these Levite/Cohenites from the Temple.

Nehemiah 13:23-25 "In those days also saw Jews that had **married** women of **Ashdod** (Canaanites/Philistines), of **Ammon** (sons of Lot), and of **Moab** (sons of Lot): and their children spake half in the speech of Ashdod, and could not speak in the Jew's language (Hebrew), but according to the language of each people. And I contended with them, and cursed them, and smote certain of them, and plucked off their hair, and made them swear to God."

Old Testament.
31. Jeshua (Hag. i. 1)
32. Joiakim (Neh. xii. 10)
33. Eliashib (Neh. iii. 1)
34. Joiada (Neh. xii. 10, 22)
35. Johanan (Neh. xii. 22)
36. Jaddua (Neh. xii. 22)
37. ....

(**Above**) Jeshua, Joiakim, Eliashib, Joiada, Johanan and Jaddua are **the last** recorded Levite/Cohenite (Aaronite) "**High Priests**" recorded after the Israelites came back to Israel after their Babylon Exile/Captivity.

Ironically, the last book about the Israelites in Israel in Chronological Order of the Hebrew Old Testament would be **Nehemiah**. The Books of Ezra-Nehemiah are included at the bottom of the Hebrew "**Eleven Books of the Writings (Kesuvim)**" but Chronicles is at the end (although 2 Chronicles talks about earlier Hebrew events like when the House of Israel and House of Judah were still in Israel). After Nehemiah drove the Children of the heirs of Eliashib out of the Temple, it would appear that the rest of the High Priests (Aaronites) under Eliashib would have no place in the Temple. **Where did they go?** The Bible doesn't say because this is when the Old Testament history in Israel comes to an end. **After the Book of Nehemiah there would be no more documented High Priests and Prophets in the Bible**. Even in the Book of **Esther** there is no documented Israelite prophet, no High Priest, no "**Hebrew Tetragrammaton**", no "**Thus Saith the Lord**", and no "**The Lord came unto me saying**". In addition, the Book of Esther was not even found to be included in the Hebrew Dead Sea Scrolls of the Old Testament dating back to 400 B.C. When the Edomite Herodian clan was in power they appointed High Priests as they saw fit every couple years just like voting for a President. Greek King Antiochus Epiphanes IV nominated his own High Priests as stated in Flavius Josephus' "Antiquities 12.5 and 2 Maccabees Chapter 4. In those days, the High Priesthood title could be bought with a price, just as our U.S. Presidential Candidates are "**bought and paid for**" into office, meaning the candidate with the most campaign money backed by the Jewish Banking Cartel is usually the one that wins (**i.e. Obama vs McCain 2008**). It is believed that collectively between **Herod the Great, Herod Archelaus, Herod Agrippa I, Herod Chalcis**, and **Herod Agrippa II** they nominated **10 fake** Jewish Gentile High Priests.

2 Maccabees 4:7-11 "When Seleucus had departed this life and Antiochus styled Epiphanes had succeeded to the kingdom, Jason, brother of Onias, usurped the High Priesthood: **he approached the king with a promise of three hundred and sixty talents of silver, with eighty talents to come from some other source of revenue**. He further committed himself to **PAYING ANOTHER HUNDRED AND FIFTY**, if the king would empower him to set up a gymnasium and youth center, and to register the Antiochists of Jerusalem. When the king gave his assent, Jason, as soon as he had seized power (of High Priest), imposed the Greek way of life on his fellow-country men (i.e. **the Gentile Greek Jews and thus the beginning of "Hellenistic Judaism"**).

The "**Antiochists**" were a cultural society formed in Jerusalem to practice the Greek way of life, centered upon their favorite past-time place, the "**Gymnasium**". So with a large amount of money Jason bribed the Greek King Antiochus Epiphanes IV to "**make him**" a Jewish High Priest. The Hebrew Israelite High Priests duties of "priesthood" were usually passed down to the sons, granted the Levites Aaronites didn't mix their seed with other nations. This is also demonstrated in **Numbers 35:25-28**.

So Jason, as new "**High Priest**", would commit to building a Greek gymnasium in Jerusalem to train up the Gentile Greek Jews in the fashion of their heathen ways and to enroll these newly "**Hellenized Greek Jews**" as "**Antiochians**". They started sacrificing on the altar to Zeus instead of the God of Israel, which they really didn't care about at that time since they were not real Israelites to being with.

2 Maccabees 4:23-24 "When three years had passed, Jason sent Menelaus, brother of Simon mentioned above, **to convey the money to the king** and to complete negotiations on various essential matters. But Menelaus, on being presented to the king, **flattered him** by his own appearance of authority, and so secured the High Priesthood for himself, **OUTBIDDING JASON BY THREE HUNDRED TALENTS OF SILVER**."

This proves the Jewish "**High Priesthood**" could be bought in those days and therefore did not consist of "**Real Aaronite Israelites**" who are High Priests by "**Birthright**". This further proves that the

Maccabees that would come along later would be no more than Greek Gentile Jews who wanted to worship the God of Israel without any Greek influence. So what happened to the Israelite High Priests? Does anybody know? **Did they go into Africa?**

IS THE COHENITE PRIESTLY TRIBE LOST IN AFRICA?

So the bible says the son of one of the sons of **Joiada** (High Priest) was removed from the Temple by Nehemiah and banished from Judah, however nothing suggests that Joiada's family (which we have no record) received this punishment too. So who was the son of **Joaida** per the bible? Was it **Jonathan** (aka. **Johanan**)? **Jeshua** was the first High Priest of Israel after the return of the Israelites under the Persian King Cyrus and Ezra.

Nehemiah 12:10-11 "And **Jeshua** begat Joiakim, and Joiakim begat Eliashib, and Eliashib begat Joiada, and **Joaida begat Jonathan**, and **Jonathan begat Jaddua.**"

Did the remaining Israelite High Priests flee into Africa? Or did they flee into Europe? The majority of Ashkenazi and Sephardic Jews today from Europe claim ancestry from **Judah, Benjamin and Levi**. They claim that the Jews commonly migrated to Europe when leaving Israel and eventually **"turned white"**. They never say their descendants migrated into Africa. So do we have any clues as to where these Israelite High Priests went after being banished from Judah/Judea, Israel?

(Above). ISLAND OF YEB, AKA "ELEPHANTINE ISLAND",
Egypt. Off the Nile River.

Among the "**Elephantine Papyri**" a collection dating back to 400 B.C. there was found Hebrew Manuscripts from the Jewish community at **Elephantine Island** in Egypt. In one of the Hebrew Manuscripts a letter was found in which the name "**Johanan**" is mentioned. **Jonathan/Johanan was not an Egyptian name in those times**. The Letter is dated, "the 20th of Marshewan, year 17 of King Darius", which corresponds to 407 B.C. It is addressed to Bagoas, the governor of Judah, and is a request for the rebuilding of a Jewish temple at Elephantine, which was destroyed by Egyptian pagans. The letter includes the following passage:

"We have also sent a letter before now, when this evil was done to us, to our Lord and to the **High Priest Johanan** and his colleagues the priests in Jerusalem and to Ostanes the brother of Anani and the nobles of the Jews, **Never a letter have they sent to us.**"

So could it be that some of the Jews were still in Egypt after fleeing there during the Babylon invasion in the 6th century as written in Jeremiah? Maybe they didn't know that Johanan was banished from the Temple and this is why no one from Jerusalem ever responded back to the Jews living on Elephantine Island. Or was Johanan re-instated after being "**purified**"?

In 500 B.C. it is believed that some of the Israelites settled on Elephantine Island, an Island in the middle of the Nile River in South Egypt. After the fall of Jerusalem to the Babylonians in 586 B.C some of the Israelites went to Egypt with Jeremiah although some people believe the Israelites left much earlier by way of the 10 lost tribes of the Northern Kingdom of Israel who were deported by the Assyrians in 722 B.C. They believe the Israelites traveled from Assyria to Babylon (Iraq) and then to Egypt along the Nile River landing on Elephantine Island. Other "**people groups**" like the Lemba Jews claim to have left Israel for Arabia around this time. The Book of Mormon also claims that some Israelite tribes (Nephites and Lamanites) left Israel prior to the full scale attack on Judea by the Babylonian. These Israelites would eventually make their way to the "New World" in the Americas/Caribbean. The Mormons, Jesuits and Freemasons would call them "Indians."

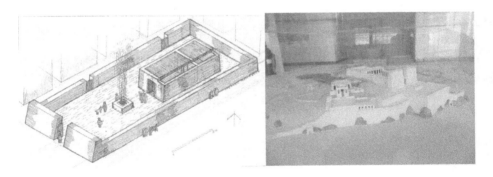

(**Right**) Shiloh Temple. (**Left**) Elephantine Temple resembled the Shiloh Temple built by the 10 tribes in Northern Kingdom of Israel. They kept the Holy days and followed the Torah (First 5 books of the bible) and not the Talmud of which Judaism uses. The temple and the people were overtaken by Egyptian Rebels in 410 B.C.

Jeremiah 44:14 "So that none of the remnant of Judah, **WHICH ARE GONE INTO THE LAND OF EGYPT TO SOJOURN THERE**, shall escape or remain, that they should return into the land of Judah, to the which they have a desire to return to dwell there: for none shall return but such as shall escape."

This is proof that the Children of Judah also ventured into Africa. So we have biblical proof in Jeremiah 44:14 and extra-biblical proof in the **"Elephantine Papyri"** Hebrew manuscripts. Now we have to ask the question, "If all the Ashkenazi Jews mainly claim to be from the Tribe of Judah, how come they don't look Black?" The Israelites in the Bible were **"indistinguishable"** from the Egyptians. What about the Levite children and their seed who are descendants of Moses and Zipporah the Cushite? Moses and Zipporah had children. If the Sons of Moses were black, then it is a good chance that the sons of Aaron were also Black. At the end of the day the Aaronites and Levites were cousins, sharing the same ancestral father. So if the Aaron and Moses both had a Black father, this would mean that the Israelite High Priests should be black, considering the High Priests didn't intermarry outside their race, just like the Brahman priests in India.

Herodotus also quotes:

"As for me, I judge the Colchians to be a colony of the Egyptians because, like them, they are black with wooly hair"

(Above) Egyptian Pharaoh Sesostris (aka. Senusret I), the 2nd Pharaoh of the Twelfth Egyptian Dynasty who ruled from 1971 B.C. till 1926 B.C.

"For the fact is as I soon came to realize myself, and then heard from others later, that the Colchians are obviously Egyptian. When the notion occurred to me, I asked both the Colchians and the Egyptians about it, and found that the Colchians had better recall of the Egyptians than the Egyptians did of them. Some Egyptians said that they thought the Colchians originated with Sesostris' army, but I myself guessed their Egyptian origin not only because the Colchians are dark-skinned and curly-haired (which does not count for much by itself, because these features are common in others too) but more importantly because Colchians, Egyptians and Ethiopians are the only peoples in the world who practice circumcision and who have always done so."

Herodotus

Xenpohanes, another Greek historian/philosopher who lived during 500-400 B.C quoted this about the Egyptians:

"The men of Egypt are mostly brown and black with a skinny desiccated look"

The remains of the Elephantine Temple, build by the Jews and destroyed by Egyptians in 400 B.C.

Exodus 2:15 **"Now when Pharaoh heard this thing, he sought to slay Moses. But Moses fled from the face of Pharaoh, and dwelt in the land of Midian: and he sat down by a well. Now the priest of Midian had seven daughters: and they came and drew water, and filled the troughs to water their father's flock. And the shepherds came and drove them away: but Moses stood up and helped them, and watered their flock. And when they came to Reuel their father, he said, How is it that ye are come so soon to day? And they said, <u>AN EGYPTIAN DELIVERED US</u> out of the hand of the shepherds, and also drew water enough for us, and watered the flock."**

Fact: *In the Book "**The Sign and the Seal**" Graham Hancock, there is jaw-dropping evidence to prove that many Israelites left Israel and ventured into Africa (Egypt-Nubia). On the **Island of Tana Kirkos** in Ethiopia, there are hollowed stones that have been used to collect the blood during sacrifices in the presence of the Ark of the Covenant. The Ethiopian monks there claim the Ark of the Covenant remained on the Island of Tana Kirkos for eight hundred years until it was taken to its current location in Axum, Ethiopia. The "**guardian of the ark**", a Ethiopian man named "**Gebra Mikail**" has to tough job of* *living and never leaving the **Church of Our Lady Mary of Zion** in Axum, Ethiopia for as long as he lives.*

WHAT ABOUT THE PRIESTHOOD? WAS THAT "HIJACKED" TOO BY IMPOSTERS?

(Above) Onias II (High Priest). According to the literary work "**Antiquities of the Jews**" by Gentile Jewish Roman historian **Flavius Josephus**, Onias II was the "**Greek**" High Priest of Israel during the Maccabean period during the years 240 B.C. to 218 B.C. According to 2 Maccabees, Onias III was the High Priest from 185 B.C. to 175 B.C. In 175 B.C. Antiochus Epiphanes IV sold the "**High Priesthood**" to Onias's (III) brother Jason for 440 talents of silver. **We already know that in the Bible, the High Priesthood of the Israelites is not something that can be bought with the money of man.**

THEY "SYNAGOGUE OF SATAN" INFILTRATED THE TEMPLE AND THE SANHEDRIN. THIS IS HOW THEY CHANGED THE LAWS TO COME UP WITH THEIR OWN SATANIC DOCTRINES....CALLED "BABYLONIAN" TALMUDIC JUDAISM.

Mysteriously the last High Priest of the Bible before the Babylonian invasion of Israelites was **Jehozadak** the son of Seraiah (High Priest). This is supported in 1 Chronicles 6:14-15 around 500 B.C. The last book of the Bible Malachi stops around 400 B.C. Mysteriously Josephus Flavius has the list of ALL the Jewish High Priests all the way to the High Priests that delivered **YAHUSHA** up to be crucified. It is said that under the Herodians and Romans during the time of Yeshua birth in the 1st century they appointed their own High Priests. In Herod's temple there was **NO** Ark of the Covenant or Stone Ten Commandments. Therefore, the Most High was not in there. Any Sacrifices done during the Herodian rule was done in vain/waste. Around 300 B.C the Greeks sacked EGYPT, Judea and extended their territory all the way to India/Afghanistan. The people in Judea and the High Priests at this time were mostly GENTILES. All, if not many of Levite records were lost and burned during the destruction of the temples. Ezra had a hard time finding LEVITES to do the temple duties. He needed help from the fake "LEVITES" called "Nethinims". Note: the last time the Ark of the Covenant was mentioned was in the Book of Samuel, prior to Queen Sheba's visit to King Solomon's in Israel. After Queen Sheba met up with King Solomon, and got pregnant with child (Menelik), the Ark was no more to be talked about. Many believe it is because the Ark was taken by King Solomon's son Menelik to Axum, Ethiopia where it is believed to be resting today. Ethiopia is also the only African Country to not be fully colonized by the Europeans.

CHAPTER 30

EDOM AND THE GENTILES, CAN THEY WIN TOGETHER?

(Above) Ashkenazi Jew and Hungary-native, **Theodore Herzl**, is known by the Jews as the founder of "**Zionism**". In the late 1800's he wrote a book called "**Judenstaat**" which proposed for a Jewish State in either **Argentina, Uganda or Palestine**. At the end of his book he states:

"Therefore I believe that a wondrous generation of Jews will spring into existence. **The Maccabeans will rise again**. Let me repeat once more my opening words: The Jews who wish for a State will have it."

Theodore Herzl

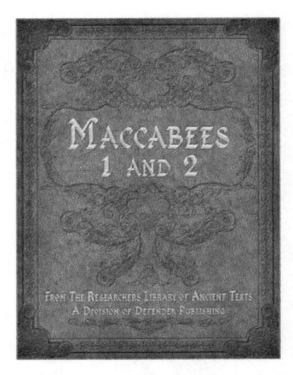

1 MACCABEES 3:48 "And laid open the book of the law, wherein the heathen had sought to paint the likeness of their images."

The First Book of the Maccabees covers the period of forty years from the accession of the Greek Ruler Antiochus (175 B.C.) to the death of Simon the (Greek) Maccabee (135 B.C.). Its contents contain brief historical introduction, the rise of the Greek Maccabean revolt, the Maccabean struggle under Judas and more. Prior to this time the Hellenistic Greek Dynasty under Alexander the Great was in control of Egypt and Judea/Israel for almost 300 years. Most of the so called "Jews" living in Judea at this time were Gentiles Jews by conversion. It was these Gentiles living in Judea that wrote Book of Maccabees". The Book of Maccabees had no prophet and Josephus Flavius admits that for a good period of time there was not one High Priest to be found. What! So was the Book of Maccabees "God-Inspired?" Let's see if God led the author to write this Catholic Bible Book. Here is how the Book of Maccabees closes (ends):

2 Maccabees 15:37-38 "So ends the episode of Nicanor, and as, since then, the city has remained in the possession of the Hebrews, I shall bring **MY OWN WORK** (not God's) to an end here too. **IF IT IS WELL COMPOSED AND TO THE POINT, THAT IS JUST WHAT I WANTED. IF IT IS WORTHLESS AND MEDIOCRE, THAT IS ALL I COULD MANAGE.**"

Does God do "**worthless**" and "**mediocre**" work when speaking through his Israelite prophets? Nope! This book is not a book from God.

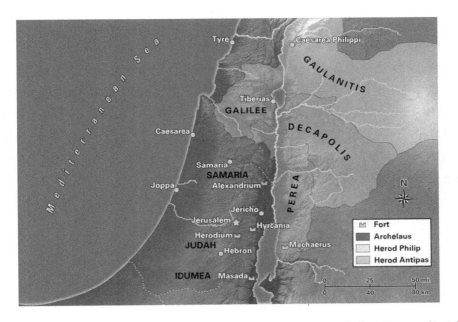

(**Above**) During the 1st Century B.C., Edomite Herod the Great divided up the Land of Canaan between his sons, **Herod II (aka. Herod Philip), Herod Archelaus, Herod Antipas and Aristobolus IV**. Herod Philip got "**Gaulanitis**" or Modern day Syria, Herod Antipas got "**Galilee**" which included the city Tiberius and Nazareth. Herod Archelaus got the territory of "**Samaria, Judah and Idumea (Edom)**".

Herod the Great tried to issue a decree to kill all the male babies so that **Yahusha Hamashiach** would not be born. The Edomites in the past had mixed their bloodline with the Kenite (supposed children of Cain). Herod the Great had 3 wives. His first wife **Mariamne I,** was a Hasmonean/Maccabean. His second wife was Doris. His third wife was Mariamne II, the daughter of Simon Boethus, the High Priest and founder line of the **Sadducees.** Herod the Great had many children but his child with the Greek Hasmonean Mariamne I was **Aristobolus IV** who was of Edomite/Greek stock.

Aristobolus IV had five children: **Herod II (Chalcis, some say Herod V), Herod Agrippa I, Mariamne III (daughter), Aristobolus minor and Herodias (daughter)**. Herod II ruled the kingdom north of Judea called "**Chalcis**". After Herod Agrippa I died, Herod II was given the responsibility of managing the 2nd Temple in Jerusalem which the Herodian family had finished (Ezra started it centuries prior). Herod II appointed his own High Priests, going against what the bible said. Therefore, during the Maccabean and Herodian Era there were no **ISRAELITE PROPHETS** and no "**REAL AARONITE HIGH PRIESTS**". Herod II appointed two high priests that would be crucial in Yahusha's (Jesus) crucifixion, Joseph, the son of Carnus, and Ananias (Acts 23).

The "**Pontias Pilate Stone (limestone)**" written in Latin to Roman Emperor Tiberius Caesar Augustus. Pontias Pilate was the Roman Prefect of Judea and on this block is reads "**Tiberivm, Pontivs Pilatvs, Praefectvs Ivdaeae**." Since the letter "v" was used in place of the letter "u" back in those times it would read today:

"Tiberium (Roman Emperor Tiberius Caesar Augustus), Pontius Pilatus, Prefect (Governor) of Judaea".

It would be Herod Antipas, the brother of Aristobolus IV who would be a key factor in the death of John the Baptist and Yahusha (Jesus of Nazareth). **Pontias Pilate**, the Roman governor/ambassador of Israel (Judea) did not want Yahusha's death on his hands and so he said, "**I find no wrong**" in Yahusha. He even tried to give Yahusha (Jesus) to **Herod Antipas** who was the ruler over the province of Galilee, where Yahusha (Jesus) was mostly found, but was sent back as Antipas couldn't find any fault in Yahusha either. However, the Gentile people

635

of Judea and the Sanhedrin would rather have Barabbas set free than see Yahusha live.

John 18:38 "Pilate saith unto him. What is truth? And when he had said this, he went out again unto the Jews, and saith unto them, **I find in him no fault at all.**"

(**Left**) Idumea or "Edom" is south of Judea. The area where the Ethiopian Jews, Sephardic Jews, Mizrahi Jews and Cochin Indian Jews (Bene Israel) reside today are in the ancient South Idumean city of Beersheba. This was during the time period of the Greek Maccabees and the Edomite Herodians in the 2nd to 1st Century B.C. when "Idumea" encroached upon the Southern border of the Territory of Judah. Beersheba sits between Palestine (Gaza) and the Dead Sea. Now it is considered South Israel in the Negev Desert. The **African Hebrew Israelites** live 20 miles south of Beersheba in a city called **Dimona, Israel**. (**Right**) Esau's mansion cave dwellings. Edom's beginning was in the caves in the Nabataean area known as Petra (modern day Jordan/North Arabia). The architectural design of the White House in Washington D.C., Rome (Italy), the Vatican and London, England is fashioned after Edom's mansions. Coincidence?

It is a known fact that there were no real boundaries between Idumea (land of Edom) and Judea in ancient times. Idumea was right below Judea, just like Ohio is right below Michigan. Idumea was close in proximity to the land given to the Tribe of Judah and Simeon. During 100 B.C the Gentile Romans and the Gentile Greeks were in control of Egypt and Judea (Israel). Less than 100 yrs. after the destruction of Solomon Temple in 70 A.D, John Hyrcanus I, was a high priest and ruler of the Jewish Nation of Judea/Samaria. He was a Hasmonean (Maccabean) as he was the son of Simon Maccabaeus, who was the son of Mattathias ben Johanan.

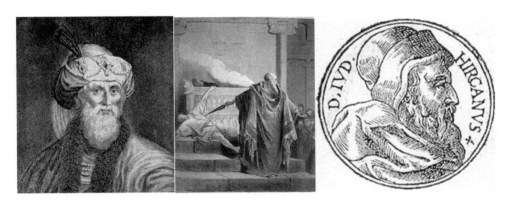

(**Left**) Gentile "Roman" Jewish convert and historian, "**Josephus Flavius**". (**Middle**) Greek "convert-to-Judaism" Maccabean Mattathias killing the priest of King **Antiochus IV (Epiphanes)** afterwards saying "**Let everyone who has zeal for the Torah and who stands by the covenant follow me!**" – Greek Septuagint, 1st Maccabees 2 (**Right**) Greek Maccabean **Jewish convert** John Hyrcanus I.

John Hyrcanus I was a Gentile Jewish Ruler that practiced Judaism but was not a Hebrew Israelite. He was a Greek-Roman by blood with Greek names given to his children because his offspring was half Greek and half Roman. His son, **Judas Aristobolous was Greek** as you can tell by his Greek name. He assumed the power of the (Hasmonean) kingdom after his father's death around 105 A.D. Judas Aristobulus had himself crowned king, taking the title "**Aristobulus I**" after he died his brother Alexander Jannaeus took over the throne from 103 B.C. to 75 B.C.

In the single year (104 A.D.) that he reigned, he seized the Galilee region in Northern Israel and compelled the inhabitants, many of whom were of **Roman**, **Syrian and Greek** descent, to become Jews by converting to Judaism.

Wait there is more!

Maccabean **John Hyrcanus I** (father of Aristobolus I) also took Dora and Marissa, cities of Idumea, and subdued all the **Idumeans.** He permitted them to stay in that country, **only if they would circumcise their genitals, and make use of the laws of the Judaism;** and they were so desirous of living in the country of their forefathers, that they submitted to the use of circumcision, and the rest of the Jewish ways of living. After this they were called no other than "**Jews**". This so-called High Priest or Levite/Aaronite "converted" the known enemy to Jews (Edomites), fought battles (which High Priests were not to do), and he made treaties with the Romans.

The Apostle Paul even admits that Aristobolus was a Roman by expressing greetings to his household during his ministry in Rome, Italy.

Romans 16:10 **"Salute Apelles approved in Christ. Salute them which are of Aristoboulous' household."**

THE MUSLIM DECEPTION: THE ANTICHRIST (LUCIFER/SATAN) IS COMING. GET YOUR SOUL RIGHT WHILE YOU HAVE A CHANCE. JUDGEMENT IS COMING.

Before we get started in dealing with Islam, Allah and Muhammad we must get clear that the name of the God of Abraham, Isaac, Jacob and Israel is not "**Allah**". The name of God is listed over 7,000 times in the bible, more than **Elohim, Ahayah** and **Allah**. We see in Genesis 4:26 that Seth, the Son of Adam **KNEW** and **CALLED UPON** the **NAME** of **THE LORD**. In our English bibles the word "**THE LORD**" is used to cover up the real name of God which is "**YAHUAH**". There is no "**V**" or "**W**" letter or pronunciation in Paleo-Hebrew and the Hebrew letter "**Vav**" has a "**oo**" pronunciation, not a "**v**" or "**double-you**" pronunciation as in the English letter "**W**". The Hebrew word "**Yahu/Yehu**-Hebrew Strong's #3058" for the English word "**Jehu**" is spelled from right-to-left: **Yod-Hey-Vav-Alef**. The Alef letter in Hebrew usually has no sound pronunciation and when used at the end of a word it represents a "**Gluttal stop**". So the word "**Yahu**" is basis for the word "**Yahuah**" as one can see that if we remove the "**alef**" from the Hebrew word "Yahu" and add a Hebrew "**Hey**" letter we will simply get the sound pronunciation "**Yahu-AH**". The same example can be done by deleting the "**Dalet**" Hebrew letter from the Hebrew word "**Yahudah**-Hebrew Strong's #3063" for the English word "**Judah**". You will end up with Hebrew pronunciation "**Yahuah**" every time.

Genesis 4:26 "And to Seth, to him also there was born as son; and he called his name Enos: then began men to **CALL UPON THE NAME OF YAHUAH (THE LORD)**."

As you can see here it says "**The Name**" or "**HaShem**" if we were using Hebrew.

In the case of Exodus 3:14-15 we need to take this approach. The word "**Shem**-Hebrew Strong's #8034/8035" in Hebrew means "**Name**". So we should see the word "**Shem**" whenever someone is saying "**My name is**". The Hebrew word "Shem" is seen in **Genesis 4:26** but it is not seen in **Exodus 3:14**. The Hebrew word "**Hayah**-Hebrew Strong's #1961" for **I AM** (or To Be) is simply a verb. Typically, a person cannot have a verb for a name. We see later in the next verse (Exodus 3:15) that God uses the word "Shem" in his statement which includes his name. Let's approach it like this, when someone admitted in the Hospital is ordered by the Doctor to go to get a CT scan or MRI they have to usually be taken there by a transporter. When the transporter walks into the room, he/she would typically enter the room saying, "**I'm the transporter, my name is…….**". The person identifies himself by his/her name and title when entering the patient's room. This is the same if someone from housekeeping was to enter a patient's room. In Exodus 3:14-15 God gives his **name, title**, and even says "**this is my name**". But he doesn't do so until "**Exodus 3:15**". In Exodus 3:14 God tells Moses "**I will be what I will be**" or "**I exist**". But we know that is **NOT** God's name. Moses knew that God's name was not "**I am that I am**". But God continued further to tell him his name and his title. He did this after saying the word "**MOREOVER**", which is like saying "**further**" or "**in addition to what has been said**". In **Exodus 3:15**, God says "**This is my Name (SHEM) FOREVER**". That scripture seals the deal folks.

Exodus 3:14-15 "And God said unto Moses, **I AM THAT I AM**: and he said, Thus shalt thou say unto the Children of Israel, I AM hath sent me to you. And God said **MOREOVER** unto Moses, Thus shalt thou say unto the Children of Israel, **YAHUAH** (The Lord) **Elohim** (God) of your fathers, the God of Abraham, the God of Isaac, and the God of Jacob, hath sent me unto you: **THIS IS MY SHEM** (NAME) **FOREVER**, and this is my memorial unto **ALL GENERATIONS**.

Not only did God give his title 4 times as "Elohim" in Exodus 3:15, but he gave a noun for his name (Yahuah) and he said, "This is my **NAME**

FOREVER". God repeated exactly what he said in Exodus 3:14 by saying "Thus shalt thou say unto the Children of Israel" followed by "Yahuah Elohim of your fathers, the God of Abraham, the God of Isaac, and the God of Jacob, hath sent me unto you: **THIS IS MY NAME FOREVER."**

Let's look at one last scripture since people say that the name "Yahuah" was inserted into the Bible by the Masoretes. Can man insert or replace something that comes out the mouth of God?

Exodus 34:5-6 "And **YAHUAH** descended in the cloud, and stood with him (Moses) there, **AND PROCLAIMED THE NAME OF YAHUAH**. And **YAHUAH** passed by before him, and **PROCLAIMED, YAHUAH, YAHUAH ELOHIM**, merciful and gracious, long suffering, and abundant in goodness and truth."

Here we see the name "Yahuah" **PROCLAIMED** (announced officially or publicly) 4 times in one verse!

Proclaim means – to declare something one considers important with due emphasis, declare officially or publicly to be.

How many times in the Bible is the word "**Ahayah**" or "**Allah**" proclaimed? It's a no contest.

Many Israelites battle and debate over what to call the name of God (Creator). This is just another one of Satan's tools to creative "**Division**" in the midst of God's People waking up. You will hear people talking about **Ahayah** vs **Yahuah** vs Yahawah. Then we will debate about whether to say **Jesus, Yeshua, Yahushua, Yawahashi, Yashaya or Yahusha** when we pray. However, God's Eternal name is also seen in the Hebrew Dead Sea Scrolls version of the **written in Paleo-Hebrew**. In Isaiah 42:8, God says "**Yahuah**" is his name. There no room for any "**error**" on this one. The "**Dead Sea Scrolls**" and the "**Ketef Hinnom**" Silver scrolls predate the Masoretes. The Silver Scrolls date back to 600 B.C. and the Dead Sea Scrolls date back to 400 B.C. They are written in Paleo-Hebrew. The Masoretes were Jewish scribe-scholars who worked between **500-900 A.D**. We can easily do the math and see that something engraved on silver or penned on papyrus paper over 1,000 years prior to the Masoretes cannot be a "forgery". The verse below from the Isaiah Dead Sea Scrolls also includes the word "**Shem/Shum**" which means "**Name**" in Hebrew.

(Above) Isaiah 42:8 shortened in Hebrew. It reads from right-to-left, "I am **YAHUAH**, that is my **SHEM (NAME).**"

(Above) Here we can see the name of the **Creator (Father)** in Paleo-Hebrew. These four Hebrew Letters make up the "**Tetragrammaton**". It appears on the **Moabite Stone**, aka the "**Mesha Stele**" dated back to 840 B.C. It lines up to the Bible in **2 Kings 3:4-8**. On this stele, can be found the words "**House of Omri**". Omri was the sixth King of Israel after Jeroboam. **King Ahab** would succeed Omri to the throne of Israel. Omri reigned over the House of Israel around the 8th Century B.C. The stele, written in Hebrew (because the Moabites were Hebrew) states how a man named "Mesha", son of Chemosh-Gad, a Moabite was having a hard time dealing with Omri (King of Israel) who was taking his cities. The Stele mentions "**YAHUAH**", "**House of David**" and "**Israel**".

In the New Testament HaMashiach (The Christ) said to his disciples in **John 5:43** "I am come in my **FATHER'S NAME**, and ye receive me not: if another shall come in his own name, him ye will receive."

So know that we know the "**Father's name**" in Hebrew, we should be able to decipher what the name of the Son of God (HaMashiach) would've been when Christ walked the earth 2,000 years ago. We know that Jesus name is derived from the English name "**Joshua**" so using an Old Testament Hebrew-English Translation Bible, we should be able to find this out easily.

So in more than one area in the Bible, God says directly that his name is "**Yahuah**"; one in **Exodus 3:15**, one in **Isaiah 42:8** and other time in Exodus 6:3. In Exodus 3:14, God does not say in same sentence "I AM is my name".

Isaiah 42:8 "I am **YAHUAH (The Lord)**, **THAT IS MY SHEM (NAME)**; and My glory will I not give to another, neither My praise to graven images."

Exodus 6:3 "And I appeared unto Abraham, Isaac, and to Jacob, by the name of God Almighty (El-Shaddai), but by **MY NAME YAHUAH** was I not known to them."

The Sumerians called the God that created the Flood, "**Huwawa**" which is similar to "**Yahuah**". The Sumerians disliked the God that "dwelled in the Mountains" called "**Huwawa**". The were unhappy with the fact that he sent the flood to destroy the earth. It's funny how "**Huwawa**" sounds like "**Yahuah**" and this is coming from a civilization that lived almost 6,000 years ago and had to have had ancestors who survived the flood (**Shem, Ham, Japheth and their children**). In order to know about the "**Great Flood**" their ancestors had to have survived the Flood.

Fact 1: *This face according to the Sumerian work, the "**Epic of Gilgamesh**" is the paganized version of the Creator God that sent the "**Great Flood**" the "Epic of Gilgamesh" talks about. According to "Gilgamesh's Epic (who many say is actually Nimrod), the face belongs to "**Huwawa**". In the Sumerian* records, Gilgamesh and his half-man/half-beast buddy *"Enki-du"* kills *"Huwawa"* by decapitation. Gilgamesh tells all of his people that he went up into the mountains (i.e. Mount Sinai) to find *"Huwawa"*, the God behind unleashing the "Great Flood" on mankind. Gilgamesh later comes back with a story that he was successful at killing him and that they would not have to worry about the terrible *"Huwawa"* no more. If Gilgamesh is the biblical *"Nimrod"* he fits the meaning of the name *"Nimrod"*, which means "Tyrant" or "Rebel". Nimrod was the son of **Cush** and the great-grandfather of **Noah**. So it is possible that the Children of Nimrod and the Children of Shem were the Ancient Sumerians. After all, Nimrod did rule over Africa and Mesopotamia (**Land of Shem**) according to the Bibl.

Genesis 10:10 *"And the beginning of his (**Nimrod's**) kingdom was Babel (**Babylon**), and Erech (**Uruk**), and Accad (**Akkad**), and Calneh, in the Land of Shinar (**Sumer-Sumeria**). All of these are cities in Ancient Sumeria (Iraq-Babylon).*

Nimrod would rebel against God, getting all the nations to build the Tower of Babel to Heaven, which God of course stops. The word Cush and Erech are in the Bible. **Kish**, the **Flood** and the Sumerian city **Uruk** are in the Epic of Gilgamesh.

Fact 2: *In the Bible, **Yahuah** appears over 7,000 times compared to <1,000 times for "I AM/Ahayah". In the Hebrew Old Testament (Tanakh), the Hebrew letters for "Yeshua", "Yahushua" and "Yahusha" all appear.* **Yahushua appears only twice.** *"Yahusha" appears more times in the Old Testament than both "Yeshua" or "Yahushua" combined.*

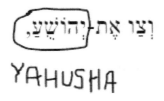

(**Above**) The words in Hebrew, "**BUT CHARGE JOSHUA (YAHUSHA**)." In most Hebrew versions of the New Testament, the

word they are actually using for the Christ is "Yeshua" and not "Yahusha". This is likely because most of the earlier New Testament versions from the 1st-3rd century A.D. are written in Aramaic, and of course Greek.

Deuteronomy 3:28 "**BUT CHARGE JOSHUA**, and encourage him, and strengthen him; for he shall go over before this people, and he shall cause them to inherit the land which thou shalt see."

"**Sha**" is the primary root of "**Yasha**-Hebrew Strong's #3467" in masculine form. It means salvation, save, deliver, or savior. Hebrew Strong's #7769 "**Shua**" means "**cry out for help**".

"**Yahusha**" is the name of the "father" combined with the Hebrew letters "**Shin**" and "**Ayin**". So in completeness it reads "**Yod-Hey-Uau-Shin-Ayin**".

"**Yahushua**" means "**Yah cries out**". This incorrect with the simple addition of the "**u**". Take out the "**u**" and we have "**Yahusha**". "**Yahusha**" means "**Yah is Salvation**". This is correct.

In Hebrew the word "**Allah**" is listed under the Hebrew Strong's lexicon **#427** as "**An Oak**". It is pronounced (al-law) in Hebrew, the language of Abraham and Ishmael. Therefore, if Abraham or Ishmael would've called out or prayed in Biblical times saying the word "Allah", they would be calling out to an Oak Tree.

In Hebrew the word "**Alah**" is listed under the Hebrew Strong's lexicon **#423** as "**to Swear, or to Curse**". It is pronounced (aw-law) in Hebrew. So back in Biblical times, if Abraham or Ishmael were to say "aw-law" they would essentially be cursing or swearing at something, not calling on God. God the "Creator" has a name, and the Bible says we should proclaim his name. Not call him a title. Even the pagan gods of Egypt, Greece, Canaan, Cush and Rome has names. So why does the "**youngest**" religion on the planet give mankind an "**ambiguous**" title and not a name? Why switch things up after 6,000 years? Osiris had a name 4,000 years ago. It doesn't make any sense. In the bible as we all know the word "Yahuah" is replaced with "the LORD". By not recognizing, calling upon God's name and not praising God by his name, we are disobeying what the Bible says. Even when we say "Hallelu-**YAH**" we are giving praises to God as "**YAH**-Hebrew Strong's #3050". **YAH AND YAHUAH** is the name of the Creator/God of Israel. It is found in the Hebrew Torah in Exodus 15:2. Despite this, European Jews only refer to God as "**the Almighty**", "**The One Above**", "**Hashem (the Name)**", "**Lord of Hosts**", or "**Adonai/Adonay**".

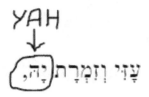

FROM THE BEGINNING OF EXODUS 15:2.

EXODUS 15:2 "The LORD (**YAHUAH**) is my strength and song, and He is become my salvation; this is my God, and I will glorify Him; my father's God, and I will exalt Him.

Deuteronomy 32:3 "Because I will publish the name (**Shem**) of **YAHUAH** (the LORD): ascribe ye greatness unto our God."

Isaiah 12:4 "And in that day shall ye say, **PRAISE YAHUAH** (the LORD), call upon his **SHEM** (NAME), declare his doings among the people, make mention that his name (**Shem**) is exalted."

Psalms 105:1 "O give thanks unto **YAHUAH** (the LORD); call upon his **SHEM** (NAME): make known his deeds among the people."

CHAPTER 31

WHAT IS THE MARK OF THE BEAST? HAS IT ALREADY COME OR IS IT AROUND THE CORNER? DON'T BE FOOLED!

(**Above**) The **Crescent Moon and Star** was used by other civilizations as the symbol for "**pagan worship**". The **Yeha Temple** in Ethiopia is one of the oldest temples in Ethiopia dated back to 600 B.C. when the **Sabaean** (Semitic) script was used prior to "**Ge'ez**", which is the language of the Ethiopian Orthodox Church and the Ethiopian Jews. The Yeha Temple in Ethiopia was known to worship the **Crescent Moon, the Star and the Sun**, 1,000 years before the pagan Arabs would worship these "Creations" of God. But what about in very ancient times? Did they worship the Sun, Moon and stars then? Who promoted and facilitated this pagan worship? The Fallen demonic angels with Lucifer/Satan promoted this, going against what God commanded. So in essence, the worship or use of the **Sun, Star and Moon** in any Religion is a form of Satanic pagan worship. In the Book of Jubilees (Little Genesis), penned by Moses while on Mount Sinai, it talks about how the "**Watchers-Fallen Angels**" were promoting this kind of Satanic/pagan worship to mankind before the flood and after the flood. Prior to the "**Dead Sea Scrolls**" discovery in Qumran, Israel dated back to 400 B.C., written in Paleo (Ancient) Hebrew, the only people know to have a complete canon of the Book of Jubilees were the

Ethiopians. So what does the Book of Jubilees written in Ancient Hebrew say about this worship of the Crescent Moon, Star, and Sun?

Book of Jubilees 8:1-4 "In the twenty-ninth jubilee, in the first week, in the beginning thereof **Arpachshad (Son of Shem)** took to himself a wife and her name was Rasu'eja, the daughter of Susan, the daughter of **Elam**, and she bare him a son in the third year of this week, and he called his name **Kainam**. And the son grew, and his father taught him writing, and he went to seek for himself a place where he might seize for himself a city. And he **FOUND** a writing **which former generations had carved on the rock**, and he read what was thereon, and he transcribed it and sinned owing to it; for it contained **THE TEACHING OF THE WATCHERS** (Fallen Angels) in accordance with which **THEY USED TO OBSERVE THE OMENS OF THE SUN AND MOON AND STARS IN ALL THE SIGNS OF HEAVEN**. And he wrote it down and said nothing regarding it; for he was **AFRAID TO SPEAK TO NOAH ABOUT IT LEST HE SHOULD BE ANGRY WITH HIM ON ACCOUNT OF IT**.

So whose descendants "**after the flood**" initially found the teachings of the Fallen Angels/Watchers who came from heaven? It was "**Kainam**", the son of **Arpachshad**, the son of **Shem! What ancient civilization first wrote about the "Watchers" aka the "Fallen Angels" who came from heaven?** The Sumerians with their writing about the "Annunaki"! Some say the word "**Annunaki**" means "**those who from the heavens came**". Others say it means, "**princely seed**" or "**princely blood**". Either way, the Sumerians believed they were the creation of the Father of all Gods, "**Anu**", hence where we get the word "Annunaki" from and possibly where the Shemitic Hebrews got the word "**Sons of Anak (Giants)**" from. The Sumerians also wrote about the "Great Flood" in the Epic of Gilgamesh! The Sumerians cuneiform script writing would be the ancestor writing style of the Israelites, the Babylonians, the Assyrians, the Persians and the people in South India whose writing derives from Cuneiform Sanskrit (which has also been found in Cameroon and Ethiopia). So where did these Sumerians live?

In Mesopotamia, the **LAND OF SHEM**! In ancient times, according to the Book of Jubilees the land of Shem started from the whole land of **Eden (Northeast Africa/Ethiopia)** all the way across the **Red Sea (Arabia)**, encompassing the land known as the "**Middle East**" and also **India**. Wow!

Book of Jubilees 8:11 "And he knew that a blessed portion and a blessing had come to **SHEM** and his sons unto the generations forever- the whole **LAND OF EDEN (ETHIOPIA)** and the whole land of the **RED SEA (ARABIA)**, and the whole land of the **EAST (MIDDLE EAST)** and **INDIA**...."

So because we know that Shem's descendants lived in Mesopotamia-Arabia we should not be surprised that the descendants of Ishmael (Shemites), the sons of Joktan (Shemites), the Moabites (Shemites), and the Ammonites (Shemites) would be caught up in "**Celestial worship**"

Deuteronomy 17:3 "And hath gone and served other gods, and worshipped them, either the **SUN**, or **MOON**, or any of the **HOST OF HEAVEN**, which I have not commanded."

Deuteronomy 4:19 "And lest thou lift up thine eyes unto heaven, and when thou seest the **SUN**, and **THE MOON**, and **THE STARS**, even all the **HOST OF HEAVEN** (Planets), shouldest be driven to **WORSHIP THEM**, and **SERVE THEM**, which the Lord thy God hath divided unto all nations under the whole heaven."

The **Kaaba Black Cube** that the Muslims circumnavigate (counter-clockwise) was in ancient times believed by the Arab pagans to house all the pagan gods during that time. The Cube represented "**Saturn**" in Roman mythology and "**Satan**" in modern religion. The Muslims keep this pagan symbol alive and well by praying towards the east in its direction in Mecca, Saudi Arabia, despite the Quran speaking against this pagan practice.

Quran Sura 2:177 "Righteousness is not that you turn your faces towards the **EAST OR THE WEST**, but true righteousness is in one who believes in **Allah**, the **LAST DAY**, the **ANGELS**, the **BOOK (BIBLE?)**, **AND THE PROPHETS (ISRAELITES)** and gives wealth, in spite of love for it, to relatives, orphans, the needy, the traveler, those who ask for help, and for freeing slaves; and who establishes prayer and gives Zakah; those who fulfill their promise when they promise; and those who are patient in poverty and hardship during battle. Those are the ones who have been true, and it is those who are the righteous."

So we have a couple things in confusion here. There 5 things Muslims are to believe in.

1. **Allah**.
2. The **Last Day**, aka the "**Return of Yahusha HaMashiach** (Jesus Christ)".
3. The **ANGELS**.
4. The **BIBLE**.
5. The **PROPHETS**.

Muslims don't believe God has an actual name. They don't believe God can have a son (or daughter). They don't believe the Bible is true because it has been tampered with so much that it is in error, thus justifying that mankind needs to follow the "untampered" pure word of God, The Noble Quran. They are told to believe in the "Israelite Prophets" but elevate Muhammad to the "**Greatest and Last Prophet of God**" despite the Quran telling us in **Sura 29:27** that Ishmael was **NOT** a prophet.

So we know who the Angels are and what the Bible is. We also know about the "**Last Days**" in the Book of Revelation in the Bible. Muhammad could easily insert this into the Quran because he knew of the Old Testament and New Testament. What about the Prophets? Who are they according to Islam and the Quran?

651

Sura 29:27 Al-Ankabut (The Spider) "And We (Allah & Angels) gave to him **ISAAC, AND JACOB AND PLACED IN HIS DESCENDANTS** (not Ishmael's descendants) **PROPHETHOOD AND SCRIPTURE.** And We gave him his reward in this world, and indeed, he is in the Hereafter among the righteous."

So here we see that the Prophets of this world are **ALL** Hebrew Israelites, not Arab Muslims. So why is anyone following Muhammad if he is not a Prophet according to their Religious Book?

It gets deeper!

The Bible says in the Book of Revelation that many followers of Christ will be beheaded. It says that these people will reign with Christ for 1,000 years. Will these people be Israelites or Gentiles? It is hard to say. But Revelation 20:4 says that many will be beheaded for not taking the "**Mark of the Beast**". The Antichrist will be involved in facilitating all of this. Take heed to these words because it is about to get **DEEP**!

Revelation 20:4 "And I saw thrones, and they sat upon them, and judgment was given unto them: and I saw the souls of them that were **BEHEADED** for the witness of Jesus, and for the **WORD OF GOD**, and which had **NOT WORSHIPPED THE BEAST**, neither his **IMAGE**, neither had received his **MARK UPON THEIR FOREHEADS**, or **IN THEIR HANDS**, and they lived and reigned with Christ a thousand years."

So according to the **Abrahamic Religions** (Judaism, Christianity, Islam), which religion is persecuting by the method of "**Beheading**"? Currently it is Islam, but many people believe that Judaism will also play a factor in "**beheading**" under the "**Noahide Laws**" in which the worship of "Yahusha (Jesus)" will be a violation of this law. So in essence, there could be two religions that punish any person on earth that worships "**Yahusha**" as God. How will this be done? By creating a "**One World Unified Religion**" under the **NWO/Antichrist**. Call it "**Chris-Lam**" or the religion of the Freemasons (**which is also**

Christianity, then Islam according to the Freemason Moslem Shriners).

Where will the Antichrist's throne be at? In the **Third Temple** that the Gentile "fake" Jews will build! How will they build it if the Arabs currently possess **Temple Mount** aka "**Mount Moriah**"? There has to be an "**Event (i.e. weather, nuclear, United Nations Law)**" that will clear the way for the Jews to build this Third Temple or there has to be an "**agreement**" between both parties (Jews-Arabs). Will the evil spirit of Satan (Antichrist) trick the Jews and the Arabs into allowing this to happen? Time will tell.

So how do we know that Islam will be one of the religions that the Antichrist will follow behind?

In **ISAIAH 14:12** one aspect of **Lucifer's/Satan's** name is left out. But why? Here is how our King James Bible reads this verse:

Isaiah 14:12 "How art thou fallen from Heaven, O Lucifer, **SON OF THE MORNING!** How art thou cut down to the ground, which didst weaken the nations."

One problem is.....**Lucifer** is a made-up name in English. Lucifer's real name in Hebrew is "**Heylel-Ben-Shachar-YALAL**". The Hebrew word "**Yalal**" was left out of our bibles for a reason! **Hebrew Strong's #3213** "Yalal" means "**to howl or howling.**" So what does "**Son of the Howling Moon**" represent? We shall see!

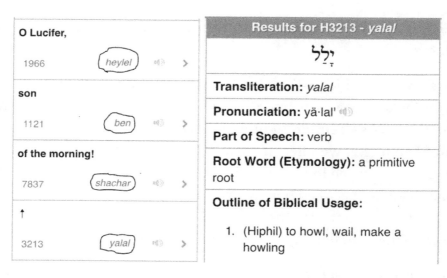

O Lucifer,		Results for H3213 - *yalal*
1966	heylel	יָלַל
son		**Transliteration:** *yalal*
1121	ben	**Pronunciation:** yä·lal'
		Part of Speech: verb
of the morning!		**Root Word (Etymology):** a primitive root
7837	shachar	
↑		**Outline of Biblical Usage:**
3213	yalal	1. (Hiphil) to howl, wail, make a howling

(**Above**) In Isaiah 14:12 Lucifer is described as "**Heylel**", SON OF THE HOWLING MORNING. The word "**Yalal**" was left out of our King James Bible". Why? Because they didn't want us to connect the dots between Lucifer and Islam. But how so? The **Crescent Moon and Star** are not unique to Islam. It has been used as Satan's "**Mark**" throughout time. **The Egyptians used it, the Ethiopians used it (Yeha Temple), and the Indians used it (Hindu-Shiva the Destroyer).**

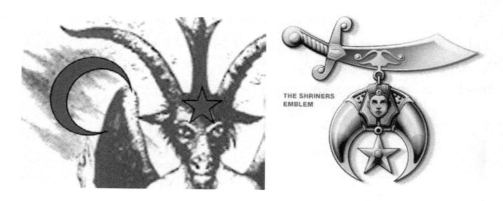

THE SHRINERS EMBLEM

(**Left**) The symbol for Satan in the Church of Satan is the "**Baphomet-Sabbatic Goat**" Half-man, Half-Goat figure. Don't believe me? Research **Eliphas Levi**, **Aleister Crowley** and **Andrew Chumbley**. Notice the "**Crescent Moon**" and "**Star**". This is not a coincidence that

Eliphas Levi drew up and inserted in this picture. (**Right**) Notice the Freemasons "**Moslem Shriner**" Emblem with the **Crescent Moon and Star.** Notice the Egyptian Pharaoh head. Why do the Freemasons use these particular symbols? In the Bible "**Hiram Abiff of Tyre**", founder of the Freemason sect was an "**Israelite**". The Israelites didn't adorn a Crescent Moon or Star. Nor were they supposed to worship the pagan gods of Egypt. It was forbidden by God. In Arabic the word "**Hilal**" means "**Crescent Moon**". It is the small part of the moon that we see after the "**New Moon**". The Islamic Calendar or Muslim Calendar (**Hijri Calendar**) is a "**Lunar Calendar**". It is 11 days shorter than our "**Solar-Gregorian Calendar**". Our year is 365 days long. The Muslim year is 354 days long. Arab Muslims use the appearance of the "**Crescent Moon**" as the mark of "**The beginning of each Islamic month**". They also use it to start their Holy Month of "**Ramadan**". In the "pre-Islamic" Era, the Arabs would climb to the top of mountains to worship the Moon God "**Hubal**". Remember, Satan always does the "**opposite**" of God. Today the Muslims use the Celestial body that is essentially a "**Dark Planetary Body**" as the basis of their calendar and symbol of their religion. The Bible never says that the Moon "**emits**" its own light but it does say it "**gives**" light to the earth. How? **By reflecting the light given off the sun to the earth**. Based on the rotation of the moon in position to the earth and sun we see different variations in the shape of the moon which is always spherical (**crescent moon, half-moon**), never straight!

Genesis 1:14-17 "And God said, Let there be lights in the firmament of the heaven to divide the day from the night; and let them be for signs, and for seasons, and for days, and years. And let them be for lights in the firmament of the heaven to **give light** upon the earth: and it was so. And God made two great lights; the greater light to rule the day, and the lesser light to rule the night: he made the stars also. And God set them in the firmament of the heaven to **give light upon the earth.**"

Note: *If the moon were a light source, instead of simply a light, there would be no night for it to govern. If we reflect the sun's light using a mirror into* *someone's eye it can temporarily blind them. If we direct enough of the sun's rays using a mirror onto a piece of paper, that piece of paper will eventually possibly start to catch fire and burn!*

So I have to repeat this important fact: **The "Crescent Moon and Star" are not unique to Islam.** We see it was also used in other civilizations: Ancient Egypt, in Hinduism (Shiva), the Ethiopians (Yeha Temple), Pre-Islam (Hubal), in Satanism, in Wicca witchcraft, and in Freemasonry. The Freemasons know this as their symbol embraces Egyptian culture and the Crescent Moon, plus the Star. Every major country and its government is controlled by the Freemasons. This can be seen in the United States Government, African Governments (i.e. Nigeria), the Royal Family in England, the Vatican/Catholic Church, Israel, Egypt, Saudi Arabia and Australia. All 33-degree Grand Master Mason Shriners know that they swear their oaths on the **Quran** (instead of the Bible) and the God they acknowledge is "**Allah**", not **Yahusha HaMashiach** (Jesus Christ). They even greet each other by saying "**As-salamu alaykum**" meaning "**Peace be upon you**" in Arabic. Freemasons who worship Allah are known as "**Moslem Shriners**". Some of our United States Presidents have been worshippers of "**Allah**". President Bush is even a firm believer in the Quran. Here is an oath of the Moslem Shriners for those who need proof.

"In willful violation whereof may I incur the fearful penalty of having my eyeballs pierced to the centry with a three-edged blade, my feet flayed and I be forced to walk the hot sands upon the sterile shores of the Red Sea until the flaming Sun shall strike me with a livid plague, and may **ALLAH**, the god of the **ARAB, MOSLEM AND MOHAMMEDAN**, the **GOD OF OUR FATHERS**, support me to the entire fulfillment of the same."

What has Presidents had to say about Islam?

"Well, first of all, I believe in an Almighty God, and I believe that all the world, whether they be Muslim, Christian, or any other religion **prays to the same God**. That's what I believe. **I believe that Islam is a great religion that preaches peace.**"

Said by President George Bush, during an interview with Al Arabiya reporter Elie Nakouzi in November 2003.

"The future MUST NOT belong to those who slander the Prophet of Islam"

Said by President Barack Obama speech to United Nations September 25, 2012.

Let's know expose if this statement is valid?

Sura 8:12 Sahih International Al-Anfal (**The Spoils of War**)

"Remember when your Lord inspired angels, "I am with you, so strengthen those who have believed. **I will cast terror into the hearts of those who disbelieved, so strike them upon the necks and strike from them every fingertip.**"

So if the Quran is a religion that preaches **peace** then we shouldn't see any verses in the Quran that promotes "**fighting**" or "**destruction**". However, the following verses in the Quran say otherwise:

- Sura 2:244
- Sura 2:216
- Sura 3:56
- Sura 3:151
- Sura 4:74

657

- Sura 4:76
- Sura 4:89
- Sura 4:95
- Sura 4:104
- Sura 5:33
- Sura 8:12
- Sura 8:15
- Sura 8:39
- Sura 8:57
- Sura 8:67
- Sura 8:59-60
- Sura 8:65
- Sura 9:5
- Sura 9:14
- Sura 9:20
- Sura 9:29
- Sura 9:30
- Sura 9:88
- Sura 9:111
- Sura 61:4

And the list goes on and on, even in the Hadith. This can researched for yourself on www.quran.com.

NEED I SAY MORE?

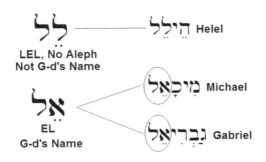

לֵל
LEL, No Aleph
Not G-d's Name
———— הֵילֵל Helel

אֵל
EL
G-d's Name
מִיכָאֵל Michael
גַּבְרִיאֵל Gabriel

(**Above**) Satan's/Lucifer's name is "HEYLEL". **Lucifer is known as "Heylel-Ben-Shachar-YALAL". He is an angel like Michael and Gabriel but notice the difference in Lucifer's Hebrew name "Helel" or "Heylel" in comparison to the names of the other "Good" angels the bible lists.** The Angels and the Prophets all have the word "God" on the end of their names as "EL" or the Hebrew Characters "**Aleph**" and "**Lamed**". For example, "Ezeki-**EL**", "Dani-**EL**", "Jo-**EL**", "Gabri-**EL**", "Micha-**EL**" and "Rapha-**EL**", and "Uri-**EL**". However, Lucifer's Hebrew name has **NO** "**Aleph**" in his name. The **Aleph** character has no sound of its own and means "**Master**" or "**Lord**" in Hebrew. The "**Aleph**" Character is found at the beginning of the words: **Adom, El, Elohim, Eloah, Ehyeh Asher Ehyeh, Adonai, and El Elyon**.

The Adhan

The Muslim Call to Prayer

(**Left**) The Wolf "**Howling**" to the Moon. (**Right**) The Muslim "**Adhan**" is the daily call to prayer that is played in Mecca, Saudi Arabia and every Mosque across the world. It is played through **loud speakers** (so

659

everyone can hear it) and is usually started in the "**MORNING**" at sunrise as the first of "**five**" calls to prayer as Muslims are required to pray 5 times a day. Ramadan is also started with a "**Muslim call to prayer**" upon seeing the "**Crescent Moon**" in the sky at sunrise. Lucifer is known in Hebrew as "**Heylel**", **SON OF THE HOWLING MORNING (DAWN).** According to Islam, Allah's Apostle said:

"Carry on taking your meals (east and drink) till "Ibn Um Maktum (companion of Muhammad)" pronounces the "**Adhan**", **for he does not pronounce it till it is dawn (MORNING)."**

This verse is based off the pre-dawn Ramadan meal, after which Muslims couldn't eat until after Sunset. In the Quran Allah states:

Quran 2:187 "Eat and drink until the white thread becomes distinct to you from the black thread of the dawn. Then resume the fast till nightfall (Sunset).

So here we see that the Muslims do not "**sound off**" their "**Prayer song**" until the morning. To some listeners this may be heard as a "**Long**" **Loud noise**, which we know sometimes causes wolves and other dogs to "**HOWL**". But the Muslims do this in **THE MORNING**. So did the Prophet Isaiah through the "**Word of God**" reveal to us that under the religion of Islam, Lucifer/Antichrist would influence radical Muslims to "**persecute the Saints-Christians**" in the Last Days? We need to take heed to these clues.

Note: Former Palestinian Muslim "**Walid Shoebat**", founder of www.shoebat.com and **Stephen Pidgeon**, founder of the "**Cepher Bible**" have also pointed out the name of Lucifer, "Helel Ben Shachar Yalal" aka "**Lucifer, Son of the Howling (Dawn/Morning)**" is connected to the Crescent Moon and Star used in Islam.

- Hebrew Strong's #3213 word for HOWL or "**Yalal**" consists of a "**Yod-lamed-lamed**".
- Hebrew Strong's #1966 word for **MORNING/SHINING ONE** or "**Helel**" consists of a "**Hey-yod-lamed-lamed**".

Let's see this in the scriptures.

Isaiah 14:12 "How are thou fallen from heaven, O **Lucifer (Shining One)**, son of the morning (dawn)! How are thou cut down to the ground, which didst weaken the nations!"

The pagan religions of the world worship the greater light (sun) and the lesser light (moon). The Egyptians worshipped both the Crescent Moon and the Sun. At dawn, the moon and the sun can often be seen at the same time!

(**Above**) Ancient Sumeria worship of the Sun and Crescent Moon. Ancient Egypt worship of the Sun and Crescent Moon. Islamic Mosque with the Sun/Star and Crescent Moon. Coincidence?

(**Left**) The **Catholic Eucharist Wafer** represents the Sun god, which is placed on a crescent moon in the Monstrance. This represents the Sexual union of the Sun god "**Nimrod**", the Moon god "**Semiramis**" and their son Tammuz (**Antichrist**). Satan loves to "**copycat**" and do the opposite of the **Most High**. (**Middle**) Many images of the Catholic Virgin Mary show her standing over a crescent moon. Sun worship images can be seen at St. Peter's Basilica at the Vatican. (**Right**) Islamic mosques have the crescent moon representing the moon god and a star for the Sun god. Many times the sun rises in the morning for the first Muslim call to prayer and can be seen cradling the crescent moon symbol on the top of the mosques. Is this a coincidence?

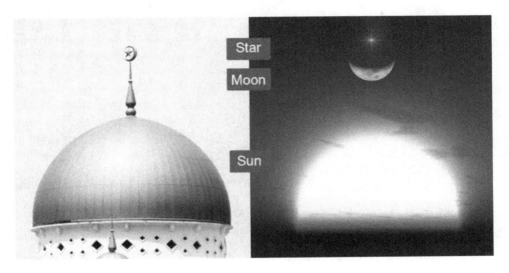

(**Above**) Are Mosques made to represent the **Host of Heaven**? According to the Torah, the "**Host of Heaven**" are not to receive adornment with buildings (graven images) or receive worship.

Deuteronomy 4:19 "And lest thou lift up thine eyes unto the heaven, and when thou seest the **SUN, AND THE MOON, AND THE STARS, EVEN ALL THE HOST OF HEAVEN**, should be driven to **WORSHIP THEM** and **SERVE THEM**, which they Lord thy God hath divided unto all nations under the whole heaven."

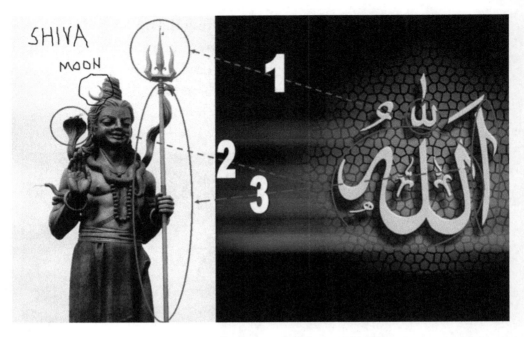

(**Left**) Hindu God **Shiva the Destroyer** (also known as Set or Shatan/Satan) mysteriously has symbols on her/him that are included in the symbols of Islam. (**Right**) The Arabic symbol for "**In the name of Allah**". Like Ancient Sumerian, Egyptian, and Canaanite religions Hinduism also has their "Trinity" gods, "**Shiva**", "**Khrisna**" and "**Vishnu**". Satan is the "**Great Copycat**".

Notice the similarities of the symbols seen on the Hindu God Shiva: The "**Trident**" on top of the staff, the "**staff with the hook**" which is also used in Egypt (Was staff), the **Serpent/Snake**, and the **Crescent Moon**. Is this a coincidence? Like the Baphomet, Shiva is an ambiguous figure appearing to be **male and female**. According to many Hindu and Christian Indians, Shiva represents the equivalent of "**Satan/Lucifer**".

Note: *Shiva the destroyer also sits outside the CERN Large Hadron Collider facility in Europe (Switzerland) were many conspiracy theorists believe the Elite of this world are trying to open up the portals/gateways to Hell or the realm of Demons.*

(**Left**) The "**666**" hand sign. (**Right**) The "**Horned**" hand sign. These hand signs are **well known** in the Satanic Occult world. By simply typing these words in your "Google" or "Yahoo" search engine you can see how many celebrities are doing it. They are not doing this for no reason. They are not doing for fun. By doing these hand signs in public for the world to see they are showing their allegiance to "**Satan**" and also letting other "Satanic" members in the world, "**They are down with Satan's team**".

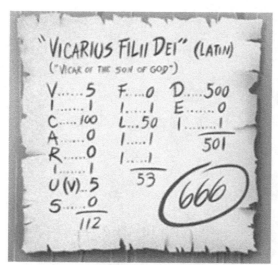

"VICARIUS FILII DEI" (LATIN)
("VICAR OF THE SON OF GOD")

V.....5   F....0   D....500
I.....1   I....1   E......0
C....100   L...50   I......1
A.....0   I....1   ─────
R.....0   I....1   501
I.....1
U (V)..5   ──
S.....0   53   (666)
──
112

It is said that the numerical value of "**Vicarius Filii Dei** "in **Latin, Greek, Roman and Hebrew** is the number "**666**". If so, is that a coincidence? There are some striking similarities to the number "**666'** and Islam. Let's see!

NOTE HOW 666 WAS WRITTEN BY THE APOSTLE JOHN WHICH MATCHES THE ISLAMIC CROSSED SWORDS AND ALLAHU AKBAR

Codex Vaticanus - A.D. 350

In The Name of Allah

The Greek number 666

(**Above**) The Greek numbers for the number "**666**" in the **Greek Codex Vaticanus**. The Codex Vaticanus is the most "**Prized**" possession of the Vatican library. It is believed one of the oldest and complete copy of the Greek Bible in existence. However, the Book of Genesis, Revelations and part of the Book of Hebrew are missing coincidentally. The Codex Vaticanus Manuscript was found in 1481 in the Vatican Library in Rome, Italy. The **Egyptian "Codex Sinaiticus"** dating back to the 4th Century A.D. also has deleted scriptures in it such as Matthew 6:13, Mark 16:9-20, Mark 1:1, and Luke 24:51.

Note: *However, the Ethiopic Bible which predates many Bibles today has these scriptures in it preserved).*

The interesting thing that scholars noted when reading the Greek Codex Vaticanus bible was that the word **"Six hundred and Sixty-Six"** in **Revelations 13:17** appeared to be the same as the Arabic words for **"In the name of Allah"**. This was a crazy find considering the **"Codex Vaticanus"** was written in Greek (which is older than Arabic), and is supposed to be the oldest manuscript of the Greek Bible dating back to 300 B.C.

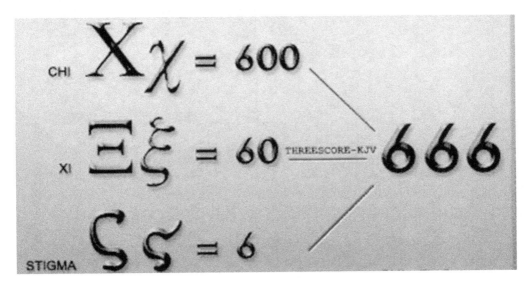

(**Above**) The Greek words that make up the number **"666"** is the **"Chi-600"**, **"Xi-60"** and **"Stigma-6"** letters.

Aramaic Peshitta New Testament- Revelations 13:15-17

"And it was given to him to give spirit to the image of the beast of prey, **(that the image also of the beast of prey should speak)** and to cause that all those whosoever who worshipped not the image of the beast of prey should be killed. And he caused all, small and great, and rich and poor, and sons of freedom and slaves, to have given to them A **SIGNATURE UPON THEIR RIGHT HANDS,** or upon their foreheads. As that no man might be able to buy or sell, unless, he had the **SIGNATURE** of the name of the beast of prey, or the number of his name. Here is wisdom. He that hath understanding, let him count the number of the beast; for it is the number of man: and his number is **Six hundred and sixty-six.**"

So what is this "Signature of the Beast". Is this also a clue? Was John trying to tell Bible readers the true identity of the "**Antichrist**" and his "**Beast New World Order System**"?

(**Left**) Personal Check. (**Right**) Credit/Debit Card.

In America, in order for **ANY** money transaction to be completed, a "**Signature**" is required. On a "**Check**" this is a "**Hand Signature**". On a Credit Card, this is a computerized "**Signature**" with a "**stylet**". On a Debit Card, this is a "**Personalized 4-digit Pin-code**" that serves as our "**Personalized Signature**". By 2017, all Americans will be forced to receive and use a "new" Debit/Credit Card with a **RFID chip. BY 2017 ALL PLACES OF BUSINESS WILL HAVE THEIR "CARD READERS" UPGRADED TO ONLY ACCEPT CARDS WITH THE**

RFID CHIP. See how easy it is for the Government to establish Laws and Rules, which we follow without hesitation or resistance? So what will be next? What will mankind be forced to accept to use in order to Buy or Sell goods? Or even drive a car, travel outside the state/country, or perhaps even live? The next thing they will do is drop the Credit/Debit card for use as payment of goods and **USE OUR PHYSICAL BODIES (Biometrics)**. They already have "**Virtual Bank Teller**" Kiosks at major banks in select states in the U.S.A. Some of these "upgraded" ATM's offer assistance even if you don't have a Debit Card. How is it possible to make an ATM transaction without a Debit/Credit Card? With Eye Scans, Hand Scans and implantable Chips! Many ATM's in Asia are already using Palm scans and Eye Scans for transactions. All under the name of "Cybersecurity and Identity Theft". As long as we have to carry wallets and cards, Americans are always at risk of having their information (monetary, credit, personal, health) stolen and used. So the next step is for "Man's Government" to mark every human being like sheep or like "goods on the shelf of a store".

Revelation 13:15 "And he (Antichrist) had power to give life unto the image of the beast, that the image of the beast should both speak, and cause that as many as would not worship the image of the beast should be killed."

Revelation 20:4 "And I saw thrones, and they sat upon them, and judgement was given unto them: and I saw souls of them that **WERE BEHEADED** for the witness of Jesus, and for the Word of God, and which had not **WORSHIPPED THE BEAST**, neither his image, neither had received his "**SIGNATURE**" upon their foreheads, or in their hands; and they lived and reigned with Christ a thousand years."

Many say that the New Testament was written in **Aramaic** first by the apostles and then was written in Greek. Well, in the Aramaic Peshitta version of Revelations 13:15-17 it uses the word "**Signature**" instead of "**Mark**" that people will be required to use or have in order to buy, sell or trade. In the Hebrew version the Hebrew letter/word here is "**Tav or Tavah-Strong's #8420/8427**". Both these words can mean "**SIGNATURE**" or "**MARK**". It was used back in the day as a sort of way of saying, "**My written Mark/signature in attestation.**" In 1933 around the same time the Social Security number was created and the U.S.A. went Bankrupt causing the passing of Bill HR 1491 & HR 4960, the UPC barcode was invented. It was later modified for use on all our goods courtesy of the Jewish Rothschild family. The Dollar Bill used to be backed by Gold (which the Rothschild's control via the amount Gold is worth on the market) but after the Bretton-Woods Act, the dollar lost its gold-backing. So money was legit for "**Legal Tender**" for purchasing all goods or paying off all forms of debts. So then they gave us "**checkbooks**" which we could use to pay for things, but only after we authorize its use with our "**Personalized Signature**". Our signature is the agreement that an institution can take a specified dollar amount out of our bank account.

LET THE BUYER BEWARE! After, we started using Checks, they came out with Credit/Debit cards. Credit/Debit cards can be swiped using the Devices at every check-out register. Now they have inserted "**RFID**" chips into our Credit/Debit Cards so that we no longer have to "**swipe**" our cards but instead have to "**Insert**" our cards into the machine as above. For both methods you have to use a "**Signature**" or a personalized "**Numerical Pin Code Signature**" in order to complete the money transaction. But they are not done! Banks like Citibank and HSBC are already running trials on getting us to do away with Cash/Debit-Credit cards. The next step is Biometrics (**hand scans/retinal scans**) or an "**Implantable RFID**" chip.

Be part of the future.

Your DNA will be your data.

HSBC

Scan to finally reveal the Mark of the Beast

(**Above**) Different Banks (**Wells Fargo, HSBC-Hong Kong Standard Bank of China**) and Credit Unions have all started incorporating "retinal scans" to access online banking/ATM's or "Hand/Fingerprint Scans". Countries like China are pulling their Gold out of all foreign vaults and are dropping U.S. Treasury Bonds. Wake Up. We will essentially be no different than the Electronic Goods and Groceries we buy at the Store. This was not God's Plan for human kind. But don't worry, in the end, everything will be made "right".

BIOMETRICS? PRECURSOR FOR THE MARK OF THE BEAST?

When John had his vision on the Island of Patmos west of Turkey and south of Greece, he probably did his best to describe some 2,000 years ago how people would be buying or selling things in the future. Whose future? **OUR FUTURE!** In today's world, most people are "**right-handed**" so it would make sense that John had a vision where he saw people using their "**Right Hand**" to make transactions. This is probably why he didn't write in the scriptures anything about people using "**Both Hands**" or their "**Left hand**".

(**Left**) Biometrics, like **Hand** Scans are being used today. Don't get it twisted. Soon everyone will be required to use them or **THEY WILL NOT** be able to work or get paid. No more swiping a badge down a magnetic strip, waving badges over some device (Near-Field Communication/NFC) or inserting a badge/card. (**Right**) Retinal Eye scans are also here. Just like John said in the Book of Revelation, for retinal scans to work, the "**Forehead**" has to be aligned so that the scan can hit both eyes (retinas). Tilting your head to the left or right will result in a "**improper eye scan**". What better way to prevent this "error" by using a "forehead placement"? Was John on the Island of Patmos, describing "**Retinal Scans**" and "**Hand Scans**"? Is this what John saw in his vision? That we would eventually be moved to a "**Cash-less, Debit/Credit Card-less**" monetary system where everything we do would be "**electronic**". This means our "Identity" will be a number in some program or supercomputer. This is essentially being fulling plugged into "**The Matrix**", except we don't have plug sockets in the back of our head. Once Cash and debit/credit cards are a thing of the past, humans will all be connected to the internet.

Electronical Medical Health Records, our Driver's License, Passports, Car insurance, Bank Accounts, Credit Cards, Loans, Government EBT and Social Security will all be tied into the World Wide Web. Externally we will be monitored via Satellites, "Smart-devices", facial recognition, "Blue Tooth", NFC and RFID technology. Just like in the Movie Terminator: Genisys, we are moving into a "**Mark of the Beast System**".

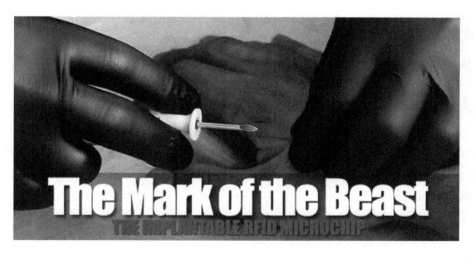

The New World Order Agenda is for **SATAN** to **CONTROL US** and for us to worship him (**Antichrist**) instead of the Creator. Once they

(Satan and his workers) have complete control they can manipulate our lives as they see fit. They can cut your finances, your passport, your medical health insurance and other valuable things "**electronically**." There will be no "**Freedom**" and "**Nowhere to Hide**" from the "**All-seeing Eye**" of Satan. Satan is not "**Omnipotent**" and "**Everywhere**" like God is. Satanists know this important fact about the difference between the Creator and Lucifer/Satan. Satan needs **WORLDWIDE SURVEILLIANCE**, the control of our basic needs (food, water, energy, housing, health, education), religion and money to get make man "bow down" to his "Beast System". All of the years man has been on this earth since the Great Flood (from Nimrod to now), Satan has desired to be like the "**Most High**" using "**Technology/Knowledge**", "**mankind**" and "**pagan gods**" to **CONTROL US**. Wake up! The Bible is a prophetical book giving us instructions on how to get to the Kingdom of Heaven but it is also a Book of "**Warning**" through "**Prophecy**". As we are seeing statues of the Baphomet, Anubis and Baal being erected in America, we are also seeing increasing "immorality" around the world. The signs that we are in the "**Days of Noah**" are evident. Open Satanic worship, worldwide "movements" to promote homosexuality or transgenderism as an "alternative" lifestyle choice, gay marriage, bestiality brothels, cloning (animals, plants, humans), Genetically Modified Foods which are causing an increase in cancer, the call for unification of all religions by the Pope, and 17 Global Goals initiated by the United Nations should be enough to cause concern in most people who are followers of the Bible. But we seem to be asleep, not aware of what is going on. We must take heed to how close we are to Bible prophecy unfolding as John envisioned it on the Island of Patmos when he wrote the Book of Revelation. We must remember that in the "Last Days" more of mankind will be deceived to worship everything else but the "**Creator**". This means Osiris, Thoth, Anubis, Horus, Amen-Ra, Enki, Satan, Baal, Allah and "Man" himself. As science and religious scholars try to prove that Yahusha or the Israelites didn't exist, we must not be deceived. We also must understand fully who "**Israel**" is because Bible Prophecy surrounds the "**Children of Israel**". Do not be deceived by Satan!

BEWARE OF SATAN AND THE FOLLOWERS OF PAGAN-INSPIRED RELIGIONS!

"WHO CHANGED THE TRUTH OF GOD INTO A LIE, AND WORSHIPPED AND SERVED THE CREATURE MORE THAN THE CREATOR, WHO IS BLESSED FOR EVER. AMEN."- ROMANS 1:25

Thank You for taking the time to read this Book. Stay tuned for Hebrews to Negroes 2: Volume 3!

God Bless and Shalom!

For more information visit www.thenegronetwork.com or email me at nicodemusdaltonjr@yahoo.com. Stay tuned for Volume 3 and many more Hebrews to Negroes Books exposing the **TRUTH!**

CPSIA information can be obtained
at www.ICGtesting.com
Printed in the USA
BVHW052241040319
541706BV00002B/16/P